POPULAR RELIGIOUS MAGAZINES OF THE UNITED STATES

POPULAR RELIGIOUS MAGAZINES OF THE UNITED STATES

Edited by

P. Mark Fackler and Charles H. Lippy

Historical Guides to the World's Periodicals and Newspapers

Greenwood Press
Westport, Connecticut • London

016.2005
P 831

Library of Congress Cataloging-in-Publication Data

Popular religious magazines of the United States / edited by P. Mark
  Fackler and Charles H. Lippy.
      p. cm.—(Historical guides to the world's periodicals and
newspapers, ISSN 0742–5538)
   Includes index.
   ISBN 0–313–28533–0 (alk. paper)
    1. Religious newspapers and periodicals—United States.
  I. Fackler, Mark. II. Lippy, Charles H. III. Series.
  PN4888.R4P67   1995
  016.2'005—dc20   94–7427

British Library Cataloguing in Publication Data is available.

Library of Congress Catalog Card Number: 94–7427
ISBN: 0–313–28533–0
ISSN: 0742–5538

First published in 1995

Greenwood Press, 88 Post Road West, Westport, CT 06881
An imprint of Greenwood Publishing Group, Inc.

Printed in the United States of America

The paper used in this book complies with the
Permanent Paper Standard issued by the National
Information Standards Organization (Z39.48–1984).

10 9 8 7 6 5 4 3 2 1

Contents

Preface

In 1986, Greenwood Press published *Religious Periodicals of the United States: Academic and Scholarly Journals*, a reference work that profiled more than one hundred titles, which were formerly or currently in print, that were of primary interest for their scholarly content. The preface to that volume noted it was not always easy to classify religious periodicals as being predominantly of academic interest or of general interest. The movement among scholars to form professional societies in the latter part of the nineteenth century brought the establishment of numerous journals promoting the individual intellectual focus of the various societies. These religious periodicals naturally targeted a rather narrow readership—mostly specialists in a given field. But a much larger number of magazines with a religious bent have sought a much wider audience. In some cases, members of a particular religious group comprised the intended audience; in others, the design was to reach anyone interested in a particular topic such as missions, women's issues, or social reform. Most of these appealed to a more general readership or a mass audience, and their content has frequently lacked the scholarly sophistication characteristic of the other journals. Some of these more popular periodicals, especially those no longer in print, claim the interest of researchers and scholars because their content illuminates particular movements or trends in the overall American religious landscape; several of these were described in the earlier volume.

This book, however, focuses directly on those American religious periodicals, past and present, directed toward a popular, general readership. Since the early Victorian era, periodical literature has served both to shape and to reflect the consciousness of Americans on many subjects, including religion. Hence, our purpose is to provide a reference work that will introduce users to the range of popular religious periodical literature that has flourished in the United States. Some magazines are valuable mostly for charting the development of the religious body that has served as the sponsoring agency; others provide insight into popular religious movements of their time. Some seek to promote personal piety and devotion; others serve as vehicles to gain adherents to a particular religious group or perspective. All offer important signals of the forces that have influenced and that continue to influence the ways in which ordinary men and women go about the business of creating their personal religious beliefs and values, and, in many cases, they show how those beliefs make a difference in the public arena.

Seven criteria guided the selection of titles for inclusion in the earlier book on academic and scholarly journals:

1. The publications of a representative grouping of academic, scholarly, and professional societies in the disciplines that constitute the field of religion
2. The range of religious groups—Protestant, Catholic, Jewish, humanist, sectarian—that publish journals
3. The variety of institutions, such as theological seminaries and universities, that sponsor periodicals
4. A concern to draw on current research in religion in materials geared to a lay audience
5. A mixture of popular and academic fare in their articles
6. Types of journals no longer in print but that disseminated scholarly work in the past
7. Matters that are currently of interest primarily to scholars but were not necessarily so when they were being published[1]

Obviously, these criteria required adaptation for a book concentrating on popular magazines. We have endeavored to offer a representative sampling that reflects the range of religious groups that have found a niche in American life and the variety of organizations that have developed periodicals on religious themes of popular interest. As before, we have included some titles that are no longer in print but that in their day were reflective of the diversity of popular religious periodical literature. We have been less concerned with scholarly content but are very much concerned with identifying titles that would open windows into the popular religious sensibilities of Americans past and present.

Even so, since more than ten thousand titles were candidates for inclusion, selection was a difficult process. In some cases, titles that we had hoped to include were abandoned because contributors could not locate complete publication runs or they found location sources obscure. In other cases, writers who were familiar with particular journals suggested additional titles. In order to keep the book to a reasonable size, many worthy titles had to be eliminated. Hence, the editors take ultimate responsibility for the titles finally included, but we are all too aware of hundreds of others that we would have profiled if we had no limits to consider.

The profiles follow a standard format, but they also reflect the analytic and critical perspective of the individual authors. Each profile offers a brief history of the periodical, which seeks to place its contents and contribution to popular religion in its proper context. Each author also indicates the kind of articles characteristic of the magazine, often highlighting representative pieces in order to give readers a feeling for the magazine's general contents. Citations refer readers to noteworthy articles that appeared in the pages of each periodical as well as to other readings that will supplement overall understanding. In addition, each profile identifies index sources, if available, and places where a complete publication run is available either in print or microform. Endmatter for each profile summarizes any title changes that might have transpired during a periodical's history, its publishers and places of publication, a listing of editors, and circulation figures.

As a rule, profiles use the current or final title for each magazine to determine alphabetical listing, unless a different title is more commonly known. All other titles used by each magazine appear in the alphabetical ordering, with a notation indicating the title for readers to use to locate the entry. An appendix groups the titles profiled on the basis of religious or thematic orientation.

We received assistance from many individuals and institutions in preparing this book for publication. Our primary debt is to the more than sixty scholars who have written the individual essays. Several contributed to the earlier volume on academic and scholarly journals, and many suggested names of other individuals who in turn became part of the overall enterprise. Many scholars involved in graduate programs in religious studies and communications studies also suggested both titles and potential contributors. In this regard, we especially appreciate the encouragement that we received from Professors Mark Noll of Wheaton College and Martin Marty of the University of Chicago. Several editorial assistants at Wheaton College—undergraduates, graduate students, and staff—did much of the work involved in keeping track of essays and writers, preparing edited materials for submission and caring for a variety of other tasks. They include David Malone, David Craig, Bill Hill, Christopher Hudson, Andrew Gross, Diane Krusemark, and Pat Wright. Without their labors, we could not have done our work. Mark Fackler received support from Wheaton College in the form of an Aldeen Grant. The frequent contact required between editors located in Illinois and South Carolina introduced both of us to the wonders of electronic mail. Marilyn Brownstein and Alicia Merritt of Greenwood Press offered constant encouragement, support, and helpful suggestions for strengthening the book.

Note

1. Charles H. Lippy, ed., *Religious Periodicals of the United States: Academic and Scholarly Journals* (Westport, CT: Greenwood, 1986), viii.

Introduction

With standard directories listing approximately three thousand titles of religious periodicals currently published in the United States, one cannot minimize the importance of the religious press in American culture. Indeed, since the emergence of periodical publications geared toward a mass market, religious titles have accounted for a substantial percentage of the total; for much of the nineteenth century they outnumbered strictly secular magazines, newspapers, and cognate periodicals.

Many periodicals, including religious ones, have targeted specialized audiences. *Christian History*, for example, a periodical that appeared briefly in the 1740s, had a relatively narrow focus. The growth of colleges and universities in the nineteenth century, along with the rise of professional institutions such as theological schools and seminaries, led to the appearance of periodicals that reflected the intellectual thrust of the sponsoring agencies. Seminary-based publications such as the *Biblical Repertory*, forerunner of the *Princeton Review*, appealed primarily to theologians, biblical scholars, and pastors, many of whom were alumni. As professional groups and societies with a religious focus became organized, they readily joined with their secular counterparts in publishing periodicals, usually quarterlies, whose appeal was likewise restricted primarily to those whose interests coincided with those of the sponsoring agency. In this category fall periodicals such as the *Journal of Biblical Literature*, originating in 1882 as the organ of the professional organization now known as the Society of Biblical Literature. There have also been numerous periodicals designed primarily to serve the needs of persons engaged in religious occupations. The Roman Catholic *Homiletic and Pastoral Review*, for example, has addressed issues of specific concern to priests in parish ministry since its founding in 1900.

Alongside these periodicals have been countless others intended to serve a larger audience—one primarily composed of laypersons. Some have promoted the interests and beliefs of particular denominations; others have reflected issues such as missions or social reform endeavors that cut across group boundaries. Some have advanced a particular theological perspective without denominational sponsorship; others with a distinct theological or denominational base have sought primarily to convince others of the correctness of a particular doctrinal viewpoint or religious persuasion. It is this vast periodical literature oriented to a lay audience, a popular audience, that forms the focus for the profiles that follow. In the colonial period, the most popular form of periodical literature was no doubt the annual almanac. While scholars suggest that ordinary people prized almanacs for their astrological information, they also call attention to the frequency with which articles on biblical and religious themes appeared in their pages. As newspapers began to appear in the larger colonial cities in the eighteenth century, usually on a weekly basis (at most), some coverage was given to religious news, though "intelligence," as news was often called, consisted primarily of brief summaries of events in Europe or North America. The travels through the North American colonies of evangelist George Whitefield in the 1740s, for example, received mention in newspapers in several of the larger cities where he preached. Those few eighteenth-century magazines with a distinctly religious tone, such as *Christian History* or the *Arminian Magazine* published in 1789–90 in Philadelphia, had a relatively heavy theological bent and, thus, a relatively limited appeal.

In the United States, the opening decades of the nineteenth century witnessed considerable growth in publishing of all sorts and the development of what we might regard as the first enduring popular periodicals, or periodicals designed to appeal to a mass audience rather than one with a limited professional or theological interest. Several factors account for that growth and also illuminate the range of periodicals that appeared. The end of the colonial epoch forced virtually all American religious groups to reorganize or at least rethink their connections with parent groups in Europe. The absence of government endorsement of any one religious group as an established church paved the way for a competitive, market-driven approach to religion—what historian Nathan Hatch has called the "democratization" of American Christianity.[1] The rise of the Protestant denomination as a distinct form of religious organization in turn led to the emergence of periodicals that echoed the beliefs, programs, and social agenda of the individual denominations. American Methodists, for example, in 1818 revived the *Methodist Magazine*, first published between 1796 and 1798, and, until it became a more intellectually oriented quarterly in 1830, printed sermons, biographical sketches, and miscellaneous religious news to promote commitment among its denominational constituency. But when the periodical took on a more scholarly tone, other periodicals quickly took its place in targeting the lay Methodist audience, many of them geared to a regional audience and most carrying the designation *Christian Advocate* in some form in their titles. Presbyterians were especially prolific in using the magazine format, offering over the decades *Presbyterian, Presbyterian Survey, Presbyterian Journal*, and after the denomination split over the matter of slavery, *Presbyterian of the South.* The *Herald of Gospel Liberty* had Congregationalist connections, though much later the *Congregationalist* would become one of several other voices for that group; in the twentieth century there would be the *United Church Herald,* which merged with the Presbyterian *A.D.* before declining circulation forced both denominations to suspend publication. Other denominations embarked on similar publishing ventures, most with the dual purpose of edifying their own adherents and providing clergy with what a later age would call continuing education in theological and ecclesiastical matters. Some, such as the *Connecticut Evangelical Magazine,* had lacked formal denominational ties but reflected more the evangelical style that undergirded much popular Protestantism of the day.

Another force feeding the expansion of the religious press stemmed largely from a broadly based Protestant concern to create a culture in the United States based on evangelical values. The impetus to reform society resulted in part from the separation of church and state; without explicit government endorsement of a particular religion, leaders from many denominations recognized that some cooperation was necessary if religion was to exert a strong cultural influence despite the denominations' competing with each other for adherents. The most well known of the host of voluntary societies that sought to impress a Protestant stamp on American culture were those calling for the abolition of slavery. There were a host of others, however, organized to promote causes ranging from the distribution of Bibles to temperance. Some, such as the American Bible Society with its *American Bible Society Record,* still endure. As interest in missions, both domestic and foreign, boomed in the first half of the nineteenth century, numerous missionary societies produced their own periodicals. Those emphasizing foreign missions offered accounts, often exaggerated, of the religious life indigenous to other nations and the hardships encountered by the missionaries as they sought to take the Christian gospel across the globe. The well-known *Massachusetts Missionary Magazine* that began publication in 1803 is typical. Over the years it was joined by many others, including the *Baptist Missionary Magazine.*

The religious ferment that marked the adolescence of the United States also generated a spate of religious periodicals. New religious movements spawned journals that trumpeted their own versions of religious truth. Alexander Campbell and the Restorationist movement that coalesced into the Disciples of Christ, for example, in 1830 launched the *Millennial Harbinger,* itself the successor to a periodical titled the *Christian Baptist.* American Unitarians, after emerging by 1819 as a religious institution separate from New England Congregationalism, were particularly prolific in founding magazines and journals that promoted their alternative to orthodox Protestant thinking. The *North American Review,* originally a Unitarian publication, did not restrict its vision to the Unitarianism of its founders, but until 1940 carried pieces by major literary figures, voices for social reform, and advocates of new ways of religious thinking. Intrigue with millennialist thinking in the 1840s led not only to the formation of several new religious movements but also to the appearance of several magazines. Having roots in the enchantment with biblical prophecy that was a hallmark of the millennialist fascination are such periodicals as *Adventist Review* and *Prophetic Times*. Jehovah's Witnesses, rooted in the Adventist movement of midcentury, would later establish its *Watchtower* to keep adventist fervor alive, and continuing interest in decoding biblical prophecy would bring about periodicals such as the *American Millennial and Prophecy Review*. Joseph Smith's Church of Jesus Christ of Latter-day Saints, better known as the Mormons, has offered numerous periodicals, some such as *Ensign* designed more for the Mormon faithful and others geared to a non-Mormon audience or those with interest in special aspects of Mormon life and history. The Holiness movement that swept across Protestant America on the eve of the Civil War saw its main mover Phoebe Palmer and her husband establishing the *Guide to Holiness* as a vehicle for promoting their insistence that a second blessing followed on conversion; it brought believers to new peaks of devotion and sanctification. Advancing interest in the Pentecostalism that brought renewed interest in gifts of the Spirit like glossolalia around the turn of the century are popular publications such as *Pentecostal Evangel*. Scores of other titles, many with brief publication histories, mirror the diversity that came to mark American religious life by midcentury.

Then, too, immigration and westward expansion contributed to the surge of religious publication. Many denominations began to produce newspapers and magazines to serve constituents in areas newly settled by Euro-Americans. The *Western Recorder*, for example, owed its genesis to the desire of Baptists in Kentucky to have their own literary voice. In some areas, the first newspapers were often produced by religious bodies and contained a blend of secular and religious news. Such was particularly true in the old Northwest and then a bit later in California and areas farther west. For a time it seemed as if every denomination had its own state newspaper. Some still do, though by the late twentieth century most have become more obviously house organs of denominations and no longer carry secular news. The *Baptist Recorder*, the voice of Southern Baptists in North Carolina, reflects that transition in its own history.

Immigration patterns brought increasing numbers of non-Protestants to American shores. Roman Catholics accounted for the largest number, and while there were a few periodicals targeted for a Catholic audience in the early years of the nineteenth century, the *U.S. Catholic Miscellany* that debuted in Charleston, South Carolina, in 1822 became a prototype for an array of diocesan and regional papers and magazines, such as *Catholic New York* and the prominent *Pittsburgh Catholic*. In time, various Catholic orders organized their own journals. The work of some of these orders was focused on the American church, itself regarded as a missionary enterprise until 1908. But the increasing maturity of American Catholicism and the expanding work of Catholic orders brought about magazines highlighting Catholic mission activity worldwide. Representative of periodicals reflecting the work of the many Catholic missions are *Maryknoll*, *Columban Mission*, and *Ligourian*.

As the nineteenth century progressed and more and more immigrants from non-English-speaking areas of Europe came to the United States, periodicals and papers published in a host of other languages quickly appeared. Not all were Catholic. American Lutherans, for example, at one time produced periodicals in German, Swedish, Norwegian, and other languages that were more familiar to their constituency than English. The *Augustana and Lutheran Companion* is but one example of this genre, but *Lutheran, Lutheran Observer*, and *Lutheran Witness* also have deep roots in the immigrant experience. The value of periodical literature in cementing bonds between individual believers and religious groups was so widely accepted that by midcentury the relatively small number of Jews living in the United States had also begun to publish their own magazines. Perhaps the most important of the early American Jewish periodicals was the *American Israelite*, begun in 1854 by Isaac M. Wise, a primary voice for the Reform movement within Judaism. But American Jews have also sustained the *American Hebrew, Reform Judaism Magazine*, and for a brief period a magazine addressing issues of particular concern to Jewish women, the *American Jewess*.

Frank Luther Mott, in his five-volume *History of American Magazines*, noted that in the two decades following the Civil War the number of religious periodicals published in the United States nearly doubled.[2] Many, of course, appeared as a result of factors that we have already noted, such as immigration and the denominational growth that followed national expansion. But several new genres of periodicals, many with a heavy religious tone, became prominent during this period. Ann Douglas has called attention to the increasing feminization of American culture in the middle third of the nineteenth century,[3] and numerous other scholars have emphasized the emergence of a "cult of domesticity" that marked the American understanding of family and gender as the Victorian era began to assume a distinctive cast. At the same time, increased reliance on mass production from the middle third of the century onward had flooded the literary market with "cheap" novels—popular fiction that aroused suspicion among many religious leaders for its presumably frivolous character. But the shift in the understanding of family and gender and the greater availability of secular literature helped stimulate not only the appearance of periodicals targeted especially toward women but also the production of magazines and cognate materials that could be used in the religious nurture of children. If Americans were going to devour popular literature regardless of warnings from the clergy, better to make literature accessible that would at least reflect acceptable moral and religious values. Among periodicals designed to appeal to Victorian women were *Godey's Lady's Book, Ladies' Repository*, and *Christian Parlor Magazine*, journals that echoed Protestant values of the day even in articles on nonreligious themes. One could devote an entire book to the scrutiny of Sunday School materials and other periodical literature intended for use by children: the *Child's Paper* is but one example.

One consequence of seeing religious nurture as part of the domestic sphere was the increasing privatization of religious experience, and periodical literature that could be read and pondered in the confines of the Victorian home helped buttress that interiorization of piety. From 1865 to 1969, for example, *Ave Maria* encouraged American Catholics to focus personal devotional life on the Blessed Virgin; the *Reign of the Sacred Heart* was also intended to bolster Catholic devotional life. Both were designed as Catholic family magazines, but gradually they began to address issues broader than private devotion as Catholics themselves moved from the periphery to the mainstream of the social order. But the need to provide devotional literature was not restricted to Catholic circles. By the early twentieth century, a spate of Protestant devotional magazines began to appear. Perhaps the most well known are *Our Daily Bread* and the *Upper Room*, a bimonthly magazine of daily devotions and suggested Bible readings that began under Methodist auspices. Both boast a readership that crosses denominational and national boundaries.

Social and religious currents of the twentieth century have led to the demise of many religious periodicals while stimulating the publication of new ones. As secular newspapers and magazines burgeoned, many religious ones saw their circulation dwindle to the point where publication became a financial impossibility. Then, too, many religiously based magazines lagged behind others in taking advantage of technological improvements that allowed more attractive layout and design, use of color and graphics, and other features that enhanced the attractiveness of a magazine to potential readers. Assimilation of immigrants and the decline in the number of immigrants entering the nation after World War I diminished the need for periodicals in languages other than English. Denominational mergers, a major theme in twentieth-century ecclesiastical history, led to the merger of magazines. In many cases, denominational magazines geared to a lay audience disappeared, victims of competition from secular sources, though those targeted toward religious professionals generally survived.

This does not mean, however, that publication of popular religious periodicals in the United States has necessarily declined in importance. Popular religious leaders and new religious movements still look to periodicals as a vehicle for promoting their causes. *Decision*, the magazine of the Billy Graham Evangelistic Association, for example, retains a respectable circulation and popularity. Norman Vincent Peale introduced *Guideposts* in 1945, a popular monthly that echoes Peale's approach to positive thinking but that bills itself as an interfaith periodical in order to reach as wide an audience as possible. New religious movements come and go, as do their periodicals. But those that have dotted the religious landscape in recent decades have provided periodicals like *Back to Godhead*, the voice of the International Society for Krishna Consciousness (better known as the Hare Krishna movement) or the *Bridal Call*, inspired by the popular midcentury evangelist Aimee Semple McPherson. Herbert Armstrong's World Wide Church of God continues to offer its *Plain Truth* free of charge; it may well be one of the most widely distributed religious periodicals today (though distribution and readership figures may vary widely). Religious news commentary continues to reach hundreds of thousands through publications such as *Commentary, Commonweal, Christianity Today,* and *Christian Century.* Seeking to respond to social change that has brought the rethinking of the role of women are periodicals like *Daughters of Sarah,* which probe theological and biblical themes from a feminist perspective. *Today's Christian Woman* matches any comparable nonreligious journal in its slick layout and eye-catching design. Of course, there remain countless periodicals published by various religious judicatories, whether regional bodies such as dioceses or statewide agencies.

From the eighteenth century to the present, popular periodicals have been a major means of promoting personal religious commitment and of nurturing individual piety while advancing causes of denominations, new religious movements, and agencies calling for social reform and rooted in religious values. There is little reason to doubt that as new technology, especially electronic publication, changes the way in which information is disseminated, popular religious publications will remain vital to the periodical industry in the United States.

Notes

1. Nathan Hatch, *The Democratization of American Christianity* (New Haven: Yale University Press, 1989).

2. Frank Luther Mott, *A History of American Magazines,* 5 vols. (Cambridge, MA: Harvard University Press, 1938–1968).

3. Ann Douglas, *The Feminization of American Culture* (New York: Avon Books, 1977).

PROFILES OF POPULAR RELIGIOUS MAGAZINES

A

A.D.

The most appropriate metaphor for the general audience magazines of the United Church of Christ is a bridge. Both *United Church Herald* and its successor *A.D.* were designed to span historic differences and to seek more effective communication.

United Church Herald was launched on 9 October 1958 with the explicit goal of helping a brand-new denomination discover its oneness. Even before the Evangelical and Reformed Church had united with the General Council of the Congregational Christian Churches on 25 June 1957, leaders of the two U.S. communions had decided to publish a common magazine. Duly appointed representatives were instructed to study the possibility of uniting the *Messenger*, official journal of the Evangelical and Reformed Church, with the Congregational Christian journal, *Advance*.[1]

Their goal, according to a report to the Second General Synod, was "to help implement and bear forward this ecumenical concern" represented in the formation of the new United Church of Christ. After more than a year of "prayerful and painstaking consideration," the joint publication committee voted "that these bodies presently responsible for publishing the *Messenger* and *Advance*—until superseded by specific action at a later date under the authority of the UCC—shall cooperate in the publication, pro tempore, of a single journal to be known as the *United Church Herald*."[2]

As the first common enterprise of the new Church—and a detailed and highly visible one at that—the publication became something of a battlefield on which different philosophies in the Churches were worked out. Unwilling at that time to appoint a single editor, coeditors were named: Dr. Theodore C. Braun, who had edited the *Messenger*, and Dr. Andrew Vance McCracken, who had edited *Advance*.

The members of the joint committee quickly agreed, however, that "there was need as soon as possible [for] concrete, visible evidence of the union" and that there was "no more effective way of proclaiming the fact of the union, or reproclaiming it every two weeks, and of carrying the news of it into many homes of the people of the UCC [United Church of Christ]" than a single publication.[3]

In the first issue, McCracken wrote an editorial promising that the magazine "will help interfuse and integrate our many local churches, or various boards and state organizations, and the members of our United Church of Christ both at home and overseas—drawing them into a common enterprise committed to the service of God and to the building of a Christian world community."[4] The initial editorial promised much more; the staff certainly worked diligently to provide what McCracken called "how-do-you-do" articles, designed to introduce members of the Evangelical and Reformed Church and the Congregational Christian Churches to each other and to their common activities. In that regard each issue for nearly a generation was intentional as the new Church discovered its own identity and as the two major streams in the life of the United Church of Christ were blended together.

By the time that the Third General Synod met in Philadelphia in July 1961, that national body declared that the *Herald* "has been an effective and distinguished instrument in behalf of the consummation of the union" and spoke of the high literary quality and varied intellectual and devotional content.[5] Such progress was not without pain, however. The *Messenger* had been both more Church-centered and oriented to a popular audience. Its larger circulation was based on promotion throughout the denomination of the "every home plan" with a special subscription price for so-called 100 percent congregations. *Advance* was printed on glossier paper, focused more on philosophical and theological issues, and by intent reached an audience of local, regional, and national Church leaders.

These differences in style were acute, as Martin Marty noted. *United Church Herald*, he observed, "met with considerable resistance, some of it highly vocal from midwestern Evangelical and Reformed churchmen who complained that the 'city slickers' of New York had urbanized their organ beyond recognition and made it too 'ecumenical.' Too much of the folksy chit-chat had disappeared." In Marty's view, however, "actually the *Herald* represents an at-homeness in the post-Protestant culture which others will have to seek."[6]

It was not easy for coeditors McCracken and Braun to work in two distant cities, New York and St. Louis; for several years there were actually two identical editions—one printed and mailed from New York to Congregational Christian subscribers and the other printed and mailed from the Evangelical and Reformed Church's Eden Publishing House in St. Louis. It was not until printing contracts expired in 1963 and J. Martin Bailey had been elected as the editor that the economic savings of a single publication were possible.

Bailey's election followed the death of McCracken and the retirement of

Braun. A Congregational Christian, Bailey had studied both journalism and theology. While attending Eden Theological Seminary in St. Louis, he had worked as editorial assistant at the *Messenger* and was well known among the Evangelical and Reformed national staff.

From the very beginning, *United Church Herald* sought not only to help consummate the union of the two Churches but to look beyond the United Church of Christ. The very first issue included an article by Henry Pitney Van Dusen, president of Union Theological Seminary, on "The Great New Fact of Our Era" as he called the ecumenical movement.[7] In 1968, the *Herald* announced that its platform included a goal "to promote religious harmony, including creative forms of cooperation and church union."[8]

Editorially, the magazine supported the Church's participation in the conciliar movement, even when the National Council of Churches and the World Council of Churches were under attack. In 1971, when the *Reader's Digest* published critical articles about the World Council's program to combat racism in October and about the participation in the World Council of Churches of the Russian Orthodox Church in November, *United Church Herald* explained the charges and declared that "the World Council of Churches and its Programme to Combat Racism deserve our wholehearted and continued support."[9]

As conversations with the Christian Church (Disciples of Christ) led to a partnership between the two denominations, the *Herald*—and, later, *A.D.*— urged closer ties and helped members of the United Church of Christ learn about the Christian Church. Similarly, the magazine covered the development of the Consultation on Church Union from the outset, publishing Eugene Carson Blake's historic "Proposal Toward the Reunion of Christ's Church," along with an editorial urging "serious, discerning and understanding attention."[10] A decade later, when many Christians were beginning to yawn with the slow progress of the consultation, the *Herald* called for "a committed willingness to explore— openly with other churches—the most effective ways to minister to local and world-wide needs. Such determination will eventually lead to a broad-based unity which is far more desirable than any narrow-gage uniformity. Don't sell COCU [Consultation on Church Union] short!"[11] The consultation led to the formation of a consortium of editors who met regularly to plan the "Interchurch Features" that appeared regularly in the publications of as many as eight denominations. The friendship and mutual confidence that developed within that consortium was a factor leading to the birth of *A.D.* magazine in 1972.

In 1958 the new *United Church Herald* took its place in a long line of publications that had served the two denominations that had merged into the United Church of Christ. The magazine's genealogy goes back to the *Missionary Herald* and the *Christian's Magazine*, both of which circulated briefly in 1804, and to the *Herald of Gospel Liberty*, first published in 1808, which claimed to be the "first religious newspaper in the world."[12] The claim of *United Church Herald* that it was the publication with the longest uninterrupted circulation in the United States is disputed, especially by American Baptists who trace their magazines, including *Missions*, back to the *Massachusetts Baptist Missionary Magazine* that began in 1803.

Regardless of which was the first Church newspaper or magazine to be published, the *Herald* proudly proclaimed its lineage: the *Missionary Herald* (1804), the *Herald of Gospel Liberty* (1808), the *Reformed Church Messenger* (1827), the *Congregationalist* (1840), the *Christian Missionary* (1894), the *Messenger of Peace* (1902), the *Outlook of Missions* (1909), the *Evangelical Herald* (1914), the *Messenger* (1934), and *Advance* (1941).[13]

This proclamation was in part a recognition of the history of the groups that had come together to form the United Church of Christ. The Congregational Christian Churches brought together Congregationalists (largely British immigrants) with the Christian Church (indigenous to America) in 1929. In 1934, the Evangelical and Reformed Church had joined the Reformed Church in the United States, made up of immigrants from the Palatinate region of Germany who settled in New York, New Jersey, Pennsylvania, Maryland, and Virginia in the early eighteenth century, and the Evangelical Synod of North America, which included pious German people who settled along the Mississippi River in the mid–nineteenth century. Each of these religious groups relied on periodicals to maintain their identity and to communicate the faith. One such publication, *Der Friedensbote* (*The Messenger of Peace*), published by the Evangelical Synod, was so profitable that the excess income was used to support missionary work at home and abroad.[14]

United Church Herald was itself a bridge to later publications. In 1972, after nearly a year of careful planning, the *Herald* and *Presbyterian Life* began an experiment of joint publication in which members of the United Church of Christ and the United Presbyterian Church in the United States received *A.D.* in one of two editions. The editors, the publisher, and the *A.D.* publishing committee assumed that their readers were more alike than different and dared to hope that other denominations would join them in the publishing effort. That none did was a disappointment; nevertheless, members of the two churches for more than a decade received a professionally produced and colorful journal that sought to meet both their individual denominational interests.

When the United Presbyterian Church in the U.S.A. and the Presbyterian Church in the United States reunited in 1983, it was decided that the needs of a new church dictated a single new publication. *A.D.* was terminated, and Presbyterians were invited to subscribe to *Presbyterian Survey*, a magazine that had served the Presbyterian Church in the United States. Members of the United Church of Christ were offered a tabloid newspaper entitled *United Church News*.

In the final issue of *A.D.*, published in July/August 1983, editor Bailey wrote:

Over the years we published 126 issues; double that number if you count the two editions of each issue. From the beginning we discovered common concerns. Presbyterians and members of the UCC [United Church of Christ] alike were affected by a hunger for faith. Their churches shared a biblical heritage and missionary zeal. Their assemblies generally held similar views of social issues. In countless towns and cities, congregations worked side by side. And for every issue we also found people and news that were unique to the UPC [United Presbyterian Church] or UCC.[15]

The *Herald* and *A.D.* also provided something of a bridge to other forms of communication that were beginning to serve the churches. When readers became accustomed to highly visual publications like *Look* and *Life*, the *Herald* in September 1966 began a bold use of color and illustration. Everett A. Thiele of Peterborough, New Hampshire, wrote to the editors: "The new format makes the magazine considerably more exciting visually and you are giving your readers professional religious journalism." Pastor Carl F. Kemper of West Burlington, Iowa, "waved it from the pulpit, like it was fresh off Gutenburg's press."[16]

The use of visuals was noted in academic circles as well. Professor Roy Paul Nelson of the University of Oregon, reproduced ten pages from the *Herald* with a caption, "*United Church Herald* art director Raymond Waites, Jr., was able to devote five spreads to a section from an oratorio. . . . For most spreads he devoted one page to copy (reversed on black) and one page to art. Note how art comes up strong at the end. No color, all black and white."[17]

When *A.D.* folded, the United Church of Christ not only launched a tabloid newspaper but intensified its publication of specialized newsletters and journals that served relatively small caucus and interest groups. That mirrored a trend in secular publishing.

United Church Herald and *A.D.* were published at a time when a social revolution was sweeping the United States. If the United Church of Christ and the United Presbyterian Church were predominantly made up of members whose roots were in the British Isles and Northern Europe, the churches also began affirming their own cultural and ethnic diversity and calling for racial and social inclusiveness.

The first editorial that Bailey wrote for the *Herald* dealt with President John F. Kennedy's first civil-rights message to the Congress. People were claiming, "You can't legislate brotherhood." The editorial called the proposed laws "logical and efficient methods to overcome delays and resistance in guaranteeing to Negroes their right to register and vote." An article in the same issue featured a Tampa, Florida, church that was working with the Tampa Urban League, "a local social-work and community service agency, to better understand and help solve some of the community's most pressing problems."[18]

Within months, the magazine chronicled the formation of the National Conference on Religion and Race, covered the historic Fourth General Synod that created a Committee for Racial Justice Now, and reported on the March on Washington led by Martin Luther King, Jr.[19] The magazine became a vocal advocate for political liberties and social justice. The platform published in 1968 cited three goals:

To champion the right and responsibility of churchmen and citizens to voice their convictions with courage. Recognizing that controversy often is creative, we affirm that the church needs the interaction of differing points of view and also that Christians have a special ministry of reconciliation.

To work for human justice and peace in the church, in the community and in the world.

To express the inclusive nature of the church in terms of race, creed, nationality and educational or economic position.[20]

This approach to church journalism met with both applause and scorn. Many subscriptions were canceled because of what readers termed "political action." But others cheered and encouraged a forthright effort to report the prophetic witness of the Church. In the early 1960s, the editor of the magazine with a predominantly white readership in a mostly white Church decided to include a photo of a "Negro Christian" in every issue. By the end of the 1970s both the United Church of Christ and the United Presbyterian Church were intentionally describing themselves as multicultural and were affirmatively seeking to place African American ministers in key administrative positions. One should not claim that this happened as a result of editorial policy, but it may be fair to suggest that the magazines were at least ahead of the Churches' democratic processes.

Another area in which the magazines sought to influence their constituencies was in the area of globalization. Throughout the 1960s and 1970s *United Church Herald* and *A.D.* deliberately described the Churches' world mission in non-chauvinistic terms. The magazines interpreted the United Church of Christ's partnership with overseas Christians and their Churches. Articles and editorials affirmed the United Nations and sought to help readers reflect an enlightened patriotism. Editorials took a propeace stance and early on opposed U.S. military involvement in Vietnam—but did so while respecting but not advocating pacifism.[21]

Both *United Church Herald* and *A.D.* also looked for theological insights in the contemporary arts. A series on "Preaching from Unexpected Pulpits" was often surprising to persons who anticipated a church magazine to feature only overtly religious themes. Reviews of books like Saul Bellow's *Herzog* and of films like *The War Game* were carried in an effort to help Christians think theologically about the world in which they lived.[22] Many works of art were reproduced and discussed. Two photo essays in *A.D.* especially reflected this position. The Christmas issue in 1973 devoted nine pages to photos and interpretations of art selected by the directors of ten U.S. art museums.[23] The Easter issue in 1974 featured selections by eleven theologians.[24] Both groups were invited by the compiler, Jane Day Mook, to reflect Paul Tillich's statement that "authentic art . . . is implicitly religious if it expresses, in whatever fashion, the artist's sensitive and honest search for ultimate meaning and significance in terms of his own contemporary culture."[25]

Martin Marty commented that "since the *United Church Herald* represents the merger between Congregationalist churches and the Evangelical and Reformed Church, one should take cheer from this thoroughly professional magazine. I would without diffidence give it to anyone—Protestant, Catholic, Jew, agnostic—for a portrait of the kind of Protestant witness I would like to see prevail."[26] Perhaps that is another way of saying that the magazine was about building bridges.

Notes

1. Minutes, The Second General Synod of the United Church of Christ, Oberlin, Ohio, July 5–9, 1959, Appendix 16, 184.

2. Ibid.

3. Ibid., 185.

4. *United Church Herald* 1:1 (9 October 1958): 2.

5. Minutes, Third General Synod, "Report of the Review Committee" as adopted, 40.

6. Martin Marty, *The Religious Press in America* (New York: Holt, Rinehart, and Winston, 1963), 46.

7. Henry P. Van Dusen, "The Great New Fact of Our Era," *United Church Herald* 1:1 (9 October 1958): 4.

8. "Goals," *United Church Herald* 11:1 (January 1968): 2.

9. "World Council Attacked," *United Church Herald* 14:12 (December 1971): 44.

10. Eugene Carson Blake, "A Proposal Toward the Reunion of Christ's Church," *United Church Herald* 3:6 (29 December 1960): 4; "Dr. Blake's Proposal," *United Church Herald* 3:6 (29 December 1960): 7; joint statement issued by United Church of Christ copresidents Fred Hoskins and James E. Wagner in San Francisco following Dr. Blake's proposal, *United Church Herald* 3:6 (29 December 1960): 2.

11. "COCU: Quiet Determination," *United Church Herald* 14:12 (December 1971): 44.

12. Elias Smith, *Herald of Gospel Liberty* 1:1 (1 September 1804).

13. Masthead, *United Church Herald* 11:1 (January 1968).

14. *UCC History and Program* (New York: United Church Press, 1974), 4–35.

15. "*A.D.* 1983: As in the Beginning," *A.D.* (July–August 1983): 4.

16. "Interaction," *United Church Herald* 9:6 (October 1966): 7.

17. Roy Paul Nelson, *Publication Design* (Dubuque, IA: William C. Brown, 1972), 2–3.

18. "To Legislate Or Not . . . " *United Church Herald* 6:2 (April 1963): 7; Arthur Allen, "Witness Through Service on the Racial Front," *United Church Herald* 6:2 (4 April 1963): 17.

19. "Nationwide Progress Reported on Religion and Race Program," *United Church Herald* 6 (4 July 1963): 3; special issue on Fourth General Synod, *United Church Herald* 6 (25 July 1963); "The March on Washington for Jobs and Freedom," *United Church Herald* 6:5 (19 September 1963): 2–3.

20. "Goals," *United Church Herald* 11:1 (January 1968): 2.

21. See "An Indispensable Tool," *United Church Herald* 7 (15 June 1965): 24; "Their Bodies to be Burned," *United Church Herald* 8:6 (1 December 1965): 38.

22. See Lionel A. Whiston, Jr., "A Man for Our Seasons," in "Between the Lines," *United Church Herald* 8:1 (15 February 1965): 29; William E. Wimer, "Views and Reviews," *United Church Herald* 10:7 (July 1967): 54.

23. Jane Day Mook, comp., "Director's Choice: A Portfolio of Religious Art," *A.D.* 2:12 (December 1973): 35–43.

24. Jane Day Mook, comp., "Theologians Choice: A Portfolio of Religious Art" *A.D.* 3:4 (April 1974): 19–29.

25. Paul Tillich quoted in "Director's Choice," *A.D.* 2:12 (December 1973): 35.

26. Marty, *Religious Press in America*, 46.

Information Sources

INDEX SOURCES: Each volume contains an index of authors and articles by subject matter, including news items.

LOCATION SOURCES: Files of *United Church Herald* and *A.D.* may be located in the archives of the United Church of Christ at Lancaster Theological Seminary, Lancaster, Pennsylvania; Eden Theological Seminary, Webster Groves, Missouri; Congregational Library, Boston, Massachusetts. Files of *Presbyterian Life* and *A.D.* are located at the Presbyterian Historical Society in Philadelphia, Pennsylvania.

Publication History

MAGAZINE TITLE AND TITLE CHANGES: *United Church Herald* (1958–1972); *A.D.* (1972–1983).

VOLUME AND ISSUE DATA: *United Church Herald* 1:1 (9 October 1958)–15:7 (July–August 1972). Published semimonthly until September 1966; published monthly thereafter. Some issues were combined issues. *A.D.* 1:1 (September 1972)–12:7 (July–August 1983). Published monthly. Some issues were combined.

PUBLISHER AND PLACE OF PUBLICATION: *United Church Herald*: Joint Publication Committee and later Franklin I. Sheeder or Thomas D. Garner for the United Church Board for Homeland Ministries, New York (with an editorial office in St. Louis until 1963). *A.D.*: Robert H. Heinze and later Roy A. Lloyd for the A.D. Publishing Committee, New York.

EDITORS: *United Church Herald*: Theodore C. Braun and Andrew Vance McCracken (1958–1963), Theodore C. Braun (1963), J. Martin Bailey (1963–1972). *A.D.*: Robert J. Cadigan and J. Martin Bailey (1972), J. Martin Bailey (1973–1983).

CIRCULATION: *United Church Herald*: 141, 461 (1963); *A.D.*: 700,000 (1973).

J. Martin Bailey

ADVANCE. *See* A.D. and CONGREGATIONALIST

ADVENTIST REVIEW

In 1848 Ellen White said to her husband, an emerging leader of the 100 or so adherents: "You must begin to print a little paper and send it out to the people. Let it be small at first; but as the people read, they will send you means with which to print, and it will be a success from the first. From this small beginning it was shown to me to be like streams of light that went clear around the world.''[1]

One of America's older religious publications, the *Adventist Review*, has been published continuously since 1850.[2] The periodical has perpetually combined the two key theological principles of the Seventh-Day Adventists: the keeping of a literal Sabbath and the Second Advent of Jesus Chirst.

The theological foundation for the Adventists was based on the teachings of William Miller, a Calvinistic Baptist, who claimed to predict the end of the present age.[3] This is where the Adventists claim their name—the Second Advent of Jesus Christ on earth. A second distinctive feature of this branch of the Adventist movements is Sabbatarianism. Joseph Bates, a Millerite, claimed that the Sabbath should be celebrated on the seventh day of the week (Saturday) and not on the first day of the week (Sunday) as traditionally acknowledged by other Protestant groups.[4] Thus, the Seventh-Day name combined with Adventist belief yielded a uniquely American religious denomination: the Seventh-Day Adventists.

Ellen White and her prophetic visions gave energy and strength to the early Adventist movement. Indeed, the publishing work of the Seventh-Day Adventists resulted from a vision that Ellen White experienced in 1848 while attending a Sabbath conference at Dorchester, Massachusetts.[5] Mrs. White recalled that the vision was like being "given a view of the proclamation of the sealing message, and of the duty of the brethren to publish the light that was shining upon our pathway.''[6] She instructed her husband as follows: "I have a message for you. You must begin to print a little paper and send it out to the people. Let it be small at first; but as the people read, they will send you means with which to print, and it will be a success from the first. From this small beginning it was shown to me to be like streams of light that went clear around the world.''[7]

James White did begin "to print a little paper" called the *Present Truth*. The first issue of one thousand copies was printed in Middletown, Connecticut, in July 1849. It was mailed out with the hope that readers would voluntarily contribute enough money to pay the printing bill. The people did respond, so that little by little circulation expanded. In 1850 the periodicals *Present Truth*, emphasizing the Sabbath doctrine, and the *Advent Review*, stressing the 1844 Millerite Advent experience, were united into the *Second Advent Review and Sabbath Herald*.[8] Two forces drove the publication and the movement forward: James White's ambition that "present truth" be made universally available and Ellen White's prophecy that the printed word go "clear round the world.''[9]

Since Adventists were geographically scattered and lacked formal organization until 1863, the *Review* provided a forum for discussion, a platform to present Seventh-Day Adventist doctrine, a vehicle of apologetic, and a strong spiritual link between diverse groups. Moreover, the *Review* was a major instrument of religious education in the early formative years. It reflected the Whites' conviction of the importance of the printed word in expressing and disseminating religious views.[10]

As James White and his wife moved from town to town in the interests of the fledgling church, the publication address moved with them. In December 1849, it was Oswego, New York; in the summer of 1850, Centerport, New York; then in November of that year Paris, Maine; the next summer, Saratoga Springs, New York. All this printing was done by whatever print shop was locally available. Finally, in 1852, White raised the money for a Washington handpress, type, and other equipment. Shop quarters consisted of the back room of a house in Rochester, New York, that the Whites rented for $175 a year.[11] Financial problems, however, plagued the enterprise, for securing support for the publication of the periodical and cognate publications depended almost entirely on the promotional talents and energies of James White.[12]

The *Review* continued from its "home" in Rochester until late 1855 when it was moved to Battle Creek, Michigan.[13] The move to Battle Creek was hastened by the burning of the Rochester location. In 1856 an editor, Uriah Smith, was hired to take on the work of James White and the rest of the staff. For nearly fifty years articles above the familiar initials "U.S." nurtured the movement. As well, Smith became the first secretary of the General Conference in the spring of 1863.[14] Smith and the *Review* symbolized the cohesion coming to the Adventist movement.

In 1855 at Battle Creek, James White, Uriah Smith, and C. W. Kellogg invested in and built the first home of the *Review and Herald*, owned by the magazine.[15] Oddly enough, the *Review and Herald* left Battle Creek and moved to Washington, D.C., because its facilities (like those in Rochester) were destroyed by fire on 30 December 1902.

The fire itself brought controversy. Adherents firmly believed that the Battle Creek blaze signaled the judgment of God because Adventists were printing secular material on the religiously sanctioned printing presses to raise revenue.[16] Not until recently has the *Review and Herald* produced anything but Church-related publications.[17]

When the Seventh-Day Adventists set up a formal structure, denominational leaders took steps to assure continued publication of the *Review*. Historian Booton Herndon noted:

A general meeting of interested persons from several states was called in Battle Creek in September of 1860. On October 1 the delegates agreed to become an official church body; the name Seventh-Day Adventist was adopted as most closely descriptive of the beliefs of the members of the new church. The following spring the Seventh-Day Adventist Publishing Association was organized and incorporated under the laws of Michigan.[18]

Thereafter, the *Review* no longer operated independently but according to guidelines and policies established by a denominational publishing committee. If the

Review had acted as the mother institution, the fostering body for all other Seventh-Day Adventist institutions and activities,[19] it was now the official organ of a denomination.

Writing in the *Review* when the publishing association started, H. A. Morrison identified the purpose of all print endeavors of the Seventh-Day Adventists, specifically including the *Review*: "This Association shall be denominated the Advent Review Publishing Association, the object of which shall be the publication of periodicals, books, and tracts, calculated to convey instruction on Bible truth, especially the fulfillment of prophecy, the commandments of God and the faith of Jesus."[20]

The *Review* is thus a public forum for the Church to teach its adherents, as well as an evangelistic outreach to bring others into the Adventist fold. The *Review* has therefore given the movement a sense of identity. Historically, according to Adventist writer Milton R. Hook, the publication has served a variety of purposes:

The papers bound the membership together and were read in lieu of attendance at church services by many. The back page announced plans of itinerating pastors and carried their meeting schedule. The publications also reported what other Adventist groups were doing, and they issued warnings of charlatans posing as prophets and preachers. But their primary purpose, which was twofold, was implied in the name of the major publication, the *Advent Review and Sabbath Herald*. Not only did they review the past Advent movement, adding continuing warnings of the signs of the times, they also constantly expounded Sabbathkeeping as present truth.[21]

As a religious proclamation, the *Review* has carried earnest and solemn exhortations to godly living and renunciations of the world with all its sin, folly, and wickedness. Articles have encouraged believers to press out into the world with the Adventist message of salvation and the coming of Jesus.[22]

Today, the *Review* continues in the tradition of its earlier years by providing Church members with Church announcements and plans and by providing a variety of articles on doctrine and belief, healthful living and living the Christian life, world Church news and official pronouncements regarding Church doctrine and belief, and social and political issues.[23]

In addition, readers' letters give personal viewpoints on the Church and world issues.[24] The *Review* and the Seventh-Day Adventist Church have traditionally stayed clear of advocating specific political positions, except when situations threaten the separation of church and government.

According to *Review* editors, the primary purpose for today's *Review* is to build up the unity of the Adventist people (nearly 8 million) worldwide. It provides an understanding of the Church's twenty-seven fundamental beliefs, hope in the second coming of Christ, help in daily Christian living, and a glimpse of the global needs and mission of Seventh-Day Adventist Christians. As one past editor said, the *Review* "is the heartbeat of Adventism."[25]

Notes

1. Ellen G. White, *Life Sketches of Ellen G. White* (Mountain View, CA: Pacific Press, n.d.), 125.

2. Booton Herndon, *The Seventh-Day: The Story of the Seventh-Day Adventists* (New York: McGraw-Hill, 1960), 57.

3. Herbert S. Bird, *Theology of Seventh-Day Adventism* (Grand Rapids, MI: Eerdmans, 1961), 42.

4. Bird, *Theology of Seventh-Day Adventism*, 14.

5. *The Story of Our Church* (Mountain View, CA: Pacific Press, 1951), 381.

6. White, *Life Sketches,* 125.

7. Ibid.

8. Donald F. Yost, quoted in Gerard P. Damsteegt, *Foundations of the Seventh-Day Adventist Message and Mission* (Grand Rapids, MI: Eerdmans, 1977), 193.

9. Donald F. Yost, "The Power of the Press," *Adventist Review,* 160: 37, pp. 11–13.

10. Roy E. Graham, "James White: Initiator," in *Early Adventist Educators,* ed. George R. Knight (Berrien Springs, MI: Andrews University Press, 1983), 16.

11. *Facsimile Reproductions of the Present Truth and The Advent Review* (Washington, DC: Review and Herald Publishing Association, 1946), 10.

12. Yost, "Power of the Press," 12.

13. Godfrey T. Anderson, "Sectarianism and Organization: 1846–1864," in *Adventism in America,* ed. Gary Land (Grand Rapids, MI: Eerdmans, 1986), 44.

14. Anne D. Jordan, *The Seventh-Day Adventists: A History* (New York: Hippocrene Books, 1988), 77.

15. Arthur W. Spalding, *Footprints of the Pioneers* (Washington, DC: Review and Herald Publishing Association 1947), 162.

16. Arthur White, "The Story of the *Review and Herald* Fire," *Adventist Review,* 154:49, pp. 3–5. See also Land, *Adventism in America,* 124.

17. *Facsimile Reproductions,* 11.

18. Herndon, *Seventh-Day,* 58.

19. Eugene F. Durand, *Yours in the Blessed Hope, Uriah Smith* (Washington, DC: Review and Herald Publishing Association, 1980), 76.

20. H. A. Morrison, "The Birth and Growth of the Review and Herald Publishing House," *Review and Herald,* 126:18, p.10.

21. Milton R. Hook, *Flames Over Battle Creek* (Washington, DC: Review and Herald Publishing Association, 1977), 18.

22. J. L. McElhaney, "What Lessons Does This Country Teach Us?" *Review and Herald,* 126:18, p.6.

23. Land, *Adventism in America,* 45.

24. Malcolm Bull and Keith Lockhart, *Seeking a Sanctuary: Seventh-Day Adventism and the American Dream* (New York: Harper and Row, 1989), 180.

25. Yost, "Power of the Press," 3.

Information Sources

INDEX SOURCES: The early issues are not indexed, but the more recent issues have a yearly content and author index.

LOCATION SOURCES: All issues of the *Review* are accessible at Andrews University, Berrien Springs, Michigan, in the Ellen G. White Reading Room and also in the University Archives Collection.

Publication History

MAGAZINE TITLE AND TITLE CHANGES: *Second Advent Review and Sabbath Herald* (November 1850–August 1851), *Advent Review and Sabbath Herald* (August 1851–December 1870), *Advent Review and Herald of the Sabbath* (December 1870–January 1876), *Advent Review and Sabbath Herald* (January 1876–May 1961), *Review and Herald* (May 1961–March 1971), *Advent Review and Sabbath Herald* (March 1971–January 1978), *Adventist Review* (January 1978).

VOLUME AND ISSUE DATA: 1:1 (November 1850)–1:13 (June 1851); 2:1 (July 1851)–2:14 (March 1852); 3:1–8:26 (May 1852-October 1856), each volume with 26 issues. Starting 9:1 (November 1856) and continuing through 45:26 (June 1875), volumes are numbered in six-month periods and almost without exception have 26 issues each. 46:1 (July 1875)–58:25 (December 1881) have 25 issues each. Starting with 59:1 (January 1882)–71:50 (December 1894), volume numbers are by calendar year with 50 issues each. 72:1 (January 1895)–present, published weekly in annual volumes with a few scattered exceptions.

PUBLISHER AND PLACE OF PUBLICATION: Various local printshops in Maine and New York (1850–1852); from the home of editor James White, Rochester, New York (1853–1855); Battle Creek, Michigan with no publisher identified, (1856–1861); Review and Herald Publishing Association, Battle Creek, Michigan (1861–1902) and Washington, DC (1902–1983); General Conference of Seventh Day Adventists, Silver Spring, Maryland (1983–present).

EDITORS: James White (1850–1855), Uriah Smith (1855–1861), James White (1861–1864), Uriah Smith (1864–1869), John Andrews (1869), Uriah Smith (1870), James White (1871), Uriah Smith (1872), James White (1873–1877), Uriah Smith (1877–1880), James White (1880), Uriah Smith (1881–1897), A.T. Jones (1897–1901), Uriah Smith (1901–1903), W. W. Prescott (1903–1909), W. A. Spicer (1909–1911), F. M. Wilcox (1911–1944), W. A. Spicer (1945), F. D. Nicholl (1945–1966), Kenneth Wood (1966–1982), William Johnsson (1982–1992).

CIRCULATION: 280,000 (first week's issue of each month) and 41,000 (the second, third, and fourth week's circulation).

Timothy J. Detwiler

ADVENT REVIEW. *See* ADVENTIST REVIEW

ADVENT REVIEW AND HERALD OF THE SABBATH. *See* ADVENTIST REVIEW

ADVENT REVIEW AND SABBATH HERALD. *See* ADVENTIST REVIEW

AMERICAN BAPTIST

In the year 1910, the *Baptist Missionary Magazine* merged with *Home Mission Monthly* and *Good Work* to form *Missions: An International Baptist Monthly*. The journal would continue under various titles until its demise in 1992. Throughout these years the publication sought to adequately reflect the commitments of one of the most theologically diverse denominations in the country. All of this was done throughout the most tumultuous years in American church history.

Missions spoke unwaveringly and unapologetically to such controversial issues as race relations, the involvement of the United States in two world wars, the eventual split of the denomination, and the absence of Southern Baptists from ecumenical dialogue. Its editors met, at times, with protest. They never encountered censorship.

When Howard B. Grose took over as the editor of *Missions* in 1910, it had an annual subscription rate of 75 cents and a circulation of 30,000. Throughout the next eighty-two years it would reach a maximum circulation of over 150,000 and would decline to 24,000 upon its closing.

When Grose took over, he saw it as his goal to reflect the original mission of the *Massachusetts Baptist Missionary Magazine*: to provide an accurate account of Baptist home and foreign missions. As a merger of home and foreign missionary journals, it would cover the international and domestic work of American Baptist missionaries. "*Missions* has an inclusive scope," the magazine stated. "It knows no geography, no divisions in terms, no race or national barriers. Its motto is *Missions*, one and indivisible covering every land and every human interest. Month by month it should bring a world survey, setting important events in their relation to the Kingdom of God and its progress."[1]

The magazine's goal was to put everyday people in touch with foreign and home missionaries, to encourage their support and foster a general missionary concern throughout the denomination. "A chief purpose of *Missions* is to make its readers feel they have come into personal contact with the missionaries, so that they can enter sympathetically into the experiences of a mission field in any part of the globe."[2] Grose was the author of several books on foreign missions and immigration.[3] His editorial efforts reflected these concerns.

An issue of *Missions* included several general articles dealing with various topics in missions and sections specifically devoted to current news on the home and international fronts. The home missions portion of the magazine contained discussions of the work by American Baptists to minister to the most needy people in the country: immigrants, African Americans, and Native Americans. The commitment to ministering to immigrants contained elements of social service as well as education and evangelism. The magazine avoided viewing foreign immigration as a problem and argued for the Church to minister to the needs of the foreign population. Unless it responds to this crisis of faith, Richmond Hill argued, "in a few years the oncoming rush and swirl of alien population will simply daze and paralyze the church, from which she will not recover for a century."[4] The focus on Native American ministries addressed the long-standing commitment of American Baptists to ministry with them. Institutions such as Bacone College and others were the primary focus of the discussion.

The commitment to minister to those most in need also led to extensive work with African Americans. The commitment to education and social service was no less vibrant here than it was with the Native Americans. In addition, the magazine supported the inclusion of blacks into American society and criticized the feelings of many white Christians toward African Americans. *Missions* was calling for an end to segregation as far back as the first decade of the twentieth century. At the behest of the editor, Mordecai Johnson delivered this challenge to white American Christians in the October 1928 issue of *Missions*:

Is it in the heart of white America that it *really* desires the Negro to become a full-fledged man [sic] with all the rights and opportunities and encouragement that any other American man may reasonably expect? Will the Negro be encouraged still further in his contribution to his own education? or will there be an unholy program and plan to abort the development that has thus far come to the American colored man?[5]

The discussion of foreign missions was also extensive. There were articles about southeast Asia (the cradle of American Baptist missions) Africa, and elsewhere. This was a period of growth for American Baptist foreign missions, and *Missions* kept its readers informed through regular disclosures of financial statements of the different missions boards. There were also brief articles about different events on the foreign-mission field in the section "From the Far Lands." These brief passages covered a variety of events and were published to give a more personal account of the events in the mission field. This section also included lists of people who were appointed to the mission field, those en route to mission posts, and those who recently arrived at various missions.

Upon the retirement of Grose, William Lipphard began his full editorship of *Missions* in 1933. He had already been associated with the magazine since 1913. When Lipphard finished his work with the magazine in the 1960s, he had been connected with it for over fifty years. He probably exerted the most influence on the direction of the periodical throughout the twentieth century. His work as the full editor would last through the Great Depression and World War II. It would also encompass the doctrinal disputes that would eventually lead to the split of the Conservative Baptist Association from the Denomination. Circulation would drop as low as 26,000 during the Great Depression and would reach a height of 53,313 in 1947. Lipphard's work was not without controversy. He had inflamed many tempers with his stances on U.S. involvement in World War II and on other issues. Nevertheless, as Lipphard stated, "I was given complete editorial freedom."[6]

Lipphard was pointed in his criticism of Hitler. However, he continually argued for a noninterventionist policy in regard to World War II. This was in good standing with most of his readership until the attack on Pearl Harbor. In his editorial "Not Hatred but Penitence," Lipphard said the following: "For more than two years this magazine has opposed America's entry into the war. But now the editorial position is clear. There will be no shirking of civic obligation, no interference with patriotic duty."[7] He went on to state that Christian diplomacy might not survive the chaos and ruin that the war brought about.

His opposition to the war brought Lipphard under investigation by the FBI. It appears that a reader may have reported him to the Bureau.

It became clear that my repeated warnings against Russia had been interpreted as pro-Nazi and pro-Japanese sentiments. Fortunately I had the bound volumes of *Missions* in the office. I called the investigators' attention to numerous articles and editorials, as far back as my article, "The Dangers of Hitlerism," in December, 1933, in which I warned against Hitlerism long before American newspapers had sensed its dangers in the world.[8]

The magazine also came under attack for the way in which it dealt with other Baptist denominations. Lipphard was a committed ecumenist. He was committed to Baptist representation in the National and World Council of Churches. Because of this, he was harshly critical of the Southern Baptist refusal to participate in the organizations. He stated time and again that the lack of full representation by Baptists hurt their Church at large. During the postwar years there were some ongoing discussions between Southern Baptists and American Baptists for joint theological education in postwar Europe. Toward this end, Dr. Charles H. Maddry, the head of the Southern Baptist Foreign Mission Board, made it clear that continuing this negative editorial policy might hinder further negotiations. He also indicated to the American Baptist General Board that a reprimand was in order. To pacify Maddry a reprimand was drawn up. "Ironically, the much-to-be-desired co-operation in theological education in Europe did not materialize, proving once again that appeasement seldom accomplishes its purpose. But Dr. Maddry was mollified and the editor was reprimanded. Even so, my editorial freedom was in no way curtailed."[9]

Lipphard reached mandatory retirement age in 1950 but stayed on as editor for another two years so that his replacement, John Calvin Slemp, could go on an extended tour of American Baptist Missionary sites. Lipphard would continue as editor emeritus long into the 1960s. For most of that time, he would continue to write an editorial entitled "As I See It." His commitment to ecumenism and Baptist principles of religious liberty and freedom of conscience would remain a hallmark of the magazine until the last issue.

The work of John Slemp was, in many ways, a continuation of the work that Lipphard had been doing. There still was the commitment to ecumenism and religious liberty. There were a few additions to the magazine, however. During the 1950s the race issue came much more into the spotlight. There were numerous articles dealing with different aspects of black empowerment, from editorials against segregation to discussions of black theological education. The magazine pushed throughout this period for cooperation between Baptist denominations for black ministerial training.[10]

The magazine's commitment to ecumenism created some structural changes in the magazine. The section entitled "News from the World of Missions" dealt with work done by other denominations as well as by American Baptists. There also were sections devoted to inter-Baptist and interdenominational relations.

Slemp would continue his service to the magazine until his retirement in 1967. In his place would be Norman Depuy. When Depuy became editor, the magazine underwent an immediate face-lift. Gone was the Times-style print and the mild-mannered appearance. In its place was a new look, in tune with the modern publishing style. It included a variety of different typefaces and modern designs in the background. The magazine also had a new title: *The Mission*.

During this period of time the magazine took a more radical, controversial approach to social issues and missions. The magazine openly discussed the black power movement and the Baptist stance on abortion rights.[11] It declared an end to "the Constantinian era of Christianity" in which the Church was no longer powerful but was in solidarity with the powerless.[12] All in all, the magazine may have been too radical for its readership. It had a sudden name change to *American Baptist*. It took on a more mild-mannered appearance and began to focus more directly on denominational activities again. DePuy moved on to a pastorate in 1974. During his editorship, the magazine had seen its highest readership: over 150,000 in the early 1970s.

Taking over for DePuy in 1974 was Phil Jenks. He would be the last editor of *American Baptist*. The structure of the magazine changed under Jenks to more adequately reflect the various departments of the American Baptist Convention. Each division—Home Ministries, International Ministries and Educational Ministries—would have a section devoted to it in every issue. There would also be several features, usually spotlighting a specific ministry or church within the American Baptist Convention.

The magazine's foreign-missions articles reflected the growing commitment of the American Baptist Convention to indigenous leadership development. Gone were the discussions of the exploits of American missionaries evangelizing "foreign lands." In their place were discussions of how American Baptists are working with the indigenous churches, under the local leadership, for specific tasks.

After the early 1970s, the circulation of the magazine began to dwindle. By 1992 it had dropped to 24,000, lower than the circulation during the Great Depression. It was for this reason that the following announcement was put in the *American Baptist*: "It is with much sadness that I write to tell you that this will be the last issue of *American Baptist*. . . . Because of rising production costs and dwindling circulation, denominational officials have decided that it is no longer cost effective to publish a monthly magazine."[13] In its place, there would be the newsletter *American Baptists: In Mission,* but it would not continue in the publication line of the old magazine. The nation's longest running periodical had finally left the scene.

Notes

1. Howard B. Grose, *Missions* 1 (January 1910): 4.
2. Ibid.
3. See *Advance in the Antilles* (New York: Young Peoples Missionary Movement, 1910) and *Aliens or Americans* (New York: Young Peoples Missionary Movement, 1906).
4. Richmond Hill, *Missions* 2 (January 1911): 32.
5. Mordecai Johnson, *Missions* 19 (October 1928): 530.
6. William Lipphard, *Fifty Years an Editor* (Valley Forge: Judson Press, 1963), 17.
7. William Lipphard, *Missions* 32 (January 1942).
8. Lipphard, *Fifty Years an Editor*, 137.
9. Ibid., 21.
10. See *Missions* 153 (January 1953): 16–17.
11. *The Mission* 168 (January 1968): 27.
12. Ibid., 19.
13. *American Baptist* 190 (July–August 1992): 2.

Information Sources

INDEX SOURCES: Each volume contains its own index.
LOCATION SOURCES: A complete set of the magazine can be found in the Archives of the American Baptist Churches in Valley Forge, Pennsylvania.

Publication History

MAGAZINE TITLE AND TITLE CHANGES: *Missions* (1910–1967); *The Mission* (1967–1970); *The American Baptist* (1970–1992).
VOLUME AND ISSUE DATA: All titles were published monthly. The volume numbers started at 1 in 1910 and continued until 1948 when they were changed to reflect the original volume numbers of the magazine. The volumes began with 146 in 1948 and ended with 190 in 1992.
PUBLISHER AND PLACE OF PUBLICATION: The American Baptist Publication Society, New York and then Valley Forge.
EDITORS: Howard Grose (1910–1932), William Lipphard (1933–1953), John Calvin Slemp (1953–1967), Norman DePuy (1967–1974), Philip Jenks (1975–1992).
CIRCULATION: 30,000 (1910); 50,000 (1911); 75,000 (1917); 26,000 (1932); 53,313 (1947); 150,000 (1972); 24,000 (1992).

Glenn Brown

A.M.E. CHRISTIAN RECORDER. *See* CHRISTIAN RECORDER

AMERICAN BAPTIST MAGAZINE AND MISSIONARY INTELLIGENCER. *See* BAPTIST MISSIONARY MAGAZINE

AMERICAN BIBLE SOCIETY RECORD

On 2 July 1818, the Board of Managers of the American Bible Society observed that "a paper issued in the name of the American Bible Society would do more to arrest public attention towards us, than any intelligence imparted through other channels." The American Bible Society (ABS) had been established in 1816 to promote "a wider circulation of the Scriptures without note or comment," and it constituted a key institution in antebellum America's "benevolent empire" of pandenominational Protestant reform organizations. Located in New York City, the society formed the nucleus of a nationwide voluntary effort to place the Scriptures in the hands of every American. To accomplish this goal, it united over one hundred local auxiliary Bible societies, organized in counties and cities throughout the United States. Administering a national philanthropy in a profoundly local and sectional culture, however, presented formidable organizational and informational difficulties. As a first step toward merging its local supporters into a national movement, the board approved the publication of "a paper issued in the name of the American Bible Society," and the first number of its *Quarterly Extracts* appeared in August 1818. The ABS thus launched the longest continuously running popular religious periodical in United States history.[1]

Several impulses, reflecting other common threads in the Society's early history, prompted the board to begin this new publication venture. First, as in most matters of structure and organization, the ABS borrowed heavily from the British and Foreign Bible Society's (BFBS) example. The BFBS, founded in 1804, began publishing its *Monthly Extracts* in August 1817 to promote the Bible cause, and the ABS's board acknowledged in 1818 that "the publication of their monthly extracts of correspondence . . . has answered their expectations." In initiating the new periodical, the managers announced their intent to follow "in the steps of the British and Foreign Bible Society" and their wish "to realize benefits similar to those which have resulted in Britain and on the continent of Europe." The ABS's managers crafted their new publication to serve three broad purposes. First, they viewed their publication as an essential public relations tool: "This Society has lost much by not taking more effectual measures for increasing its publicity or notoriety in every part of the United States," the board observed. Second, the managers hoped to increase monetary contributions and to use the publication for fund-raising purposes: They believed that Christians would not "refuse or hesitate to aid the National Institution of their own country, when they see the high place which under the blessing of Heaven it is likely to assume." Finally, the ABS viewed the *Quarterly Extracts* as an essential informational resource for American Christians: According to the managers, the publication would serve as "an object of great importance both to the community at large and to the interests of this Society."[2]

The *Quarterly Extracts* initially appeared in August 1818 as a compact thirty-two–page, 8-by-5-inch pamphlet with a press run of fifteen hundred copies. Early articles included accounts of the proceedings of the ABS's Board of Managers, lists of financial contributions to the Society, extracts from the reports and correspondence of auxiliary Bible societies, printed speeches prepared for the organization's annual meetings, and reprints from articles appearing in the BFBS's own publications. Title and frequency of publication varied throughout the antebellum period. *Quarterly Extracts* became *Monthly Extracts* in 1821, and the board changed the name to simply *Extracts* in 1833, reflecting the publication's somewhat sporadic appearance. Production delays resulted from myriad causes, including New York City's cholera epidemic in 1822, the society's move to a new depository, problems with printers and binders, and staff turnover. In 1843, the managers adopted the name *Bible Society Record*, which endured until 1970. In 1849, a more rigorous publication schedule was established, and the *Record* appeared every month through 1932.

Content and format also varied during the antebellum years. By the late 1820s, the Society increasingly relied on paid, traveling Bible agents to raise funds, distribute Scriptures, and stimulate local auxiliaries. These agents provided the New York office with monthly narrative reports from the field, and their observations and experiences provided a constant supply of anecdotal *Record* stories. As the ABS began expanding its overseas commitments in the 1830s, reports from Protestant missionaries and appeals from translators and distributors abroad occupied increasing prominence and space. The Society's own corresponding secretaries compiled and edited agent and auxiliary reports for the *Record*, taking care to delete controversial passages offensive to the organization's broad-based Protestant constituency.

Radical format changes occurred in 1849. For the next six and a half years, the *Record* resembled a newspaper, as the managers altered its size to 11 by 17 inches, its length to four pages, and its publication schedule to monthly. Circulation policy changes accompanied this new format. The Society still sent free copies to financial contributors and auxiliary Society officers, but they now established an individual subscription rate of twenty-five cents per year. Further, auxiliaries wishing additional copies for local distribution were now required to pay twelve and a half cents per copy.

Content remained relatively constant, with board minutes, contributor lists, and correspondence from agents and auxiliaries constituting the core articles. The ABS also underscored its policy of publishing only those communications "not too long" and those "pertaining in catholic spirit to the Bible Society work." The board carefully avoided denominational controversy, political stances, and theological argument. Admittedly, these policies tended "to lessen the variety of matter in the periodical, and perhaps prevent a very extensive sale," but the board remained convinced that the prohibitions would "render [the *Record*] more useful to those who seek light and aid in this particular branch of Christian benevolence."[3]

Experimentation with the newspaper format ended in 1856, when the managers finally settled on a standard 6½-by-10-inch format, with issues running sixteen pages. Dissatisfaction with the newspaper format centered around the fact that "in the view of many, the work thus assumes an ephemeral character, and, like other newspapers, is soon destroyed." The Society increasingly viewed its publication as a permanent "record" in many ways, preparing an annual index and fixing on a format that it considered "more easily preserved and used for reference." This new format, with minor changes in masthead and motto, remained constant until the turn of the century.[4]

Some subtle editorial changes altered the publication's character. Acknowledging that the Society "has now an extensive correspondence abroad with missionaries and with its own Agents," the managers concluded in 1856 that the *Record* would "increase in interest and value as the great work of spreading the Gospel advances." Articles describing the ABS's overseas labors increased greatly in number and dominated the *Record* throughout the late nineteenth and early twentieth centuries. The managers also invited pastors to contribute "incidents as to the usefulness of the Scriptures, or the abuse of them," and showed some disposition to approach more controversial issues. For example, the Rev. Joseph Holdich, a prominent Methodist and corresponding secretary of the ABS, prepared a series of critical articles attacking the Douay Bible throughout 1856.[5]

Monthly circulation reached its nineteenth-century peak of 40,126 in 1868, but the periodical also continued to run large deficits of between eight thousand and nine thousand dollars throughout the 1860s and 1870s. By 1875, in the midst of a great financial depression and decline in the Society's own monetary resources, the managers halved the circulation list to 16,500. They eliminated gratuitous distribution to contributors, resolving to send the *Record* only to "such persons as make annual request that it may be forwarded to them." Individual subscription rates were increased to thirty cents per year, and "clubs" now received a twenty-five–cent annual charge, payable in advance. Editorial responsibilities remained with the ABS's three corresponding secretaries throughout the period, and these individuals contributed most articles and edited relevant external communications.[6]

Beginning in 1900, the *Bible Society Record* underwent a series of stylistic transformations that brought a more modern, magazinelike appearance to the venture. The introduction of photographs (1900), heavier grade covers (1900), dual colored-ink covers (1904), more streamlined financial information (1906), special thematic issues (1906), higher quality paper (1907) and similar innovative measures testify to the managers' desire to expand the *Record*'s popular appeal. High production costs and minimal subscription income limited the board's efforts and occasionally caused the managers to scale back innovations.

Some tension existed between the publication's professed purpose and the need to excite the readership and remain competitive in the religious-publishing field. The managers cautioned readers in 1901 to remember that the periodical "is a 'record' primarily, intended to inform the members of the society, its officers, and supporters of what it has actually done," and they advanced the notion that "it is, therefore, debarred from attempting to be a merely popular magazine." Nevertheless, they simultaneously observed that a principal focus of the *Record* involved cultivating "a wider popular sympathy" for the Society's work, and they noted the importance of molding "the facts into such a form and to accompany them with such statements" to attract general support. At times, they apologized to the readership that "it must contain, from month to month, statements of business detail and statistics, the acknowledgment of contributions, and other similar matter." Recognizing the futility of "bringing it into competition with larger and more expensive publications," they nevertheless explored ways "to make its pages attractive to the general religious community." The *Record* generally pursued its conservative course throughout the early twentieth century, eschewing controversy and preferring to err on the side of the routine and the mundane.[7]

Beginning in the 1920s and accelerating rapidly by the 1940s, the Society dramatically increased the *Record*'s press run and disseminated the publication more widely. Auxiliary Bible societies occupied an increasingly marginal status within the movement after 1900, and the ABS looked largely to the churches and small contributors for ongoing support. In addition to subscribers, the Society expanded the *Record*'s mailing list to include annual donors whose contributions exceeded one dollar (1923), offered special long-term subscription rates (1941), and provided complimentary copies to all Protestant ministers in the United States (1959). Circulation figures soared. *Newsweek* polled seventy representative religious journals and reported that the *Record* showed the largest circulation growth between 1941 and 1947, increasing 500 percent to 210,000. By the 1960s, over 1 million copies per month were distributed.[8]

Efforts to personalize the publication and to tie its production more closely to the ABS's "Education and Information" department accompanied this circulation change. Traditionally, editorship of the *Record* remained anonymous, with responsibility resting among the corresponding secretaries and general officers. As late as 1967, the journal's staff box listed only "The Secretaries" as "editors." Beginning in that year, however, the ABS started identifying specific individuals as editors. Various ABS officers contributed bylined articles, photographs proliferated, and a more "popular" approach to articles ensued. In 1970, the ABS officially changed the journal's name to *American Bible Society Record* to identify more explicitly the publisher and to avoid confusion with competing Bible societies in the United States. March 1972 brought another format change, as the *Record*'s editors introduced a more compact, 5¼-by-7¾-inch "digest" format. Readability, tighter and more condensed articles, and an effort to create a "more complete, sectional presentation of the worldwide Bible cause" remained the motivating factors behind the new changes.[9]

By the 1970s and 1980s, the publication settled into a relatively standard and routine format. The *Record*'s managing editor viewed his charge as providing a report of the Society's stewardship to its donors. Editorial autonomy diminished somewhat in 1973 when the ABS's officers reverted to former practice and referred to themselves as "editors." A careful internal review process insured editorial input from ABS officers prior to publication, and the public-relations employee who produced the journal operated with the title "managing editor." Articles emphasized the Bible Society's work in third-world countries, and advertisements promoted the ABS's annuity, donor, and volunteer programs. Coupons, placed inside the magazine, served as fund-raising tools and as mechanisms for ordering ABS products. Circulation stabilized at approximately 250,000 to 300,000 per month, as computerization helped the Society weed its subscription lists and eliminate duplication. All donors contributing more than three dollars per year, as well as a large number of complimentary subscribers, constituted the principal recipients. Despite the introduction of computerized typesetting and minor design innovations, the format remained relatively constant. As the twentieth century draws to a close, this venerable publication appears designed primarily as a means of reaching the Bible Society's own internal constituency rather than as a vehicle for broadening and expanding the ABS's audience.

Notes

1. Minutes of the meeting of the Board of Managers, 2 July 1818, American Bible Society Archives, New York: *The Constitution, Charter, and By-Laws of the American Bible Society* (New York: American Bible Society's Press, 1853). On the American Bible Society's efforts to create a national institution and balance it with local commitments, see Peter J. Wosh, "Bibles, Benevolence and Emerging Bureaucracy: The Persistence of the American Bible Society, 1816–1890" (Ph.D. diss., New York University, 1988). Standard histories of the nineteenth-century "benevolent empire" include Clifford S. Griffin, *Their Brothers' Keepers: Moral Stewardship in the United States, 1800–1865* (New Brunswick: Rutgers University Press, 1960) and Charles I. Foster, *An Errand of Mercy: The Evangelical United Front, 1790–1837* (Chapel Hill: University of North Carolina Press, 1960). For the most recently published history of the American Bible Society, see Creighton Lacy, *The Word-Carrying Giant: The Growth of the American Bible Society (1816–1966)* (South Pasadena: William Carey Library, 1977); but students would also do well to consult Henry Otis Dwight, *The Centennial History of the American Bible Society* (New York: Macmillan, 1916).

2. Minutes of the meeting of the Board of Managers, 2 July 1818, ABS Archives. The British and Foreign Bible Society's predecessor publication is discussed in William Canton, *A History of the British and Foreign Bible Society* (London: John Murray, 1904), 1:325.

3. American Bible Society, *Annual Report* (1850), 66.

4. *Bible Society Record* 3:6 (December 1855): 22.

5. Ibid. 1:1 (January 1856): 1.

6. Minutes of the meeting of the Board of Managers, 2 July 1874. Circulation statistics, as well as a variety of other useful information, can be found in two unpublished

sources: Dorothy U. Compagno, "Public Relations, Financial Promotion, and Support, 1861–1900," ABS Historical Essay, no. 17, pt. 5, pp. 8–20 (1966), ABS Archives; and John H. Zimmerman, "Public Relations, Financial Promotion and Support, 1901–1930," ABS Historical Essay, no. 17, pt. 5, pp. 19–60 (1967), ABS Archives.

7. American Bible Society, *Annual Report* (1901), 13; (1902), 11; (1903), 33; (1910), 21.

8. John H. Zimmerman, "Public Relations: Promotion and Publicity Service to the Bible Cause, 1931–1966," ABS Historical Essay, no. 17, pt. 6-I, pp. 22–45 (1968), ABS Archives.

9. *American Bible Society Record* 117:3 (March 1972): 4.

Information Sources

INDEX SOURCES: Each annual volume contains its own partial index, beginning with 1856.

LOCATION SOURCES: The most complete copies of all volumes are located at the American Bible Society Archives, 1865 Broadway, New York, New York 10023. The American Theological Library Association offers a microfilm edition of the *Record* through its Preservation Filming in Religion program.

Publication History

MAGAZINE TITLE AND TITLE CHANGES: *Quarterly Extracts* (1818–1821), *Monthly Extracts from Correspondence of the American Bible Society* (1821–1833), *Extracts from Correspondence of the American Bible Society* (1833–1843), *Bible Society Record* (1843–1970), *American Bible Society Record* (1970–present).

VOLUME AND ISSUE DATA: No. 1 (August 1818)–No. 9 (January 1821); No. 1 (July 1821)–No. 47 (August 1826); No. 1 (November 1826)–No. 64 (April 1834); No. 1 (May 1834)–No. 55 (September 1843); No. 1 (November 1843)–No. 35 (May 1849), 1:1 (July 1849)–3:6 (December 1855); 1:1 (January 1856)–present. The publication was intended as a quarterly from 1818 until January 1821 and monthly from July 1821 until 1833. In fact, publication was irregular, and many numbers were published together throughout this period. *Extracts* appeared irregularly between 1833 and 1839, and bimonthly from 1839 to 1849. It was published monthly between September 1849 and December 1932, nine times annually in 1933 and 1934, and ten times annually beginning in 1935 and continuing through the present.

PUBLISHER AND PLACE OF PUBLICATION: American Bible Society, New York, New York (1818–present).

EDITORS: Agents and Corresponding Secretaries (1818–1967), Homer B. Ogle (1967–1968), Benjamin A. Bankson (1968–1972), Clifford P. MacDonald (Managing Editor) (1973–present).

CIRCULATION: 1,500 per month (1818); 2,000 per month (1821); 30,000 per month (1858); 34,000–40,000 per month (1860–1874); 16,000–20,000 per month (1875–1923); 26,000–33,000 per month (1924–1938); 62,000 per month (1941); 80,000 per month (1942); 97,500 per month (1943); 200,000–255,000 (1945–1950); 325,000–500,000 per month (1953–1957); 750,000–1,000,000 per month (1960–

1964); 500,000–600,000 per month (1966–1970); 250,000–300,000 per month (1985–1990).

Peter Wosh

AMERICAN CHURCH MONTHLY

The *American Church Monthly* was an independent religious periodical published in the first half of the twentieth century by lay and clerical members of the Protestant Episcopal Church.[1] The Protestant Episcopal Church, often called the American Church, is the American section of the International Anglican Communion. Despite its name, the *American Church Monthly* had no official connection or sponsorship with any American church. It first appeared in March 1917 and continued without interruption until January 1939, when it ceased publication. For one year only, from January 1938 until January 1939, it appeared with a new name, the *New American Church Monthly*. Throughout its twenty-two–year history, the *American Church Monthly* was dependent on revenue from subscriptions and on an increasing amount of advertising. The magazine ceased publication because it ran out of operating funds.

The main purpose of the *American Church Monthly* was to advocate the "Anglo-Catholic" position within the American Church. In the beginning and for several years thereafter, the magazine did not make this purpose explicitly known. In fact, it blandly called itself "a magazine of comment, criticism, and review dealing with questions confronting the Anglican Communion and more especially the Church in the United States."[2] However, the editorials and the articles left little doubt that the editors sought consistently to advocate one position with regard to all the issues they discussed. By 1922, this purpose was set forth clearly and unequivocally. The magazine declared that it proposed "to set forth the cause of the Catholic religion in the Anglican communion and particularly in the American Episcopal Church." Furthermore, it declared that its pages were not intended to constitute "a forum of debate" nor "to represent all schools of thought in the Episcopal Church."[3] Simply put, the editors and contributors had no interest in using their independent publication to promote general discussions. For them, the American Church had one preeminent mission: to reunite with the Roman Catholic Church.

The *American Church Monthly* was predominantly written by and for scholarly clergymen and academics,[4] and far and away the greater amount of space in each number was taken up by scholarly articles. So, despite the magazine's claim that it sought a lay audience, it rarely catered to the tastes of most lay people. At times, it did include pieces that either appealed to or were submitted by lay people who were not scholars. For example, poetry occasionally appeared, and there were some articles describing the work of army chaplains during World War I and settlement workers in the urban areas. But these pieces were always very short compared to the very lengthy articles submitted by scholars.

Over its publication life, the monthly had three editors-in-chief. In the first volume (March 1917), the magazine listed no one person as editor, but rather the members of an editorial council. One year later, the publication announced that Selden Peabody Delany, D.D., a clergyman originally from the Midwest, was now the primary editor. At the time that he assumed the editorship of the *American Church Monthly*, Delany was associate rector of the Church of St. Mary the Virgin in New York City. In October 1929, he gave up his position with the magazine to another midwestern clergyman, Charles Carroll Edmunds, D.D. One year later, Delany converted to Roman Catholicism and in 1934 was ordained a Catholic priest. He died the next year.[5] In November 1934, Edmunds assumed the position of associate editor, giving up his position as editor to Granville Mercer Williams, S.S.J.E, S.T.D.

Under the editorial direction of Delany and Edmunds, the *American Church Monthly* was a staid, decorous, and often arid publication with a consistently pro-Catholic point of view. Under Williams, the magazine was still pro-Catholic, but it became livelier, at least in the editorials, which were often witty, even satirical. For example, Williams referred to the lengthy debates within the Church of England as "learned palaver" and poked fun at the "Monster Pageant of Chaos" at the New York World's Fair, that he feared might dazzle him so much that for him "the edge might be taken off Paradise." He reckoned he would have to leave town, for, as he said, "if we stayed in New York and attended this pageant we should become so enamoured of modern civilization *à la Manhattan* as to lose all taste for Heaven."[6] However, if the editorials became witty, the articles remained as dry as ever. The first number of the "new" magazine carried a short but formidable article entitled "Axioms of Catholic Christology" that contained passages in Greek.[7]

Over the years, the *American Church Monthly* discussed many issues of importance to the American Church; these issues included modernism,[8] secularism, feminism, racism, World War I, psychology, and fascism. But the magazine's main preoccupation was to promote Anglo-Catholicism and, as an ancillary mission, to condemn Protestantism. Incidentally, the magazine's writers never referred to the American Church as the Protestant Episcopal Church, which was its official name. As far as they were concerned, the true American church had little in common with Protestant denominations like the Presbyterians, Baptists, Methodists, or the various ethnic Reformed churches. They called their church the "Episcopal Church," the "American Church," or even the "Catholic Church."

Anglo-Catholicism in twentieth-century America traced its roots back to the Oxford Movement in nineteenth-century England. Beginning in 1833, a small but influential group of clergymen and professors at Oxford University urged the Church of England to reform its ritual, liturgy, decoration, and music in a Catholic direction.[9] The style of Anglo-Catholicism that characterized the *American Church Monthly* was more or less that of the Oxford people, except that the magazine's writers sought less to reform the Church than to convince Catholics and especially other Episcopalians that the Anglican Communion was already Catholic in its essentials. They not only sought imminent reunion with Rome, but they considered themselves already in spiritual brotherhood with Roman Catholics. Delany called Episcopalians "Anglican Catholics" and Roman Catholics "old Catholics." Williams even referred to the Pope as the "Holy Father," something no Protestant would ever have done.[10]

Like the Oxford men, the *American Church Monthly* people argued that true Christianity dated back before the Protestant Reformation. On the positive side, they promoted the upgrading of church music, the study of church history, and even the revival of monasticism and holy orders.[11] On the negative side, they decried Protestantism and criticized any Episcopalians who cooperated with Protestants, even when they sought to promote Christian unity. In 1932, Edmunds condemned outright all of the Episcopal clergy who had participated with Protestant clergy in a combined worship service at the St. Louis conference of the National Christian Unity League. Edmunds confessed to be "quite at a loss to understand how [the Episcopalians] . . . could participate in such a service. They ought to know . . . such action was clearly contrary to Catholic teaching and practice and a scandal and affront to the great body of members of the Episcopal Church."[12] To their credit, the editors and writers of the *American Church Monthly* understood perhaps better than many others that the American Church was losing out in its struggle to win the hearts and minds of Americans, losing out to the fundamentalist preachers and to rising secularism as well. In 1938, Williams openly admitted that as the general American population grew, the vital statistics of the American Church decreased: There were fewer baptisms, fewer confirmations, and fewer Sunday school teachers than the year before.[13] The magazine's writers believed that the American Church was losing out because it tolerated a variety of opinion about central elements of the Christian religion, especially the sacraments and certain rituals. As a result, people did not know exactly what the Church stood for. The irony was that the definition they sought to bring to the American Church was a form of Christianity that appealed to very few in their society. The rarefied piety of men like Delany, Edmunds, and Williams belonged to a slower, quieter time than the fast, loud America of the Jazz Age, an age that preferred Billy Sunday, an age that preferred, to Williams's chagrin, the "Monster Pageant of Chaos."

In 1961, in a conscious attempt to rekindle the Anglo-Catholic flame and pick up where the *American Church Monthly* left off, a group of Episcopalians in New York City called the American Church Union founded the *American Church Quarterly: A Theological Review*. Granville Williams was on the editorial board. The magazine promoted itself as "a missionary activity for the teaching and defense of the historic Catholic and Apostolic Faith of the Church." In 1970, it altered its name to *Church Theological Review*, but it was essentially the same magazine. It apparently ceased publication that same year.

Notes

1. The *American Church Monthly* had no direct connection with an earlier Episcopalian magazine of the same name, published in the mid–nineteenth century. The earlier *American Church Monthly* appeared from January 1857 through June 1858 and issued only three volumes of six numbers each. The magazine was owned by Reverend J. H. Hobart Brown, was published in New York City successively by Edward P. Allen and William N. Dunnell, and was edited by Reverend Henry N. Hudson, M.A. The *American Church Monthly* (1857 version) directly succeeded an earlier magazine called the *True Catholic*, which evidently was also Episcopalian in its point of view and affiliation. The former editor of the *True Catholic*, Hugh Davey Evans, LL.D., was a regular and independent contributor to the *American Church Monthly* (1857 version). Unlike the *American Church Monthly* that later would appear in 1917, the *American Church Monthly* of the 1850s did not take sides in the various controversies in the American Church; instead, the editor consciously sought to publish a diversity of opinion. A complete microfilm copy of this magazine is housed at the Harold Washington Library Center in Chicago.

2. *American Church Monthly* (March 1917): 1.

3. Ibid. (November 1922): 337.

4. For example, the initial 1917 editorial board was loaded with D.D.'s and Ph.D.'s. Moreover, one issue in 1938 listed among its nine contributors three clergymen, two professors, one former missionary, and one divinity student. The two remaining contributors were a poet and the wife of a priest. *American Church Monthly* (March 1917); *New American Church Monthly* (March 1938).

5. Delany (1845–1935) was born in Fond du Lac, Wisconsin, and was educated at Harvard and at the Western Theological Seminary in Chicago. As a practicing clergyman, he had served churches in Massachusetts and Wisconsin. Delany's published writings included *Difficulties of Faith* (1906), *The Ideal of Christian Worship* (1909), *The Value of Confession* (1913), *The Religion of the Prayer Book* (1919), *Christian Practice* (1920), *The Parish Priest* (1926), and *Why Rome* (1930). Edmunds was born in 1858 in Green Bay, Wisconsin, and was educated at Trinity College, Connecticut, and at General Theological Seminary in New York City. By the time he became editor of the *American Church Monthly*, he had served churches in New York, New Jersey, and Connecticut and had been a professor of literature and New Testament interpretation at General Theological Seminary. He also had served four times as a delegate to the General Convention of the American Church. His published writings included *Book of Devotions* (1895) and *Gospel Manuscripts of the General Theological Seminary* (with W.H.P. Hatch) (1917). *Who Was Who in America with World Notables* (Chicago: A. N. Marquis, 1942), 1:312; 4 (1961–68): 279.

6. *New American Church Monthly* 43: 3 (March 1938): 99; ibid. 43: 6 (June 1938): 248.

7. Ibid. 43: 1 (January 1938): 3.

8. Modernism was a religious point of view that gained adherents in the first two decades of the twentieth century. Modernists argued that modern science, biblical scholarship, and archaeology should be seen as authoritative in the instances where their conclusions conflicted with a literal interpretation of the Bible.

9. Chief among the Oxford group were John Keble and John Henry Newman; New-

man eventually converted to Catholicism. R. K. Webb, *Modern England*, 2d ed. (New York: Harper and Row, 1980), 233–34.

10. *American Church Monthly* 1 (May 1917): 4; ibid. 12 (September 1922): 7, 12; *New American Church Monthly* 44 (August 1938): 53.

11. *American Church Monthly* 12 (September 1922): 34.

12. Ibid. 32 (July 1932): 5.

13. Ibid. 43 (January 1938): 4.

Information Sources

INDEX SOURCES: Each volume is indexed.

LOCATION SOURCES (complete): University of Chicago Library; Cleveland Public Library; University of Illinois, Urbana; New York Public Library; Princeton Theological Seminary Library.

LOCATION SOURCES (incomplete): American Antiquarian Society, Worcester, Massachusetts (vols. 29, 36–43; some volumes incomplete); Andover-Harvard Theological Seminary Library (vols. 1–45; vol. 1 incomplete); Bard College Library, New York (vols. 1–4, 9–10, 13–23, 25–45); Carnegie Library of Pittsburgh (vols. 10–13, 24–25; some volumes incomplete); Detroit Public Library (vols. 3–15); Free Library of Philadelphia (vols. 1–30, 34–45; some volumes incomplete); Library of Congress (vols. 1–45; some volumes incomplete); Louisiana State University Library (vols. 1–27, all volumes incomplete); University of Michigan Library (vols. 1–27; some volumes incomplete); Milwaukee Public Library (vols. 1–23, 32–44); Minnesota Historical Society, St. Paul (vols. 1–44); Nashotah House Library, Nashotah, Wisconsin (vols. 1–42); Enoch Pratt Library, Baltimore (vols. 37–45); Seabury-Western Theological Seminary Library, Evanston, Illinois (vols. 1–42); Smith College Library, Massachusetts (vols. 15–43); all volumes incomplete); University of Texas Library, Austin (vols. 42–45; some volumes incomplete); Yale University Library, New Haven, Connecticut (vols. 1–45; some volumes incomplete).

Publication History

MAGAZINE TITLE AND TITLE CHANGES: *American Church Monthly* (1917–1937); *New American Church Monthly* (1938–1939).

VOLUME AND ISSUE DATA: *American Church Monthly* 1:1 (March 1917)–42:6 (December 1937); *New American Church Monthly* 43:1 (January 1938)–45:1 (January 1939).

PUBLISHER AND PLACE OF PUBLICATION: Temple Publishing Corporation, New York City (May 1917–April 1919); New Brunswick, New Jersey (May 1919–May 1922); New York City (June 1922–December 1928); Concord, New Hampshire (January 1929–May 1930); Menasha, Wisconsin (June 1930–December 1931); Staten Island, New York (1932); Concord, New Hampshire (January 1933–January 1939).

EDITORS: Seldon Peabody Delany, D.D. (1918–1929); Charles Carroll Edmunds, D.D. (1929–1934); Granville Mercer Williams, S.S.J.E., S.T.D. (1934–1939). CIRCULATION: Unknown.

David Mulder

AMERICAN CHURCH QUARTERLY: A THEOLOGICAL REVIEW. *See* AMERICAN CHURCH MONTHLY

AMERICAN EXAMINER. *See* AMERICAN HEBREW

AMERICAN HEBREW

When the first issue of the *American Hebrew* appeared on Friday morning, 21 November 1879, its anonymous editors declared: "We represent that class of the citizens of this happy Republic who are proud to designate themselves as well by the appellation men of old bestowed on that great wandering preacher of Monotheism who came from Chaldean Ur." American Jews were wanderers no more, in the view of these men, since they were now residents in this "hospitable land of liberty and equality."[1] Yet between the years 1879 and 1956, with this periodical's explorations of Christian America's hostility toward Jews, the pages of the *American Hebrew* would reveal the limits of that initial optimism. But at the same time the magazine proudly chronicled the lives of Jews, among them the poet Emma Lazarus and the composer George Gershwin, whose contributions to American culture encouraged others to knock on opportunity's door.

When *American Hebrew* first appeared on New York's newsstands in November 1879, Philip Cowen, a local printer, was listed as the magazine's publisher, but the identity of the editors was not revealed. In his memoirs, Cowen explained, "We wanted no individual member to be held responsible for any utterance in the paper." Credibility was also an issue. The editorial board was composed of young upstarts like Max Cohen, Solomon Solis Cohen, Samuel Greenbaum, Daniel P. Hays, H. Pereira Mendes, Jacob Fonesca da Silva Solis, Cyrus Sulzberger, and Frederic De Sola Mendes, the circle's most influential figure.

These men were daring enough to challenge the *Jewish Messenger* and the *Hebrew Leader*, the two established New York Jewish weeklies. They hoped to bring a fresh vibrancy to Jewish journalism but feared their youth and inexperience would work against them. To maintain the aura of secrecy, contributing editors often signed articles with pseudonyms like "Philos" and "the Maccabean." The secret became a guessing game that was played until *American Hebrew*'s thirty-third anniversary when the names finally were revealed.[2]

The Jewish community was not the exclusive audience of the *American Hebrew*. Cowen, publisher from 1879 to 1905, hoped to appeal to "the world outside.'' In his memoirs he wrote, ''Our presentation of the life and activities of our people was to be complete and dependable . . . .We wanted our paper to be sought by the best classes of non-Jews.''[3] On the occasion of *American Hebrew*'s sixtieth anniversary, Max Cohen, one of the original editors, noted the periodical's large number of non-Jewish subscribers, who included, in Cohen's words, ''thousands of Christian ministers, educators, and laymen who earnestly seek to know and understand their fellow-citizens of the Jewish faith.''[4]

There is no way to measure adequately the success of those attempts to reach outside the Jewish community, but *American Hebrew* editors never flagged in their efforts to increase understanding between Jews and Christians. Through tongue-in-cheek dispatches, *American Hebrew* at times played up the sheer inanity of bigots and their petty hypocrisies. At other times, in more serious tones, they invited prominent Christians to reflect on the nature and origins of anti-Semitism. Perhaps the most notable result was a special Passover issue printed in April 1890 entitled ''Prejudice Against the Jews: Its Nature, Its Causes, and Its Remedies, A Consensus of Opinion by Non-Jews.'' Among the respondents were James Cardinal Gibbons, a Roman Catholic; Edward Everett Hale, Boston Unitarian; Washington Gladden, a Social Gospel leader; Charles Eliot, President of Harvard; and Teddy Roosevelt, a rising political star. Their replies reveal much about the subtleties of anti-Semitism among the elites of Gilded Age America.[5]

In 1919, when Rabbi Isaac Landman took over as editor, this concern for Jewish-Christian relations reached its zenith. Landman was a liberal in religious affairs. He was endowed with an optimistic outlook and looked toward the advent of a universal faith—a conviction that might explain in part his ardent anti-Zionist views. Landman worked closely with the Federal Council of Churches to promote dialogue and used the editorial power of the *American Hebrew* in his efforts to build bridges between Jews and Christians.[6]

Despite these forays into interfaith religious concerns, *American Hebrew*'s primary focus remained the life of American Jewry. In the first issue the domestic news column announced a lecture series on Jewish history in Montgomery, Alabama, and the formation of a new congregation in Bradford, Pennsylvania. That column remained an *American Hebrew* staple throughout its history. Hearing about Jews in such exotic places as Oklahoma and Wyoming helped to create a national network of mutual support that aided small communities in overcoming isolation.'

American Hebrew also carried international news. At times traveling friends filed dispatches from abroad, but most often editors clipped those reports from European Jewish journals. News from England, Germany, Austria, Romania, Russia, and Palestine gave Jewish Americans, especially recent immigrants, a chance to follow events in the old country and helped to forge a sense of a worldwide Jewish community. But the news from abroad was not always received with joy. Reports of the happy accomplishments of European Jewry and the progress of Theodore Herzl's Zionist movement competed with stories about entire villages fleeing persecution. By the late nineteenth century, in response to pogroms in Russia, the editors gave the foreign column the ominous title "The Oppressor's Rod."

The old country's violence sent many refugees to American shores. Those arriving in New York's harbor after 1886 were met by Bartholdi's Lady Liberty, the "New Colossus" celebrated in the verse of Emma Lazarus that graced the statue's pedestal. A native New Yorker long active in Jewish affairs, Lazarus enjoyed a close relationship with the *American Hebrew*. Along with *Century* and *Lippincott's*, *American Hebrew* frequently published Lazarus's poetry and prose, including an important series of essays that later appeared in book form as *Epistle to the Hebrews*. When Lazarus died in 1888, *American Hebrew* devoted its weekly issue to her memory, printing black-bordered columns to mark her passing. For Lazarus's celebration of Jewish identity and her concern for the plight of Europe's refugees, the editors eulogized her as "the sweet singer of Israel." The editors also saw Lazarus as a progressive example of women's changing role in American culture, extolling her as "a luminous illustration of the now more widely credited fact that woman can occupy the higher intellectual and cultured plane as well as man."[7]

American Hebrew carried news from around the globe, but throughout its history the magazine remained very closely identified with New York City. On the occasion of the magazine's silver jubilee in 1904, the editors noted a momentous shift in Jewish history. Within the course of the magazine's lifetime, the center of world Jewish life had moved to America—more precisely, to New York. Joining earlier German Jewish immigrants, waves of Eastern European Jews arrived in the city looking for new opportunities and new identities as Americans. Together, these groups formed the largest Jewish population in the world. The pages of the *American Hebrew* follow their passage into the American mainstream.

News of important congregations like Temple Emanu-El and Temple Beth-El grace issues of the *American Hebrew*, revealing much about the personalities and issues of religious life in New York's Jewish community. But the details of life outside the temple reveal even more about New York's turn-of-the-century Jewish community. The magazine's back pages offer a mother lode of minutiae about social groups, fraternal organizations, and charity societies, attesting to the energy and organizational brilliance of the city's Jewish community. Those back pages also carry fascinating sweeteners such as Hebrew translations of nursery rhymes like Humpty Dumpty and Little Bo Peep.

Another revealing feature of *American Hebrew*'s back pages is its advertisements. According to Philip Cowen's memoirs, food advertisements conflicting with dietary laws were rejected, and so were advertisements deemed frivolous, including those from *schadchen*, the Jewish community's matchmakers. All ads had to measure up to "straitlaced ideals."[8] Like any periodical of the same era, advertisements in the *American Hebrew* attest to the birth of an urban commercial culture and its full flowering in the twentieth century. Early advertisements featured headache remedies, cooking wares, horse harnesses, and parlor organs. They also included advertisements targeted solely to a Jewish audience, including advertisements for religious books, mohel services, and such Passover items as matzos and kosher wines. By 1929, *American Hebrew*'s pages featured Steinway pianos and talking pictures, including one full-page spread for "Disraeli," a Warner Brothers' film starring George Arliss. The shift in advertisements reflects in part the upward economic movement of an immigrant community.

In November 1905, not quite one year after *American Hebrew* celebrated its silver jubilee, the magazine marked the 250th anniversary of the arrival of Jews in America with a stunning two-hundred-page special edition. Using photographs and other illustrations and featuring long essays on such topics as Jewish philanthropy, the Jew as tiller of American soil, Southern Jews in the Civil War, and Jewish women in America, the issue charted the contributions of the Jewish people, from the original Sephardic community of New Amsterdam to the German and Russian Jews of more recent arrival. Although *American Hebrew* lasted another half century, its past and future concerns were brought together here in perhaps its most impressive issue. No better words capture the spirit of the *American Hebrew* than the ones that graced the editorial page that day: "Self-sacrificing in war; law-abiding in times of peace; devoted to progress and social welfare during periods of strife and turmoil—the American Jew has always been an exemplary citizen."[9]

Notes

1. *American Hebrew* 1 (21 November 1879): 5.
2. Philip Cowen, *Memories of an American Jew* (New York: International Press, 1932), 41–45.
3. Cowen, *Memories*, 50.
4. *American Hebrew* 146 (8 December 1939): 4.
5. Ibid. 42 (4 April 1890).
6. See Lance S. Sussman, " 'Toward Better Understanding': The Rise of the Interfaith Movement in America and the Role of Rabbi Isaac Landman," *American Jewish Archives* 34 (April 1982): 35–51.
7. *American Hebrew* 33 (25 November 1888): 5.
8. Cowen, *Memories*, 64.
9. *American Hebrew* 77 (24 November 1905).

Information Sources

INDEX SOURCES: Most later volumes include a partial index.
LOCATION SOURCES: Partial holdings in many libraries, most on microfilm.

Publication History

MAGAZINE TITLE AND TITLE CHANGES: *American Hebrew* (1879–1902), *American Hebrew and Jewish Messenger* (1903–1922), *American Hebrew* (1922–1932),

American Hebrew and Jewish Tribune (1932–1935), *American Hebrew* (1935–1956). Absorbed *Jewish Chronicle* (1880), *Jewish Reformer* (1886), *Jewish Tidings* (1895), *Jewish Messenger* (1903), *Jewish Tribune* (1932), and *Jewish Daily Bulletin* (1935). Merged with the *Jewish Examiner* in 1956 to form the *American Examiner.*

VOLUME AND ISSUE DATA: 1:1 (21 November 1879)–166:20 (14 September 1956). Published weekly, with various monthly supplements.

PUBLISHER AND PLACE OF PUBLICATION: American Hebrew Publishing Company, New York, New York, (1879–1956).

EDITORS: Frederic De Sola Mendes, representing an editorial collective (1879–1906); Joseph Jacobs (1906–1916); Herman Bernstein (1916–1919); Isaac Landman (1919–1937). After Landman there was a quick succession of editors, including Louis Rittenberg, Joseph Biben, and Leo Glassman.

CIRCULATION: Unknown.

Jesse T. Todd, Jr.

AMERICAN ISRAELITE

Until the radio and television era many American preachers reached beyond the limited audience of the traditional sermon through print journalism. Isaac Mayer Wise (1819–1900), the father of the Reform movement in American Judaism, was no exception. "It seems that the pen is not only mightier than the sword, but also mightier than the pulpit," Wise once wrote, "for the audience is limited to hundreds while the journal speaks to tens of thousands."[1] A tireless advocate of reform within Judaism, Wise founded the *Israelite* in 1854 and used the weekly to stir up interest in his ideas. The paper was Wise's pulpit until his death in 1900. Wise began calling his journal the *American Israelite* in 1874, and that has remained its name ever since. The oldest Jewish newspaper in America, the *American Israelite* is still published on Main Street in Cincinnati.

Part of Wise's vision was his embrace of America as a promised land for Jews, a notion no doubt related to his own experience as an immigrant. Wise was born in Bohemia and served as a rabbi there before he left for the United States at the age of twenty-seven. In America he found his first job as a rabbi at Albany's Beth El synagogue. After a short and stormy tenure there, Wise joined a generation of other young Americans who headed west to find new opportunities. He settled in Cincinnati, accepting an appointment at Bene Yeshurun synagogue. There Wise remained for the rest of his life.

Like a Methodist circuit rider, Wise used Cincinnati as a base to visit settlements all along the Anglo-American frontier. "He traveled up and down the roads and rivers to scores of cities," the historian Marc Lee Raphael has written, "founding congregations, lecturing, and spreading the message of Reform Judaism wherever there were German Jews and their children."[2] Wise knew the importance of forging mutual ties between himself and his far-flung network of reform-minded Jews. His movement needed a voice, and the *Israelite* proved to be the ideal medium.

Wise published the first issue of the *Israelite* on 15 July 1854. The masthead featured a sunburst with the words in Hebrew and English, "Let there be light." On the front page, Wise printed the first installment of "The Convert," a novel that the rabbi himself had written. The issue also included a reprint of his Fourth of July sermon delivered at Bene Yeshurun. This remarkable sermon reveals Wise's embrace of the notion of America's manifest destiny. The nation's founding represented, for Wise, "the resurrection of mankind from a long and death-like sleep." It was the beginning of a new age of liberty, one that Jews should observe faithfully because "we ought to know best how to appreciate the blessings which the declaration of independence brought to us and for mankind."[3]

Wise continued his explorations of American identity on the editorial page of that first issue. Intending to prove that Jewish faith was perfectly compatible with good citizenship, Wise defined the Jewish American as having "practically demonstrated that the firmest attachment to the cardinal points of his religion comports well with the duties he owes as a good and law-abiding citizen." In his view the "American Israelite" was a supporter of progress, enlightenment, and liberal religion, a person willing to live "under the aegis of republican institutions" while "independent of the mass of expediences and conventionalities, that compose the great bulk of the discipline and liturgy of the synagogue."[4]

Opponents of Wise's reform program received the newspaper with little enthusiasm. Isaac Leeser, editor of the *Occident*, a Philadelphia-based journal with traditionalist leanings, forecast a brief life for Wise's paper. Leeser wrote that Wise's paper "will in all likelihood prove a creature of a day, and will soon go the way of flesh."[5] In the early days it seemed as if Leeser's words might prove prophetic. Despite Wise's aggressive efforts to market his newspaper, he was unable to enroll more than five hundred subscribers for the first issue. In the first year the paper lost six hundred dollars, forcing Wise to tap personal funds to continue publication. That investment soon paid off. Wise began to draw readers with his staunch defense of the faith and his fiercely partisan views. "I promised Judaism a sharp weapon," he recalled in his memoirs, "I promised progress, enlightenment, spiritual striving, a fearless organ."[6] Wise was engaged in a war on two fronts. He denounced proselytizing by Christian missionaries and also struggled with fellow Jews over the definition of American Judaism.

Wise's activities transformed Cincinnati into the American capital of the Reform movement in Judaism. The Union of American Hebrew Congregations (1873), Hebrew Union College (1875), and the Central Conference of American Rabbis (1889) represented the three institutional pillars of Wise's reform efforts, and he established them all in Cincinnati. Every issue of *American Israelite* traces their historical development, the fruit of Wise's brilliant organizational efforts. *American Israelite* also set its sights beyond Cincinnati's limits and reported the news from the frontier communities that Wise had visited. "It is the purpose of a Jewish gazette, to report faithfully each and every thing, that is going on in the Jewish community at large," Wise claimed.[7] Thus, along with dispatches from New York, Philadelphia, Paris, Berlin, and Frankfurt, Wise printed announcements of births, engagements, weddings, deaths, synagogue picnics, and Young Men's Hebrew Association athletic contests from places like Birmingham, Dallas, Fort Wayne, Bay City, and Wichita.

Two decades into the newspaper's history, Wise marked its success with a new typeface, new headings, and a new title. For Wise, the title change signalled the success of his efforts to "naturalize" American Jews. "Twenty years long *The Israelite* has fought the battles of the Lord in this blessed land, for truth, reform, progression, light, and charity," Wise remarked. And now the strife was over. "The Hebrew is Americanized, and his religion naturalized," Wise wrote. "They are no longer stranger: they are perfectly at home in this blessed country."[8] These remarks represent the high-water mark of Wise's efforts to promote the United States as a secular Zion, a promised land where Jews finally might live in peace.

Despite Wise's efforts to promote "Americanization," the German language continued to tug at the hearts of many of his followers. From July 1855 until his death in 1900, Wise reached these readers through *Die Deborah*, a German-language supplement to the *American Israelite*. Intended especially for women, this paper featured serialized novels, biographies, and poetry as well as news and commentary. "In its columns appeared Wise's more intimate articles," according to Max May, Wise's grandson, "and he frequently spoke of the paper as his waste basket."[9] From 3 July 1874 to 11 August 1875, *Die Deborah* carried Wise's reflections on his first decade in America. Those passages served as the basis for Wise's *Reminiscences*, published posthumously in March of 1901.

On 29 March 1990, *American Israelite* was published with black-bordered columns to mark the death of its founder. A simple announcement appeared on the editorial page: "Isaac M. Wise died on Monday afternoon at six o'clock, at his home on Mound Street, Cincinnati."[10] The next issue included a memorial supplement featuring a review of Wise's life and work. It also included a reprint of the funeral oration, delivered by Louis Grossman, junior rabbi at Cincinnati's Plum Street Temple. Wise was a visionary, in Grossman's words, who saw America as a "land of promise; homes, warm and pure, and clean altars of God and the dawn of a new day."[11] Wise's death was a sad moment for the Reform movement in America but it was hardly a fatal blow. His stunning organizational achievements insured the continuity of Reform ideas and institutions.

After Wise's death responsibility for the *American Israelite* passed to his son Leon. Under the new editor, the publication remained the voice of reform. Its pages reflected the concerns of the movement, including sabbath observance, the resettlement of new Jewish immigrants from Eastern Europe, and the fierce debates concerning the efforts of Jewish nationalists in Palestine. On 5 January 1928 Jonah Wise marked *American Israelite*'s seventy-third anniversary with a restatement of the journal's principles. He acknowledged that his generation had "outlived many of the perils and the problems of the immediate past." But the divisions within Judaism that had troubled his father also concerned Jonah. He pledged to use *American Israelite* as a vehicle "to rise above faction and remain free of querulous meddling."[12]

On 23 February 1956, almost a year and a half later than the actual date of the centenary, *American Israelite* published a sixty-four-page issue to celebrate its hundredth anniversary. Congratulating the *American Israelite* for its patriotic devotion, President Eisenhower sent a telegram, a reproduction of which appeared on the first page. The anniversary issue includes testimonials from readers praising the *American Israelite* for its historical role in the formation of American Judaism. Priscilla Ginsberg's brief history of the newspaper, also included in that issue, says little about the periodical after Wise. That omission suggests that the paper's golden age ended with its founder's death in 1900.

In the same special issue an article by S. D. Tempkin, a British lawyer and Jewish lay leader, echoed concerns that Wise himself once had expressed. Tempkin praised America "as the land of opportunity for the Jew." He was struck by the energy and optimism of American Jews but was hardly sanguine about their spiritual health. The synagogue, the historical focus of Jewish faith in the Diaspora, was the primary object of his concern. "Not only does the Synagog appear to command the allegiance of a smaller proportion of the community," Tempkin wrote, "but instead of standing on a different plane to secular institutions, it has to compete and compete fiercely for a place with them."[13]

Tempkin could not comprehend the vast transformations taking place in American Judaism in that period—changes reflecting larger currents in American culture. Some of those trends are clearly visible in the advertisements of *American Israelite*'s centenary issue—a veritable catalog of goods and services for American suburban life in the 1950s. These advertisements pitch "Cincinnati's Finest Ranch Homes," new autos, and shopping malls far from Main Street. They provide a fine visual accompaniment to one of the issue's most interesting articles: a syndicated piece by P. Nibur on suburbanization and the future of American Judaism.

The movement of American Jews to the suburbs, Nibur admitted, marked the abandonment of urban Jewish neighborhoods. But was it a threat to the faith? Nibur said no. The isolation of suburban life might lead, in his view, to a Jewish renaissance. Young couples bereft of the old neighborhood ways would realize "that they must seek out fellow Jews, if they are to retain some of the emotional ties which [formerly] bound them."[14] Jews then would forge new ways of community life. Suburbanization indeed often meant the reorientation of Jewish life around an entirely new institution known as the Jewish Community Center.

A glance through recent issues of *American Israelite* reveals a vibrant Jewish life in greater Cincinnati. The paper continues to publish announcements of births, bar and bat mitzvahs, weddings, and obituaries. Now the listings are mostly local, a fact rooted in part in Wise's successful itinerant preaching. Many of the small towns that Wise visited over a century ago have grown into cities with their own local Jewish press. *American Israelite* lists the activities of Cincinnati's Jewish Community Center along with the services of the area's many synagogues, including Lubavitch, Orthodox, Conservative, Traditional Conservative, and Reform. The periodical that was once Isaac Mayer Wise's fiercely partisan advocate of reform also includes meditations by an orthodox rabbi—a vivid reminder of the ecumenism of American Judaism in the late twentieth century.

Notes

1. *American Israelite* 44 (1 July 1897): 4.
2. Marc Lee Raphael, *Profiles in American Judaism* (San Francisco: Harper, 1985), 14.
3. *The Israelite* 1 (15 July 1854): 3.
4. Ibid., 5.
5. Quoted in Isaac Mayer Wise, *Reminiscences*, trans. and ed. David Philipson (1901; reprint, New York: Arno Press, 1973), 269.
6. Wise, *Reminiscences*, 267.
7. *The Israelite* 2 (10 August 1855): 36.
8. *American Israelite* 1 (3 July 1874): 4.
9. Max B. May, *Isaac Mayer Wise: The Founder of American Judaism* (New York: Putnam's, 1916), 252.
10. *American Israelite* 46 (29 March 1900): 4.
11. Ibid., Memorial Issue (5 April 1900): 2.
12. Ibid. 74 (5 January 1928): 1.
13. Ibid. 101 (23 February 1956): 1:14.
14. Ibid., 3, 7.

Information Sources

INDEX SOURCES: Many issues include a partial index.
LOCATION SOURCES: Partial holdings in many libraries. Complete microform copies are available from the American Jewish Periodical Center, 3101 Clifton Avenue, Cincinnati, Ohio 45220.

Publication History

MAGAZINE TITLE AND TITLE CHANGES: *The Israelite* (1854–1874) and *American Israelite* (1874–present). German-language supplement: *Die Deborah* (1855–1900).
VOLUME AND ISSUE DATA: 1:1 (15 July 1854)–present. Published weekly, with occasional special issues and supplements. Some volumes and issues are irregularly numbered.
PUBLISHER AND PLACE OF PUBLICATION: Isaac M. Wise (1854–1900); American Israelite Publishing Co., Cincinnati, Ohio (1900–present).

EDITORS: Isaac Mayer Wise (1854–1900), Leon Wise (1900–1929), Jonah Wise (1929–
    1930), Henry Segal (1930–1985), Phyllis Singer (1985–present).
CIRCULATION: Unknown.

Jesse T. Todd, Jr.

AMERICAN JEWESS

Like other nineteenth-century women's periodicals, including the *Ladies'
Home Journal* and *Godey's Lady's Book,* the *American Jewess* helped invent
and perpetuate the image of woman as queen of the domestic realm, the guardian
of hearth and home. "The man must earn the funds," one advice columnist
reminded readers in the first issue of *American Jewess* in April 1895, "and the
woman, in the office at home, must invest these funds with prudence and intelligence."[1] For a dime an issue, or one dollar for a yearlong subscription, a
reader found advice on how to shop, cook, clean, and care for her husband and
children. Yet the *American Jewess* also reflected the importance of women's
lives beyond the home's threshold. Under the guidance of Rosa Sonneschein,
editor and publisher during the periodical's brief life span from 1895 to 1899,
the *American Jewess* served as a forum for Jewish women's voices on matters
of economic, political, and religious importance.

Born in Hungary in 1847, Sonneschein came to the United States in 1869
with her husband, Rabbi Solomon Hirsch Sonneschein, and their four children.
They settled in St. Louis, where Rabbi Sonneschein took charge of a congregation affiliated with the liberal Reform movement of Isaac Mayer Wise. The
Sonnescheins divorced in 1893, and two years later Rosa founded the *American
Jewess.*[2] A tireless advocate of women's rights, Sonneschein used her monthly
periodical to showcase progressive views on such issues as universal suffrage
and the ordination of women as rabbis.

Rosa Sonneschein launched her publishing career at a time when women had
begun to reevaluate their roles within American Judaism. In 1893 Hannah
Greenbaum Solomon had founded the National Council of Jewish Women
(NCJW) as a result of women's exclusion from a Jewish conference at the
World's Parliament of Religions in Chicago. The council provided an independent forum for women's involvement in social, political, and religious matters. Its members promoted a number of progressive-era causes, including
public-health and sanitation improvements and educational reforms. The organization also led efforts to strengthen Jewish identity through the study of Jewish
history and culture.[3] Although there was never a formal connection between the
American Jewess and the NCJW, Sonneschein published news about the council
and its activities in a regular column. Reports from local NCJW chapters provided readers of the *American Jewess* with a record of the growing influence of
women in Jewish communities across the nation.

In the late Victorian era, middle-class Jewish women, like their Catholic and
Protestant sisters, shouldered the expectation of saving not only their own in-

dividual households but also the nation—even the world. Men often wrote about this burden of womanhood. In the inaugural issue of the *American Jewess*, Adolph Moses declared that the American woman was the midwife of a new age. "There is in the American woman an idealism," Moses wrote, "a deep religious sense, an almost mystical yearning after spiritual illumination." Moses saw women's involvement in progressive causes, in charity work and moral reform, as evidence of a higher calling. "The American woman is the coming type of womanhood throughout the civilized world. It is her manifest destiny to form womanhood in her own image and after her likeness."[4]

In that same issue Emile G. Hirsch explained how Judaism's past and future were linked to the liberation of women. For Hirsch, modern Judaism was the creation of a peaceful revolution against ignorance and superstition. Jews had thrown off the fetters of what Hirsch called "home Orientalism" and "religious rigorism" in order to establish an egalitarian and universal faith. Women were the vanguard of a Jewish renaissance. "Let her place her new culture into the service of her old faith," Hirsch wrote of the emancipated Jewish woman, "and the winters of indifference will yield to springtides of young and hopeful life."[5] Two years later Rabbi David Philipson joined the chorus of male voices. In a six-page essay entitled "The Ideal Jewess," Philipson defined the Jewish woman as the paragon of spirituality. "She makes her life a sermon," Philipson wrote, "wherefrom may be drawn the choicest lessons of the traits beautiful."[6]

This idealization of Jewish womanhood also was expressed in the magazine's illustrations. The cover of the first issue of the *American Jewess* was a Victorian fantasy, complete with gilded boughs and torches surrounding a portrait of a "classical Jewess." It was an image suggesting refinement and respectability, two characteristics considered to be cardinal feminine virtues in this period. Sonneschein saw these social graces not only as ends in themselves but also as weapons in a war against discrimination and bigotry. In "The Woman Who Talks" advice column in May 1895, editor Sonneschein tackled the brute fact of continuing discrimination against Jews in summer resorts. For Sonneschein, the mission of the "ideal Jewess" was to destroy through respectability dangerous and harmful stereotypes. "The Jewess represents a race; the Christian an individual," Sonneschein wrote. "Hence it does not suffice for the Jewess to be as refined as her Christian sister; she must outdistance her in every desirable social quality."[7]

Sonneschein also used her magazine to celebrate Jewish life and culture. "Going under the Chupah," an article by an Eastern European immigrant, offered an insider's account of a traditional Jewish marriage ceremony on Manhattan's Lower East Side.[8] Sonneschein herself wrote a fascinating piece recounting a Yom Kippur service that she witnessed in the Turkish village at the World's Columbian Exposition in Chicago in 1893. Under a canopy of rugs and tapestries, Sonneschein saw "hundreds of men of our ancient faith, clad in Oriental splendor, worshipping . . . the God of Israel . . . Imagine, amidst the most glorious achievements and products of science, history and modern industry . . .

stood a handful of Oriental Jews."[9] That pride was also expressed in the serialized fiction that Sonneschein published. Since popular novels often portrayed Jews in a manner that reinforced degrading stereotypes, many Jews had never read fair representations of their lives. In the fiction department of the *American Jewess* readers met Jewish women and men who were sympathetic, believably human, and sometimes heroic characters.

Political reportage figured prominently in every issue of the *American Jewess*. Of particular interest are Sonneschein's dispatches from the 1897 Zionist Congress at Basle. Her reports capture some of the energy and excitement that many Jews experienced at the prospect of a homeland in Palestine. An ardent feminist as well as a Zionist, Sonneschein harshly criticized the congress for refusing to grant women a voice and vote. "And strange to say," Sonneschein wrote, "with this strong craving for liberty and equality, the Zionists began their proceedings by disenfranchising women."[10] A year later Sonneschein was able to report that future gatherings could not as readily ignore women, especially since New York City's delegation to the next Zionist Congress included a Mrs. R. Gottheil.[11]

On the occasion of the third anniversary of the *American Jewess* in 1898, its editor proudly reflected on her magazine's achievements. "We have created a bond of sisterhood," Sonneschein wrote, "doing our share to weaken existing prejudices against the Jewess by bringing to public notice the Jewess of today." In that piece she also boldly called for the ordination of women to the rabbinate. "We have shouldered the burden of journalism," Sonneschein wrote, "because we believe the time has come when Jewish women will play an important part in the Synagogue; that they are fully as capable to fill the pulpit as the pew; and that woman's life, purer and nobler than that of man, is worthy to be devoted to the sacred cause of religion."[12] Sonneschein's appeal went unheeded until 1972, when Sally Preisand was ordained a Reformed rabbi. But long before the pulpit was available to women, the *American Jewess* had given women a forum to comment on Scriptural texts. In articles like Ida Elizabeth Skinner's "At Haran's Well," women became de facto interpreters of the word.[13] In addition, the *American Jewess* often reprinted sermons, many of them anonymously submitted. It is indeed possible that some of these texts were written by women, perhaps even by Sonneschein herself.

Even as Sonneschein marked the fourth anniversary of the *American Jewess*, it was clear that the magazine was in financial trouble. The summer edition of 1898 notified readers that the periodical was under new management. Rosa Sonneschein would continue writing for the journal, it was announced, but a corps of professionals would manage its business affairs. The new owners seemed determined to advance the magazine's progressive views. "The time is ripe for Jewish women to play a most important part in Jewish life," readers were told, "The Jewish woman must have her own vehicle of communication with the world, that she may proclaim and demand her rights."[14] But that conviction was not enough to save the monthly. After a brief life of only four years, the final issue of the *American Jewess* was published in August 1899. In a bitter

"Publisher's Valedictory," Israel Zangwill upbraided certain "unscrupulous individuals" who had not paid their subscriptions. But he finally placed responsibility for the periodical's demise at the feet of "so-called 'enlightened' Jews" who "are ashamed to have their neighbors and the letter carriers know that they are interested in Jewish matters."[15]

Like other women's magazines of the period, The *American Jewess* showcased the home as the sphere of women's greatest influence. Its "Household Notes" section featured hints on how to remove stains from tablecloths, how to fix a sewing machine, even tips on how to drive away mice. The magazine also offered sketches of the latest ready-to-wear dresses in its column entitled "London and Paris Fashions." But Sonneschein took her readers far beyond domestic concerns. In the short span of the magazine's lifetime, Sonneschein, her guest columnists, and the readers who contributed opinion pieces helped define the concerns and goals of the nascent women's movement in American Judaism.

Notes

1. "The Woman . . . Who Talks," *American Jewess* 1 (April 1895): 39.

2. Jack Nusan Porter, "Rosa Sonneschein and *The American Jewess* Revisited: New Historical Information on an Early American Zionist and Jewish Feminist," *American Jewish Archives* 32 (November 1980): 125–31.

3. See "National Council of Jewish Women," in *Jewish-American History and Culture: An Encyclopedia,* ed. Jack Fischel and Sanford Pinsker (New York: Garland, 1992), 450–51.

4. Adolph Moses, "The Position of Woman in America," *American Jewess* 1 (April 1895): 15, 19–20.

5. Emile G. Hirsch, "The Modern Jewess," *American Jewess* 1 (April 1895): 11.

6. David Philipson, "The Ideal Jewess," *American Jewess* 4 (March 1897): 260.

7. "The Woman . . . Who Talks," *American Jewess* 1 (May 1895): 90.

8. "An Immigrant Going Under the Chupah," *American Jewess* 7 (April 1898): 13.

9. Rosa Sonneschein, "Yom Kippur in the Midway," *American Jewess* 3 (September 1896): 618–20.

10. Rosa Sonneschein, "The Zionist Congress," *American Jewess* 6 (October 1897): 20.

11. *American Jewess* 8 (September 1898): 5.

12. Rosa Sonneschein, "A Word to Our Readers," *American Jewess* 7 (April 1898): 13–14.

13. Ida Elizabeth Skinner, "At Haran's Well," *American Jewess* 2 (August 1896): 580–85.

14. The American Jewess Co., "To Our Readers," *American Jewess* 7 (July–August 1898): 64.

15. "The Publishers' Valedictory," *American Jewess* 8 (August 1899): 3.

Information Sources

INDEX SOURCES: An index follows every volume.
LOCATION SOURCES: Complete microform copies are available from the American
    Jewish Periodical Center, 3101 Clifton Avenue, Cincinnati, Ohio 45220.

Publication History

MAGAZINE TITLE: *American Jewess* (1896–1899).
VOLUME AND ISSUE DATA: 1:1 (April 1895)–8:8 (August 1899). Published monthly.
PUBLISHER AND PLACE OF PUBLICATION: Rosa Sonneschein (1895–1898), Rosa
    Sonneschein Co., Chicago; Israel Zangwill (1899), American Jewess Publishing
    Co., New York, New York.
EDITORS: Rosa Sonneschein (1895–1898), Israel Zangwill (1899).
CIRCULATION: Unknown.

Jesse T. Todd, Jr.

AMERICAN JUDAISM. *See* REFORM JUDAISM

AMERICAN LADIES' MAGAZINE. *See* GODEY'S LADY'S BOOK

AMERICAN MILLENARIAN AND PROPHETIC REVIEW

American dispensational premillennialism was catalyzed in the 1870s by John
Nelson Darby and the Niagara Bible and International Prophecy conferences.
However, the social and theological contours of that movement had been
sketched a generation earlier by a small but highly articulate group of Americans
who had begun to disseminate the views of English and Scottish premillennialists such as Edward Irving, Lewis Way, William Anderson, James Begg, and
Henry Drummond, associated with the Albury Park conferences of the 1820s.
These Americans followed their British mentors in calling themselves "millenarians" or "literalists," and they countered prevailing postmillennialist views
by arguing that a proper, "literal" interpretation of Scripture showed that
Christ's second coming would inaugurate, not conclude, the millennium. By the
1840s, a decade after the British movement had peaked, millenarianism had
established a relatively widespread and close-knit following in America, and
was promoted by several popular publications.[1] One of these, edited by Isaac
P. Labagh, was the *American Millenarian and Prophetic Review*, published in
at least two volumes from 1842 to 1844 (a third volume may have been issued
in the following year).

Isaac P. Labagh, born in 1804 in Leeds, New York, was a son of the Dutch
Reformed pastor and trustee of Queens (later Rutgers) College, Peter Labagh
(1773–1858). The younger Labagh attended Dickinson College and New Brunswick Seminary. After the seminary, he took pastorates at Dutch Reformed
churches in Rochester and then Gravesend, New York.

Trouble arrived in 1842. In February of that year Labagh, apparently influenced by British millenarians republished by Orrin Rogers and Joel Jones in the *Literalist* (1840–1842), delivered "A Sermon on the Necessity of the Personal Return and Reign of Christ on the Earth" before the Premillennial Advent Association of New York City.[2] The Gravesend pastor delivered his sermon at a time when more radical Adventists like William Miller and George Storrs had cultivated a mood of fascination in America with things eschatological. Advocates of the "British-American strain of millenarianism,"[3] such as Labagh, differed sharply on social as well as theological points from the Millerites, whom they dubbed "Second Advent brethren,"[4] and they took great pains to point out those differences. Millenarians, while happy to speculate about "times and seasons," discouraged any prediction of the "day and hour" of Christ's return. They differed with Adventists also on several technical points of doctrine (no less important to the disputants for their technicality) relative to the Second Advent, the millennium, the consummation of all things, and the return of the Jews to Palestine. Social and ecclesiological differences were equally pronounced. Millenarians tended to be affluent, well-educated Calvinists or Episcopalians with strong intellectual ties to British authorities. Some, like Labagh, were drawn to high-church ecclesiology—which may help explain the meager influence of John Nelson Darby on antebellum premillennialism in America.

Yet despite their differences, millenarians and Adventists shared a common set of concerns, used similar vocabulary, and invoked some of the same authorities. Such affinities won the millenarians both the wider public hearing and the heightened ecclesiastical censure afforded the Adventists. In the impassioned climate of the times, Labagh was promptly suspended for his millenarian views. He was not alone. The Scots Presbyterian John Lillie, who later served the millenarian cause as editor of the *Jewish Chronicle* from 1844 to 1848, gave a similar lecture before the same body in the same year and was tried for heresy by the New York presbytery.

Following his suspension, Labagh joined the Episcopal Church, where millenarian views had the backing of respected clergy like J. P. K. Henshaw, bishop of Rhode Island (*Inquiry into the Meaning of the Prophecies* [1842]), Edward Winthrop, rector of St. Paul's, Cincinnati (*Lecture on the Second Advent of the Messiah* [1843]), and George Duffield (*Dissertations on the Prophecies Relative to the Second Coming of Christ* [1842]). He was soon appointed rector of Calvary Episcopal Church, New York.[5]

Labagh wasted little time, publishing the first issue of *American Millenarian and Prophetic Review* in mid–1842. The stated purpose of the journal was to recover the prophetic passages of Scripture, which the editor felt was sadly neglected, and to promote the principle of interpretation, "literalism," by which those passages might be rightly divided. No set of the first volume exists, but it apparently began in the summer and was issued monthly in a newspaper format. The second volume, published in New York City beginning in June 1843, featured a new 8 1/2-by-5-inch pamphlet or journal format. Two reasons were given for the change. First, the new format made the publication better able to escape the ravages of time. Unlike newspapers, the more durable journals could be collected to form small reference libraries. Second, the new format made it easier to circulate a single issue among multiple readers. The *American Millenarian* was a "popular" journal, and it was expected that each issue would be passed from hand to hand, to friend or foe, to confirm or confound. Like other nineteenth-century journals, the *American Millenarian* was both a social and an ideological instrument. It served to consolidate and instruct the faithful, and it supplied the ammunition with which the faithful engaged their critics.

The layout of the journal was clean and without ostentation. Each number contained sixteen to eighteen pages of single-column text, with no illustrations. A page heading, in italics, announced the general theme of each page. The contents consisted largely of correspondence with the editor, editorial articles, and reprints of sermons and articles by British and American authors on millenarian themes. Authors often followed the pious custom of publishing articles without attribution or under clever pseudonyms. Each issue concluded with a list of the journal's agents and a list of other millenarian works available from the publisher. Later issues carried pleas from the editor that the one-dollar annual subscription fee, though due in advance, might at least be paid by volume's end. All of the issues were later collected in a single volume, which opened with maps of the ancient Holy Land, as it was divided by Joshua and as it would be divided in the Restoration, and with a map of the restored sanctuary drawn according to the prophecy of Ezekiel. The maps were followed by a comprehensive table of contents. No information on the number of subscribers was given, but Labagh listed agents in New York, New Jersey, Connecticut, Rhode Island, Massachusetts, Ohio, Pennsylvania, Tennessee, and Michigan.

Although Labagh abandoned his original goal of expanding to a bimonthly and then weekly publication schedule, he did project a third volume. This third volume was to be enlarged to thirty two pages per issue and sold for two dollars, double the previous subscription rate. It was to be essentially a republication in twelve parts of Old Testament expositions by Edward Irving. No evidence exists that the third volume was ever published in journal form. Labagh was by this time increasingly involved in the evangelization of Jews in New York City. He did, however, publish in book form in 1845 the collected expositions of Irving on which the third volume was to be based as *Interpretations of Old Testament Prophecies Quoted in the New, by a Celebrated English Divine.* The book was well bound, but printed on poor-quality paper. It consisted of spartan republication devoid of advertisement, epilogue, or attribution (Irving was only alluded to, not directly named). A brief prologue included the same maps attached to the beginning of volume two, mentioned above, and a title page with a brief byline for the editor, identified by name and described as a "Minister of the Protestant Episcopal Church and Missionary to the Jews." A note indicated that profits would support the mission to the Jews.[6]

In addition to his work promoting millenarianism and his involvement in the evangelization of Jews, Labagh was active in the organization of Episcopal churches in New Jersey and New York. In 1860 he moved to Illinois, where he established a female seminary and founded St. Peter's Church in Cairo. He then moved to Iowa, where he pastored St. Peter's Church, in Fairfield, until his death in 1879.

The British-American millenarianism espoused by Labagh and his journal can usefully be described as the confluence of three distinguishable interests of emphases: literalism, premillennialism, and Jewish evangelism and restorationism. The articles and correspondence appearing in the *American Millenarian* fall generally into these three categories.

The starting point in the logic of millenarianism was the hermeneutic of "literalism." Literalists felt that the interpretation of the Bible in general and of its prophetic passages in particular had been hindered by the age's tendency to look for a "spiritual" meaning behind the text. Millenarians called their adversaries "spiritualists" (a particularly misleading label after the Fox sisters' communications in 1848) and insisted that they were blinding the eyes of Christians to soon-coming events. At one level, literalists simply asked that students of the Bible apply to "unfulfilled" prophecy the same principle of interpretation that they applied to "fulfilled" prophecy (e.g., prophecies relative to the birth and death of Christ). But, in fact, a wide philosophical gulf divided literalists and "spiritualists." So at another level literalists asked their hearers to choose sides in an ideological conflict. This was especially clear in skirmishes between millenarians like George Duffield and "Professor [Moses] Stuart and his German authorities."[7] A staunch defender of orthodoxy, Stuart was a renowned biblical scholar who presaged the increasing influence of German idealism and the growing sensitivity to the symbolic or figurative aspect of religious language that Horace Bushnell expressed. As one contributor to the *American Millenarian* pointed out, "The spiritualist assumes a spiritual invisible state of things, peculiar to the mind and heart of men, and incapable of being expressed in any other than analogical or allegorical language, or, as Professor Stuart . . . has it, 'the world of mind,' in contradistinction from 'the world of matter.'" By contrast, the literalist insisted that "prophecy contemplates visible realities transpiring or to transpire as historical events in this world."[8] The language of prophecy had a literal reference to concrete events in the empirical world, where "mind" and "matter" joined in sensory experience.

What literalists defended was not crass materialism, as Stuart claimed, but rather the alliance among Calvinism, commonsense realism, and Baconian science. This was nowhere more clear than in the work of David Lord. Once beyond the stage of platitudes, literalists admitted that both literal and "tropical," or "figurative," passages existed in the Bible. The problem was met in determining which principle applied to which passage. Throughout the 1850s, David Lord followed careful scientific methods to unveil a formidable array of "Laws of Symbolization," which he sought to popularize in the *Theological and Literary Review* (1848–1861) and in his *Characteristics and Laws of Fig-*

urative Language (1857). Set in the context of his theory of the "verbal" and "plenary" inspiration of Scripture, his laws proved that Baconian science and commonsense realism could guide one between spiritualism and wooden literalism.

The second component in millenarianism was a complex scheme of eschatological events. This scheme, while inspired by eighteenth-century premillennialists like William Cuninghame, has been described above. The nature and sequence of events of the last days were not as clearly defined as they would be a generation later. But, as a rule, millenarians, drawing on their analysis of prophetic texts (preeminently Daniel, Ezekiel, and Revelation) expected the following events. The last days would witness the return of the Jews to Palestine. The first truly apocalyptic event, however, would be the "rapture of the Saints . . . to meet the Lord in the air." After this "first resurrection" had removed the righteous to safety and service in the Lord's heavenly army, the "great tribulation" would be visited on the earth. At the end of the great tribulation, Christ would return with his saints to conquer and reign over an earthly kingdom centered in a restored Jerusalem.[9] During the millennium, a restored Israel would inhabit a restored Jerusalem and worship at a restored temple. Jesus would serve as both king and high priest. At the end of the millennium. Satan would be loosed for a season to instigate the "last apostasy," which would be followed by the "last," or "general," resurrection, reserved primarily for the wicked, but also for some righteous ones who died during the millennium. The "total dissolution of the earth by fire" would follow, making ready for the last eschatological event: the establishment on the purged earth of an "everlasting, spiritual, material, and visible kingdom" that would never end.[10]

The antebellum millenarians also outlined a kind of protodispensationalism. It was certainly not as detailed as that being articulated later by Darby, but it generally differentiated between antediluvian, postdiluvian, Mosaic, Christian, and millennial "dispensations."[11] Furthermore, the threefold role of Christ (prophet, priest, king) was related to the dispensational framework: Christ ministered as prophet during his life in the old covenant dispensation. He mediated as priest during the present church dispensation. In the coming millennial dispensation he would reign as king.[12]

The third ingredient in antebellum millenarianism was an earnest commitment to the evangelization of Jews and to the success of Zionism. This agenda was derived from the perceived role of the Jews in these imminent eschatological events. Lewis Way in 1815 had founded in Britain the Society for Promoting Christianity among the Jews. In 1820, Elias Boudinot organized an American equivalent, the American Society for Meliorating the Condition of Jews. Boudinot's original organization quickly declined; but, fueled by the zeal of millenarians, interest in Jewish evangelism revived in the 1840s, and "Jews Societies" were organized throughout the East. Millenarians insisted that converted Jews be allowed to continue Jewish customs, including worship on the Jewish Sabbath and the keeping of Jewish feasts. In making their argument they appealed to the Jerusalem compromise of Acts 15 that, while not requiring Gentiles to keep the Mosaic law, did not require Jews to abandon it. Indeed, according to the millenarians, the ceremonial law would be revived during the coming millennium but with a commemorative or "retrospective," as opposed to a "prospective," reference.[13] By supporting the conversion of Jews and Jewish settlement in Palestine, millenarians were hastening that day.

Antebellum American millenarianism, then, was defined, not by theology strictly speaking, but by a hermeneutic added to a belief in specific eschatological events and combined with a particular missiological and political agenda.

American millenarians faced staunch opposition from well-respected quarters. The editors of *Bibliotheca Sacra, New York Observer*, and *Methodist Magazine and Quarterly Review* were among those who frequently took millenarians to task. But, as mentioned earlier, millenarians themselves matched the social and theological profile of their most distinguished opponents. They were generally well educated, and many were individuals of means. Joel Jones, coeditor of the *Literalist*, served as mayor of Philadelphia. Edward Lord, the brother of David Lord, was president of the New York and Erie Railroad. Denominationally their strength was centered in the same Calvinist-Episcopalian nexus that would prove so essential to postbellum premillennialism. Like their counterparts in Britain, they were part of a movement that drew its enthusiasts primarily from the social elite.[14]

But if millenarians resembled their critics, they also differed from them in important ways. For one thing, they were social pessimists in an age of optimism, and they found in their premillennialism the basis for a critique of progressivism and American triumphalism. They denounced postmillennialists who imagined that Britain and America were "destined to put every thing right that's wrong in the world." The redemptive role in these last days belonged not to "Laodicean Gentile churches on either side of the Atlantic" but rather to "THE RESTORED AND CONVERTED JEWISH NATION."[15] Nor were millenarians impressed by new inventions and technological progress. "Steamboats and railroads," declared one contributor, "are no test of the progress of a people in the only sound, we mean a *religious*, morality."[16]

Millenarians interpreted contemporary missionary success as another of the age-old cycles in which the light of the Gospel had waxed strong in region after region, only to be dimmed again. If more, it was a sign, not of a gradually approaching millennium, but of Christ's suddenly approaching premillennial return. The world would be converted only by the apocalyptic intervention of Christ. Until then the present world would remain "overspread with darkness, superstition, idolatry, anarchy, tumult, and war, under the empire of Satan, and the seat of the papal, the infidel, and the Mohammedan Antichrists."[17] Yet, millenarians insisted that their pessimism about human agency did not dampen missionary enthusiasm. Millenarians would zealously serve as God's instruments in the calling out of an elect people from every nation. Moreover, they argued that their realistic expectations would prevent the disillusionment awaiting those who expected "the peaceful and progressive conversion of the world."[18]

But if millenarians were out of step with nineteenth-century American excep-
tionalism, they were in step with contemporary calls for the ''higher life''—and
thus anticipated the alliance that would develop a generation later between dispensational premillennialism and the Holiness and Pentecostal movements. Millenarians called on Christians to pursue a deeper knowledge of divine things.
Having learned the rudiments of the Gospel, sufficient to salvation, the earnest
believer should seek the exalted and exalting purposes of God found in prophecy. Furthermore, millenarians were deeply influenced by the diffuse spirit of
Romanticism, which in its protean forms inspired belief in the supernatural and
aided premillennialism and high-church ecclesiology—and, thus, they drew a
ready connection between miracles and millenarianism.[19] They criticized mainstream evangelicals who removed miracles to the distant future or the distant
past, thereby making incredible the idea of an imminent resurrection of the saints
and return of Christ. Almost eighteen hundred years, they agreed, had passed
without any visible manifestation of God's power. But this only heightened their
expectation. When four thousand years of miraculous agency were placed
against the eighteen hundred years of its dormancy, wrote one millenarian, ''why
. . . should we count it a thing improbable, that . . . such visible intercourse and
agency should again commence, and be renewed before our sight?''[20]

In their own day, millenarians stood in the shadow of Adventists like William
Miller. In present historiography they stand in two shadows: that of the Adventists and that of the later dispensational premillennialists. Indeed, the tendency to equate antebellum premillennialism with Adventism has led to the
impression that dispensational premillennialism involved a sharp break with previous forms of premillennialism in America. On the contrary, in its British-
American constituency, its Reformed-Episcopalian matrix, its common sense
and Baconian presuppositions, and in the basic contours of its eschatological
doctrine, the community of discourse reflected in the *American Millenarian and
Prophetic Review* clearly prefigured the better-known premillennialism to come.

Notes

1. My description of the broader millenarian movement is based on Robert Kieran
Whalen, ''Millenarianism and Millennialism in America, 1790–1880'' (Ph.D. diss., State
University of New York at Stony Brook, 1972). Also helpful are the early chapters in
Ernest Robert Sandeen, *The Roots of Fundamentalism: British and American Millenar-
ianism, 1800–1930* (Chicago: University of Chicago Press, 1970).

2. Isaac P. Labagh, ''A Sermon on the Necessity of the Personal Return and Reign
of Christ on the Earth'' (New York, 16 February 1842), Jenks Collection of Adventual
Materials, Aurora University Library, Aurora, Illinois.

3. This is the term that Robert Whalen used to distinguish it from the better-known
millenarianism of the Adventists.

4 *American Millenarian* 2:3 (August 1842): 37.

5. See Sandeen, *Roots of Fundamentalism*, 55.

6. Information on *Interpretations of Old Testament Prophecies* is based on a corre-

spondence with Eleanor Wilson, Library Public Services, Bryan Wildenthal Memorial Library, Sul Ross State University, Alpine, Texas.

7. *American Millenarian* 2:2 (July 1843): 25.

8. Ibid., pp. 26–27.

9. The millenarians had also, therefore, made the distinction (often credited to Darby) between the rapture (the ascension of the saints) and the second coming of Christ, with his saints, to inaugurate the millennial kingdom. See *American Millenarian* 2:9 (February 1844): 134.

10. Ibid. 2:7 (December 1843): 99–104; 2:8 (January 1844): 118–119, 126; 2:9 (February 1844): 134; 2:10 (March 1844): 147.

11. Ibid. 2:5 (October 1843): 67; 2:11 (April 1844): 161–66.

12. Ibid. 2:4 (September 1843): 52ff.

13. Ibid. 2:8 (January 1844): 126; 2:11 (April 1844): 166–88.

14. D. W. Bebbington, *Evangelicalism in Modern Britain* (London: Unwin Hyman, 1989), 104.

15. *American Millenarian* 2:5 (October 1843): 77–78.

16. Ibid. 2:5 (October 1843): 79. The author, identified as ''J. L.,'' was probably John Lillie.

17. Ibid. 2:6 (November 1843): 95.

18. Ibid., P. 93.

19. Bebbington, *Evangelicalism in Modern Britain*, 81.

20. *American Millenarian* 2:3 (August 1843): 40; See also 2:8 (January 1844): 123. Among the signs of the last days there was to be the renewal of ''*the spirit of prophecy* and other miraculous gifts,'' only partially fulfilled on the day of Pentecost.

Information Sources

INDEX SOURCES: Volume 2 contains a detailed table of contents but no index.

LOCATION SOURCES: Volume 1 is apparently not in existence. Volume 2 is included in the American Periodicals Series 2, reel 1093, University of Michigan Microfilms. A copy of the collected expositions of Edward Irving, on which volume 3 was to be based, is held in the Aldridge Collection, Bryan Wildenthal Memorial Library, Sul Ross State University, Alpine, Texas.

Publication History

MAGAZINE TITLE: *American Millenarian and Prophetic Review* (1842–1844).

VOLUME AND ISSUE DATA: 1:1 (June?, 1842)–2:11 (April–May 1844). Published monthly, with a final double issue. A third volume may have been published.

PUBLISHER AND PLACE OF PUBLICATION: Isaac P. Labagh, New York, New York.

EDITOR: Isaac P. Labagh.

CIRCULATION: Unknown.

Roger Robins

AMERICAN NATIONAL PREACHER: OR ORIGINAL MONTHLY SERMONS FROM LIVING MINISTERS OF THE UNITED STATES. *See* NATIONAL PREACHER

AMERICAN SENTINEL. *See* LIBERTY

ARENA. *See* WALTHER LEAGUE MESSENGER

ARENA ONE. *See* WALTHER LEAGUE MESSENGER

ARMY AND NAVY MESSENGER: FOR THE TRANS-MISSISSIPPI DEPARTMENT

On 12 April 1861 the shelling of Fort Sumter began the bloodiest conflict in American history. The story of the Civil War is to be found not only in the military maneuvers, the bloody battles, the heroic and tragic leadership, and the incalculable destruction of property, but also in the everyday lives of civilians and soldiers. The hopes and fears and the beliefs and attitudes of civilians and soldiers are a large part of the story, too. Such information is often revealed in letters, journals, sermons, newspapers, and magazines. The *Army and Navy Messenger: For the Trans-Mississippi Department* was one religious magazine that arose during the conflict. From 15 September 1864 until 11 May 1865, the *Messenger* carried general news, reports on revivals, health advice, and spiritual direction for the soldiers of the Confederate armies.

Wars have a way of leading people to ponder life's significant questions. The destruction and loss of life associated with military conflict often results in a profusion of writings that justify one's cause by providing divine sanction for the task at hand. The Civil War was no different. The conflict resulted in a large production of literature, much of it religious in content. In the South, at least twenty-one religious magazines were published between 1860 and 1864. Of these, six served a unique function. They were religious magazines produced for the military personnel of the Confederate armies. These six religious papers grew out of the rising evangelical movement in the South. The Presbyterians printed the *Soldier's Visitor*; the Baptists, the *Soldier's Friend*; the Methodist Episcopal Church, South, the *Army and Navy Herald* and *Soldier's Paper*; and the Evangelical Tract Society, the *Army and Navy Messenger* and the *Army and Navy Messenger: For the Trans-Mississippi Department*. In addition to providing both religious and secular news for the Confederate armies, all of these magazines sought to offer spiritual guidance to the men in the battlefield.

Several organizations were founded for the specific purpose of providing literature during the conflict. The largest of these was the Evangelical Tract Society of Petersburg, Virginia. This interdenominational organization was founded at the beginning of the war for the express purpose of supplying the Confederate armies with religious literature. General Robert E. Lee donated one hundred dollars toward the establishment of the *Army and Navy Messenger*, believing that religious instruction for the troops was of paramount importance.[1] The result was the printing of the *Army and Navy Messenger*, which was to be shipped to all of the Confederate armies. It soon became apparent that shipment to the troops on the western front would prove difficult. Large quantities had been destroyed enroute by General William T. Sherman in Mississippi. Hence, the *Army and Navy Messenger: For the Trans-Mississippi Department* was formed. Modeled after the eastern counterpart, the *Army and Navy Messenger*, the first issue for the western front was published 15 September 1864 in Shreveport, Louisiana.

The editors, Reverend W. B. Norris and Reverend H. M. Smith, stated the goals of the paper in the initial issue of the *Messenger*: "We shall furnish information of the progress of the war; current intelligence; news of the doings of our enemies; religious army news; religious correspondence; selections from standard religious writers; for we desire to make it a religious paper, and above all things, to bring our friends in the army, that knowledge, which maketh wise unto salvation."[2] Like her counterparts, the editors of the *Messenger* saw their first task at hand as an evangelistic one. Brief articles like "You Are In Danger" and "Repent Ye" boldly proclaimed the need for each soldier to make peace with God. The call rang out, "Sinner awake and repent. There is safety in Christ. Arise and pray. Flee from the wrath to come. Turn to Christ and be safe."[3] Yet, as noted, these papers also served as the primary source of news and information for the men in the field.

The *Messenger* regularly carried reports on the revivals that were occurring throughout the armies of the South. Chaplains were requested to provide information of God's work because "these tokens of Divine presence and power, should not go unheralded and unsung. . . . Let them go upon the Record to the honor of the Lord and the benefit of all who love his name."[4] Every issue contained accounts of God's working among the men of valor. Such comments as the following graced the pages of every issue of the *Messenger*: "We baptized one hundred and forty-six—many of whom had been notorious for wickedness, many more were 'almost persuaded to be Christians.' . . . Never have I seen so great a work or more glorious results."[5]

The *Messenger* also included secular information. Each issue reported on the various campaigns then going on around the country. Using a variety of general headings like "Telegraphic Dispatches," "General Intelligence," and "Summer Campaigns," the troops were kept abreast of the latest military successes and defeats. If spreading the "good news" of the Gospel to the men was the stated goal, spreading good news in general was the underlying rule that dominated the pages of the *Messenger*. Building the morale of the Confederate armies was the essential, though seldom mentioned, job of the religious press. In the initial issue of the *Messenger*, W. B. Norris stated: "When engaged in a struggle for the cause of God and humanity, much depends upon the morale of the troops as demonstrated by facts in past history."[6] Not only were successes on the

battlefield trumpeted across the pages, but defeats were presented in a manner
that would lead one to believe that all hope was not lost. One way to do so was
to give a religious dimension to almost all the news published. To achieve this
goal, the *Messenger* painted the Confederate cause as part of a bigger picture
in history. The South was not simply fighting a war against the North for the
right to hold slaves. Rather, the Confederate cause was God's cause. The Confederate way of life was simply a reflection of God's design for the universe.
The organic concept of society, which was predominant in the South, focused
on relationships. Husband and wife, parent and child, ruler and ruled, master
and slave—all were part of a system designed by God. Different persons were
ordained to do different tasks, just as various cells in a plant perform specific
functions. It was God who created this type of universe, and it was God who
would ultimately sustain it.

The providential hand of God was a reassuring theme invoked in the *Messenger*. An early editorial stated: "The designs of God in His Providence in
regard to our country will surely be accomplished, which we believe to be our
independence and dignity as a people, and His own glory."[7] In the same issue
a chaplain concluded his exhortation to the men with these words: "May your
career be marked with consummate success, and [may] you live to be the instrument in the hands of a favoring Providence in rallying thousands of our
brave Soldiers to the blood-baptized standard of the 'Captain General' of the
sacramental hosts of earth's redeemed."[8] The will of a just and righteous God
who controlled the universe would surely come to pass. According to the *Messenger*, even the North should understand that God's laws and plan would not
be thwarted.

The laws of nature and the designs of Providence cannot be resisted, without suffering
the penalty of disobedience. Universal empire is impossible; and the union of hetero-
geneous nations, under one government, leads inevitably to disruption. . . . The people
of the North ought to have recognized God's hand in the secession of the Confederate
States, and consented to their peaceable withdrawal.[9]

God's providential plan favored the Confederacy because it best represented
Christian ideals. North and South would be separate because "this is the ordering of God's Providence, which forbids the permanent union of heteroge-
neous nations. Difference of institution, climate, and mental and moral
characteristics more than compensate for sameness of language and for the want
of a mountain chain division."[10] With such an understanding, even news of
defeat could suggest positive results.

The *Messenger* skillfully portrayed the "positive" aspects of defeat. Battlefield losses were not a result of the Union's superiority, but a sign of God's
care for the Confederacy as a nation. The God of the Confederacy wanted a
pure country to fulfill a sacred mission. Similar to Jehovah's chastening of the

nation of Israel through her enemies, God might chasten the Confederacy to build a righteous nation. Moral purity and virtue became themes that dominated the pages of the *Messenger* as the battlefield losses mounted.

The end of the war in God's providence, depends on ourselves; it is put pretty much in our own hands; we can hasten it, or postpone it just as we please. This, like all wars, must end sooner or later. If our soldiers are true and faithful, it must end soon. If they are undisciplined, insubordinate, careless of duty, indifferent to public morality and private rights, straggling, deserting, skulking from the service, the end of the war is a long way off; much longer than we like to think.[11]

Final victory was assumed as part of God's bigger plan, but the armies of the Confederacy could prolong the conflict by a behavior that was iniquitous. Hence, moral suasion became a central theme in the *Messenger*. "Providence will not suffer us to go down if we show a proper devotion, a proper wisdom, and a proper courage. Let our wise men plan, let our brave men fight, and let our good men pray. God will open up a way of escape for us and will disappoint our enemies. Let our faith not fail."[12] If defeat on the battlefield seemed to belie this notion of the Confederacy's being an ambassador of God's plan, it merely indicated that the South had room for moral improvement and that the cost would be well worth it. Victory was not to the many or to the strong but to those who did right. "And peace is the fruit of righteousness. It is not only necessary that our cause *be right*—of which we are fully assured—but that we *do right*, in order that we have immediate success. . . . The war will pay for its cost in blood by the elevation of character which it must bestow."[13] Defeat should not lead to despair, but to a desire to improve the righteous character of the South. A moral South would be a victorious South.

By the time of the publication of the 16 March 1865 issue, Atlanta had fallen, Sherman had completed his devastating "march to the sea," and Lee was only weeks away from surrendering to Grant. Defeat was at hand. Yet the pages of the *Messenger* offered words of encouragement to the troops: "Grant, Thomas and Smith have been whipped so often that we need not take them into the calculation. In South Carolina Sherman is confronted by an equal force with all the natural advantages on our side. Let Sherman be destroyed, and the supremacy of the Confederacy is [*sic*] established."[14] With the final defeat of the Confederacy, the *Messenger* ceased to exist. Yet until the final issue was published on 11 May 1865, the *Messenger* dutifully promoted the Confederate cause.

Notes

1. Gardiner H. Shattuck, *A Shield and Hiding Place: The Religious Life of the Civil War Armies* (Macon, GA: Mercer University Press, 1987), 49; Henry Smith Stroupe, *The Religious Press in the South Atlantic States, 1802–1865* (Durham, NC: Duke University Press, 1956), 43.

2. *Army and Navy Messenger: For the Trans-Mississippi Department* (15 September 1864): 1.
   3. Ibid. (16 February 1865): 2.
   4. Ibid. (15 September 1864): 2.
   5. Ibid. (29 September 1864): 2.
   6. Ibid. (15 September 1864): 1.
   7. Ibid. (29 September 1864): 1.
   8. Ibid. (29 September 1864): 1.
   9. Ibid. (16 February 1865): 1.
   10. Ibid. See also ibid. (2 March 1865): 2.
   11. Ibid. (15 September 1864): 2.
   12. Ibid. (16 February 1865): 2.
   13. Ibid. (29 September 1864): 1.
   14. Ibid. (16 March 1865): 2.

Information Sources

INDEX SOURCES: None.
LOCATION SOURCES: Most complete run is at University of Texas, Austin.

Publication History

MAGAZINE TITLE: *Army and Navy Messenger: For the Trans-Mississippi Department.* (1864–1865).
VOLUME AND ISSUE DATA: Published biweekly from 15 September 1864 through 11 May 1865.
PUBLISHER AND PLACE OF PUBLICATION: Evangelical Tract Society, Shreveport, Louisiana.
EDITORS: W. B. Norris (1864–1865) and H. M. Smith, (1864–1865).
CIRCULATION: Unknown.

Kurt Berends

AUGUSTANA. *See* LUTHERAN COMPANION

AUGUSTANA JOURNAL. *See* LUTHERAN COMPANION

AUGUSTANA, LUTHERSK KRYKOTIDNING. *See* LUTHERAN COMPANION

AUGUSTANA, OCH MISSIONÄNEN. *See* LUTHERAN COMPANION

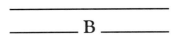

B

BACK TO GODHEAD

Airports, rock concerts, malls, highway rest areas, and other public places were common distribution points for *Back to Godhead*, the magazine of the Hare Krishna movement until the practice of *sankirtana* (public chanting, preaching, and literature distribution) began to decline in the late 1970s.

The first American issue was produced in the basement of a storefront on Manhattan's Lower East Side in 1966. The previous year, at age 70, the founder of the magazine and the Hare Krishna movement, His Divine Grace A. C. Bhaktivedanta Swami Prabhupada, arrived in New York from Calcutta, India. Determined to fulfill a mission given to him by his own spiritual guru, Prabhupada attempted to spread Krishna Consciousness throughout the English-speaking world. While in Calcutta, he discovered that one of the most effective ways of gathering disciples was through the distribution of religious literature. So he began *Back to Godhead*, published sporadically between 1944 and 1966, despite India's war-related paper shortage.[1] The first American issue of *Back to Godhead*—a simple, twenty-eight–page mimeographed and stapled piece—had a distribution of only one hundred copies.

Prabhupada described Krishna Consciousness as having four levels of faith. From the first publication, each issue of *Back to Godhead* sought to help readers attain the first two levels. The first level, the understanding one's relationship with Krishna, was especially prominent during the late 1960s and through the 1970s. The second level was to train individuals to love Krishna.[2] Recently, the magazine has emphasized this second level as readership has become more sympathetic to the faith.

At the first level, the magazine emphasized that every person is primarily spiritual, that a peaceful, blissful and fulfilled life can be found "if one seriously chants the Hare Krishna mantra and regularly reads *Back to Godhead*."[3] Because a goal of the movement is to get as many people chanting the mantra as possible, it appears in a prominent place within every issue, inviting the reader to chant, and thus begin one's relationship to Krishna. Every one of the early issues introduced the movement to uninformed readers.

As a primary tool for *sankirtana*, the magazine arose to its height of circulation in the 1970s when the founder referred to it as the ''backbone of the Krishna Consciousness movement'' (officially known as the International Society of Krishna Consciousness or ISKCON).[4] Circulation doubled each year from 1974 to 1976,[5] peaking near half a million.[6] If accurate, these figures place *Back to Godhead* in the top one hundred magazines distributed in the United States,[7] yet very few readers subscribed to the magazine in contrast to the numbers handed out for *sankirtana*.

Although the readership included devotees of the Hare Krishna faith, the target audience remained the individual on the street corner who would encounter a devotee through *sankirtana*. As a result, topics in the magazine frequently included meditation, existentialism, exegesis of Hare Krishna scripture, testimonies of converts, or philosophical discussions explaining why Krishna Consciousness is superior to other religions. Several articles condemned evolution[8] and told stories of Krishna and his appearances on earth.[9]

Although a page or two of ISKCON news appears in most issues, *Back to Godhead* never has intended to be a news magazine. It has served as a general and brief information source, not to take the place of other ISKCON news periodicals such as the *ISKCON World Review*. *Back to Godhead* has remained a philosophical magazine purporting its religious views. Any political reference, therefore, has always been discussed in a spiritual light. Discussions of current events have always turned to a spiritual agenda.[10] To show the superiority of Krishna Consciousness, the philosophies of such individuals as Jesus Christ, Thomas Aquinas, Søren Kierkegaard, and Plato have been discussed.[11]

With the death of the founder Prabhupada in 1977, the Hare Krishna movement found itself on the edge of turmoil while it struggled to reestablish under new leadership. Although never the magazine's editor, Prabhupada made crucial editorial decisions and set policy. His writings were the most frequently published, and still are, though now through book excerpts, lectures, and transcribed conversations.

The late 1970s brought new challenge to *Back to Godhead*. The anticult movement in the United States stirred distrust of *sankirtana*. Institutions formerly open to the movement, such as airports and county fairs, now sought legal means to close their doors. The movement fell out of favor in public opinion as the Hare Krishnas were often viewed as brainwashers and outright criminals.[12] *Back to Godhead* responded by reporting court victories and strongly refuting accusations of brainwashing.[13] One growing public image that *Back to Godhead* could not reverse was the perception that *sankirtana* was simply a money-making scheme. ISKCON, in fact, made considerable income from the sale of books and *Back to Godhead* and from other small businesses.[14]

Circulation began to drop off during these turbulent times for additional reasons as well. The publication fell as ISKCON discovered that small books were a cheaper way to put the views of Prabhupada before the public. The evolution of *sankirtana* made *Back to Godhead* less crucial in the process. In addition, when the first generation of Hare Krishna devotees began to have families of their own, less time would be given to traditional outreach practices. As a result *Back to Godhead* remained an effort to systematically propagate spiritual knowledge and attempted to promote Vedic culture as revealed in the *Bhagavad Gita* and *Srimad Bhagavatum*. It tried to promote a simpler life as it brought members of the society together with each other and Krishna.[15] Yet articles grew less philosophical, the writing easier to read, with more emphasis on holy writings and the general education of readers. Items such as Krishna recipes appeared, indicating the change in primary readership to those already sympathetic to the faith.

With changes in readership, a decline in circulation and an evolving format, Satsvarupa Goswami stepped down from his post as editor for health reasons. In 1989 Jayadvaita Swami, who had served as editor previously, again assumed the office. Faced with change, he deemed it necessary for the paper to take a sabbatical for a year ''so that we could improve our contents, pull our finances in order, and better organize our service to our subscribers.''[16] Reemerging in 1991, *Back to Godhead*, now with a drastically cut circulation, was for the first time subscription driven. It aimed for three audiences, each relatively equal in numbers: Hare Krishna devotees, members of the Indian community, and Westerners who, though not devotees, are sympathetic to Krishna Consciousness.[17] ''The audience focus has shifted from an emphasis on introducing the reader to Krishna Consciousness to appealing to those already interested.''[18] The goal had now completely shifted from the first level of Krishna Consciousness to the second.

The new *Back to Godhead* seeks to bridge the gap between devotees living in temple communities and those living in private homes. Articles emphasize how to live a natural life, how to practice Bhakti-Yoga at home, guidance for raising children, how to cook, how Krishna Conciousness applies to science, and what resources are available for those at home. It aims to help people distinguish between spiritual reality and distracting items of the world, and above all else it continues to present Krishna Consciousness as taught in *Bhagavad Gita* and *Srimad-Bhagavatum.*

Although originating from a mimeograph machine, *Back to Godhead* was soon in regular, color magazine format. Later editions brought about glossy paper and an easy-to-read layout. It appeared as a bimonthly from 1966 to the early 1970s, when it began to appear eleven times a year with thirty-two pages. When *Back to Godhead* reemerged in 1991, it doubled in size to sixty-four pages and became a bimonthly. Every issue of *Back to Godhead* includes a chapter from the *Srimad-Bhagavatum*, letters to the editor (and editorial responses), and a list of ISKCON Centers around the world.[19] Only official Hare

Krishna products and literature are advertised. *Back to Godhead* is always edited by a senior member of ISKCON, though it is not the official mouthpiece of the ISKCON ruling board. Every issue also contains the movement's motto[20] and calendar. Editorial guidance has come from the "Back to Godhead Handbook," a collection of quotations from Prabhupada, who said, "I will never die, I will live on in my writings."[21]

Notes

1. Umapati Swami, *Srila Prabhupada and His Magazine*, pamphlet printed by *Back to Godhead Magazine*, nd.

2. *Back to Godhead Handbook* (Philadelphia: Back to Godhead Magazine, nd.), 11.

3. *Back to Godhead*, no. 53 (1973): 1.

4. Ibid. 11:1 (January 1977): 1.

5. E. Burke Rochford, *Hare Krishna in America* (New Brunswick, NJ: Rutgers University Press, 1985), 174.

6. "ISKCON News," *Back to Godhead*, no. 60 (1973): 13. In addition, this issue reports that "Back to Godhead is now available in English, French, German, Spanish, Italian, Japanese, Gujarati, Chinese, Dutch, Swahili, and Bali." These issues seem to be in addition to the half-million English issues. In 1993 only an Italian edition was published.

7. Dan Golenpaul, ed., *Information Please Almanac, Atlas and Yearbook, 1977* (New York: Golenpaul, 1977).

8. For an example see Bali Mardan dasa, "Darwin's Mistake," *Back to Godhead* 10:10 (October 1976): 10–14.

9. For an example see Prabhupada, "The Birth of Lord Krishna," *Back to Godhead* 64 (n.d.): 3–9.

10. During the 1970s the energy crisis was discussed in a column entitled "Living in the Material World," *Back to Godhead*, no. 60 (1973): 16. In the same column in ibid., p. 28, Nixon's integrity was questioned. Later, during the Reagan years, the superiority of Krishna Consciousness was shown in Mathuresa dasa, "Star-Wars Pie," in ibid. 20: 12 (December 1985): 25.

11. For examples see "Christ Is Our Guru," *Back to Godhead* 20:12 (December 1985): 14, as well as Prabhupada and Emmanuel Jungelaussen, "Interview with a Benedictine Monk: Krishna or Christ Is the Same Name," *Back to Godhead* 11:3–4 (March-April 1977): 4–8. Aquinas is discussed in *Back to Godhead* 12:7 (July 1988): 5, and Kierkegaard in ibid. 12:11 (November 1988): 5. Similarities in Plato's thought to Krishna Consciousness are shown in Prabhupada and Syasundara, "Plato's Politics," ibid. 11:15 (May 1977): 4–8.

12. Rochford, *Hare Krishna in America*, 184–85.

13. *Back to Godhead* 12:5 (May 1988): 9.

14. Charles Lippy and Peter Williams, eds., *Encyclopedia of the American Religious Experience* (New York: Scribners, 1988), 2:693.

15. *Back to Godhead* 20:12 (December 1985): 1.

16. Jayadvaita Swami, "What Our Readers Have Told Us," Ibid. 25:1 (January–February 1991): 7.

17. Tamraparni Dasi, Subscriber Services Manager for *Back to Godhead*, interview with the author, 19 October 1993.

18. Letter from Arcida dasa to Carolyn J. Felix, 20 March 1992.

19. Although this column used to appear in every issue, it now appears only in the January–February and November–December issues because the number of centers has grown so large.

20. The motto that has appeared since the magazine's earliest days in Calcutta reads: "Godhead is light. Nescience is darkness. Where there is Godhead there is no nescience."

21. *Back to Godhead* 13:1–2 (January-February 1978): 1.

Information Sources

INDEX SOURCES: Many issues in the 1980s were author-indexed by the Back to Godhead office. Since reappearing in 1991, the publication is self-indexed in the December issue.

LOCATION SOURCES: Some of the early 1970 years are available on microfiche through University of Michigan. A near complete set is available through the movement's archives: Bhaktivedanta Book Trust Archives, P.O. Box 255, Sandy Ridge, North Carolina 27046.

Publication History

MAGAZINE TITLE: *Back to Godhead* (1944–present).

VOLUME AND ISSUE DATA: Approximately 28 issues published sporadically between 1944 and 1965. First American issue 1 (1966)–68 (December 1975) and 10:1 (January 1976)–24:10 (November 1989). Resumed publishing with 25:1 (January 1991), bimonthly through present.

PUBLISHER AND PLACE OF PUBLICATION: ISKON Press (1966–1971), Bhaktivedanta Book Trust (1971–1990) and Back to Godhead, Inc. (1990–present). Manhattan, New York (1966–1969), Boston (1969–1972), Brooklyn, New York (1973–1975), Los Angeles (1975–1979), Manhattan (1979–1981), Philadelphia (1981–1989), San Diego (1989–1993), Gainesville, Florida (1993–present).

EDITORS: Hayagriva dasa (1966–1967, 1969) and Rayaram dasa (1966, 1968), Satsvarupa dasa Goswami (1969–1974, 1977–1989), Jagannatha Suta dasa (1975–1976), Jayadvaita Swami (1974–1975, 1989–present).

CIRCULATION: 500,000 (1976); 12,000 (1994).

Christopher D. Hudson

BAHA'I MAGAZINE. *See* WORLD ORDER

BAPTIST. *See* CHRISTIAN CENTURY

BAPTIST BANNER. *See* WESTERN RECORDER

BAPTIST BANNER AND WESTERN PIONEER. *See* WESTERN RECORDER

BAPTIST BULLETIN

In January 1933, less than a year after formally organizing into an association, the leaders of a small group of fundamentalist Baptist churches needed a more efficient way of responding to a growing volume of correspondence. H. G. Hamilton, president of the fledgling association, stated that "our only apology for this publication is that so many letters come asking questions concerning this and that we thought it best to answer in this manner."[1] The reference was to a four-page publication, 8 1/2 by 10 1/4 inches, entitled the *Bulletin* and issued by the General Association of Regular Baptists (GARBC). It was edited by Hamilton and published from his church in Buffalo, New York. The masthead declared that the "object" was "to maintain a testimony to the supernaturalism of Christianity as opposed to the anti-supernaturalism of modernism." It was composed exclusively of printed matter: news from churches, regional associations, and mission agencies, as well as announcements of upcoming events and available publications. It also reprinted excerpts of varying length from past and present Christian writers.

In May 1933, at the second annual meeting of the association, "after some discussion it was voted to continue the publication of 'The Bulletin.' " Hamilton would continue as editor, though his term as president had expired. A resolution was passed by the gathering, expressing appreciation to Hamilton for his editorial work in connection with "our official organ, The Bulletin."[2] Still in publication, the magazine continues to serve the GARBC in that role.

The first volume, containing twelve issues, ran until February 1934. Apparently intended to be a monthly, the *Bulletin* was not printed if the association was "without sufficient funds to pay for the issue,"[3] which accounted for irregularity and delays. It was "distributed free of charge."[4] Beginning with the third issue (April 1933), occasional photographs were included.

The second volume—each issue still four pages long—bore the expanded name *Baptist Bulletin*. The page-one masthead declaration was altered,[5] reading "to maintain a testimony to the truth of the Bible as historically held by Baptists," thus further specifying its provenance.

In April 1934, Hamilton stated that "almost 2,000 people" received the publication. In October 1934, an appeal for contributions referred to the "several thousand copies" sent out each month.

In May 1935, two significant changes were made regarding the *Baptist Bulletin*. David Otis Fuller, pastor in Grand Rapids, Michigan, was appointed to the publication committee as editor in chief.[6] Furthermore, it was decided to place the publication on a subscription basis. The first issue under Fuller's editorship was distributed free, but announcements were included indicating that subscription rates would go into effect with the next issue. The price was fifty cents per year, reduced to twenty-five cents "in lots of 25 or more." By February 1936, there were 1,800 paid subscriptions.[7] Other changes were soon evident. The number of pages was increased, eventually reaching sixteen. The volume numbering started over, perhaps to mark the commencement of subscription financing. Above the name of the magazine, on page one, now appeared the slogan, "The Book, the Blood, the Blessed Hope," referring to the Bible, the crucifixion of Jesus Christ as the substitutionary atonement, and the personal return of Christ. A subtitle now indicated that the *Baptist Bulletin* was intended "for Bible-Believing Baptists." Issues regularly contained one or more photographs. For a time beginning in December 1935, the *Bulletin* devoted a full page to reprinting an illustrated serial drawn by Phil Saint for the *Presbyterian Guardian*, entitled "A Christian Goes to College," depicting the confrontation with modernism. Several issues between 1935 and 1938 reproduced editorial-style cartoons that graphically illustrated the threat posed by modernism, communism and/or fascism (and, in one case, by "marihuana"). Front covers were introduced for the third volume, then discontinued. During Fuller's term as editor, the *Bulletin* displayed the same aggressive, dramatic style that made him a leading figure in the GARBC for nearly sixty years. R. T. Ketcham succeeded Fuller with the July–August 1938 issue, and he remained until December 1944. He returned to the position with the December 1948 issue. Perhaps the most prominent and influential leader of the GARBC, Ketcham was a match for Fuller in aggressiveness, though he was less flamboyant. Ketcham had led local and state fundamentalist groups in Pennsylvania and Ohio and was instrumental in the establishment of the GARBC in 1932. He had been elected vice president (1933) and president (1934–1938) and would serve as national representative (1948–1960). The *Bulletin* was an important vehicle for Ketcham's exhortations to purity and service and his indictments of unorthodox theology and compromising alignments. In his introductory editorial, he promised biblical expositions (his own and others), "several pages of missionary material," and "a small section" ("Facts for Baptists to Face"), fulfilling the obligation of the publication "to let Baptists everywhere know the facts concerning the destructive work which Modernism is accomplishing in the ranks of the people called Baptists."[8] Ketcham also enlisted "an old time feature writer for a great newspaper syndicate," Barney Antrobus, an Indiana pastor, to contribute "four or five" pages each month. Antrobus was the first person of journalistic background to be associated with the *Bulletin*.

At the end of that issue, Ketcham noted, "We are not at all satisfied" with the *Bulletin*'s present state. "We may change the form of the paper and make several other changes in it." Ketcham lengthened it by eight pages (to twenty-four), introduced his previously promised features, and added a section ("Gleanings") containing news from the association's churches, edited by his assistant pastor R. F. Hamilton. In 1944, H. O. Van Gilder, from Portsmouth, Ohio, and long involved in national leadership of the GARBC, was appointed to the newly created post of national representative. He was appointed editor of the *Bulletin* as well (now with about three thousand subscribers). Ketcham and R. F. Hamilton assisted, and another Ohio pastor, George Bates, was enlisted to supply material that reminded older readers and informed newer readers of the continuing presence of theological forces inimical to traditional Baptist doctrines. This department addressed Van Gilder's concern that the passage of time and the "present happy circumstances" of the association's churches would lead people to forget the rationale for the establishment of the GARBC or to think that times had changed and conditions improved, removing the need for a separatist Baptist movement.[9] This concern was frequently expressed in later decades, as the GARBC entered its second and then third generation, increasingly fearful that its sons and daughters would fail to maintain its original stance. The *Bulletin* was a primary means for reasserting the GARBC's perspective in a changing religious landscape.

Van Gilder continued the practice, started in 1944, of devoting an issue to a listing of the association's churches and pastors. "The Yearbook Number" gradually lost its connection with the *Bulletin*, becoming a separate GARBC publication in 1952.

In 1948, Van Gilder resigned as national representative and *Bulletin* editor to assume a college presidency on the West Coast. Ketcham was selected to succeed him in both positions. In 1951, Larry Ward, a Wheaton College–trained journalist with several years' experience, was named managing editor and director of publications for the new Regular Baptist Press.[10] This milestone marked the advent of journalistic responsibility for the *Bulletin*. Ketcham's 1955 resignation ended the era of "pastoral editorship." Both of Ward's successors, Merle Hull (1955–1987) and Vernon Miller (1987–) were pastors by training and experience, but both turned to full-time journalism.

Ward highlighted individuals ("Meet our Baptist Laymen," "Pastor of the Month") and introduced features targeted for specific audiences ("Tips for Teachers," "Youth Page," "For Women Only"). A table of contents and a religious-news column were added. Improved printing technologies were employed.[11] The length had varied considerably, but in 1956 a thirty-two-page minimum was established.[12] The six thousand subscriptions of 1957 grew to thirteen thousand in 1958 and twenty thousand in 1962. Subscriptions would reach fifty thousand in 1973.

Numerous features have come and gone. Book reviews, (added by Van Gilder) remain, as do letters to the editor (a Ward addition). News from the churches and missionaries are a staple, as are reports and editorials on the wider religious scene. Now a four-color, thirty-two page publication, the *Baptist Bulletin* bears little resemblance to its 1933 forerunner.

There is considerable similarity in the purpose and the message, however, though with some developments. The stated "object" or "purpose" under H. G. Hamilton of maintaining "a testimony to supernatural Christianity" and "to the truth of the Bible as historically held by Baptists" was later enlarged by Fuller to "a three-fold aim."[13] In addition to maintaining "a testimony," he intended the *Bulletin* to inform constituents "of the conditions existing among Baptists both good and bad" and "to encourage, strengthen, and fellowship with . . . all Baptists everywhere" who had similar beliefs. Ketcham guided the publication according to a similar agenda, defending the "reading public's" "right to know" about the continuing apostasy.[14] Van Gilder wrote of his desire that the *Bulletin* be "helpful" to readers. As the GARBC grew, the help that was needed took additional forms. Under Ward, the *Bulletin* began to include material for churches who needed advice on the mechanics of designing and implementing a wide range of ministries. The *Bulletin* thus reflected the maturing of the GARBC, moving from "pioneering" to "settlement" orientation.

The message remained the same, with some important developments. "Historic Christianity" as articulated within a Baptist ecclesiology, with the addition of the premillennialism of the Bible Conference Movement (evangelical meetings for Bible study and spiritual renewal conducted at vacation sites in the East and northern Midwest) and affirmed with a militancy born of devotion to truth and opposition to error, to the GARBC necessarily implied a thoroughgoing ecclesiastical and personal separatism.

Initially the audience was composed of three, perhaps four, groups but had only two theological perspectives. On the one hand there were the "modernists." This term embraced a range of views, all unified by some variation from orthodoxy or at least by a minimizing of its importance. On the other hand there were those who affirmed orthodox Christianity (especially in its Baptist version) and opposed deviations. Three groups can be identified: churches in the GARBC, churches that had broken off all relations with the Northern Baptist Convention (NBC) but had not affiliated with the GARBC, and those that had not (yet?) left the NBC. The GARBC saw itself as the logical destiny of the other two groups and through the *Bulletin* regularly invited them.

If puzzled by the refusal of other separatist Baptists to join them, the GARBC through the *Bulletin* came to express opposition to those who espoused conservative theology but rejected the practice of ecclesiastical separation (the "new evangelicals" typified by Billy Graham from the early 1950s onward)[15] or—which was perhaps more frustrating—those who did separate, but not completely (most often represented by the Conservative Baptist Association, founded in 1947). As more positions appeared on the theological spectrum, the *Bulletin* enlarged its focus to include not only modernists but also conservatives who were not separatists of the correct form. Since the 1960s, doctrinal departure from orthodoxy within evangelicalism has been an increasing theme, accompanied by renewed warnings to watch for inroads of such drift among regular Baptists.

The *Bulletin* has consistently opposed the Roman Catholic Church, warning against its threat to religious freedom and truth. John Kennedy's 1960 presidential campaign called forth repeated declarations of the peril of Vatican domination. In this the *Bulletin* combined its anti-Catholicism with its political concerns. For most of the *Bulletin's* history, modernism and Catholicism joined with communism to form a threatening triumvirate. The *Bulletin* in various ways featured statements on the pressing social and political issues, predictably and explicitly aligned with the Right.[16] A notable exception was the editorial support for the 1962 Supreme Court ruling against governmentally imposed prayer in schools, though the next year's ban on voluntary prayer and Bible reading was strenuously opposed. The *Bulletin* also published the frequent GARBC resolutions in favor of "social concern" and "social responsibility" and advocated ministries for the disadvantaged and inner cities.

In all of this, the *Baptist Bulletin* in its role as official organ of the GARBC has exemplified the convictions of the fundamentalist Baptists who publish it, who both herald their gospel to the unbelieving culture and also sound the alarm of that culture's encroachments on the Church.

Notes

1. *Bulletin* 1:1 (January 1933): 1.
2. Ibid. 1:4 (June 1933): 4.
3. *Baptist Bulletin* 2:5 (July–August 1934): 4; ibid. 2:11 (May 1935): 4.
4. Ibid. 2:2 (April 1934): 2.
5. For its first appearance, see ibid. 2:5 (July–August 1934): 1.
6. Ibid. 1:1 (June–July 1935): 7.
7. Ibid. 1:7 (February 1936): 12.
8. Ibid. 4:1 (June 1938): 1.
9. Ibid. 10:9 (February 1945): 5.
10. Ibid. 17:2 (July 1951): 6.
11. Ibid. 17:4 (September 1951): 2.
12. Ibid. 21:10 (March 1956): 28.
13. Ibid. 1:1 (June–July 1935): 2.
14. Ibid. 10:8 (January 1945): 1.
15. For one of the first published criticisms of Graham, see ibid. 18:5 (October 1952): 4.
16. Ibid. 28:2 (July 1962): 18; ibid. 30:5 (October 1964): 7.

Information Sources

INDEX SOURCES: No general index has been compiled. A partial index to each volume, 33–37, is published in the following volume, in the October or November issue.
LOCATION SOURCES: The Historical Commission of the Southern Baptist Convention, 901 Commerce Street, Suite 400, Nashville, Tennessee 37203–3260, has a nearly complete microform of the *Bulletin* and the *Baptist Bulletin*.

Publication History

MAGAZINE TITLE AND TITLE CHANGES: *Bulletin* (1933–1934), *Baptist Bulletin* (1934–present).
VOLUME AND ISSUE DATA: Issues 1:1–2:11 (old series, 1933–1935) were published

irregularly. Issues 1:1–3:10 (1935-1938) (June-July, August-September combined) were published ten times per year. Issues 4:1 (July–August 1938)–4:10 (May 1939), 5:1 (June 1939)–37:12 (May 1971) were published monthly, including yearbook issues (1944–1952) published separately and in different formats. Eleven issues have been published per year from 1972 to present (August combined with July).

PUBLISHER AND PLACE OF PUBLICATION: General Association of Regular Baptist Churches: Buffalo, New York (1933–1935); Grand Rapids, Michigan (1935–1938); Gary, Indiana (1938–1939); Waterloo, Iowa (1939–1945); Chicago, Illinois (1945–1965); Des Plaines, Illinois (1965–1976); Schaumburg, Illinois (1976–present).

EDITORS: H. G. Hamilton (1933–1935), D. O. Fuller (1935–1938), R. T. Ketcham (1938–1945, 1948–1955), H. O. Van Gilder (1945–1948), Merle Hull (1955–1987), Vernon Miller (1987–present); managing editors: D. W. Gillespie (1937–1938) and Larry Ward (1951–1955).

CIRCULATION: 31,000 (1992).

Stephen R. Spencer

BAPTIST MISSIONARY MAGAZINE

Under various titles, the *Baptist Missionary Magazine* was the premier voice for Baptist missionary endeavors for more than one hundred years. In addition to its function as the principal instrument of missionary intelligence for American Baptists, the magazine was also a primary catalyst in the formation of the Baptist denomination in the United States. It strongly advocated the organization of the General Missionary Convention of the Baptist Denomination in the United States of America for Foreign Missions, the first Baptist body to embrace a national constituency.

Indeed, an abruptly inherited foreign missionary program brought the autonomous and often disparate Baptist congregations into formal association. In 1812, three American Congregationalists named Luther Rice, Adoniram, and Ann Judson accepted the Baptist principle of believer's baptism upon their arrival in India. Consequently unable to serve the Congregationalist cause in the Indian mission, the Judsons pushed on to Burma, while Rice returned to the United States and sought financial support. Rice found a zealous ally in Thomas Baldwin, pastor of Boston's Second Baptist Church, president of the Massachusetts Baptist Missionary Society, and editor of the *Massachusetts Baptist Missionary Magazine*. Baldwin discerned in the sudden conversions of the Judsons and Rice a providential stimulus for American Baptists. "The important question now comes up," Baldwin queried in the pages of his magazine, "Shall we support these two brethren, or must they be compelled to give over their mission, and return without having made an attempt to save the perishing souls of the heathen?"[1] With Baldwin's influential endorsement, delegates from various state conventions met in Philadelphia in 1814 and established the general convention to support the Burma mission. In 1817, the convention sanctioned Baldwin's journal, and ten years later adopted it as an official organ, a position it held until its merger with other journals in 1909 that resulted in a new periodical entitled *Missions.*

Baldwin began the *Massachusetts Baptist Missionary Magazine* in 1803 as the journal for the Massachusetts Baptist Missionary Society. For fifty cents per year, subscribers received an assortment of missionary reports and reprints from British publications that described the nascent efforts of New England Baptists to evangelize the Northeast and recounted the budding British Baptist missionary enterprise in India. The report of Judson's conversion appeared in 1813; and during the following year, the magazine led the clamor for a national missionary organization.

In 1817 Baldwin renamed the journal the *American Baptist Magazine and Missionary Intelligencer,* added Daniel Sharp and Thomas Winchell to the editorial staff, and began a bimonthly publication schedule. The principal objects of this new series of the magazine were to "propagate religious intelligence, and promote a Missionary spirit."[2] In addition to missionary letters (most of them from the Judsons) and articles in support of missions, the magazine printed notices of the "Ordination of Ministers, the Constitution of Churches, and the Opening of New Meeting-houses, with many other interesting facts . . . which otherwise might be irrecoverably lost."[3] Following its endorsement that same year by the convention, circulation jumped to ten thousand, a 150 percent increase in subscribers; Baldwin reprinted the initial numbers to supply requests for complete volumes.[4] In 1819, as the result of an increased subscription price to 75 cents per year, the journal contributed its first profits to the missionary venture.

The days of affluence, however, came to an abrupt close. When the new series began publication, it was the only Baptist periodical published in the United States and enjoyed for a time the largest circulation of any American magazine;[5] but by 1820 competition from other publications had increased to where subscriptions began a rapid decline. The 1821 annual report of the Baptist Missionary Society of Massachusetts called attention to this concern and appealed for increased circulation. The value of the magazine, according to the report, lay not only in its function as "a vehicle of authentic and interesting religious intelligence" but also in its annual contribution of five hundred dollars "clear profits" to the mission society.[6] In 1825, in an effort to answer charges that a recent rate increase to one and a half dollars per volume was simply too high, the format of the journal was changed: the title was shortened to the *American Baptist Magazine,* it became a monthly, and engravings and a new typeface were introduced. The first advertisements also appeared. Nevertheless, the journal continued to experience financial trouble and the appeals for increased subscriptions continued throughout the nineteenth century.

Another blow to the magazine occurred in August 1825 when Baldwin died unexpectedly while on a trip to Maine. The loss of Baldwin's management skills plunged the magazine into a period of editorial instability, even though such scholarly and capable men as Francis Wayland and Lucius Bolles had assumed Baldwin's mantle. The board of managers of the general convention, which assumed full control of the magazine in 1827, could not secure adequate funding for the position of editor; Bolles was the first of many editors who also served in the capacity of corresponding secretary for the board. For this double duty, the board originally appropriated one thousand dollars, but almost immediately reduced this sum (to five hundred dollars) and the profits, if any, from the magazine.[7]

The difficulty in obtaining sufficient subscribers to keep the magazine financially viable led to various changes in format, ownership, and pricing. In 1829, coverage was broadened with "articles adapted to promote the interests of Christian truth and piety," edited by Irah Chase and H. J. Ripley, while all missionary correspondence was relegated to the "Missionary Register," edited by Ensign Lincoln, which appeared at the end of each number.[8] Chase and Ripley resigned after only one year, and a new format was adopted in 1833 with smaller type and larger pages. More departments, such as "Literary Notices" of recent books, became regular features, while mission news continued to be segregated into the "Register." But in 1836, the board eliminated all articles and features except missionary news and intelligence, lowered the subscription price to one dollar per year, and renamed the journal the *Baptist Missionary Magazine* to reflect its new focus. Circulation briefly improved, but plunged again after a few years to less than five thousand.

Despite its meager circulation, the magazine remained for Baptists a convenient digest of denominational information. In addition to presenting sermons promoting the cause of missions and the sometimes tedious missionary diaries and letters (one 1846 article asked readers not to complain of missionary correspondence that contained "little else than a dry detail of labors performed with comparatively small success"[9]), the magazine was the principal depository of the official records of the general convention and its board. But even during the years in which it was limited primarily to missionary intelligence, the journal presented fascinating, though not impartial, glimpses of nineteenth-century life at home and abroad in "graphic, and frequently minute descriptions of the geography, government, religion, and manners of the countries" to which Baptist missionaries had gone forth.[10] Commentary about the growing mid-century tensions among American Baptists, however, was sparse and limited primarily to official resolutions outlining the neutral position of the board on the question of slavery and other "irrelevant" issues.[11] The "Alabama Resolutions," which brought the issue of slavery to a head, and the subsequent formation of the Southern Baptist Convention, received only reserved notice in the magazine without any attached editorial comment.

For the first time in decades, the magazine turned a profit in 1848, even though circulation continued to decline and the price remained unchanged. By the following year, the convention abandoned the hope that the journal would again produce sufficient profits for missionary undertakings and seemed satisfied to see it become self-supporting. This change in official attitude may have influenced another title change in 1850, this time to the *Missionary Magazine*, although the format remained unaltered. From then until the end of the century, circulation languished at about five thousand, while the editors agonized over what to do to boost subscriptions. "We are aware that, in the estimation of many, [the magazine] is not sufficiently miscellaneous and popular in its character to secure general attention," wrote Jonah G. Warren in 1868. "But the problem is how to popularize it without destroying its essential character; how to adjust it to the taste of those who seek after novelty and excitement, and still make it a faithful reflector of missionary life, is one of very difficult solution."[12] Finally, in 1871, the editors instituted radical changes in format and appearance that remained essentially unchanged though often improved for the next four decades. The volume for 1871 identified itself as the initial volume, the old numbering system was also maintained, and the new series designation disappeared altogether in 1873 when the title reverted back to the *Baptist Missionary Magazine*.

The most significant alterations to the format and design came during Edmund F. Merriam's tenure as editor (1800–1901). Engravings increasingly gave way to halftones; new typefaces, graphics, and printing methods were introduced (linotyping began in 1895); new departments were added; and a new rate scale was inaugurated that offered substantial savings for "club" orders (as low as thirty-five cents per volume). During 1882, each number of the magazine also contained an issue of the *Helping Hand*, a periodical published for the newly created Women's Missionary Union. In an article celebrating the magazine's centennial in 1903, Merriam claimed that he had been the first to introduce to a missionary journal an "attractive make-up and a liberal use of cuts" after the policy of "popular secular magazines," which had since been "imitated by nearly all the leading missionary periodicals of America."[13] Merriam's strategy worked; circulation slowly began to rise, and the magazine unabashedly printed letters of praise from readers such as the North Scituate, Massachusetts, pastor who wrote that "the printing is elegant; the matter is interesting and instructive; the illustrations are numerous and exceedingly helpful." One speaker at a missionary conference referred to the journal as "chapters in the modern acts of the apostles," and another pastor commented, "I would not do without the Magazine if it cost $3.00."[14]

Throughout its history, the magazine promoted its usefulness as a source of information for the "missionary concerts of prayer" held on the first Sunday evening of each month in local churches, but only with the 1886 volume did there appear as a regular monthly feature a suggested program for how the magazine could be best used for these gatherings. Popular demand brought about an increase in personal news about missionaries, and a new motto—"Missions Made Interesting"—appeared in 1903. That same year, the magazine celebrated its centennial, the first American periodical to pass the century mark.[15] Merriam contributed a short article on the journal's history in which he observed that the magazine "performed a great work in making Baptists acquainted with each other's toils and trials, hopes and triumphs, and more than any other agency served to prepare the Baptists of this country for the united action which resulted in the formation of the General Missionary Convention at Philadelphia 18 May 1814, which event marks the birth of the Baptist Denomination as a body in the United States."[16] But only six years later, the venerable journal was combined with *Home Mission Monthly* and *Good Work* to form a new journal entitled *Missions*. It was "a passing only in name," argued the final editor S. R. Warburton, but in fact America's oldest religious periodical had passed into history.

Notes

1. *Massachusetts Baptist Missionary Magazine* 3 (September 1813): 335.
2. *American Baptist Magazine and Missionary Intelligencer* 1 (January 1817): 3.
3. Ibid. 3 (January 1821): 4.
4. Ibid. 1 (July 1817): 160.
5. Neal L. Edgar, *A History and Bibliography of American Magazines* (Metuchen, NJ: Scarecrow, 1975), 65, 93–94.
6. *American Baptist Magazine and Missionary Intelligencer* 3 (July 1821): 142. The contribution from the journal represented about 25 percent of the society's annual budget.
7. *American Baptist Magazine* 7 (June 1827): 174. As a pastor in Salem, Massachusetts, Bolles had an annual salary of twelve hundred dollars.
8. Ibid. 9 (January 1829): 5–8.
9. Ibid. 26 (November 1846): 342.
10. Ibid. 24 (December 1844): 352.
11. See, for example, ibid. 21 (June 1841): 153–60.
12. *Missionary Magazine* 48 (July 1868): 217.
13. *Baptist Missionary Magazine* 83 (December 1903): 749.
14. Ibid. 78 (February 1898): 83; ibid. 82 (March 1902): 85; ibid. 79 (March 1899): 88.
15. Edgar, *American Magazines*, 93.
16. *Baptist Missionary Magazine* 83 (December 1903): 748.

Information Sources

INDEX SOURCES: Each volume contains its own index. Volume 63 (1883) contains a cumulative index of major topics for 1803–1883.

LOCATION SOURCES: A complete file is available in the archives of the American Baptist Board of International Missions, Valley Forge, Pennsylvania. A microfilm edition is available in the American Periodical Series II (American Periodicals 1800–1850), University Microfilms International, Ann Arbor, Michigan, 48106.

Publication History

MAGAZINE TITLE AND TITLE CHANGES: *Massachusetts Baptist Missionary Magazine* (1803–1816), *American Baptist Magazine and Missionary Intelligencer*

(1817–1824), *American Baptist Magazine* (1825–1835), *Baptist Missionary Magazine* (1836–1849), *Missionary Magazine* (1850–1872), *Baptist Missionary Magazine* (1873–1909). Merged with *Home Mission Monthly* and *Good Work* to form *Missions* (1910).

VOLUME AND ISSUE DATA: *Massachusetts Baptist Missionary Magazine* 1:1 (September 1803)–4:12 (December 1816); originally published semiannually, later three times a year, then quarterly with triennial volumes. *American Baptist Magazine and Missionary Intelligencer* 1:1 (January 1817)–4:12 (November 1824); published bimonthly with biennial volumes. *American Baptist Magazine* 5:1 (January 1825)–15:12 (December 1835), *Baptist Missionary Magazine* 16:1 (January 1836)–29:12 (December 1849), *Missionary Magazine* 30:1 (January 1850)–52:12 (December 1872), *Baptist Missionary Magazine* 53:1 (January 1873)–89:12 (December 1909); published monthly with annual volumes.

PUBLISHER AND PLACE OF PUBLICATION: Baptist Missionary Society of Massachusetts, Boston, Massachusetts (1803–1826); Board of Managers of the Baptist General Convention, Boston, (1827–1845); Executive Committee of the American Baptist Missionary Union, Boston (1846–1909).

EDITORS: During the periods when the magazine lacked a full-time editor, one or more of the secretaries of the board assumed editorial responsibilities, thus causing some confusion in dating. Full and part-time editors included Thomas Baldwin (1803–1825), Francis Wayland (1826), Lucius Bolles (1826–1836), Solomon Peck (1836–1841, 1847–1854), Ebenezer Thresher (1842–1846?), Samuel Francis Smith (1854–1881), Jonah G. Warren (1867–1872), George W. Gardner (1873–1876), John N. Murdock (1876–1881), Edmund F. Merriam (1880–1901), Fred P. Haggard (1901–1909), S. R. Warburton (1909).

CIRCULATION: 4,000 (1816), 10,000 (1821), 5,000 (1858), 8,000 (1871), 13,000 (1901).

Rodger M. Payne

BAPTIST WORLD. *See* WESTERN RECORD

BEAUTY OF HOLINESS. *See* GUIDE OF HOLINESS

BIBLE SOCIETY RECORD. *See* AMERICAN BIBLE SOCIETY RECORD

BOSTON PILOT. *See* PILOT

BRIDAL CALL

The *Bridal Call* is an integral part of the fascinating story of the life and work of evangelist Aimee Semple McPherson. Born in 1890 in southern Ontario and reared amid the colorful and earnest spiritual intensity of the early Salvation Army, McPherson lived in the United States from 1911 until her death in 1944. Her evangelistic activities began in 1915. By 1920, the largest auditoriums in the United States and Canada could not hold the crowds that gathered to hear her simple evangelical message and to have her pray for physical healings. The *Bridal Call* was the tool that McPherson used to mold her scattered, diverse following into a constituency. The publication gave McPherson's followers identity and purpose, called them to partnership through prayer and giving, and brought them sermons and testimonies that nurtured their faith. Most importantly, the publication bridged the considerable gaps among McPherson's followers and forged them into a recognizable, viable group.

The first *Bridal Call* (subtitled *Pentecostal Monthly*) was a four-page sheet published in June 1917 in Savannah, Georgia. For three months, a supporter, F. A. Hess, printed the paper, and McPherson with a few willing helpers prepared copy and addressed and mailed several thousand issues. In September 1917, the Christian Workers Union, a publishing concern in Framingham, Massachusetts, began publishing the *Bridal Call*. In addition to publishing tracts, pamphlets, and a magazine called *Word and Work*, the Christian Workers Union operated a mission, a faith home, and camp meetings in the area. It was the hub of a busy nondenominational network, and McPherson's access to that network increased her visibility and the support for her efforts.

McPherson was fascinated with biblical marriage themes. She chose the name *Bridal Call* from the Song of Solomon 2:10: "Rise up my love, my fair one, and come away." McPherson placed these words in the mouth of Christ, the bridegroom, calling for his bride, the Church. She used the verse as the magazine's motto and printed it under the masthead on the cover. In April 1918, she changed the motto to Revelation 22:17: "The Spirit and the Bride say Come, and let him that heareth say Come." These verses and the title of the magazine captured McPherson's sense that she lived in the last days and that Christ was calling humankind to prepare quickly to meet him.

From September through December 1919, the *Bridal Call* was sixteen to twenty pages long. Each issue contained one photograph, printed on the cover. Often it pictured McPherson or the tents that she used for preaching. Until June 1918, both Aimee Semple McPherson and her husband, Harold McPherson, were listed as editors. They separated in 1918, however; and after June 1918, Aimee Semple McPherson was sole editor.

The *Bridal Call* was printed in double columns. Each issue included transcripts of McPherson's sermons, advertisements for her publications, testimonies from her meetings, announcements of future meetings, and articles by others whom she deemed helpful in nurturing her followers in their understanding of her theme verse, Hebrews 13:8: "Jesus Christ, the same yesterday, and today and forever." The first subscription rate was twenty-five cents per year. Bundles for distribution cost two cents per issue, or twenty-five cents for twenty copies.

The magazine had two forthright purposes: to forge McPherson's disparate following into a constituency and to evangelize. Most articles invited readers to experience the content about which they read—to be saved, healed, or baptized with the Holy Spirit. In time, each issue contained at least one article on each of the themes that constituted McPherson's primary message: Jesus the Savior, baptizer with the Holy Spirit, healer, coming king. She called these four points the "Foursquare Gospel."

In January 1920, McPherson moved publication of the *Bridal Call* to Los Angeles. She had arrived there in December 1919 and had decided to locate in the city. She began publishing the *Bridal Call* herself and made several changes in its appearance. Instead of featuring a photo of herself or her tent, the cover featured a table of contents in the form of a placard supported by two angels under an illustration of the second coming of Christ. She printed photographs of meeting sites and crowds in each issue. The issues generally exceeded twenty pages. The subscription price rose to a dollar per year.

In June 1921, McPherson introduced her *Bridal Call* readers to an ambitious project that tested the strength of the network that she had carefully built. She described her plans to construct the Echo Park Revival Tabernacle and invited her readers to contribute. She was not only raising money, however; she was also intentionally distributing a sense of ownership, and she always carefully acknowledged publicly and profusely her gratitude to the thousands of readers who kept in touch only through the pages of the *Bridal Call*. Lists of many who gave were published each month, and the magazine carried pictures of the building plans. *Bridal Call* readers gave generously: When the church (known as Angelus Temple) opened its doors in 1923, the contributors had given money for general construction, the purchase of chairs, and the completion of one of the Temple's elegant stained-glass windows.

The November 1923 issue of the *Bridal Call* was the last that appeared on paper that was roughly 10½ by 7 inches. McPherson did not publish a December 1923 issue. The January 1924 issue introduced readers to a new format, a new title, and a new list of contributors. With the January 1924 issue, the *Bridal Call* became the *Bridal Call Foursquare*. Printed on larger stock (11¼ by 8 inches), it also introduced brightly colored glossy covers featuring art work inspired by the seasons of the year. McPherson generally found a way to picture Angelus Temple somewhere in the mix. McPherson still edited the magazine, and she still wrote much of the copy, but she also featured the work of some of the Foursquare personalities who helped her realize her dreams in Los Angeles. Notable among these was Frank Thompson, a retired Methodist pastor from Rochester, New York, who was best known for his publication of the *Thompson Chain Reference Bible*. Thompson retired to Los Angeles, where he became a faculty member at McPherson's thriving Bible institute, the Lighthouse of International Foursquare Evangelism (LIFE).

The alterations in the format of the *Bridal Call* reflected significant changes in McPherson's career. Although she still traveled extensively, she was committed to an ever-increasing number of projects in Los Angeles: the Temple, its branch churches, her Bible school (which quickly attracted some one thousand students), a radio station, publications, and, by the late 1920s, a commissary that organized the Temple's outreaches among the economically and socially dispossessed. All of these endeavors demanded money, and the *Bridal Call*'s role as promoter of her dreams was more important than ever. After 1926, when rumors of scandal hounded McPherson after her widely publicized six-week disappearance, the magazine also served as the vehicle through which she vindicated herself and her ministry. And as graduates of her Bible school extended her efforts, the magazine devoted more coverage to the work of the growing number of branch churches in the United States and missionary work elsewhere. As McPherson's work assumed a more denominational character, the *Bridal Call* did too. Throughout the 1920s, the *Bridal Call Foursquare* was available at newsstands around Los Angeles.

After a decade as the *Bridal Call Foursquare*, on 4 July 1934 the magazine title was changed to the *Foursquare Bridal Call Crusader*. Published on newsprint, the magazine no longer sported glossy colorful covers. Perhaps reflecting financial constraints related to the Depression, the magazine was shorter and was printed in three columns. Published weekly on Wednesdays, it was more of a newspaper than the *Bridal Call Foursquare* had been. It still carried sermons, but it also provided information written as news updates, with date and place lines and short headings. McPherson remained editor and publisher, but she wrote fewer of the articles. The magazine focused increasingly on news from the branch churches and the mission fields. It also promoted events at Angelus Temple and McPherson revivals. To help with the cost of publication, the magazine carried advertisements from Los Angeles area businesses alongside missionary news and Bible studies.

The final edition of the *Foursquare Bridal Call Crusader* was published in December 1935. With the 1 January 1936 issue, the title was shortened to *Foursquare Crusader*, a title that lasted until June 1944, when it was changed to *Foursquare Magazine*. In January 1939, the magazine became a monthly again, and it has remained a monthly since.

Aimee Semple McPherson died in September 1944. Her son, Rolf McPherson, replaced her as head of the International Church of the Foursquare Gospel and as editor in chief of the *Foursquare Magazine*. He retained those roles until his retirement in 1988, when he was replaced by John R. Holland. Under Rolf McPherson's supervision, in September 1964, the *Foursquare Magazine* became the *Foursquare World Advance*, the title that it carries today. Its circulation around the globe in 1993 was 98,000.

Information Sources

INDEX SOURCES: There is no index to the *Bridal Call.*

LOCATION SOURCES: There are no known copies of the first three issues of the *Bridal Call.* The best collection, although incomplete, is at the Heritage Center of the International Church of the Foursquare Gospel. For information, contact International Church of the Foursquare Gospel, Founders' Ministries, 1100 Glendale Boulevard, Los Angeles, California 90024.

Publication History

MAGAZINE TITLE AND TITLE CHANGES: *Bridal Call Pentecostal Monthly* (June 1919–November 1923), *Bridal Call Foursquare* (January 1924–June 1934), *Foursquare Bridal Call Crusader* (July 1934–December 1935), *Foursquare Crusader* (January 1936–May 1944), *Foursquare Magazine* (June 1944–August 1964), *Foursquare World Advance* (September 1964–present).

VOLUME AND ISSUE DATA: It has been published monthly, with some early numbers (before 1923) published together; it was published weekly from July 1934 to December 1935.

PUBLISHER AND PLACE OF PUBLICATION: F. A. Hess, Savannah, Georgia (June–August 1917); Christian Workers Union, Framingham, Massachusetts (September 1917–November 1919); Aimee Semple McPherson, Los Angeles, California (1920–1944); International Church of the Foursquare Gospel, Los Angeles (October 1944–present).

EDITORS: Coeditors Aimee Semple McPherson and Harold McPherson (June 1917–June 1918), Aimee Semple McPherson (1920–1944), Rolf McPherson (1944–1988), John R. Holland (1988–present).

CIRCULATION: 98,000 (1993).

Edith Blumhofer

BRIDAL CALL FOURSQUARE. *See* BRIDAL CALL

BRIDAL CALL PENTECOSTAL MONTHLY. *See* BRIDAL CALL

BRIDGE: THE WALTHER LEAGUE. *See* WALTHER LEAGUE MESSENGER

BULLETIN. *See* BAPTIST BULLETIN

C

CAMPUS LIFE

"Geared to the Times, But Anchored to the Rock" was the motto of Youth for Christ, a key organization in the "new evangelical" movement that arose during the 1940s. That same motto is useful as a thumbnail description of *Youth for Christ Magazine* and *Campus Life*, the periodicals that the movement spawned. Trendy in style and subject matter but conservative in theology, *Youth for Christ Magazine* and *Campus Life* have, since the mid–1940s, provided evangelical teens entertaining reading, counsel, and a bridge to the larger evangelical subculture.

Youth for Christ (YFC) emerged from a series of scattered fundamentalist youth rallies that sprang up independently in various cities, including Detroit, Indianapolis, New York, and St. Louis, during the late 1930s and early 1940s. Led by youthful evangelists dissatisfied with the ossified routines of traditional revivalism, the rallies emphasized lively music, silly skits, contests, and fiery preaching. Encouraged by each other's successes and bombarded with requests from across the country to organize similar programs, leaders began informal association and cooperation during 1944. In January 1945 a temporary committee met in Detroit to discuss future organizational possibilities. At that meeting the committee authorized the publication of *Youth for Christ Magazine* (hereafter *YFCM*).

The committee chose Clyde Dennis, a Chicago printer, as the first editor. *YFCM* inherited its title and a subscription list of about eight hundred from Roger Malsbary's Indianapolis-based YFC organization. Dennis's appointment was only temporary, and within a few months Ken Anderson, a young writer who specialized in fiction, replaced him. In 1946 the magazine took over the subscription list of Philadelphia-based *Youthcast* magazine. With this addition and a new subscription rate of about three hundred per month, the magazine was on solid-footing by 1947, serving as the primary product of YFC's Chicago-based youth publications department.[1]

In its early years, the digest-sized magazine served mainly as a YFC organ. Its glossy pages and abundant photographs were filled with the comings and goings of YFC leaders and reports on rallies and activities in various cities across the country. Special evangelistic thrusts overseas, like a YFC blitz of Cuba in early 1949 and YFC refugee work in Europe, received a particularly prominent place, as did the early successes of ex-YFC evangelist Billy Graham.[2] Periodically, special constituencies such as servicemen and prominent concerns like YFC's role in the local church were put in a special issue or in a "YFC Symposia."[3]

What is perhaps most surprising about the tone and content of *YFCM* in its early years, especially in light of its later direction and incarnation as *Campus Life*, was its peculiarly adult bearing. Into the early 1950s, *YFCM* was virtually indistinguishable from mainstream fundamentalist/evangelical periodicals like *Moody Monthly*, *King's Business*, or *Sunday School Times*. Neither its layout nor articles, centering on Christian service, conversion stories, and missions, made much concession to its youthful audience. Its only distinguishing mark was a predilection toward fiction of the type that editor Anderson hoped to make a more viable presence in the evangelical community. Short fiction pieces like "Miracle in Ward Six" (about a death-bed conversion) and "One Yard Short of Pay Dirt" (Laz Marlbough, star fullback for Cotters Valley High School encounters Christ) were regular features that one was hard pressed to find in less "frivolous" evangelical periodicals of the *Moody Monthly* stripe.[4]

As the 1950s moved on, however, it was increasingly clear that *YFCM*'s focus was changing. Symbolic of America's cultural move to the suburbs, YFC moved its headquarters in 1953 to the western Chicago suburb of Wheaton. Later that same year, Mel Larson took over as managing editor as Ken Anderson became an associate editor and moved into a new career as a Christian filmmaker.[5] *YFCM*'s graphics became flashier, and in July 1954 the magazine moved to a larger format. While it still devoted a good deal of space to local YFC chapters (Hi-School Clubs), rallies, and campaigns, its appeal gradually broadened. This was most noticeable in *YFCM*'s attempt to identify with the interests, pastimes, and fads of the wider American youth culture. Articles about revivals, missions, and evangelism decreased in number. In their place were features on Christian filmmaking, Christian sports heroes such as pole vaulter Bob Richards and UCLA quarterback Donn Moomaw, and born-again media celebrities like Roy Rogers and Redd Harper, star of Billy Graham films.[6] Also indicative of the new thrust of *YFCM* in the 1950s were articles like "Baby Sitting for Christ," "Can a Christian Kid be Popular?" and "Acne—Youth's Mysterious Enemy," aimed at teens' day-to-day concerns and social insecurities.[7] There was also a conscious effort to protect young people from the rise of juvenile delinquency and the attendant assault on evangelical moral, social, and entertainment taboos. Parking, petting, dancing, drinking, and smoking were all targeted as dangers.

Alternative goals and behavior for *YFCM* readers came in articles on marriage and career alternatives and in a YFC campaign to supplant the high-school prom with its own banquets.[8]

The late 1950s and early 1960s saw relatively frequent turnover in *YFCM*'s leadership. Mel Larson stepped aside as editor in early 1958 and was replaced by Vernon McLellan, an editor for the Assemblies of God periodical entitled *Christ's Ambassadors Herald*. McLellan moved on in late 1959, his place taken by associate editor Warren Wiersbe. In early 1962, Ron Wilson, previously the editor of *Moody Monthly*'s "Youth Supplement," became *YFCM*'s fourth editor in four years when Wiersbe left to accept a pastorate in Covington, Kentucky. Through the mid-1960s the magazine's content remained focused on white, suburban, middle-class teenage life. Relationships between the sexes were frequent topics in articles like "Should We Have a Minimum Dating Age?" and "There Is a Way to Dump Her Gracefully."[9] "Letters on Loveliness," a column by Charlene Johnson, gave fashion and grooming tips for teenage girls that supplemented features like "Expert Advice on How to Keep Your Hair Pert and Pretty."[10] For male readers, there were features on Christian athletes such as football's Raymond Berry and Bill Glass and baseball's Bobby Richardson and Albie Pearson.[11] The major exception to the otherwise upbeat tone was a grim, foreboding brought on by a new spate of articles that reflected the heightened tensions of the Cold War. Sandwiched between articles such as "Pointers for Good Punting" and "The Case for Chastity," *YFCM* readers found stories with titles like "Mistletoe and Missiles," "Teen-Age Fanatics Who Want to Kill America" and "Watch Out for Communists on Campus."[12]

The year 1965 marked a major turning point for *YFCM*. In January of that year, Sam Wolgemuth, former director of YFC's overseas operations, became the organization's new president. Wolgemuth wanted to broaden YFC's appeal beyond its comfortable niche within the evangelical subculture. As part of his plan, he put Ron Wilson in charge of an effort to create a South American YFC magazine and appointed Harold L. Myra as *YFCM*'s new editor. Myra, a young, scholarly Presbyterian, had been with *YFCM* as an associate editor since 1961, shortly after his graduation from college. To bring *YFCM* up to date, he promptly introduced four-color covers and photographic spreads, used more photos with professional models, and began including more travel, adventure, and hobby articles. In line with YFC's recently adopted name for its high-school clubs, the magazine's name changed in late 1965 to *Campus Life*. But, YFC connections became almost an afterthought as the magazine increasingly became a general-interest, Christian, teen magazine.[13]

More profound changes became evident in content. Topics for articles were indicative of the severe crises that plagued American culture during the turbulent 1960s and early 1970s. Drug use and the sexual revolution came in for much criticism in articles like "Freakout" and "Sex without Hang-Ups." Myra's bolder, more open-minded approach often produced articles that no other evangelical magazine of that time would have dared to print, including a debate on the "Playboy Philosophy" between Hugh Hefner associate Anson Mount and a YFC staffer.[14]

YFCM sidestepped civil rights and the problem of racism until late 1964 when Ron Wilson made the decision to begin including pictures of black teens mingling with whites and articles dealing with racial prejudice. Under Myra, *Campus Life* continued the more open stance, despite criticism from local YFC directors who claimed that the articles would hurt fund raising and local church support. In the following years *Campus Life* went out of its way to feature whole issues on racism, articles by black evangelists and youth workers, and fiction dealing with racial themes.[15]

The war in Vietnam and the divisive backlash it unleashed in the United States also figured prominently in the pages of *Campus Life*. Given the constituency's conservative, patriotic bent, coverage into the mid–1960s was understandably supportive, featuring articles that documented missionaries' and chaplains' efforts, what draftees might expect in basic training, and Christian teens' experiences in the war. As the war dragged on, however, the attitude changed to one of marked ambivalence; positive articles were gradually balanced by Myra's troubled editorials, real-life tales of maimed and killed GIs, and articles like "They Watch in Terror as We Burn," a reprint of a soldier's letter describing a raid on a suspected Viet Cong–controlled hamlet.[16]

The countercultural Jesus Movement moved center stage in the early 1970s. Despite its tendency to anti-intellectualism and the specter of growing "Jesus-mania" in the larger culture as evidenced in pop vehicles like "Jesus Christ Superstar" and a tide of "Jesus" merchandising, the editors were strongly supportive of the movement. Positive articles like "Middle America Meets the Jesus Freaks" and a look at Jesus rocker Larry Norman were given prominent berth.[17] More importantly, the rise of the Jesus People and their attendant championing of "Jesus Rock" signaled the vindication of *Campus Life*'s approach to the world of popular music. Through the mid–1960s, the magazines mirrored the larger evangelical subculture's negative attitudes toward rock 'n' roll, in teen panel discussions such as "Is Rock 'n' Roll on the Way Out?" and articles like "Rock 'n' Roll: Music or Madness?"[18] The editors apparently realized, however, that music was too large a force in the youth culture to ignore. Beginning intermittently in 1954, the magazine published record reviews in columns like "Platter Chatter" and "Spins and Needles," touting a sanctified alternative in albums by gospel euphonium soloists and in collections of the hymns of Fanny Crosby. By 1962, *YFCM* was sponsoring "Platter Parties" for small groups of teens who would rate records like Ralph Carmichael's "Hymns at Sunset."[19] The more progressive-minded Myra, however, backed off from the antirock stance. In the spring of 1967, he authored "The Sound!" a bold article that featured a young man listening to the Beatles' "Revolver" album and weighing the merits of each song. The protagonist's decision to "sift out the bad, just like in books and TV . . . to evaluate music, performers, lyrics, to be aware of innuendos . . . cut out what keeps him from becoming what he wants to be" became the new credo of *Campus Life*.[20] Lyrics and references to rock groups and songs began to appear more frequently. With the rise of the Jesus Movement, "Jesus Rock" and its successor "Contemporary Christian Music" became a fixture in the magazine.

In 1975, Harold Myra moved on to become the president and CEO of Christianity Today, Inc. Under Myra's tutelage, *Campus Life*'s circulation had grown from 30,000 to 160,000, and the magazine's outreach stretched far beyond its original YFC constituency. Philip Yancey, managing editor since 1971, took over the reins as editor. Through the balance of the 1970s and into the 1980s, *Campus Life* reflected the times in both the evangelical subculture and American society more generally with a shift toward personal, therapeutic concerns and a decreased emphasis on broader social ills. The successful formula that balanced humor, adventure, teen issues, and entertainment with advice columns for general ("I Never Promised You a Disneyland," "Person to Person") and sexual (Tim Stafford's "Love, Sex, and the Whole Person") problems carried circulation over the 200,000 mark by the late 1970s.[21]

Despite these successes, the late 1970s and early 1980s proved to be a stressful time for the magazine. The most serious problems were inflation and constantly rising postal rates. Under pressure to meet expenses, yearly subscription rates rose from $8.95 to $14.95 between 1978 and 1982 and the price per copy doubled from $1 to $2. The magazine began accepting advertisements from sources such as the Columbia Record and Tape Club that, along with its coverage of secular and Christian rock, drew heavy fire from some in its constituency.[22] Leadership was also a problem. Yancey, whose 1977 book *Where Is God When It Hurts?* had drawn critical and sales success, decided to concentrate on freelance writing in 1979 and stepped back from most of his duties. During the next year and a half the key positions at *Campus Life* shuffled back and forth with Steve Lawhead and Gregg Lewis alternately in charge until Lawhead's departure in early 1980 to begin a record company.

Spurred by the twin problems of finance and leadership, YFC brought Yancey back as vice-president of publishing during the summer of 1980. Finances continued to be a problem, however, with questions raised within the editorial staff and within YFC about the relation between *Campus Life* and YFC and the magazine's future direction. On 1 November 1981 *Campus Life* became an independent publishing concern "affiliated with Youth for Christ" with Yancey as publisher and Lewis as editor.[23] This situation proved short-lived because of continuing financial problems, and in mid-1982 the magazine was purchased by former editor Harold Myra's Christianity Today, Inc., thus becoming the third magazine in what would be a powerhouse stable of evangelical periodicals.[24]

The new arrangement provided the financial and administrative equilibrium that *Campus Life* needed, stabilizing subscription rates for over a decade and trimming excess circulation. Additionally, there emerged a steady editorial team that remained intact into the 1990s under Gregg Lewis, Jim Long, Christopher Lutes, and Ruth Senter. *Campus Life* maintained its position as the premier evangelical youth magazine into the 1990s, an era of declining demographics for youth as part of the overall American population. Advice, teen fiction, splashy photo features, colorful graphics, and an emphasis on music and entertainment continued a predictable, but winning, format that went back over a quarter of a century. While *Campus Life* was still directed toward white, middle-class kids, an undercurrent of Christian compassion and social responsibility pervaded the magazine in features like "Making a Difference."[25]

YFCM and *Campus Life* represent a major shift in evangelical attitudes toward youth culture in the post–World War II era. Its pages document not only a revolution in evangelicals' attitudes toward recreation and entertainment but also a remarkable shedding of traditional prohibitions against worldly amusements. Despite these changes, the magazines represented more than evangelicalism's enslavement to larger cultural norms. They functioned as an influential voice for traditional notions about the Bible, morality, piety, and service for evangelical youth bombarded by an ever-multiplying array of contrary messages. Overall, *YFCM* and *Campus Life* are and continue to be a testimony to the flexibility and energy that make evangelicalism an enduring force within American cultural life.

Notes

1. Mel Larson, *Youth for Christ: Twentieth-Century Wonder* (Grand Rapids, MI: Zondervan, 1947), 84, 95.

2. John A. Huffman, "Cuba Invaded!" *YFCM* 7:1 (April 1949): 50–53, 70–74; Mabel Moore, "Refugee Work Continues Unabated," *YFCM* 7:2 (May 1949): 54–55, 58. For examples of coverage of Billy Graham's activity, see Billy Graham, "I Tasted Revival!" *YFCM* 7:10 (January 1950): 10–13, 79–80. Most issues during 1950 devoted a great deal of coverage to Graham and to other reports of revival happening across the country.

3. "YFC and the Local Church," *YFCM* 10:2 (May 1952): 28–37. The May 1953 issue of *YFCM* was a special "Serviceman's Issue."

4. Carroll E. Kennedy, Jr., "Miracle in Ward Six," *YFCM* 7:6 (September 1949): 12–14; Christopher Sarby, "One Yard Short of Pay Dirt," *YFCM* 7:7 (October 1949): 14–16, 52–54.

5. *YFCM* 11:9 (December 1953): 5.

6. See, for example, Mel Larson, "Pole Vaultin' Parson [Bob Richards]," *YFCM* 10:3 (June 1952): 16–21; Donn Moomaw, "Life Is Like Football," *YFCM* 11:7 (October 1953): 12–16; Redd Harper, "Real Talk from Real Life," *YFCM* 11:10 (January 1954): 16–19; "Who's Who in Religious Films," *YFCM* 11:10 (January 1954): 31–37; Mel Larson, "In God's Corral [Roy Rogers]," *YFCM* 11:11 (February 1954): 37–39; "Wheaton's All-American Burnham Scores in Classroom and Pulpit, Too," *YFCM* 12:8 (November 1954): 8–9; Mel Larson, "Forging Ahead on the Film Frontier," *YFCM* 13:3 (June 1955): 18–21, 42.

7. Robert A. Cook, "Can a Christian Kid Be Popular?" *YFCM* 11:11 (February 1954): 18–24; Paul de Kruif, "Acne—Youth's Mysterious Enemy," *YFCM* 15:3 (July

1957): 21–22; Hazel B. Howard, "Baby Sitting for Christ," *YFCM* 15:9 (February 1958): 19–20.

8. See, for example, Connie Doyle, "Christian Youth Answers Kinseyism," *YFCM* 12:1 (April 1954): 35–38; William J. McDermott, "Why Be a Stink-O? [antismoking]" *YFCM* 13:4 (August 1955): 10–12; William J. McDermott, "Guard That Brain of Yours [antialcohol]," *YFCM* 13:7 (October 1955): 12–14; Jack Hamilton, "Parkin' and Pettin'," *YFCM* 14:12 (April 1957): 16; Jim Smith, "Well, What About Dancing?" *YFCM* 15:5 (September 1957): 11, 33; Dwight H. Small, "The High Cost of Petting," *YFCM* 16:4 (September 1958): 6–7. For a look at YFC's attempts to counter the popularity of high-school proms, see "It's Reception Time," *YFCM* 12:2 (May 1954): 14–15.

9. Dave Richardson, "There Is a Way of Dumping Her Gracefully," *YFCM* 20:3 (August 1962): 13; "Should We Have a Minimum Dating Age?" *YFCM* 20:9 (February 1963): 28–31.

10. Marian Hamon, "Expert Advice on How to Keep Your Hair Pert and Pretty," *YFCM* 20:10 (March 1963): 38–39. Charlene Johnson's "Letters on Loveliness" column ran monthly from April 1962 until mid–1970.

11. See, for example, Mel Larson, "Flingin' Francis [Fran Tarkenton]," *YFCM* 17: 12 (May 1960): 12–13; Mel Larson, "World's Greatest Athlete [Rafer Johnson]," *YFCM* 18:5 (November 1960): 18–19; "Christian All-Star Team [baseball]," *YFCM* 20:5 (October 1962): 9–11; Franklyn Miller, "Two Persistent Pros [Raymond Berry and Don Shinnick]," *YFCM* 21:5 (October 1963): 22–24; Jim Hefley, "Mighty Little Angel [Albie Pearson]," *YFCM* 23:3 (August 1965): 11–13.

12. See, for example, Dave Breese, "Mistletoe and Missiles," *YFCM* 16:7 (December 1958): 10–11; Ted W. Engstrom, "Watch Out for Communists on Campus," *YFCM* 18: 11 (April 1961): 34–35, 39; Dave Foster, "Could You Bear Brainwashing?" *YFCM* 19: 9 (February 1962): 19, 32, 36, 38; Gordon McLean, "A Communist Leader Talks," *YFCM* 20:1 (June 1962): 6, 36–37; "Teen-Age Fanatics Who Want to Kill America," *YFCM* 20:3 (August 1962): 10–12, 24–25; "When the Commies Hold a Youth Conference," *YFCM* 20:6 (November 1962): 11–13.

13. *YFCM* 22:10 (March 1965): 4–5; James Hefley, *God Goes to High School* (Waco, TX: Word Books, 1970), 86–87, 90.

14. See, for example, C. A. Roberts, "Sex and the New Sophistication," *Campus Life*, 24:6 (November 1966): 8–10; Gordon R. McLean, " 'Turn On—Tune In—Drop Out,' " *Campus Life* 25:1 (June 1967): 44–46; Dean Merrill, "Junkie!" *Campus Life* 25:3 (August 1967): 6–11, 15, 26; Larry Christenson, "Psychedelic Christmas," *Campus Life* 25:7 (December 1967): 6–9, 22; Larry Richards, "God Made Something Beautiful," *Campus Life* 27:4 (November 1969): 12–25. For the debate between the *Playboy* and *Campus Life* philosophies, see the February 1969 issue, 18–31.

15. The first articles that tackled racial issues in *YFCM* were by Larry Fuhrer, "Prejudice and the Christian Teenager," 22:4 (September 1964): 18–20, 29; and by Joyce Starks, "I Want My Rights for Christmas: An Interview With a Negro Teenager," *YFCM* 22:7 (December 1964): 10–11. In subsequent years, *Campus Life* featured a number of articles on racial issues and themes. For example, see Bill Pannell, "The Real Race Issue," *Campus Life* 24:6 (November 1966): 26–27; Tom Skinner, "The Roughest in Harlem," *Campus Life* 24:9 (February 1967): 52–54; Phyliss Naylor, "Seven Scenes From the Life of Willie John Prather," *Campus Life* 25:11 (April 1968): 12–14, 25; "Blue Eyes," *Campus Life* 26:3 (August 1968): 4–5; Jack Olson, "The Black Athlete: A Cruel Deception [reprinted and condensed from *Sports Illustrated*]," *Campus Life* 26:

6 (November 1968): 26–37; " 'Poverty': Are You Sure You Know What It Is?" *Campus Life* 26:7 (December 1968): 28–30; Reynaldo Murazzi, "The Latins around You," *Campus Life* 27:5 (December 1969): 18–21; Dean Merrill, "Indian," *Campus Life* 28:8 (March 1971): 66–69. The June–July 1969 issue of *Campus Life* was specifically devoted to the problems of racism.

16. Many Vietnam-related articles that appeared in *Campus Life*, especially the early articles, were positive in nature. For example, see Sam Wolgemuth, "The Highest Badge of Courage," *Campus Life* 23:12 (May 1966): 32–33; Don Mardock, "And the Training . . ." *Campus Life* 24:1 (June 1966): 10–11; Sam Wolgemuth, "Saigon Interview," *Campus Life* 24:2 (July 1966): 22–23, 25; Ken Overstreet, "For Teen Men Only" column, *Campus Life* 24:2 (July 1966); Ken Overstreet, "For Teen Men Only" column, *Campus Life* 24:6 (November 1966); Phil and Louie Palermo, "From Saigon to Ban Mé Thuot," *Campus Life* 26:3 (August 1968): 34–38. Increasingly this sanguine view changed, as evidenced in such articles and editorials as "Laughter in the Morning," *Campus Life* 25:3 (August 1967): 16–17; Harold Myra, "Is Vietnam a Good Thing?" *Campus Life* 26:3 (August 1968): 3; Chaplain Ray Johnson, "Postmark: Mekong Delta," *Campus Life* 26:5 (October 1968): 8–14, 82–85; "They Watch in Terror as We Burn," *Campus Life* 26:6 (November 1968): 52–53; Harold Myra, "It Ought to Hurt," *Campus Life* 27:8 (March 1970): 26–30; "Campus Life Forum on Vietnam," *Campus Life* 28:1 (June–July 1970): 3–6; Harold Myra, "Evil in the USA," *Campus Life* 28:2 (August–September 1970): 21–25; Darcy Miller, "How Can I Wish You a Merry Christmas?" *Campus Life* 28:5 (December 1970): 20–21.

17. The first articles that publicized the Jesus Movement in *Campus Life* appeared in early 1970: "Good Vibes Penetrate the New Left/Good Vibes Penetrate the Rose Bowl Parade," *Campus Life* 27:8 (March 1970): 20–22, 51. See also "Middle America Meets the Jesus Freaks," *Campus Life* 29:1 (June–July 1971): 12–17, and Donna Day and Thomas Diggs, "Travelin' With Jesus," *Campus Life* 29:1 (June–July 1971): 18–20; Philip Yancey, "The Norman Sound of Jesus Music," *Campus Life* 29:2 (August–September 1971): 58–61; Bob Cording, "The Son Worshippers," *Campus Life* 29:6 (January 1972): 58–62; "Will Exuberant Jesus Freaks and Traditional Churches Collide?" *Campus Life* 29:7 (February 1972): 8–10, 12; Bob Combs, "Genuine, Natural-Grown Electronic Music Man ["Jesus dj" Scott Ross]," *Campus Life* 30:6 (December 1972): 60–62, 64–66. *Campus Life* editors were not naive about the problems of trendiness that the Jesus People presented. For example, see "See Us on TV!" *Campus Life* 29:1 (June–July 1971): 62.

18. For a look at *YFCM*'s treatment of the subject of rock 'n' roll, see such articles as Gunnar Urag, "Singing in the Holy Spirit," *YFCM* 14:12 (April 1957): 26–27; "Blessing or Blasphemy?" *YFCM* 15:3 (July 1957): 11; Marlin "Butch" Hardman, "Rock n' Roll: Music or Madness?" *YFCM* 16:5 (October 1958): 10–12; Norman E. King, "Teen-Age Idol Worship," *YFCM* 16:10 (March 1959): 6–7; Marlin "Butch" Hardman, "The Real Scoop on Rock 'n' Roll," *YFCM* 17:5 (October 1959): 10–12; "The Last Time I Saw Elvis," *YFCM* 17:10 (March 1960): 4–5; "YFC Teen Panel: Is Rock n' Roll on the Way Out?" *YFCM* 17:10 (March 1960): 14–15. Many within evangelicalism were still uncomfortable at this point with the idea of lush, orchestral scores and instrumentation for sacred music; see Thurlow Spurr, "Mr. Music," *YFCM* 18:8 (February 1961): 43.

19. For examples of record reviews see "Platter Chatter," *YFCM* 17:2 (July 1959),

and "Mr. Music" column, *YFCM* 19:11 (April 1962): 33. For an account of a "Platter Party," see *YFCM* 20:5 (October 1962): 28–29.

20. Harold Myra, "The Sound!" *Campus Life* 24:11 (April 1967): 42–46. For other examples of *Campus Life* use of secular rock with an eye to spiritual benefit see "The Sounds of Music," *Campus Life* 26:8 (January 1969): 12–19, 34–40; Dave Foster, "Cliff Richard—Number One!" *Campus Life* 26:12 (May 1969): 20–26; Dave Jackson, "Rock From Nazareth," *Campus Life* 27:7 (February 1970): 55–60. After the early 1970s, record reviews and articles dealing with rock and Christian rock stars become regular features of *Campus Life*.

21. Circulation information cited in biographical sketches of Harold Myra and Philip Yancey is available from Christianity Today, Inc., Carol Stream, Illinois.

22. Regarding these troubles, see "A Special Message to the Friends of CAMPUS LIFE," *Campus Life* 39:4 (October 1980): 9, and "Time to Celebrate!" *Campus Life* 41:1 (July–August 1982): 22.

23. See "40 Years and Counting," *Campus Life* 40:9 (April 1982): 50.

24. Stephen Board, "Moving the World With Magazines," in *American Evangelicals and the Mass Media*, ed. Quentin J. Schultze (Grand Rapids, MI: Zondervan, 1990): 130–31.

25. For example, see "Making a Difference," *Campus Life* 45:7 (February 1987): 44–46.

Information Sources

INDEX SOURCES: There is currently no indexing information available.

LOCATION SOURCES: The early volumes of *Youth for Christ Magazine* are rare. The best collection is located at Bob Jones University in Greenville, South Carolina. Other good collections are those at the Billy Graham Center Library, Wheaton College, Wheaton, Illinois, and at the Moody Bible Institute in Chicago. *Campus Life* magazine is available rather widely. Issues since 1972 are available on microfilm from University Microfilms, Ann Arbor, Michigan.

Publication History

MAGAZINE TITLE AND TITLE CHANGES: *Youth for Christ Magazine* (1944–1965), *Campus Life* (1965–present).

VOLUME AND ISSUE DATA: *Youth for Christ Magazine* 1:1 (1944)–23:4 (September 1965). *Campus Life* 23:5 (October 1965–present). Published monthly, except during the summer; ten issues a year.

PUBLISHER AND PLACE OF PUBLICATION: Youth for Christ, Indianapolis, Indiana (1944); Youth for Christ, International, Chicago, Illinois (1945–1953); Youth for Christ, Wheaton, Illinois (1953–1975); Youth for Christ, Carol Stream, Illinois (1975–1981); Campus Life Publications, Inc., Carol Stream, (1981–1982); Christianity Today, Inc., Carol Stream, (1982–present).

EDITORS: Roger Malsbary (1944), Clyde Dennis (1945), Ken Anderson (1945–1953), Mel Larson (1953–1958), Vernon McLellan (1958–1959), Warren Wiersbe (1959–1962), Ron Wilson (1962–1965), Harold Myra (1965–1975), Philip Yancey (1975–1979), Steve Lawhead and Gregg Lewis (1979–1980), Gregg Lewis

(1980–1982), Gregg Lewis and Jim Long (1982–1988), Jim Long (1988–1993), Christopher Lutes and Ruth Senter (1993–present).
CIRCULATION: 800 (1945); 30,000 (1965); 160,000 (1975); 176,000 (1982); 146,000 (1992).

Larry Eskridge

CATHOLIC NEAR EAST

The Catholic Near East Welfare Association (CNEWA) was established on 11 March 1926 by Pope Pius XI. The association's formation was the result of a papal decision to bring together all of the American organizations providing aid to Russia and the Near East (including the Holy Land), those contributing to the work of the Eastern Catholic churches, and those promoting unity between the Roman Catholic and Orthodox Churches. The responsibility for administering and supervising the new organization was given to the archbishop of New York, who was charged by the pope to "work on behalf of Russia and the Christian East—that is, those lands in which from ancient times the majority of Christians are members of the various Eastern churches."[1]

CNEWA's mandate extended from Central and Eastern Europe to India and included all Eastern Christians. The association has worked in Afghanistan, Albania, Armenia, Azerbaijan, Belarus, Bulgaria, Cyprus, Egypt, Eritrea, Ethiopia, Georgia, Greece, India, Iran, Iraq, Israel, Jordan, Kazakhstan, Kyrgyzstan, Lebanon, Palestine, Russia, Syria, Tajikistan, Turkey, Turkmenistan, Ukraine, and Uzbekistan. As a nongovernmental, international organization, CNEWA encourages and assists programs of "pastoral support, humanitarian assistance, interfaith communication and public awareness."[2]

The work of CNEWA began in the years following World War I, when Greek, Russian, Armenian, Assyrian, and Chaldean refugees all converged on Constantinople (Istanbul). The city was unable to handle the enormous influx of population and asked relief organizations for assistance. One of the first to respond was Bishop George Calavassy, the Greek Catholic exarch of Constantinople and an early advocate of the union of the Orthodox and Roman Catholic Churches. In 1922, Calavassy was introduced to Msgr. Richard Barry-Doyle, chaplain to the English-speaking Catholic community of Constantinople. Barry-Doyle readily agreed to raise funds to help support the bishop's relief efforts.

Barry-Doyle came to the United States later in 1922 and immediately initiated a fund-raising campaign. He traveled across the United States, giving a lecture entitled "The Call of the East" in a successful effort to generate more funds. In 1924, Barry-Doyle and five Catholic laymen formed the first organization to have the name Catholic Near East Welfare Association.

These same years witnessed a growing concern about the fate of Russian refugees arriving in Berlin, Paris, and Vienna, many of whom were in need of material assistance. The Catholic hierarchy of Europe believed that the refugees needed spiritual relief as well as financial help and thought this could only be accomplished by convincing them to convert to Roman Catholicism.

The result of this belief was the formation of the Catholic Union, and Augustine Count Von Galen, O.S.B., was sent to the United States by the Congregation for the Oriental Churches to raise money for the new organization. In 1925, Von Galen established an office of the Catholic Union in New York City with the permission of Patrick Hayes, archbishop of New York. One of the goals of the organization was to raise money to support Byzantine Catholic seminarians. It was hoped that when these seminarians were ordained they would work for the reunion of the Bulgarian, Romanian, Russian, and Ukrainian Orthodox Churches with Rome.

In March 1926, Pius XI merged Barry-Doyle's CNEWA with Von Galen's Catholic Union, retaining the name of the former group. The new group was placed under the direction of Edmund A. Walsh, S.J., former director general of the Papal Relief Mission to Russia. The United States bishops endorsed CNEWA in September 1926 and gave it the sole authorization to solicit funds for Catholic interests in Russia and the Near East.

Msgr. Thomas J. McMahon, national secretary of CNEWA, was notified by Pope Pius XII in 1949 that he was being named president of a special mission for Palestine to be known as the Pontifical Mission for Palestine. The new mission was the result of the pope's concern that conditions in Palestine were deteriorating to the point that Arab Christians and the sacred shrines of Christianity were jeopardized. Displaced Palestinians needed to be provided with food, medicine, and housing. "In such a volatile political situation an independent mission of emergency relief was essential. The Holy Father wanted to unify the humanitarian and charitable efforts of the Church among the refugees in the Holy Land."[3]

Beirut was chosen as the field headquarters for the new pontifical mission. Local committees were formed for Arab Palestine (West Bank), Egypt, Lebanon, Syria, Jordan, Israel, and Gaza. The function of the Pontifical Mission for Palestine has been to make "resources available for humanitarian relief and development in the name of the Holy Father."[4] The mission currently has offices in Beirut, Amman, and Jerusalem. In addition to its other work, CNEWA serves as the primary fund-raising vehicle for the pontifical mission. Msgr. John G. Nolan was named national secretary of CNEWA in 1965 and retained this position until 1987. In 1974 Nolan established *Catholic Near East*, "a quarterly magazine that narrates the stories of the people of the East,"[5] because he had concluded that his columns, syndicated in various Catholic newspapers throughout the United States, were not contributing to the work of the organizations. In the first issue of the magazine, Nolan wrote:

Through *Catholic Near East* magazine may you draw still closer to the mission effort and charity of the Church there. May you become better acquainted in its pages with those you aid by your prayers, alms, and sacrifices! The people, countries, and rites of the East are real, vibrant, struggling, and growing in spite of all handicaps and hindrances.[6]

Nolan hoped that *Catholic Near East* would educate its readers about the work of CNEWA and the Pontifical Mission for Palestine. Hence, the magazine regularly publishes articles detailing the association's various projects. Nolan also believed, however, that people needed to be educated about the history and faith of those served by CNEWA and the pontifical mission. This conviction has led to features on various countries and the faiths of the residents (e.g., an article might focus on Orthodox, Eastern, or Oriental Catholics), as well as occasional "spiritual pieces."

The first issue of *Catholic Near East* reflected Nolan's goals by including articles entitled "Our Lady's Advent," "Christmas at Bethlehem," and "Christmas in India." The second issue (Spring 1975) contained pieces entitled "The Holy City" and "The Melkites Today." The latter did not focus exclusively on Melkite Catholics (Syrian Catholics who do not accept the Christological definitions of the council of Chalcedon) in Arab lands, but also profiled those living in the United States. The editors of the magazine hoped that features such as "The Melkites Today" would make U.S. Catholics and Protestants aware of the presence and needs of Arab Christians.

CNEWA and the Pontifical Mission for Palestine neither offer relief based on one's religious beliefs nor criticize these beliefs. Indeed, the goal is to promote understanding between Eastern religions and Roman Catholicism. In a column entitled "The Pontifical Mission—for Palestine?" Msgr. Robert L. Stern wrote:

Who are these brothers and sisters?
—Arab Catholics? Yes, Armenians, Chaldeans, Copts, Ethiopians, Latins, Melkites, Maronites, and Syrians.
—Other Arab Christians? Yes, Orthodox and Protestant.
—Muslims? Yes, Sunni and Shi'ite.
—Druze? Yes.
—Jews? Yes, Ashkenazim and Sephardim.
—Those with no religious profession? Yes, believers, agnostics, atheists, all.[7]

The editors of *Catholic Near East* have published articles with such titles as "The Baha'is: One of the World's Newest Religions" (Fall 1983) and "Origins of Ethiopia's Black Jews" (Fall 1986). The Fall of 1982 issue was devoted to exploring Hinduism from a historical and contemporary perspective.

Most issues of *Catholic Near East* contain at least one article devoted to theological and spiritual issues. "Hunger and the Eucharist" appeared in the Spring 1976 issue. Father Romanos V. Russo contributed a piece in July 1991 entitled "A Prayer of the Heart," in which he related his visit to the Monastery of the Transfiguration in Ellwood City, Pennsylvania. The article provided an enlightening glimpse of the prayer life of the monastery's nuns. In 1984 the magazine published a special issue focusing on the topic of suffering. The phenomenon of suffering was examined from the perspective of John Paul II's letter on the subject; from a physical, spiritual, and sociological perspective; and from the perspective of the suffering that results from war.

The relief work of CNEWA and the Pontifical Mission for Palestine is reflected in the people and countries chosen for inclusion in the magazine. An article entitled "They Have Nothing to Eat" (Summer 1985) was published at a time when Ethiopia was suffering from a severe famine. An article by Michael J. L. LaCivita entitled "Where Do We Go from Here?" (July 1991) focused on the rise of ethnic and religious tensions in the Balkans. LaCivita attempted to increase readers' awareness of how different the Yugoslav situation was from that of the United States. "A cultural marvel, Yugoslavia is a historical nightmare, a testimony to intolerance. This nation, rooted in Roman, Byzantine, Venetian, Ottoman and Austro-Hungarian traditions, is a melting pot whose contents never blended. How unlike our own experience in the United States."[8]

Despite the fact that CNEWA provides relief in an area that extends from Eastern Europe down through the Levantine, including India and North Africa (e.g., Ethiopia), it receives most of its attention from its work in the Middle East. Although both CNEWA and the Pontifical Mission for Palestine continually assert that they are interested in neither political nor religious problems unless suffering people are involved, both have been accused of being pro-Palestinian and anti-Semitic when the question of Israel is raised. Indeed, it is assumed that the Israeli government merely "tolerates" the presence of both organizations in Jerusalem. The tension has lessened somewhat as a result of the dialogue that John Cardinal O'Connor of New York has established with both the national and international Jewish community.

Throughout the history of *Catholic Near East*, attempts have been made to address the question of Israel and the Palestinians. In a 1991 article, "Title Searches," Msgr. Robert L. Stern implied that there was no definitive answer to the question of to whom the Holy Land belongs. "To the children of Abraham, because God promised it to him four thousand years ago? . . . Is it the land of the Assyrians or the Babylonians, the conquerors of the ancient Israelite kingdoms? Of the Persians, Greeks, Romans, Arabs, Seljuk Turks, Crusaders, Mamluks or Ottoman Turks that conquered the same land, each in turn?"[9] Two years earlier, Stern addressed the Vatican's reluctance to recognize the state of Israel. Stern noted that even though Israel had not been recognized, special needs of the people of that region were being addressed through CNEWA and the Pontifical Mission for Palestine.

Each issue of *Catholic Near East* contains a regular feature entitled "Our World." The focus of this section has changed over the years, but currently highlights the work of the sponsoring organizations. A 1991 "Our World," for instance, included items on the pontifical mission's efforts to deliver food and medicine in north-central Iraq, the testimony of Msgr. Robert Stern before the U.S. Congress on the issue of aid for Lebanon, and the visit of Bishop Serapion of the Coptic Orthodox Church to CNEWA.

In 1992, circulation of *Catholic Near East* approached approximately 90,000. Every Catholic institution in the United States (parishes, colleges, elementary and secondary schools, religious houses of study, and novitiates), donor, and member of the Catholic hierarchy in Rome receive a copy.

When the magazine first began publication, it accepted freelance articles. Over the years, it has moved away from this policy and toward one that solicits articles on themes and issues selected by the editors.

Since 1989, the length of *Catholic Near East* has been thirty-two pages, and its size is six by nine. Color photographs and glossy text have been a part of the magazine since its inception.

There are other magazines published in the United States that deal with Catholic relief work and missionary activities. *Maryknoll, Holy Land Magazine*, and *Common Life* (published by the Society of St. Edmund) are cognate publications.

Notes

1. *Catholic Near East* 18 (April 1992): 30.
2. Ibid.
3. Ibid. 15 (Summer 1989): 10.
4. Ibid.
5. Ibid. 17 (October 1991): 23.
6. Ibid. 1 (Winter 1974): 2.
7. Ibid. 15 (Summer 1989): 30.
8. Ibid. 17 (July 1991): 11.
9. Ibid. 17 (January 1991): 30.

Information Sources

INDEX SOURCES: None.
LOCATION SOURCES: Bound volumes may be found at Catholic Near East Welfare Association, 1011 First Avenue, New York, New York.

Publication History

MAGAZINE TITLE: *Catholic Near East.*
VOLUME AND ISSUE DATA: 1 (1974–present). Published quarterly.
PUBLISHER AND PLACE OF PUBLICATION: Catholic Near East Welfare Association, New York, New York.
EDITORS: Ronnie Treanor (1974–1976), Virginia Rohan (1977–1978), Claudia McDonnell (1978–1981), Regina Clarkin (1982–1984), Claudia McDonnell (1985),

Michael Healy (1985–1989), Thomas McHugh (1989–1991), Michael LaCivita (1992–present).
CIRCULATION: 90,000 (1992).

Margaret M. McGuinness

CATHOLIC NEW YORK

A wide variety of Catholic newspapers has been published in New York City since the nineteenth century. Representatives of this genre include publications that appealed to specific ethnic groups (*Gaelic American, Katholische Kirchenzeitung*), those that were circulated on a national and/or international basis (*Catholic Worker, McGee's Illustrated*), and some that were primarily of local interest (*Catholic News, New York Weekly Register*). An overview of these papers provides the historian, theologian, and sociologist with a sense of how American Catholics have viewed local, national, and international religious and political issues over time.

American Catholicism encompasses a wide range of ethnic, regional, and economic groups. But a newspaper hoping to appeal to the Catholic population of a certain geographic area must focus on issues of interest to that community. Some issues will be of general concern to Catholics, such as abortion, the role of parochial schools, and the position of politicians on issues that may shape the future of American Catholicism. A local Catholic newspaper, however, must also report items of interest primarily to the immediate community, such as significant anniversaries of priests and parishes, clergy reassignments, and profiles of important regional figures. *Catholic New York*, the newspaper of record for the archdiocese of New York, disseminates both types of information to its readers.

In 1981, Terence Cardinal Cooke, archbishop of New York (1967–1983), announced plans to establish an archdiocesan newspaper. The New York Catholic community was then served by the *Catholic News*, which also functioned as the Catholic newspaper for the archdiocese of Newark. *Catholic News*, published by the Ridder family, was losing subscribers, and Cooke was concerned that the Roman Catholics of his archdiocese had no common vehicle of communication.

Cooke knew that the archdiocese of New York, then the third largest diocese in the United States, contained a diverse population. The archdiocese covers the urban boroughs of Manhattan, the Bronx, and Staten Island, as well as rural Orange, Suffolk, and Dutchess counties.

In the inaugural issue of *Catholic New York* (27 September 1981) the archbishop wrote that *Catholic New York* was to be an "all-important effort of evangelization and communication in the life of our local church."[1] Cooke went on to say that "with God's help, *Catholic New York* will reflect the rich diversity of the ten counties which make up the Archdiocese."[2]

The first issue of *Catholic New York* demonstrated the editors' awareness of the diversity present among its readers. The paper profiled the seventeen vicariates of the New York archdiocese to illustrate the complexity of New York Catholicism. *Catholic New York* has consistently published feature stories on aspects of Catholic life in New York. Early cover stories, for instance, included a focus on the urban ("Serving the City: Risks and Rewards," 25 October 1981), as well as the rural ("The Church's Presence at West Point," 1 November 1981).

In an article commemorating the birth of the paper, Cooke addressed the issue of whether the staff of *Catholic New York* would be able to treat controversial issues within the Catholic Church. The cardinal wrote that the staff has the "ability to report and to analyze those aspects of modern life of particular concern to Catholics. In a spirit of faith, they will do this with respect for and loyalty to the teachings of Christ and His Church."[3] The staff was expected to demonstrate a "commitment to an objective and factual reporting of events and to providing a forum for Catholic opinion and productive dialogue."[4]

William Reed, a writer for the New York *Daily News*, addressed this same issue in a column on the op-ed page. Reed wrote that he expected *Catholic New York* to be a "real" newspaper, not a house organ for the chancery. Issues of the paper have proved Reed correct. The first issue, for example, featured stories on the scandals emanating from the archdiocese of Chicago over the financial affairs of John Cardinal Cody. The paper continued to cover the activities of Chicago's chief prelate until the issue was resolved.

In 1982, an article appeared in the *New York Times* entitled "Lay Catholic Editors Enjoy Papers' Freedom." The story focused on the editorial freedom enjoyed by the staffs of *Catholic New York* and the official publication of the diocese of Brooklyn, the *Tablet*. The article quoted Gerald Costello, first editor in chief of *Catholic New York*: "The role of a diocesan paper is to enlighten, not indoctrinate, the Catholic reader."[5] Costello pointed out that his paper included all stories of interest to New York Catholics, including "stories about groups critical of the bishops, columns questioning papal pronouncements and letters lamenting the decline of the Latin mass or the absence of women priests."[6]

Cooke hoped that *Catholic New York* would increase its readers' awareness of the need for social justice in both the United States and the world. He wrote that *Catholic New York* would "attempt to motivate all Catholics and people of every faith with whom we are joined, to feed the hungry, to shelter the homeless, to heal the sick, to be advocates of social change for those who suffer injustice."[7] The second issue of the paper indicated that the editorial staff agreed with the cardinal. The cover story of that issue focused on the homeless population of New York City, a group that was just beginning to receive attention in the media.

New York's archdiocesan newspaper continues to report on local Catholic responses to contemporary social problems. *Catholic New York* has featured stories on the opening of Incarnation Children's Center in Manhattan for babies born with AIDS, parishes in "fashionable neighborhoods" (St. John the Evangelist) that provide shelter to the homeless, and the implementation of Project Rachel, a healing and reconciliation program for those troubled by abortion.

The staff has not hesitated to report news that could generate criticism of the Catholic Church. In the tenth-anniversary issue (26 September 1991) the editors noted that "one of the most painful long-running stories"[8] that the newspaper had ever covered concerned the departure of Father Bruce Ritter from Covenant House in the wake of allegations concerning financial and sexual abuse.

As the "newspaper of record" for the archdiocese of New York, *Catholic New York* also publishes the full text of all papal encyclicals and all official "teaching" letters issued by the archbishop. The second issue, for example, contained John Paul II's "Laborem Exercens" ("On Human Work").

The editors recognize that the paper is often the only source of local Catholic news. An important regular news item includes clergy reassignments and profiles of new ordinands. This allows Catholics living in one section of the archdiocese to learn what has happened to a priest who served formerly in their parish. Parishes celebrating significant anniversaries are often singled out for feature articles.

Terence Cooke died on 6 October 1983 and was succeeded as archbishop by John J. O'Connor. Shortly after his installation, the new archbishop announced that his top priority would be working to end legalized abortion. O'Connor received national attention as a result of public pronouncements on this issue. A reporter from *Catholic New York* covers O'Connor's Sunday homily at St. Patrick's Cathedral to ensure that any newsworthy statements are accurately reported. In addition, editorial policy allows the archbishop to write a column as often as he chooses. O'Connor has used his column to promote his views on such issues as abortion, the 1992 racial tension in the Washington Heights section of Manhattan, and the contribution of African-American Catholics to their church.

Catholic New York contains several other regular features, including an op-ed section that publishes columns dealing with scriptural, theological, and contemporary issues discussed by a variety of authors. Gerald M. Costello began an editor's column in the first issue. Anne M. Buckley, Costello's successor, has continued the practice.

Letters to the editor are published regularly. They reflect all viewpoints relating to issues or events reported in the paper. Since Cardinal O'Connor is an important New York City leader, the editors receive many letters relating to his pronouncements on abortion, homosexuality, and the role of religion in politics. The policy is to publish letters whether they agree or disagree with Catholic teaching as long as they are not obscene or incomprehensible.

By 1992, each issue also contained at least one page of news relevant to the Hispanic community of the archdiocese. Important statements issued by the pope and the archbishop often appear in both Spanish and English.

Approximately one hundred awards have been conferred on the newspaper since its first issue appeared in 1981. It has received two awards for general excellence from the Catholic Press Association. *Catholic New York* tied for the 1985 "Best Interview" award of the Catholic Press Association for an interview with New York's governor, Mario Cuomo ("Cuomo and the Church," 26 April 1984).

The staff of *Catholic New York* requested a Gallup survey of its readership in 1987; the results were reported in the paper on 12 November of that year. The readers of the paper view themselves and their archdiocesan newspaper as political, social, and theological conservatives. There is some indication that they consider themselves slightly more conservative than the paper. They do, however, want and expect the paper to present all sides of any controversial issues of interest to New York Catholics. The average reader is over fifty years of age. The survey noted that the most frequently read stories were those relating to archdiocesan news.

Issues of *Catholic New York* average forty-eight pages. The archbishop of New York, as head of the Communication Corporation of the archdiocese, is the titular publisher. Advertising is welcomed. There is currently a circulation of approximately 130,000. The paper is distributed through subscriptions (in 1992 subscriptions were twenty dollars for one year) and is also made available in local parishes and institutions of the archdiocese.

Notes

1. *Catholic New York* 1 (27 September 1981): 3.
2. Ibid.
3. Ibid.
4. Ibid.
5. *New York Times* (10 October 1982): 59.
6. Ibid.
7. *Catholic New York* 1 (27 September 1981): 3.
8. Ibid., 10 (26 September 1991): 21.

Information Sources

INDEX SOURCES: None.
LOCATION SOURCES: A complete bound collection of *Catholic New York* can be found at the newspaper's offices, 1011 First Avenue, New York, New York.

Publication History

MAGAZINE TITLE: *Catholic New York.*
VOLUME AND ISSUE DATA: 1:1 (27 September 1981–present). Published weekly.
PUBLISHER AND PLACE OF PUBLICATION: Archbishop of New York, Ecclesiastical Communications Corporation, New York, New York.

EDITORS: Gerald Costello (1981–1991), Anne M. Buckley (1991–present).
CIRCULATION: 130,000 (1992).

Margaret M. McGuinness

CENTRAL PRESBYTERIAN. *See* PRESBYTERIAN OF THE SOUTH

CHARISMA. *See* CHRISTIAN LIFE

CHARISMA AND CHRISTIAN LIFE. *See* CHRISTIAN LIFE

CHICAGO-BLADET. *See* EVANGELICAL BEACON

CHILDLIFE. *See* WORLD VISION

CHILD'S PAPER

Children: They should be seen and not heard. This age-old statement exemplified the Victorian nineteenth century. Children grew up early in those brutal times when child-labor laws were rare. These laws were not nationally enacted until after the *Child's Paper* discontinued circulation. Children had no voice and were powerless. But the American Tract Society (hereafter known as ATS) saw that children were important, that they were a significant constituency and an important mission field. Reach the children, and you will reach the families thought the ATS. They believed that an immigrant family could be evangelized through its English-speaking children. The ATS's ministry, though directed at individuals, did not forsake larger social structures.

When the national ATS began in 1825, the result of a merger between the American Tract Society in Boston (formerly the Evangelical Tract Society) and the New York Tract Society to provide a stronger and broader base of operation, there were twelve children's tracts and seventy-five children's books being produced by the New York branch alone. In 1827 the ATS launched a concerted effort to reach children, mainly through the printing and distribution of books and tracts. By 1850 the number of children's tracts had increased to more than two hundred different titles.

According to Margaret Cutt in *Ministering Angels*, "Without the printings of the Tract Societies, children's libraries in the poorer homes of the last century would have been scanty indeed, and the self-education of the newly-literate adult would have often stopped short for lack of cheap books."[1] As a by-product, publications like the *Child's Paper* served to educate as well as convert.

Many branches had their own publications; local groups filled the gap left by the increasing demands upon the national society. In Albany, New York, an auxiliary of the ATS published the *Child's Friend*. The ATS began its own periodical devoted wholly to children in January 1852. The *Child's Paper* originated because the previous method of devoting space to children within the pages of the ATS's *American Messenger* was insufficient.

The main purpose of the *Child's Paper* was to reach the thousands of children in the growing nation with the message that they were sinners in need of a savior. The ATS sought the old and young, the immigrant and the long-time resident, hoping to convert them to Christianity of an evangelical sort. Even though there were other publications serving this constituency, the ATS realized that there were many children who were not being reached and that one more children's paper might bridge the gap. The price of the paper was so inexpensive—a penny apiece—that subscribers often purchased multiple copies to use as a means of evangelism.

Another purpose, though more as a result, was that the *Child's Paper* also served to keep the ATS before the public. It helped spread the news of the ATS's work. The work of the ATS relied on the ever-present support of the Christian public. Most of their publications, with tracts constituting the largest amount, were given gratis. No one was refused material owing to their ability to pay.

The *Child's Paper* was printed on an efficient Adams press. The ATS had mastered the methods of producing cheap reading material, and its first printer, Daniel Treadwell, was the first to utilize steam power to run his presses, doing this in 1822. The ATS had to build a new printing building because the old wooden structure could not handle the powerful shaking presses. Isaac Adams improved upon Treadwell's success. Adams modified Treadwell's designs to produce his own patented presses in 1830 and 1836. Both presses used a bed and platen system, where the bed with type was raised to an inked platen.

The *Child's Paper* was primarily distributed through the mail. It was specifically produced in such a size so that it was less costly to mail than were other similar publications. The ATS purposefully made this newspaper four pages in length so that it would cost only a quarter of the price of postage that was charged on larger monthly newspapers. The ATS had perfected the art of marketing their products and circulating them to the greatest amount of individuals at the least amount of cost.

Owing to the cost of mailing letters in the mid-nineteenth century, costing often ten to twenty-five times greater than periodicals,[2] newspapers were often used to send along messages to friends and family. Many would circle words or letters in a certain order to produce a message and simply remail the newspaper.[3] Therefore, a newspaper's circulation may have been larger, with this secondary form of distribution, than is usually thought.

Colporteurs also helped expand the circulation of the *Child's Paper*. For example, John Wesley Osborne, the eventual bishop of the Methodist Episcopal Church, while a colporteur for the American Tract Society, recruited 117 new subscribers in 1857.

The annual reports of the ATS contain a wealth of information concerning the activities of this integral part of the nineteenth century's "Benevolent

Empire.'' In 1854 the ATS was circulating 300,000 copies monthly of the *Child's Paper*, and the Boston depository of the ATS distributed over 816,000 copies that same year. By 1869 the *Child's Paper* had increased its monthly circulation to 355,000. But by its demise in 1897, it was circulating only about 33,000 per month.

However, from the beginning of this venture, the *Child's Paper* reached beyond the borders of this country to other English-speaking lands to spread the ''good news.'' In its inaugural year it had a circulation of nearly seven thousand in England.

In order to reach children, the ATS learned what children liked: stories. The *Child's Paper* survived on the use of the story, usually three hundred words or less, within its pages. Some of its content was biography, some was fiction. Biographies of individuals like John Wesley and John Bunyan and moral stories telling of the effects of drinking were regular fare in the *Child's Paper*.

The fiction of the *Child's Paper* consisted of stories with a religious lesson extolling the virtues of faith and righteousness. The popular press was full of romance and fiction, and the ATS sought to battle that trend. Much of what was available, like the works of Maria Edgeworth, did not reject religion or speak against it but simply left it out. For the ATS this was a sin of omission. The ATS wanted to give an alternative to that readily available material and produce stories that included religion and that fostered faith.

Fiction . . . lamentably pervades our own country: deluding our youth with dreams of unreal bliss; pandering to the taste of the licentious; seducing the innocent; profaning all sacred things; prostituting the press; and sacrificing the welfare, temporal and eternal, of thousands, for the sake of pecuniary gain . . . .This misnamed ''literature'' has demoralized thousands of unsuspecting, and it's known to have been the occasion of ruin to many of both sexes by its polluting pages.[4]

The shape of Victorian literature began to change. Sensational novels and other forms of fiction began to emerge. British forms of literature influenced the styles used in the states. A mock advertisement placed in *Punch* highlighted a new journal entitled *Sensation Times and Chronicle of Excitement* that would be ''devoted chiefly to the following objects; namely, Harrowing the Mind, Making the Flesh Creep, Causing the Hair to Stand on End, Giving Shocks to the Nervous System, Destroying Conventional Moralities, and generally Unfitting the Public for the Prosaic Avocations of Life.'' Among the regular highlights were to be numbered ''some extraordinary revelations of the habits and actions of exceeding Low Life.''[5] Though the advertisement was most likely an exaggeration, the trend emphasized was exactly what the ATS was seeking to combat. ''Having long regretted that the limited columns of the American Messenger excluded a proper amount of reading adapted to children, the question of issuing a child's paper was seriously considered; and after careful deliberation a little monthly sheet, with neat engravings, entitled 'The Child's Paper' was commenced.''[6]

Along with stories, which were to stimulate the mind, the ATS included wonderful, clear engravings to stimulate the eyes. These engravings often enveloped half of the front page and were also interspersed throughout the paper in smaller sizes.

Engravers like Edwin Davis French, noted for his bookplates, helped to illustrate the pages of the *Child's Paper*. Others who helped the ATS were B. Ross Bogart, Alexander Anderson, and Robert Roberts. "Suffice it to say that the art work of the American Tract Society was constantly improved until it led the way for other American publishers in the 1850s and 1860s.''[7]

Since ATS laborers never received acclaim for their work, explicit mention of editors within the pages of the *Child's Paper* publications is very difficult to find. The stewards were usually noted simply as "the editors,'' or the contributors were recognized with their initials. However, some have shown through by their diligence.

In its early years the paper was shaped by the work of R. S. Cook and William A. Hallock, who were with the ATS from the beginning. These two men worked together for a few years before Helen Knight took the editorship.

Helen Cross Knight was one of the earliest editors of the *Child's Paper*. She began this task in 1857, holding it for five years. Knight, along with editing the *Child's Paper*, wrote a biography of long-time ATS general secretary William Hallock and also edited the *Illustrated Family Christian Almanac*. Oliver Addison Kingsbury was a later editor of the *Child's Paper*. Kingsbury's father, Oliver R. Kingsbury, was a member of the ATS board of directors for many years. The younger Kingsbury served as editor during the years 1875 to at least 1882 (records beyond that are difficult to locate).

From the beginning the ATS sought to be a national organization. The structure of the ATS included depositories and auxiliaries. Depositories were owned and operated by the ATS, whereas auxiliaries were independent organizations that were able to purchase materials in volume at a discount. Each of these institutional arms helped disseminate the *Child's Paper*.

The ATS had printing operations in most major U.S. cities and eventually had operations from coast to coast. But to maintain their national scope and to continue working amid various ethical, denominational, and social differences, a middle road often had to be taken. The ATS had to steer clear of anything or any topic that did not "receive the general approbation of all Christians.''[8]

The ATS, like other institutions of its time, was rife with dissention and factionalism over the issue of slavery. Just as it had torn asunder bonds of cooperation in denominations, churches, and organizations, so, too, slavery broke the ATS.

In 1859, after many years of proclaiming their dislike for the general lack of pronouncements against slaveholders and slavery, the Boston depository separated from the national organization to become the ATS, Boston. Since it had no legal right to any of the publications of the other ATS (New York), the Boston society began the *Child at Home*, which was published from 1863 to 1873. In an attempt to garner subscribers from the ATS (New York), the Boston society made its pictures colored and opened an office and distribution center in New York. Conversely, the ATS (New York) set up operations in Boston.

The existence of two ATSs has left much confusion for those researching the history of this influential organization. The two societies eventually reunited in 1878 after many years of personal and national bitterness and strife produced by the volatile issue of slavery.

The *Child's Paper*, in its forty-five years of operation sought to change the lives of individuals and families for the better through moral stories and articles located within its pages. Its distributors, in their annual reports, often told of the great zeal and excitement that attended the delivery of the *Child's Paper*. At times, schools were released early so that children could rush to receive their copies.

The ATS sought to mold children through the ideas and doctrines of nineteenth-century evangelicalism, devotion to Scripture, a personal faith that interacts with daily life, and the amelioration of social conditions while working for the eradication of social evils. For this the *Child's Paper* began.

Notes

1. Margaret Nancy Cutt, *Ministering Angels* (Herts, England: Five Owls Press, 1979), 31.

2. Wayne Fuller, *The American Mail: Enlarger of the Common Life* (Chicago: University of Chicago Press, 1972).

3. Richard B. Kielbowicz, *Origins of the Second-Class Mail Category and the Business of Policymaking, 1863–1879* (Columbia, SC: Association for Education in Journalism and Mass Communication, 1986).

4. American Tract Society, *Instructions from the Executive Committee to the Agents and Colporteurs of the American Tract Society* (New York: American Tract Society, n.d.), 8.

5. Quoted in Winifred Hughes, *Maniac in the Cellar: Sensation Novels in the 1860s* (Princeton: Princeton University Press, 1980), 3.

6. American Tract Society, *A Brief History of the Organization and Work of the American Tract Society, Instituted in Boston, 1814* (Boston: American Tract Society, 1855), 13.

7. Lawrance Thompson, "The Printing Activities of the American Tract Society from 1825 to 1850," *The Papers of the Bibliographic Society of America*, 35:2 (1941): 102. Thompson's work gives insight into the evolution of the artwork and engravings for the Society's publications.

8. Edwin Gaustad, ed., *American Tract Society Documents, 1824–1925* (New York: Arno Press, 1972), 9.

Information Sources

INDEX SOURCES: Unknown.
LOCATION SOURCES: Boston Public Library holds volumes 1–20. The Library of
    Congress, Cleveland Public Library, Oberlin College (Ohio), American Baptist
    Historical Society (Pennsylvania), and the American Tract Society (Garland,
    Texas) all contain partial runs.

Publication History

MAGAZINE TITLE: *Child's Paper.*
VOLUME AND ISSUE DATA: 1:1 (January 1852)–46:8 (August 1897). Published
    monthly.
PUBLISHER AND PLACE OF PUBLICATION: American Tract Society, New York.
EDITORS: William A. Hallock and R. S. Cook (1854–1855), Helen Cross Knight (1857–
    1867), William A. Hallock and Helen C. Knight (1869–1874), Oliver Addison
    Kingsbury (1875–1882?).
CIRCULATION: 300,000 (1854); 230,000 (1861); 355,583 (1869); 350,099 (1871);
    33,750 (1897).

David B. Malone

CHRISTIAN ADVOCATE

During the nineteenth and early twentieth centuries, an age when "the daily
or weekly tabloid knew no real rival as the prime source of information for the
American mind," no publication challenged the influence of the *Christian Advocate* in all its permutations.[1] Launched in 1826 by the Book Concern, the
official publishing house of the Methodist Episcopal church (MEC), the *Advocate* was for much of its nearly 150 year history the most popular weekly periodical in the United States.

The origins of the *Christian Advocate* are found in the appearance of *Zion's
Herald* (1823). The *Herald* reflected the growing conviction of MEC bishops
that American Methodism must devote itself more fully to "the cultivation of
the human mind."[2] During its first year of operation, the *Herald*, published by
Moore and Prowse of Boston, had a very spartan appearance with no regular
departments. Only news items from the MEC, letters, reprints of sermons, and
personal notices were included.

In its second year, under the editorship of Barber Badger, *Zion's Herald*
became a significant force in the popular religious press. Expanded to an imperial size, the "new" *Herald* maintained its original four page/four column
structure while employing a larger banner and larger point type. Possessing over
5,000 subscribers within three years of its creation, the *Herald* proudly promoted
itself as "the only weekly paper in America devoted to the interests of the
Methodist Church."[3]

In September 1826, Badger suddenly departed for New York to assume the editorship of a new Methodist weekly launched by the Book Concern under the name "Christian Advocate." Despite the humiliation of losing his helmsman to an upstart periodical, Solomon Sias, the publisher of the *Herald*, was generous in his praise of the *Advocate* saying, "We feel deep satisfaction in hailing the new paper as a sister—engaged in the same glorious cause with ourselves."[4]

Little did Sias realize that the *Christian Advocate* would soon shatter records for circulation figures, with 28,000 subscribers in 1828 and 120,000 readers before 1841.[5] Unlike *Zion's Herald*, the *Advocate* was entirely a creation of the Book Concern and its remarkable leader, Nathan Bangs. Bangs, whose decorous view of the Christian faith was as far removed from the prevailing Methodist revivalism as day from night, viewed the *Advocate* as "the main act" in his grand strategy "to rescue our [Methodist] institutions from reproach and to preserve our plans of procedure from being frustrated."[6]

Although Bangs was the creator and eventual editor (1828–32, 1834–36) of the *Advocate*, its first two volumes were the handiwork of Badger.[7] In fact, the early *Advocate* was almost a mirror image of *Zion's Herald* at the time of Badger's departure: the folio format of four pages/four columns on imperial size paper and regular departments on news items, home tips, anecdotal cures for every manner of illness, personal notices (marriages, births, and obituaries), and a four page miscellaneous section (including departments for ministers, parents, children, ladies, and poetry lovers).

Because it was published under the aegis of the Book Concern, the *Advocate* enjoyed a status that *Zion's Herald* could never hope to achieve.[8] Accordingly, the *Advocate* was packed with information concerning MEC conference and circuit news, missionary updates, and reports of camp meetings and revivals. Not one to gamble, Bangs further ensured the *Advocate*'s success by distributing a free copy to every Methodist preacher whose address could be confirmed.[9] Soon almost every Methodist in America was familiar with the "Prospectus" of the *Advocate*: "This will be a general Religious Newspaper. . . . It will be conducted on liberal Christian principles, and is designed to be an entertaining, instructive, and profitable family visitor. . . . [N]o reasonable pains or expense will be spared to make it worthy of its patrons."[10]

The success of the *Advocate* was immediate and absolute. Letters of praise poured into the Book Concern offices. A letter from Berks County, Pennsylvania was typical of the platitudes offered: "It is admitted by all within the circle of my acquaintance, that the size, quality, typography, general contents, and price [$2.00 a year, if paid in advance; $2.50 within six months] of the 'Advocate' are calculated to give very extensive satisfaction."[11] The *Advocate* was so popular that the Book Concern was forced to reprint old issues for the loyal readers who might have missed them.

Although the *Advocate* was the first magazine in America to have a circulation as high as 20,000, it grew through absorption as well as by expansion of readership. On 17 March 1827, the *Advocate* merged with the *Wesleyan Journal* of

Charleston, SC and for a short time became known as the *Christian Advocate and Journal.*[12] Early in 1828, the *Religious Messenger* of the Philadelphia Conference surrendered to the *Advocate* and sold out to the Book Concern. But the real prize for the Book Concern and the final obstacle in Bangs's strategy to monopolize Methodist journalism was *Zion's Herald*, which resolutely resisted the Book Concern's advances until late 1828.

The decisive factor that finally brought the two papers together was economic. Simply put, the *Herald* found it increasingly difficult to compete with the astounding popularity of the *Advocate*. On 5 September 1828, the merger was consummated and the *Advocate*'s new banner read, *Christian Advocate and Journal and Zion's Herald*. It was a Pyrrhic victory; exactly five years later, *Zion's Herald* would once again be publishing in Boston independently of the *Advocate*.[13]

By 1833, however, the *Advocate* was the uncontested information weekly of the MEC. The official mouthpiece of the MEC, the *Advocate* emphasized the objectives of the general conference. During its early days the *Advocate* addressed such issues as the resettlement of freed slaves in Liberia,[14] various types of moral reform,[15] the institutionalization of American Methodism, as seen primarily in the creation of Sunday schools,[16] and the endorsement of a growing sectarian spirit within American Methodism which attacked Calvinists, Universalists, "Romanists," Millerites, Mormons, and even Baptists with equal fervor.[17]

The *Advocate* set a new standard for American tabloid journalism; it also attracted an unprecedented number of readers (120,000 by 1841). Success encouraged competition. Between 1834 and 1836, the general conference of the MEC authorized regional *Advocates* for Cincinnati, Charleston, Richmond, and Nashville.[18] Although designed as complementary editions of the "mother (New York) paper," to some extent all the regional *Advocates* were competitors. For the MEC, the success of the various *Advocates* contributed to the rapid growth of American Methodism in the first half of the nineteenth century. Unfortunately, the quarter century prior to the Civil War was also a period fraught with dissension. Specifically, antebellum Methodism faced conflicts over higher education, abolitionism, and schism.

Despite the efforts of Nathan Bangs, Methodism retained a strong dose of anti-intellectualism. Consequently, when John Dempster began a "theological education movement" within the MEC in the 1840s, controversy ensued. Not only conservatives opposed the establishment of centers of biblical and theological studies. Methodist college presidents feared that seminaries would siphon off monetary support for their own schools. Throughout the 1840s, the *Advocate* mirrored the debate. The consensus was so against the theological education movement that *Advocate* editor Thomas E. Bond (1840–1848; 1852–1856) felt constrained to carry an insert that he and his paper disavowed the movement and its objectives. Widespread support for Methodist seminaries would have to wait until after the Civil War.[19]

Debate over theological education was intense but orderly in comparison to the firestorm that erupted over abolition. Reflecting its moderate stance as the MEC's official organ, the *Advocate* initially assumed a hostile attitude toward the "radical abolitionists," like Orange Scott, within northern Methodism. Only when the MEC was on the verge of schism in 1844 did Thomas Bond open the pages of the *Advocate* for a full discussion of the slavery issue. His hesitancy illustrated the equivocation that paralyzed and eventually rent the MEC into northern and southern divisions. For most anti-slavery Methodists, schism became inevitable when the 1840 general conference issued a strongly pro-slavery resolution. The ill-feeling toward southern Methodists, reflected in many issues of the *Advocate*, from late 1844 on, only served to confirm the "Plan of Separation" that solidifed what became a ninety-five year split within American Methodism.[20]

The turmoil did little to weaken the paper's grip on devoted Methodists. In addition, the paper gradually evolved from a magazine format to something akin to the modern tabloid. Prior to the Civil War, the original four page layout was retained. The need for more space was simply accommodated by the addition of more columns per page and smaller type: five columns in 1828, six columns in 1838, seven columns in 1845, and eight columns in 1857.

As its creation, the early *Advocate* was also a vehicle for selling the wares of the Book Concern. This caused little uproar. Much more contentious was the use of non-religious advertising.[21] By the late 1850s, under the guidance of senior book agent and publisher, Thomas Carlton (1852–1872), the *Advocate* began to hawk every conceivable product. Carlton steadfastly defended such a strategy as the best way to keep the cost of the *Advocate* within the reach of all Methodists.[22] Still, the outcry over "profane advertising" was loud and long. Especially troublesome were the medicinal ads about which the *Advocate* warned in 1863: "We do not recommend them any more than we guarantee the pianos, sewing-machines, insoluble cements, bells, and railroads named in our advertising department."[23]

For American Methodists, the denomination's split over slavery in 1844 was a grim preview of the later War Between the States. Paradoxically, during the nation's blackest hours, the *Advocate* further enhanced its journalistic prestige with a weekly "Progress of the War" news summary and first-hand reports of the conflict, most of them contributed by William Strickland, the *Advocate*'s assistant editor who enlisted as a chaplain in the Union Army in 1861.[24]

After the war, circulation hit an all-time high of 63,000 in 1878, and the paper became an icon of bourgeois America.[25] Continued success allowed the Book Concern to move from its offices at 200 Mulberry Street to its lavish new facilities at 805 Broadway Street. Under the leadership of its most influential editors, Daniel Curry (1864–1876) and James Monroe Buckley (1880–1912), the *Advocate* became a staunch "conservator of home life" in late Victorian America.[26] Buckley, especially, campaigned long and hard in favor of moral issues like temperance and against all forms of intellectual "agnosticism," like the theories of Charles Darwin.[27]

However, articles and editorials of the late nineteenth century *Advocate*, betray a clear uneasiness that belies the paper's many platitudes of strident self-confidence. Increasingly outflanked by the new secular newspapers, the *Advocate* saw its readership and economic viability slowly draining away. For every decade after the 1870s, circulation fell by 10,000 or more (reaching the low 30,000s by the year 1900) and the paper faced annual deficits. Plush new offices in Manhattan and state-of-the-art printing presses could not disguise the fact that by 1912, "The people [were] not interested enough even to dislike the paper."[28]

By the beginning of the twentieth century, the *Advocate* was forced to remake itself. It had to answer the question, "What is a specifically *religious* newspaper?" The answer led the *Advocate* into a period of social advocacy as it became the conscience of a wealthier, better educated, and more sophisticated Methodism. It had supported the rights of free blacks after the Civil War,[29] but now, after initial opposition to the trade union movement, the paper became a solid defender of the laboring class.[30] In the 1920s, with James R. Joy at the helm (1915–1936), the *Advocate* forged a powerful presence in its opposition to child labor, racial prejudice, and materialism.[31]

Still the twentieth century *Advocate* was not strictly a vehicle for social reform. Its most enduring role was as the official paper of the MEC. To that end, any *Advocate* issue was full of information on annual and general conferences, revivals, and various goings on within Methodism. Historically, the modern *Advocate* reflected and promoted the spirit of ecumenism that resulted in the creation of the Methodist church from the MEC and MEC, South on 10 May 1939.

Despite the prominence of American Methodism among Protestant denominations, the *Advocate* began to suffer from a decline in circulation that even special consultants could not arrest.[32] The embrace of all varieties of "responsible advertising" proved only a temporary corrective.[33] Even the long-sought Methodist unification of 1939, which reorganized the *Advocate* by removing its various regional competitors and by placing it under an executive-style board of publication, could not save the sinking ship.[34]

The unavoidable fact was that the *Advocate* had become an anachronism. It was conceived early in the nineteenth century to be many things to many people: a source of hard news, a conduit for church opinions, a vehicle for moral and social consciousness, a source of entertainment, and more. In addition, it was to be sold to a vast audience for as low cost as possible. To its credit, the *Advocate* succeeded brilliantly for nearly a century. By the mid-twentieth century, however, it was a victim of the ills that put many newspapers and magazines out of business: high costs, a lack of focus, and the inability to compete in the marketplace with other media.

The *Advocate* did not die without a struggle. Imaginative and resourceful editors like Roy L. Smith (1940–1948), T. Otto Nall (1948–1960), and Ewing

T. Wayland (1960–1973) introduced rigid accounting principles, increased the price of the paper, tinkered with its format (introducing a *New Christian Advocate* [1956–59] directed specifically at Methodist clergy in a new digest size of 5¼" × 7⅜"), and enlisted prominent contributors like Reinhold Niebuhr, Henry P. Van Dusen, and Georgia Harkness. Nor was focus a problem with Smith who stated that the function of the *Advocate* was: "To educate Methodists to churchmanship, to inspire and deepen them in their spiritual life, to challenge them with the world task of Christianity, to inform them about the church and its program, and to serve as the spokesman for the church."[35] But when the board of publication of the United Methodist church met in January 1973, the *Advocate* was a desperately-ill publication that defied all remedies. Circulation, once astronomic, had fallen to 10,000 in 1972. Publication finally halted with the 28 March 1973 issue.

In its various incarnations the *Advocate* probably reached more people than any other single religious newspaper.[36] If the genius of early American Methodism was, as Philip Schaff stated in 1854, its ability to embody many characteristics associated with the "typical American," then the genius of the *Christian Advocate* was its ability to occupy a place in the consciousness of many in the nineteenth and early twentieth centuries as the most characteristically American of popular religious periodicals.[37]

Notes

1. James P. Pilkington, "Methodist Publishing in Historical Perspective, 1865–1939 [Section 6]," in Emory S. Bucke, ed., *The History of American Methodism*, (New York and Nashville: Abingdon Press, 1964), 3:191. The appellation "Christian Advocate" is the most popular in Methodist history. The "mother" *Advocate*, published in New York from 1826–1940 and in Chicago from 1941–73 endured at least seven name changes. In addition, many other American Methodist periodicals have used the title "Christian Advocate" with some regional designation. The United Methodist church entered the 1990s with five national or state newspapers that employed the title "Christian Advocate." Throughout this paper *Advocate* will designate the *Christian Advocate* (1826–1973) in all its variations.

2. James P. Pilkington, *The Methodist Publishing House: A History*, vol. 1: *Beginnings to 1870* (Nashville: Abingdon Press, 1968), 199.

3. *Zion's Herald* 2 (1 January 1824): 1.

4. *Zion's Herald* 4 (13 September 1826).

5. Nathan Bangs, *A History of the Methodist Episcopal Church*, 2d ed. (New York: Mason & Lane, 1841), 4:434. The figures cited were estimates of Bangs.

6. Bangs, 2: 351.

7. J. M. McClintock asserted that from 1826–28 Badger was little more than the "nominal" editor of the *Christian Advocate* with most of the editorial matter "chiefly furnished by Dr. Bangs." Abel Stevens, *The Life and Times of Nathan Bangs* (New York: Carlton & Porter, 1863), 243. Noting the great similarities between *Zion's Herald* in 1826 and the new *Advocate*, I believe that McClintock seriously underestimates Badger's initial influence on the *Advocate*.

8. The Methodist general conference in May 1828 adopted the *Christian Advocate* as the official paper of the MEC.

9. Pilkington, *Methodist Publishing House* 1: 202.

10. *Christian Advocate* 1 (9 September 1826): 3.

11. *Christian Advocate* 1 (23 September 1826): 10–11.

12. The name changed in 1828, but reappeared on the banner of the *Advocate* from 30 August 1833 until 28 December 1865.

13. The New England conference was never happy with its "subordination" to the New York Book Concern. Consequently, in 1833, the trustees of Wesleyan Academy purchased the name "Zion's Herald" from the Book Concern and began publishing anew at Wilbraham, MA. The refurbished *Zion's Herald*, published until 1975, established itself as an unrelenting force for social justice within American Methodism. Before the Civil War, it was especially renowned for its support of William Lloyd Garrison, Orange Scott, and other radical abolitionists.

14. Although the *Advocate* spoke against the "inhumanity of the slave trade" in 1829, it did not advocate abolition until the MEC divided into northern and southern factions in 1844. *Christian Advocate and Journal and Zion's Herald* 4 (23 October 1829): 30.

15. The *Advocate* was quintessentially Victorian in its preoccupation with "personal vice." The temperance movement received an endorsement in the 31 July 1829 issue and a regular "Temperance Department" on 22 April 1831. By 1833, the *Advocate* had also denounced sabbath breaking, prostitution, and theater going. Of swearing, an 1856 issue stated: "That profane swearing is incompatible with the character of a gentleman . . . scarcely 'the vilest of the vile' will deny." *Christian Advocate and Journal* 31 (10 April 1856): 15.

16. With its third issue, the *Advocate* started a regular column devoted to "Sabbath Schools." Eventually, this column consisted of various "Scripture Questions" to be used by Sunday School teachers all over the country.

17. Contrast this attitude with the "Prospectus" of the first *Advocate* which professed to adhere to "liberal Christian principles." *Christian Advocate* 1 (9 September 1826): 3. See also the articles against Calvinism and Universalism by Wesleyan University president Wilbur Fisk that ran in the *Advocate* for much of 1833.

18. The papers were the *Western Christian Advocate* (Cincinnati, 1834); *South-Western Christian Advocate* (Nashville, 1836); *Richmond Christian Advocate* (Richmond, 1836); and *Southern Christian Advocate* (Charleston, 1836). The Cincinnati endeavor was published directly by the Book Concern. The others were published by conference committees, but underwritten to some degree by the Book Concern. Of these papers, the most prominent was the one housed in Nashville, which became the major periodical for the MEC, South, 1845–1939.

19. Despite post–Civil War urbanization and the clamor for settled and better educated pastors in the northern and eastern U.S., the *Advocate* argued that itinerants on the model of rough hewn Peter Cartwright best guaranteed a "fervid pulpit" and a prophetic ministry. *Christian Advocate and Journal* 39 (28 April 1864): 132.

20. See Thomas E. Bond's pungent editorial in the *Christian Advocate and Journal* 26 (20 November 1851): 186. The split was especially grievous for the Book Concern because the Plan of Separation mandated an "equitable division of property" between the MEC and MEC, South. Pilkington, 1: 321–23.

21. Until the mid–1840s, the *Advocate* advertised only the products of the Book Concern. When the denomination divided regionally, Book Concern revenues fell off precip-

itously. This situation opened the door to ''non-religious'' advertising. However, this advertising was temporarily discontinued from 1851–59 because of the criticism from *Advocate* readers. *Christian Advocate and Journal* 25 (27 June 1850): 102.

22. *Journal of the General Conference, 1860* (New York: Carlton & Porter, 1860), 344.

23. *Christian Advocate and Journal* 38 (19 November 1863): 372.

24. Pilkington, 1: 427–38. For an example of Strickland's work, see *Christian Advocate and Journal* 37 (9 January 1862): 9.

25. Walter N. Vernon, Jr., *The United Methodist Publishing House, A History.* Volume II: *1870–1988* (Nashville: Abingdon Press, 1989), 210.

26. Vernon, 2: 61. For example, Buckley editorialized against secular reading on the sabbath and the involvement of women in affairs outside the home. *Christian Advocate* 60 (12 February 1885): 173 and (5 March 1885): 248.

27. Temperance was the favorite cause of late nineteenth century Methodists. The *Advocate* even endorsed the 1888 Presidential candidacy of Prohibition Party leader Clinton B. Fisk. *Christian Advocate* 61 (30 September 1886): 1078. Discussion was split over the compatibility of Darwinism and Christianity, but Buckley had a famous run-in with agnostic Robert Ingersoll in 1891. *Christian Advocate* 66 (24 December 1891): 1634.

28. In 1912, 1500 pastors were asked why the *Advocate* was failing. 53% said the price was too high, and 38% disagreed with the paper's content. The findings of the survey were collected in the MEC pamphlet, *Why They Failed.*

29. *Christian Advocate* 43 (9 April 1868): 114.

30. *Christian Advocate* 61 (17 June 1886): 375. By 1932, the New York *Advocate* workers were unionized. Vernon, 2: 311.

31. For example, see the *Christian Advocate* 87 (14 November 1912): 1991.

32. Vernon, 2: 179.

33. By the 1880s, all previous reluctance to solicit advertising had dissipated. With the turn of the century, however, the Book Concern did develop some self-imposed restrictions on advertising: (1) no liquor, wine, or beer ads; (2) no cure-all medicine ads; (3) no stock speculations; (4) no ministerial certifications, testimonials, etc. of products; (5) nothing vulgar; and (6) no medicines containing alcohol or narcotics. Vernon, 2: 211.

34. In order to cut costs, the Book Concern sold its New York property in 1938. Thus, from 17 March 1938 through 26 December 1940, the ''New York'' *Advocate* was published in Cincinnati.

35. Vernon, 2: 425–26.

36. The special centennial issue of the *Christian Advocate* estimated that from 1826–1926, no less than 200 million copies of the paper had been produced. *Christian Advocate* 101 (9 September 1926), Part 2: 23.

37. Jaroslav J. Pelikan, ''Methodism's Contribution to America,'' in Bucke, 3: 597.

Information Sources

INDEX SOURCES: Each volume is self-indexed.

LOCATION SOURCES: Through 1916 in *American periodical series, 1800–1850.* The most complete print collections are in Bird Library, Syracuse University, and the United Methodist Publishing House Library, Nashville.

Publication History

MAGAZINE TITLE AND TITLE CHANGES: *Christian Advocate* (9 September 1826–10 March 1827); *Christian Advocate and Journal* (17 March 1827–29 August 1828); *Christian Advocate and Journal and Zion's Herald* (5 September 1828–23 August 1833); *Christian Advocate and Journal* (30 August 1833–28 December 1865); *Christian Advocate* (4 January 1866–27 September 1956); *New Christian Advocate* (4 October 1956–24 September 1959); and *Christian Advocate* (1 October 1959–28 March 1973).

VOLUME AND ISSUE DATA: *Christian Advocate* 1:1 (9 September 1826)–1:27 (10 March 1827); *Christian Advocate and Journal* 1:28 (17 March 1827)–2:52 (29 August 1828); *Christian Advocate and Journal and Zion's Herald* 3:1 (5 September 1828)–7:52 (23 August 1833); *Christian Advocate and Journal* 8:1 (30 August 1833)–39:52 (28 December 1865); *Christian Advocate* 40:1 (4 January 1866)–131:36 (27 September 1956); *New Christian Advocate* 131:37 (4 October 1956)–134:36 (24 September 1959); and *Christian Advocate* 134:37 (1 October 1959)–148:12 (28 March 1973). From 4 January 1866 until 2 January 1941, the *Christian Advocate* usually carried the designation, "New York" to distinguish the paper from its regional counterparts.

PUBLISHER AND PLACE OF PUBLICATION: Nathan Bangs (1826–28), John Emory (1828–32), Beverly Waugh (1832–36), Thomas Mason (1836–40), George Lane (1840–52), Thomas Carlton (1852–72), Reuben F. Nelson (1872–80), John M. Phillips (1880–89), Sandford Hunt (1889–96), Homer Eaton (1896–1913), John H. Race (1913–16, 1921–24), Edwin R. Graham (1916–21), and George C. Douglas (1924–40) for the Methodist Book Concern of the Methodist Episcopal Church, NY. B. A. Whitmore (1940–46), Fred D. Stone (1946–48), Roy L. Smith (1948–52), J. Edgar Washabaugh (1952–60), and Lovick Pierce (1960–68) for the Board of Publication of the Methodist Publishing House, Chicago. Lovick Pierce (1968–70) and John E. Procter (1970–73) for the Board of Publication of the United Methodist Publishing House, Nashville.

EDITORS: Barber Badger (1826–28); Nathan Bangs (1828–32; 1834–36); John Durbin (1832–34); Samuel Luckey (1836–40); Thomas E. Bond (1840–48; 1852–56); George Peck (1848–52); Abel Stevens (1856–60); Edward Thomson (1860–64); Daniel Curry (1864–76); C. H. Fowler (1876–80); James M. Buckley (1880–1912); George P. Eckman (1912–15); James R. Joy (1915–36); Harold P. Sloan (1936–40); Roy L. Smith (1940–48); T. Otto Nall (1948–60); Ewing T. Wayland (1960–73).

CIRCULATION: 5,000 (1826); 28,000 (1828); 63,000 (1878); 27,400 (1912); 266,000 (1941); 345,000 (1946); 244,000 (1954); 34,000 (1970); 10,000 (1972). Figures through 1912 for only the "New York" *Christian Advocate*; from 1941 on, totals include figures for what had been the "New York" *Advocate* plus what had been the other five regional *Advocates*.

Robert H. Krapohl

CHRISTIAN ADVOCATE AND JOURNAL. *See* CHRISTIAN ADVOCATE

**CHRISTIAN ADVOCATE AND JOURNAL AND ZION'S
HERALD.** *See* CHRISTIAN ADVOCATE

CHRISTIAN ADVOCATE: WESTERN EDITION. *See* WESTERN
CHRISTIAN ADVOCATE

CHRISTIAN BANNER. *See* CHRISTIAN CYNOSURE

CHRISTIAN BAPTIST. *See* MILLENNIAL HARBINGER

CHRISTIAN CENTURY

A retrospective view would dictate that no rational person would have the
audacity to predict a one-hundred-year period as "Christian." But then neither
would most be willing to take on the breadth of issues that the *Christian Century*
("refounded" in 1908) did.

The *Century*, characterized by its outspoken opinions on every aspect of contemporary life, grew to be one of the most influential religious periodicals in
the United States. Consistently seeking to be the prophetic voice of Christian
liberalism, it has attacked unpopular issues, willing to take a stand and daring
to be wrong. Through time and the guidance of six editors, the *Century*'s understanding of liberalism has undergone considerable change. Its editorial policy
has moved from dogmatism to an awareness of the "ambiguities of the human
predicament" and from "absolutist espousals of positions to a probing of the
complexities of issues." For, notes editor James Wall, "different eras call forth
different responses."[1]

The *Christian Century* traces its origins to the *Oracle*, which began 12 July
1884 in Des Moines, Iowa, as a Disciples of Christ magazine under the editorship of George A. Campbell. In 1891, however, it moved to Chicago, Illinois,
where Campbell found encouragement from Herbert L. Willett of the University
of Chicago Divinity School and other Disciples leaders in the city. The credit
for its survival and ultimate success, however, is given to Charles Clayton Morrison.

When Campbell could no longer pay the printing bills for the magazine,
renamed *Christian Century* in 1900, Charles Clayton Morrison was asked to be
the temporary editor. Morrison began preaching at a Disciples of Christ church
in Chicago in the late 1890s. He had also pursued graduate study in philosophy
at the University of Chicago where he was greatly influenced by John Dewey's
empiricism and developed a curiosity for the relation between religion and culture. Then in September of 1908, Morrison, the progressive optimist, bid fifteen
hundred dollars for the *Century* at a sheriff's auction. With funding assistance
from a variety of people, Morrison became permanent editor and remained so
until 1947.

Initially, Morrison intended to keep the *Century* within the Disciples denomination, but he soon changed his editorial policy to "minimize but not avoid controversial subjects."[2] Morrison promptly turned the *Century* into a voice for the Social Gospel, adding a column called "Social Survey" and including material from writers such as Walter Rauschenbusch and Jane Addams. The *Century* exhibited an interest in the arts and religion by establishing regular columns like "Poems of the Social Awakening" and "Book World." The progressive optimism of the times was also reflected in the column entitled "The World Is Growing Better."

Additionally, Morrison broadened the scope of the journal by turning away from strictly midwestern concerns to include national and international concerns, though at first this was primarily a focus on missions. Theologically, the *Century* moved away from its denominational ties. In 1910, Morrison added the subtitle "A Constructive Weekly," but in 1917 he changed it to "An Undenominational Journal of Religion" to reflect the Disciples of Christ's lack of support for denominations. As the *Century* moved away from a denominational identity, readership began to grow dramatically.

Increased circulation expanded coverage of volatile issues such as civil liberties (including suffrage), prohibition, and war. The *Christian Century* was an ardent defender of civil liberties and spoke against illegal arrests, holding of political prisoners, and deportation of aliens at a time when the United States was in the grip of the Red Scare. Additionally, the *Century* battled capital punishment, condemned racism, defended freedom of speech, and supported organized labor's demands for the right to strike, minimum wage, and eight-hour days. For the *Century*, the Depression affirmed the need for radical economic change, and it found itself supporting the socialist movement. The era also saw the birth of the now familiar "How My Mind Has Changed" series to which prominent theologians were asked to contribute.

The *Century* was also concerned about justice for women on the issue of suffrage. It showed sensitivity to feminist concerns long before such became fashionable by adding a female editor, Ida Withers Harrison, and a column entitled "Modern Womanhood."

Although Morrison demonstrated an openness to many cultural changes, he was adamant about the harmful effects of alcohol, calling liquor the country's "worst menace."[3] The *Century* waged a campaign in favor of the Volstead Act and allowed this issue to influence its editorial opinions on causes of moral decline as well as its endorsement of politicians.

One of the most divisive issues for the editors—one faced several times—was war. When World War I began, Morrison, though sympathetic to the pacifist movement, was reluctant to line up with that camp and eventually supported U.S. involvement. But the sense of betrayal that he felt by the "unjust and vicious"[4] terms of the Versailles treaty led him to join the movement to outlaw war. Morrison was committed to the ideal of world peace and strongly supported the formation of the League of Nations and, later, the United Nations.

Despite his apparent positioning, however, the *Century* often served as a forum for diverse opinions about war. Nevertheless, a rift eventually developed between Morrison and Reinhold Niebuhr, a gifted contributing editor, over Morrison's lack of support for U.S. involvement in World War II. Prior to Pearl Harbor, the *Century*'s editors, although upset by Hitler's aggressiveness, argued vehemently for neutrality. Niebuhr left the *Century* over these differences and in 1941 founded *Christianity and Crisis*, but his views continued to have a shaping influence on the magazine's content.

Related to the war was the question of a Jewish homeland. The *Christian Century* has been criticized for its editorial position in the 1940s opposing the establishment of such a homeland. Martin Marty, a long-time staff member, has defended the policy by explaining that although it now seems wrong, the *Century* was listening to passionately anti-Zionist leaders of Reform Judaism.[5]

The *Century* demonstrated its ability to change its position on war in light of the Korean conflict. Convinced of the dangers of communism, editorials argued that some situations, like Korea, required use of force. When Dwight Eisenhower became president, the *Century* sang his praises for his role in bringing peace to Korea but even more for his anticommunism. However, the *Christian Century* was an early and vocal opponent of Senator Joseph McCarthy and his efforts to root out presumed Communists from positions in the government and the military.

In 1947 Morrison retired, and Paul Hutchinson became the new editor. At that time Protestantism's cultural hegemony was slipping. The *Century* feared the emerging pluralism, most especially the Catholic ''menace.'' To the *Century*, Protestantism was fundamental to American democratic society, and it was the Church's responsibility to assert itself in that society, calling the secular to ''religious revival.''

Under the editorship of Harold E. Fey (1956–1964), the periodical moved toward a more realistic understanding of Protestantism's minority position in society. With that pluralistic understanding came a guarded openness to other faiths, particularly Catholicism, while maintaining the ideal of Christian unity. However, that openness did not come easily. When it first appeared likely that there would be a Catholic president, the editors feared that the influence of the ''hierarchy of the Roman Catholic Church'' would endanger the American tradition of separation of church and state.[6] Although it later supported John F. Kennedy, the *Century* maintained its support for the separation of church and state but noted that ''the First amendment separates the institution of the church and the institution of the state . . . not religion and politics.''[7]

In 1963 the *Century* changed its look, noting that ''we have dropped ungraceful and negative 'undenominational' and substituted graceful and positive 'ecumenical' as our front-page sub-title.''[8] This change was perhaps indicative of the changing attitude toward pluralism in general and Catholics in particular.

Always an advocate of civil liberties, the *Century* supported the Supreme Court's 1954 decision to ban segregation but expressed patience toward the South. However, as early as 1917 it had spoken on behalf of American Negroes.

In 1958 the *Century* announced that a previous contributor, Martin Luther King, Jr., was becoming an editor-at-large. And in 1963, the *Christian Century* was the first national publication to print the entire ''Letter from Birmingham Jail'' that gave impetus to the civil-rights movement. In addition, Fey wrote a significant series of five articles calling for justice for Native Americans and for the U.S. government to live up to its responsibilities to tribal peoples in the nation.

Kyle Haselden became editor in 1964 and promptly issued an editorial endorsement of Lyndon B. Johnson's presidential candidacy. The move cost the *Century* a one-year revocation of its tax-exempt status. But Haselden soon became disillusioned with Johnson because of the growing American military involvement in Southeast Asia. The *Century* took a strong stand against military intervention and for humanitarian aid to Vietnam. Haselden also joined the *Century*'s voice to those of war protesters and became a defender of the right to disagree.

In 1972 James A. Wall took over the editorial reins from Alan Geyer, who had succeeded Haselden in 1968. Geyer had continued the process of change in editorial tone from idealism to realism, from dogmatism to pluralism, from absolutism to a recognition of the complexity of the human condition. The *Century* now counts among its readers and contributors not only liberal Protestants, but also Jews, Roman Catholics, and even the once-marginalized evangelicals.

While the *Century* has always been a forum for poetry, book reviews, and film reviews, Wall has significantly increased that coverage, noting how religion intersects with film and literature. His goal has been to ''cover it as art, not as a purely sociological statement.''[9]

Historically, the *Christian Century* has taken strong positions. Under Wall, however, that advocate voice has diminished—although by no means disappeared—and is being replaced with a complex, pluralistic voice. Thrilled with the ending of the Cold War, the *Century* has turned greater attention toward emerging Third World countries. The *Century* continues to give high priority to matters of social justice, especially for minorities and women. The *Century* was an ardent supporter of the Equal Rights Amendment, arguing that ''the ERA is a necessary step in that long process to liberate both women's and men's minds from the cultural hang-ups of sexual stereotypes which have served to perpetuate women's subordinate status.''[10] The *Christian Century*, Wall has said, ''will continue to do what we can to preach justice and truth in each particular time and place.''[11]

Earlier *Century* editors foresaw a potential problem when they argued against the creation of an Israeli state—namely, a developing Arab-Israeli hostility. Wall followed in those editors' footsteps when he wrote against the ''hardline attitude taken by Israeli supporters on the matter of Palestinian nationalism'' and ''the subtle manner in which Christians who defend Palestinian rights are tabbed as covertly anti-Semitic.''[12]

For all of its changes over the years, the *Century* has in significant ways remained the same. It consistently challenges the Church to raise its social conscience by championing unpopular causes—hammering, probing, prophesying. In the words of James Wall,

The tune we have been banging for 100 years and hope to continue playing throughout another century comes from Scripture, tradition and experience. It also arises from the society we seek to serve, for this magazine has insisted that its task is to stand poised at the intersection of religion and society, . . . ready to report, analyze and propose solutions for the events occurring at that intersection.[13]

Notes

1. James M. Wall, interview with author, 15 December 1992.
2. Linda-Marie Delloff, Martin E. Marty, Dean Peerman, and James M. Wall, *A Century of the Century* (Grand Rapids, MI: Eerdmans, 1987), 8.
3. Ibid., 24.
4. Ibid., 22.
5. Martin E. Marty, "The Century and the Holocaust: Setting the Record Straight," *Christian Century* 102 (10 April 1985): 350–52.
6. Delloff et al., *Century*, 97.
7. "A Wall, Not a Sieve," *Christian Century* 81 (15 January 1964): 68.
8. "Typographically Your Century," *Christian Century* 80 (2 January 1963): 4.
9. Wall, interview with author.
10. " 'I Didn't Raise My Little Girl To Be a Soldier': Sense and Nonsense about the ERA," *Christian Century* 89 (25 October 1972): 1058.
11. "A Second Century," *Christian Century* 101 (4–11 January 1984): 4.
12. James M. Wall, "Paying a Price for the Status Quo," *Christian Century* 95 (1–8 February 1978): 91–92.
13. James M. Wall, "One Hundred years of Pot-Banging," *Christian Century* 101 (4–11 July 1984): 651–52.

Information Sources

INDEX SOURCES: Periodicals are self-indexed in the last issue of June and December annually and in *Reader's Guide to Periodical Literature*, *Guide to Social Science and Religion in Periodical Literature*, *Religion Index One*, *Religious and Theological Abstracts*. Book reviews are in *Book Review Digest* and *Book Review Index*; media reviews in *Media Review Digest*; poetry in *Index of American Periodical Verse*.

REPRINT EDITIONS: University Microfilms International, Bell and Howell Micro Photo Division.

LOCATION SOURCES: Partial collections are widely available. *Union List of Serials* lists complete collections only at Andover-Harvard Theological Library and University of Vermont. The Christian Century Archives are held in Special Collections, Morris Library, Southern Illinois University.

Publication History

MAGAZINE TITLE AND TITLE CHANGES: *Christian Oracle* (1884–1899), *Christian
   Century of the Disciples of Christ* (1899–1901), *Christian Century* (1902–   ).
   Absorbed *Christian Tribune* (1900), *Christian Work* (1926), *Baptist* (1933), and
   World Tomorrow (1934).
VOLUME AND ISSUE DATA: *Christian Oracle* 1:1 (July 1884)–26:47 (November
   1899); *Christian Century of the Disciple of Christ* 26:48 (December 1899)–28:
   52 (December 1901); *Christian Century* 29:1 (January 1902–present). Published
   weekly, except biweekly for the first two weeks of January and February, the last
   two weeks of March, the third week of May through September, and the last two
   weeks of November and December.
PUBLISHER AND PLACE OF PUBLICATION: Christian Century Foundation, Chicago.
EDITORS: George A. Campbell (1884–1908), Charles Clayton Morrison (1908–1947),
   Paul Hutchinson (1947–1955), Harold E. Fey (1956–1964), Kyle Haselden
   (1964–1968), Alan Geyer (1968–1972), James M. Wall (1972–present).
CIRCULATION: 35,000 (1992).

Annalee Ward

CHRISTIAN CENTURY OF THE DISCIPLES OF CHRIST. *See*
CHRISTIAN CENTURY

CHRISTIAN CYNOSURE

The *Christian Cynosure* originated in 1868 as the fortnightly organ of a Chicago-based evangelical Protestant organization, the National Christian Association Opposed to Secret Societies.[1]

Among the multitude of voluntary associations joined by nineteenth-century
Americans, none provoked more controversy than so-called secret societies, organizations with covert oaths and esoteric rituals epitomized by the Masons. The
best-known outbreak of hostility toward such groups occurred in the 1820s with
the emergence in New York of an anti-Masonic movement that attracted enough
popular support in the North to field a third-party presidential candidate in 1832.[2]
Anti-Masonry receded as an organized movement shortly thereafter, though a
residue of animosity toward secret societies remained among evangelicals. In
1868 a Chicago-area coterie of evangelical social reformers led by Jonathan
Blanchard (1811–1892), president of Wheaton College, renewed their attack on
secrecy by creating the National Christian Association and the *Christian Cynosure*.

Blanchard, who edited the paper for its first twenty-four years, was a minister
and educator likened by one admirer to the "ancient prophets of God" for his
bold application of religious truth to such social issues as slavery, intemperance,
and Sabbath breaking.[3] Prior to the Civil War, he had been one of the West's
foremost evangelical abolitionists, an indefatigable crusader who mixed social

reform, revivalism, and a compelling vision of Christ's coming kingdom in a potent message that attracted numerous followers. But he also made many enemies with his decided opinions and an often sharp and unyielding manner. Blanchard first attacked secret societies in the 1840s during his years as pastor of Cincinnati's Sixth Presbyterian Church when he became alarmed by the formation of the Sons of Temperance, an organization that employed Mason-like rituals and regalia in the fight against liquor.[4] Secret societies continued to preoccupy him after his move to Illinois, where he turned Congregationalist and in 1846 assumed the presidency of Knox College. In 1860 Blanchard founded and became the first president of Wheaton College.[5]

Blanchard's apprehensions about covert and oath-bound organizations became especially acute with the outbreak of civil war, the violence and irrationality of which seemed inexplicable apart from insidious and clandestine influences. Shortly after the war, he announced that secret societies had replaced slavery as the primary target of his reforming zeal, and in 1867 he organized an antisecrecy convention that led the following year to the creation of the National Christian Association. The association was chartered by the state of Illinois in 1874 as a nonprofit corporation ''to expose, withstand, and remove secret societies, Freemasonry in particular, and other anti-Christian movements in order to save the churches of Christ from being depraved and to redeem the administration of justice from perversion, and our Republican government from corruption.''[6]

The *Cynosure*'s primary focus throughout its entire 115-year history was antisecrecy. Arguments against secret societies, exposés of their activities, and news of the National Christian Association's work against them thus filled its columns. The *Cynosure* published reports from association lecturers and agents as well as accounts of annual conventions and other gatherings. The paper also relied heavily, especially in the beginning, on the pre–Civil War movement against secret societies by publishing articles by aging reformers and reprinting pieces that had first appeared in the 1820s and 1830s. But so prolific was the multiplication of secret societies in late–nineteenth-century America that the *Cynosure* was never without targets. The publication not only criticized such long-familiar foes as the Masons and Odd Fellows but also attacked college fraternities, the Ku Klux Klan, the Grand Army of the Republic, the Patrons of Husbandry, the Noble Order of the Knights of Labor, and many of the other Gilded Age organizations that adopted esoteric oaths and rituals.

While the specific target varied, the basic message remained constant. With the appearance of each new secret society in a culture that *Cynosure* sympathizers feared was becoming mesmerized by the allure of hidden truth and concealed intimacy, the paper published articles reprising long-familiar accusations of political and spiritual subversion. The *Cynosure* declared that oath-bound members of Masonic lodges and other covert associations conspired in illegitimate and often criminal ways to evade democratic and legal processes. And even worse were the eternal consequences. The paper charged that Masonry and its imitators were really false religions based upon an Enlightenment-derived intellectual and spiritual syncretism hostile to Christianity but concealed and rendered seductive to unsuspecting victims by ornate regalia, secret passwords, and elaborate mythologies.

The paper's first number appeared on 25 July 1868 as the *Christian Banner*, a title dropped after only one issue in deference to a Boston periodical of the same name. The next issue came out on 8 September 1868 as the *Christian Cynosure*, a name probably suggested by Jonathan Blanchard, whose fascination with the image of a fixed and eternal emblem of truth dated from his youth.[7] Six volumes of the fortnightly *Cynosure* in its original four-page, twenty-three-by-seventeen-inch format were subsequently published, the last number appearing on 17 March 1874. A weekly edition in the same format was launched on 7 September 1871 and for several years ran concurrently with the fortnightly. After the fortnightly expired, the weekly expanded to a sixteen-page format measuring 14½ by 10⅕ inches, a size that remained relatively constant until the paper became a monthly in 1897. Subscribers originally paid a dollar per year, a cost that had risen to three dollars by 1897. The *Cynosure*'s circulation was never large, apparently reaching its late–nineteenth-century peak in 1874 at 4,780.[8] Its editorial offices from 1883 to 1981 were located in a Chicago building given to the National Christian Association by a wealthy Chicagoan named Philo Carpenter, a friend of Jonathan Blanchard and a like-minded evangelical social reformer.[9]

Jonathan Blanchard controlled and defined the *Cynosure* during his many years as editor, assisted by his family and members of the Wheaton College community. The paper operated, in fact, very much as a Blanchard family enterprise, and it was closely and publicly linked to the college in what Blanchard believed to be a mutually advantageous alliance devoted to promoting Christ's earthly kingdom. Articles by Wheaton College faculty members, students, and graduates appeared regularly in its columns, as did advertisements for the school and news of its progress. Blanchard's family was also much in evidence. The first *Cynosure* publisher was a Blanchard son-in-law, Ezra A. Cook, whose Chicago publishing house offered a variety of antisecrecy books and pamphlets. Moreover, Ezra's wife, Elizabeth Blanchard Cook, along with another of Jonathan's sons-in-law, Henry Lyman Kellogg, handled the paper's day-to-day operations throughout much of the later nineteenth century.[10]

The *Cynosure* was more than a single-issue reform newspaper under Jonathan Blanchard. An effort was made, for example, to turn it into a religious family newspaper when it expanded to a sixteen-page weekly in 1874 by broadening its appeal with new departments devoted to general religious and secular news, home life, farming and gardening, Sunday schools, and other appropriate topics.[11] Blanchard, moreover, used the *Cynosure* as a vehicle for fostering a broad-based Christian movement to reform American society that went far beyond antisecrecy. A prolific writer, he filled its columns with letters, sermons, editorials, and reminiscences featuring his decided opinions on a wide range of religious, political, and social issues.

In the 1870s, Blanchard used the *Cynosure* to launch a political movement aimed at restoring American society to what he believed were the fundamental principles of the Declaration of Independence. Blanchard's American Party nominated presidential candidates in the elections of 1872, 1876, 1880, and 1884, and *Cynosure* articles covered party activities and expounded its platform.[12] That platform called for the proscription of secret societies, a constitutional amendment recognizing the United States as a Christian country, Sabbath observance, Bible study in the schools, a prohibition on the importation and sale of intoxicating drinks, a guarantee of the rights secured to all Americans by the Civil War amendments, international arbitration for peace, an end to monopolies, protection of the public credit, justice for the Indians, free trade, and abolition of the electoral college.[13]

Following Blanchard's death in 1892, his successors at the *Cynosure* found it difficult to sustain his energy and vision. In 1897 the paper became a monthly greatly reduced in size and scope. No longer a religious family newspaper promoting a general platform of social reform, it was announced that it would be "devoted exclusively to the defence of the kingdom of Christ from the assaults of the secret lodges."[14] The first issue of the new monthly, dated May 1897, measured 9½ by 6½ inches. It had thirty-two pages and a cover, a format that remained substantially unchanged until 1931, although occasional special issues included more pages. The Great Depression, however, forced a reduction in the number of pages to sixteen, a size that remained relatively constant until the *Cynosure* ceased publication with the Autumn 1983 issue.[15] In 1976 the paper was reduced in frequency to a quarterly.[16] In 1903 about 5,000 copies of the *Cynosure* were being printed each month. That number had fallen to 2,700 by 1924, and in 1980 the paper had a paid circulation of only 1,958.[17] Yearly subscriptions for the monthly began at a dollar in 1897 and went up to one and a half dollars in 1920.[18]

Despite its narrowly defined mission, the monthly *Cynosure* occasionally went beyond antisecrecy to cover a wider range of religious and social issues. The paper, for example, expressed opposition to labor unions in the first decades of the twentieth century, and during the 1920s, numerous articles appeared that were written from a fundamentalist perspective.[19] The Moody Bible Institute and Wheaton College, both fundamentalist schools, endorsed the antisecrecy movement and Wheaton especially maintained close ties to the paper. Articles by the college's second and third presidents, Charles Blanchard and J. Oliver Buswell, Jr., appeared regularly in its pages.[20]

The monthly *Cynosure* changed editors frequently. But one editor, William Irving Phillips, a Congregational minister who had graduated from Wheaton College in 1873, became the paper's moving force until he retired in 1925. Phillips served as the National Christian Association's general secretary from 1881 until 1925, often doubling during that time as the *Cynosure*'s editor and publisher.[21] Following Phillips' retirement and the death of Jonathan Blanchard's son Charles in 1925, the influence of Wheaton College gradually receded in the

Cynosure's pages, although the school retained some ties to the paper until it ceased publication.[22]

The Christian Reformed Church gradually emerged during the 1920s as the paper's mainstay. That denomination's general synod regularly recommended the National Christian Association to its local churches as a worthy benevolence, and by 1935 more Christian Reformed pastors were subscribing to the paper than were clergy from any other denomination.[23] A Christian Reformed pastor from Chicago, Benjamin Essenburg, became editor in 1936 and held that post until his death in 1976.[24] His successors, Edward J. Masselink and the *Cynosure*'s last editor, Fred Van Houten, were both Christian Reformed pastors.[25]

Notes

1. Histories of the National Christian Association include *A Brief History of the National Christian Association* (Chicago: Ezra A. Cook, 1875); Clarence N. Roberts, "The Crusade Against Secret Societies and the National Christian Association," *Journal of the Illinois State Historical Society* 64 (Winter 1971): 382–400; and Robert Wayne Smith, "A Study of the Speaking in the Anti-Secrecy Movement, 1862–1882, with Special Reference to the National Christian Association" (Ph.D. diss., State University of Iowa, 1956).

2. A recent account is Paul Goodman, *Towards a Christian Republic: Antimasonry and the Great Transition in New England, 1826–1836* (New York: Oxford University Press, 1988).

3. *Christian Cynosure* 24 (2 June 1892): 1.

4. Jonathan Blanchard, "Secret Societies. A Discourse Delivered in the Sixth Presbyterian Church, Cincinnati, Sept. 7, 1845," *Sermons and Addresses*, by Jonathan Blanchard (Chicago: National Christian Association, 1892), 57–71.

5. Blanchard's life is recounted in Clyde S. Kilby, *Minority of One: The Biography of Jonathan Blanchard* (Grand Rapids, MI: Eerdmans, 1959).

6. Certificate of Incorporation, National Christian Association, 28 February 1874, Corporation Department, Secretary of State, State of Illinois.

7. See Blanchard's poem "To the Polar Star," dated 1830 in the diary that he kept as an undergraduate at Middlebury College, in the Jonathan Blanchard Collection, Special Collections, Buswell Memorial Library, Wheaton College, Illinois. The poem later appeared in print several places, including Blanchard, *Sermons and Addresses*, 136–37.

8. *Christian Cynosure* 6 (18 June 1874): 16.

9. Ibid. 15 (4 January 1883): 8; ibid. (Winter 1981): 22.

10. Ibid. 11 (3 October 1878): 8; ibid. 47 (April 1915): 369.

11. Ibid. 6 (2 April 1874): 8.

12. Ibid. 14 (13 April 1882): 5; ibid. 16 (26 June 1884): 4–5, 9.

13. *Brief History*, 9–12; *Christian Cynosure* 11 (14 November 1878): 13.

14. *Christian Cynosure* 29 (1 April 1897): 8.

15. Ibid. 64 (November 1931): 195.

16. Ibid. (June 1976).

17. Ibid. 36 (June 1903): 40; ibid. 57 (June 1924): 37; Statement of Ownership, Management and Circulation, 11 October 1980, "*Christian Cynosure* Publication, 1978–

1980'' folder, National Christian Association Collection, Special Collections, Wheaton College, Illinois.

18. *Christian Cynosure* 30 (May 1897); 52 (January 1920).

19. Ibid. 32 (April 1900): 403–4; 56 (September 1923): 156–57.

20. Ibid. 36 (July 1903): 75–84; ibid. 42 (August 1909): 99–103; 59 (July 1926): 67–75.

21. Ibid. 52 (November 1919): 196–97; ibid. 66 (December 1933): 115–20.

22. For example, Wheaton's chaplain, Evan D. Welsh, remained on the paper's advisory board until it ceased publication. See ibid. (Autumn 1983): 2.

23. Ibid. 61 (June 1928): 38; ibid. 67 (January 1935): 133.

24. Ibid. (Winter 1976): 3–4.

25. Ibid. (Winter 1981): 2; ibid. (Autumn 1981): 8–12.

Information Sources

INDEX SOURCES: No comprehensive index exists, although a small file citing selected topics from the paper's earliest years is available in Special Collections, Buswell Memorial Library, Wheaton College, Illinois.

LOCATION SOURCES: The most complete file is found in Special Collections, Buswell Memorial Library, Wheaton College. The years 1937–1957 are, however, missing from the Wheaton file.

Publication History

MAGAZINE TITLE AND TITLE CHANGES: *Christian Banner*, 25 July 1868; *Christian Cynosure*, 8 September 1868–Autumn 1983.

VOLUME AND ISSUE DATA: 1:1 (25 July 1868)–6:16 (17 March 1874), published fortnightly; 1:1 (7 September 1871)–3:24 (26 March 1874), published weekly; 6:25 (2 April 1874)–29:34 (29 April 1897), published weekly; 30:1 (May 1897)–(June 1976); (Winter 1976)–(Autumn 1983), published quarterly.

PUBLISHER AND PLACE OF PUBLICATION: National Christian Association, Chicago, Illinois (1868–1872, 1883–1981); Phoenix, Arizona, and Orland Park, Illinois (1981–1983); Ezra A. Cook, Chicago (1872–1882).

EDITORS: Jonathan Blanchard (1868–1892), Henry M. Hugunin (1893–1895), M. A. Gault (1895–1899), William Irving Phillips (ca. 1899–1915, ca. 1920–1923, 1924–1925), James Edwin Phillips (1915–ca. 1920), A. H. Leaman (1923–1924), Gerhard H. Doermann (ca. 1925–1934), G. M. Van Pernis (1934–1936), Benjamin Essenburg (1936–1976), Edward J. Masselink (1977–1981), Fred Van Houten (1981–1983).

CIRCULATION: 4,780 (1874); 2,700 (1924); 1,958 (1980).

Richard S. Taylor

CHRISTIAN DIGEST. *See* ETERNITY

CHRISTIAN DISCIPLE. *See* CHRISTIAN EXAMINER

CHRISTIAN EVANGEL. *See* PENTECOSTAL EVANGEL

CHRISTIAN EXAMINER

Unitarians, as the old saying goes, believe in "the Fatherhood of God, the brotherhood of man, and the neighborhood of Boston." The *Christian Examiner*, and its predecessor the *Christian Disciple*, celebrated all three; yet it was much more than a regional magazine designed to advance denominational doctrine. It was one of the most ambitious and expansive literary and religious periodicals of the day. Contemporaries praised its high quality, and a leading chronicler of the history of magazines called it "one of the most important American religious reviews."[1] The *Christian Examiner* was distinguished not only by its quality and breadth, but also by its long list of gifted contributors. It remains an especially useful historical source because in its pages readers can trace the shifting contours not only of Unitarianism but, more broadly, of American religion and culture in the nineteenth century.

Unitarianism, with which the *Examiner* was associated, emerged as a distinct movement within New England Congregationalism when the Unitarian Controversy erupted in 1805. A passionate debate ensued that year because some Trinitarian Congregationalists grew angry when a moderate Calvinist was replaced by a liberal, Henry Ware, as Hollis Divinity at Harvard University. They feared that a diluted and dangerous form of Christianity—one rejecting the doctrines of original sin, the trinity, vicarious atonement, and election—would flourish in the leading institution for training ministers in eastern Massachusetts. William Ellery Channing articulated the nature of the disagreement eloquently in his widely-circulated sermon "Unitarian Christianity," which he delivered in Baltimore in 1819. Channing's manifesto provided Unitarians with a coherent statement of faith.

Unitarians formed an association, though not yet a full-blown denomination, when the constitution for the American Unitarian Association was adopted on 26 May 1825. Against the wishes of some radicals, Unitarianism was defined in explicitly Christian terms and given denominational form when the National Conference of Unitarian Churches was established in 1865. Another split, a smaller one, occurred at this time, as radicals fled because they felt constricted by the association's explicitly Christian platform. During the latter half of the nineteenth century, those who remained in the association focused much of their attention on building and defining the new denomination.

Denominational history is reflected in the pages of the *Examiner* and its predecessor, the *Christian Disciple* (1813–1823), which is really part of the same file.[2] Only a change of name and the adoption of new volume numbering distinguish them. Without missing a beat, the *Examiner* continued the legacy of the *Disciple*. The latter's motto was "Speaking the truth in love." Overall that accurately described the tone of the review. It contained summaries of Unitarian faith, such as "The Fundamental Doctrines of Christianity" or "Objections to Unitarian Christianity Considered," as ministers who wrote for the magazine in its early years sought to define themselves over and against their Trinitarian opponents.[3] They sympathetically summarized and favorably reviewed sermons by Channing and other leading spokespersons for the tradition.[4] But the early editors and contributors rarely turned to sarcasm or caricature. They made it clear that they felt pushed from the Congregational churches, and they expressed disappointment at the rancor of the debates. The prospectus for the *Disciple*, on the other hand, proclaimed that authentic Christianity was a "pure and mild religion." The prospectus championed "charity and forbearance" and aimed "to soften the violence of party."[5]

The *Examiner* took over the *Disciple*'s motto and continued to advocate courteous but rigorous argument as it published works on Unitarian theology and practice. The *Examiner* was the most influential periodical of Unitarianism during its "Golden Age" (1835–1865), and most of its leading figures contributed to its pages, including William Rounseville Alger, Henry Whitney Bellows, William Ellery Channing, James Freeman Clarke, Octavius Brooks Frothingham, Frederick Henry Hedge, and Henry Ware, Jr. Clarke, for instance, continued the liberal assault on Calvinist doctrine. In 1854 he offered a nuanced comparison of "Polemical Theology" and "Irenic Theology" of Calvinism and Unitarianism. After acknowledging that Calvinism contained some truths, Clarke, in an essay entitled "Polemics and Irenics," repeated the usual criticisms of "the Trinity, the Vicarious Atonement, the doctrines of Election, Depravity, and Everlasting Punishment." He then argued that the central principle of Unitarianism—that Christianity is a reasonable and progressive religion whose essence is "life not creeds"—provided the best foundation for continuing progress in theology.[6]

The reader also can trace intradenominational debates in the pages of the *Examiner*. An article by George Ripley in the November 1836 issue proposed that Christian truths could be supported without appeal to miracles. That piece opened a long battle—known as the "miracles controversy"—between conservative Unitarians and Transcendentalists. Not only Ripley but also Ralph Waldo Emerson, Theodore Parker, and other Transcendentalists contributed pieces during the second third of the century, but the status of their views was hotly contested. When the "miracles controversy" broke out, the *Examiner*'s editor, William Ware, aimed for moderation, and he succeeded in that he managed to frustrate partisans in both camps. Between 1857 and 1861, as Frederick H. Hedge and Edward Everett Hale assumed management, the *Examiner* embraced Transcendentalism's leading ideas and voices.

During the mid–1860s, controversy erupted again as many Unitarian leaders wanted to provide the association with a denominational structure and a clearer, more explicitly Christian identity. The *Examiner*'s editors during this period, Joseph H. Allen and Henry W. Bellows, sided with the more moderate and conservative elements, and that penchant shaped the character of the periodical and its coverage of this debate.[7] It also helped to divide Unitarians further by, as the radicals might have put it, muffling dissenting voices. By 1857 about one fifth of the *Examiner*'s subscribers had abandoned the review, and this contributed to financial difficulties that in turn led to the *Examiner*'s demise and the start of a new magazine, *Old and New*, at the end of 1869.[8]

That the review mirrored denominational shifts is of interest to the historian of Unitarianism, but that is not why the periodical deserves the attention of scholars or why it might be called "popular." The *Disciple* and *Examiner* were "popular" magazines in the sense that they aimed at wide coverage and broad readership. The editors of the *Disciple*, for instance, directed their efforts at "the great mass of Christians," from "the man of business to the husbandman and mechanic."[9] To reach those readers the managers vowed to keep the periodical inexpensive and broad ranging. Found in the pages of these magazines were discussions of history, philosophy, science, education, reform, literature, as well as religion.

Contributors chronicled contemporary religious events and addressed the pressing issues of the age. They did not encourage readers to reach the emotional heights evident at the revivals on the rural frontier, but the influence of the Second Great Awakening was clear in the contents of the *Disciple*, which tried to "rouse professors [of Christianity] from their slumbers, to breathe into them a spirit of mild but earnest devotion."[10] In the pages of the *Disciple* and *Examiner*, Unitarian leaders also confronted the major intellectual challenges of the day. They defended historical criticism of the Bible and led the way in the American discovery of Asian religions. Editors published "religious intelligence" about recent developments in Boston, America, and the world. Perhaps in part because their own experience as dissenters had sensitized them to the problems of the marginalized, Unitarian authors also denounced the "extermination" of the Indians, announced "the mournful honor of adding a new department to the literature of civilization—the autobiographies of escaped slaves," and defended Roman Catholics just as anti-Catholic sentiment swelled.[11]

The editors of the *Examiner* valued literature, broadly conceived, and they published a number of noteworthy essays and reviews. One of the most important and often overlooked essays in American literary history was reprinted in its pages in 1830. That piece, William Ellery Channing's "Remarks on National Literature," was ostensibly a review of C.J. Ingersoll's *Discourse Concerning the Influence of America on the Mind*, but Channing took the opportunity to describe the current literary crisis and fashion as a call for change.[12] Channing exhorted American writers to overcome subservience to Europe and usher in cultural independence, just as their ancestors had fought for political autonomy earlier. Channing was a precursor of the "American Renaissance" that followed in the 1840s and 1850s, and the *Examiner* evaluated new works by participants in that broad literary movement—Nathaniel Hawthorne, Herman Melville, Ralph Waldo Emerson, Henry David Thoreau, and Walt Whitman. One *Examiner* contributor was "grieved and disgusted at the amount of idle, ephemeral, useless fiction" that women's magazines were pouring out, but liberal female writers such as Catharine Maria Sedgwick and Maria Susanna Cummins found their books reviewed in the magazine.[13] Reviewers also considered the work of mainline Protestant novelists like Harriet Beecher Stowe. A brief assessment of Stowe's influential *Uncle Tom's Cabin* lavishly praised her skill as a novelist and accurately predicted that no other publication would be "more effective in the service of a holy but perilous work."[14]

That "holy work," of course, was the abolition of slavery, and from the start, the *Disciple* and *Examiner* devoted attention to the various antebellum movements aimed at uplifting individuals and reforming society. As in other areas, Unitarians helped to lead the way.[15] Contributors advocated abolition and temperance. They condemned dueling and capital punishment. The *Examiner* also published fifty-five articles dealing with education and its reform. Because Noah Worcester, the *Disciple*'s first editor, was a leader in the antebellum peace movement, the *Disciple* was filled with articles on war and peace. In fact, the topic received so much treatment that readers began to complain that it was eclipsing religious issues, and Worcester felt compelled to apologize to readers in 1819.[16] The *Examiner* continued to deal with the issue, especially before, during, and after the Civil War.[17]

The *Examiner* survived only a few years after the Civil War ended. Before its demise in 1869, it had survived financial difficulties, a series of intradenominational debates, and a long list of able but inattentive editors. Yet the *Disciple* and *Examiner* left an ample inheritance to the editors, contributors, and readers of *Old and New* and the *Unitarian Review* (1874–1891), which continued the legacy. The *Disciple* and *Examiner* published some weak issues and articles, of course; and the sober and scholarly style limited their appeal to some extent. Few religious magazines in America, however, can boast of their list of contributors. Few have matched their quality or scope.

Notes

1. Frank Luther Mott, *A History of American Magazines* (Cambridge: Harvard University Press, 1938), 1:284.

2. Ibid., 285.

3. *Christian Disciple* 1:6 (1813): 180–81; ibid., n.s., 1 (1819): 436–48.

4. Ibid. 1:2 (1814): 44–47.

5. Ibid. 2:1 (1814): iii–v.

6. *Christian Examiner* 57 (September 1854): 170, 176, 180, 181.

7. For examples of articles that set a conservative tone, see "National Conference of Unitarian Churches," *Christian Examiner* 78 (May 1865): 409–30; "The Unitarian Movement," *Christian Examiner*, n.s., 1 (May 1866): 289–303; and "The National Conference of Unitarian Churches," *Christian Examiner* 81 (November 1866): 388–400. One article that stirred controversy was written by E. C. Towne "Christianity and Pseudo-Christianity," *Christian Examiner*, n.s., 3 (March 1867): 133–60.

8. For further details, see Joseph Henry Allen, "Editor's Note Book: The 'Christian Examiner,'" *Unitarian Review* 27 (April 1887): 363–67.

9. *Christian Disciple* 2:1 (1814): v.

10. Ibid., p. iv.

11. For examples of articles in which these issues were discussed, see "Reflections on the Decrease of American Indians," *Christian Disciple* 6 (April 1818): 136–41; "Narratives of Fugitive Slaves," *Christian Examiner* 47 (July 1849): 61–93; and "Reactions in Favor of the Roman Catholics," *Christian Examiner* 23 (September 1837).

12. *Christian Examiner*, n.s., 2 (January 1830): 269–95.

13. Ibid. 36 (January 1844): 141.

14. Ibid. 52 (May 1852): 451.

15. On Unitarians' preeminence in reform, see Daniel Walker Howe, "At Morning Blest and Golden-Browed: Unitarians, Transcendentalists, and Reformers, 1835–1865," in *A Stream of Light: A Short History of American Unitarianism*, ed. Conrad Wright (Boston: Unitarian Universalist Association, 1975), 39.

16. *Christian Disciple*, n.s., 1 (January–February 1819): 1–2.

17. Concerning the issue of war and peace, see "The War," *Christian Examiner* 71 (July 1861): 95–115; "The Peace Policy: How It Is Urged, and What It Means," *Christian Examiner* 74 (January 1863): 113–32; and "The Nation's Triumph, and Its Sacrifice," *Christian Examiner* 78 (May 1865): 430–43.

Information Sources

INDEX SOURCES: William Cushing, *Index to the Christian Examiner* (Boston: J. S. Cushing, 1879), lists by author and subject. A copy of that index also appears in Kenneth Walter Cameron, ed., *Research Keys to the American Renaissance* (Hartford, CT: Transcendental Books, 1967), 3–82. It is also indexed in *Poole's Index to Periodical Literature*.

LOCATION SOURCES: The *Christian Examiner* is available on microfilm from University Microfilms International, Ann Arbor, Michigan. A complete run is housed at Andover-Harvard Theological Library, Cambridge, Massachusetts.

Publication History

MAGAZINE TITLE AND TITLE CHANGES: *Christian Examiner and Theological Review* (1824–1828), *Christian Examiner and General Review* (1829–1844), *Christian Examiner and Religious Miscellany* (1844–1857), *Christian Examiner* (1857–1869).

VOLUME AND ISSUE DATA: Bimonthly. 1824–1828, one volume yearly (1–5); 1829–1843, two volumes yearly (6–35) (even-numbered volumes contain March, May, July; odd-numbered contain September, November, January); 1844–1869, two volumes yearly (36–87) (even-numbered volumes contain January, March, May; odd-numbered contain July, September, November). There are some irregularities. Volume 9, December 1830, was substituted for January 1831, which was omitted. To make the voluming regular, there were two January 1844 numbers, one belonging to volume 35 and one to volume 36.

PUBLISHER AND PLACE OF PUBLICATION: All of the following publishers were located in Boston, except for the last named. Cummings, Hilliard Co. (1824–1826), Bowles and Dearborn (1827), Gray and Bowen (1830–1832), Charles Bowen (1833–1837), James Munroe and Co. (1837–1843), William Crosby

(1844–1857), H. P. Nichols (1848–1857), Thomas B. Fox (1857–1863), Joseph H. Allen (1863–1869) William R. Alger (1865–1869), James Miller and H. W. Bellows, New York (1866–1869).
EDITORS: John G. Palfrey (1824–1825), Francis Jenks (1826–1830), James Walker and F. W. P. Greenwood (1831–1839), William Ware (1839–1844), Alvan Lamson and Ezra S. Gannett (1844–1849), George Putnam and G. E. Ellis (1849–1857), F. H. Hedge and E. E. Hale (1857–1861), Thomas B. Fox (1862–1864), Joseph Henry Allen (1863–1865), Henry W. Bellows (1866–1869).
CIRCULATION: Unknown.

Thomas A. Tweed

CHRISTIAN EXAMINER AND GENERAL REVIEW. *See* CHRISTIAN EXAMINER

CHRISTIAN EXAMINER AND RELIGIOUS MISCELLANY. *See* CHRISTIAN EXAMINER

CHRISTIAN EXAMINER AND THEOLOGICAL REVIEW. *See* CHRISTIAN EXAMINER

CHRISTIAN FUNDAMENTALIST

The "enemies" were gaining ground, and something had to be done. People needed to be organized, and theological positions clearly argued. In response to those enemies of modernism, rationalism, and higher criticism of the Bible, the *Christian Fundamentalist* was written, and the World's Christian Fundamentals Association (WCFA) was established. The first issue of *Christian Fundamentalist* appeared in July 1927, and the final issue was published in October 1932.

An understanding of the *Christian Fundamentalist* would not be complete without knowing of its editor in chief, William Bell Riley. He was born in Indiana in 1861 to a family deeply involved in the slavery issue, and because William's father sympathized with slave owners, the Rileys moved to Kentucky. Riley "yielded his heart to Christ" at age seventeen, and he changed his career plans from the law to being a defender of his faith.[1] In preparation for theological battle, Riley was graduated fourth in his class and first in debate at Hanover College in Indiana.[2]

Riley's center of influence was the First Baptist Church of Minneapolis, Minnesota, where he served as primary pastor for forty-five years (1897–1942). During Riley's stay, First Baptist's membership grew from 585 to 3,600—a sevenfold increase, while the population of Minneapolis had only tripled.[3] Although Riley lived a long and active life until his death in 1947, his theology remained remarkably consistent, though considered dogmatic by his critics.

Riley developed a conservative, biblical theology labeled "fundamentalist" after the 1910 series of books entitled *The Fundamentals*. For fundamentalists, the word of God as given in the Bible is central to all beliefs. As Riley later preached, "The one way of salvation is by the Word; the one way of reaching others is by the Word; the one way of victory against the Adversary is by the Word."[4]

Although Riley argued for Christ as the ultimate solution to societal problems, he was not apathetic in responding to political controversies. Riley traveled to various college campuses to debate political issues, and he lobbied for several congressional bills by traveling to Minnesota churches and seeking legislative support.[5]

The fundamentalist cause suffered many setbacks in America during the 1930s and 1940s, but Riley's strong influence continued in the Midwest region. William Trollinger has argued that Riley established a "regional empire" in Minnesota even if fundamentalism had waned elsewhere.[6] Riley was a vocal defender of the faith on many fronts, including the *Christian Fundamentalist*.

The title page of the first issues stated that the *Christian Fundamentalist* was a "monthly magazine published in the interest of 'Christian Fundamentals' by the World's Christian Fundamentals Association, Minneapolis, Minn., and devoted to the cause of evangelical Christianity and orthodox theology."[7] The first issue was devoted to defining fundamentalism and setting forth the objective of the WCFA.

In the first year of the journal, space was given to minutes of WCFA meetings, theological essays that further elucidated the fundamentalists, and reports from foreign-mission fields. As the magazine became more clearly defined, its pages became a battleground against liberalism and modernism. For example, in the October 1927 issue, Riley argued that Carleton College of Minnesota was a "vendor of false and anti-Christian philosophies."[8] Often Riley would discuss teachings and course offerings by schools to illustrate the enemy's foothold in the educational system.

During the life of the publication, the format became somewhat standardized: announcements of upcoming conferences, minutes of past meetings, various theological editorials, an essay by Riley, reports from the foreign-missions field, and commentary on the "denominational world" (Presbyterian, Baptist, Episcopal, Lutheran, and Methodist).

Advertising in the magazine dealt mainly with books (many written and recommended by Riley) and with the Northwestern Bible and Missionary Training School founded in 1902 by Riley. The school still exists today as Northwestern College in Roseville, Minnesota, a suburb of St. Paul.

Christian Fundamentalist ceased publication in 1932 for three main reasons: Riley's health suffered, Riley wanted to embark on a national teaching campaign, and the financial commitments to the magazine waned. In a column titled "Discontinuing This Magazine" in the final issue, the writer suggested that "there are now many efficient Fundamental magazines; we feel that this one can be spared without great injury to the Cause."[9]

Actually, the voice of the fundamentalist cause was passed on to another publication, the *Pilot*, originating in 1920 and produced by the Northwestern Bible and Missionary Training School. In October 1932, readers of the *Christian Fundamentalist* received the first issue of volume 13 of the *Pilot* instead of the *Christian Fundamentalist*. The enemies continued to be fought, but this time on a different front.

Notes

1. William Bell Riley, "Youth in Search of God," in *Problems of Youth*, by William Bell Riley (Grand Rapids, MI: Zondervan, 1941), 107–23.
2. Allyn C. Russell, *Voices of American Fundamentalism: Seven Biographical Studies* (Philadelphia: Westminster Press, 1976), 82.
3. Lloyd B. Hull, "A Rhetorical Study of the Preaching of William Bell Riley" (Ph.D. diss., Wayne State University, 1960), 133.
4. William Bell Riley, "Youth's Victory Lies This Way," in *Youth's Victory Lies This Way* by William Bell Riley (Grand Rapids, MI: Zondervan, 1938), 131.
5. Marie Acomb Riley, *The Dynamic of a Dream* (Grand Rapids, MI: Eerdmans, 1938). Marie Riley, William Riley's wife, discussed his "political evangelism" around the state.
6. William Vance Trollinger, Jr., "One Response to Modernity: Northwestern Bible School and the Fundamentalist Empire of William Bell Riley" (Ph.D. diss., University of Wisconsin at Madison, 1984).
7. *Christian Fundamentalist* 1:1 (July 1927): 3.
8. Ibid. 1:4 (October 1927): 3.
9. Ibid. 6:4 (October 1932): 34.

Information Sources

INDEX SOURCES: A contents page accompanies each issue. No general index was published during the magazine's life; however, a loose paper index has been tucked into the front covers of the bound volumes dated July 1927–June 1930.

LOCATION SOURCES: All issues are housed in the W. B. Riley Memorial Library Archives at Northwestern College, Roseville, Minnesota.

Publication History

MAGAZINE TITLE: *Christian Fundamentalist* (1927–1932).

VOLUME AND ISSUE DATA: 1:1 (July 1927)–4:4 (October 1932). Published monthly.

PUBLISHER AND PLACE OF PUBLICATION: William B. Riley, Minneapolis, Minnesota.

EDITORS: William B. Riley (1927–1932), coeditor with Paul W. Rood (July 1929–March 1932), with associate editors Paul W. Rood and Harry Rimmer (April 1932–October 1932).

CIRCULATION: Unknown. Prices for the magazine were given in dollars ($1.50), shillings, francs, and belga, suggesting that the magazine had some international circulation.

Todd J. Rasmuson

CHRISTIAN HERALD

A recent article on Christian publishing identified some major problems facing those producing reading material for a Christian audience:

People want a religion based less on theology and more on their own experiences, religion as lived and not as it ought to be lived. They want a religion that speaks to the everyday problems of contemporary life, not one that tells them what to think and feel. They want to connect the internal religious experience with external realities, to experience the holy not as an intellectual exercise but as something they can bring into their lives to provide healing and wholeness.[1]

In many ways, the demands of today's religious audience are similar to those facing the audience of the first issue of the *Christian Herald and Signs of Our Times*, later shortened to *Christian Herald* in 1899. "Entered, according to Act of Congress, in the year 1878, by Benj. Jas Fernie and Joseph Spurgeon, in the Office of the Librarian of Congress, at Washington,"[2] and ended with the third issue in volume 115 (1992), *Christian Herald* was founded "to give the right hand of fellowship to all engaged in the circulation of a pure Gospel, and hope from all such the recognition and greeting usually accorded a fellow-laborer in the same field."[3] At four cents per copy, or $1.50 for a year's subscription, Fernie and Spurgeon asserted that the magazine had "no pecuniary gain in view, as the price clearly evidences."[4] *Christian Herald* gave practical advice to those engaged in everyday activities, as well as those laboring in Christian service. Among *Christian Herald*'s firsts: The Pollyanna fiction stories were originally published as a serialized story in it, the first red-letter edition of the Bible was published by *Christian Herald*, Fanny Crosby published many of her hymns for the first time in it, and the *Christian Herald* Singers released an album of Christmas music in the 1950s.[5]

Christian Herald was originated as a weekly magazine, moving to monthly service in 1931 and to bimonthly issues in 1989. The first issue promised the following items every week:

A Portrait and Biography of some eminent person—A Sermon by the Rev. C. H. SPURGEON, of London—A Sermon by the Rev. T. DE WITT TALMAGE, of Brooklyn, or some other American Preacher—An Article elucidatory of the Prophecies of Holy Writ, written by Clergymen who have made the subject their especial study—A Study of Current Events and Religious Intelligence—A Serial Tale and Short Anecdotes, etc.— Also, once a month, a Sermon by the Eminent Methodist Minister, Dr. W. MORLEY PUSHON.[6]

Dr. Louis Klopsch purchased *Christian Herald* in 1889. Continuing with the same format as its originators, he desired to increase circulation of the magazine (thirty thousand at the time of purchase). Klopsch also wanted to make the magazine "a medium of American bounty to the needy throughout the world."[7] His particular mark on the magazine was its contribution to the growth of rescue missions throughout the world. He would publicize disasters in graphic detail in the (accurate) belief that readers would respond to the needs of those in disaster areas and would support rescue missions that provided aid. Because of Klopsch's publicity and encouragement, *Herald* readers also helped to sponsor the Bowery Mission in New York and the Mont Lawn Camp, located in the Poconos, for inner-city children. In addition, *Christian Herald* spearheaded a national drive in 1894 to keep Moody Bible Institute open and campaigned to have "In God We Trust" restored to American coins in 1907. Of his activism, Klopsch wrote in 1892: "How grand will be the result in the last day for those who have consecrated the printing press to high and holy objects! God will say to them, 'You broke off a million chains, you opened a million blind eyes, you gave resurrection to a million of the dead.' "[8]

Klopsch's vision and fervor never diminished over the years, despite changes in publishers and editors. The words "A Voice for the Layman" appeared under the title in September of 1964 and continued through the June 1969 issue, indicating the magazine's target audience. A 1985 edition of *Religious Writer's Marketplace* describes *Christian Herald* as an "evangelical family magazine about Christian faith in everyday life, designed to exalt Jesus Christ as Savior and Lord and to make disciples for him."[9] And the 1992 *Magazines for Libraries* noted that *Christian Herald* "carries articles for a popular audience on general religious and ethical topics . . . all from a conservative viewpoint intended for the whole family."[10]

The family emphasized in *Christian Herald* is a traditional one. Catherine Marshall, who joined the staff as "woman's editor" in 1958, wrote an open letter to the readers in January 1960, informing them that her recent marriage to Len LeSourd, then editor of *Guideposts*, made it necessary for her to concentrate on the career of wife and mother and to cut back her activities at the magazine. She continued as a contributing editor, writing such articles as "Why Segregate the Sexes in Church Work?" Despite the liberal tone of the article's title, most advice on the family in *Christian Herald* concentrated on traditional divisions of labor between husbands and wives, although there is rarely any indication that such a division puts men in a superior role, as this advice from the 1 January 1908 issue shows:

Husbands are to love their wives as Christ loves the Church. A modern husband, whose ideal of domestic life is that he is an autocrat and his wife a person subject to his authority, will signally fail in carrying out his endeavors, and will succeed in making his home a place of wretchedness. Married people should first of all be congenial friends; they are comrades on the road.[11]

Christian Herald carried a wide variety of articles, some simple and some thought provoking, but almost always containing a moral that was enduring. This note, for example, appeared in the 22 June 1982 issue:

The treasures collected by a mouse were unearthed a few days ago at Newton, Mass. In pulling down the piazza of an old hotel the nest of a mouse was found which contained over a quart of pins, hairpins, and needles, a few small silver and copper coins, and a railroad ticket between Auburndale and Boston. It was a strange collection, which must have been gathered with no little difficulty and labor. We do not know to what extent animals have the power of reasoning, but it is evident that this little creature could not have been very largely gifted in that direction or it would not have taken so many pains to hoard articles it could not possibly use. But then we may be told and very justly too, that men often do the same thing. (Eccles. 4:8)[12]

Other social concerns revolved around popular culture. In 1946, *Christian Herald* asked its readers to vote on the best motion picture of the year. In 1960, the last year, readers were told that voting was even more important because of the increase in movies with "questionable values." *Christian Herald* also took issue that year with the promotion of the film *Solomon and Sheba*. The producers had run advertisements in Christian magazines, touting the film as an exciting means of teaching Bible history. A promotional kit, offered free to churches, included a fifty-four–frame filmstrip, a fact sheet on Solomon and Sheba, topics for discussion, a bibliography, and a map of Israel at the time of the story. Promotion of the movie outside Christian audiences, however, emphasized the lurid nature of the film: a "realistic" orgy scene, the seduction of Solomon by Sheba, Sheba's bathing in the scented milk of asses, and pagan revels. A March 1960 editorial in *Christian Herald* chided the producers of the film, asking them how a movie could be offered to two different audiences in such disparate ways. The editorial urged *Christian Herald* readers to boycott the film. More recently, *Christian Herald* has done interviews with artists like singer Amy Grant, who has come under fire from some church members for "selling out" her Christianity through secular music.[13]

Concern for purity of beliefs and pure evangelical witness led *Christian Herald* to comment on various cults and competing beliefs in modern society. In 1968, Jerome Ellison asked "Why Is Astrology So Popular?" as astrology columns began to appear frequently in newspapers.[14] Ellison debunked many of the claims of astrology, a topic that *Christian Herald* returned to in both 1985 and 1990 in order to help readers explain why Christianity was superior to those who were enamored of astrology.[15] As more of its readers voiced concerns regarding their witness to various "cult" groups and New Age thinkers, *Christian Herald* began a series of articles called "The Mars Hill Collection" that told readers how to talk to representatives of groups like Mormons, New Agers, Jehovah's Witnesses, Muslims, and the Worldwide Church of God.[16]

Christian Herald gave consistent voice to the political concerns of its readers.

In 1910, *Christian Herald* commented on the decision of the Illinois Supreme Court to exclude the Bible from public schools, asking, "Now that the first serious blow against the freedom of God's Word has been struck, who can tell how far the assault may be carried?"[17] The tone of such commentary changed, however, with the introduction of such articles as Bill Jack's "The First Amendment Works for Christians Too."[18] In order to help put faith into action, *Christian Herald* introduced a six-page, pull-out "Christian Action Guide," with contact names and telephone numbers for people who wanted to take Christian action in their community, such as starting services for the handicapped, providing Bible studies, or even writing to decision makers about topics of concern to Christians.[19] World events were also of concern: On the eve of World War II, Daniel A. Poling wrote in *Christian Herald*: "Never again can the Church bless war itself and be worthy of survival. The Christian Church must denounce the war method and those who invoke it. But the Church must also comfort and strengthen her children. . . . For the Church there is no isolation and no room for negative pacifism. We are all in this war."[20]

Typically, articles reflected concerns of the times. During World War I and World War II, the magazine was consistently optimistic about the role that America was playing; during the Depression, *Christian Herald* helped its readers keep a "stiff upper lip" with the message that bad times would soon pass. In 1968, *Christian Herald* addressed problems surrounding the Vietnam War and the effect that American withdrawal would have on the Church there. *Christian Herald* maintained a patriotic position over the years, demonstrating through its writings that Christians must work to uphold the principles on which America was founded. Contributors to *Christian Herald* included such notables as FBI director J. Edgar Hoover, who wrote a piece titled "America's Future and Yours" for the November 1967 issue. Most recently, lead stories have concerned "heroes of the faith": people working to make a difference in the world through their Christian commitment. Consistently, articles focused on the necessity for ordinary people to find ways to change the world around them through their faith. As Pat Robertson noted in "The American Church at the Crossroads":

Consider these facts: The majority of born-again evangelicals in the United States define success as the acquisition of a secular position and material wealth; some 40 percent express no clear-cut position on abortion; more than half believe that divorce is an acceptable solution when the marriage partners are incompatible. In short, the Christian in the United States, while professing a biblical faith in the Lordship of Jesus Christ, in practice affirms a humanistic view of life and reality.[21]

In 1986, *Christian Herald* created the "James 1:22" award, given to people who were making a difference in the world. Among the recipients was Randall Terry, founder of the antiabortion group Operation Rescue. Although most readers applauded the award, later issues ran several letters from people who were angered by it and who canceled their subscriptions as a result. Some argued that, despite the fact that Terry is making a difference in the world, his notion of civil disobedience contradicts the admonition in Romans 13 to be obedient to the law of the land. Other recipients of the award included Virgil Gulken, founder of Love INC (In the Name of Christ). The organization was originally an outreach to the homeless, but now also helps people with a variety of problems who are having difficulty connecting with appropriate agencies for assistance.

Graphically, *Christian Herald* was a mainstream magazine, revealing little innovation in design or the use of color. Louis Klopsch introduced some color into the magazine, and as technology advanced the covers showed a bit more complexity. For the most part, covers reflected designs standard for the time: Until the 1960s, cover designs were illustrations rather than photos, with many covers looking much like the standard church bulletin used by a variety of churches. By the end of the 1960s, covers were more often photographs of people or places in the lead articles. In 1986, *Christian Herald* underwent a radical design change, with the use of varied types (e.g., one that appeared to be scrawled by hand for the headline title and some headlines inside), more white space, and color. The response was not overwhelmingly positive from readers, some of whom preferred the traditional, conservative look once worn by the magazine; but the design changes lasted to the end.

The *Christian Herald* ceased publication in the month after the anniversary issue marking its 115th year, transferring its subscription list to the *Christian Reader*. With the exception of its issue identification (appearing as volume 115, no. 3, 1992, rather than May–June 1992) no indication of the end of publication was apparent. *Christian Herald* subscribers received nothing until the November–December 1992 issue of the *Christian Reader*, announcing its selection as the "publication best suited to carry on the long and faithful ministry of CHRISTIAN HERALD magazine"[22] and encouraging readers to continue their support of the various Christian Herald Association and ministries.

Notes

1. Barbara Hofert, "Spiritual Guidance," *Library Journal* 115 (1 November 1990): 58.

2. *Christian Herald* 1 (24 October 1878): Cover.

3. Ibid.

4. Ibid.

5. Ibid. 115 (March–April 1992): 45.

6. Ibid. 1 (24 October 1878): Cover.

7. Ibid. 115 (March–April 1992): 23.

8. Ibid., p. 27.

9. William H. Gentz, ed., *Religious Writer's Marketplace* (Philadelphia: Running Press, 1985), 27.

10. Bill Katz and Linda Sternberg Katz, eds., *Magazines for Libraries* (New Providence, NJ: R. R. Bowker, 1992), 979.

11. *Christian Herald* 115 (March–April 1992): 29.

12. Ibid., p. 24.

13. Ibid. 114 (September–October 1991): 17–21.

14. Ibid. 91 (May 1968): 18–22ff.

15. For articles critical of astrology, see Gordon Dalbey, "The Beast in the Beauty of the Stars," *Christian Herald* 108 (September 1985): 56–62; and Robert Morey, "Mars Hill Collection: When Christians Meet Astrology," *Christian Herald* 111 (December 1988): 22–25.

16. See, for example, James R. Spencer, "The Mars Hill Collection: When Christians Meet Mormons," *Christian Herald* 111 (February 1988): 46–49; Bob and Gretchen Passantino, "The Mars Hill Collection: When Christians Meet New Agers," *Christian Herald* 111 (February 1988): 50–53; Rick Townsend with William M. Alnor, "The Mars Hill Collection: When Christians Meet Jehovah's Witnesses," *Christian Herald* 111 (April 1988): 36–40; Victor Khalil and Deborah Khalil, "The Mars Hill Collection: When Christians Meet Muslims," *Christian Herald* 111 (July–August 1988): 42–46; Eric Pement, "The Mars Hill Collection: When Christians Meet the World Wide Church of God," *Christian Herald* 111 (October 1988): 40–42ff; Robert Morey, "Mars Hill Collection: When Christians Meet Astrology," *Christian Herald* 111 (December 1988): 22–25.

17. Ibid. 115 (March–April 1992): 30.

18. Ibid. 111 (1988): 16–19.

19. Ibid. 112 (1989): Special Insert.

20. Ibid., p. 35.

21. Ibid. 108 (March 1985): 23.

22. *Christian Reader* (November–December 1992): Cover.

Information Sources

INDEX SOURCES: *Christian Periodical Index*, Volume 7 (1982)–Volume 17 (1992); *Guide to Social Science and Religion in Periodical Literature* (1964)–Volume 29 (1992).

LOCATION SOURCES: Christian Herald Association, Chappaqua, New York; Library of Congress.

Publication History

MAGAZINE TITLE AND TITLE CHANGES: *Christian Herald and Signs of Our Times* (1878–1899), *Christian Herald* (1899–1992). Absorbed into *Christian Reader.*

VOLUME AND ISSUE DATA: 1:1 (October 1878)–115:3 (1992). Published weekly until 1931, monthly until 1989, bimonthly through 1992.

PUBLISHER AND PLACE OF PUBLICATION: Michael Baxter (1878–1890), Louis Klopsch (1890–1910), Otto Koenig (1910–1918), Graham Patterson (1918–1927), Ford Stewart (1946–1966), Laurence S. Heely, Jr. (1968–1971), Kenneth Wilson (1971–1973), Frederick Loomer (1973–1985), David Kucharsky (1985–1991), Edward H. Morgan (1991–1992). Published in New York City through 1973; published in Chappaqua, New York, 1973–1992.

EDITORS: Benjamin James Fernie (1878–1879), Benjamin Aitken (1879–1881), Ben-

jamin James Fernie (1881–1890), T. De Witt Talmage (1890–1902), Louis Klopsch (1902–1910), G. H. Sandison (1910–1918), Charles Sheldon (1918–1927), Daniel Poling (1927–1966), Ford Stewart (1966–1967), Kenneth Wilson (1968–1978), David Kucharsky (1978–1986), Dean Merrill (1986–1990), Bob Chuvala (1990–1992), Vicki T. de Vries (1992).
CIRCULATION: 30,000 (1889); 165,000 (1992).

Roxane Salyer Lulofs

CHRISTIAN HISTORY

Christian History, the only magazine devoted to the history of Christianity that has been directed toward the general reader, was literally born in a barn. In 1982, A. Kenneth Curtis, bucking the advice of experts in periodical publishing, launched the magazine in a barn that he turned into an office complex. It would not work, he was told, because interest to sustain such a publication was lacking.[1] Undaunted, Curtis proceeded and then watched the magazine grow in popularity.

More than ten years before founding *Christian History*, Curtis, who holds a Ph.D. in communications from Walden University, founded Gateway Films. This award-winning, Christian filmmaking enterprise was the catalyst for the concept of a popular magazine devoted to Christianity's past. The seeds were planted when Curtis committed the company to producing a series of films on key figures in the history of the Church.[2]

The first film in the series on Bohemian reformer John Hus was well received, but Curtis quickly learned from both laity and clergy that the study of Christianity's past had been seriously neglected. "I realized," said Curtis, "that we contemporary Christians have little idea where we came from. Lay people are nearly totally unaware of our past, and ministers receive only a semester or two of church history, hardly enough to get a good grasp of the past."[3]

From the beginning, Curtis has believed that knowledge of Christianity's past is essential to its life. "Our conviction," he wrote, "is that the Lord of history will continue to direct and lead his people to new levels of understanding and obedience in the future as he has in the past. We believe that we are better prepared to discern his leading as we are grounded in our heritage."[4]

Curtis essentially suggests that the threefold benefit gained from understanding the history of Christianity is an awareness of historical precedents, a sharpened contemporary perspective, and a sense of the future purposefulness of God's involvement in human affairs. As we uncover precedents for how God has worked, reasons Curtis, we gain a new perspective on the present and, by extension, the future unfolding of God's plans. The end result, he concludes, is that "we will develop a sense of continuity and see how the unfolding of God's purposes transcends any single generation, century, denomination, geography, or ideology.[5] In short, Curtis views Christianity's past as the key to understanding her present and future condition and character.

With these convictions and an awareness of the general lack of knowledge of Christian history, Curtis made the decision to prepare a resource guide rich in background information to accompany the Hus film.[6] The purpose of this guide and of the magazine that evolved from it was to tutor laity in Christian history using a popular format and to provide students of Christian history with a resource for materials not readily available elsewhere. In both cases, the ultimate objective was to generate a desire to learn more about Christianity's past.[7]

The Hus guide was followed by a magazine-style upgraded guide for the second film (on Count Zinzendorf) in the series. When this was enthusiastically received, plans were made to produce similar guides for the third and fourth films, on John Wesley and John Wycliffe respectively—and *Christian History* was born. The announcement that *Christian History* would make the transition from an "occasional" publication to a quarterly[8] came in 1984 with issue four, on Swiss Reformer Ulrich Zwingli. In the following year, that objective was achieved.

From its inception, *Christian History* has followed the same basic format. Each issue has featured four or five main articles devoted to a key person (e.g., St. Augustine or C. S. Lewis), a group of people (e.g., the Baptists or the Waldensians), a movement (e.g., Pietism), or a topic (e.g., "Persecution in the Early Church" or "Spiritual Awakenings in North America"). Occasionally, a "special" issue (e.g., "The 100 Most Important Events in Church History," or *Heritage of Freedom*, a 124-page hardbound book) has signaled a departure from the usual format.

Most issues of *Christian History* have begun with a "Did You Know?" collection of "little-known or remarkable" facts about the subject, in order to pique the readers' interest. Other regular features have included a "gallery" of friends and foes (biographical sketches of people related to the topic), an historical time line of subject events, excerpts from original writings, and a bibliographical resource section to assist in further exploration of the topic. From the start, a mainstay of the magazine has been its graphics. Every issue has been a visual feast of illustrations and charts designed to give "an accurate glimpse into the period" under consideration.[9]

Production and editorial responsibilities in the early years were shared by several people on a part-time basis. There were numerous single-issue editors, editorial coordinators, and consultants. Until issue 16 (1987) when a full-time person came on board, only Curtis, managing editor Mark Tuttle, and art director Robin Heller had worked on each issue.

With issue 22 (1989), ownership of the magazine passed from the Christian History Institute, the magazine's parent corporation, to Christianity Today Incorporated (CTi). Curtis wrote that the magazine "became more than we could handle. It began taking us away from our film work, and we felt we had something unique to contribute there."[10] A second reason for the sale, according to Curtis, was the realization that "the magazine had more potential than we could help it realize. We had the magazine well established, but it would take someone with more expertise to raise it to new heights." That "someone" came in the person of Harold Myra, president of CTi. At a meeting of the Evangelical Press Association, a chance encounter between Curtis and Myra led to the eventual transfer of ownership. Now, says Curtis, "we're able to reach four or five times as many readers."[11]

Surveys have shown that the magazine's audience is generally within the evangelical Christian camp. Almost half of *Christian History*'s readership has graduate or seminary degrees, and nearly one in six holds an earned doctorate. Their common bond is a basic enjoyment of learning about Christianity's past.[12]

In spite of *Christian History*'s predominantly evangelical audience, the magazine has steadfastly held to a nondenominational, nonsectarian presentation of the Christian history. Curtis has explained the rationale for this approach:

Our evangelical commitment continues to drive us forward as we research and report on our rich Christian heritage. Yet we aim to maintain a non-partisan, non-denominational stance, seeking to serve the whole Body of Christ. We feel that faithfulness to Christ means practicing an uncompromising integrity in our handling of history. Accordingly, we do not use only writers of our own background and persuasion. We will publish the work of writers who, in our judgment, best interpret the subject matter at hand.[13]

Curtis went on to say that the quest for truth required a willingness to "criticize ourselves and our own tradition."[14] This quest for truth and a willingness to turn the light of criticism upon Christianity's past and traditions has been carried on by Kevin A. Miller, who became editor in 1990.

Notes

1. *Christian History* 11:4 (1992): 4.
2. Ibid. 1:1 (1982): 2.
3. Ibid. 11:4 (1992): 43.
4. Ibid. 2:1 (1983): 2.
5. Ibid. 1:1 (1982): 2.
6. Ibid.
7. Ibid. 11:4 (1992): 43. The current "Christian History Mission Statement" outlines the objectives of the publication:

To communicate church history in an accurate yet visual and engaging way; to highlight people who served God faithfully, despite their human failings and the difficulties of their times; to help contemporary Christians feel part of, and understand their place in, the historic church; to encourage appreciation for the diversity of Christianity in different eras and cultures; to provide historical background on issues facing contemporary church leaders.

8. Ibid. 3:1 (1983): 3.
9. Ibid., "Writer's Guidelines."
10. Ibid. 11:4 (1992): 44.
11. Ibid., p. 45.

12. Ibid., "Writer's Guidelines."
13. Ibid. 7:1 (1988): 3.
14. Ibid.

Information Sources

INDEX SOURCES: *Christian History*'s request for inclusion in the *Religion Index One* is currently pending. A list of single issue themes may be requested directly from *Christian History*, 465 Gundersen Drive, Carol Stream, Illinois 60188.
LOCATION SOURCES: A majority of back issues of *Christian History* are currently available from *Christian History*, Past Issue Sale, P.O. Box 550-A, Church Hill, Maryland 21690.

Publication History

MAGAZINE TITLE: *Christian History* (1982–present).
VOLUME AND ISSUE DATA: 1:1 (1982)–Issue 1; 2:1–2 (1983)–Issues 2–3; 3:1 (1984)–Issue 4; 4:1–4 (1985)–Issues 5–8; 1986-present published quarterly. 5:1 (1986) was also designated *Heritage of Freedom*; 9:4 (1990) was designated as special issue on "The 100 Most Important Events in Church history."
PUBLISHER AND PLACE OF PUBLICATION: Christian History Institute, Worcester, Pennsylvania (1982–1989); Christianity Today, Inc., Carol Stream, Illinois (1989–present).
EDITORS: Mark Tuttle (managing editor, 1982–1987), A. K. Curtis (publisher/editor (1987–1989), Key F. Payton (managing editor (1987–1988), A. Vinoy Laughner (managing editor, 1988–1989), Kevin A. Miller (editor, 1990–present), A. K. Curtis (senior editor, 1990–present).
CIRCULATION: 50,000 (1992).

Larry V. Crutchfield

CHRISTIAN HOME AND PARLOR. *See* CHRISTIAN PARLOR

CHRISTIAN INDEX

The Baptist denominations have birthed, adopted, published, and terminated hundreds of religious periodicals ranging from Bible study curricula and devotional guides to theological journals and newspapers. Of these, the religious newspapers have been the focus of the most intense discussion and controversy—and, arguably, of the greatest denominational pride.

Most of these newspapers survived for only a limited span, for the viability of most Baptist newspapers has been linked to the personality of their founders and editors. Many, if not most, of these papers died with their founders. The exceptions have almost universally been linked to the defined constituencies of established denominational bodies. In the case of some papers, these constituencies may have shifted over time.

Among the survivor papers must be numbered the *Christian Index*, currently the official news journal of the Georgia Baptist Convention. For more than 170 years, the paper has served the Baptist cause and denominational purpose.

The paper was born in the midst of the missionary movement that swept the Baptist denomination and others in the early nineteenth century. Its founder was Luther Rice, one of the most famous Baptists of his century and the founder of a host of Baptist causes and institutions.

Commissioned a Congregationalist missionary in 1812, Rice set sail for Calcutta, only to convert to Baptist convictions during the long sea voyage. His well-known compatriots, Adoniram and Ann Haseltine Judson, had preceded him in this decision during the journey. Rice was charged to return to the United States in order to establish relations and support with the Baptist denomination back home.

Rice soon became the central organizer and advocate of the Baptist missionary cause and the catalyst for a missionary movement that quickly shaped the Baptist denomination. His efforts resulted in the 18 May 1814 establishment of "General Missionary Convention of the Baptist Denomination in the United States of America, for Foreign Missions," more commonly known as the Triennial Convention.

Rice was charged to establish a monthly news journal in order to extend and promote the missionary cause, and the *Latter Day Luminary* began publication in 1817. By the next year, the newspaper numbered more than 8,000 readers. Nevertheless, by 1822 the need for a weekly publication with a broader assignment was evident, and Rice launched a new endeavor with his new periodical entitled *Columbian Star*, which began publication on 2 February 1822.

The paper's name was directly related to Luther Rice's other great project, Columbian College, established as a Baptist educational institution in Washington, D.C. (now George Washington University). James Knowles, a tutor at the college, was the first editor, but much of the material bears the mark of Rice's pen and heart. The comprehensive scope of the new paper's mission was made clear in its inaugural editorial:

Our main design is to render the paper an authentick [*sic*] repository of missionary and other religious intelligence, as well as a medium for inculcating sound theological doctrines, and pure moral precepts. We shall also present to our readers a compendious summary of the passing tidings of the times; inform them of the progress of the sciences, and all those liberal and useful arts which embellish society, and meliorate the condition and economy of life; and we shall be pleased, if our *Star* shall be able to throw an occasional beam upon the path of classical and elegant literature.[1]

In fact, the paper was seldom able to give much attention to "classical and elegant literature," its pages filled with material related to the growing Baptist cause and with news of missionary and religious interest.

The *Columbian Star* was staunchly Baptist, but irenic in tone and spirit. The theological convictions of the paper matched the firm and vibrant Calvinism of most Baptists on the Atlantic seaboard, and the editors commonly addressed doctrinal issues from both polemical and apologetic postures. The paper resounded with themes of Christian orthodoxy, and controversial issues (including such issues as imputation, the *ordo saludis*, and ecclesiology) were debated in article and letter exchanges.

The goal of the paper and its editors was evident: to build a new denominational consciousness among the Baptist people, who by practice and inclination were avowedly independent. Rice and his partners were convinced that the Baptist cause would never reach critical mass without the development of such a denominational consciousness, and they saw the paper as the central instrument of consciousness raising.

The *Columbian Star* was published from a house near Columbian College for five years, providing Baptists with news of mission developments, church reports, and (often sensationalized) items of common interest. T. Baron Stow, a prominent Baptist figure, edited the paper from 1825 to 1827, just as Luther Rice entered a period of great controversy and distress. Rice was a genuine visionary, but his dreams far outstripped his ability to see his causes through to maturity. Crisis came over funds for the mission boards and, later, over the collapse of the college.

The paper rose to new heights of readership and scholarship under the editorship of W. T. Brantly (1827–1833), a leading Baptist theologian and churchman. Brantly changed the name of the paper (which moved to Philadelphia during his editorship) to the *Columbian Star and Christian Index*, apparently in an effort to indicate its religious character. With the issue of 2 January 1831, the name was shortened to the *Christian Index*, as it has continued.

During Brantly's editorship, the paper took a decided turn toward Georgia in both readership, agents, and news interest.[2] A problem common to many Baptist newspapers has been the lack of a defined constituency. This clearly plagued the *Index*, and the turn to Georgia was most likely more a pragmatic response to interest than a calculated strategy. That is, the turn to a focus on Georgia indicates that the publishers recognized a growing concentration of subscribers in the South's most populous state. Better to belong to Georgia than to risk belonging to no one. Brantly served as editor with distinction, providing solid substance and judicious insight. But he proved unable to operate the paper on a solid financial base, and the issue of 29 March 1833 carried the announcement that the *Index* was moving to Washington, Georgia, to be edited by Jesse Mercer.

This was the great turning point in the early development of the *Christian Index*. In Jesse Mercer, the paper was finally in the hands of an editor who combined fierce determination, a superior grasp of the writing craft, solid theological substance, and personal financial means. Mercer is the towering figure of Georgia Baptist history—a combination of statesman, political theorist, hymn composer, Reformed Baptist theologian, master organizer, and business entrepreneur. Mercer was established as the most frequent external contributor to the *Christian Index* and the *Columbian Star* from its inception, and he had been the prime mover behind the establishment of the Georgia Baptist Convention in 1828.

Mercer began his charge with the 14 September 1833 issue, and included in his first editorial this statement:

We now enter immediately on our duties as editor of a religious Journal, and begin to feel them of mountain weight. In the first, chief place, how to please God, the Judge of All, otherwise than by the presentment of truth, frankly and candidly expressed, according to his conscientious views of His Holy Word, he knows not: but in doing this, in the second place; how to most please his patrons . . . in their various and conflicting sentiments; and in the peculiarity of mode in which, these sentiments in different sections are clothed, is a herculean task indeed.[3]

These "various and conflicting sentiments" ranged from views on the education of women to matters of missionary and ecclesiastical debate. Looming over the entire enterprise was the issue of slavery, which had already begun to divide the nation—and, with it, the major denominations. The relocation of the paper to Georgia came with the recognition that to do so would be to lose significant numbers of Northern readers. But, on the other hand, both Brantly and Mercer had high hopes for a dramatic increase in subscriptions throughout the South.

After its recovery and reestablishment under Mercer (also the founder of Mercer University), the paper was assumed by the Georgia Baptist Convention in 1841, under the editorship of W. H. Stokes, who had served as Mercer's associate editor. By now the paper reflected a clear Southern bias and was dominated by Georgia Baptist news, though departments related to other states were periodically added in an attempt to boost circulation outside the state. The paper went through a succession of editors in the next two decades, until the advent of the Civil War threw all Southern institutions into disruption and disarray.

In the crisis, the paper was sold once again, this time to Samuel Boykin and C. M. Irwin of Albany, Georgia. The *Index* continued publication throughout the war, except for a seven-month interruption in 1865. When the paper reappeared, it was evidently owned by J. J. Toon of Atlanta, where the paper moved and remained. The first editorial published under Toon's ownership included this explanation:

The good ship, *Index*, after being tossed about and battered by rough storms on Confederate seas, was driven into port. For many and weary months, her friends knew not what had become of her, and fears were entertained that she had floundered at sea and was lost. We are able to relieve all apprehensions concerning her safety. True, her rigging was pretty well used up, and her masts broken, but her *hull is sound*. Her timbers are the very heart of live oak, and are as firm and solid as when the good ship was first launched on her eventful voyage, forty-four years ago.[4]

The paper established a new reputation and format during the last half of the nineteenth century and thrived under the skilled editorship of Henry H. Tucker (1866, 1878–1882, 1885) and several others. The next major turn for the paper came in 1907, when B. J. W. Graham, then coowner and coeditor of the paper, established the Index Printing Company with ten thousand dollars in capital stock. This company met with some measure of success, printing numerous other state papers and periodicals of other denominations, as well as the *Christian Index*.

But Graham sold the paper to the executive committee of the Georgia Baptist Convention in 1919 because of his conviction that "the paper will become more useful to the denomination in the promotion of its enterprises."[5] With this move the paper came once again into the hands of the Georgia Baptist Convention, and it did so just as similar developments took place in most of the other large state conventions. The 1920s were the decade of dramatic Baptist centralization in the South. The state conventions established permanent organizational structures, called full-time denominational executives, and sought to bring the state papers under the official aegis of the denomination—with promotion of the denominational program the paramount concern.

The *Index* emerged on 1 January 1920 with a new editor, Louie D. Newton, a new owner, and a new format. The convention had purchased the assets of the paper, the most important of which was the list of twenty-two thousand subscribers. Newton was one of the paradigmatic figures of Baptist life in the twentieth century. He established a prominence shared by no more than five or six contemporaries and was often known as "Mr. Baptist" in Georgia and beyond. He had been a reporter with the *New York Daily World* while earning a master's degree in journalism at Columbia University and was a born wordsmith and promoter. Under Newton's ten-year editorship the paper achieved national prominence. Newton was not theologically trained, and his editorials were most often promotional in nature or tied to major national or world events. He was a native Georgian and had traveled almost every mile of the state's roadways while an agent for the denomination prior to his assumption of the editorial office.

Newton left the office in 1929 to assume the pastorate of Atlanta's distinguished Druid Hills Baptist Church. His successor, O. P. Gilbert (1930–1947), was a much-respected Georgia pastor, who bore the burden of seeing the paper through the trials of the Great Depression. Gilbert was followed by John Jeter Hurt (1947–1966), an Associated Press newsman, who brought his background in secular journalism to the paper. Hurt was followed by another trained journalist, Jack U. Harwell (1966–1987).

Harwell's editorship ended in the midst of the controversy that had erupted within the Southern Baptist Convention during the late 1970s. Harwell's editorial stance and writing style were isolated and criticized by conservatives within the denomination. During Harwell's last years, the board of directors of the *Index* established an editorial review board, an unprecedented development.

This editorial review board and Harwell clashed over editorials that were charged to be divisive and over news coverage that conservatives attacked as unfair and politicized. By the late 1980s, Harwell had become a regular issue at meetings of the Georgia Baptist Convention, where conservatives and moderates clashed over an entire range of issues. Increasingly, the *Index* and its editor became the central focus.

The issues came to a climax in 1987, when Harwell announced his resignation, which was then accepted by the board of directors. Just a few weeks later, the convention met and passed a resolution asking that Harwell be reinstated. But the convention's executive committee declined to do so in December 1987.

Jack P. Lowndes was named interim editor, and he served until 1989, when R. Albert Mohler, Jr., a theologian and seminary administrator was elected editor. Mohler served until 1993, when he was elected president of the Southern Baptist Theological Seminary in Louisville, Kentucky. William T. Neal, a former associate editor, was elected to succeed Mohler as editor.

At its peak in the 1960s and 1970s, the paper numbered over one hundred thousand subscribers, mostly organized through church budget subscriptions (mass subscriptions through local churches). In 1993, subscribers numbered close to eighty thousand.

The role and purpose of state Baptist papers is again in question as the 1990s unfold. Increasing tensions between some state conventions and the Southern Baptist Convention threaten the denominational solidarity that nourished the papers during the period from 1925 to 1975. Changes in reading habits and an aging readership pose new problems as well. Nevertheless, the *Index* has emerged from trials in the past and now stands as one of the oldest survivors among American religious periodicals.

Notes

1. *Columbian Star*, 1:1 (2 February 1822). Quoted in Jack U. Harwell, *An Old Friend with New Credentials: A History of the Christian Index* (Atlanta: Executive Committee of the Baptist Convention of the State of Georgia, 1972), 28. This volume, written by an editor of the paper, is the best source of historical background and documentation. Much of the material in this essay is based upon material found in Harwell's volume.

2. This turn is well documented in James Adams Lester, "A History of the Christian Index" (Master's thesis, New Orleans Baptist Theological Seminary, 1955).

3. Quoted in Harwell, *Old Friend*, 63.

4. Editorial, *Christian Index* 44:47 (9 November 1865). Quoted in Harwell, *Old Friend*, 97.

5. *Christian Index* 99:52 (29 December 1919): 2.

Information Sources

INDEX SOURCES: No published index exists.
LOCATION SOURCES: Hard copies of most volumes are held at the *Christian Index*,

Atlanta, Georgia. Microfilm copies of the entire published series are available through the Historical Commission of the Southern Baptist Convention, 901 Commerce Street, Nashville, Tennessee.

Publication History

MAGAZINE TITLE AND TITLE CHANGES: *Columbian Star* (1822–1827), *Columbian Star and Christian Index* (1827–1831), *Christian Index* (1831–present).

VOLUME AND ISSUE DATA: 1:1 (2 February 1822)–present. Some numbering anomalies mark earlier volumes. Published weekly since 1822, with some numbers missing from 1865 owing to war and some later volumes missing owing to financial emergencies.

PUBLISHER AND PLACE OF PUBLICATION: Luther Rice, Washington, D.C. (1822–1827); W. T. Brantly, Philadelphia, Pennsylvania (1827–1833); Jesse Mercer, Washington, Georgia (1833–1841); Georgia Baptist Convention, Washington, Georgia (1841–1860); Samuel Boykin and C. M. Irwin, Washington, Georgia and other cities (1860–1865); J. J. Toon and others, Atlanta, Georgia (1865–1919); Executive Committee of the Baptist Convention of the State of Georgia, Atlanta, Georgia (1920–present).

EDITORS: James D. Knowles (1822–1825), T. Baron Stow (1825–1827), W. T. Brantly (1827–1833), Jesse Mercer (1833–1840), W. H. Stokes (1840–1842), Joseph S. Baker (1842–1848), B. M. Saners (1849), J. F. Dagg (1850–1855), J. S. Walker (1857–1859), E. W. Warren (1859), Samuel Boykin (1860–1865, 1888), Henry H. Tucker (1866, 1878–1882, 1885), David Shaver (1867–1873, 1888), David E. Butler (1874–1878), M. B. Wharton (1882–1884), G. A. Nunnally (1889), Lousing Burrows (1890–1891), I. R. Branham (1892), J. C. McMichael (1892–1895), A. C. Ward (1895), T. P. Bell (1896–1915), I. J. Van Ness (1896–1900), B. J. W. Graham (1901–1919), Louie D. Newton (1920–1929), O. P. Gilbert (1930–1947), John Jeter Hurt (1947–1966), Jack U. Harwell (1966–1987), R. Albert Mohler, Jr. (1989–1993), William Neal (1993–present).

CIRCULATION: 2,000 (1823); 78,500 (1993).

R. Albert Mohler, Jr.

CHRISTIANITY TODAY

By the mid–1950s, the "neo-evangelical" movement in America had gathered considerable momentum. Propelled in part by the rising popularity and influence of Billy Graham, this major party within American fundamentalism had been slowly moving away from the increasingly sectarian and antagonistic stance of its conservative Protestant peers vis-à-vis moderate and liberal Protestantism and the American cultural and political establishment. Intent on infiltrating and transforming American culture rather than separating from it, the neo-evangelicals had been constructing a network of institutions and organizations that would promote traditional evangelical doctrines and mores within the major Protestant denominations and also within higher education, politics, and the media.[1]

Graham, who had become a world-renowned revivalist virtually overnight during his 1949 evangelistic "crusade" in Los Angeles, took advantage of his own popularity and the resurgence of interest in evangelical Christianity to found *Christianity Today* in 1956. As Graham would remember later, "I was awakened one night at about 2 A.M. I went to my desk and wrote out ideas about a magazine similar to the *Christian Century*, one that would give theological respectability to evangelicals. . . . I thought the articles should appeal especially to men who were open to the biblical faith in the mainline denominations, but the magazine had to be thoroughly evangelical."[2] *Christianity Today* would prove to be a medium unparalleled in promoting the message of the new evangelicalism and in reflecting the cultural and religious attitudes of its constituency.

Graham found immediate support for this journalistic venture from his father-in-law, L. Nelson Bell. A medical missionary from 1916 to 1941, Bell had served as chief surgeon at Tsingkiangpu General Hospital, the largest Presbyterian hospital in China. Bell was a staunchly conservative Southern Presbyterian who, upon returning to the United States in 1941, led in the founding of the *Southern Presbyterian Journal* in 1942 (called the *Presbyterian Journal* after 1959), a staple for conservatives within the Presbyterian Church in the United States.[3] On Christmas day 1954, Graham shared his vision for a new evangelical magazine with Bell. It was to be similar to the *Southern Presbyterian Journal* in theological orientation, but national and interdenominational in scope. Soon the two men were laying plans.

Graham asked Wilbur Smith, a friend and founding faculty member of the Fuller Theological Seminary in Pasadena, California, to serve as the first editor of *Christianity Today*. Though Smith had been interested in religious journalism for some time and had long been looking—and even planning—for a journal such as this, he declined Graham's offer. Soon thereafter, however, Fuller's Harold Lindsell suggested Carl F. H. Henry for the position. Henry, Fuller's primary theologian, seemed ideally suited for the job. He was a prolific author and had begun his career as a journalist and newspaper editor in Long Island prior to his evangelical conversion.[4] After some deliberation on both sides, Henry became the magazine's founding editor.

The purpose of *Christianity Today* at its inception was very much in tune with the larger neo-evangelical agenda. The magazine's founders hoped to infuse America's religious and cultural life with conservative evangelical thought and values. An editorial entitled "Why 'Christianity Today?'" in the magazine's first issue stated this purpose boldly: "Neglected, slighted, misrepresented—evangelical Christianity needs a clear voice, to speak with conviction and love, and to state its true position and its relevance to the world crisis." It went on to argue that "theological liberalism has failed to meet the moral and spiritual needs of the people. Neither the man on the street nor the intellectual is today much attracted by its preaching and theology."[5] This contradistinction to Protestant liberalism was also in tune with the neo-evangelical agenda and provided the magazine with an ideological raison d'être. Evangelicals had been growing wary of the liberal Protestant departures from Christian orthodoxy for many years. They believed that these departures had contributed significantly to what they regarded as the deterioration of America's moral fabric and that a revival of evangelical conviction might yield a revival of conservative social and political practices as well. Carl Henry once described the founding of *Christianity Today* as an attempt to give the *Christian Century* "a run for its biases." As the journalistic centerpiece of what many evangelicals conceived as the liberal Protestant establishment, the *Century* constituted both a model and an ideological counterpart for the founders of *Christianity Today*. In a letter to James DeForest Murch, a conservative Disciples of Christ minister, Henry wrote, "I understand that the circulation of *Christian Century* is on the decline and this is our most opportune moment to strike."[6]

To support their goal of producing a magazine that would infiltrate American culture with conservative evangelicalism, the founders secured financial backing, especially from board member and Sun Oil magnate J. Howard Pew, but also from the Billy Graham Evangelistic Association, board member Maxey Jarman of the General Shoe Corporation, and others. *Christianity Today*'s founders determined to grant complimentary subscriptions to every Protestant minister in the United States (or at least as many as could be identified).[7] Some of these two hundred thousand ministers were eventually dropped from the magazine's subscription list, and the policy of granting free subscriptions was ultimately abandoned in March 1967. Most copies of *Christianity Today*, however, were distributed free of charge well into the 1960s.[8]

The generous financial support that helped initially to make *Christianity Today* so readily accessible also threatened for a time to undo the magazine. Just a few weeks prior to the press date of the first issue, Carl Henry learned from Harold John Ockenga—founding president of Fuller Seminary, pastor of Boston's historic Park Street Church, and now chairman of the magazine's board— that J. Howard Pew had requested to review advance proofs of the first issue. Apparently Pew, an ardent capitalist, felt that he had been betrayed in the past by organizations such as the National Council of Churches that had asked him for money and then used it for causes that he did not support. Henry found Pew's request an affront to his editorial freedom and wrote to Bell (who would serve as the magazine's administrative officer under the title of executive editor for eighteen years), threatening to resign. Not only did Pew's request reveal an unacceptable lack of trust in Henry (whom Pew secretly suspected of socialism), but Henry also wanted to avoid the appearance that his editorials were controlled by Pew's money. In the course of a complex and somewhat volatile struggle, Bell supported Henry, and Billy Graham ultimately persuaded Pew to withdraw his request to review proofs of the magazine's subsequent issues.[9]

Christianity Today has developed stably in the years since this rather rocky beginning, undergoing a few significant changes but maintaining its evangelical posture and rather steady circulation levels. Carl Henry served as editor of the magazine until 1968, establishing it as perhaps the most highly regarded evangelical periodical in the United States. Upon Henry's somewhat mysterious departure from the magazine,[10] Harold Lindsell, the one who had first recommended Henry as editor, was appointed to replace him. By the time of Lindsell's editorship, the ideological commitments of American evangelicals had diversified considerably. Many evangelicals had moved away from the doctrine of biblical inerrancy, for example, and others had abandoned conservative politics. These trends worried Lindsell, who is perhaps best known for his defense of biblical inerrancy in *The Battle for the Bible* (1976). Like Henry, he was interested in engaging the broader culture from an evangelical point of view, but Lindsell tended to focus his attention as much on shoring up the evangelical populace against internal threats as on engaging more cosmopolitan or "mainstream" concerns. On 27 September 1968 when Lindsell took over the magazine, it had forty-seven contributing editors, most of whom were intellectuals with wide-ranging interests. The first issue published during Lindsell's tenure featured an article by two Old Testament scholars on the value of the Revised Standard Version of the Bible. By 28 July 1977 when the magazine moved its headquarters from Washington, D.C., to Carol Stream, Illinois, however, it had only twelve "editors-at-large" (it no longer used the title "contributing editor") and featured an article by an evangelical pastor entitled "The Family Church: Any Place for Singles?"[11] The magazine's move to Carol Stream at the end of Lindsell's tenure symbolized this change of priorities at *Christianity Today*. Carol Stream and its neighbor town, Wheaton, have for many years represented the heartbeat of the evangelical subculture in America. Housing dozens of evangelical institutions and organizations, these towns have constituted the nerve center of the evangelical network since World War II.

Kenneth S. Kantzer, then dean of Trinity Evangelical Divinity School in Deerfield, Illinois, became editor of *Christianity Today* upon its move to the Chicago suburbs. Kantzer shared Lindsell's commitment to biblical inerrancy but had a more irenic temperament than Lindsell and proved more interested in nurturing the evangelical community intellectually and spiritually than in battling with other evangelicals. At the beginning of his tenure as editor, Kantzer stated that "it is important to heal [intraevangelical relationships] rather than to alienate." While he promised not to "compromise" the magazine's commitment to orthodoxy or "condone any departure from biblical authority," he also promised that "on the other hand, no personal vendetta will be carried out against those who may disagree with us."[12] Kantzer also showed an interest in providing the magazine's readers with more sophisticated theological content than they had grown accustomed to under Lindsell. During his brief tenure as editor (1978–1982), Kantzer helped to bring *Christianity Today* and the evangelical community out of an era that had proved turbulent for all Americans. V. Gilbert Beers, who had been converted under the preaching of Harold Lindsell, succeeded Kantzer and served as editor from 1982 to 1985. A prolific author of a variety of evangelical literature, Beers had become best known for his children's books. Though three years was hardly enough time to leave a distinct mark upon a magazine the size of *Christianity Today*, Beers faithfully maintained the course set by Kantzer and steered the magazine into even calmer waters.

In 1985 *Christianity Today* underwent a structural change. Harold L. Myra, who had been serving the magazine as ''publisher and president,'' became ''publisher and executive editor.'' With the help of ''executive editors'' George K. Brushaber and Terry C. Muck, Myra now led a committee of ''senior editors'' (originally Brushaber, Dennis F. Kinlaw, J. I. Packer, and former editors Kantzer and Beers) in shaping the magazine's editorial content. Under Myra, who is more of a businessman/journalist than a theologian, *Christianity Today* has attempted to keep pace from an organizational standpoint with an increasingly sophisticated market while maintaining its commitment to the evangelical mind. Thus while Christianity Today, Inc., has now become a parent company responsible for several evangelical periodicals, this corporate growth has been counterbalanced on the editorial or intellectual side by the formation of an evangelical think tank at *Christianity Today* called the Christianity Today Institute (CTI). The institute was announced by Myra in March of 1985:

We feel an increased responsibility to glean the best thinking from evangelical thought leaders and to disseminate their seasoned judgments widely. We are therefore developing a think tank called the Christianity Today Institute. . . . More than 50 fellows and resource scholars will be involved on a continuing basis, and their work will periodically appear in this magazine in the form of special institute supplements.[13]

While ''the best'' evangelical thinking is now usually reserved for these special CTI supplements, the intent of *Christianity Today*'s founders to infiltrate American culture with a credible and intellectually sophisticated evangelical witness has not been entirely forsaken.[14]

In the nearly forty years since its founding, *Christianity Today*'s fundamental commitment to traditional evangelical doctrine and praxis has supported various developments in editorial tone, administrative structure, circulation policy, layout, and graphics. The United States and its cultures have undergone many remarkable permutations since 1956, and, like many other popular religious magazines, *Christianity Today* has attempted to adapt to the changes that have affected its market while remaining faithful to the vision and direction given the magazine by its founders. This has not always been an easy task. Through the years *Christianity Today* has become more popular in orientation and less influential at the national level than at least some of its founders had hoped. And as the evangelical movement has grown and diversified it has become nearly impossible for any single voice to speak for or to all evangelicals.[15] Despite such changes, however, *Christianity Today* has managed to remain, as one recent author has phrased it, ''the most widely read serious religious journal in the nation.''[16]

Notes

1. For an introduction to the neo-evangelical movement, see Joel A. Carpenter, *Revive Us Again: The Recovery of American Fundamentalism, 1930–1950* (New York, forthcoming); and George M. Marsden, *Reforming Fundamentalism: Fuller Seminary and the New Evangelicalism* (Grand Rapids, MI: Eerdmans, 1987).

2. *Christianity Today* 25 (17 July 1981): 26.

3. For more on Bell, see John C. Pollock, *A Foreign Devil in China: The Story of Dr. L. Nelson Bell, an American Surgeon in China* (Minneapolis: Zondervan, 1971).

4. For more on Henry, see his own *Confessions of a Theologian: An Autobiography* (Waco, TX: Word Books, 1986).

5. *Christianity Today* 1 (15 October 1956): 20.

6. Henry, *Confessions of a Theologian*, 144; see also Carl F. H. Henry to James DeForest Murch, 26 November 1955, folder 35, box 1, collection 8, Records of *Christianity Today*, Billy Graham Center Archives, Wheaton, Illinois.

7. Those who did purchase the magazine paid the same price, twenty-five cents per issue or five dollars per year, from its first issue in October of 1956 until February of 1968, when the price was raised to forty cents per issue or six dollars per year. In 1992 the magazine sold for over two dollars per issue or almost twenty-five dollars per year.

8. The circulation totals of *Christianity Today* have fluctuated throughout its history between a low of 120,000 and a high of 250,000. For these statistics, I have drawn upon Daryl Alan Porter's "*Christianity Today*: Its History and Development, 1956–1978" (Master's thesis, Dallas Theological Seminary, 19?8), 56 ff.

9. For details of this controversy, see Henry, *Confessions of a Theologian*, 160–63.

10. Henry's relationship with the magazine's board had become somewhat strained by 1968. For details of his departure, see Porter, "*Christianity Today*," 36–42.

11. *Christianity Today* 12 (27 September 1968); ibid. 21 (29 July 1977).

12. See Kenneth S. Kantzer, "Of Prophetic Robes and Weather Vanes: An Interview with Kenneth Kantzer," *Christianity Today* 22 (7 April 1978): 23, 25. Kantzer was not a journalist by background, but tried to build on his strengths as a scholar. While he admitted that "it *is* a handicap not to have been an editor or professional writer," he also noted, "my years of teaching the history of Christian thought and systematic theology provide me with a background that I consider immensely valuable for the editing of a thought journal like *Christianity Today*. . . . I believe that my lifelong role as an educator will help me direct the theological and ecclesiological impact of the publication. Perhaps it will mean that the magazine will be more instructive than evangelistic in its approach to troublesome issues facing the church today"(23).

Indeed, the magazine did become more educative under Kantzer. Soon after assuming the leadership of *Christianity Today*, he published articles on such meaty theological themes as process theology (2 June 1978), the historical relationship between Christianity and Judaism (18 August 1978 and elsewhere), the epistemological controversy between David Hume and Thomas Reid in the age of Enlightenment (22 September 1978), biblical criticism (20 October 1978), and the thought of Friedrich Schleiermacher (15 December 1978). Later he would take up a broad range of such topics, from liberation theology (19 October 1979 and elsewhere) to the theology of history (2 May 1980) and just war theory (7 November 1980).

13. *Christianity Today* 29 (1 March 1985): 11.

14. While the issues that have been addressed by the Christianity Today Institute are not as theoretically sophisticated as those addressed in *Christianity Today*'s earlier years, the institute has not shied away from thorny issues or pandered to the more trendy or fashionable tastes of its constituency. The first five CTI supplements dealt with "The Christian as Citizen" (19 April 1985), "Into the Next Century: Trends Facing the Church" (17 January 1986), "Biomedical Decision Making: The Blessings and Curses of Modern Technology" (21 March 1986), "Women in Leadership" (3 October 1986), and "South Africa: Can the Church Mend the Anguish of a Nation" (21 November 1986). Later supplements dealt with such topics as "Great Sex: Reclaiming a Christian Sexual Ethic" (2 October 1987), "Rich Wisdom: New Testament Teachings on Wealth" (12 May 1989), "The Remaking of English Evangelicalism" (5 February 1990), and "Why Is Latin America Turning Protestant?" (6 April 1992).

15. Several of *Christianity Today*'s founders and all of its editors remain alive and well, and most of them are quite concerned about the evangelical movement's development. As sociologist James Davidson Hunter has shown in *Evangelicalism: The Coming Generation* (Chicago: University of Chicago Press, 1987), many within the coming generation of American evangelicalism have abandoned or at least significantly altered the original neo-evangelical goal to infiltrate and transform American culture with conservative Protestant thought and values.

16. William Martin, *A Prophet with Honor: The Billy Graham Story* (New York: Morrow, 1991), 211.

Information Sources

INDEX SOURCES: *Reader's Guide to Periodical Literature, Christian Periodical Index, Religion Index One: Periodicals*, and *Religious and Theological Abstracts, Book Review Index*.
REPRINT EDITIONS: University Microfilms International.
LOCATION SOURCES: Library of Congress, numerous college and university libraries.

Publication History

MAGAZINE TITLE: *Christianity Today* (1956–present).
VOLUME AND ISSUE DATA: 1:1 (15 October 1956)–21:3 (5 November 1976), published fortnightly; 21:4 (19 November 1976)–21:17 (3 June 1977), published semimonthly; 21:18 (17 June 1977)–21:20 (29 July 1977), published fortnightly, except 6 May, 8 and 29 July, 9 and 30 December; 21:21 (12 August 1977)–22:17 (2 June 1978), published semimonthly; 22:18 (23 June 1978)–24:20 (21 November 1980), published semimonthly (monthly in July and August—22 issues per year); 24:21 (12 December 1980)–26:10 (21 May 1982), published semimonthly (monthly in July, August, and December—21 issues per year); 26:11 (18 June 1982)–27:9 (20 May 1983), published semimonthly (monthly in June, July, August, and December—20 issues per year); 27:10 (17 June 1983)–34:12 (10 September 1990), published semimonthly (monthly in January, May, June, July, August, and December—18 issues per year); 34:13 (24 September 1990–present), published monthly (semimonthly in April, October, and November—15 issues per year).

PUBLISHER AND PLACE OF PUBLICATION: Today's Publications, Washington, D.C. (1956–1957); Christianity Today, Washington, D.C. (1957–1977); Christianity Today, Carol Stream, Illinois, (1977–present).
EDITORS: Carl F. H. Henry (1956–1968), Harold Lindsell (1968–1978), Kenneth S. Kantzer (1978–1982), V. Gilbert Beers (1982–1985), George K. Brushaber and Terry C. Muck, executive editors (1985–1990/91), Harold L. Myra, editorial director (1991–present).
CIRCULATION: 180,000 (May 1992).

Douglas A. Sweeney

CHRISTIAN LIFE

Following World War II, American Christianity underwent significant transformations. Returning soldiers took advantage of the GI Bill and the expanding postwar economy to get an education and to marry and move their families off the farms and out of the cities to the suburbs. Mass-produced housing, the building of a nationwide highway system in the 1950s, and the promotion of middle-class domestic ideology shifted attention to the suburbs. Suburban communities were focused around the nuclear family that included more children than during the 1930s and early 1940s. New churches needed to be built in the suburbs, and congregations had to learn how to accommodate young, growing families. For conservative Christians, postwar America meant their initial entrance into the suburban middle class. No longer isolated in rural, agrarian communities, fundamentalists and evangelicals responded to a modern consumer economy.

In order to reach the suburban family, conservative Christian publishing houses created literature appropriate for such a readership. The lifting of war-induced paper rationing meant that companies could begin to experiment with innovative publishing ventures. In 1946 Clyde H. Dennis began publishing *Christian Life and Times*, a small-format magazine for evangelicals. A young man of thirty-two, Dennis had spent the previous eight years publishing fundamentalist tracts and now served as president of Good News Publishing Company. *Christian Life and Times* would be published by Good Books, Inc., a book and magazine publisher not associated with any particular denomination but owned by a group of Christian businessmen from Chicago. Dennis hoped that his magazine would serve the same readers as *Moody Monthly*, which had a readership of eighty-five thousand. Distributed initially in the Midwest, *Christian Life and Times* had an initial first print run of thirty-five thousand copies.

Dennis intended the magazine to bridge the gap between the secular and religious worlds. *Christian Life and Times* would be "a news magazine, photo magazine, book condensation magazine, and a magazine full of significant general interest and devotional articles."[1] He wanted to publish a Christian magazine that combined the format of *Life* and *Time*. At the same time, the magazine would be fully Christian, with a fundamentalist orientation. For Dennis, as with other conservative Christians of this period, secular forms could be used to promote evangelical messages.

Christian Life and Times contained condensed novels in the same vein as *Reader's Digest*. It also published photo spreads of inspirational scenes. Majestic mountains, young people in love, and old people, all graced its pages. Articles carried titles such as "This Month's Bible Chat," "Why I Must Return to the Dark Continent" (by an African missionary), and "How a Bible Student Lives." The tone of the magazine was upbeat, inspirational, and chatty.

Christian Life and Times was sold to subscribers by door-to-door salesmen and women. When individuals subscribed to the magazine, they received a box of Scripture stationery as a premium. The magazine employed some reporters, but also relied on readers to contribute stories, paying twenty dollars for stories about "people who have changed my life." Advertisements within the magazine reflected the developing market for conservative Christian goods and services. Books and objects produced by Good News Publishers, the company that owned the magazine, were advertised. Good News Publishers sold not only books, but also a "Gospel Coin" that Christians were to keep in their pockets or give away as a testimony to their faith. Bible games, Christian greeting cards, Bible conferences, and religious music were all advertised during the first years of the magazine's publication.

In 1948 a change in ownership occurred. *Christian Life and Times* was combined with *Sunday Magazine* to form *Christian Life*. Clyde Dennis became the associate editor and Robert Walker the editor. Walker, a graduate of the Northwestern University School of Journalism, was an assistant professor of journalism at Wheaton College (1941–1951). He directed the Christian Writer's Institute, a correspondence school in Christian journalism organized from Wheaton College. In 1949 Clyde Dennis's name no longer appeared on the masthead. The copyright of the magazine was held by Sunday Magazine, Inc. until 1959, when it was taken over by Christian Life, Inc., which also published *Choice* (a magazine dealing with consumer purchases) and *Christian Bookseller*. In 1964 the *Christian Life* offices were moved from Chicago to Wheaton, Illinois. Robert Walker remained editor until 1987 when *Christian Life* merged with *Charisma*, owned and published by Stephen Strang.

Under the editorship of Robert Walker, *Christian Life*'s orientation became evangelical rather than fundamentalist. A 1959 "statement of faith" explained that the editorial slant of the magazine assumed that the Bible was the inspired, infallible, and authoritative Word of God. Millenarian and dispensational orientations, however, did not figure in the statement.[2] Feature articles reflected this commitment. In a 1971 article entitled "What's Behind the Mid-East Crisis?" the author asserted that "to answer these questions, we need simply to turn to the Bible, the most comprehensive book on the Mid-East crisis."[3] *Christian Life* did include articles by nonevangelicals, including one by a Catholic nun entitled "Fascinated by Christ."[4]

Under Robert Walker's editorship, the format was enlarged and the inclusion of condensed books was dropped. By the late 1960s a color format was adopted. Articles covered general themes (Christian education, missionaries, money), news (international, national), feature articles (such as "Christmas in Nebraska"), and profiles of notable Christians. Photographs remained important, especially to illustrate news events. News of a secular nature was barely reported. Instead, news articles combined issues of current interest with evangelical messages. For instance, in "Was the Peace Corps for Our Polly?" the author concluded that although Polly completed Peace Corps training, she eventually decided that she was "too strongly imprinted with conservative living patterns to be comfortable trying to conform to another." For Polly, social change came only through the "regenerative power of the Christian gospel."[5] *Christian Life* published articles that applied evangelical notions of individual salvation, biblical inerrancy, and conservative morals to contemporary social events. It showed a preference for inspirational stories that revealed personal holiness. *Christian Life* consistently reported on Billy Graham's evangelical crusades. Columns on practical activities ("Your Good Health," "All in a Woman's Day," "Tips on Crafts/Hobbies") reflected its family orientation.

Advertisements in the 1950s and 1960s indicate that the magazine was marketed to Protestant pastors. Advertisements for church furnishings, organs, pews, choir robes, films and film strips, and sound systems accompanied articles on church and Sunday-school management. In the 1970s, the target audience of advertisements shifted back to the lay person and away from the clergy. Advertisements for folding chairs and tape recordings disappear, and their place is taken by publicity for religious books, music, and missions. This shift reflects the reassertion of fundamentalism after the election of Jimmy Carter and the rise of the new religious Right. Evangelicals, not merely their pastors, became the consumers of religious goods and services.

From 1953 into the early 1970s, *Christian Life* carried a series of combined advertisements and articles that featured church buildings. Early in the 1950s, Robert Walker had joined with Rev. Joseph Kimbel to produce a series of low-cost plans for preengineered churches and parsonages. Kimbel, pastor of United Missionary Church in Elkhart, Indiana, and a part-time teacher of art at the denomination's Bethel College also maintained a firm called Church Enterprise, specializing in evangelical church design. *Christian Life* published stories of pastors who built churches based on designs or materials bought through the magazine. The "Wildwood" church, for instance, seated two hundred and when built with local contractors cost only thirty-five thousand dollars. The church-parsonage building packages were produced and stored in Weyerhaeuser warehouses. Prefabricated churches could also be ordered. Once they arrived, they could be erected in two days at a cost of between 10 and 15 percent less than the preengineered churches. These church-building articles not only point out the weak boundary between the magazine's spiritual and commercial endeavors, but they also serve as an index for popular notions of religious architecture during the rapid growth of suburban Protestantism.

Robert Walker edited *Christian Life* for forty-three years. In 1986, the board of directors of Christian Life Missions, which published *Christian Life*, arranged for Stephen Strang, publisher of *Charisma*, to take over the magazine. At first it was felt that both magazines would find their appropriate market: *Charisma* for charismatics and *Christian Life* for evangelicals. A new staff was hired, and more color graphics were included in *Christian Life*, but the publication apparently did not do as well as expected. The following year, the two magazines were combined. The name *Christian Life* was initially retained, and Strang included articles from both magazines, giving *Christian Life* a more charismatic orientation. According to Strang, the new publication would make "it one of the largest paid circulation evangelical magazines in the world."[6] Robert Walker continued to contribute articles to the new publication. However, Strang eventually came to believe that a new journal would have better marketing potential. Thus, later in 1987, *Christian Life* ceased to be published, and the new journal *Charisma and Christian Life* replaced it.

Notes

1. *Christian Life* 1 (July 1946): 20.
2. Ibid. 21 (May 1959): 1.
3. Ibid. 33 (May 1971): 21, 52ff.
4. Ibid. 29 (July 1967): 28–33.
5. Ibid. 29 (April 1968): 32f, 59–62.
6. *Charisma and Christian Life* 12:11 (June 1987): 6.

Information Sources

INDEX SOURCES: None.
LOCATION SOURCES: Available at evangelical Christian colleges such as Wheaton College, Illinois, or Moody Bible Institute, Illinois.

Publication History

MAGAZINE TITLE AND TITLE CHANGES: *Christian Life and Times* (1946–1948), *Christian Life* (1948–1987), *Charisma and Christian Life* (1987–present).
VOLUME AND ISSUE DATA: 1:1 (May 1946)–3:6 (June 1948); 10:1 (July 1948)–48:12 (April 1987); 12:11 (June 1987–present). At each merger, *Christian Life* assumed the volume and issue data of the absorbing magazine.
PUBLISHER AND PLACE OF PUBLICATION: Good Books, Inc., Chicago, Illinois (1946–1948); Sunday Magazine, Inc., location unknown (1948–?); Christian Life Missions, Inc., Wheaton, Illinois (1959–1986); Strang Publications, Altamonte Springs, Florida (1986–present).

EDITORS: Clyde H. Dennis (1946–1948), Robert Walker (1948–1986), Stephen Strang
(1986–present).
CIRCULATION: 200,000.

Colleen McDannell

CHRISTIAN LIFE AND TIMES. *See* CHRISTIAN LIFE

CHRISTIAN MESSENGER

At Cane Ridge, Kentucky, in August 1801, a revival fire was set that burned throughout the West, led to the modern Disciples of Christ and Christian Church movements, and spawned several religious publications, among them the *Christian Messenger*, edited for all save its final year of publication by Barton W. Stone.

Stone's career in Kentucky is part of the saga of religious revivalism in the South. Converted by the preaching of James McGready, Stone was ordained a Presbyterian but subscribed to the Westminster Confession only so far as he "saw it consistent with the Word of God."[1] Following the Cane Ridge meetings, which Stone estimated drew up to twenty-five thousand people for seven days, Stone came under suspicion for harboring "free will" notions in contrast to the obligatory Calvinist doctrine of predestination. Stone withdrew from the presbytery rather than stand trial. For a short time in 1803–1804 Stone and five other clergy organized the Springfield Presbytery, but it was dissolved in 1804 when Stone adopted the label "Christian" and resolved to follow no creed or text but the Bible.

Early on, his movement toward ecclesiastical independence and biblical literalism was threatened by the loss of followers to the Shaker faith of Mother Ann Lee, but Stone's revival preaching kept the "Christian connexion" growing until its adherents, by the time he began publishing the *Messenger*, numbered 3,350 in Kentucky and almost 13,000 throughout the Midwest and South.[2]

The *Messenger* first appeared on 25 November 1826, printed in Georgetown, Kentucky, on one sheet of paper, cut and folded into twenty-four pages, 7 ½ by 4 ½ inches, with no illustrations and solid 9-point type from front to back. The masthead bore Paul's words from 1 Thessalonians 5:21, "Prove all things; hold fast that which is good." Stone was identified as editor and "An Elder in the Church of Christ." Subscribers were promised twelve monthly issues for one dollar; agents in seven states received a one-issue bonus for every ten subscribers they enrolled. From the beginning and throughout the fourteen volumes, contents were sermons, expositions of doctrine pertinent to Stone's movement, excerpts from correspondence, obituaries, and "religious intelligence" or news of baptisms and revivals.

Stone's movement is part of the larger phenomenon of Restorationism. He advocated a cleansing of the Church of all creeds and confessions, "restoring" Christianity to its primitive New Testament basis. To that end, the *Messenger* was dedicated to "the ancient religion of Christ—the religion of love, peace, and union on earth." Truth was to be restored in "her heavenly, captivating robes, unadorned with the tinsel of human wisdom in compliance with God's will and the pious wishes of every honest Christian."[3]

Enemies there were aplenty, chiefly the Presbyterians (whence Stone had emerged), the Baptists (whose associations, Stone maintained, denied the doctrine of local church sovereignty for which Baptists had long stood), Catholics, and Shakers. About Stone's old Presbyterian colleagues, the *Messenger* blasted "their bitter strife and uncharitable opposition—their pride and worldly spirit—their death and cold formality,"[4] but always it was the ominous creeds that kept people from truth and union. "If the Bible will not stand upon its own intrinsic worth, let it die. . . . Take away human creeds and a fair prospect opens for a union among the people of God."[5] With biblical literalism came an assortment of rationalism and romanticism. Stone believed that "the Bible was addressed to rational creatures, and designed by God to be understood for their profit."[6] Hence, clergy educated in their systems and traditions were superfluous to true religion and hurtful to its genuine advance. He also insisted that rationally precise doctrines would never create genuine unity; only the spirit of Jesus could overcome divisiveness and competition.

The *Messenger* gave Stone's adherents a sense of community, confidence that their recovery of true religion was God's purpose on earth, and solace in grief. During the Kentucky cholera epidemic of 1833, the *Messenger* published several stories of deathbed scenes: mothers calling children to their bedside for a last appeal to live true to faith; fathers expiring without regrets for lost years or fortunes; children dying. There was obvious sermonic value in such accounts, but they also captured a strong sense of the frailty of human life and the normality of faith amid uncertainties—a sense utterly lost in modern obituaries.

Stone used the *Messenger* to explain his denial of orthodox teachings on the Trinity, substitutionary atonement, divine election, and Christ as the eternal second person of the Godhead. Long articles of syllogistic and exegetical reasoning speak of the theological acumen of the "average reader" in the antebellum South. Popular religious editors today would faint at the material that Stone produced, often running from one issue to another, then after a brief respite, picking up the topic again in response to a correspondent. Stone was writing to an audience schooled in the catechisms, as alert to the discipline of systematic theology as modern churchgoers are to television serials. His was an educated audience, narrowly so. Yet Stone's writing is not merely explanatory; it is a highly charged rhetoric surrounded on all sides by naysaying adversaries. Stone was a revivalist, not an armchair theologian.

Rarely did Stone elaborate ideas on how his followers' Christian faith might impose on matters of public policy. On slavery, he was careful to distance his magazine from the abolitionists and formally opposed emancipation. But Stone put his journal's full weight behind the recolonization movement and urged readers to provide money for passage of "free people of color" to Liberia and so "secure the blessing instead of the curse of our greatly injured fellow-creatures."[7] Finally in 1835, following his move from Lexington to Jacksonville, Illinois, Stone published a long "Address to the People of the United States on Slavery," calling slavery "the darkest cloud that hangs over America" and noting that "the danger of a servile and a civil war is gaining every day."[8] Despite Stone's proximity to Alton, Illinois (where editor and minister Elijah P. Lovejoy fell to a mob in 1837 for opposing slavery), and the increasing tensions over states' rights and emancipation, the *Messenger* was quiet on slavery after 1835.

However, Stone was rarely quiet about the slowness of subscribers' payments or agents' remittances or postal overcharges. The editor seemed downright indignant in his columns, especially toward subscribers who complained about his price: "Did they know the vast number of delinquents—the time and labor spent in writing and preparing for the press—the money paid for postage of letters, etc., they would not make such an insinuation."[9]

In early 1832, Stone achieved a partial alliance with Alexander Campbell of the Disciples. Though they disagreed on several theological and practical concerns, they shared the revival spirit, opposition to denominations, and a capacity to publish and produce periodicals. Volume 6 of the *Messenger* lists John T. Johnson, a Disciples minister, as coeditor. This arrangement survived until Stone's move to Jacksonville, when Johnson founded the *Christian Advocate* and the *Messenger* shrank to sixteen pages per issue. It appears that Stone tried to clear the *Messenger* of debts by raising subscriptions to $1.25 in 1836, but soon fell back to the standard dollar a year. He also sought help as "the infirmities attendant to old age" began to limit his considerable energies.[10]

Volume 11 lists elders Thomas M. Allen and Jacob Creath, Jr., of Missouri as coeditors. In 1843 Stone purchased a press with D. P. Henderson, who became the *Messenger*'s coeditor and who finished volume 14 following Stone's death in November 1844.

In many respects, Stone's restoration of Christianity to its primitive roots, always the purpose of his preaching and writing, was also a blending of theology with nineteenth-century liberalism. Stone dismissed original sin as unfair: God requires only what the human person can do. "To demand more would be tyrrnnical [*sic*] injustice."[11] He never compromised on local church autonomy ("Let every attempt made by our conference to form laws and rules for the government of the church . . . be frowned at indignantly by all."[12]), and he insisted on egalitarianism with respect to the privileges of faith, God being the "common father."[13] For all the *Messenger*'s esoteric theological distinctions, the magazine was also a very human journal of life's poignant moments, a journal of the important issues that face each person, written by a man who had in his bones both Elijah's fire and David's passion—the surety of God's judgment and the mystery of God's benevolence. The *Messenger* at its peak had only eighteen hundred subscribers, but the magazine gave Stone's Christian churches a point of connection, a sense of the larger whole, and a clearer picture of the enemies of the faithful. Stone's readers knew that beyond their hardscrabble church halls was a war of ideas and words that traded on issues of ultimate concern. Those isolated by forest and field were nonetheless a family of faith. On a frontier where poor roads and icy rivers delayed paper and hindered circulation, the *Christian Messenger* gave new birth to old religious impulses.

Notes

1. Stone, quoted in John B. Boles, *Religion in Antebellum Kentucky* (Lexington: University Press of Kentucky, 1976), 33.
   2. Ibid., p. 42.
   3. *Christian Messenger* 1 (25 November 1826): 1.
   4. Ibid.
   5. Ibid. 1 (25 June 1827): 180.
   6. Ibid. 1 (25 November 1826): 4.
   7. Ibid. 1 (25 April 1827): 140.
   8. Ibid. 9 (April 1835): 82.
   9. Ibid. 5 (January 1831): 1.
   10. Ibid. 12 (November 1841): 1.
   11. Ibid. 1 (25 January 1827): 68.
   12. Ibid., p. 54.
   13. Ibid. 1 (25 November 1826): 8.

Information Sources

INDEX SOURCES: Each volume contains its own partial index. A general index is published with volume 14 in the Star Bible Publications reprint edition, 1978, Fort Worth, Texas.

LOCATION SOURCES: The best copies of all volumes were collected in 1978 for a reprint edition, published by Star Bible and Tract Corp., Fort Worth, Texas.

Publication History

MAGAZINE TITLE: *Christian Messenger* (1826–1845).

VOLUME AND ISSUE DATA: 1:1 (November 1826)–14:12 (April 1845). Published monthly, with some numbers published together.

PUBLISHER AND PLACE OF PUBLICATION: Barton W. Stone, Georgetown, Kentucky (1826–1833); Jacksonville, Illinois (1834–1845).

EDITORS: Barton W. Stone (1826–1844); Coeditors John T. Johnson (1832–1834), Thomas M. Allen and Jacob Creath, Jr. (1840–1841), D. P. Henderson (1843–1845).

CIRCULATION: 1,800 (1836).

P. Mark Fackler

CHRISTIAN NEWSETTE. *See* ETERNITY

CHRISTIAN ORACLE. *See* CHRISTIAN CENTURY

CHRISTIAN PARLOR MAGAZINE

Founded in 1844 by Darius Mead, a New York clergyman, the *Christian Parlor Magazine* was intended to be what its title indicated—a magazine for the parlor in Christian homes. It was primarily a Christian literary magazine meant to provide a morally superior alternative to secular literary journals of the day. Indeed, part of the rationale given in the opening issue was to stay "the tide of unsound morals" driven by the mass of unseemly publications.[1] It was published monthly and also bound and sold as a complete book at the end of each volume. In its first years the *Christian Parlor Magazine* included moralist fiction and poetry along with instructive biographical sketches and a piece of Christian music in each month's thirty-two-page issue.

The magazine's editors advised potential writers that their contributions needed to improve the magazine's readers or at the least provide them with beneficial amusement, otherwise their submissions would be refused. Abstract lectures on morality and religion would be rejected, and writers of "sickly love stories" should not apply.[2] The editor asked potential contributors to remember that the magazine was intended for "persons of different evangelical creeds, scattered all over the Union." Hence, anything that was the least bit critical of any sect had to be avoided.[3]

Founding editor Darius Mead left his position at the close of the third volume in 1847, moving on to an editorial post with the *Home Magazine and Fireside Reader*. Under the direction of its new editor, Joel T. Headley, the *Christian Home and Parlor* (sometimes called "Headley's Magazine")[4] furnished readers with more to choose from. In addition to its original goal of filling "a place in lighter literature without the objectionable features too often connected with it,"[5] Headley expanded the correspondence section, used materials from a wider range of sources, included descriptions of foreign places (mostly European), provided short book notices, and printed literary news from Europe and America. The magazine published a series of engravings (each issue included a plate of a Bible scene and one of nature—either a flower, bird, or landscape) and printed portraits of an issue's biographical subjects.

In a column on "Ourselves and Our Readers," editor Headley claimed that from the start the goal of the magazine was to provide "literature of the lighter class for the family circle, and especially for young ladies and gentlemen," aiding them in "healthful development of the mind," which, in his view, included taste and the affections along with the intellect.[6] Women, it was assumed, would not be interested in the tawdry subject of politics presented in the newspapers. This journal would be more congenial to a woman's "taste and habits of thought." Fiction, however, needed to be dealt with carefully since it posed both potential value and danger. The magazine informed its readers that it did not publish love stories or fairy tales, nor any works of fiction except those that had "the purpose of illustrating and enforcing truth."[7] Thus, it presented translations of European poems such as Schiller's "The Lady of the Bell," gave advice on how to make a happy home, and republished old and recent English poems. Early contributors included Noah Porter, Anne C. Lynch, Jacob Abbott, Lyman Beecher, and T. S. Arthur.

Ordinary literary magazines were criticized for trying to "please the fancy" without "cultivating the feelings or enriching the mind." Because of that "evil," because of the "exciting love tales which arrest and inflame the youthful heart . . . apt to create an ideal world for the early dreamer, which renders practical life insipid, and its duties irksome," many had condemned all light reading. But Headley defended it on the grounds that Christians also needed relaxation, that not everything they did needed a utilitarian motive. Of course, Headley recognized the increasing popularity of magazines and their power to transmit ideas and to convey "thought and expression."[8] He thought it unwise for the religious and moral realm to surrender that world without at least a fight.

Headley proved that he was ready to defend Protestantism and American democracy. Under his editorship the magazine pursued a more forceful intolerance of Roman Catholicism. In an essay on "Pope Pius IX and Italy," Headley reported on a trip to Italy and the antipapal attitudes that he claimed to find there prior to Pius IX's coming to power. He described at length the reforms that Pius brought to Rome and the attempts by the Austrian government to overturn them.[9] Despite the good he did, in the end the Pope was still a monarchical despot opposed to liberty. Headley claimed that the whole policy of Europe was to "keep out the leaven of republicanism."[10] His defense of the American democratic system came out in comments on other European events, notably the revolutions of 1848.[11] Headley despaired of any attempts at self-government not based on religious principles acknowledging God as sovereign. He also saw a dim future for the divine right of kings throughout Western Europe. Only the maintenance of Protestant Christian principles would maintain America's free institutions since such ideas were the bedrock of American liberty.[12]

The magazine also profiled famous Americans. Lyman Beecher, the New School Presbyterian minister and president of Lane Seminary in Cincinnati, was praised as a simple and unpretentious preacher whose sermons lacked thunder and anecdotes but allowed listeners to take away new ideas. "John Smith," the essay's author, described a sermon that Beecher gave at Fireman's Hall in Cincinnati (on the relation of conscience to moral government) when a fire alarm went off. Beecher's "spell" was not broken, and scarcely a half-dozen people left the hall for what turned out to be a false alarm. When a second alarm followed, Beecher continued as if nothing happened.[13] A profile of artist Thomas Cole by Daniel Huntington suggests the magazine's tendency to find religious value in biography. As with other short biographies of artists, the piece on Cole emphasized his paintings with religious themes, such as an illustration of the Twenty-third Psalm and the unfinished "Pilgrim of the Cross and the World." His later works were praised as being "in complete harmony with the teachings of our Divine Master.'' Finding ''no stain'' on the great landscape painter's moral character, Huntington praised Cole with typical midcentury rhetoric.[14]

Historical articles like Lyman Beecher's ''The Puritans and Their Institutions'' were also relatively common.[15] The colonists turned out, in Beecher's writing, to be a lot like mid-nineteenth-century Presbyterians in their piety, form of government, and theology. Beecher's appreciation for the Puritans runs far enough to credit them with laying the basic framework for American government. Indeed, applying and observing the ''Puritan elements of our Republic'' would assure God's continued protection and blessing. A series of other articles in the magazine concerned the quest for wealth, some of them, such as ''Literature and Business'' using the subject as a forum for exploring ways to ''ennoble'' a greedy age.[16] Literature, the essayist claimed, would prevent people from becoming misers. It would instead help people be better and lead them to greater success, as the proper combination of the two had done for Ricardo and Roscoe. Others, such as the editor's comments on the California gold rush, gave familiar commentary on the dangers associated with rapid accumulation of wealth.[17] J. Maltby contributed an essay on secular progress and Christianity, urging a vague Christianization of the age and the concept of progress.[18]

In 1855 the *Christian Parlor Magazine* merged with *Happy Home* to form the *Happy Home and Parlor Magazine*, although the first issue only appeared in 1856. While the *Christian Parlor Magazine* was, especially under Headley's editorship, similar to other literary magazines, particularly *Graham's*, it tried to map out a distinctive niche for itself as the literary magazine for Christian homes. It seems not to have done particularly well. The *Christian Parlor Magazine* generally refrained from pushing any of the important antebellum reforms, although it did, especially in its last years, criticize the acquisitive ethic. It was at bottom a comfortable literary magazine aimed at a broad upper-middle-class Christian audience and lacked any unusual doctrinal or political markings. Historians interested in Christian literature and responses to ''secular'' magazines in the middle of the nineteenth century will find a useful source in the *Christian Parlor Magazine*.

Notes

1. *Christian Parlor Magazine* (May 1844):2.
2. See, for instance, Ibid. (June 1848): 60.
3. Ibid.
4. Frank Luther Mott, *A History of American Magazines, 1741–1850* (New York: Appleton, 1930).
5. *Christian Parlor Magazine* (May 1847): 1.
6. Ibid. (May 1848): 1–3.
7. Ibid. (April 1848): 352.
8. Ibid. (May 1847): 1.
9. Ibid. (March 1848): 289–92.

10. Ibid. (April 1848): 321–24.
11. Ibid. (May 1848): 27–30.
12. Ibid. (July 1848): 92.
13. Ibid. (April 1848): 362–64. See also the May 1848 issue.
14. Ibid. (September 1850): 143–46. A good discussion of Ralph Waldo Emerson can be found in *Christian Parlor Magazine* (July 1851): 271–74.
15. Ibid. (May 1850): 3–6.
16. Ibid. (February 1851): 278–79.
17. Ibid. (March 1851): 297–98.
18. Ibid. (February 1849): 284.

Information Sources

INDEX SOURCES: Located at the end of each annual volume except volumes 1 and 9.
LOCATION SOURCES: Microfilm edition from University Microfilms, *American Periodical Series, 1800–1850,* 2 reels. OCLC lists over 60 libraries holding the microfilm edition. Full runs of the periodical are widely available at college and university libraries throughout the United States.

Publication History

MAGAZINE TITLE AND TITLE CHANGES: *Christian Parlor Magazine* (1844–1855). Merged with *Happy Home* to form *Happy Home and Parlor Magazine* (1856–1859). Also issued as an annual with the title *Christian Parlor Book.* Sometimes the annual was issued as a gift volume with the title *Gems for the Fireside.*
VOLUME AND ISSUE DATA: 1:1 (May 1844)–11:12 (December 1854); published monthly. The compilation of the previous year's issues sold as a gift book with an 1855 publication date.
PUBLISHER AND PLACE OF PUBLICATION: Darius Mead (1844–1847), E.E. Miles (1847–1852), George Pratt (1852–1854), James Pratt (1855). All in New York City.
EDITORS: Darius Mead (1844–1847), Dorus Clarke (coeditor, 1845–1847), Joel T. Headley (1847–1855).
CIRCULATION: Unknown.

David O. Yntema

CHRISTIAN READER. *See* CHRISTIAN HERALD

CHRISTIAN RECORDER

While the *Christian Recorder* became the official organ of the African Methodist Episcopal (A.M.E.) Church in 1852, it actually began in 1848 when the denomination authorized its general book agent, Reverend Augustus R. Green, to purchase the Pittsburgh-based *Mystery Press* from Martin R. Delany, an abolitionist and African emigrationist. It became Green's responsibility to transform the Delany newspaper into the *Christian Herald*, an A.M.E. quarterly.

Although Green drew sixteen hundred subscribers to the *Herald* by 1852, the publication was unsuccessful for financial reasons. Green's resignation and subsequent relocation to Canada gave the General Conference of 1852 an opportunity to reorganize the *Herald*.[1]

At the Annual Conference in New York, Reverend M. M. Clark seized that initiative. Born in Delaware in 1807, Clark was graduated in 1835 from Jefferson College in Canonsburg, Pennsylvania. His interest in the *Herald* grew out of his previous experience as general book agent, a position he attained at the 1844 General Conference. Clark believed that the publication needed a clearer focus and a different format. At the 1852 General Conference he proposed that the newspaper, now renamed the *Christian Recorder*, become a weekly and devote itself to religion, morality, science, and literature. The denomination accepted his prospectus and elected Clark the first editor. He published fewer than twenty issues before he resigned in 1854. The financial difficulties that troubled Clark also hindered the second editor, Jabaz Pitt Campbell, who sporadically printed the *Christian Recorder* during his tenure.[2]

Despite these early difficulties, the newspaper played a crucial role for the denomination and the African-American population during the Civil War. For a time, between 1859 and 1861, publication of the *Christian Recorder* had been suspended because of irregular oversight. Since Campbell had taken a pastorate, Elisha Weaver, then editor and general book steward, reported to the General Conference of 1864 in Philadelphia that after two years "we commenced the republication of this paper on the 1st of January, 1861, and have been enabled to keep it in the field ever since." He further noted that "we are now issuing every week . . . 3,560 copies." Weaver reported revenues of $4,908.45 and expenses of $4,708.38. He told delegates that no indebtedness encumbered the newspaper and that "we have now cash remaining in hand . . . amounting to four hundred dollars."[3]

While A.M.E. officials were pleased that their decade-long wait for financial stability in the *Christian Recorder* was over, the African-American population also had reasons to cheer the role of this denominational publication. From the pages of the *Christian Recorder*, Blacks received vital information about the Civil War and the prospects for emancipation. As slaves became contraband owing to war, the *Christian Recorder* challenged "our people and churches" to help homeless Blacks with food, clothing, and schools. In an editorial in 1863, Weaver lauded the Emancipation Proclamation and observed that "we thank God and President Lincoln for what has been done." Although the edict initially applied only to those areas in rebellion against the federal government, Weaver hoped that Congress would manumit slaves in those border states still in the Union.[4]

The General Conference of 1864 elected John M. Brown to succeed Weaver as editor. Brown, an A.M.E. missionary assigned to the wartime South, declined to serve. He told delegates that without time "to wind up my affairs in my field of labor in Virginia" he could not discharge those dual responsibilities. Hence,

James Lynch replaced Brown in 1866 and served until 1867 when he too went South to organize A.M.E. congregations. Weaver immediately became editor until the General Conference of 1868 in Washington, D.C., chose Benjamin T. Tanner as the next editor. With Tanner, the *Christian Recorder* continued as a major organ for the A.M.E. Church and for the Black population in general.

Tanner, who served until 1884, won numerous plaudits from those within his denomination. The General Conference of 1884 in Baltimore praised Tanner because he had done "all that a man of his varied learning could do by the press and by his eloquence, by his personal piety and by the pulpit to secure popularity and a wide circulation for the *Recorder*." Tanner's tenure coincided with a period of militant Black activism. Like Weaver during the Civil War, Tanner used the newspaper to cover pressing issues that confronted African Americans. When the venerable Frederick Douglass spoke at Bethel A.M.E. Church in Baltimore at an 1879 meeting that sought Black teachers for the city schools, Tanner featured the event in the *Recorder*. Since Tanner launched the quarterly entitled *A.M.E. Church Review* in 1884, Benjamin F. Lee, the president of Wilberforce University, succeeded him at the *Recorder*.[5]

Richard R. Wright, Jr., who became de facto editor in 1909, had a major influence on the *Christian Recorder*. During the 1908–1912 quadrennium, John H. Collett, the general manager of the A.M.E. Book Concern that published the newspaper, died on 8 April 1909. Henry T. Johnson, who had become editor in 1892, died on 23 July 1910. The health problems of Collett and Johnson had already caused the *Christian Recorder* to cease publication in late December 1908. On 3 March 1909 Wright assumed dual duties as managing editor of the *Recorder* and of the Book Concern, and publication of the *Christian Recorder* resumed. The General Conference of 1912 in Kansas City, Missouri, elected Wright as editor in his own right. In 1916 he reported to the General Conference in Philadelphia that the *Christian Recorder* had been published once weekly since the 1912 general conference. It regularly contained eight pages that included a news department, a woman's page, sermons, Sunday School lessons, Christian Endeavor topics, and editorials. By 1924, features had expanded. A health column, for example, featured Dr. D. A. Bethea, "a physician of public spirit and fine professional standing," a current events section provided a "review of the principal events in the secular world," and there were now "notes of racial progress" that Wright took from various Black newspapers. "The most important and unusual things are clipped from these papers," Wright noted, "and condensed in single paragraphs, so that our readers may keep abreast with our own race progress."[6]

Wright, who served as editor until he became a bishop in 1936, revived the *Recorder*'s tradition of addressing crucial issues that faced African-Americans. The edition of 1 February 1917, for example, encouraged the wartime Black migration from the agricultural South to Northern industrial areas. From his Philadelphia office Wright declared that "every community in the North" should help "to get jobs for our friends in the South." He wrote, "Let a million come. In coming the negroes will get higher wages. They will get first-class schools, running nine months a year." He felt that for these advantages it was worth leaving the South.[7]

While the *Christian Recorder* has been the principal newspaper of the A.M.E. Church, it has shared denominational support with three other publications: the *Southern Christian Recorder*, founded in 1886 by Bishop Henry M. Turner; the *Western Christian Recorder*, officially launched in 1900 by J. Frank McDonald; and the *South African Christian Recorder*, founded in 1902 by Carlton M. Tanner. The *Southern Christian Recorder* and the *Western Christian Recorder* merged at the General Conference of 1952 in Chicago and became the *Southwestern Christian Recorder*. Then at the General Conference of 1960 in Los Angeles, the *Southwestern Christian Recorder* merged with the *Christian Recorder*.[8]

The General Conference of 1980 in New Orleans changed the *Christian Recorder* from a weekly newspaper to a fortnightly, published, sometimes in color, every other Monday.[9] The A.M.E. Sunday School Union Publishing House in Nashville, Tennessee, has been the official publisher of the *Recorder* since 1960. Until then, the now defunct A.M.E. Book Concern published the *Recorder* in Philadelphia.

During the tenure of Robert H. Reid, who has served as editor since 1976, the *Christian Recorder* continued to cover local, national, international, secular and religious news, as well as in-house activities of the many A.M.E. congregations around the world. The *Recorder* remains one of the connecting links between the denomination's leadership and membership. As in the past, the newspaper presents news and events to African-Americans that other presses often neglect and omit. Timely editorials on relevant religious, political, economic, and other subjects appear in every issue. Some have been reprinted elsewhere. For example, *World Parish*, the international organ of the World Methodist Council, reprinted a 1977 *Christian Recorder* editorial on Anwar Sadat following the Egyptian president's historic peace trip to Israel. Other editorials by Reid have dealt with similarly important topics.[10] Some recent articles have included "South African Dutch Reformed Church Comes of Age—Now Calls Apartheid by its Proper Name: Sin," "Black on Black Crime and Drug Proliferation: Giant Enemies of the Black Society," "Black Churches Must Prepare Posthaste to Attend and Counsel AIDS Victims," and "Neo-Pentecostalism in African Methodism Produces Phenomenal Membership Growth for Churches Embracing It."[11]

The editor of the *Christian Recorder* holds the rank of general officer in the two-million-member A.M.E. Church. Some of the editors have also written books related to the A.M.E. Church and to the African-American population. Benjamin T. Tanner published *An Outline of our History and Government for African Methodist Churchmen* (1884). Richard R. Wright, Jr. produced *Who's Who in the General Conference of 1912* (1912), *Centennial Encyclopedia of the African Methodist Episcopal Church* (1916), and *Who's Who in the General Conference 1924* (1924). Robert H. Reid, Jr. wrote *Irony of Afro-American*

History: An Overview of A.M.E. History and Related Developments (1984).[12] Additionally, editors who were elected bishops in the denomination included Jabaz P. Campbell in 1864, Benjamin T. Tanner in 1888, Benjamin F. Lee in 1892, and Richard R. Wright, Jr. in 1936. John M. Brown, who was elected but did not serve as editor, attained the episcopacy in 1868.[13]

Officially established as an A.M.E. publication in 1852, the *Christian Recorder* is the oldest African American newspaper still in existence. Since the denomination includes congregations in the Americas, Africa, and Europe, the *Christian Recorder* regularly reaches an international constituency.

Notes

1. Daniel A. Payne, *History of the African Methodist Episcopal Church* (Nashville: Publishing House of the A.M.E. Sunday School Union, 1891), 278; Gilbert A. Williams, *Christian Recorder* (Nashville: A.M.E. Sunday School Union, n.d.), 3.

2. Payne, *History*, 172, 278–79; *Minutes of the Tenth General Conference of the African Methodist Episcopal Church* (Philadelphia: William S. Young, 1852) 4–5; Richard R. Wright, Jr., *Encyclopedia of African Methodism* (Philadelphia: Book Concern of the A.M.E. Church, 1947), 571; Williams, *Christian Recorder*, 3–4.

3. *Thirteenth General Conference of the African M.E. Church* (Philadelphia: William S. Young, 1864), 48.

4. James M. McPherson, *The Negro's Civil War* (New York: Vintage Books, 1965), 51, 133.

5. *Thirteenth General Conference*, 44; Wright, *Encyclopedia of African Methodism*, 352; *Journal of the 18th Session and 17th Quadrennial Session of the General Conference of the African Methodist Episcopal Church in the World* (Philadelphia: James C. Embry, 1884), 205; John W. Blassingame and John McKivigan, eds., *Frederick Douglass Papers*, 1st ser., vol. 4 (New Haven: Yale University Press, 1991), 542–546; Wright, *Encyclopedia of African Methodism*, 352.

6. *Proceedings of the Quadrennial Session of the General Conference of the African Methodist Episcopal Church* (Nashville: Publishing House of the A.M.E. Sunday School Union, 1912), 54–55, 272–73; *Journal of the Twenty-fifth Quadrennial Session (Being the Centennial Session) of the General Conference of the African Methodist Episcopal Church* (Nashville: A.M.E. Sunday School Union, 1916), 344–347; *Journal of the Twenty-seventh Quadrennial Session of the General Conference of the African Methodist Episcopal Church* (Philadelphia: A.M.E. Book Concern, 1924), 363.

7. Emmett J. Scott, *Negro Migration During the War* (New York: Oxford University Press, 1920), 164–65.

8. Wright, *Encyclopedia of African Methodism*, 509–10; James H. Smith, *Vital Facts Concerning the African Methodist Episcopal Church* (Philadelphia: A.M.E. Book Concern, 1939), 154; *Combined Minutes of the General Conferences, African Methodist Episcopal Church, 1948, 1952, 1956* (Nashville: A.M.E. Sunday School Union, 1956), 230; *The Official Minutes of the Thirty-sixth Session of the General Conference of the African Methodist Episcopal Church* (Nashville: A.M.E. Sunday School Union, 1960), 122.

9. *The Combined Minutes of the Forty-first Session of the General Conference of the African Methodist Episcopal Church* (Nashville: A.M.E. Sunday School Union, 1970), 108.

10. *World Parish* 17 (February 1978): 1, 6.

11. Robert H. Reid, Jr., *The Quadrennial Report of the A.M.E. Christian Recorder: The 42nd Session of the General Conference of the African Methodist Episcopal Church, July 8–15, 1984, Kansas City, Missouri* (Nashville: A.M.E. Sunday School Union, 1984), 3; Robert H. Reid, Jr., *The Quadrennial Report of the A.M.E. Christian Recorder: Forty-fourth Session of the General Conference of the African Methodist Episcopal Church, July 8–16, 1992, Orlando, Florida* (Nashville: A.M.E. Sunday School Union, 1992), 6–9.

12. Benjamin T. Tanner, *An Outline of Our History and Government for African Methodist Churchmen* (Philadelphia: [A.M.E. Book Concern], 1884); Richard R. Wright, Jr., *Who's Who in the General Conference of 1912* (Philadelphia: [A.M.E. Book Concern], 1912); *Centennial Encyclopedia of the African Methodist Church* (Philadelphia: [A.M.E. Book Concern], 1924); Robert Henry Reid, Jr., *Irony of Afro-American History: An Overview of A.M.E. History and Related Developments* (Nashville: A.M.E. Publishing House, 1984).

13. Reid, *Irony of Afro-American History*, 86; *Thirteenth General Conference*, 44; Wright, *Encyclopedia of African Methodism*, 566.

Information Sources

LOCATION SOURCES: Microfilm copies of the *Christian Recorder* at Mother Bethel African Methodist Episcopal Church, Philadelphia, Pennsylvania; also at Drew University (New Jersey), Indiana University, and other academic libraries.
INDEX SOURCES: Unknown.

Publication History

MAGAZINE TITLE AND TITLE CHANGES: *Christian Herald* (1848–1852), *Christian Recorder* (1852–present). Appeared sometimes as *A.M.E. Christian Recorder.*
VOLUME AND ISSUE DATA: 1:1 (1 July 1852)–129:51 (28 July 1980), published weekly; 129:52 (11 August 1980)–present, published biweekly; 1854–1856, appeared irregularly; 1859–1861 and late December 1908–March 1909, publication suspended.
PUBLISHER AND PLACE OF PUBLICATION: Book Concern of the A.M.E. Church, Philadelphia, Pennsylvania (1852–1952); A.M.E. Sunday School Union, Nashville, Tennessee (1952–present).
EDITORS: Molliston Madison Clark (1852–1854), Jabaz Pitt Campbell (1854–1860), Elisha Weaver (1861–1864), A. L. Stanford (1861), James Lynch (1866–1867), Elisha Weaver (1867–1868), Benjamin Tucker Tanner (1868–1884), Benjamin Franklin Lee (1884–1892), Henry Theodore Johnson (1892–1909), Richard Robert Wright, Jr. (1909–1936), George Arnett Singleton (1936–1944), David Norris (1944–1950), Fred Hughes (1950–1960), Benjamin Julius Nolen, Sr. (1960–1964), Lawrence Sylvester Odom, Sr. (1964–1966), Benjamin Julius Nolen, Sr. (1966–1973), A. Lewis Williams (1973–1976), Robert H. Reid, Jr. (1976–present).
CIRCULATION: 7,000 (1993).

Dennis C. Dickerson and Robert H. Reid, Jr.

CHRISTIAN'S MAGAZINE. *See* HERALD OF GOSPEL LIBERTY

CHRISTIAN'S MAGAZINE, REVIEWER, AND RELIGIOUS INTELLIGENCER. *See* HERALD OF GOSPEL LIBERTY

CHRISTIAN STANDARD AND GUIDE TO HOLINESS. *See* GUIDE TO HOLINESS

CHRISTIAN TRIBUNE. *See* CHRISTIAN CENTURY

CHRISTIAN WORK. *See* CHRISTIAN CENTURY

CHRISTIAN WORKER'S MAGAZINE. *See* MOODY MAGAZINE

CHURCH ADVOCATE

The *Church Advocate* is the monthly religious magazine of the Churches of God, General Conference, with editorial offices located in Findlay, Ohio. The *Advocate*, together with its immediate predecessor, the *Gospel Publisher*, has been the primary religious periodical of the Churches of God since 5 June 1835.

The origins of the *Advocate* are found in the influences of a religious movement, commonly called the Second Great Awakening, on the primarily German population found in eastern and central Pennsylvania in the 1820s. John Winebrenner (1797–1860), pastor of the Harrisburg Reformed charge in the early 1820s, became convinced that a spiritual awakening was needed within his churches and the community. In order to promote an experiential Christianity centered on a "new birth" in the life of each individual, he adopted a number of religious practices associated with the Second Great Awakening. Frequently termed the "new measures," these practices included praying for sinners by name, holding "experience meetings" late at night, and using the "mourner's bench"—instead of the catechism—for repentant sinners.

These measures and the highly charged emotionalism associated with them were rejected by the vestries and some of the parishioners of the Harrisburg charge, and by 1825 the doors of the churches in the charge had been locked against him. Consequently, Winebrenner and his new-measures parishioners organized an independent congregation in Harrisburg that adopted a name popular among Pennsylvania German pietists, the "Church of God." This movement was also part of a wider endeavor among some Protestants to eliminate denominational labels and "restore" Christianity to its New Testament structures.

Many Christians in the Harrisburg area, including some who belonged to independent churches, soon began to look to Winebrenner for leadership. Additional Churches of God were established. Winebrenner took this as a sign that primitive, Biblical Christianity was being restored in his time. He assumed, as did many of his contemporaries on the American church scene, that the New Testament, rightly read, provided the plan (both theological and governmental) as well as the proper name for the Church. An "eldership" was organized in

October 1830, consisting of six "teaching elders" (ministers) from Churches of God in the area. Several new elderships were formed over the next twenty years as the Church of God movement spread rapidly to the West, into western Pennsylvania and into Ohio, Indiana, Illinois, Iowa, as well as south into Maryland— generally following Pennsylvania German settlement patterns.

The theological stance of Winebrenner and most in the Church of God was similar to that of free-church Protestant evangelicalism of the time, but with some subtle differences. Christian conversion experience was central, and a watershed event, in the Christian's life. Upon receiving Christ through an experience of a new birth, the Christian was automatically a member of God's Church. For Winebrenner, therefore, a converted person, regardless of denominational affiliation, was in reality a member of the Church of God, although (unfortunately) wearing a "sectarian" label.

Freedom of the will was emphasized against a predestinarian theology. Winebrenner rejected the Calvinistic approach, found in a number of German and English denominations in America, that God does not will the salvation of all. Only the elect would be saved. Rather, frequently quoting appropriate Scripture, Church of God ministers emphasized that salvation was a gift of God available to all who chose, of their own free will, to repent and accept the lordship of Christ in their lives.

Believers' baptism by immersion was the accepted practice, although from the beginning there were those members who insisted that inasmuch as the new birth was the only essential criterion for Church membership, baptism was unnecessary. Scriptural precedent was used to justify the adoption of footwashing as a "third ordinance," although here again many members regarded the washing of the saints' feet and even the Lord's supper only as desirable, but not essential, practices. This high degree of individualism and emphasis on standards of personal piety in the Christian life have given the Church of God a strong pietistic flavor since its inception. With the establishment of the first eldership in 1830, the Church of God adopted a presbyterian polity, one that emphasizes the authority of the eldership or conference in matters of faith and practice and in the appointment of ministers. However, in practice, many churches have tended to be more congregational, regarding the local congregation as the highest authority.

In the early 1830s Winebrenner and others conceived the idea of a paper to promote the views of their Church and Christian practice, provide a forum for Church of God pastors and laity, and establish a central connecting point for the expanding Church of God movement. Consequently, on 5 June 1835, the *Gospel Publisher and Journal of Useful Knowledge* first appeared—published, printed, and distributed by John Winebrenner. It was a four-page, fifteen by ten inch tabloid, printed by a conventional bed-and-platen press. The cost was $1.50 per year if paid in advance; $1.75, if paid in the first six months; and $2.00 if not paid within the year. Inasmuch as $1.50 was roughly equivalent to three-days' wages for a laborer in the 1830s, getting the *Publisher* was not an inexpensive proposition. There were five hundred to eight hundred subscribers in the late 1830s and the 1840s, many of whom received the paper on credit. This engendered a debt that hung heavily over the *Gospel Publisher* (and *Church Advocate*) for the next fifty years or so.

Winebrenner was a man of wide-ranging interests. He was first and foremost a preacher (in both English and German), but also a businessman, small farmer, inventor, traveler, and social reformer. Publishing, printing, and editing were not his first love, a fact that he made known to his readers from time to time. Therefore, in 1840, in order to preach more and tend to the needs of an expanding denomination (though Winebrenner would not use that word since he believed it denoted a corruption of the Church), he turned the *Publisher* over to John Weishample, an independent-minded Church of God preacher and printer. Weishample enjoyed his work. He wrote more editorials than Winebrenner and added a page, more or less, in German for the readership more comfortable with that language than with English. But Weishample had interests in starting another Church paper, and in 1844 he turned the *Publisher* over to Reverend George McCartney to edit, while continuing as printer. The arrangement did not work well. In addition, the "ruinous credit system" was putting the paper more deeply in debt. Finally, on 13 August 1845, the *Gospel Publisher* was discontinued. It was briefly resurrected for an issue on 12 December 1845 in order to publish the minutes of the East Pennsylvania eldership of the Church of God, and then, once again, fell silent for several months.

At this point John Winebrenner stepped in, convinced of the need for a Church paper. On 1 May 1846, the Church of God paper reappeared as the *Church Advocate*, with Winebrenner again as publisher, printer and editor. Winebrenner saw the *Advocate* as a continuation of the *Gospel Publisher*, so the first year of the *Advocate* was listed as volume 11. The rationale for the name change was theological.

Since 1 May 1846, the *Church Advocate* has been in continuous publication in various sizes (largest, 21 ¼ by 18 ½ inches; smallest, 8 ½ by 11 inches), with as few as four pages, and as many as forty-eight. The few occasions when the *Advocate* has not been printed on schedule have been the result of press breakdowns, a printer's illness, change in editors, short-term financial restructuring, or the push of Robert E. Lee's Army of Northern Virginia into the Harrisburg area in June of 1863, just before the battle at Gettysburg. For the first 145 years, the *Gospel Publisher* and *Church Advocate* were published and printed in various locations in central Pennsylvania (including Harrisburg, Carlisle, Mt. Joy, and Lancaster), but most often (125 years) in Harrisburg. Since 1979 the *Advocate* has been published in Findlay, Ohio.

Between 1835 and 1992 the Church of God paper had only eleven editors. For 70 years, between 1869 and 1939, there were only two editors (C. H. Forney, 1869–1909, usually regarded as the theologian and historian of the nineteenth-century Church of God; and Sherman Grand Yahn, 1909–1939). Since the Civil War, up to 1992, there have been only seven editors.

Generally, but not exclusively, the *Gospel Publisher* and *Church Advocate* have reflected the outlook of conservative, evangelical Protestantism in America. The continuing pietist emphasis in the Churches of God has sometimes operated to diminish extremes of doctrinal debate within the pages of both papers, although a strident, fundamentalistic rhetoric was commonplace in the issues of the *Advocate* in the first part of the twentieth century. Of special theological interest was the John Winebrenner–John Williamson Nevin (of Mercersburg Theology fame) correspondence, carried in the *Gospel Publisher* in the early 1840s. In opposition to the emphasis of Winebrenner and others on "the anxious bench" (where "mourners" sometimes gathered to pray for salvation) and "new measures" revivalism, Nevin began to stress the "catechetical system" and an antiindividualistic, "organic" view of the church.

In the pre–Civil War period, the *Gospel Publisher* and *Church Advocate* were both oriented to social reform as well as theological issues. In the first issue of the *Publisher* Winebrenner printed an article in opposition to smoking, suggesting that it was a well-known fact that smoking tobacco caused cancer. In the 1830s Winebrenner was an abolitionist of note, and the *Publisher* was considered an "abolitionist rag" and was burned in the streets of Charleston, South Carolina. Both the *Publisher* and *Advocate* were also "temperance" papers. At the same time, Winebrenner did not equate temperance with abstinence and on occasion ran recipes for the making of wine in the *Advocate*, much to the disgust of some others in the Church of God. Before the Civil War both papers had a certain pacifistic overtone. Winebrenner was vehemently opposed to the war between Mexico and the United States and counseled his readers not to support it. Widespread support of the Civil War by the mostly Northern Church of God ended pacifist inclinations in the *Advocate*.

In the post–Civil War period, as the Church of God turned inward (with the rest of the country), social reform was downplayed. Much more emphasis was placed upon evangelism, education, missions, and minute formulations of Christian and Church of God doctrine. There was a temperance column, and antialcohol articles increased as America moved toward its experiment with Prohibition in the 1920s. Some concern was expressed over labor-management and immigration issues in the late nineteenth century. Most writers for the paper, representing small towns and rural areas, tended to be critical of the labor movement and suspicious of the large number of immigrants coming to the United States from central and southeastern Europe—many of whom were seen as a threat to the prevailing Protestant ethos as well as American democracy.

Of some interest during this period was the editorship of C. H. Forney (1869–1909). Educated for a time at Oberlin, he attempted to reconcile the Christian faith to the rising interest in evolution and German higher criticism of the Bible. A primary person in the establishment of Findlay College (now the University of Findlay), Forney defended the liberal arts against an exclusively biblically oriented approach to education. A postmillennialist in a generally premillennialist Church in the late 1800s, editor Forney exuded a genteel, cultured openness as he went about his editorial duties.

Under editor S. G. Yahn (1909–1939) the developing fundamentalist movement in the Churches of God was reflected in editorials and articles in the *Advocate*. Strict adherence to "fundamental" Christian doctrine, especially the literal inerrancy of Scripture, was urged. At the same time, the pietist-experiential emphases from the nineteenth century continued. The *Advocate*, like the Churches of God as a whole, both grimly and enthusiastically supported American involvement in World War I against Germany and the Central Powers, making clear that even though the Churches of God had German roots, its membership, including editor Yahn, was patriotic to the core.

During the second half of the twentieth century the Churches of God gradually became associated with the growing evangelical movement and reaffirmed a more-or-less neofundamentalist doctrinal position (that is, an approach emphasizing the fundamentals in a more reasoning and less strident way). The *Church Advocate* reflected to some extent this theological direction but, at the same time, was less oriented to doctrinal exposition than earlier. Coverage of Churches of God news continued, and considerable space was allocated to world Christian concerns. In addition to presenting material urging the development of higher standards of Christian piety, editors used the *Advocate* to promote values associated with Christian family formation and life, including concerns about marital problems, divorce, abortion, adoption, homosexuality, death, drugs in the home, families with AIDS, and age and gender issues.

In the nineteenth century and well into the twentieth, most *Publisher* and *Advocate* editors considered themselves spokespersons for the Churches of God. Some considered their editorial opinion as orthodoxy for the church. In more recent years, especially during the tenures of Jack Parthemore (1960–1979), David Draper (1979–1982), and Linda Draper (1983–   ), editors have tended to emphasize more their role as servants of, rather than leaders in, the Church.

Information Sources

INDEX SOURCES: Generally each volume of the *Gospel Publisher* and *Church Advocate* contains its own index. Nineteenth-century indexes, especially before the Civil War, tend to be erratic and partial.

LOCATION SOURCES: A complete file of copies of the *Gospel Publisher* and *Church Advocate* is on microfilm or in bound volumes in the libraries of the University of Findlay and Winebrenner Theological Seminary, both located in Findlay, Ohio.

Publication History

MAGAZINE TITLE AND TITLE CHANGES: *Gospel Publisher* (5 June 1835–12 December 1845); *Church Advocate* (1 May 1846–present).

VOLUME AND ISSUE DATA: *Gospel Publisher* 1:1 (5 June 1835)–10:3 (13 August 1845); published monthly, one issue, 12 December 1845. *Church Advocate* 11:1 (1 May 1846)–present; published monthly.

PUBLISHER AND PLACE OF PUBLICATION: While published in behalf of the

Church of God, until 1878 the editor of the *Gospel Publisher* and *Church Advocate* was usually the publisher, printer, and distributor as well. In 1878, the committee on publication of the Church of God became publisher of the *Advocate*. In 1992, the publisher of the *Church Advocate* was the Churches of God, General Conference, headquartered at 700 East Melrose Avenue, Findlay, Ohio 45840.

For the first 145 years, the *Gospel Publisher* and *Church Advocate* were published in various localities in central Pennsylvania (including Harrisburg, Carlisle, Mt. Joy, and Lancaster), depending in large part upon the location of the Church of God congregation that the editor was also pastoring. For about 125 years of the 145, the paper was published in Harrisburg. Since 1979 the *Advocate* has been published in Findlay, Ohio.

EDITORS: John Winebrenner (1835–1840), John Weishample (1840–1843), George McCartney (1844–1845), John Winebrenner (1846–1857), James Colder (1857–1859), E. H. Thomas (1859–1869), C. H. Forney (1869–1909), S. G. Yahn (1909–1939), Roy Schreiner (1939–1960), John Parthemore (1960–1979), David Draper (1979–1982), Linda Draper (1983–present).

In the nineteenth century, especially prior to the Civil War, there were numerous assistant and associate editors who assumed the editorial chair when the editor was ill, on an extended trip, or holding a protracted revival meeting.

CIRCULATION: For the *Gospel Publisher* in the 1830s and 1840s the circulation was (paid and credit) between 500 and 800. In 1992, the paid circulation of the *Church Advocate* was around 6,500.

Richard Kern

CHURCH THEOLOGICAL REVIEW. *See* AMERICAN CHURCH MONTHLY

COLUMBAN FATHERS MISSIONS. *See* COLUMBAN MISSION

COLUMBAN MISSION

In June 1908, Pope Pius X promulgated a new constitution, a communication of general authority that a pope issues in his own name, entitled *Sapienti consilio*, which, among other things, removed the Catholic Church in America from the jurisdiction of *Propoganda Fidie*, the Roman curial office that oversees missionary churches, and placed it under the Sacred Consistoral Congregation, which carried out administrative duties on behalf of cardinals and the pope and was responsible for the appointment and discipline of missionaries going overseas from Europe.[1] This move reflected the growing strength, importance, and affluence of the Catholic Church in the United States. Even though the Church in America continued to receive tens of thousands of immigrant Catholics from Europe each year until the Immigration Restriction Act went into effect in the 1920s, it was not long before the former missionary Church itself began to recruit and send missionaries to Asia, Africa, and South America.

On St. Patrick's Day, 17 March 1918, Father Edward Galvin, a priest of the diocese of Cork, Ireland, arrived in Omaha, Nebraska, searching for an American headquarters for the Columban Fathers, a missionary society for service in China that he and a group of fellow priests had founded in Ireland in 1916. Weary of the kind but firm rejections from members of the U.S. hierarchy, Galvin sought the aid of Father Patrick Judge, pastor of Omaha's Sacred Heart Church, who introduced him to Archbishop Jeremiah J. Hasty of Omaha, a former missionary in the Philippines. After hearing Father Galvin's plan for establishing an American branch of the Columban Fathers, Archbishop Hasty expressed only one reservation about inviting the society to establish itself in his archdiocese. "I am afraid," the archbishop said, "that Omaha is not big enough for your work."[2] After all, Galvin and the other founders of the Columban Missionary Fathers had enormous plans: to call the Irish Catholic faithful the world over to supply the resources necessary for a major missionary effort in China.

From the time that Edward Galvin discerned his priestly vocation, he felt called to missionary work. Born in 1882 in County Cork, Galvin's first obstacle to realizing his missionary vocation was his father, who insisted that there was plenty of work for a young priest in Ireland. But after his ordination in 1909, Galvin was informed that the diocese had no pastoral positions available. He was encouraged to serve a parish in the United States, where clergy were badly needed, and then return to Ireland in three years.[3]

The United States was not the mission field of which Galvin had been dreaming, but he accepted the challenge and set off for the diocese of Brooklyn, New York, where he had a number of Irish friends and where he became curate at Holy Rosary Church. Toward the end of his three-year stint in America, Galvin met a Canadian Lazarist missionary from China who had come to Brooklyn to solicit funds, and Galvin decided to follow the missionary back to China.[4] Despite initial objections from family, friends, and Church superiors, Galvin left for China in 1912 and began a four-year apprenticeship with the mostly French Lazarist community in and around Hangzhou. He learned Chinese and local customs, while discovering the possibilities and limitations of missionary work in China. Galvin returned to Ireland in 1916, intent on founding an Irish missionary society for work in China. Seven priests joined Galvin's successful petitions to the Irish hierarchy for permission to form the Missionary Society of St. Columban.[5] Then came fund-raising money, establishing a headquarters and missionary seminary, and petitioning the Holy See for a missionary vicariate in China.

Galvin then returned to the United States to establish an American branch of the society. Once settled in Omaha, Father Galvin determined to establish a periodical to inform the faithful about the mission work in China and to raise urgently needed funds. Without a magazine, Galvin realized, there would be no revenue. Using a secondhand typewriter in a tiny rented office, Father Galvin banged out the first issue of the *Far East*, named after the society's Irish magazine in April 1918. A local printer gave Galvin credit for two thousand copies of the *Far East*, which he sent to friends in Brooklyn, to other Irish expatriates, and to seminary classmates serving in America.[6] Father Galvin filled this first issue with colorful stories of his own experiences in China as well as his dreams for the future of the mission, which then had only four men in the field.

Edward Galvin's friends responded generously. Contributions permitted the group to move into its first permanent U.S. headquarters in November 1918. But Galvin longed to return to the China mission. So in August 1920, eleven Columban priests, with Galvin as their superior, arrived at their new missionary vicariate at Hanyang in central China.[7]

Galvin became a legend among Catholic missionaries in China, first as a priest and, after 1927, as a bishop. The *Far East* faithfully recorded his adventures, although for four years during the Japanese occupation he was unable to communicate with his supporters outside China.[8] Bishop Galvin remained in China for four years after the Communist takeover, trying to minister to his flock while the Church was being persecuted by the government. In September 1952, Galvin was expelled from China, never to return. Suffering from leukemia, he spent the last years of his life in Ireland, writing and lecturing as he was able to on behalf of the Columbans, who by that time were serving in eleven nations in Asia and Latin America. He died on 2 February 1956.[9]

The *Far East* became a popular monthly periodical in Catholic homes during the 1920s and 1930s. From the beginning, Galvin used photographs as well as the personal stories of Columban missionaries to convey to the magazine's readership the nature of missionary work. Catholics throughout the nation were able to read inspirational and often enlightening articles in the *Far East* about Chinese peasant life, the poverty of city dwellers in the Philippines, and the struggle for social justice on the part of Latin Americans. Galvin's successors as editor have all been Columban priests, most with experience in the missionary field.[10] This background has given the magazine over the years an authenticity to which the readership has readily responded.

In 1967, the name of the periodical was changed to *Columban Fathers Missions* to reflect the expanded fields of the order's missionary endeavors. Missions in Korea, the Philippines, Burma, India, and Japan had been added while Galvin was still serving in China. During the 1950s and 1960s the Columban Fathers extended their work to Peru, Chile, Taiwan, Fiji, Brazil, Jamaica, and Belize. Gradually, use of the word "Fathers" in the periodical's title was deliberately reduced until in 1971 it was dropped altogether, and the magazine became known simply as *Columban Mission*.[11]

During the 1960s, the editorial approach of the periodical also changed. Although personal testimony from active missionaries still played a prominent role in *Columban Mission*, a new attitude reflecting the ecclesiology of Vatican II was clearly seen. By dropping "Fathers" in the magazine's title, the editors hoped to convey that evangelization was not a ministry reserved for clergy but was the responsibility of all the faithful. The relationship between the "home" and "missionary" churches became more that of sister communities and less one of dependency as before. There was also a significant shift in attitude toward non-Christian religions. A new spirit of acceptance, understanding, and dialogue, especially with regard to the religions of Asia, can be seen in the pages of *Columban Mission*. Although social-justice issues had always been a significant part of the magazine, these took on a new urgency after the Second Vatican Council. Liberation theology—which calls on the Church to identify with the struggle of the poor and dispossessed for justice and peace in a radical way— became a recurring focus.

Although fund-raising remains an important function of *Columban Mission*, by 1992 its primary purpose was to inform readers about the ongoing work of evangelization and to interpret the cultures, aspirations, and needs of people in missionary lands. *Columban Mission* seeks to explain the continuing need for Christian missions in a pluralistic world and to shed light on the current missionary process through articles on human rights, non-Western cultures, mission theology, mission spirituality, and interfaith dialogue.[12]

Columban Mission continues to reach a wide audience with a circulation of 189,180, down from an all-time high in 1986 of 242,600. It is published monthly, except for June and August, by the Society of St. Columban. The annual subscription price is ten dollars.[13] Although *Columban Magazine* has developed into a very professional, sophisticated publication, it remains true to the spirit of founder Edward Galvin.

Notes

1. *Acta Sanctae Sedis* 41 (1908): 425–40.
2. William E. Barrett, *The Red Lacquered Gate* (New York: Sheed and Ward, 1967), 117.
3. Ibid., pp. 24–26.
4. Ibid., p. 55.
5. Ibid., p. 98.
6. Ibid., pp. 118–19.
7. Ibid., p. 153.
8. Ibid., ch. 29.
9. Ibid., ch. 31.
10. Interview with Father Richard Steinhilber, editor of *Columban Mission*, 6 October 1992.
11. Richard Steinhilber to the author, 4 May 1992.
12. *Statement on the Role and Function of Our Magazine*, issued by the Columban Fathers Superior General and his Council, 1980.
13. Statistics obtained from Father Richard Steinhilber.

Information Sources

INDEX SOURCES: Each volume contains a partial index. A general index is also available through the Columban Missions Office (St. Columbans, Nebraska).

LOCATION SOURCES: Widely available in Catholic university, college, and seminary libraries; complete run available at the Columban Mission Office, St. Columbans, Nebraska, 68056.

Publication History

MAGAZINE TITLE AND CHANGES: *Far East* (1918–1967), *Columban Fathers Missions* (1967–1971), *Columban Mission* (1971–present).
VOLUME AND ISSUE DATA: 1:1 (April 1918–present). Published monthly, except for June and August.
PUBLISHER AND PLACE OF PUBLICATION: Society of St. Columban, St. Columbans, Nebraska.
EDITORS: Edward Galvin (1918), E. J. McCarthy (1919–1923), Patrick O'Connor (1923–1945), Edward Depresio (1946–1955), Donald O'Mahony (1956–1966), Owen MacElroy (1967), Joseph Hanrahan (1968–1972), Peter McPartland (1972–1980), Richard Steinhilber (1980–present).
CIRCULATION: 189,180 (1991).

Mark B. Sorvillo

COLUMBIA

Columbia is a monthly publication of the Knights of Columbus, a fraternal association of Roman Catholic laymen that was founded over a century ago. The stated purpose of the magazine, according to its sponsors, is "to inform and motivate Catholic laymen and their families."[1] Members of the Knights receive the magazine automatically. The order produces the publication in three different languages: English (for the United States and anglophone readers in Canada); French (mainly for the Canadian province of Quebec); and Spanish (for Mexico, regions of the Caribbean, and Central America). Its circulation of approximately one and a half million qualifies *Columbia* as the largest Catholic monthly in North America.[2]

The association that supports *Columbia*, the Knights of Columbus, was founded in New Haven, Connecticut by the Reverend Michael Joseph McGivney (1852–1890). At the group's inaugural meeting in February 1882, about sixty interested men gathered in the basement of St. Mary's Church, where McGivney worked as assistant to the pastor. The young priest had grown concerned that Catholic men were increasingly drawn to a host of secret societies that the Church had officially condemned.

Such secret societies possessed both a social and a practical lure: The groups typically composed elaborate oaths and ornate rituals of initiation and advancement, all of which served to bind the men together into a close fellowship. In addition, many operated a rudimentary system of life insurance by assessing small fees that were collected and distributed to survivors upon the death of a member. These patterns of organization were not overlooked by Father McGivney. "Our primary object," he explained in a letter introducing the Knights to fellow Catholic clergy in Connecticut, "is to prevent our people from entering *Secret Societies* by offering the same if not better advantages to our members."[3]

Accordingly, among the initial actions of the new society were the creation of a series of degrees of membership, each with its accompanying ritual, and the establishment of a mutual benefit insurance plan. At first, all new members of the order were enrolled in the insurance program. In fact, so intimately related were the spiritual and the actuarial aims of the Knights of Columbus in its embryonic days that a form for medical certification of good health was printed directly on the reverse side of application blanks and membership was limited to men below the age of forty-five, who were assumed to be the best insurance risks.

But there was also a powerful symbolic impetus to the efforts of McGivney and his lay collaborators—namely, a symbolism conveyed in the order's name. In an era when the attachment of Catholic Americans to their country and its principles was frequently questioned, the Knights claimed the exploration of the North American continent "as the Catholic baptism of the nation," for "Columbus was the symbol par excellence of the Catholic contribution to American culture."[4]

Immigrant Catholics and their children, regardless of ethnic or linguistic differences, could appeal to the legacy of Columbus to legitimate their connection to America and thereby offset nativist prejudices. As one charter member of the Knights stated, Catholics "were entitled to all rights and privileges" in the New World "due to such a discovery by one of our faith."[5] With Columbus as their symbolic precursor, nineteenth-century Catholics could be considered not so much newcomers to the American scene as merely later arrivals. "Just as the heirs of the Pilgrims invoked the Mayflower as the Protestant symbol of their pedigree as early Americans," contends historian Christopher J. Kauffman, "so the Knights invoked the Santa Maria as the symbol for the Catholic pedigree."[6]

The original Knights of Columbus in New Haven were fairly prosperous, upwardly mobile Irish politicians and businessmen for whom the "Catholic ghetto" gleamed with a gilded edge. Nevertheless, these men were no strangers to anti-Catholic bigotry and the cultural insecurities that it bred. For example, the *New York Times* almost three years earlier had complained on its front page that St. Mary's "blemished" the broad thoroughfare where it stood along with the residences of the president of Yale University and of at least one *bona fide* millionaire.[7]

It is hardly surprising, then, that New Haven's Irish, lacking social standing on a par with their affluence, would seek solidarity in brotherhood. Nor is it a surprise that to the cornerstone trio of Columbian virtues—"Charity, Unity, and Fraternity"—would soon be added a fourth: "Patriotism." This last commitment distinguished the Knights of Columbus from other mutual-benefit societies, which often drew on ethnic loyalties, and placed the group amid the variety of voluntary associations in American society.

Monthly publication of *Columbia* commenced in August 1921. The magazine replaced a related periodical, the *Columbiad*, which preceded *Columbia* by nearly thirty years and was directed toward the same readers, although it was separately owned. An early description called *Columbia* "an international modern magazine, containing up-to-date fiction, verse, editorials, articles on business, sport, art, literature, sociology, religion, and the ordinary interests of the ordinary man."[8] *Columbia* may have been modern, but "ordinary" it deliberately was not.

At the start, *Columbia* established an air of social ease and cultural sophistication, while preserving ties to its Catholic roots. Repeatedly the magazine argued for Catholic interests wherever they were denigrated or ignored, asserting that discrimination on the basis of one's creed, although prevalent, was inconsistent with American ideals and was the result of ignorance and falsehoods.[9] *Columbia* also underlined the sacrifices endured by notable Catholics for the United States and the world.[10] This feature continues in the 1990s in profiles of Catholics well known in politics, the arts, and professional sports.[11] But the publication's maturity derived from more than historical boasts.

Through first-person reporting, *Columbia* promoted travel, especially to Catholic settings like Ireland and Quebec. It occasionally published devotional poetry and mediocre short stories with a pronounced moralistic bent but balanced this fluff with essays by leading figures in the Catholic literary orbit. During the 1920s and 1930s alone, Hilaire Belloc (1870–1953), G. K. Chesterton (1874–1936), and the team of Francis J. "Frank" Sheed (1897–1981) and Maisie Ward (1889–1975)—whose byline the editors supplemented with the note that she was "also Mrs. F. J. Sheed"—all contributed to *Columbia*.[12]

Clearly the editors had lofty intellectual and social aspirations for their readers. One issue even devoted three pages to the intricacies of "Polo: Sport of Thoroughbreds,"[13] as if the pursuit would be a natural avocation for masses of American Catholic laymen. "*Columbia* projected a cosmopolitan image," observes Kauffman, "as it published articles by representatives of the Catholic intellectual elite, the American hierarchy, and the political and academic establishments."[14] Nevertheless, this veneer of elitism in time yielded to a more popular appeal as the contents of the magazine increasingly concentrated on two of the Knights' long-term concerns: rooting out indecency and immorality in American institutions and strengthening those institutions against the perceived onslaught of secular and materialistic values.

In agreement with Catholic moral teaching, *Columbia* has always editorialized strongly in opposition to the use of artificial means of contraception and the legal availability of abortion. Beginning in the 1930s, the magazine sought to undercut the idea that drastic limitations on births were necessary for economic comfort and social advancement.[15] A 1931 editorial predicted that the endorsement by a committee of the Federal Council of Churches of "the careful and restrained use of contraceptives" constituted "a long step toward the final disintegration of Protestantism."[16] By the outbreak of World War II, the language of *Columbia*'s contributors had become somewhat more heated. One writer counted the ideology of planned parenthood as a "home grown species of Hitlerism,"[17] thus linking defeat of the movement for "birth prevention" with combat against the Axis powers.

More recent commentaries in *Columbia* have criticized plans to permit public schools to distribute contraceptive devices,[18] while longer features have touted the sole modes for regulating conception approved by the Catholic Church: the "Billings" and the "sympto-thermal" methods.[19] There is little explicit discussion of abortion in the earliest volumes of *Columbia*, but since the U.S. Supreme

Court handed down its decision in *Roe v. Wade* in January 1973, the Knights have frequently devoted the first issue of *Columbia* in the year to the antiabortion cause.[20] In addition, the magazine often reprints denunciations of legal abortion excerpted from addresses made by political leaders at the Knights of Columbus' convention each summer.[21]

Columbia has also condemned sexually provocative messages in the magazines, music, and movies that dominate popular culture. The Knights first took up this campaign during the 1930s in response to the contemporary motion-picture industry. For example, William Cardinal O'Connell (1859–1944), archbishop of Boston, offered a blistering blast at the "riot of rotten, disgusting play acting that is going on in the film industry." He found most offensive "obscene and immoral moving pictures, with their unutterably filthy plots and their unspeakably brazen presentation. These are undermining the moral life of your children," O'Connell warned, "and perhaps even of your own selves."[22]

The Knights'—and, hence, *Columbia*'s—concern with identifying the threat to American institutions posed by Communists, foreign and indigenous, is as old as the magazine itself. In the 1920s, the order engaged speakers to barnstorm service luncheons, school assemblies, and local Knights of Columbus council meetings across the country, throwing light on the evil intentions of purported subversive movements in America and exposing with logical acuity the perceived flaws in leftist thinking.

One such hired itinerant was David Goldstein (1870–1958), a self-described "Christian Israelite" who made a reputation for himself as a fierce orator, a prolific pamphleteer, and a regular columnist for *Pilot*, the newspaper of the Boston archdiocese. *Columbia* circulated reports of Goldstein's travels in what he termed "a constant drive for the recognition of Catholic principles as they apply to the vital interests of life—to intellectual, moral, civic and economic affairs." Goldstein was careful, he said, to proclaim to his audiences that "the principles set down as our basic law, our American concepts of civil liberties, our rights and duties of the body politic, are derived from Catholic teachings down the ages."[23]

Of course, *Columbia* cast widely to enlist allies in the fight against "Reds" who had no religion. Its editors even applauded the appearance (on May Day, 1933) of the first edition of *Catholic Worker*, a radical pacifist newspaper still issued. The *Worker*, they argued, "takes from the Communists the thunder they have stolen" by their battles against injustice in the workplace. Because of this, they wrote, the newspaper is "useful and deserving of all success."[24]

The magazine also kept one eye fixed on international affairs. Fifteen years after the Bolshevik Revolution, for example, it published a critical three-part assessment of "The Russian Riddle" by a Vatican diplomat.[25] "Today a nation of a hundred and fifty million souls must bring up their children without thought of God," the author lamented, "save the derision of His name, taught them from their tenderest years."[26] Like many other American Catholic organs, *Columbia* later lent words of favor to the Spanish government of Francisco Franco

(1892–1975), which it viewed as a bulwark against the foes of "Christian civilization."[27]

Yet it was not until after World War II that the Knights of Columbus and their periodical embarked on what without exaggeration has been labeled "a militant anti-Communist crusade."[28] In 1952, *Columbia* reprinted an address from the national convention of the Knights that summer in which Francis Cardinal Spellman (1889–1967), archbishop of New York, verbally assailed secularism.[29] In 1954, *Columbia* sought recognition of some "Limits of Academic Freedom." As "a matter of self-protection, inoculation against a virus," its contributor reasoned, "it is the obligation of schools and colleges . . . to remove those whose primary loyalties and obligations belong to agencies which would eliminate freedom from the earth."[30] Throughout the decade and into the next, the magazine's favorite targets included Communist regimes abroad and their suspected sympathizers at home, liberal critics of federal law-enforcement agencies and their methods of hunting Communists, and strict separationists such as Protestants and Other Americans United (or, in general, anyone who balked at inserting the phrase "under God" into the Pledge of Allegiance).[31]

By 1957, then, *Columbia*'s editor could feel justified in devoting most of his column for that month to the death of a Fourth Degree member of Father Fitzmaurice Council No. 607 in Appleton, Wisconsin. Senator Joseph R. McCarthy (1908–1957) was eulogized in the official publication of the organization to which he belonged as "the victim of the most shameful, deliberately contrived and unrelenting attack ever directed against a loyal citizen of the United States." McCarthy deserved better, the editorial explained, for "at a time when his country was being ever so politely, graciously and ignorantly betrayed, he blew the police whistle—loudly and rudely and effectively and right in the middle of a fatally soothing program of chamber music, with a Moscow motif, being rendered by some of the nicest people."[32]

Strident though this anti-Communist rhetoric may seem, it illustrates a distinctive characteristic of the conservatism espoused by the Knights of Columbus and *Columbia* during the first half of the century. As Kauffman put it, "It was not political conservatism but rather cultural conservatism."[33] Or it was at least a conservatism with a powerfully populist and morally traditional element. In the 1950s, time-honored Americanism seemed under attack: Who, in actual fact, had delegated the leadership of the common culture to the effete functionaries of the American Association of University Professors? And who held cherished civic ceremonies hostage to the tidy church-state theories of a few privileged Protestants? In a time of fear that the country was being delivered into captivity by "some of the nicest people," patriotic Knights praised the steadfast anti-Communism of a rough-and-tumble Joe McCarthy and the starched-collar rectitude of an unsmiling J. Edgar Hoover (1895–1972).

Ironically, *Columbia*'s basic conservatism sometimes led it to adapt neatly to a religious environment within the Catholic Church that was growing steadily more progressive. Nowhere is this pattern of reliance upon increasingly liberal

Church teaching more evident than in the magazine's treatment of changes in ecclesial life that were wrought by the papacy of John XXIII and the opening of the Second Vatican Council (1962–1965).[34] Without exception, reports in *Columbia* emanating from Rome during the 1960s spoke with a joyful accent and communicated in a hopeful tone. A newspaper editor described for the magazine a new kind of Catholic being born: "The new Catholic will be more relaxed. He will be more sociable. He will be more at home in the world . . . He will be positive rather than negative, and outgoing and open rather than defensive."[35] An American priest who worked as a press officer at the Vatican summarized the pivotal nature of the period: "The significant lesson of the Second Vatican Council," he wrote in *Columbia*, "is that the one, holy, catholic and apostolic Church is a Church in change."[36] The Knights of Columbus followed the lead of the Holy See and embraced these changes. There ensued a series of extended articles in the magazine dealing with such subjects as appreciation for the doctrines of other religions and the value for the Catholic Church of ecumenical dialogue.[37]

As profound as have been the changes in the Catholic Church over the past thirty years, certain components of *Columbia* have remained remarkably stable. The particular contents of special features aside, the magazine has carried running columns devoted to instruction in fundamental items of Catholic doctrine; celebration of family life; stimulation of religious vocations; and opinion on policy developments from the Vatican, Washington, and other Western capitals. But by far the central recurring segment of *Columbia* (called "What Knights Are Doing," "K. of C. Roundup," "Knights of Columbus News Roundup," "KC Report," or "Knights in Action") dramatizes in words and pictures the manifold good works of local councils in the United States and around the world.

Admittedly, some of the news that enters *Columbia* through this section is, in the words of two critics, "a thoroughly American variety of activities— charity donations, banquets, and athletic contests."[38] The accompanying illustrations are mostly of the sort derided by professional photographers as static "grip-and-grab" shots (i.e., ones picturing a handshake and a presentation). Over the years, *Columbia* has surely depicted thousands of Communion breakfasts, ribbon cuttings, dedication speeches, installations of officers, and checks changing hands. Its readers have thereby visited countless parish halls, church gymnasiums, hockey rinks, and restaurants.

Hostile jabs notwithstanding, however, here perhaps more than anywhere else in the magazine one senses fully the spirit and scope of the Knights of Columbus and, with them, the vitality of lay Catholic life over the course of the twentieth century.

Notes

The author is grateful to Richard McMunn, current editor of *Columbia*, for assistance in verifying some facts.

1. See *Columbia*, in *1992 Catholic Press Directory* (Rockville Centre, NY: Catholic Press Association, 1992), 97.

2. See "Knights of Columbus," in *1991 Catholic Almanac*, ed. Felican A. Foy, O. F. M. Avato and Rose M. Avato (Huntington, IN: Our Sunday Visitor, 1990), 575.

3. Quoted in Christopher J. Kauffman, *Faith and Fraternalism: The History of the Knights of Columbus, 1882–1982* (New York: Harper and Row, 1982), 19.

4. Christopher Kauffman, "The Knights of Columbus: A Historical Portrait," *Columbia* 62 (June 1982): 4. See also Christopher J. Kauffman, "Columbianism and the Knights of Columbus,"*Columbia* 72 (August 1992): 11–14.

5. Quoted in Kauffman, *Faith and Fraternalism*, 16.

6. Kauffman, "Knights of Columbus," 4.

7. "An Unprofitable Church: Roman Catholic Troubles in New Haven," *New York Times*, 28 July 1879, 1, as reproduced in Kauffman, "Origins of Columbianism," 10.

8. "Activities of the Order," *Columbia* 9 (August 1929): 29.

9. Francis M. Crowley, "Religious Prejudice and Catholic Teachers," *Columbia* 9 (November 1929): 5–7, 45; Richard Reid, "They Hate What Is Not," *Columbia* 10 (January 1931): 14–15.

10. Typical offerings include John L. Considine, "His Light Shone Among Men" [on Roger Brooke Taney (1777–1864), a Chief Justice of the United States Supreme Court], *Columbia* 8 (September 1928): 28, 49–50; Joseph Gurn, "Sons of a Great American" [on the descendants of Charles Carroll of Carrollton (1737–1832), a signer of the Declaration of Independence], *Columbia* 8 (October 1928): 16–17, 47; Joseph Gurn, "Catholic France Our First Ally," *Columbia* 32 (February 1953): 7, 15–16; and Doran Hurley, "Lincoln's Catholic Kinship" [which numbered as Catholics the sixteenth president's stepmother and his father, who was rumored to be a convert], *Columbia* 37 (February 1957): 21–22, 41.

11. Recent examples include Paul F. Healy, "Speaker of the House" [on John William McCormack (1891–1981)], *Columbia* 44 (March 1964): 9–11, 36; Thomas A. Sander, "Knight in the White House" [on President John Fitzgerald Kennedy (1917–1963)], *Columbia* 46 (November 1966): 8–13; and Wally Carew, "Mike Ditka: Chicago Coach Far from Bearish about His Faith," *Columbia* 72 (November 1992): 10–12.

12. Among others, see Hilaire Belloc, "The Danger in Europe. I: Origins," *Columbia* 13 (March 1934): 7, 20–21; idem, *Columbia* 13 (April 1934): 4, 12; F. J. Sheed, "A Non-Euclidean Morality: It Would Be Good To Be Good," *Columbia* 18 (November 1938): 2, 18–19; Maisie Ward, "Principles Are Not Enough: For Cows You Need Technique," *Columbia* 18 (December 1938): 5, 18–19.

13. Arthur J. Lea Mond, "Polo: Sport of Thoroughbreds," *Columbia* 8 (September 1928): 20–21, 42.

14. Kauffman, *Faith and Fraternalism*, 254–55.

15. Constantine McGuire, "Population and Prosperity," *Columbia* 10 (August 1930): 5–6, 37; and Matthew S. Redling, "The Bogey of 'Overpopulation': Calamity Is Not Imminent," *Columbia* 32 (August 1952): 4, 19.

16. Editorials, "Another Surrender," *Columbia* 10 (May 1931): 19.

17. John S. Kennedy, "Saboteurs of Democracy: The Greatest Single Peril to Our Future," *Columbia* 21 (March 1942): 5, 18.

18. Elmer Von Feldt, "Comment: Pushing Pagan Values in Public Schools," *Columbia* 67 (January 1987): 2; Elmer Von Feldt, "Comment: Family Values and Public Policy," *Columbia* 67 (April 1987): 2–3; Russell Shaw, "Washington: Are Free

Contraceptives for Teen-Agers Acceptable?'' *Columbia* 67 (April 1987): 5; and Russell Shaw, ''Washington: Missing the Point on AIDS,'' *Columbia* 67 (May 1987): 4.

19. Joan Grenon, ''Discovering the Natural Way to Family Planning,'' *Columbia* 67 (April 1987): 8–15.

20. For examples, see *Columbia* 69 (January 1989) and *Columbia* 71 (January 1991).

21. See, for example, Ronald Reagan, ''Crucial Values,'' *Columbia* 62 (October 1982): 24–28; idem, ''The Importance of Fundamental Values,'' *Columbia* 66 (October 1986): 22–23; and J. Danforth Quayle, ''The Address of the Vice President: Dan Quayle Calls for a Family Perspective in Public Policy,'' *Columbia* 69 (October 1989): 13–16.

22. William Cardinal O'Connell, ''The Scandal of the World,'' *Columbia* 13 (July 1934): 4. More than twenty years later, *Columbia* was also highly critical of the release of *Baby Doll*, a film based on a screenplay written by Tennessee Williams.

23. David Goldstein, ''Making the Truth Known,'' *Columbia* 8 (August 1928): 40.

24. Editorials, ''The Thieves of Thunder,'' *Columbia* 13 (October 1933): 13.

25. Louis J. Gallagher, S.J., ''The Russian Riddle,'' *Columbia* 10 (March 1931): 5–7, 32; idem, *Columbia* 10 (April 1931): 7–9, 31; and idem, *Columbia* 10 (May 1931): 16–17, 23.

26. Gallagher, ''Russian Riddle,'' 16.

27. Kauffman, *Faith and Fraternalism*, 332–33. The most prominent exception to this pattern of support for Franco in the Catholic press was the lay journal *Commonweal*.

28. Kauffman, ''Knights of Columbus,'' 8.

29. Francis Cardinal Spellman, ''Secularism: Road to Communism,'' *Columbia* 32 (October 1952): 7, 14, 23.

30. Francis P. Kilcoyne, ''Limits of Academic Freedom,'' *Columbia* 33 (February 1954): 4, 22–23.

31. A representative piece from the period is a boilerplate essay by J. Edgar Hoover, the long-reigning director of the FBI, entitled ''The Deadly Contest,'' *Columbia* 41 (August 1961): 20, 36.

32. Editorial, ''Watchman of the Citadel,'' *Columbia* 37 (June 1957): 22.

33. Kauffman, *Faith and Fraternalism*, 367.

34. For example, see Monsignor Vincent A. Yzermans, ''Vatican II: Where Now?'' *Columbia* 46 (January 1966): 14–16.

35. Joseph A. Brieg, ''A New Catholic A-Coming,'' *Columbia* 44 (December 1964): 21.

36. Edward L. Heston, C.S.C., ''Vatican II's Church of the Future,'' *Columbia* 46 (February 1966): 12.

37. See, for example, Rabbi Arthur Gilbert, ''Understanding Judaism in America,'' *Columbia* 47 (August 1967): 6–15.

38. Edward Wakin and Joseph F. Scheuer, *The De-Romanization of the American Catholic Church* (New York: Macmillan, 1966), 215.

Information Sources

INDEX SOURCES: Individual volumes are not self-indexed. Some are indexed in *Catholic Periodical Index* (1930–1966) and in *Catholic Periodical and Literature Index* (1967–).

LOCATION SOURCES: Archives of the Knights of Columbus Supreme Council, New

Haven, Connecticut. The Archives also owns complete sets of the predecessor publication, *Columbiad*, dating from 1899, and scattered materials from before that date.

Publication History

MAGAZINE TITLE AND TITLE CHANGES: *Columbia* (August 1921–present). Preceded from November 1893 by an independent publication, the *Columbiad*.

VOLUME AND ISSUE DATA: 1:1 (August 1921)–present. Published monthly.

PUBLISHER AND PLACE OF PUBLICATION: Supreme Council of the Knights of Columbus, New Haven, Connecticut. Until November 1923, editorial and advertising offices were located in New York City.

EDITORS: John B. Kennedy (1921–1924), Myles Connolly (1924–1928), John B. Donahue (1928–1965), Elmer Von Feldt (1965–1988), Richard McMunn (1988–present).

CIRCULATION: Nearly 1,500,000 (1992).

Kevin J. Christiano

COLUMBIAD. *See* COLUMBIA

COLUMBIAN STAR. *See* CHRISTIAN INDEX

COLUMBIAN STAR AND CHRISTIAN INDEX. *See* CHRISTIAN INDEX

CONGREGATIONALIST

For eighty-five years, from 1849 to 1934, the *Congregationalist* was a weekly newspaper published in Boston and written primarily by and for New England Congregationalists. This did not mean, however, that its interests were strictly parochial. Religious and secular topics alike found their way into the pages of the *Congregationalist*. National and international news were reported, as well as regional and local matters of interest. News and opinion were supplemented by theological discussions, historical articles, travel essays, literary features, and a miscellany of other writings. In spite of wide-ranging interests and a shifting religious terrain over its eighty-five-year life span, however, the *Congregationalist* did maintain a consistent and describable character.

In one sense, the purpose of the *Congregationalist* was as specific as its name suggests. From start to finish it existed in part to advance the interests of Congregationalists. It is no accident that the paper originated at a time when Congregationalism as a movement was in search of both identity and structure and that it went out of existence at the time when a merger with the Christian Church produced a new denomination.

Since 1801 Congregationalists and Presbyterians had been operating under a Plan of Union that allowed newly formed congregations outside New England to choose either polity and to be served by ministers ordained in either tradition. In addition, cooperative agreements had been reached in the New England states, and voluntary organizations such as the American Home Missionary Society served the common interests of Presbyterians and Congregationalists. Such practical arrangements stood as a significant experiment in Christian unity. They had succeeded, at least to the extent of lasting longer than many might have thought possible in a competitive religious environment.

By midcentury, however, union was no longer the order of the day. Old School Presbyterians, increasingly organized and aggressive through the 1830s, carried out a successful attack upon the Plan of Union at the general assembly in 1837. The resulting schism in the Presbyterian Church left both sides trying to define themselves as the true Presbyterians. Gradually New School Presbyterians and Congregationalists also abandoned the Plan of Union. Identities that had become blurred over the years now needed to be recovered.[1]

From the outset the *Congregationalist* clearly saw its task as one of helping to redefine and clarify the principles and practices of Congregationalism. One concern was polity. Sandwiched in among the vaguer and loftier-sounding goals put forward during the first year was a commitment to promote the ecclesiastical principles of Congregationalism. There was still a place, advocates said, for a paper "associated with scriptural [read *congregational*] church polity."[2]

Polity was not simply a question of which form of Church government was most efficient, most convenient, or even most scriptural. Congregational polity defined the Congregational Churches as being fully in tune with, and the chief representatives of, "the democratic spirit of the age."[3] If the United States was, in Sidney Mead's phrase, a "nation with the soul of a church," Congregationalism was here understood as the institutional embodiment of that soul.

Theology was naturally a concern as well. Initially the stance was articulated in a general way as reflecting traditional Puritan thought as advanced by Jonathan Edwards and others. A more descriptive, but also more carefully worded, statement came about a year later: "We advocate distinctively but not aggressively or illiberally, the theology of New England as it has been maintained by the schools of Edwards, Smalley, Bellamy, Hopkins, Dwight, and Emmons."[4] Clearly, the *Congregationalist* was involved in the delicate task of trying to provide definition without being divisive.

Mention of names associated with the New Divinity of Edwards and his theological heirs might serve in part to distinguish the position of the *Congregationalist* from a more rigid Calvinism of the Old School, but the real danger was perceived as coming more from the theological "left." Unitarianism had reared its head at Harvard early in the century, resulting in the founding of Andover Seminary in 1808 to combat its influence. At the time of the *Congregationalist*'s founding more than forty years later, that battle was still being fought. It is hardly surprising that a paper published in Boston would have many graduates of Andover on its editorial staff. Nor is it surprising that they would continue to see themselves charged with defending evangelical orthodoxy against Unitarian heterodoxy. This battle was joined often and openly in the pages of the *Congregationalist.*

Apologetics came to be less noticeable, however, as time went on. As Congregationalism became better organized and more firmly established as a denomination, it was as if a formal, theoretical defense were no longer necessary. Now the cause was served more by community building. The *Congregationalist* kept the faithful abreast of what was going on, primarily in the sphere of New England Congregationalism. Meetings were announced and reported on, important occasions in the lives of persons and congregations were celebrated, and ministerial comings and goings were duly reported. News from the Congregational hinterland was also included. If such news was generally brief, it could at least portray an image of a denomination that was alive and well in distant regions.

What the *Congregationalist* also communicated, however, was a religious stance that transcended denominationalism: "We are fully persuaded that the great work of Christianity in regenerating human society . . . is but begun. Its mission will not be fulfilled till idolatry, caste, slavery, political despotism, intemperance, impurity, and all other abominations of sin are swept from the face of the earth."[5] Such a statement should not be understood as separate from, but rather as providing the context for, more specifically denominational concerns. Congregationalism was not to be defined solely by its position on sectarian issues but also by its continued commitment to bringing about a "new age" when Christian values would permeate American society.

Antislavery sentiment was apparent from the beginning, both in the writing and in the leadership of the *Congregationalist.* Of the original editors, the best known was Edward Beecher, respected member of the famous Beecher family, former president of Illinois College, and then pastor of Salem Street Church in Boston. Beecher had become prominently associated with the antislavery cause while in Illinois, largely because of his association with the abolitionist Elijah Lovejoy and because of the book that he had written following Lovejoy's martyrdom in 1837. When Edward's sister Harriet became an associate editor following the publication of *Uncle Tom's Cabin,* the symbolism was further strengthened.[6]

It was, however, the patriarch of the Beecher clan, Lyman Beecher, who more accurately represented the overall spirit of the publication. By 1850 Lyman Beecher was seventy-five years old, in poor health and no longer publicly active, but the broad program of the "evangelical empire" with which he had been identified found an echo in the pages of the *Congregationalist.* Indeed the *Congregationalist* traced its origin to one of the earliest of religious periodicals, the *Recorder,* which had begun in 1816 and which saw itself as a voice for the same expansive Protestantism that Beecher championed.

In the antebellum period, temperance had come to be almost a universal cause among Protestant reformers, and it was an issue to which many clung as symbolic of a value system that was often felt to be under attack in the world that emerged after the Civil War. The *Congregationalist* never wavered in its support for the cause of temperance. It campaigned at the level of personal decision, local option, state law, and constitutional amendment. Even as the *Congregationalist* breathed its last, it was still bemoaning the repeal of Prohibition.[7]

On other issues the *Congregationalist* proved to be more flexible. The perceived need to fight and win a battle with the Roman Catholic Church was very evident in the early days. The political and ecclesiastical despotism popularly associated with Catholicism was roundly and equally condemned. Catholicism was directly pilloried, and scorn and pity typically attended news from "Catholic countries," which were pictured as superstitious and barbarian. Anti-Catholic sentiment did not die easily or quickly, but over time attitudes seemed to soften, or became better disguised.

Sabbath observance was another issue that had once been considered by many, including Lyman Beecher, as a kind of behavioral test of orthodoxy. Though the *Congregationalist* never gave up on the general desirability of Sabbath observance, it did modify its position both as to what constituted observance and whether it should be enforced by law. Allowance was made, for instance, for immigrant groups that had different notions of the Sabbath, or none at all.[8]

Some issues, of course, were new, and the pages of the *Congregationalist* chronicle changes in both Church and society. In the midst of the Civil War, at the same time that the Emancipation Proclamation was celebrated and the death of Lyman Beecher mourned, there were also articles warning of the dangers of mass immigration and the growth of cities.[9] The *Congregationalist* seemed to be aware quite early that the emergence of an urban, industrial society would pose serious challenges to the churches.

For the next forty years, however, the response of the *Congregationalist* to new social realities was cautious. Two people who received prominent and frequent mention were Joseph Cook and Dwight L. Moody. Cook was a Congregational minister in Boston whose popular noontime lectures espoused a mild and conservative form of social Christianity. Moody, of course, was the premier urban revivalist of the time, and was not only immensely popular but also a favorite son of Massachusetts. His career was followed closely, and his death dominated the news as none others had. Washington Gladden, on the other hand, received much less attention. Gladden spoke for a more prophetic form of social Christianity. Although he spent most of his career in Columbus, Ohio, he had begun in Massachusetts and was a Congregational minister who also might have laid some claim to being a native son. It was not until the twentieth century that the *Congregationalist* moved to identify itself more strongly with social Christianity.

On some issues the *Congregationalist* clearly saw itself as providing a forum for the discussion of issues on which Christians might legitimately disagree. This was the case, for instance, with regard to Darwinism and higher criticism. On other issues, however, it found itself taking the lead. In opposing the participation of the United States in World War I, for instance, it espoused a pacifist position right up to the time of entry and continued to defend the rights of conscientious objectors.[10] It also focused attention on racial issues even when social Christianity largely avoided them and when, later in the 1920s and 1930s, civil rights was hardly a popular cause.

Other changes were also evident. The *Congregationalist* was originally published in folio editions, four pages, small type, no photographs. After 1870 the size was reduced to nine by thirteen inches, but it increased in 1899 to twelve by sixteen inches. The number of pages gradually increased to thirty-six after 1900, and cover photos were added.

The *Congregationalist* sometimes mirrored, sometimes championed, change in Church and society, but it saw itself throughout as an instrument for the advancement of a Christian civilization. That was an ideal that the publishers of the weekly felt Congregationalists ought to hold. It was an ideal that had long been implicit in most of evangelical Protestantism in the United States. It was an ideal that the *Congregationalist* still held in 1934 as it passed the baton to another paper, the *Advance*.

Notes

1. For a summary of the story regarding the Plan of Union and its disintegration, see Sydney E. Ahlstrom, *A Religious History of the American People* (Garden City, NY: Doubleday, 1975), 1:551–71.

2. *Congregationalist* 1 (7 December 1849): 113.

3. Ibid., p. 114.

4. Ibid. 2 (8 February 1850): 21.

5. Ibid. 1 (7 December 1849): 113.

6. The announcement that Harriett Beecher Stowe had been made a contributing editor appeared in the issue of 3 December 1852.

7. *Congregationalist* 119 (4 January 1934): 13.

8. Ibid. 31 (18 February 1880): 52.

9. Ibid. 14 (6 February 1863): 21.

10. Ibid. 102 (11 January 1917): 37.

Information Sources

INDEX SOURCES: None.

LOCATION SOURCES: A complete collection is held in the Congregational Historical Society Library in Boston. The collection at the Chicago Theological Seminary library is almost complete, lacking only a few of the early volumes.

Publication History

MAGAZINE TITLE AND TITLE CHANGES: *Congregationalist* (1849–1867), *Congregationalist and Boston Recorder* (1867–1870), *Congregationalist* (1870–1900), *Congregationalist and Christian World* (1901–1917), *Congregationalist and Advance* (1917–1920), *Congregationalist* (1921–1930), *Congregationalist and Herald of Gospel Liberty* (1930–1934).

VOLUME AND ISSUE DATA: 1:1 (May 1849)–1:32 (December 1849); 2:1 (January 1850)–50:52 (December 1898); 84:1 (January 1899)–119:34 (March 1934); published weekly. When it merged with the *Recorder* in 1899, it assumed the volume numbers of the *Recorder.*

PUBLISHER AND PLACE OF PUBLICATION: James Fay (1849–1855), Galen James and Edward Fay (1856), Galen James and Company (1857–1870), W. L. Greene and Company (1871–1898), W. A. Greene and Company (1899–1901), Pilgrim Press (1902–1934). All issues published in Boston.

EDITORS: Edward Beecher, Joseph Haren, Jr., Increase Tarbox (1849–1850), Edward Beecher and Richard Storrs (1851–1854), Henry Dexter (1852–1854), R. S. Storrs, H. M. Dexter, A. L. Stone (1855–1856), Henry Dexter (1857–1860), Galen James, C. A. Richardson, W. L. Greene (1861–1870), no editor listed (1871–1910), Howard Bridgman (1911–1921), William Gilroy (1922–1934).

CIRCULATION: None available.

James F. Bundy

CONGREGATIONALIST AND BOSTON RECORDER. *See* CONGREGATIONALIST

CONGREGATIONALIST AND CHRISTIAN WORLD. *See* CONGREGATIONALIST

CONGREGATIONALIST AND HERALD OF GOSPEL LIBERTY. *See* HERALD OF GOSPEL LIBERTY

CONNECTICUT EVANGELICAL MAGAZINE

Suspended between the euphoria accompanying the rekindling of revivalistic fires and the horrifying prospect of "ye awful infidel" Thomas Jefferson ascending to the presidency, fifteen Congregational clergymen from across Connecticut consciously launched the *Connecticut Evangelical Magazine* in July 1800 to advance a "counter-reformation." Published monthly during the next fifteen years (with one six-month lapse during the second half of 1807), upwards of 3,000 copies of the *Connecticut Evangelical Magazine* were distributed to paid subscribers and, less regularly, were distributed by traveling missionaries free of charge to others. The magazine disseminated two broad types of religious knowledge. First, it communicated varied forms of "religious intelligence," including narratives of revivals, reports of missionary and other voluntary societies, and other news documenting the vitality of evangelicalism. Second, through unsigned submissions from its editorial staff, focusing on specific aspects of doctrine, lay behaviors, and clerical practices, the magazine informally codified the essential tenets of a "New Divinity."

Spearheaded by Rev. Nathan Strong, minister of the First Congregational Church of Hartford, and Yale President Timothy Dwight (who joined the editorial staff in 1801), publication followed on the heels of several earlier actions intended to reverse "the tide of infidelity" fed during the preceding quarter century by the heady spirit of revolution and independence. In 1792, Strong successfully lobbied the General Association of Connecticut to form a committee on missions, an action that six years later culminated in the formation of the Missionary Society of Connecticut and the despatching of clergymen to provide for "the welfare of the regions beyond."[1] Shortly thereafter, in the fall of 1798, revivals originating in two Litchfield county churches had, by early 1800, swelled into a general "awakening" across western Connecticut.

The format of the magazine, modeled after British religious journals, remained unchanged throughout its lifetime. With dimensions of 8 1/2 by 5 inches, the magazine promised at least forty pages of reading per edition. Readers were further advised, in a lengthy introduction to the first edition and on the cover page of all subsequent editions, that profits arising from the sale of the magazine were to be placed in a fund, the interest to be appropriated to the Missionary Society of Connecticut. Profits and contributions to this fund totaled $11,520 in 1815.

Examination of the first edition proves instructive. Following the editors' lengthy statement of purpose, missionary activity is highlighted, first with the reprinted copy of the London Missionary Society's 1795 charter and its endeavors in Africa and other areas of the world and then in an elaboration of activities sponsored by the newly chartered Missionary Society of Connecticut to convert the "heathen" in Vermont and New York's newly settled frontiers.

Three ministerial narratives next describe "the late wonderful outpourings of the Holy Spirit" in Somers, West Britain, and Torringford, Connecticut. Notwithstanding considerable variation in length, they all reflected an approach to revivals reminiscent of Jonathan Edwards's description of the evangelical awakening of the 1740s. References to the "surprising" nature of the work, the "unexpected" targets, the reversal of religious lethargy, and the imposition of new moral standards underscored strict adherence to the magazine's editorial policy: furnishing the "means to discriminate between experimental godliness, both from the fancies of fanaticism and the coldness of formality."[2] Errors plaguing the first Great Awakening were to be consciously avoided.

Consistent with a desire to awaken its readers' spirituality while concomitantly guarding against error, the *Connecticut Evangelical Magazine* interspersed its religious intelligence with topical essays addressing issues of doctrinal and practical concern. During its first two years, titles included "The Use of Means," a reference to methods for sustaining revivals advocated by Jonathan Edwards, "The Importance of Doctrinal Preaching," "Justification by Faith," "How the Gospel Should Be Reported," and "On Social Worship." Directed toward a clerical audience, these essays were self-consciously constructed to provide systematic practices, effective sermons, and other means to facilitate the spread of revivals.[3]

In all but a handful of cases, pseudonyms were used to protect the identity of the writers, and each word scrupulously avoided denominational references.

Both policies reinforced the magazine's panevangelical goal, to minimize denominational differences and propagate "the peculiar principles of Christianity."[4]

Likewise, the magazine steered clear of political partisanship. Nonevangelicals were treated as a homogeneous entity, and their "irreligion" inevitably linked to "immoral behavior." Dispensing with subtleties, "Confessions of an Infidel" and heart-wrenching deathbed accounts of famous (e.g., Jean Jacques Rousseau) and common nonbelievers were juxtaposed with the calm and knowing repose exhibited by ministers, their wives, and others.

While these sorts of articles, together with annual reports of the general association and the Connecticut Missionary Society (and occasional reports of other missionary societies), occupy the lion's share of the magazine's pages, the *Connecticut Evangelical Magazine* also illuminates issues of contention and shifts in evangelical attitudes over time.

In regard to the former, the *Connecticut Evangelical Magazine* printed several essays critical of the behavior exhibited by some recent converts. One example involves an essay entitled "Misconduct of Professors," printed during the peak of the first revivalistic surge in June 1801, which rebuked the overzealous tendencies of recent converts to judge others. Comparable behaviors, the author recalled, had proved deleterious to the first Great Awakening.[5] Equally noteworthy was a December 1802 article titled the "Imperfection of Young Converts," in which the anonymous author exhorted clerical colleagues to end the new practice of accepting teenagers into full Church membership.[6]

"Different sentiments" were also voiced over the camp-meeting revivals then unfolding on the Kentucky frontier. While acknowledging "the circumstance of persons falling down under religious impressions" to be "strange" by New England standards, a spirited defense of immediate conversion was proffered anonymously in a June 1802 essay. Citing scriptural episodes to verify the authenticity of their conversion, the author warned all "enemies" to desist from calling the camp meetings "the work of Satan."[7]

Shrinking numbers of revival accounts appearing during the five years after 1801 underscore the pattern of revivalism's ebb and flow. Lulls in local activity, however, did not undermine the editors' faith in the historic character of the times. Annual New Year's addresses, typically six to eight pages in length, reveal the editors' unyielding determination to invoke a millennial perspective when interpreting events of the previous year. Evangelicalism, they insisted, remained on the rise, borne out through the revivals and missionary labors occurring around the world. Setbacks, too, fired the apocalyptic yearnings of the editors. The 1802 report of the "reestablishment of Popery in France," construed as "mischievous and repugnant to the liberty and happiness of mankind," substantiated "the signs of the times [that] the days which are to come will be days of trouble.[8]

No explanation accompanied the magazine's decision to halt publication during the second half of 1807. Resumption of the magazine in January 1808, with no changes in its editorial staff, acknowledged that the "distracted state of the old world" had caused "interruptions of intercourse between our own and distant countries." Calling these "the darkest times," a veiled reference to the strong Federalist leanings of its constituency, the *Connecticut Evangelical Magazine* nurtured the theme of millennial expectancy reverberating from the imposition of Jefferson's unpopular embargo and the subsequent war.

That theme pervades the magazine throughout its final seven years of publication. Missionary reports describe the redoubling of efforts to provide traditional missionary services to new settlements and to disseminate books, with almost ten thousand alone (including 384 copies of the magazine) distributed in 1808. Apocalyptic images also grew starker, as in the January 1809 essay "Thoughts on the Millennium," which prophesied the intensification of "the present state of convulsion" as part of a "great overturning" necessary for "the introduction and spread of the gospel."[9] Revival narratives from across Connecticut and Massachusetts similarly reinforced the millennial imagery, as did regularly published reports from European missionary groups citing efforts in Japan, Africa, and Latin America aimed at converting "worshipers of idols, of priests, [and] heavenly bodies."

The outbreak of war in 1812 produced several noteworthy pieces. A fast sermon, delivered in Hartford by principal editor Nathan Strong was reprinted in the journal. Carefully adhering to editorial conventions that required the opening disclaimer, "I do not address you in the character of a politician," Strong then proceeded, in an uncharacteristically partisan reference, to praise Connecticut's Federalist leadership, declaring that "the oath of the Lord is upon them."[10]

Even more dramatic was a November 1812 article titled the "State of Parochial Clergy as to Residence," which proffered a startlingly revisionist perspective of New England history. Rather than the traditional image of Puritans escaping persecution in their quest to form Massachusetts Bay, the author asserts that the original settlers erroneously exaggerated the rift between themselves and the Church of England. "The thirty-nine Articles of the English church as established by the law of the realm," the author observed, "[today] would be judged correct by the greater part of the churches in New England."[11]

Embargoes notwithstanding, missionary reports from the London Missionary Society appear in the September 1813 issue, as do those of the British and Foreign Bible Society. Likewise, doctrinal commentaries, revival narratives, and other traditional fare continued to be interspersed with bold millennial prophesies. The Reverend Nehemiah Prudden, in an uncharacteristically signed address to the Connecticut Missionary Society, reported that "we are near the close of the days of sorrow. The first five vials are poured out, the six and seventh only remain."[12] Again, in January 1814, the editors in their annual address advised readers that "whatever evils await a sinful world, the darkest times of the church are undoubtedly past," with prospects imminent "of the approach of a period of universal peace and prosperity to the world."[13]

Millennial visions die extremely hard. Following the Treaty of Ghent, the

Connecticut Evangelical Magazine buried its enthusiasm for the Hartford Convention under a series of articles advocating a new spirit of pacifism. In the April and May issues, an article titled "A Solemn Review of the Custom of War" stressed the "demoralizing and depraving effects of war" both on and off the battlefield. Pointing to the "wanton devaluing of human life," the author inquired, Was not humanity "sufficiently enlightened to apply the principles of the gospel for the abolition of war?"[14]

Shortly thereafter, in its July 1815 issue, the *Connecticut Evangelical Magazine* published the Louisiana Bible Society's report accepting a generous donation of 100 pounds sterling to form the "most noble institution of modern times," the British and Foreign Bible Society.[15] Anxious to put the war behind it, the editors continued to applaud the work of voluntary societies in furthering the propagation of the Gospel.

Following publication of its December 1815 edition, the *Connecticut Evangelical Magazine* abruptly folded without explanation to its readers, a casualty of editor Nathan Strong's deteriorating health and the burgeoning public condemnation of the clergy's leadership role in opposing the "unrighteous war." In June 1816, the *Religious Intelligencer* was launched by Nathan Whiting in New Haven where, for twenty-two years, it continued the *Connecticut Evangelical Magazine*'s policy of disseminating information on revivals, missions, and voluntary societies.

The *Connecticut Evangelical Magazine* promulgated the adage, "Think globally, act locally." Born of the desire to fan the flames of a newly begun Second Great Awakening, the magazine provides an unparalleled peek into the clergy's self-conscious efforts to inculcate its constituency with a global justification for local action. While modern readers inevitably suffer from the *Connecticut Evangelical Magazine*'s policy not to identify authors, it remains a veritable gold mine for examining the evolution of New England orthodox thought and action during the explosive years between 1800 and 1815.

Notes

1. Elaboration of their activities in Vermont appears in Paul Jeffery Potash, "Welfare of the Regions Beyond," *Vermont History* 46 (1978): 109–28.

2. *Connecticut Evangelical Magazine* 1 (July 1800): 4.

3. Donald M. Scott elaborates upon the ministry's obsession with developing "revival workshops" through which they could "share techniques and particularly effective sermons and map out joint campaigns." See Scott, *From Office to Profession: The New England Ministry, 1750–1850* (Philadelphia: University of Pennsylvania Press, 1978), 37.

4 *Connecticut Evangelical Magazine* 1 (July 1800): 4.

5. Ibid. 1 (June 1801): 450–51.

6. Ibid. 2 (December 1802): 214–19.

7. Ibid. 2 (June 1802): 475–76.

8. Ibid. 2 (January 1802): 243.

9. *Connecticut Evangelical Magazine and Religious Intelligencer*, n.s., 2 (January 1809): 22.

10. An excellent analysis of this speech appears in William Gribbin, *The Churches Militant: The War of 1812 and American Religion* (New Haven: Yale University Press, 1973), 28.

11. *Connecticut Evangelical Magazine and Religious Intelligencer*, n.s., 4 (November 1812): 431–32.

12. Ibid., n.s., 6 (November 1813): 409.

13. Ibid., n.s., 7 (January 1814): 6–7.

14. Ibid., n.s., 8 (May 1815): 169–70.

15. Ibid., n.s., 8 (July 1815): 275.

Information Sources

INDEX SOURCES: An annual index appears in the concluding edition of each volume (June of each year between 1801–1807; December for the series running between 1808–1815).

LOCATION SOURCES: All fifteen volumes have been microfilmed as part of the American Periodical Series: Volumes 1–7 (July 1800–June 1917) of the first edition appear on APS II, Reel 14; the second series [referred to as the new series], volumes 1–8 (January 1808–December 1815) appear as APS II, Reels 127, 128 and 129.

Publication History

MAGAZINE TITLE AND TITLE CHANGES: *Connecticut Evangelical Magazine* (July 1800–June 1807), *Connecticut Evangelical Magazine and Religious Intelligencer* (January 1808–December 1815).

VOLUME AND ISSUE DATA: 1:1 (July 1800)–7:12 (June 1807); new series, 1:1 (January 1808)–8:12 (December 1815); published monthly.

PUBLISHER AND PLACE OF PUBLICATION: *Connecticut Evangelical Magazine*: Hudson and Goodwin, Hartford, Connecticut. *Connecticut Evangelical Magazine and Religious Intelligencer*: Peter Gleason and Co., Hartford (1808–1813); Gleason and Oliver D. Cooke (1814–1815).

EDITORS: Charles Backus, A.M. (1800–1807), James Cogswell, D.D. (1800–1801), Jeremiah Day, A.M. (1800–1807), Timothy Dwight, D.D. (1801–1807), David Ely, A.M. (1800–1807), Zebulon Ely, A.M. (1800–1807), Abel Flint, A.M. (1800–1807), Levi Hart, A.M. (1800–1807), Isaac Lewis, D.D. (1800–1807), Samuel J. Mills, A.M. (1800–1807), Elijah Parsons, A.M. (1800–1807), Nathan Perkins, A.M. (1800–1807), John Smalley, A.M. (1800–1807), Nathan Strong, A.M. (1800–1807), Benjamin Trumbull, D.D. (1800–1807), Joseph Washburn, A.M. (1802–1807), Moses C. Welch, A.M. (1804–1807), Nathan Williams, D.D. (1800–1807).

The "new series" of the *Connecticut Evangelical Magazine and Religious Intelligencer* (July 1808–December 1815) did not reveal its editors. With the exception of Nathan Strong, other editors remain unknown.

CIRCULATION: 3,000 (1800–1807); 3,730 (1808–1815).

P. Jeffrey Potash

**CONNECTICUT EVANGELICAL MAGAZINE AND RELIGIOUS
INTELLIGENCER.** *See* CONNECTICUT EVANGELICAL
MAGAZINE

CONSECRATED LIFE AND GUIDE TO HOLINESS. *See* GUIDE
TO HOLINESS

COR. *See* REIGN OF THE SACRED HEART

COVENANT COMPANION

On 20 February 1885 a group of Swedish-American Mission Friends gathered in Chicago and decided to form a denomination that they called the Swedish Evangelical Mission Covenant of America. Although all but two or three of the sixty-three assembled delegates supported the motion to organize themselves, opinions in the years prior to that action had been anything but united. Having endured a generation of controversies with the Lutheran Church of Sweden and having immigrated to the United States during the preceding decades, many of them were reluctant to submit themselves to another Church organization. Yet they also cherished their Lutheran heritage and recognized the dangers of isolation in the new land. The question of organization and numerous other issues enlivened debates among the Mission Friends in a plethora of Swedish-language periodicals published during the last decades of the nineteenth century. It is not an exaggeration to say that the religious press was one of the most influential forces in the formation of the Mission Covenant Church.

Like many immigrant groups, the Swedes used the medium of print to the fullest in their attempts to unify and nurture their fellow immigrants. In the area of publications, the Mission Friends took second place to none. In 1935, E. Gustav Johnson of North Park College in Chicago noted fifty periodicals that the Mission Friends had issued during their sixty-year history in the United States. Ranging from the idiosyncratic leaflets published by individuals to widely representative magazines with large circulations, these publications became the medium for the expression of everything from sophisticated political or theological views to diatribes against the decline in American morality. The first paper published among the Mission Friends was *Zions Banér*, which first appeared in July 1871. Edited by Rev. C. Anderson, pastor of a Lutheran congregation in Galesburg, Illinois, this paper became for all practical purposes the organ of the Lutheran Ansgar Synod until it was absorbed by another Swedish-language paper, the *Chicago-Bladet*, in October 1879. In 1874, another group of Mission Friends, organized as the Mission Synod, began publication of their official organ, *Missions-Vännen*. During the next decade as the immigrants wrestled with the issue of whether or how their church would be organized, the *Chicago-Bladet* and the *Missions-Vännen* served as the primary forums for the frequently harsh debate. The *Chicago-Bladet* had strongly opposed organization on the basis of a combination of dispensationalist and antidenominational views. The editors and writers of *Missions-Vännen* just as forcefully urged the Mission Friends to unite in a denomination. With the formation of the denomination, the controversy continued. The annual meeting of 1886 naively urged the *Chicago-Bladet* and the *Missions-Vännen* to merge or at least to cease their fighting. The controversy continued, however, and it became clear that the antidenominational attitudes expressed in the *Chicago-Bladet* would prohibit it from serving the Mission Covenant Church.[1] At the same time, while in favor of the organization and enjoying a wide circulation among members of the Mission Covenant, the *Missions-Vännen* served as the unofficial organ of the new denomination, but for a variety of reasons failed to achieve official status.

The publication of a new periodical, *Missionären*, by two professors at the Covenant's new college, North Park, further alienated the editors of the *Missions-Vännen*, who became outspoken opponents of the college. *Missions-Vännen* drifted further from the center of the Covenant by aligning itself with the emerging fundamentalist movement during the early decades of the twentieth century. It continued until 1960 as an independent Swedish-language paper that was frequently hostile toward the Covenant.[2]

Meanwhile, the denomination adopted *Missionären* as its official organ in June 1895. Edited by David Nyvall, president of North Park College, during its first two years as the Covenant's paper, *Missionären* was a sixteen-page monthly. In 1897 it was enlarged to tabloid size under the editorship of Axel Mellander and remained such until it ceased publication in 1905.

The denomination did not have another official paper until 1911 when a semimonthly magazine, *Missionsförbundets Ungdomstidning* (*The Mission Covenant's Young People's Paper*), began publication. It is this publication that is the earliest direct ancestor of the denomination's current official magazine, the *Covenant Companion*. In December 1915, the denomination expanded its publication to a weekly eight-page regulation-size newspaper, renamed *Förbundets Veckotidning* (*Covenant Weekly*).

The Covenant's focus on young people emerged as the immigrants recognized that their offspring faced issues far different than they had in their youth. In addition, it was becoming increasingly clear that despite efforts to maintain their Swedish heritage and language, these Swedish-Americans had to make accommodation to the language and culture of their adopted homeland if they were to keep their churches relevant to the coming generations. Antiforeign sentiments during World War I also pushed Covenanters toward the use of the English language. Thus, in the early 1920s the Covenant developed a bilingual system of Sunday-school lessons and in June 1922 began publication of a monthly titled the *Teacher's Companion*, its first English-language effort, to help teachers implement the new lessons.[3] Edited by Nathaniel Franklin, the *Teacher's Companion* began as a sixteen-page paper in magazine format. Gradually it increased to twenty pages, then to twenty-four. The next year the Covenant expanded the scope of the magazine to include adolescents as well as children, renamed it the *Covenant Companion*, and lengthened it to thirty-two pages, one half general reading material for young people, and the other half materials for Sunday-school teachers. Franklin spoke of the transition as one of great promise. The *Teacher's Companion* could retire from the scene since "a stronger and better Companion" was prepared to take over and expand the work. "For as the larva in the cocoon is changed into the beautiful butterfly, so the Teacher's Companion ceases to be, but will be born again into the greater and better Mission Friend magazine, The Covenant Companion."[4]

An attractively designed and well-edited magazine, the *Covenant Companion* became increasingly successful and expanded to forty-eight, then fifty-two, and finally sixty-four pages. One of the magazine's distinctive features was an extensive use of art, both on its cover and interior. A regular contributor for fourteen years was Warner Sallman who also served for a number of years on the denomination's board of publications. Later Sallman would become known around the world for his art, especially his "Head of Christ." A charcoal sketch of what later became the oil portrait of the "Head of Christ" first appeared on the cover of the February 1924 issue of the *Covenant Companion*.[5] Encouraged by increasingly positive accounts of the denomination's acceptance of the magazine, in October 1928 the editors began to issue the magazine as a biweekly and finally in November 1930 as a sixteen-page weekly. The future of publishing in the Covenant had never looked brighter.

Yet in late 1930 signs of the massive effect of the Depression began to appear. Numerous subscribers were forced to cancel their subscriptions, businesses could no longer purchase advertisements, and the denomination became less and less able to support its ministry of publishing. By 1934 it had become clear that the progress of the past few years could not be sustained; in fact, serious and damaging cuts became necessary. Financial pressures forced the merger of the Covenant's two periodicals, *Förbundets Veckotidning* (*Covenant Weekly*) and *Covenant Companion* into one newspaper. There was no magazine format with its original artwork and high-quality paper when the two publications were issued on 16 January 1934 as two parts of the one newspaper, a six-page Swedish section edited by Erik Dahlhielm and a six-page English section edited by G. F. Hedstrand. A month later, each section had been expanded to eight pages, but by the next year, the editorial staff had been reduced, and Hedstrand became sole editor of the combined paper, which thereafter included only four pages in Swedish.[6] Hedstrand tried to put the best face on the changes:

Here we are, dressed in a comely house dress of gingham. Gone are the days of silk stockings, satin slippers, and evening frocks. But we expect to retain that "sweet school-girl complexion," and the spirit of youth and enthusiasm. Those are intangible things that an economic depression can not touch. And they are the essential things in a paper. The appearance appeals to the eye, but the content makes the paper. It is pleasant to eat from expensive plates, but it is the food which constitutes the meal.[7]

In 1933, the Covenant board of publications had summarized the editorial policy of the *Covenant Companion* in a way that reflected the ongoing tension between the Swedish pietistic heritage and the American context. The board insisted on the following:

1. The *Covenant Companion* should serve as a denominational medium for contact with those who must be reached through the English language.
2. It should give special emphasis to the needs of our young people.
3. It should be representative of the spiritual and devotional interests of our people in accordance with our pietistic heritage.[8]

The tabloid format continued until 1959 when the name of the publication was changed to the *Covenant Companion* and the editors returned to a twenty-four–page magazine format. Carl Philip Anderson had replaced Hedstrand as editor in 1955, and from that time strenuous effort had been exerted to return the *Covenant Companion* to some of its former glory. Although resuming the magazine format, the editor had to apologize to readers who urged the use of better quality paper. He asked for patience, since improvement in paper stock would require different printing equipment and would double production costs. Occasionally, issues of special significance appeared with higher quality paper. Finally, the editors took the plunge; and with the 31 July 1964 issue, higher quality paper once again became standard.

By the late 1950s, the editorial policy of the magazine had come to reflect the changing circumstances in the denomination and more clearly echoed the concerns of mainstream American Protestantism. The three objectives stated by the board of publications no longer spoke of either issues of language or heritage, nor any effort specially to address concerns of youth. Now the three objectives were to propagate the gospel, promote a Christ-like life among the denomination's churches and its members, and apply the principles of the Gospel in every area of life.[9]

As part of an ongoing and highly successful effort to increase subscriptions, in 1959 the editorial staff developed a club subscription plan, eventually named the Every Member Plan, whereby churches would purchase enough subscriptions to give the *Covenant Companion* to all their families. By October 1960, fifty-five churches had joined the plan and 175 churches had come on board by June 1966. The peak of the program came in the mid–1970s when as many as 287 churches, or 53 percent of the total church membership, subscribed. Since that time, as financial pressures on local congregations and growing local concerns took precedence over denominational issues, subscriptions to the plan and overall circulation have steadily declined.

With the 1 January 1965 issue, the *Covenant Companion* again became a biweekly, expanded from twenty-four to thirty-two pages, with an upgraded paper stock that allowed color printing. In 1984, the magazine was again changed, becoming a forty-eight page monthly. In 1988 the editors redesigned the magazine, and in June 1990 covers were printed in full color. With the February 1993 issue, in response to financial pressures, the *Covenant Companion* was reduced to forty pages.

The character of the magazine has remained basically unchanged since the 1960s, with regular news features on events in the Covenant Church and the larger world Church, forums for discussion of issues especially pertinent to the Covenant, letters to the editor, devotional articles, regular guest columns, Bible studies, and editorials. One change of significance occurred after 1965 when the *Companion* began to include conference and department newsletters as special sections.

In the early 1980s, the editorial staff of the *Covenant Companion* informally adopted a new mission statement that emphasized the role of the magazine to inform, stimulate thought, and assist its readership in wrestling with contemporary issues of theology and Christian life. The statement also stressed the role of the *Companion* as a unifier for Covenant people, "to gather the church it serves by putting Covenanters in touch with each other." In recent reports to the annual meeting, the editor has regularly stressed the magazine's goal to bring Covenanters together in mind and spirit.[10]

The *Covenant Companion* subscribes to the Religious News Service and is a member of the Associated Church Press and Evangelical Press Association.

Notes

1. Many of those associated with the *Chicago-Bladet* eventually helped form the Association of Free Congregations that ultimately became the Evangelical Free Church.

2. In his review of Karl A. Olsson's history of the Covenant church, Conrad Bergendoff expressed wonder that the Covenant could survive "with a journal in its own ranks constantly hampering it." See "History Brings Various Emotions" [review of *By One Spirit*], *Covenant Companion* 52 (19 April 1963): 8–9.

3. The name "Companion" was drawn from a sermon by F. M. Johnson at the founding meeting of the denomination, using the text of Psalm 119:63, "I am a companion to all who fear you, of those who keep your precepts" (NRSV). See Karl A. Olsson, *Into One Body . . . by the Cross*, 2 vols. (Chicago: Covenant Press, 1985–1986), 1:164.

4. Nathaniel Franklin, Editorial, *Teacher's Companion* 2 (November 1923) : 2.

5. See David Morgan, "Imaging Protestant Piety: The Icons of Warner Sallman," *Religion and American Culture* 3 (Winter 1993): 29–47; and Jack R. Lundbom, "Warner E. Sallman: A Centenary Tribute to a Covenant Artist," *Covenant Companion* 81 (July 1992): 8–11, 40.

6. Not until 1956, however, was the Swedish section completely eliminated.

7. G. F. Hedstrand, "Our New Paper," *Covenant Weekly: Covenant Companion Section* 23 (16 January 1934): 2.

8. Board of Publications, Minutes, 27 February 1933, Box 31, folder 4, Carl Philip Anderson Collection, Covenant Archives and Historical Library, North Park College and Theological Seminary, Chicago. Used by permission of Covenant Publications.

9. "Objectives of *The Covenant Companion*," Box 1, folder 1, Anderson Collection.

10. "Companion Mission Statement," position paper written during a consultation at the Phoenix annual meeting in 1983, Box 1, folder 1, Covenant Publications, General collection, Covenant Archives and Historical Library, North Park College and Theological Seminary, Chicago.

Information Sources

INDEX SOURCES: Indexed yearly in each December issue (since 1959).

LOCATION SOURCES: Covenant Archives and Historical Library, North Park College and Theological Seminary, 3225 West Foster Avenue, Chicago, Illinois 60625.

Publication History

MAGAZINE TITLE AND TITLE CHANGES: *Missionsförbundets Ungdomstidning* (1911–1915), *Förbundets Veckotidning* (1915–1934), *Teacher's Companion* (1922–1923), *Covenant Companion* (1923–1934), *Covenant Weekly* (1934–1959), *Covenant Companion* (1959–present). *Covenant Weekly* combined *Förbundets Veckotidning* and *Covenant Companion*.

VOLUME AND ISSUE DATA: *Missionsförbundets Ungdomstidning* 1:1 (19 December 1911)–4:24 (30 November 1915); *Förbundets Veckotidning* 4:25 (7 December 1915)–23:2 (9 January 1934); *Teacher's Companion* 1:1 (June 1922)–2:6 (November 1923); *Covenant Companion* 2:7 (December 1923)–13:1 (6 January 1934); *Covenant Weekly* 23:3 (16 January 1934)–47:52 (26 December 1958); *Covenant Companion* 48:1 (2 January 1959)–present. *Covenant Weekly* adopted the volume and issue numbers of *Förbundets Veckotidning*.

PUBLISHER AND PLACE OF PUBLICATION: Covenant Press, 3200 W. Foster Avenue, Chicago, Illinois 60625.

EDITORS: Nathaniel Franklin (1922–1923) (*Teacher's Companion*), G. F. Hedstrand (1923–1955), Carl Philip Anderson (1955–1970), James R. Hawkinson (1970–present).

CIRCULATION: 34,000 (1975); 22,000 (1993).

Stephen R. Graham

COVENANT WEEKLY. *See* COVENANT COMPANION

D

DAUGHTERS OF SARAH[1]

Daughters of Sarah had its modest beginnings in Chicago, Illinois, in September 1973. Its origins lie in a yearlong Bible study that met to discuss the role of women in their Church. At the same time, the role of women in general was at the forefront of American society. The founding members consisted of eight women who were students and wives of faculty and students at North Park (Evangelical Covenant) Theological Seminary community: Gwen Bagaas, Bonnie Borgeson, Carol Brown, Sharon Hughes-Tremper, Frances Mason, Grace Nelson, Doreen Olson, and Lucille Sider Dayton [Groh] (who became the first editor of *Daughters of Sarah*).[2] The founding members decided that other women might be interested in what they had discussed, so they decided to create a newsletter and collected 30 dollars to pay for postage and copying costs. The first issue, mailed in November 1974, was four type-written 8½-by-11-inch mimeographed pages. It was sent to about two hundred women, many of whom were friends and acquaintances of the original members. The first issue contained a brief article on Catherine Booth (wife of Salvation Army founder William Booth), a biblical article about woman as companion to man, and a discussion on gender stereotyping.

The purpose of *Daughters of Sarah* has been simply and clearly stated from the beginning: ''We are Christians; we are also feminists. Some say we cannot be both, but Christianity and feminism for us are inseparable.''[3] The magazine name *Daughters of Sarah* has an interesting origin:

The name *Daughters of Sarah* was chosen to parallel the designation ''sons of Abraham'' for Christians. Sarah was a strong woman, very human, and equally called by God to a new land of promise. Only through Sarah's aged body and her faith in God's impossible doings could the promise be fulfilled. We are her daughters today, as Paul says, not of flesh, but of promise. We are considered worthy to be co-heirs of God's kingdom.[4]

It appeared, even at its formative stages, that *Daughters of Sarah* was addressing a felt need among women. Lucille Sider Dayton described the amazement about the positive responses after the first mailing. "We almost panicked . . . when some of our subscribers sent us a two-year subscription. They seemed to be taking us more seriously than we were taking ourselves!"[5] *Daughters of Sarah* has strived to be both nondenominational and inclusive of the various, yet still maturing, views of feminism.

Some have questioned the apparent lack of men at the initial stages of *Daughters of Sarah*,[6] and, as Sider noted, it was necessary since "we needed time to develop ourselves apart from men. We were quite defensive back then, and were not always easy to live with. We weren't sure of ourselves, so we fought doubly hard."[7] This exclusivism was a necessary stage in *Daughters of Sarah*'s development; however, presently, there are regular male contributors to the magazine.

The magazine, although written in a popular style, maintains a high level of academic integrity. Noted scholars like Nancy Hardesty, Letha Scanzoni, Virginia Ramey Mollenkott, and David Scholer often contribute insightful historical and exegetical articles on women. In its early stages the magazine was divided into five parts: (1) biblical articles demonstrating the need to "reread" traditionally patriarchal texts, as shown by Thomas Finger's intuitive article "Husbands, Submit to Your Wives," which challenges the conventional interpretation of Ephesians 5:18b–33; (2) practical articles dealing with the role of women in the home, society, and Church, as exemplified by Sheryl Lee Oslen's article "Singleness: Moving beyond Categories," a plea for accepting "singleness" as an authentic lifestyle; (3) historical articles illustrating how women have played significant roles in Church and society;[8] (4) "Dear Daughters"—a question and answer section about biblical feminism; and (5) "The Grapevine"—a news bulletin board of current items (conferences, newly published books, etc.) and people that would be of interest to the readership.

Daughters of Sarah, as a religious publication, places itself within the evangelical tradition, although the periodical avoids using this label. Reta Halteman Finger, the present editor, in a recent survey article on feminist theologies, has noted: "*Daughters of Sarah* has generally represented the . . . biblical position of Christian feminism. We try to include a range of positions within this broader category, as well as drawing many insights from writings with a liberationist perspective."[9] In many ways, *Daughters of Sarah* avoids glib categorizing; it prides itself on serious engagement with the Bible along with an openness to the many voices within a Christian and feminist framework. A recent purpose statement reflects this disposition: "We find it necessary to *agree* to *disagree* that we may create a true forum for a wide range of viewpoints that are both Christian and feminist."[10]

Daughters of Sarah's audience is a consistent group, as indicated by the results of its yearly surveys. Most readers are highly educated women (over 50 percent have done postgraduate work) between the ages of twenty-three and thirty-five who are affiliated either with a specific Church (denomination) or who identify themselves as "Christian."[11] There has been a slight increase over the years in male subscribers. Beyond demographics, the yearly surveys also accomplish another important task: an evaluation of the magazine by its readers. Questions ask what area(s) of the magazine readers would like to see expanded and what area(s) they find troubling about the magazine. One of the many strengths of *Daughters of Sarah* continues to be its yearly reader surveys.

The number of subscribers began with roughly fifty (those who responded to the initial mailing of two hundred) and within a year grew to a thousand. Subscriptions have continued to grow. As of 1993, there were fifty-five hundred subscribers. The price of the magazine in 1974 was two dollars for a four-issue subscription. In 1993, the cost was eighteen dollars.

The format of the magazine has also evolved. As previously noted, the first issue in 1974 was an 8½-by-11-inch mimeographed newsletter. The second issue (January 1975) took the form of a 6½-by-8½-inch booklet. In 1979 the magazine began to include color and artwork. By 1980, the publication again changed size. It became smaller (5½-by-8½-inch) to help reduce printing costs and to conform more to standard magazine sizes, although the actual number of pages increased. Since then, the format and design of the magazine have basically remained the same.

Daughters of Sarah began as a bimonthly publication and continued as such for nearly eighteen years. It was forced to change to a quarterly publication because of the new postal rates introduced in February 1991.[12] Nevertheless, *Daughters of Sarah* maintained its character by expanding to sixty-four–page issues to compensate for the loss of two issues.

The contents of the magazine have also developed. Magazine topics have grown more progressive. For instance, topics like women in the Third World, domestic violence, abortion, rape, homosexuality, sexism, and racism were not examined in the early days of the publication but are now routine fare. The magazine regularly includes book reviews, review essays, poetry, photographs, artwork, and, at times, cartoons.

It is important to recognize that *Daughters of Sarah* was conceived as and continues to be a group effort.[13] Although some women are historically referred to as "founding mothers," no member claims credit for *Daughters of Sarah*'s inception. There is also a recognition of diversity within the core group, as indicated by Reta Halteman Finger's comment on a recent staff retreat: "We do not all agree on what seem like basic issues; yet we struggle to understand each other and provide space for each other to grow."[14] This diversity is reflected by the various viewpoints that are offered when a controversial topic is discussed (e.g., abortion or homosexuality).

The many ways in which the magazine communicates to its constituency also stimulates community. In 1990, for example, a "Kindred Spirits" column was created in the hope of assisting *Daughters of Sarah* readers to network with each other.[15] A year later, a column called "Segue" was started "to support women who belong to fundamentalist or evangelical churches, who want to stay there but who struggle to grow as whole persons in places where gender roles seem oppressive."[16] More importantly, entries for "Segue" are written by and for readers. These efforts and many others demonstrate the importance of creating a readership community for *Daughters of Sarah*. The idea of community began *Daughters of Sarah*, and this idea still continues today.

Notes

1. The author would like to thank Reta Finger (editor) and Jeanne Baly (business and circulation manager) of *Daughters of Sarah* for reading and commenting on an earlier draft of this article. Reta also offered historical data on *Daughters of Sarah* and assisted in articulating the particular type of feminism that *Daughters of Sarah* represents.

2. While there was no formal relation with North Park Theological Seminary, except that Lucille Sider Dayton's then-husband Donald Dayton was librarian there, it nevertheless provided an evangelical milieu for the creation of the magazine.

3. *Daughters of Sarah* 1:1 (November 1974): 1. Interestingly, in 1988 a logo was designed to symbolize the mission statement. It is a picture of a tree, with a woman with outstretched arms as the trunk. Underneath her are two thick supporting roots that are appropriately labeled: Feminism and Christianity. The logo now appears in the magazine's masthead and on stationery.

4. *Daughters of Sarah* 9:4 (July–August 1983): 2.

5. Ibid. 6:1 (January–February 1980): 9.

6. Reta Finger brought to the author's attention the fact that Donald Dayton wrote a number of articles for *Daughters of Sarah* in its early stages and, moreover, was the one who originally suggested the magazine idea to Lucille.

7. *Daughters of Sarah* 10:6 (November–December 1984): 7.

8. For example, the entire September–October 1984 issue was devoted to exemplary women, such as Puah, Hilda of Whitby, and Hannah Whitall Smith.

9. *Daughters of Sarah* 10:6 (November–December 1984): 6.

10. Ibid. 19:2 (Spring 1993): 3.

11. The results of yearly surveys are printed in the magazine.

12. See *Daughters of Sarah* 17:4 (July–August 1991): 32.

13. There are often magazine advertisements asking local members and those visiting the Chicago area to attend the monthly potluck dinners held in *Daughters of Sarah*'s office.

14. *Daughters of Sarah* 8:1 (January–February 1982): 2.

15. See Ibid. 16:1 (January–February 1990).

16. Ibid. 17:2 (March–April 1991): 21.

Information Sources

INDEX SOURCES: From 1974 to 1986, indexing for editorials, articles, and book reviews was done in the winter issue for the previous year. Beginning in 1987, articles are indexed in *Religion Index One: Periodicals*, and book reviews are indexed in *Index to Book Reviews in Religion*.

LOCATION SOURCES: Copies of *Daughters of Sarah* can be found in most college/university libraries. Volumes 1 to 15 (1974–1989) are bound journals. Copies are on microfilm, beginning with volume 16 (1990).

Publication History

MAGAZINE TITLE: *Daughters of Sarah* (1974–present).
VOLUME AND ISSUE DATA: 1:1 (November 1974)–present. Published quarterly.
PUBLISHER AND PLACE OF PUBLICATION: Daughters of Sarah, Inc., Chicago, Illinois.
EDITORS: Lucille Sider Dayton [Groh] (1974–1976), Reta Halteman Finger (1976–present).
CIRCULATION: 5,500 (1993).

Joseph B. Modica

DECISION

Editors of religious and secular magazines alike cannot help but envy the enormous popularity of *Decision*. First published in November 1960, *Decision* reached a United States circulation of 2.1 million by 1965, with additional editions available in Canada, Britain, and Australia, and translations available in French, Spanish, and German.[1] By 1975, *Decision*'s U.S. circulation hit the 5 million mark, being distributed to more American homes that year than *Time* magazine. The spectacular growth of this magazine makes it one of the more amazing success stories in the publishing industry. One cannot attribute the success of *Decision*, however, solely to its content. Rather, this magazine's popularity is inextricably tied to the extraordinary popularity of its nominal editor in chief, evangelist Billy Graham. To understand the success of *Decision*, we must understand the person of Billy Graham and something of the times that produced him.[2]

Billy Graham first caught national attention in 1949, during a series of revival meetings in Los Angeles. Two days before the start of those meetings, President Truman announced that Russia had detonated its first atomic bomb, an event we now refer to as the start of the Cold War. Graham already positioned himself as a bitter opponent of communism, and in his first sermon he wasted no time raising the specter of nuclear destruction. He pounced on his listeners' anxiety about nuclear attack and Communist takeover, warning that the nation's only true protection lay in regaining God's favor, which required renouncing our sinful ways and returning to the path of righteousness. Such rhetoric brought

Graham to the attention of another bitter opponent of communism, William Randolph Hearst. Hearst liked what he heard about Graham so much that he issued the following career-changing order to his huge newspaper conglomerate: "Puff Graham." His support, along with the sensational conversions of two Hollywood celebrities and a wiretapper from Mickey Cohen's organized crime gang, brought to the revivals swarms of reporters, who in turn brought Graham's name into every American home.[3]

Immediately, invitations to hold evangelistic meetings in communities across the United States and around the world poured into Graham's mailbox. Within a few months of the Los Angeles revival, Graham founded the Billy Graham Evangelistic Association (BGEA) to manage his rapidly expanding activities. Over the next two years, Graham's ministries included weekly "Hour of Decision" radio broadcasts, daily publication of a question-and-answer newspaper column titled "My Answer," and production of feature-length evangelistic films such as "Mr. Texas." During this period, Graham also refined his revival-meeting practices to include an extensive follow-up program for all who made "inquiries" at his meetings (called "crusades"). It was also during this period that Graham began his close association with political figures, beginning with Governor Strom Thurmond of South Carolina and eventually including President Truman and all White House occupants thereafter. By the end of the decade, Graham's dossier included the authorship of several best-selling books, the founding of *Christianity Today* (an evangelical counterpart to the *Christian Century*), regular television broadcasts of his evangelistic crusades, and the launching of *Decision* magazine.[4]

To what did Graham owe his enormous popularity? Though some might stress his personal charisma, his international stature, or the drama of his crusades, much of Graham's popularity (and concomitantly *Decision*'s popularity) lies in the appeal of the particular version of Christianity that he has expounded and exemplified. Many Christian fundamentalists disliked Graham intensely because he identified with "neo-evangelicalism," a movement that rejected the separatism, anti-intellectualism, and militancy that characterized much of fundamentalism. Neo-evangelicals (now known simply as "evangelicals") wished to be known solely for their emphasis on belief in the Gospel of Jesus Christ, the inerrancy of the Bible, and the urgency of spreading the Gospel to the entire world.[5] Therefore, when Graham encouraged the participation of all Christian Churches in his crusades, including the Roman Catholic Church and liberal Protestant Churches, he was acting as an exemplary evangelical. This same act brought Graham the wrath of many fundamentalists. To Graham's way of thinking, if Roman Catholics or liberal Protestants supported the Gospel as he preached it, they were welcome.

The evangelical Christianity that Graham championed appealed to a wide variety of people. First, it appealed to persons from fundamentalist backgrounds who were disillusioned with the strict separatism and rigid behavioral codes of fundamentalism. Second, it appealed to members of liberal Churches, who may have found their denomination's emphases on humanity's inherent goodness and the social Gospel untenable in light of World War II, the horror of the Third Reich, and the spread of communism. Third, it was attractive to people of various denominations who saw their own Churches strengthened as a result of a Graham crusade in their hometown. Fourth, it appealed to anyone who found in evangelicalism's simple message of personal faith in Jesus, unencumbered with additional dogma or requirements, a persuasive answer to their personal situation.

The key to understanding *Decision*'s popularity and its significance, then, lies in locating *Decision* first within the immediate phenomenon of Billy Graham, and second within the broader framework of the neo-evangelical movement. *Decision* is popular because it provides a monthly, symbolic link between its readers and Billy Graham. In each issue, readers find sermons, articles, and news reports that affirm and proclaim the evangelical faith, challenge the reader to do the same, and report the success of Graham and his organization in promoting the Gospel. (The last is to be expected since the majority of *Decision* recipients are either regular BGEA contributors or crusade inquirers.[6]) At the same time, *Decision* links the reader to the broader evangelical movement by emphasizing evangelicalism's central tenets. Each issue is carefully constructed to include news from various denominations and contributions by denominationally diverse authors and to avoid any topic that might divide readers otherwise supportive of the evangelical cause. The underlying, but not subtle, message is this: The proclamation of the Gospel is primary; all else is secondary.

The basic structure of *Decision* has remained virtually unchanged since its inception. Each issue begins with a printed sermon (almost always by Graham), which is then followed by six to nine additional articles. These articles tell of people's conversions, encourage readers to engage in personal evangelism, assure readers about their faith, report the successes of evangelistic crusades, provide a Bible study on some aspect of evangelical belief, and challenge readers to greater levels of faith and commitment. Each issue also includes several regular features, consisting of a page of devotional prose or Scripture, a schedule of BGEA crusades, letters from readers, brief news reports on evangelistic events throughout the world, and an editorial. *Decision* abounds with photographs and illustrations and has followed standard layout techniques to maintain visual interest and attract attention to its articles.[7] Notably absent from the magazine are discussions of political or social issues; such issues are mentioned only briefly and serve mostly as illustrations of worldly evil.[8] Though *Decision* changed its format in 1985, articles and regular features have remained remarkably similar in style and in the range of topics covered since the inaugural issue.

Graham's sermon, which almost always occupies the first page,[9] has changed little in emphasis since November 1960. Though Graham varies his sermon's introduction to touch on some pressing contemporary concern,[10] the body of his sermon follows one of two patterns. It either makes a direct evangelistic appeal, or it calls readers to lead a Christian evangelical life. ''Rising Beyond Conformity," Graham's first message in November 1960, is typical of the hundreds that followed. It challenged readers who felt pressured to conform to "the patterns of this world" to reject society's pressures and choose instead to live a non-conformist lifestyle of complete surrender to Christ. Such a lifestyle is a "constant rebuke" to people who do not live according to God's law and need to hear the "message of Christ." Graham concluded by explaining how those who do surrender to Christ will ultimately receive God's favor. The sermon is usually the only piece that Graham himself contributes and it rarely extends to more than one and a half tabloid pages. Since *Decision* refuses outside advertising, the bulk of the magazine consists of contributions by other authors.[11] About half the time, these authors are from Graham's staff; the rest of the time they are drawn from the broader evangelical movement.

Though the authors have changed over the years, articles appearing in *Decision* have stayed within a narrow range of formats. One staple that readers could count on appearing monthly was a testimony by persons of public prominence about their conversions. The first issue, for example, included the conversion account of David Rowlands, M.D., billed as "one of the most remarkable conversions of the mid-century." Rowlands recounted how he gave up his religious skepticism and his prosperous medical practice after "surrendering to Christ" at a Graham crusade. Immediately, Rowlands began speaking of Christ to everyone, and eventually he moved to New Zealand so that he could "reach the masses and win them to Christ."[12] Another *Decision* staple is the Bible study. This feature typically includes a written commentary on a biblical text and closes with an assignment for readers to do on their own. Articles that touch on some general aspect of conversion (e.g., assurance of God's forgiveness) appear monthly, as do articles encouraging the reader to engage in evangelism personally. Finally, one or two articles about everyday living as a Christian (e.g., being a leader, deepening one's prayer life) round out the typical issue.

A few minor changes are perceptible over the years. Most obvious to contemporary eyes is the more gender-inclusive language of current issues compared to early issues. Articles by women or about women now appear regularly, which did not happen in earlier years.[13] *Decision* has also become more accessible to less-educated readers over the years. The current typeface is about two points larger than the original, sentences have become shorter and less demanding, and only words that are widely understood are included. As well, *Decision* has undergone layout and format changes to keep pace with publishing standards, most notably switching from a tabloid to a full-color magazine format in 1985.[14]

Decision has remained committed to its original mission since its inception. It has not altered its commitment to its founding mission: "To take the Gospel to as many people as possible."[15] What the future holds for *Decision* is unclear. Although Graham is aging and faces greater health problems, there is no heir apparent in the wings at BGEA. *Decision*'s circulation has been declining. As of 1992, it circulated to 1.7 million readers, one of the largest audiences for a religious magazine in the United States but only one third of its 1975 readership. How BGEA will maintain *Decision*'s place at the top of religious publishing after Graham's death is uncertain, though the organization has the resources to do so.

Notes

1. By contrast, *Newsweek* had 1.7 million subscribers, *Time* had 3 million, and the *New Yorker* had less than 500,000. Figures are taken from N. W. Ayers and Sons' *Directory of Newspapers and Periodicals, 1960–1969.*

2. It is important to point out that only one fourth of *Decision*'s circulation is delivered to paid subscribers; the majority of the magazine's recipients are Graham's donors, who pay for their subscription more indirectly.

3. Marshall Frady, *Billy Graham: A Parable of American Righteousness* (Boston: Little, Brown, 1979), 197.

4. Charles H. Lippy, ''Billy Graham,'' *Twentieth Century Shapers of American Popular Religion*, ed. Charles H. Lippy (Westport, CT: Greenwood Press, 1989), 179–86.

5. See George M. Marsden, *Reforming Fundamentalism* (Grand Rapids, MI: Eerdmans, 1987), for an excellent discussion of the growth of ''neo-evangelicalism'' out of, and as a correction to, fundamentalism.

6. It should be noted, however, that articles in *Decision* make no financial requests for BGEA. Requests for financial support are mailed separately to donors in monthly letters. The one exception to this is a small advertisement for a booklet explaining how to plan one's estate and how to include gifts to BGEA in that estate.

7. *Decision* used two colors (black and another color) beginning with its first issue (November 1960). By the second issue, the magazine began to vary the second color from page to page. By 1962, full-color photographs and illustrations appeared, and they continued to appear with greater and greater frequency until 1985, when *Decision* switched to a complete full-color magazine format.

8. During the 1960s and 1970s, Graham did frequently condemn communism because of its atheism and its restrictions on religious activity. These condemnations were almost always used to introduce his sermons. Yet Graham became the very first Western minister to preach in a Communist country in the early 1980s, despite protests by President Reagan and many evangelicals that he was being used as a propaganda tool. This act indicated his opposition to communism was primarily a result of communism's opposition to evangelism, for once he and others were allowed to preach freely in Communist countries, his criticism vanished. Graham also condemned the student and racial violence of the 1960s. His opposition to the former stemmed from the student movement's affront to biblical morality. Graham's opposition to the latter, however, stemmed not out of bigotry, but out of his support for the nonviolent approach of Martin Luther King, Jr. Graham's sermon introductions of recent years indicate not only his concern for evangelism worldwide, but also his growing interest for international peace and freedom. Beyond brief mentions of issues like these in Graham's sermons, however, *Decision* is devoid of political and social comment.

9. When Graham's sermon is not on the first page, it appears on the center pages.

On those occasions, the first page features a sermon by an associate BGEA evangelist, the sole exception being a transcription of Richard Nixon's speech to the audience at his Presidential Prayer Breakfast (April 1969), where Graham also spoke. After the embarrassment of Watergate, however, *Decision* downplayed Graham's association with political figures.

10. For example, after President Kennedy's assassination, Graham's cover sermon began by expressing shock at the suddenness and horror of Kennedy's death. His sermon then shifted, however, to emphasizing the brevity of life and the need to prepare for the life to come. During the turmoil of 1969, Graham began many sermons with references to campus and urban violence. But again, Graham rapidly shifted to a discussion of the need for conversion in order to bring America real peace. Different introductions, same conclusion.

11. Although *Decision* refuses outside advertising, as BGEA grew and diversified, advertisements for books, evangelistic movies, schools of evangelism, and summer Bible conference retreats from groups operating under the BGEA umbrella were given two pages in the back to solicit readers.

12. *Decision* 1:1 (November 1960): 4.

13. On the contrary, articles by Christians of any race have been a part of *Decision* since its inception. Graham was considerably ahead of his Southern peers in his attitudes toward race. Graham (and *Decision*) never condemned bigotry directly in the early years, however. Graham considered the conversion experience the only effective antidote to hatred. Therefore, Graham emphasized the Gospel; his racial views could be gathered only from his actions—such as sharing the platform with members of all races, hiring employees of all races, refusing to segregate seating at his crusades, and associating freely with all races. *Decision* adopted the same pattern: emphasizing the gospel, but readily including stories, photographs, or news reports by or about members of all races.

14. Prior to 1985, full-color pages were most likely to appear in December (Christmas), April or May (Easter, which is dated a month in advance), July (Independence Day), and special anniversary editions (e.g., the tenth-anniversary edition of *Decision*).

15. Quoted from the mission statement, provided to the author by Dr. Roger C. Palms, 30 June 1992. The complete mission statement is: "The purpose of *Decision* magazine is to continue the emphasis of the evangelistic ministry of Billy Graham through the printed page: to take the Gospel to as many people as possible."

Information Sources

INDEX SOURCES: *Decision* produced a twenty-five–year cumulative index in 1986, covering 1960 to 1985. In 1991, *Decision* released a five-year index covering 1986 to 1990. *Decision* is also indexed in the *Catholic Periodical Index.*

LOCATION SOURCES: Bound copies of all issues are available at the Billy Graham Evangelistic Association offices in Minneapolis and the Billy Graham Center Archives, Wheaton College, 500 East College, Wheaton, Illinois 60187. Copies are available on microfilm from University Microfilms International, 300 North Zeeb Road, Ann Arbor, Michigan 48106–1246. Some university and seminary libraries have bound or microfilm holdings.

Publication History

MAGAZINE TITLE: *Decision*.
VOLUME AND ISSUE DATA: 1:1 (November 1960)–present. Published monthly, with combined July–August edition.
PUBLISHER AND PLACE OF PUBLICATION: Billy Graham Evangelistic Association, Minneapolis, Minnesota (1960–present).
EDITORS: Billy Graham (editor-in-chief, 1960–), Sherwood E. Wirt (editor, 1960–1976), Roger C. Palms (editor, 1976–present).
CIRCULATION: 295,000 (1960); 950,000 (1963); 2,100,000 (1965); 3,270,000 (1968); 4,000,000 (1970); 5,000,000 (1975); 3,000,000 (1980); 2,000,000 (1990); 1,700,000 (1992).

Timothy T. Clydesdale

DER VEREINSBOTE. *See* WALTHER LEAGUE MESSENGER

DIMENSION. *See* REFORM JUDAISM

DIMENSIONS IN AMERICAN JUDAISM. *See* REFORM JUDAISM

DOOR

The *Door* is most often characterized as a Christian magazine of humor and satire. It is compared to the *National Lampoon* and other renowned sources of satire for its sharp wit and biting commentary. But to present this magazine only in this manner is to miss the seriousness of its intent and of much of its composition. Although a good deal of the content is satirical humor couched in everything from essays to cartoons, much is also serious commentary, interviews, and editorials.

This magazine grew out of a four-page mimeographed sheet called the *Wittenberg [sic] Door*, created in 1968 by Gary Wilburn and Paul Sailhammer, for distribution to youth workers in Southern California. It was sold for a minimal subscription price, but by 1971 the author/publishers were unable to maintain their commitment to the magazine. At that time, the staff of Youth Specialties in El Cajon, California was also considering putting out a magazine for youth workers. Wilburn and Sailhammer sold their title, concept, and subscriptions to Youth Specialties for the cost of their debts, and the first issue in magazine form was published in June 1971. (Youth Specialties is a closely held corporation, founded in 1969, that publishes material and trains youth workers through seminars and conventions.) The owners of Youth Specialties were Mike Yaconelli, Wayne Rice, and Denny Rydberg. They joined with Ben Patterson to produce the *Wittenburg Door*. Over the years they have been known generically as ''the Keepers of the Door'' and have given themselves various titles in the editing/publishing hierarchy. In the fifth-anniversary issue, Rice, Yaconelli, and Patterson are identified as starting the *Door*.[1] Rice is designated as the art director and credited with misspelling *Wittenburg* on that first issue, a mistake that was noticed but, in the true spirit of the magazine, never corrected. By the sixth issue (April–May 1972), Rydberg is identified as editor, and he held that position until 1979.

The "Keepers of the Door" began to disperse from El Cajon in 1976 when Yaconelli moved to Yreka, California to assume the pastorate of a church. He continued as one of the owners of Youth Specialties and an editor of the magazine. Rice has remained an owner and staff member of Youth Specialties. Rydberg and Patterson have moved on to other ministries. In 1979, Yaconelli became the editor of the *Wittenburg Door*. In 1987, Bob Darden, who had been a contributing editor to the magazine, became part of the editorial staff. In the December 1987–January 1988 issue, Darden is listed as an editor with Mike Yaconelli. By the April–May edition of 1988, Yaconelli is designated as senior editor with Darden as executive editor. By the next year, Karla Yaconelli is listed as managing editor.

In its current configuration, the *Door* is an excellent example of contemporary publishing technology. Assignments are made and articles screened by Darden in Waco, Texas. He sends the material by fax or electronic mail to the Yaconellis in Yreka, California, where it is edited and sent back to Waco for layout, design, and printing. Distribution is handled by a subscription service in Mount Morris, Illinois.

True to its origins on a mimeograph machine, the *Wittenburg Door* has, until recently, had the look of an underground newspaper. It is in an 8½-by-11-inch format, usually thirty-two pages in length (including the back cover) and is stapled twice on the spine. It was customarily printed on beige-colored unpolished paper and either typed or typeset to look like it was done on a typewriter. Occasionally the editors would depart from their regular format by adding color to a cover to make a point, as in the issue on Catholics (no. 67), which portrayed a stained glass bingo card in full color, or the one on evil (no. 74), in which the whole magazine was printed with white ink on black paper.

In 1989, with issue number 104, it was decided to abandon the counterculture look and adopt a new format to take the magazine into the 1990s. The name was changed from the *Wittenburg Door* to just the *Door* since that was the way most of its devotees referred to it. The size remained the same, but both the cover and the interior were done on polished paper with two or three colors of ink. The copy was now typeset and the layout had a more open and crisp feel. With the September–October 1991 issue, presumably for cost reasons, the magazine reverted to plain white paper and one color of ink for the interior content while retaining the full-color, polished appearance on the cover.

The magazine continues to be published by Youth Specialties in El Cajon. It is supported solely by subscriptions. A subscription for six issues annually cost twenty-four dollars in 1993. As a matter of principle, the publishers have never accepted advertising, feeling that to do so might compromise their ability to challenge the established icons of the Christian subculture. The magazine was marketed primarily through direct mail to persons on the Youth Specialties mailing list and through various incentives for subscribers to "spread the word." This is the kind of magazine that quickly turns an avid subscriber into an advocate, and its reputation is often spread by word of mouth. The circulation of the magazine reached a high of over twenty-three thousand in the early 1980s, at which point the publisher stopped promoting it, and subscriptions slipped to approximately nine thousand in 1993. A renewed advertising and promotional campaign then got under way.

"The *Door* 1992 Readers Survey" provides insight into the audience for this magazine. The bulk of subscribers falls into the thirty to fifty age range. The audience is almost exclusively Caucasian (98 percent) and mostly male (74 percent). Ninety to ninety-five percent are affiliated with a Church, and those affiliations range from fundamentalist to liberal, with the largest group (42 percent) identifying themselves as evangelicals. Ninety-eight percent have some college education, and two thirds have baccalaureate degrees or higher. Seventy-one percent are married, and 30 percent of the readers work for a Church or Christian organization in some capacity.

One is hard pressed to find a clear statement of purpose for this magazine. However, there are glimpses of insight into the reason for its existence hidden in various articles and interviews throughout the years. The first edition of the magazine, when it was still a mimeographed paper, had a column titled "To Wrinkle The Sta-Prest Mind," itself a statement of purpose. The column was reprinted in part in the tenth-anniversary issue and states, "It will be the editorial policy of this publication to seek ways in which to honor the truths of our heritage and apply their essence to the situations faced in contemporary society. Through satire, review, reporting, cartooning, humor, and feature articles we will attempt to 1) stimulate creative thought, 2) evaluate and review methods and materials of the past, the present and the future, and 3) create a respected critical opinion."[2] The methods and materials referred to likely pertain to youth work since the magazine was originally intended to be a professional journal of youth ministry. One of the original editors, Paul Sailhammer, is quoted as saying, "I've always thought of the *Door* as a mirror reflecting what is going on in the name of Jesus."[3]

In "Interview: Keepers of the Door," the editors were asked, "Do you guys have a philosophy for achieving reform and renewal through the *Door*?" They responded:

I think we have a philosophy but its not written down anyplace. We couldn't pick out a file and say "This is the philosophy." But we're trying to shoot down sacred cows that maybe shouldn't be sacred cows in the church. We're trying to get the church to look at issues that maybe they've just skimmed over in the past because "everybody else is doing it.'' We're trying to ask questions perhaps that some people aren't asking. We're trying to give frustrated people a platform from which to speak. And we're trying to do it all with a sense of humor.[4]

Later in the same interview the editors confessed:

All of us are committed to Jesus Christ. All of us love the church although we have some feelings that the church may not be heading in the right direction. . . . We struggle with whether you can be a cynic and a Christian at the same time. . . . Basically we're across the board anti-institutional. The evangelical church is highly institutionalized. So naturally they're going to get a lot of flak from us. . . . We treat ourselves pretty much like we treat everybody else. We laugh at ourselves. We print the rotten letters that come in. We don't think of ourselves as a big professional magazine.[5]

The tenth-anniversary issue (no. 61) contained another interview with the editors. When asked, ''What are you trying to do with the *Door*?'' they responded that they were trying to

change the church. Save it from itself because too many churches take themselves too seriously. . . . We love the church but we do not love those things which contradict the gospel we believe. There ought to be a place for some form of laughter in any institution. Christianity certainly needs that. . . . It is easy to fall into various forms of idolatry, so the function of the *Door* is simply to be someplace where people can say, ''This is funny, this is ridiculous, this is not nearly as important as you think it is.''[6]

Another important aspect of the editorial purpose is revealed in the same interview. ''The *Door* has a ministry to those people who are somewhat cynical and yet have never felt comfortable in the church. They are helped when they discover there are others who have seriously questioned the church, yet are still part of it. There are also a lot of people who have been hurt by the church and need an outlet to express how they feel. The *Door* provides that.''[7] The current (1993) senior editor, Mike Yaconelli, indicated that the purpose of the magazine had mellowed somewhat over the years. While still seeking to reform and renew Christian Churches through the use of humor, an increasing emphasis was being placed on educating readers about the real meaning of the Gospel and encouraging Christians frustrated by institutional religion to remain committed.

The difficulty of accomplishing these purposes through the use of satire was painfully acknowledged by Yaconelli in his editorial, ''Satire Is Risky Business'':

One cannot satirize with integrity without loving those whom he satirizes. The satirist must be able to feel the pain that satire causes. . . . There have been so many times when I have come to this typewriter and slashed at the keys in a frenzy of anger and hostility,

never once sensing the pain of those affected by these words. That doesn't mean that
many of the words did not need to be said. It simply means that if I am not willing to
experience the pain my words cause, I have no right to say them.[8]

Risky business indeed!

But this magazine has been able to walk that thin line with varying degrees
of success for twenty-five years. The major vehicles for accomplishing these
purposes are the same ones with which the editors began: articles and interviews,
cartoons and features, editorials and reviews, and letters to the editor. The interview has always been the mainstay of the publication. Every issue since the
beginning has had "The *Door* Interview," and the list of those interviewed
reads like a "Who's Who" of contemporary Christendom and beyond. Subjects
have included Billy Graham and Mark Hatfield; authors such as Madeleine
L'Engle, Malcolm Muggeridge, Calvin Miller, and Walter Wangerin; and theologians like Martin Marty and Henri Nouwen. The list was not limited to
evangelical Christians. Malcolm Boyd, the gay-activist Episcopal priest, was
included, as was Maggie Kuhn of the Gray Panthers and authors Richard Selzer
and Neil Postman. Indeed, the magazine even interviewed Rienhold Niebuhr
posthumously, using quotes from his writing as responses to the questions. There
are relatively few articles as such in the magazine, but it has attracted such
notable contributors as Frederick Buechner, Robert Capon, and Thomas Howard.

A significant amount of space is given in each issue to letters received in
response to given issues. Each issue has a theme such as "Marriage and the
Ministry," "Jocks for Jesus," "Charismatics," or "Preachers." More recent
issues address current themes such as "Counseling," "Co-Dependency," and
"The Men's Movement." Particular issues would yield a huge response in the
mail with both accolades and irate demands for cancellation of subscriptions.
The issue on "Sex," whose cover featured a couple in bed over which hung a
picture of a blindfolded Jesus, resulted in such an outcry that critical letters to
the editor were published in several successive issues. Sometimes the editors
would comment on letters, but often the mere publication of a letter would serve
the purpose of holding a mirror up to Christian Churches better than any comment could.

A major feature of the magazine almost since its inception has been the award
of "The Loser of the Month." In each issue the editors present "the coveted
Green Weenie" to that person or organization that best illustrates the foolishness
in which Christian Churches sometimes engage. The *Door* has never had to go
searching far for potential winners. The network of admirers and subscribers
apparently sends the magazine an ample number of candidates from which the
editors choose. Most often the award goes to an average aberration in the Christian subculture, such as a chapel decorated completely with likenesses of the
Precious Moments figurines, or the Church that offered a money-back guarantee
on tithing. Sometimes, however, the "Loser of the Month" would be a major
figure like Robert Schuller. The *Door* awarded him the "green weenie" for

building the Crystal Cathedral while pointing out what else could have been done with the fifteen million dollars that was spent on the building.

Various other features have come and gone throughout the history of the magazine. "Truth Is Stranger Than Fiction" is a collection of real—albeit bizarre—advertisements, such as the enticement to come to church to see the minister kiss a pig, or the ad for Jasper the singing dog who was available for children's ministries. "News Briefs" are hypothetical stories of whimsical news events, but the "Not So Good News Department" contains excerpts from real newspaper stories from the bizarre to the frightening. "The *Door* Dare" is a challenge to readers to respond to a request such as "Take a photo of someone asleep in church" or "Send us the goofiest thing you can find at your local Christian bookstore." In its earlier days, the *Door* regularly reviewed music, books, and movies, sometimes Christian but most often secular offerings that were having an effect on the culture. This feature has been dropped from the magazine in recent years.

Cartoons appear regularly in the magazine, and some, such as "Pastor Biddle" and "Dogs Who Know The Lord," become regular features. There are no real advertisements in the *Door*, but occasionally they are run for hypothetical products such as "AGlow—the holy roll-on deodorant for worshippers who raise their hands during worship."

The *Door* is a magazine that set out to shine the bright lights of sanity and reason on an institution that claims to have and to proclaim the truth. It is an awesome responsibility to presume to have the truth and certainly risky business to reveal the foibles of hallowed institutions with the razor edge of wit and satire. That has been the task of the *Door*. This magazine seems to be always questioning itself just as it questions everything else, continually asking if it has outlived its usefulness or if Christian satire is just too risky a business. In a guest editorial entitled "An Unabashedly Philosophical Justification for the Existence of 'That Magazine,'" James Sennett wrote:

The *Wittenburg Door* . . . [is] a weapon in the continual struggle against arrogance. The *Door* keeps an eye on us, lest we begin to assume that we have God and truth all wrapped up and in our hip pockets. If our ideas can be stretched to the point of ridicule . . . they may be acceptable, useful, and even necessary for a given point in our growth. But we must never deify the wineskins. As long as the "Off The Wall Gang" in El Cajon is perusing our mailers and pilfering our sacred cows, we will seldom be so tempted. (The threat of a "Green Weenie" is the greatest guardian of orthodoxy since the Spanish Inquisition.)[9]

Notes

1. *Wittenburg Door*, no. 31 (June–July 1976): 16.
2. Ibid., no. 61 (June–July 1981): 44.
3. Ibid., p. 11.
4. Ibid., no. 31 (June–July 1976): 7–13.

5. Ibid.
6. Ibid., no. 61 (June–July 1981): 3.
7. Ibid.
8. Ibid., no. 88 (December 1985–January 1986): 31.
9. Ibid., no. 87 (October–November 1985): 5.

Information Sources

INDEX SOURCES: There is no comprehensive index. Each issue contains its own partial
    index. Every five years the magazine does a somewhat whimsical retrospective,
    listing each issue and its highlights for the preceding five years.
LOCATION SOURCES: Copies of all issues are available from Youth Specialties, 1224
    Greenfield Drive, El Cajon, California 92021.

Publication History

MAGAZINE TITLE AND TITLE CHANGES: *Wittenburg Door* (1971–1989), *Door*
    (1989–present).
VOLUME AND ISSUE DATA: 1 (June–July 1971)–present. Usually published bi-
    monthly. Numbered by issue; no volume numbers are used.
PUBLISHER AND PLACE OF PUBLICATION: Youth Specialties, 1224 Greenfield
    Drive, El Cajon, California 92021.
EDITORS: Denny Rydberg (1972–1979), Mike Yaconelli (1979–1987), Mike Yaconelli
    and Bob Darden (1987–present).
CIRCULATION: 23,000 (1980s); 9,000 (1993).

Richard A. Morrow

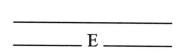

E

EDGE. *See* WALTHER LEAGUE MESSENGER

ENSIGN OF THE CHURCH OF JESUS CHRIST OF LATTER-DAY SAINTS

> You have no idea what it means to our family so many miles away from
> Church headquarters to receive the *Ensign*. It was so thrilling to discuss in
> this week's family home evening this last issue and the general conference
> talks given by our prophets.

This letter, like many from around the world that pour into the magazine
offices of the Church of Jesus Christ of Latter-day Saints (LDS) (Salt Lake City,
Utah), is significant in what it says about the nature of Latter-day Saints, their
Church, and members' relationship to the *Ensign*, their monthly magazine established in 1971. Latter-day Saints, or Mormons, believe that they are led by
a modern prophet, the president of the church, as well as by other living prophets. These leaders constitute the church's First Presidency (the president and his
counselors) and Quorum of the Twelve Apostles.

Consequently, the *Ensign*'s purpose is to provide a means for English-
speaking Mormons worldwide to receive timely counsel from their prophet-
leaders. Two of the twelve monthly issues (May and November) are devoted to
reporting the news and the complete texts of the thirty or more addresses given
at each of the Church's April and October general conferences. These conferences are held in Salt Lake City's tabernacle on Temple Square and are broadcast by satellite to more than three thousand chapels in the United States and
Canada and sent worldwide by videotape to all other Church units. These twice-
yearly *Ensign*s, liberally apportioned with photographs of the conferences, av-

erage 112 pages. The other ten issues yearly, each 80-pages long, reflect a diverse editorial format designed to meet the needs of members and the Church.

Surveys show that the most widely read article is the lead "First Presidency" message, written monthly by one of the three members of the "First Presidency." This high readership stems from the use of the "First Presidency" message in a monthly activity that takes place among Mormons. Each Mormon family is assigned two lay male home teachers, and each woman is assigned two female visiting teachers as well, from their ward or Church branch. The male home teachers visit member families monthly and discuss the "First Presidency" message with them. The female visiting teachers come to homes monthly to talk with women about an *Ensign* "Visiting Teacher" message. Thus, the *Ensign* provides material that is brought monthly into LDS homes to guide Mormons relative to Church teaching on spiritual and temporal matters.

In addition to these well-used features, *Ensign* readers are presented monthly with more than twenty-five other articles in their ten nonconference issues that include discussions of Church scripture and doctrine; pieces on marriage, parenting, and the challenges facing single adults; the "Mormon Journal" (with its first-person accounts of members' applying doctrinal principles in everyday life); pieces on social issues; articles on Mormon history; stories that showcase LDS-produced artwork; pieces designed to serve as resources for missionary work and to spur family history research; and Church-related news.

Each January *Ensign* features articles discussing the Scripture that Church members are asked to study that year. This Churchwide scriptural study activity rotates quadrennially among the Bible, the *Book of Mormon*, as well as two other volumes regarded as "scripture" by Mormons, namely, the *Doctrine and Covenants* and the *Pearl of Great Price*. Each December *Ensign* features an index to assist members in selecting articles from the year's issues for their weekly Church-encouraged family home evening discussions on doctrinal teachings and daily life. Surveys report that 86 percent of *Ensign* subscribers read more than half of each magazine, with 15 percent reading less than half.

With a 1994 circulation of 680,000 among English-speaking readers, including audiocassette and Braille editions, the *Ensign* is one of the world's most widely circulated denominationally produced magazines, with subscriptions increasing annually at about 3 percent. Articles from the *Ensign* are also translated into more than thirty other languages, with a combined non-English circulation of 250,000 (1994). These non-English LDS magazines, collectively known to Mormons as the "International Magazines," contain a selection of articles from the *Ensign*; the *New Era*, an LDS monthly for teens; and the *Friend*, a Church-produced monthly for children. The *Ensign* carries no advertising, but is self-sustaining from its subscription income (in 1993, ten dollars annually). The leadership of each local Church unit annually conducts, at no expense to the magazine, a campaign among local Church members to secure subscriptions.

The *Ensign* was formed in 1971 when the "First Presidency" amalgamated several English-speaking periodicals that had their roots in LDS Church history.

Between 1830 and the 1840s, Joseph Smith and his followers moved from New York to Ohio, Missouri, and then Illinois, seeking to build a latter-day community of Zion. The Mormons arrived in Utah in 1847 and established the region they called Deseret. Three years later the *Deseret News* was established in Salt Lake City as a daily newspaper. As years advanced, the *Deseret News* increasingly served secular functions for the Utah Territory. Consequently, monthly publications were created for purposes of religious instruction: the *Juvenile Instructor* for Sunday-school teachers in 1866, the *Woman's Exponent* in 1876, the *Young Woman's Journal* in 1889, the *Improvement Era* for young adult males in 1897, and the *Children's Friend* in 1902. These magazines or their journalistic posterity merged in 1971 to create the present *Ensign* for adult members, *New Era* for youth, and *Friend* for children. Since 1971, the *Ensign* has undergone continuous refinement but has not changed in purpose. It remains the worldwide English-magazine voice of the Church of Jesus Christ of Latter-day Saints.

Information Sources

INDEX SOURCES: Self-indexed in the December issue each year.
LOCATION SOURCES: Available from the Church Historical Department, Church of Jesus Christ of Latter-day Saints, Salt Lake City, Utah 84150.

Publication History

MAGAZINE TITLE: *Ensign* (1971–present).
VOLUME AND ISSUE DATA: 1:1 (1971)–present. Published monthly.
PUBLISHER AND PLACE OF PUBLICATION: Corporation of the President of The Church of Jesus Christ of Latter-day Saints, 50 East North Temple Street, Salt Lake City, Utah 84150.
EDITORS: Doyle L. Green (1971–1976), Dean L. Larsen (1976–1978), James E. Faust (1978–1979), M. Russell Ballard (1979–1984), Carlos E. Asay (1984–1986), Joseph B. Wirthlin (1986), Hugh W. Pinnock (1987–1989), Rex D. Pinegar (1989–present), Joe J. Christensen (1993–present).
CIRCULATION: 680,000 (1994).

Jay M. Todd

EPISCOPALIAN. *See* SPIRIT OF MISSIONS

ETERNITY

After a serious dispute in mid–1949 with the Board of Directors of *Revelation* magazine, Donald Grey Barnhouse (1895–1960), fundamentalist pastor of the prestigious Tenth Presbyterian Church of Philadelphia and world-renowned biblical expositor, relinquished his position as editor of *Revelation*, a post he had held since the monthly's inception in January 1931. Barnhouse grieved the

forfeiture of the national publication he had helped to found, and many readers
mourned the loss of their inspirational journalist-minister. Devoid of its powerful
animating spirit, the circulation of *Revelation* quickly evaporated; and by early
1950, it folded. For his part, Barnhouse launched a new monthly magazine in
April 1950 entitled *Eternity*, which was also published in Philadelphia at a rate
of three dollars per year but which had a larger paid circulation (almost fifteen
thousand) than its predecessor.[1]

Eternity thus represented *Revelation* resuscitated, with few changes in appearance or format and absolutely no transformation in its strict editorial policy
of advocating conservative Protestant theology and practice. *Eternity*, like its
forerunner, consisted of forty-eight pages, but it was appreciably smaller in size
(10¾-by-8½ inches versus 11¾-by-8¾ inches), its pages possessed a new
glossy finish, and occasional black-and-white photos augmented the former standard of clip art illustrations. With the exception of religious instruction specifically for young people, *Eternity* resumed its predecessor's format. This included
lengthy editorials, sermons, Bible studies, Sunday-school lessons, devotional
meditations, prophecy studies, news of religious events from around the world,
book reviews, and feature articles by some of the most famous fundamentalists
of the day, such as Oswald J. Smith, G. Campbell Morgan, Vance Havner,
Wilbur M. Smith, Harold J. Ockenga, Merrill F. Unger, and *Eternity*'s celebrated
editor, Donald Grey Barnhouse. As he had with *Revelation*, Barnhouse tightly
controlled the ideological slant of *Eternity* and maintained a firm adherence to
Protestant orthodoxy during his tenure as editor from 1950 until his death in
November 1960. In fact, *Eternity* was such an expression of Barnhouse that it
is impossible to speak responsibly about the magazine during its first formative
decade without consideration of its founder and his thought.

Barnhouse imbibed traditional Protestant beliefs and practices early. Born on
28 March 1895 to devout Methodist parents in Watsonville, California, he
earned degrees from the Los Angeles Bible Institute (now Biola University) and
Eastern Baptist Theological Seminary. He also attended the University of Chicago, Princeton Theological Seminary, the University of Grenoble (France), and
the University of Pennsylvania. From 1919 to 1921, he labored as a missionary
with the Belgian Gospel Mission. He later pastored two Philadelphia churches:
Grace Presbyterian Church from 1925 to 1927 and Tenth Presbyterian Church
from 1927 to 1960. In addition, throughout his forty-one year ministry, he spoke
at many fundamentalist Bible conferences around the world, preached regularly
over hundreds of radio stations, taught religion occasionally on national television, wrote over a dozen books, and published hundreds of journal articles, most
of them in *Revelation* and *Eternity*.[2]

His theology consisted of a complex mixture of modified dispensationalism,
Calvinism, and fundamentalism.[3] Barnhouse studied dispensationalism at the
Los Angeles Bible Institute under such notable proponents as Reuben A. Torrey,
Arno C. Gaebelein, and Cyrus I. Scofield. He selectively appropriated some of
its major components into his doctrinal system—embracing, for example, the

ideas of the pretribulational rapture of the Church and the premillennial return of Jesus but rejecting the notion of God's changing and conditional covenants with humankind. *Eternity* offered a regular column as well as many feature articles on biblical prophecy and the interpretation of current world events in light of scriptural "predictions." The Reformed theological underpinnings in Barnhouse's thought can be traced to his two years of graduate study at Princeton Theological Seminary from 1915 to 1917. Under the tutelage of professors such as Benjamin B. Warfield, Robert D. Wilson, and John Davis, Barnhouse warmly embraced Calvinistic notions of the sovereignty of God, human spiritual depravity, and divine election. In Barnhouse's words, his Calvinism basically emphasized "man's complete ruin in sin and God's perfect remedy in Christ."[4] As a lifelong minister in the Presbyterian Church in the United States of America, Barnhouse steadfastly supported its hallmark doctrinal affirmation, the Westminster confession of faith. His fundamentalism grew out of his personal study of Scripture that stressed a highly literal program of interpretation. As a consequence, he adamantly underscored not only the authority of Scripture as the only standard for a Christian's faith and practice, but also the plenary (full) inspiration of the Old and New Testaments. Such Calvinistic and fundamentalist teachings suffused the pages of *Eternity* during Barnhouse's term as editor.

The combination of these three conservative Protestant theological systems by Barnhouse was manifested in corresponding public or social policies in *Eternity*. In general, the magazine advocated the evangelization of American society and the world, rather than its Christianization, suggesting that the dispensational premillennial worldview prevailed against Calvinistic notions of church and culture. Traditional family values and patriarchy were enthusiastically affirmed, and divorce and women's ordination opposed. Communism was a frequent target of attack, but the magazine's writers often considered anticommunists more hazardous than their opponents. Anti-Catholicism was a prevalent theme, especially during John F. Kennedy's successful presidential campaign in 1960. *Eternity* maintained a strong position of support for Israel and its right to self-rule in Palestine as a condition for America's future favor with God and as a precursor of the restoration of the kingdom of God. Racism was scorned as inimical to God's purposes, and the magazine displayed progressive attitudes toward full legal justice on civil-rights issues. Surprisingly, *Eternity* spoke sympathetically of Pentecostalism, usually an anathema for fundamentalists of the time. Not surprising, however, were the magazine's frequent assaults upon religious liberalism and its advocacy of separation from such elements. Yet, after Barnhouse published his New Year's resolution of 1953, this characteristically fundamentalist trait of exclusion mellowed somewhat in the pages of *Eternity*.[5] In his personal decree, Barnhouse pledged to be less disputatious and more cooperative with religious adversaries in the future. Consequently, ecumenism received less caustic coverage as an evangelical or nonseparatist tone began to emerge from the magazine. However, this was not so much a doctrinal change as one of social practice. Theologically, *Eternity* continued to be—without apology—a Reformed, fundamentalist, and semidispensationalist journal.

During the Barnhouse era, *Eternity* absorbed the readership of three declining fundamentalist-evangelical magazines: in 1954, the *Christian Newsette*; in 1956, the *Christian Digest*; and in 1958, Arno C. Gaebelein's fervently premillennial *Our Hope*. Nevertheless, circulation fell precipitously after 1956. Thousands of readers cancelled their subscriptions in protest of *Eternity*'s sometimes unfashionable or unpredictable editorial views, such as the endorsement of Seventh-Day Adventism as an orthodox Christian denomination and the unusual support for Mao's domestic policies in China.[6]

Modest but significant changes in the midst of continuity characterized Russell T. Hitt's tenure as editor of *Eternity* from 1960–1975. Hitt was a former editor of *Christian Life* magazine and author of the best-seller *Jungle Pilot*, a biography of the twentieth-century missionary-martyr Nate Saint. Minor alterations in fiscal policy, appearance, and format evolved slowly. Subscription rates went from four dollars to seven dollars for twelve monthly issues with a concomitant increase in the average number of pages from forty-eight to sixty-four. Its size remained unchanged and would continue unaltered until the magazine's demise. Black-and-white feature photos remained the norm, with occasional color advertisements. Articles and columns shrank in length and number to accommodate greater advertising and illustrative art work. Bible and prophecy studies, Sunday-school lessons, and devotional-inspirational pieces became rare. New annual features arose. In the mid–1960s, a yearly "summer sampler" appeared in each July issue, featuring a potpourri of important selections from Christian literature. And in 1968, an annual survey of Christian institutions of higher education became enormously popular with readers. Overall, *Eternity*'s subscribers must have been extremely pleased with these and other modifications because circulation reached an all-time high of fifty thousand in 1975.[7]

Some of these gradual "external" changes reflected more momentous transformations in the magazine's theological and social slant. Evangelical and Calvinistic emphases prevailed over the former dominant fundamentalist and dispensational proclivities. "Evangelical" rather than "fundamentalist" quickly became the magazine's label of choice. Barnhouse's earlier softening of separatist rhetoric after 1953 was accelerated as *Eternity* sympathized with the Jesus movement, the charismatic renewal, and interfaith cooperative efforts among conservatives. Bland disdain for religious liberals and ecumenism continued but with increasing restraint. Toward the late 1960s, even *Eternity*'s previous anti-Catholicism diminished. Reformed views of church and society, which traditionally called for the direct and active engagement of culture by the church, displaced earlier dispensationalist notions of the abandonment of cultural institutions in favor of purely ecclesiastical work. There was a proliferation of articles on the religious interpretation of "secular" topics of the time, such as nuclear weapons, American foreign aid, the civil-rights movement, Vietnam, capital punishment, the countercultural revolution of the 1960s, and Watergate.

In sum, *Eternity* during this time moved increasingly toward mainstream Reformed evangelicalism and sought to apply aggressively "all of God's Word to all of life"—a masthead slogan that appeared at the end of Hitt's term as editor, but which summarizes the enormous changes in the magazine's theological and social outlook of the previous fifteen years.[8]

William J. Petersen, who served as editor from 1975–1986, and James Montgomery Boice, who succeeded him in 1987 as *Eternity*'s fourth and final editor, continued this evangelical Calvinistic orientation, stressing the church and its impact upon culture. Two topical trends appeared with greater frequency after 1975. Petersen, who had served since 1958 under both Barnhouse and Hitt as managing editor and executive editor, expanded *Eternity*'s global coverage of Christianity. Frequent features of religious news and missions activities in Latin America, Africa, Asia, and Europe related those and other international developments to American readers. Another trend was the increased attention to evangelical participation in politics, especially at the national level, reflecting the rise of the religious Right during the 1970s and 1980s. Boice, a successor of sorts to Barnhouse as pastor of Tenth Presbyterian in Philadelphia and speaker for the Bible Study Hour radio broadcast, assumed editorial responsibilities of *Eternity* as its circulation dwindled (from 50,000 in 1975 to 35,500 in 1987) and its subscription costs spiraled (from $7 in 1975 to $18.90 in 1987). In an effort to save expenses and boost revenues, Petersen had combined the July and August issues beginning in 1980 and initiated a bond sale in Pennsylvania in 1983. In order to stave off extinction, *Eternity* announced at the start of Boice's tenure a "repositioning" of its topical focus without compromising its Calvinistic doctrinal integrity.[9] The magazine endeavored to devote itself to Christian commentary on the secular news and cultural trends of the times. The venture to create a more secure niche for *Eternity* in the competitive American market of Christian periodicals, however, ultimately failed. The magazine succumbed in January 1989, a casualty of ever-increasing costs, especially postal expenses, and of continually shrinking circulation despite a 21 percent reduction in its subscription rate.

Notes

1. *Eternity* 1 (April 1950): 13; see also William J. Petersen, "Twenty-Five Years of Eternity," *Eternity* 26 (April 1975): 12–13.

2. Ronald Thomas Sexton, "A Critical Examination of the Preaching of Donald Grey Barnhouse" (Th.D. diss., New Orleans Baptist Theological Seminary, 1984).

3. See C. Allyn Russell, "Donald Grey Barnhouse: Fundamentalist Who Changed," *Journal of Presbyterian History* 59 (Spring 1981): 33–57.

4. Ibid., p.41.

5. See the inside front cover, *Eternity* 4 (January 1953).

6. *Eternity* 9 (January 1958): 2, 5; see also Donald Grey Barnhouse, "Postscript on Seventh-Day Adventism," *Eternity* 8 (November 1957): 22ff., 47ff.

7. See William J. Petersen, "The Magazine That Lived," *Eternity* 26 (May 1975): 22–24, 64–65.

8. Ibid. 25 (January 1974): 11.

9. Ibid. 37 (December 1986): 9.

Information Sources

INDEX SOURCES: A complete index for each volume can be found at the back of the year's December issue. No general or multiyear occasional index was published.

LOCATION SOURCES: All volumes can be located at the Library of Congress, Princeton Theological Seminary, the State Historical Society of Wisconsin (Madison), Concordia Seminary (St. Louis), Wheaton College (Illinois), Westminster Theological Seminary (Philadelphia), and Fuller Theological Seminary (Pasadena, California).

Publication History

MAGAZINE TITLE: *Eternity* (April 1950–January 1989).

VOLUME AND ISSUE DATA: 1:1 (April 1950)–40:1 (January 1989). Published monthly, except 1980–1988 when the July and August issues were combined.

PUBLISHER AND PLACE OF PUBLICATION: Evangelical Foundation, Philadelphia (April 1950–January 1977), Evangelical Ministries, Philadelphia (February 1977–May 1988), Foundation for Christian Living, Pawling (New York) and Philadelphia (June 1988–January 1989).

EDITORS: Donald Grey Barnhouse (editor, 1950–1953; editor in chief, 1953–60), Russell T. Hitt (executive editor, 1953–1960, editor, 1961–1975), William J. Petersen (editor, May 1975–February 1986), James Montgomery Boice (editor, January 1987–January 1989).

CIRCULATION: 15,000 (1950); 20,000 (1953); 35,000 (1956); 30,000 (1960); 50,000 (1975); 48,000 (1979); 39,000 (1985); and 35,500 (1987).

Michael T. Girolimon

EVANGELICAL BEACON

In understanding the history of the *Evangelical Beacon,* it is useful to modify a sentiment expressed by the *Evangelical Beacon*'s first editor, Roy A. Thompson, namely, that it is inconceivable that any such movement as the Evangelical Free Church could have existed apart from the influence of its publications.[1] Indeed, the best sources on the history of the Evangelical Free Church (EFC) of America are the Norwegian-Danish Free Church publications, the *Evangelisten* and *Evangelist*, and the Swedish Free Church *Chicago-Bladet* and *Evangelical Beacon*. Both the *Evangelist* and the *Evangelical Beacon* are the English-language children of their immigrant language parents (*Evangelisten* and *Chicago-Bladet*).

The founders of the EFC were immigrants from Sweden, Norway, and Denmark. They brought the traditions, beliefs, and memories of their religious experiences in their respective countries to the United States after the American Civil War. Victor L. Walter has identified four "springs" within these immigrants from which the "distinctly American Evangelical Free Church" would arise.[2] First, the immigrants gathered in homes for Bible reading as a protest against the "dead orthodoxy" of the state Lutheran churches (in Scandinavia). Second, they were caught up in the pietist movement from the University of Halle that surged from Helsinki to Civil War America. Third, they were warmed by the revival fires of the Moravian Brethren and Methodist groups. Fourth, they were part of the political, economic, and religious ferment that was unleashed upon the shores of the United States.[3]

To this list, one other "spring" is important for understanding the birth of the *Evangelical Beacon*. Regarding the Scandinavian immigrants and members of the Evangelical Free Church of America, Dr. Roy A. Thompson has commented: "Their appreciation of good Christian literature and their absorption with it were responsible for the nickname often given them. They were *lasare* (readers), identified with the 'Readers' Movement,' which was well known in the 17th and 18th centuries in the Scandinavian countries."[4]

The founding date for the EFC is arbitrarily considered to be 1884.[5] By then, groups of Scandinavian believers had collected themselves into local church fellowships in the United States. In particular, Swedish immigrant farmers in the Illinois, Iowa, and Nebraska corn and livestock belt sent delegates from twenty fellowships to Boone, Iowa, to convene from 14 to 19 October 1884. The conference, initiated by the *Chicago-Bladet*, a Swedish-language newspaper, discussed the Bible's view of the Church. That same year the first two Norwegian-Danish Free Church congregations were founded by Norwegian sailor families on opposite sides of the continent in two of America's harbor cities—Tacoma (Washington) and Boston. "So 1884, the official founding date, tells us two things—the EFC began spontaneously in two streams defined and separated by language."[6] It would be from these Swedish and Norwegian-Danish roots that the *Evangelical Beacon* would emerge in 1931.

Three years (1887) after this first conference, the Swedish group of Free Churches voted to commission H. J. Von Qualen as missionary to China and commended him to the churches for support. The Swedish Free Churches began calling themselves the "Swedish Evangelical Free Church" in 1890. The following year, the meeting in Chicago of the Norwegian-Danish group of Free Churches began the formation of what they were to call the "Western Association" to aid ministry and fellowship among groups in the western and eastern United States. This began the Free Church tendency to work through districts. In 1894, the Swedish Evangelical Free Church formed a national ministerial association. Also at that time, the pattern of ordination was established—with sponsorship by local church, district examination, national ministerial approval, and ordination by the district with the local church.[7]

Thirteen years (1897) after the Boone conference, the Swedish group set up the first formal school for the training of converts and Christian workers. Meeting at Oak Street Hall in Chicago, the subject matter was the Bible. This and the earlier (1884) Norwegian-Danish department at Chicago Theological Seminary were the forerunners of the present Trinity Evangelical Divinity School and Trinity College. In 1908, the Women's Missionary Society of the EFC was founded by Josephine Princell as the Free Church Missionary Society (in the Swedish group). One year later (1909), the Norwegian-Danish Free Churches reversed their decision to be two regional associations and formed a single organization. As part of that union, they adopted the first American Free Church statement of faith. Until 1919, national and regional-conference credentialing had been based on voluntary contributions to the associations or missions programs. Formerly membership and voting rights in the associations was of individuals; now, it would be of congregations. That year, the Eastern Association of the Norwegian-Danish group voted to base credentialing on delegates elected by individual congregations.[8]

Although efforts toward union were officially undertaken as early as 1935, in 1950 there was a merger of the Evangelical Free Church Association (Norwegian-Danish) led by President E. A. Halleen and the Evangelical Free Church of America (Swedish) led by Arnold T. Olson. At the merger, the Swedish name was taken, and E. A. Halleen was elected for a one-year term as president. It was agreed that upon Halleen's retirement, Arnold T. Olson would be president. Olson was president for the next twenty-five years.

The *Evangelical Beacon*'s history may be reviewed before the merger and after the merger. Thompson used this outline in "tracing the origin, development, and significance of the publication ministry of The Evangelical Free Church of America" throughout its first hundred years of existence (1884–1984).[9] The events in the history of the EFC have served as the ongoing content of first the Norwegian-Danish *Evangelisten* and the Swedish *Chicago-Bladet* and later of their cognate publications, the English-language *Evangelist* (Norwegian-Danish) and *Evangelical Beacon* (Swedish).

The immigrant forebears of the present *Evangelical Beacon* were the Swedish *Chicago-Bladet* (1877–1952) and the Norwegian-Danish *Evangelisten* (1890–1955). Both of these publications were published in the language of the immigrants. John Martenson, editor, outlined the content of the *Chicago-Bladet* in its premier issue: "As much news as possible concerning the progress of God's Kingdom, both in America, Sweden and other lands; also important national and international news, and news from Chicago. . . . A children's column . . . inspirational articles from well-known Christian preachers . . . which will keep the paper's content on a high spiritual level."[10]

In the first issue of the *Evangelisten*, editor R. A. Jernberg put forth the following goals for its content: "Each issue will contain two Bible lessons with commentary. A picture, as large and beautiful as the one in our initial issue will also appear. There will be short stories for children as well as something interesting and good for the whole family."[11] The *Chicago-Bladet* was started as a private publication but eventually became the official paper of the Swedish Free

Churches in 1926. The *Evangelisten* was begun as the official paper of the Norwegian-Danish Free Churches. Both would cease publication within a few years of the merger that established the EFC. However, the contents of both would live on in the *Evangelical Beacon*.

Just prior to the birth of the *Evangelical Beacon*, the English-language *Evangelist* was begun by the Norwegian-Danish Free Churches. A cousin to the *Evangelical Beacon*, the *Evangelist* began in the later 1920s as the English edition of the *Evangelisten*. In January 1930, the *Evangelist* was reborn as a separate publication of the Norwegian-Danish Free Churches.[12] The decade after World War I was a time of language transition for both the Norwegian-Danish and the Swedish Free Churches. Prior to the birth of the *Evangelical Beacon*, the Swedish Free Churches had experimented also with a Swedish- and English-section approach in the *Chicago-Bladet*. As with the *Evangelisten*, this arrangement reflected the dominance of English among the younger generations in the Free Churches. The *Evangelical Beacon* was begun as a separate English-language publication of the Swedish Free Churches in October 1931.

The role of the *Evangelical Beacon* prior to the merger of the Norwegian-Danish and Swedish Free Churches is summarized by Thompson: "We were looking forward to forthcoming events in the history of our denomination. For several years before the merger . . . there was much discussion of the subject and a considerable amount of editorializing concerning the merger, the editor [Roy A. Thompson] being a member of the merger committee and doing everything in his power to present the advantages of the merger."[13]

With remarkable unity, the Norwegian-Danish and the Swedish Free Churches merged in June of 1950. Much of the difficult task of merging schools, properties, and other ministry activities had preceded the official merger. Already by 1947 the publications of the Swedish Free Churches had been moved to Minneapolis to join the Norwegian-Danish publications.[14] While the *Evangelisten* and the *Chicago-Bladet* would continue publication for several years, the *Evangelist* and *Evangelical Beacon* merged into a single publication. Roy A. Thompson continued as editor of the combined *Evangelical Beacon and Evangelist* with Olai Urang of the *Evangelist* as associate editor. In 1958, the combined name was shortened to the *Evangelical Beacon*.

The founding editor of the *Evangelical Beacon*, Dr. Roy A. Thompson, was converted under the ministry of Pastor E. A. Halleen of the First Evangelical Free Church of Minneapolis. He was led into the field of journalism while a student at the Free Church Bible Institute and the Moody Bible Institute (Chicago). He furthered his preparation at George Washington University (Washington, D.C.), the University of Minnesota, Presbyterian Theological Seminary, and the University of Chicago. Thompson also pastored two churches in the Chicago area and was a part-time teacher at the Free Church Bible Institute.

Mel Larson was the second editor of the *Evangelical Beacon*. He joined the staff as the part-time editor of the newly added young-people's page on 28 November 1939. From the mother church of the Evangelical Free Churches in

Minnesota (First Evangelical Free Church of Minneapolis), Larson was in his last year of journalism studies at the University of Minnesota when he had suggested to Thompson the young people's page. Before taking over the editing of the *Evangelical Beacon* in 1958, Larson had edited *Youth for Christ Magazine* beginning in 1953.[15]

When Larson died of cancer, George Keck was named as acting editor. Mr. Keck had "17 years experience as editor and managing editor of the newspaper *Unit-Register* in Orland, Calif. (16 years) and now news editor of the *Central Oregonian* in Prineville, Ore. It was while editor of the paper in California that he and his wife were converted at a service in the Evangelical Free Church in Orland." His testimony appeared shortly thereafter in the *Evangelical Beacon.*[16]

Carol Madison, the present editor of the *Evangelical Beacon* was first introduced to the EFC through summer employment while she was a college student at the Beacon Bookstore located in the denominational headquarters. During her senior year at Bethel College in St. Paul, Minnesota, she worked for the *Evangelical Beacon* as an intern. Upon graduation she was hired as an editorial assistant. Three years later she transferred to the Office of Public Affairs where she headed up the division of Free Church publications. While there, she published the children's club program of the Adventure Club (now published by David C. Cook). Following George Keck's retirement, she was appointed editor of the *Evangelical Beacon*. She introduced a new magazine named *Pursuit* as a quarterly evangelistic magazine to be published instead of the *Evangelical Beacon.*[17]

The present *Evangelical Beacon* contains a half-dozen or more features, as well as departments. The features are usually thematically related within an issue. For example, the October 1993 issue followed the theme of "Profiles of Free Church Servants." The focus of the November 1993 issue is on "Mission USA," a missions strategy of the EFC. The departments are reports from the various ministry divisions of the EFC (i.e., from the president, EFC Mission, Trinity Evangelical Divinity School, and district news).

Physically, the present *Evangelical Beacon* measures 8¼ by 10¾ inches, staple-bound in a magazine format. The early issues were printed on newsprint and included line artwork and screened photographs. Color ink was introduced for covers and features during the late 1950s. In the early 1980s four-color covers began to appear. By the early 1990s, four-color printing was being employed on features. The early *Evangelical Beacon* employed a three-column format. At present, a two-column layout, often with an indented first column, is used for most features and important departments. The balance of an issue is in three-column format. However, as with the first issues, the present graphic design accommodates a variety of techniques for adding emphasis to a given feature.

In *The Dynamic of the Printed Page in EFC History*, Thompson introduced his account of Free Church publications by asking, "Are we making as much and as good use of the tremendous facilities available in *our* generation as those so-called 'primitive' Christians did nineteen hundred years ago?''[18] Quoting Edgar Goodspeed's book, *Christianity Goes to Press*, Thompson noted that the "primitive" Christians "adopted the Greek techniques of writing and publishing and made the fullest use of them in [their efforts] to spread the gospel over the ancient world.''[19] In particular, Thompson noted the early Church's adoption of the codex, or leaf-book form, and the advent of the movable-type printing press prior to the Reformation as significant events in the "pre-history" of the *Evangelical Beacon*. The adoption of modern publishing techniques was early and continual with the *Evangelical Beacon*. Thompson's challenge has continued to be answered positively with a legacy of Evangelical Press Association awards to the *Evangelical Beacon*. For example, it received an award for "Best Redesign" in 1992 for improvements over the 1991 issues. Also noteworthy is the fiftieth-anniversary issue (15 October 1981) of the *Evangelical Beacon* that was awarded the "Best Theme" citation by the Evangelical Press Association.

Summarizing the importance of the EFC's commitment to using the press, as well as the importance of the "primitive" Church and the Scandinavian forebears, Thompson commented: "Our publications have been the principal media for preserving and perpetuating the principles and purposes which have characterized our Evangelical Free Church work from the beginning.[20]

Notes

1. H. Wilbert Norton, *The Diamond Jubilee Story of the Evangelical Free Church of America* (Minneapolis, MN: Free Church Publications, 1959), 128.

2. Victor L. Walter, "Where We've Been," in *A Living Legacy: Essays on the Evangelical Free Church Movement: Past, Present and Future* (Minneapolis, MN: Free Church Publications, 1990), 20.

3. See also Arnold Theodore Olson, *Stumbling Toward Maturity* (Minneapolis, MN: Free Church Press, 1981).

4. Roy A. Thompson, *The Dynamic of the Printed Page in EFC History* (Minneapolis, MN: Free Church Press, 1981), 19.

5. Walter, "Where We've Been," 23.

6. Ibid., 24.

7. Ibid., 24–26.

8. Ibid., 26–27.

9. Thompson, *Dynamic*, 11. The before-the-merger and after-the-merger chapters were published in somewhat shortened form in the *Evangelical Beacon* (15 October 1981): 5–9. That fiftieth anniversary issue of the *Evangelical Beacon* was awarded the "Best Theme" award of the Evangelical Press Association.

10. Thompson, *Dynamic*, 150.

11. Ibid., 152.

12. Consequently, the *Evangelist* volume and issue numbering begins with 1; 1 (January 1930), although it had been previously published as the English edition of the *Evangelisten*.

13. Thompson, *Dynamic*, 38.

14. Norton, *Diamond Jubilee Story*, 232.

15. Ibid., 41–43.

16. Ibid., 57–58.

17. Interview with Carol Madison, 18 June 1993.

18. Thompson, *Dynamic*, 14.

19. Thompson, *Dynamic*, 12–13. See also Edgar Johnson Goodspeed, *Christianity Goes to Press* (New York: Macmillan, 1940).

20. Thompson, *Dynamic*, 166.

Information Sources

INDEX SOURCES: Each volume contains its own partial index. Neither a general index nor a comprehensive index has been compiled.

LOCATION SOURCES: The only complete set of all volumes is collected at the Evangelical Free Church of America corporate offices, 901 East 78th Street, Minneapolis, Minnesota 55420–1300.

A mostly intact collection of volumes is available at the Rolfing Library, Trinity Evangelical Divinity School.

Publication History

MAGAZINE TITLE AND TITLE CHANGES: *Evangelical Beacon* (1931–1950), *Evangelical Beacon and Evangelist* (1950–1958), *Evangelical Beacon* (1958–present).

VOLUME AND ISSUE DATA: Weekly publication began with 1:1 (6 October 1931); biweekly publication began with 37:32 (12 May 1964); triweekly publication began with 58:20 (2 September 1985); monthly publication began with 63:15 (1 September 1990). Throughout its publication history the *Evangelical Beacon* has often reduced the number of issues published during the summer months (July, August, and September). Publication was reduced to eight issues per year with 65:6 (May 1992). Publication remains monthly except for March, June, September, and December when *Pursuit*, a quarterly evangelistic magazine, is published instead of the *Evangelical Beacon*.

PUBLISHER AND PLACE OF PUBLICATION: Evangelical Free Church of America, 901 East 78th Street, Minneapolis, Minnesota 55420–1300.

EDITORS: Roy A. Thompson (1931–1957), Mel Larson (1958–1972), George Keck (1973–June 1990), Carol Madison (July 1990-present).

CIRCULATION: 33,302 (August 1993); largest to date was 39,919 (November 1985) prior to the separate publication of the *Canadian Evangelical Beacon*.

Ronald A. Johnson

EVANGELICAL BEACON AND EVANGELIST. *See* EVANGELICAL BEACON

EVANGELICAL FRIEND

Quakers—sometimes known as the Society of Friends, the Friends Church, or, simply, "Friends"—emerged in mid-seventeenth-century England in the seedbed of radical Puritanism. Their belief in the possibility and necessity of inward revelation, most often referred to as the "inward light of Christ," which drew persons into a right relationship to God, became a key to interpretation of the Bible and provided motivation and power to live a holy life (sanctification or "perfection"). From the start, the Quaker approach to the understanding and practice of Christianity involved implications for their style of life, dress, business dealings, and language use. For example, the well-known early Quaker pronominal usage (the refusal to use "you" in the singular and the substitution of "thee" or "thou") was not only a more truthful and grammatically accurate linguistic choice, but was also a sign of Quaker insistence on not using any symbolic form that imparted unmerited pride or promoted vainglory. "Plain speech" and other spiritually motivated cultural patterns of behavior set a Quaker apart from the rest of society, and consequently persecution became very common during the early years of Quakerism.

During their first fifty years, Quakers were a Christocentric sect with radically evangelistic goals and missionary fervor, sometimes referring to their venture as "primitive Christianity revived." They not only embraced oral rhetoric in the form of impromptu preaching to members and potential converts, but they also embraced the relatively new print technology. They enthusiastically entered the tract and pamphlet wars of seventeenth-century England and her colonies, producing 2,678 separate publications within their initial seven decades.[1] During later "quietistic" periods, Friends tended to withdraw from the world—at least they renounced the impulse to evangelize—and the American component of Quakerism was rocked with several major and minor schisms, the most sociologically and theologically significant known as the "Hicksite separation" of 1827. Nineteenth-century Quaker schisms had an enormous effect on the subsequent development of American Quakerism into virtually autonomous, but more recently communicative and cordial, groupings of Friends into separate "yearly meetings" that resembled a tree with an exceedingly complex branch structure but with common roots in seventeenth-century England. The early Quaker whole-hearted adoption of the printing press has a contemporary manifestation in the vitality of several contemporary Quaker book and pamphlet publishing houses and three popular religious magazines—*Friends Journal*, *Quaker Life*, and *Evangelical Friend*—which represent the three largest American Friends bodies and, thus, a spectrum of social and theological thought across the landscape of American Quakerism. *Friends Journal* speaks for the nearly 32,000-member Friends General Conference, the main organization of "Hicksite" Friends, who emphasize "the example of Christ and the 'inner light' which, if followed, is deemed to enable the believer to live in conformity to the will of God. The Hicksites de-emphasize attempts to win converts and champion unprogrammed meetings based upon waiting for divine guidance."[2] *Quaker Life* is the main publication of the 55,000-member Friends United Meeting, which is largely evangelical in theology and supports a wide, but not universal, paid pastoral ministry. *Evangelical Friend* represents the more than 26,000-member

Evangelical Friends International (North America Region), the branch of Quakers who stress the necessity of personal salvation, belief in the deity of Christ, the promotion of revivalism and missions, the development of a professional and paid pastorate, and who most often call themselves, collectively, a "Church."[3]

Evangelical Friend has its roots in the deliberations of the Association of Evangelical Friends (AEF) (1927), a loosely organized group of theologically conservative Quakers who became an expression of "evangelical resistance to certain theologically liberal positions within the Friends United Meeting."[4] As early as the initial 1927 conference in Cheyenne, Wyoming, AEF conferees unanimously concluded that there was a compelling need for "a church periodical that would be faithful to the doctrines and standards as held by evangelical Friends in North America."[5] However, because of sectional disputes and other pressing problems, the project did not even begin to materialize until the third AEF conference held in Oskaloosa, Iowa, in 1954, when conferees agreed to publish a quarterly entitled *Missionary Voice of Evangelical Friends* to help publicize their missionary efforts.

By 1965, the Evangelical Friends Alliance, a new organization that provided an umbrella structure for four cooperating yearly meetings (Ohio, Rocky Mountain, Kansas, and Oregon), had become a reality, existing for a time concurrently with the AEF, which finally disbanded in 1970, having accomplished its essential objective of Quaker renewal.[6] Talk of a unified magazine for evangelical Friends actually had begun to emerge at the first Coordinating Council meeting of the Evangelical Friends Alliance in 1963.[7] Finally, in 1967, the forty-year-old dream of the Cheyenne Conference of the venerable Association of Evangelical Friends was fulfilled when the Evangelical Friends Alliance initiated a joint magazine entitled *Evangelical Friend*. Initially a twenty-four–page monthly magazine, the new publication incorporated AEF's *Missionary Voice* and the individual periodicals of the four yearly meetings: *Northwest Friend* (Oregon Yearly Meeting, now Northwest Yearly Meeting), *Southwest Friend* (Kansas Yearly Meeting, now Mid-America Yearly Meeting), *Rocky Mountain Friend* (Rocky Mountain Yearly Meeting), and *Evangelical Friend* (Ohio Yearly Meeting, now Evangelical Friends Church-Eastern Region). The magazine's budget was built on the combined budgets of the four regional publications and *Missionary Voice*. The editor was to serve without pay, but with a small stipend for expenses, a fiscal practice that has persisted through the tenures of four editors.

In his initial editorial, Dean Gregory, the magazine's first editor, expressed his determination that the magazine "be broad enough . . . to permit the discussion of every important Christian concern . . . and narrow enough to eliminate from these pages trivia, fadism, and matters of little consequence.[8] An examination of the magazine under Gregory's editorship reveals significant attainment of the balance that he sought. At the outset, *Evangelical Friend* included, in addition to editorials, a very strong emphasis on missions, with a special section called "Missionary Voice," a continuation of both the name and vision of the previous publication. In each issue the new magazine also included several brief reviews of popular-audience Christian books, original articles (most of which were devotional or sermonic in nature), articles reprinted from other evangelical publications, occasional poems (beginning with the second issue), and four separate four-page "inserts" containing news originally thought appropriate only to members of each individual yearly meeting.[9]

When Gregory assumed the added responsibility of becoming superintendent of the Kansas Yearly Meeting, Jack L. Willcuts, the former editor of *Northwest Friend*, was named executive editor, and Harlow Ankeny was named managing editor. Upon Gregory's untimely death in 1970, Willcuts began a fifteen-year tenure as editor-in-chief. Under Willcuts and Ankeny, who eventually tallied twenty-five years of editorial and managerial service to the publication, the magazine significantly matured in form and content. In 1972 the four regional "inserts" were woven into a new section of the publication and thus became a regular part of the magazine—now 28 to 32 pages in length—sent to every home in the four yearly meetings.

In the April-May 1976 issue, the magazine revealed a major design change, the brainchild of Quaker artist Paul Lewis. Harlow Ankeny wrote that Lewis advised the editorial staff to "put a new boldness in the design, adding department 'gates' into the format, and urging us to think in terms of 'grabbing' the reader and offering 'life changing' content." Also introduced in 1976, the new cartoon feature, "Mr. Quaker," provided what Ankeny epitomized as "comic relief while spoofing our Quaker traditions or gently pushing a cause," an important tradition and feature that continues in the current magazine.[10]

One of the most significant contributions during Willcuts' tenure was his own editorials, frequently insightful and sometimes brilliant in both thought and style. Willcuts, who also served as superintendent of the Northwest Yearly Meeting, became a major national and international voice for evangelical Friends and one of the best-loved twentieth-century Quaker writers and servant leaders. A selection of his editorials has recently been published.[11]

Evangelical Friend again changed editors in 1986 when Willcuts retired from the position. Lon Fendall, after a year of study under the guiding hand of Willcuts, took over the reins. Fendall, a former member of Senator Mark Hatfield's Washington, D.C., staff and, at the time that he assumed the position of editor, a director of the Center for Peace Learning at George Fox College, brought a wealth of national and international experience to the task. During his four years of tenure, Fendall guided the publication through its second major design change, again with the help of Paul Lewis, and through one of the most challenging fiscal crises of the magazine's history, which resulted in the reduction of the magazine to six issues per year.

The magazine's overall content remained essentially the same under Fendall's leadership, but there were subtle changes. "The Missionary Voice" appeared irregularly as a separate feature after volume 19. There also appeared to be a discernible editorial interest in two areas. The first continued and perhaps more strongly emphasized an agenda that was set during the last half of Willcuts's tenure and that sent the magazine increasingly toward the discussion of contemporary issues with articles addressing such topics as the elderly ("Ministering in Nursing Homes," "Abuse of the Elderly"), prison ministry ("Sharing Joy Behind the Bars"), the farm crisis ("Friends and Hurting Farm Families"), and abortion ("Abortion: Not Just a Woman's Problem"). The second direction was backward toward an understanding and perhaps needed revitalization of Friends history for contemporary evangelical Quakers with the inclusion of historically oriented biographical articles ("The Struggle of Elizabeth Fry," "Thomas Chalkley and the Intervention of God") and articles that attempted to reassess contemporary evangelical Quakerism and its place both in history and in contemporary Quakerism ("Probing Questions for Quakers," "Evangelical Friends and the Richmond Declaration," "Reflections on EFA").

In his final editorial, Fendall credited the work of managing editor, Dan McCracken, who actually began his work behind the scenes on a part-time basis in 1981, for "producing a consistently high-quality magazine." Fendall also warned that "the survival of the magazine will depend on maintaining its high quality in content and appearance." He urged readers, perhaps with an evaluative backward glance to the quality of submissions received during his tenure, to give the new editor "the best of your writing (not just the articles that might not get published somewhere else)."[12]

In 1990 Paul Anderson took over as editor-in-chief. Described by Fendall as a man "superbly qualified to serve the magazine, with his demonstrated skills as a communicator" and as a person who "understands evangelical Friends and Quakers in general as well as anyone alive today," Anderson seemed an appropriate person to wear the mantle passed on by Dean Gregory and Company.[13] Thus far in his brief tenure, Anderson has continued writing insightful editorials, but has also opted to write an article for an issue instead of an editorial. His main innovation, though, has been the development of thematically oriented issues. Two recent issues are good examples. The January-February 1993 issue dealt with humor and included articles with such titles as "Funny Things Happen on the Way to the Cemetery," "Comic Reversal and Cosmic Reversal," and "Humor as a Survival Tactic." Anderson contributed an editorial entitled "A God Who Laughs . . . and Weeps." The March-April 1993 issue dealt with evil, including articles with the following titles: "Naming Evil and Doing Good," "Structural Evil," "The End of Pacifism," and "The Lamb's War."

The magazine still includes book reviews, news of Friends in the four-member yearly meetings, letters to the editor, and articles of the devotional or sermonic variety. The dominating missions emphasis of the magazine's earliest years has given way to a balance of contemporary problem orientation and traditional evangelical missionary zeal. The original several-page section with the title "Missionary Voice" is now a one-page feature titled "Our Friends Missionary Outreach." In addition, a reader may encounter an occasional article dealing with the various missionary efforts of evangelical Friends or news items relevant to Friends mission fields in a regular new feature titled "Hot Off the FAX."

Through the writing, editing and leadership skills of four editors over twenty-six years, *Evangelical Friend* has emerged as a respected denominational magazine. The publication has both influenced and reflected the tensions and polarities sensed among and between the four yearly meetings that are its constituency and the larger intellectual and spiritual geography of American Quakerism. Harlow Ankeny accurately captured the magazine's present position with regard to its readership in these words: "It is not so much an 'official' organ of EFA as it is a reflection of new unity among Friends internationally."[14]

Notes

1. Luella M. Wright, *The Literary Life of the Early Friends, 1650–1725* (New York: AMS Press, 1966), 8.

2. Ralph K. Beebe, *A Garden of the Lord: A History of Oregon Yearly Meeting of Friends Church* (Newberg, OR: Barclay Press, 1968), 2.

3. Ibid., 2. The figures are from Walter Williams, *The Rich Heritage of Quakerism* (Newberg, OR: Barclay Press), 1992.

4. Arthur O. Roberts, *The Association of Evangelical Friends: A Story of Quaker Renewal in the Twentieth Century* (Newberg, OR: Barclay Press, 1975), 1.

5. Ibid., 10.

6. Ibid., 38.

7. Harlow Ankeny, "25 Years," *Evangelical Friend* 26:5 (September–October 1992): 18.

8. Dean Gregory, "Why a New Magazine?" *Evangelical Friend* 1:1 (September 1967): 5.

9. Ankeny, "25 Years," 19.

10. Ibid.

11. *The Sense of the Meeting: Selected Editorial Writings of Jack L. Willcuts*, ed. Susan Willcuts Kendall (Newberg, OR: Barclay Press, 1992).

12. Lon Fendall, "Mantle Transfer Again," *Evangelical Friend* 22:3 (May–June 1990): 4.

13. Ibid.

14. Ankeny, "25 Years," 19.

Information Sources

INDEX SOURCES: Copies of two typed and photocopied indices may be requested directly from the Barclay Press, 600 East Third Street, Newberg, Oregon 97132–3106: (1) an index of articles by author, and (2) an index of articles by subject.

LOCATION SOURCES: Complete collections may be found at the offices of three of the sponsoring Friends groups: Northwest Yearly Meeting, Newberg, Oregon; Mid-AmericaYearly Meeting, Wichita, Kansas; and Evangelical Friends Church-Eastern Region, Canton, Ohio. In addition, several Quaker college libraries have complete collections, including: Earlham College (Richmond, Indiana), Friends

University (Wichita, Kansas), George Fox College (Newberg, Oregon), Haverford College (Philadelphia, Pennsylvania), Malone College (Canton, Ohio) and Swarthmore College (Philadelphia, Pennsylvania).

Publication History

MAGAZINE TITLE: *Evangelical Friend* (1967–present).
VOLUME AND ISSUE DATA: 1:1 (September 1967)–present. Published six times per year.
PUBLISHER AND PLACE OF PUBLICATION: Evangelical Friends International–North America Region, Newberg, Oregon.
EDITORS: Dean Gregory (1967–1970), Jack Willcuts (1970–1985), Lon Fendall (1986–1990), Paul Anderson (1990–present).
CIRCULATION: 10,000.

Michael P. Graves

EXAMINER. *See* WATCHMAN-EXAMINER

EXTRACTS FROM CORRESPONDENCE OF THE AMERICAN BIBLE SOCIETY. *See* AMERICAN BIBLE SOCIETY RECORD

F

FAR EAST. *See* COLUMBAN MISSION

FIELD AFAR. *See* MARYKNOLL

FIELD AFAR: MARYKNOLL. *See* MARYKNOLL

FIELD AFAR: THE MAGAZINE OF MARYKNOLL. *See* MARYKNOLL

FÖRBUNDETS VECKOTIDNING. *See* COVENANT COMPANION

FORTH. *See* SPIRIT OF MISSIONS

FOURSQUARE BRIDAL CALL CRUSADER. *See* BRIDAL CALL

FOURSQUARE CRUSADER. *See* BRIDAL CALL

FOURSQUARE MAGAZINE. *See* BRIDAL CALL

FOURSQUARE WORLD ADVANCE. *See* BRIDAL CALL

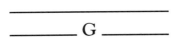

GODEY'S LADY'S BOOK

In 1837 Victoria ascended the British throne, inaugurating a sixty-four–year reign that would come to be known as the Victorian Age, a cultural era in the Anglo-American world. Across the Atlantic, that same year saw the merger of two magazines to form the "new" *Lady's Book*, a publication that for the next four decades would hold sway as the self-described "Queen of Periodicals," the authoritative voice of American Victorianism for women of the emerging middle class.

Louis A. Godey (1804–1878), a Philadelphia entrepreneur, originally began the *Lady's Book* in 1830 as a women's magazine of fashion and fiction. "The Book," as Godey often called his publication (to the consternation of those who thought the Bible was the only printed material in nineteenth-century America properly referred to by that title),[1] was primarily a business proposition. Although Godey prided himself on the magazine's high moral tone, he wished to capitalize on the growing audience of women readers, and his editorial purpose simply was to be "useful and entertaining" to that group.[2] Two years earlier in Boston, Episcopal clergyman John Lauris Blake also had established a women's publication, the *Ladies' Magazine*, and had hired a forty-year-old widow, Sarah Josepha Hale (1788–1879), as its editor. Both Godey's *Book* and the *Ladies' Magazine* were monthly publications aimed at a similar audience. But Sarah Hale was a born crusader, and from the start the *Ladies' Magazine* became the platform for what would be Hale's lifelong concern: promoting "the mental, moral, and religious improvement of women."[3]

Hale had obvious editorial skills, and Louis Godey possessed a business acumen. By 1836, Godey was planning to diversify his publishing enterprise and needed help with the editorial responsibilities of the *Lady's Book*. At the same time, what was by then called the *American Ladies' Magazine* was struggling financially. Godey offered to buy the publication, merge it with his *Book*, and hire Hale as coeditor of the new venture. Hale accepted, and one of the most successful partnerships in the history of nineteenth-century American magazines was born. Godey and Hale shared the direction of the *Lady's Book* for forty-one years. For the first two decades after the merger, circulation soared: from a respectable 25,000 in the early 1840s to 70,000 by 1850 to a high of 150,000 in 1860, making the *Lady's Book* the most widely circulated monthly magazine in antebellum America.[4]

Throughout its long life, *Godey's Lady's Book*, as the magazine came to be known in the 1840s, was identified as a women's magazine rather than a religious periodical.[5] The bulk of *Godey's* was filled with what still is standard fare for such publications: short stories, occasional nonfiction pieces, fashion news, decorating tips, recipes, and household information. Nonetheless, Sarah Hale was a staunch advocate of Victorian "true womanhood," and religion formed the cornerstone of her value system. Her views reflected influences from the Yankee Congregationalism of her early life and the Episcopalianism that she embraced in middle age. With Hale in charge of the literary content of the *Lady's Book*, the magazine championed attitudes toward women, religion, and culture that increasingly came to characterize middle-class American Protestantism. The religious side of the publication can be seen in three editorial emphases: (1) Hale's belief in a God-ordained woman's sphere of activity and the innate religious superiority of women, (2) her identification of spirituality with gentility, and (3) her advocacy of a number of specifically religious causes to advance what she perceived as women's Christianizing influence.

Hale had developed her understanding of the concept of "woman's sphere" during her years with the *American Ladies' Magazine*. When she moved to the *Lady's Book*, she used occasional articles and the "Editors' Table," her monthly column at the back of each issue, to reiterate her position, often citing books or published sermons in support of her views.[6] Hale believed that men and women were intellectual equals, but that the motivations and character of the two sexes differed radically. Men were superior physically, more stimulated than women by the physical senses, and fitted for active roles in the public arena—for example, in business, politics, or the military. Women, on the other hand, had a God-given moral superiority; they were designed with a unique ability to exert moral and religious influences over children and men. By exercising such influence within the family circle, a domain described as a woman's "empire of the heart," women functioned as chief agents in the "civilization of the world."[7]

The bedrock of feminine moral authority was piety. "In the Gospel of the Lord Jesus is her hope and strength. . . . She must be pious or she has no power to do good." From such convictions came Hale's embrace of education for women as a "holy cause." Educated women were best equipped to establish homes characterized by Christian virtue. On this foundation rested "not only individual and social happiness" but also the "national prosperity and glory" of the young American republic. Women, in other words, bore primary responsibility for the social and spiritual well-being of their families and the nation. Yet their activities were limited to the home or to certain other circles where a domestic atmosphere could be duplicated. A true woman never would be happy or useful "in the lecture room of the physician, in the forum, the pulpit, or the halls of legislation."[8]

Hale not only identified moral and spiritual superiority with womanhood but she also stressed the reciprocal relation among piety, beauty, and taste. Everything between the covers of the *Lady's Book*, she claimed, was designed to elevate a woman's taste—and, thus, her spirituality and virtue. "We must carry out our plan [in the *Book*] of the beautiful and appropriate in dress, in poetry, in fiction, in education, till all shall meet . . . in the sacred beauty of the Christian character."[9]. Hale's assumption that fashion and fiction could be enlisted, in effect, as aids to sanctification challenged the beliefs of many Protestants who associated such things with "the world," a dominion at war with God. Yet the resolute morality, not to mention the attractiveness, of the *Lady's Book* apparently won over many readers. "Though many good people condemn all 'fashion-plate' periodicals," wrote one subscriber, "I think a well-conducted one, like the *Lady's Book*, is calculated to do immense good, by presenting religious truths and the 'beauty of holiness' in company with good taste, refinement and genius."[10] *Godey's Lady's Book* was one of many influences that helped to transform the message of nineteenth-century middle-class Protestantism into the "gospel of gentility."

Hale's belief that women were the divinely appointed agents behind the "moral improvement of the world" determined the causes that she promoted in the pages of the *Lady's Book*.[11] She supported women's education and advocated women instead of men as public-school teachers. Beginning with a January 1847 editorial, she launched a persistent campaign to have Thanksgiving Day declared a national holiday.[12] Thanksgiving rituals embraced the themes of piety, patriotism, domesticity, and national unity that made the day, in Hale's mind, an ideal American holiday. In the immediate post–Civil War years, with Thanksgiving encumbered by its cultural baggage as a Yankee festival, Hale lent the magazine's influence to the popularization of the Victorian Christmas. With its celebration of love, family, peace, and good will, Christmas, too, was good for the nation.[13]

Through the pages of *Godey's*, Hale also championed such specifically religious efforts as the women's mission movement and the revival of deaconess orders among Protestants. She was an early proponent of training women to serve as medical missionaries, and in 1851 she became the first secretary of the Pennsylvania Ladies' Medical Missionary Society. *Godey's* readers shared in news of the society's progress, and by 1853 it had begun to sponsor the medical training of three women for the mission field. Denominational mission boards, however, refused to send single women, and the project was placed on hold.[14] It was revived in 1861 with the founding of an independent sending agency, the Woman's Union Missionary Society, in New York City. Hale became president of the Philadelphia branch. Bolstered by monthly solicitations in *Godey's* editorial columns, her group raised two thousand dollars during the first year, enough to support a teacher for a Burmese mission school.[15] In 1869, the initial dream was realized when missionaries in northern India asked the Philadelphia society to recruit a female doctor. Hale contacted Clara Swain, a graduate of the Women's Medical College in Philadelphia. Swain, a Methodist, left for India that same year under the sponsorship of northern Methodist Church women, and she was the first American woman to serve as a medical missionary.[16]

Hale's encouragement of such daring efforts by women pointed to tensions inherent in the ideology that she promoted through the *Lady's Book*. On the one hand, her commitment to the unique moral and spiritual power of women drove her to seek new avenues to further women's influence. On the other hand, Hale's allegiance to the "woman's sphere" acted as a conservative force, sometimes at odds with the implications of her more radical ideas. The engraved illustrations at the front of the January 1861 *Lady's Book* were one example of the mixed message. The magazine's cover paid tribute to the heroic benevolent efforts of several famous women: their exertions in visiting prisons, nursing battlefield wounded, establishing charitable institutions, improving the conditions in asylums. Yet immediately inside the magazine was the idyllic portrayal of a home scene. "We are constrained to say that these exceptional women [on the cover] are the exception, not the rule of life," Hale editorialized. "In our second picture is embodied the real worth, the true sublimity of woman's destiny and duty."[17]

In addition, while the words of the magazine extolled women's character, the popular fashion "embellishments" (hand-painted engraved illustrations) at the front of each issue fostered a different and perhaps even more powerful feminine role: women as consumers. The magazine itself was a carefully designed product. With its lavish cover and nine-by-six-inch size, a bound volume of the *Lady's Book* had the same dimensions and appearance as the popular Victorian gift books.[18] And while Sarah Hale moralized from her editorial columns, Louis Godey used "Godey's Arm Chair," his editorial space, in part to run a mail-order business. By sending cash with their requests, women could purchase silk, bonnets, earrings, patterns, and other items, with orders acknowledged in print and accompanied by Godey's chatty comments regarding the transactions. The Hale/Godey partnership exemplified the growing ties between piety and commerce among the Victorian middle class.

Godey's Lady's Book enjoyed its most vigorous years during the two decades before the Civil War. In the 1840s, it sustained a modest literary reputation, publishing works by Poe, Longfellow, Harriet Beecher Stowe, Catharine Maria Sedgwick, John Greenleaf Whittier, Lydia Sigourney, and others. During the 1850s the magazine assumed a more romanticized, sentimental tone, with a greater number of embellishments designed as tableaus to illustrate religious themes, such as the Apostles' Creed or the Lord's Prayer. Women often were portrayed as Madonna figures, the decorative centerpieces of always happy homes. Stories during this decade came from lesser-known writers; the magazine served as one outlet for Protestant women who were exploring the moral and didactic potential of popular fiction. No hint of the bitter controversies over slavery or growing sectional tensions slipped into the pages of *Godey's*. Like the woman's sphere that it represented, the *Lady's Book* was a territory unto itself, isolated from the rough and tumble of public life. Religious controversies were taboo, and Louis Godey forbade the mention of politics. Even with the outbreak of hostilities between North and South, the policy stood. There were occasional editorial allusions to "bereaved hearts" and "enmities and strifes," but the magazine never directly acknowledged the Civil War.

By the 1860s, circulation had peaked, and a gradual decline began, although the magazine still boasted a hundred thousand subscribers as late as 1873.[19] However, by this time, *Godey's* major competitor, *Peterson's Magazine*, featuring a more thoroughly secular emphasis on fashion and light fiction, had outdistanced the *Lady's Book* in circulation. Increased space in the magazine devoted to fashion news, patterns, and needlework reflected some efforts to compete, but both Godey and Sarah Hale were aging, and the *Lady's Book* with them. Overall, content in the post–Civil War period followed established patterns, with Hale occasionally reprinting earlier editorials. At the close of 1877, ill health forced Godey to step down, proud to the last that "not an immoral thought or profane word" had ever marred the pages of his magazine.[20] Then eighty-nine years old, Sarah Hale chose to leave at the same time. Her departure also marked the demise of the "Editors' Table," the column that had given the magazine so much of its moral and religious focus. The *Lady's Book* would never again have a clear editorial voice. Although the publication maintained a certain aura of late-Victorian morality, with Hale's resignation it ceased to be in any sense a distinctively religious magazine. Fashions, recipes, patterns, and parlor games became ends in themselves, apart from any "higher calling" for women.

The *Lady's Book* survived as a women's magazine under a series of different publishers until 1892. It then was moved to New York and struggled for six more years as *Godey's Magazine*, a literary and general-interest monthly.[21] However, when it had lost the forceful personalities of Louis Godey and Sarah Hale, the reign of the "Queen of Periodicals" had come to an end. During their long administration, *Godey's Lady's Book* had set the standards for nineteenth-century women. It mirrored an idealized Victorian America—a world of middle-class prosperity, "Christian" civilization, elevated womanhood, and religious earnestness. The knowledge that reality often fell far short of the promised vision apparently did not dim the enthusiasm of legions of subscribers who found the magazine "useful, ornamental and instructive," just as Louis Godey promised.

Notes

1. Ruth E. Finley, *The Lady of Godey's* (Philadelphia: Lippincott, 1931), 50.

2. *Lady's Book* 3 (December 1831): 357.

3. Ibid. 13 (December 1836): 283.

4. Circulation figures are based on Louis Godey's estimates, cited in Frank Luther Mott, *A History of American Magazines* (Cambridge: Harvard University Press, 1939), 1:581.

5. The magazine underwent a series of title changes. It was most commonly known as the *Lady's Book*, *Godey's Lady's Book*, or *Godey's Magazine*. See "Publication History."

6. Through careless typesetting and because Hale occasionally was joined by coeditors, the column often carried a plural title.

7. *Godey's Lady's Book* 14 (January 1837): 2; ibid. 34 (March 1847): 173.

8. Ibid. 14 (January 1837): 5; ibid. 33 (November 1846): 235.

9. Ibid. 14 (January 1837): 5.

10. Ibid. 35 (November 1847): 272.

11. Ibid. 23 (November 1841): 236.

12. Ibid. 34 (January 1847): 52, 53. As a result of Hale's efforts, Abraham Lincoln proclaimed the first national day of thanksgiving in 1863.

13. Ibid. 75 (December 1867): 543.

14. Ibid. 46 (June 1853): 551–54; see also ibid. 70 (May 1870): 451–54.

15. The project was first mentioned in ibid. 62 (January 1861): 78, 79, and was elaborated on in February of that year. For results, see ibid. 64 (January 1862): 93, 94.

16. Ibid. 80 (May 1870): 454.

17. Ibid. 62 (January 1861): 78.

18. Angela Marie Howard Zophy, "For the Improvement of My Sex: Sarah Josepha Hale's Editorship of *Godey's Lady's Book*, 1837–1877" (Ph.D. diss., Ohio State University, 1978), 53.

19. Mott, *History of American Magazines*, 581.

20. *Godey's Lady's Book* 95 (August 1877): 117.

21. For a more detailed discussion of *Godey's* final two decades, see Mott, *History of American Magazines*, 592, 593.

Information Sources

INDEX SOURCES: Although indexing is incomplete, *Godey's* is included in *Poole's Index to Periodical Literature*. Each volume of *Godey's* also contains a title index, usually at the front of the volume as microfilmed, occasionally also at the end of the volume. Contents of editorial columns have not been indexed.

LOCATION SOURCES: All volumes are on microfilm as part of the American Periodicals Series, listed under the heading "Godey's Magazine." Holdings of bound volumes, of particular interest for the hand-colored engravings, are included in the *Union List of Serials*. Institutions listing nearly complete holdings include Kansas State University, Library of Congress, Los Angeles Public Library, St. Louis Public Library, and Yale University.

Publication History

MAGAZINE TITLE AND TITLE CHANGES: *Lady's Book* (varies) (1830–1839), *Godey's Lady's Book and Ladies' American Magazine* (1840–1843), *Godey's Magazine and Lady's Book* (January 1844–June 1848), *Godey's Lady's Book* (July

1848–June 1854), *Godey's Lady's Book and Magazine* (July 1854–December 1882), *Godey's Lady's Book* (January 1883–September 1892), *Godey's Magazine* (October 1892–August 1898).

VOLUME AND ISSUE DATA: 1:1 (July 1830)–137:18 (August 1898). Published monthly, in two volumes per year, January–June and July-December; last volume has only two numbers.

PUBLISHER AND PLACE OF PUBLICATION: Louis A. Godey and Co., Philadelphia (1830–1877), Godey's Lady's Book Publishing Co., Philadelphia (1877–1883), J. H. Haulenbeek and Co., Philadelphia (1883–1886), William E. Striker, Philadelphia (1886–1887), Croly Publishing Co., Philadelphia (1887–1888), Godey Publishing Co., Philadelphia (1888–1892), New York City (1892–1898).

EDITORS: Louis A. Godey (1830–1836), Sarah J. Hale and Louis A. Godey (1837–1838, 1846–1877), Sarah J. Hale, Lydia H. Sigourney, and Louis A. Godey (1839–1840), Sarah J. Hale and Lydia H. Sigourney (1841), Sarah J. Hale, Lydia H. Sigourney, Morton McMichael, and Louis A. Godey (1842), Sarah J. Hale, Morton McMichael, and Louis A. Godey (1843–1846), J. G. L. Brown, Charles W. Frost, and Mrs. S. A. Shields (1878), J. Hannum Jones, A. E. Brown, and Mrs. S. A. Shields (1878–1881), J. Hannum Jones and A. E. Brown (1881–1883), J. H. Haulenbeek (1883–1885), J. H. Haulenbeek and Eleanor Moor Hiestand (1885–1886), Mrs. D. G. Croly (1887–1888), Albert H. Hardy (1892–1893), Harry Wakefield Bates (1894–n.d.), Harold Wilkinson (n.d.).

CIRCULATION: 150,000 (1860).

Kathryn Long

GODEY'S LADY'S BOOK AND LADIES' AMERICAN MAGAZINE.
See GODEY'S LADY'S BOOK

GODEY'S LADY'S BOOK AND MAGAZINE.
See GODEY'S LADY'S BOOK

GODEY'S MAGAZINE.
See GODEY'S LADY'S BOOK

GODEY'S MAGAZINE AND LADY'S BOOK.
See GODEY'S LADY'S BOOK

GOING WITH GOD.
See WORLD VISION

GOOD WORK.
See BAPTIST MISSIONARY MAGAZINE

GOSPEL HERALD

The *Gospel Herald* has been the weekly magazine of the Mennonite Church for over fifty years. Since its inception, it has reflected the issues, beliefs, tensions, and nature of that Church.

The nineteenth-century Mennonite Church in America was little different from the first group of Anabaptists that formed in the days of the Reformation. They kept themselves apart from the rest of society, maintained their own language (German) in the midst of an English-speaking nation, and lived lives of simplicity and frugality.

However, the scriptural truths that had so burned in the first Mennonites became faded and familiar with time until they were traditions. Young people were not encouraged to join the Church until they married. By that time, few had any interest in tying themselves to a Church so out of step with the surrounding culture. Mennonites had no Sunday schools for training children in the faith, and fewer and fewer Mennonite children understood sermons in German since they attended English-speaking public schools.[1] Furthermore, a sense of embarrassment about their Church and culture made Mennonites apologetic,[2] an attitude sure to repulse the next generation.

The Church itself had no central government. It had influential leaders, but lacked a vehicle to enable Mennonites to move the Church out of the sixteenth century into the present and, in the process, transform it into a cohesive unit. The group needed a voice, an official Church magazine written by Mennonites for Mennonites that would set forth Mennonite doctrine and train adherents in their faith.

Nine men, one each from various Mennonite conferences, met on 7 November 1907 in Goshen, Indiana, to "consider the advisability of establishing a publishing house to be owned and controlled by the church."[3] At that time there were three privately owned businesses serving the Mennonite Church: the Gospel Witness Company, the Mennonite Book and Tract Society, and the Mennonite Publishing Company.

The first had been in operation just three years and was headed by Bishop Daniel Kauffman, one of those in the forefront of the move toward both a central governing body and an official paper.[4] His magazine bore the name of his company, *Gospel Witness*. The tract society did not publish a periodical. The Mennonite Publishing Company had been in operation for forty-four years and was then under the leadership of Bishop John F. Funk. His magazine, the *Herald of Truth* was published bimonthly and had a loyal following. Funk also had been a tireless supporter of a general conference and Church-directed paper.[5] In fact, Daniel Kauffman had often published articles calling for such in Funk's magazine, with Funk's giving a hearty "amen" to them in editorial comments. Yet Daniel Kauffman's *Gospel Witness* had been set up in direct competition to John Funk's magazine.[6]

These men, like their papers, had many things in common. When in their early twenties, both had left the Mennonite Church and were soon on their way to successful secular careers, Funk in the lumber business in Chicago and Kauffman in politics in Missouri. Both had been school teachers and loved reading and the world of ideas. Both came to value the biblical faith of their forebearers and articulately defended it. Funk experienced salvation in a Presbyterian Church and threw himself wholeheartedly into the emerging Sunday-school movement. Contemporary and friend of Dwight L. Moody, Funk often worked alongside the former. Kauffman, a widower just two years after marrying, started thinking about religion when he contemplated his motherless son and renewed his commitment during a Mennonite evangelistic meeting.

Funk, however, was of an older generation and had had an "epiphany" experience that he cherished but rarely spoke about. Kauffman was seen as an effective and influential leader, often heading committees; Funk had difficulties with both his fellow bishops and his Church members. Perhaps their early career choices foreshadowed their styles of Church leadership. Kauffman, as a politician, understood the need for consensus and sensed when the time was ripe for change. Funk, as a businessman, made decisions and issued orders.

Mennonite historian J. C. Wenger said that Funk was

certainly the man who, more than any other, molded the modern Mennonite Church into its present form. . . . He founded the publication work of the Mennonite Church . . . through his church organ and personal influences promoted Sunday schools throughout all the Mennonite settlements of North America. He took the first steps toward the creation of the Mennonite Board of Missions. He promoted the concept of a Mennonite General conference.[7]

While Funk's endeavors had grown from proprietorship to partnership to corporation,[8] Kauffman had turned over all profits to the Church while he owned the Gospel Witness Company.[9]

When those nine men met in November of 1907, all three companies involved with Mennonite publishing offered to sell their assets to the new organization. The Gospel Witness Company asked for almost ten thousand dollars for its presses, equipment, and real estate. The Mennonite Book and Tract Society asked for four thousand dollars. The Mennonite Publishing Company asked for just over fifty thousand dollars. The committee paid the Gospel Witness Company around seven thousand dollars (they did not buy the real estate), gave the Mennonite Book and Tract Society nearly five thousand dollars, and offered the Mennonite Publishing Company eight thousand dollars for its six periodicals and list price for anything else purchased.[10] Both the Gospel Witness Company and the Mennonite Book and Tract Society asked for and got cost price, while Funk offered his equipment at present value or a reduction of 25 percent of the cost price.[11] Furthermore, the equipment purchased from the Gospel Witness Company was not sufficient to meet the needs of a publishing concern that intended to print books as well as a weekly Church magazine. But the combination of the two companies' equipment would have been adequate.[12]

Funk was faced with a choice: sell at a tremendous loss and thus rob his stockholders of their rightful return or create divisiveness in the Church. When the committee would not meet even a revised asking price of twenty-four thousand dollars, Funk agreed to the eight thousand dollars offered. The committee made a verbal agreement with Funk that he would receive five hundred dollars a year for the rest of his life regardless of whether he did anything for the new publication.[13] His family maintains that that agreement was kept for not more than two years.

The committee came up with a name for the new magazine by default. Someone suggested that the names of the two papers be combined to form *Gospel Herald*. The name did not meet with enthusiasm, but when no other name was forthcoming, it was adopted.[14]

Kauffman and Funk were named editors; however, Kauffman was clearly considered the editor and held that position for thirty-five years. Now the Mennonite Church truly had an official voice, for Kauffman was also on many of the decision-making committees for the general conference. Daniel Hertzler summarized the situation: "It was as if it did not seem right to attempt to operate a major denominational committee without him."[15] Thus, what appeared in the *Gospel Herald* reflected the position of Church leaders. In form and appearance, the *Gospel Herald* took up where the *Gospel Witness* left off: the sixteen pages were nine by twelve inches in a three-column layout. On style it reflected the unadorned, no-frills attitude of its Church: block letters in serif type on pure white paper. There were no pictures or illustrations. The first issue was dated Saturday, 4 April 1908; had an address of Scottdale, Pennsylvania; and listed three editors: Daniel Kauffman, John F. Funk, and D. H. Bender. The first issue included editorials; a report of the 8th annual American Mennonite Mission at Dhamtari, India; an article on doctrinal teaching; features entitled "Family Circle" and "Question Drawer"; youth pages; notes on denominational activities; correspondence from churches telling about local events; a listing of mission projects with articles about a few of them; commentary on current issues such as the "Negro Problem," "The Normal Life of a Woman," and world news; obituaries; and conference dates.[16]

Given the tight-knit nature of the Mennonite Church and culture, it is not surprising that its weekly Church magazine resembled a long, newsy, family letter. The practical aspects of displaying a Mennonite lifestyle are given greater space than abstract doctrinal issues. There is frequent emphasis on the Mennonite view of pacifism. For example, the lead article for the 15 October 1991 issue had in its subtitle, "A peace church cannot let the military provide the only answer."[17] In 1992, a reader wrote about making the Mennonite "peace system operational."[18]

The Mennonite heritage is a frequent subject. Two articles in the 25 September 1973 issue dealt with the Mennonite tradition.[19] A commissioned series of articles began in 1977 with the title "What is the Mennonite Church?"[20] In the 7 January 1992 issue, the lead article dealt with the question, "Is Mennonite an ethnic heritage, or is it an understanding of Christian faith?''[21] and an interested observer wrote to the magazine that she ''gets the impression that the Mennonite Church finds its primary identity in the belief of pacifism rather than in the person of Christ.''[22]

Just as Mennonites have resisted change, their magazine has rarely changed its format, design, or themes. There was an experiment with rays extending from an open Bible behind the three-dimensional letters of the magazine title in the late 1930s and early 1940s, but that was short-lived. A table of contents appears sporadically. There are still no outside advertisements, although there is an occasional announcement of a new book offered by the publishing house. In the late 1940s, pictures and ilustrations first appeared, usually of people interacting with each other. From the very first issue, women authors have been included, not just writing on topics traditionally accorded to women. A much more recent development is the use of cartoons. ''Sisters and Brothers,'' by Joel Kauffman, premiered on 4 October 1977 and ran through 24 February 1981. In 1983 ''Pontius,'' also by Joel Kauffman, was introduced. Daniel Hertzler, past editor of the *Gospel Herald*, described the magazine in this way: ''It has a small circulation by typical publishing standards—about 23,000 in the U.S. and Canada. Yet within the Mennonite Church, [it] . . . is as recognizable as *Newsweek* or the *New York Times*.''[23] Eugene Seals, vice-chairperson of the Mennonite Board of Missions, said that the *Gospel Herald* ''is the one medium which addresses virtually all aspects of Mennonite Church life, faith, and strategy.''[24]

In the early forties, Kauffman became too ill to continue as editor. The board pressured Paul Erb, an English professor at Goshen College, to accept the editorship. He did so reluctantly.[25] Careful to preserve much of the Kauffman tradition, Erb made one very significant change in the editorial page. While Kauffman had remained silent on several troubling issues such as the Civilian Peace Service in World War II, Erb saw a need to ''speak for myself'' and make the editorial page ''represent front line thinking.''[26]

Following Erb as editor in 1962 was John M. Drescher, a Mennonite pastor. His eleven years in that post spanned a ''time of turbulence and trouble for both the nation and the church.''[27] During these years, much of the fabled Mennonite resistance to change crumbled, and in the process ''the church took on the character of the world.''[28] For a decade, Drescher provided a balanced approach in the *Gospel Herald*, encouraging the charismatic movement but focusing on the fruit of the spirit, reminding the Church of its roots but warning of the danger of ''ancestor worship.''

In 1973 Daniel Hertzler became editor. Wayne North described Hertzler's contribution: ''Dan always presented a viewpoint that was insightful and often unique . . . couched in vivid, often humorous phrases.''[29] Hertzler guided the magazine until 1990 when J. Lorne Peachy assumed the post of editor.

The *Gospel Herald* is both mirror and object; it is a reflection of the state of the Mennonite Church and the attitudes, values, and beliefs of its people; but it is also through the great influence of its editors a creator and shaper of the Church and its priorities.

Notes

1. Alice K. Gingerich, *The Life and Times of Daniel Kauffman* (Scottdale, PA: Herald Press, 1952), 9, 10.
2. Helen Kolb Gates, *Bless the Lord, O My Soul* (Scottdale, PA: Herald Press, 1964), 68.
3. Ibid. 193.
4. Gingerich, *Daniel Kauffman,* 40.
5. Gates, *Bless the Lord,* 69–70.
6. Daniel Hertzler, ed., *Not by Might* (Scottdale, PA: Herald Press, 1983), 13.
7. Gates, *Bless the Lord,* 11.
8. Ibid., 70.
9. Gingerich, *Daniel Kauffman,* 60.
10. Gates, *Bless the Lord,* 194.
11. Ibid., 194–95.
12. Ibid., 195.
13. Ibid., 208.
14. Hertzler, *Not by Might,* 15.
15. Ibid., 18.
16. *Gospel Herald* 1 (4 April 1908): 1–16.
17. Ibid. 84 (15 October 1991): 1.
18. Ibid. 85 (14 April 1992): 4.
19. Ibid. 64 (25 September 1973): 732, 735.
20. Ibid. 70 (29 March 1977): 265.
21. Ibid. 85 (7 January 1992): 1.
22. Ibid., p. 5.
23. Hertzler, *Not by Might,* 157.
24. Ibid.
25. Ibid., 88.
26. Ibid., 90.
27. Ibid., 130.
28. Ibid.
29. *Gospel Herald* 83 (20 November 1990): 798.

Information Sources

INDEX SOURCES: Most volumes contain a partial index.
LOCATION SOURCES: A complete set of all *Gospel Herald* volumes can be found at the Mennonite Historical Society, Lancaster, Pennsylvania; the Historical Library of Eastern Mennonite College in Harrisonburg, Virginia; the Mennonite Heritage Center in Metamora, Illinois; and the Herald Press offices in Scottdale, Pennsylvania.

Publication History

MAGAZINE TITLE: *Gospel Herald* (1908–present).
VOLUME AND ISSUES DATA: 1:1 (4 April 1908)–present. Published weekly. Early
    issues identified Saturday as the day of publication; this was later changed to
    Tuesday and then to Friday.
PUBLISHER AND PLACE OF PUBLICATION: Herald Press, Scottdale, Pennsylvania.
EDITORS: Daniel Kauffman (1908–1943), Paul Erb (1944–1962), John M. Drescher
    (1962–1973), Daniel Hertzler (1973–1990), J. Lorne Peachy (1990–present).
CIRCULATION: 2,200 (1992).

Ruth Morris

GOSPEL PUBLISHER. *See* CHURCH ADVOCATE

**GOSPEL PUBLISHER AND JOURNAL OF USEFUL
KNOWLEDGE.** *See* CHURCH ADVOCATE

GOSPEL WITNESS. *See* GOSPEL HERALD

GUIDEPOSTS

The publishing legacy enshrined in *Guideposts* began in 1945 under the guiding hands of its founders and publishers, Ruth Stafford Peale and Norman Vincent Peale. The magazine was one medium of outreach of the ministry of the
Peales. Dr. Peale gave reason for this choice when he said, ''My choice of tools
with which to reach everyone on behalf of Jesus Christ is radio, the platform,
and the printed word; primarily the latter.''[1]

Among the many influences that shaped Norman Vincent Peale and the focus
of *Guideposts*, four would be primary: (1) Peale's personal experience and understanding of Jesus Christ, (2) nurturing parents and family, (3) good mentors,
and (4) the American dream of an Ohio country boy.

The teachings of Jesus Christ were communicated early to the young Peale.
But conversion for him was a continual process of call, recall, and many calls
besides. Ruth was sometimes the preacher's pastor. While vacationing in England in 1933, a discouraged first-year pastor of Marble Collegiate Church in
New York City sat before her. In the intimacy of table conversation, what was
to become the aim of *Guideposts*—''To help people overcome problems, to
give them encouragement and guidance''—happened for the future editor.[2]

Peale's father, Clifford Peale, had turned from a successful medical profession
to that of the Methodist parish ministry. Growing up, Norman was plagued by
a sense of inferiority. He had been asked by his father to yield this feeling of
inferiority to the Great Physician for healing. Later, amidst the uproar of the
publication of *The Power of Positive Thinking* in 1952, Norman—who at the
time had a letter of resignation from the ministry in his pocket—received from

his father's deathbed a powerful affirmation and words of encouragement. He later tore up the resignation and continued. Almost ten years after starting *Guideposts*, Norman wrote "How to Overcome an Inferiority Complex" for the February 1955 issue of *Reader's Digest*. These nurturing moments were mileposts/ guideposts of psychological healing that were incorporated into his therapeutic principles of (1) prayerize, (2) picturize, and (3) actualize.[3]

Good friends and mentors have contributed to the success of Peale and *Guideposts*. From Peale's preministerial job as a cub newspaper reporter, throughout his many years in the pastorate, and particularly at the inception of *Guideposts*, the counsel of associates provided accountability and encouragement. Newspaper journalists taught Peale to write simply and directly. Business leaders brought him out of a possible clergy-church parochialism to the larger and perhaps tougher ring of a "preacher" to business conventions with a message that did not "preach" in the derogatory sense. Peale listened like a good reporter and preached like the evangelist that he was. It was to the business community that the first years of *Guideposts* were addressed. Large companies bought the magazine and distributed it free to their workers. Only later did it become a subscriber-supported magazine.[4]

The final shaping principle grew from Peale's country roots. He brought to his long pastoral career in New York City a warmth and naturalness, honed by a fine education and by exposure to the workaday world. Always a promoter of the American free-enterprise system, he brought a conservative patriotic concern to his speeches and several excursions into the political realm. That a boy from Ohio would love the big cities was not a denying of the rootage, but rather was the bringing of the very best of a pastoral heart to a very large flock. *Guideposts*, as an inspirational magazine, always sought a wide market; neither Protestant nor Catholic, neither management nor labor, *Guideposts* was a bridge between the church and business world.

At its beginnings in 1945, *Guideposts* received much help—and perhaps some from DeWitt and Lila Wallace of the *Reader's Digest*. Grace Perkins Oursler, wife of *Reader's Digest* editor Fulton Oursler, became the editor of *Guideposts*,[5] though Oursler himself offered unofficial assistance. Raymond Thornburg, brother-in-law of newscaster Lowell Thomas, who was a neighbor of the Peales in Pawling, New York, completed the publishing team. Dr. and Mrs. Peale, after forty-six years of overseeing the magazine, in 1991 turned over control of Guideposts Associates, Inc. to a new president and CEO, John F. Temple.[6] As if in full circle, Fulton Oursler, Jr., son of the first editor, was named editor in chief in November 1992.[7]

What led the Peales to start *Guideposts*? Friends from the business community such as Branch Rickey, Lowell Thomas, J. C. Penney, Capt. Eddie Rickenbacker, suggested to Peale the need for a spiritual letter service to promote the free-enterprise system and the need for true stories to show how everyday life can be influenced by religious faith. In 1944, Rev. Peale met with newspaper-publishing magnate Frank Gannett to give focus to this new venture. It would

(1) support freedom under God; (2) motivate youth to be the great persons they can be under the American system of free enterprise, and (3) be a spiritual publication to build once again into our nation a deep faith in God.[8]

These friends also contributed financially to secure mailing lists and pay initial start-up costs. The first issue began with only four pages, in a 4½-by-6-inch folded format, not unlike the *Kiplinger Newsletter*. By August 1948, it became a stapled magazine of twenty-four pages. It was enlarged the next year, 1949, to 5 by 7¼ inches; and in 1982, to its present size of 5⅛ by 7½ inches, and to forty-eight pages.[9] *Guideposts*, the name chosen for this spiritual newsletter, was an outgrowth of Rev. Peale's ministry as well as a teaching instrument that Rev. Peale credited for teaching the principles of positive thinking and its good results. At a particularly hard time in 1950, when *Guideposts* was seeking to expand its circulation, Tessie Durlach, a director on the board of *Guideposts*, said that the problem had been an emphasis on "lack." Bemoaning a lack of subscribers had created a condition of lack. What was needed was to replace that "lack" image with a positive one of the hundred thousand subscribers they wanted.[10] Durlach's conviction combined with the biblical lesson of "as a man thinks, so is he" to become the impetus for Peale to insist that "as we think, so do we create." Two years later this notion was to find its full expression in the best-seller, *The Power of Positive Thinking*.

When *Guideposts* began, its editorial offices were rooms over a grocery store in Pawling, New York. As *Guideposts* grew into one of the most widely read inspirational magazines in the world, editorial operations moved to a nearby house on Quaker Hill and then to a complex purchased in Carmel, New York.[11] *Guideposts* had only four editors in its first forty-eight years: Grace Perkins Oursler, Leonard E. LeSourd, Arthur Gordon, and Van Varner. Following the restructuring in 1991 when the Peales retired, Fulton Oursler, Jr. was appointed editor in chief.

Guideposts was begun for business people. Traveling salespersons were a major target audience in the early years. Corporate industrialists subscribed in quantity and distributed the magazine to employees. *Guideposts* surveys conducted after the 1952 publication of *The Power of Positive Thinking* revealed that the readership was increasingly middle-class, middle-aged women.[12] A *New Yorker* contributor characterized the content of the magazine by noting: "Each month, *Guideposts* features inspiring stories of people who have walked up to adversity and kicked it."[13]

Each *Guideposts* first-person story has attempted to validate the principle ("guidepost") that with the right skills (prayer, positive thinking) and relevant knowledge, individual readers can overcome their particular crisis and move through to newness. This approach reflects Peale's well-known conviction that faith, self-help, and psychotherapy are complementary. *Guideposts* also offers a national prayer fellowship, which further binds the readers into a surrogate family.[14]

Moving from industrial bulk-rate subscriptions (down to 8 percent of the total by 1981) to individual subscriptions, the magazine's circulation rose from a half million in 1953 to one million by 1961 and to a peak in 1984 of over four and a half million.[15] *Guideposts* remains an expression of the Peales' personal philosophy: "Urging people to believe in their own worth, to understand their God-given potential, and therefore, by right thinking, decency, creative work, and God's guidance, to make something really worthwhile of their lives."[16] A statement in each issue describes it best: "*Guideposts* magazine, A Practical Guide to Successful Living, is a monthly inspirational, interfaith, nonprofit publication written by people from all walks of life. Its articles present tested methods for developing courage, strength and positive attitudes through faith in God."[17]

Notes

1. Norman Vincent Peale, *The True Joy of Positive Living: An Autobiography* (Pawling, NY: Foundation for Christian Living, 1984), 138.

2. *Guideposts* 2:7 (September 1947): sec. 4, p. 8.

3. Norman Vincent Peale, *The Power of Positive Thinking* (Pawling, NY: Center for Positive Thinking, 1987), 17.

4. Carol V. R. George, *God's Salesman: Norman Vincent Peale and the Power of Positive Thinking* (New York: Oxford University Press, 1993), 103, 108.

5. Ibid., 111.

6. *New York Times*, 26 April 1991, D16.

7. Norman Vincent Peale, "A Message from Our Founder," *Guideposts* 47:9 (November 1992): 46.

8. Peale, *Positive Living*, 170.

9. Ibid.

10. Ibid., 173–74.

11. Ibid., 176.

12. George, *God's Salesman*, 104.

13. *Contemporary Authors, New Revision Series* (Detroit: Gale Research, 1990), 29: 338.

14. George, *God's Salesman*, 105–6.

15. Ibid., 114, 123; Peale, *Positive Living*, 175.

16. Ibid., 28.

17. *Guideposts* 47:9 (November 1992): 47.

Publication History

MAGAZINE TITLE: *Guideposts* (1946–present).

VOLUME AND ISSUE DATA: 1:1 (1946)–present. Published monthly.

PUBLISHER AND PLACE OF PUBLICATION: Guideposts Associates, Inc., Carmel, New York.

EDITORS: Grace Perkins Oursler (1945–1951), Leonard E. LeSourd (1951–1974), Arthur Gordon (1974–1981), Van Varner (1981–1992), and Fulton Oursler, Jr. (1992–present).

CIRCULATION: 3,750,000 (1992).

Lawrence Thompson

GUIDE TO AND BEAUTY OF HOLINESS. *See* GUIDE TO
HOLINESS

**GUIDE TO AND BEAUTY OF HOLINESS AND REVIVAL
MISCELLANY.** *See* GUIDE TO HOLINESS

GUIDE TO CHRISTIAN PERFECTION. *See* GUIDE TO
HOLINESS

GUIDE TO HOLINESS

For more than forty years, the *Guide to Holiness* served as the leading periodical of the American Holiness movement, an instance of the American inclination toward perfectionism. This popular religious movement joined American revivalism with the perfectionist teachings of Methodist founder John Wesley. The result developed an understanding of the Christian life as including two separate works of grace, each experienced by the individual at an identifiable, specific moment and place. Adherents anticipated the first work as the new birth or conversion, whereby one became a Christian. The second work—known variously as Christian perfection, sanctification, or holiness—came when one's heart was transformed to love God perfectly.

The *Guide to Holiness* served as this movement's leading periodical from the journal's inception in 1839 until the mid-1880s, when it began a precipitous decline because of the movement's fragmentation into small sectarian groups. During its career, the *Guide* remained a privately owned monthly without a firm institutional base apart from the Methodist ties and outlook of its editors. Its early connection to Phoebe Palmer, the Holiness movement's leading exponent who edited the journal in its most influential decade from 1864–1874, accounts for the paper's wide influence and character.

Beginning in Boston as the *Guide to Christian Perfection* in July 1839, the paper in its early years depended largely on the reputation and Methodist associations of its founding editor, Timothy Merritt. Following a long itinerancy as a frontier circuit rider, Merritt had served five years with his denomination's papers, the *Zion's Herald* and the *Christian Advocate*, and had published several books showing a taste for public doctrinal debate and a pastoral concern for the experiences of conversion and sanctification. When failing health forced his retirement from the ministry at about the age of sixty, he began the paper.

Merritt acknowledged the peculiarity of a separate periodical devoted to a single doctrine and experience—that of Christian perfection. He attributed the need for such a paper to the recent interest in the doctrine outside of Methodism, referring particularly to the emergence of perfectionism at Oberlin College (Ohio) under Charles G. Finney and Asa Mahan. Timothy Merritt's intuition of the moment proved correct, locating the *Guide* on the rising crest of a broad-based religious movement in American revivalism.

The paper appeared as a plain publication of twenty-four pages containing no illustrations or graphics beyond a simple line drawn between articles whose print filled the quarto pages with a single broad column of print. The cover page presented a simple masthead atop the first article. There were no advertisements. Its only news reported on the New England Methodist conference sessions, betraying a local character despite the paper's early aspirations.

This first issue anticipated the nature and priorities of the emerging Holiness movement. It included a reprint of a sermon by John Wesley, three narratives of the sanctification experience, two apologetic statements, and an article on how to attain the experience. Two editorials defended the journal and appealed for support, with a specific call to women authors.

Unfortunately, Merritt's declining health prohibited him from seeing the *Guide* much beyond its first year. D. S. King, a friend of Merritt's and also the publisher of Asa Mahan's *The Scripture Doctrine of Christian Perfection* (1839), appeared as joint editor and publisher with the second volume. King soon assumed full responsibility. He dropped the term ''perfection'' from the title, believing the name *Guide to Holiness* would increase circulation outside Methodist circles. King ended his term as editor with a circulation listed between twenty-five hundred and three thousand.

When the journal's publisher (Waite, Pierce and Co.) became ''embarrassed in their affairs,'' seeking to sell off their less profitable commitments, Reverend H. V. Degen purchased the journal in 1851 ''as a business venture'' but one that Degen regarded as a movement of Divine providence. The *Guide*'s new editor and publisher had previously served as head bookkeeper for the Methodist Book Concern in New York City and had charge of accounts for Methodism's *Christian Advocate*.[1]

Under Degen, the *Guide to Holiness* became one of the nation's leading religious monthlies. In 1852, the journal received several improvements in its appearance. A new title page ornamented and illustrated with woodcuts replaced the plain appearance of the earlier covers. Degen introduced new type and a double column and enlarged the magazine from twenty-four to thirty-two pages. He further loosened the ties to Methodism, asserting that ''holiness is not sectarian, but Christian,'' and allowed theological language differing from Wesley and the Methodists. The journal occasionally criticized the denomination and opened its pages more fully to testimonies and articles from Congregationalists, Episcopalians, Baptists, and others. The most notable of these was Congregationalist scholar T. C. Upham of Bowdoin College (Maine).[2]

B. W. Gorham joined Degen as associate editor in 1854. Gorham united a call to revitalize the Methodist camp meeting with a call to revive Wesley's distinctive doctrines. Degen published Gorham's *Camp Meeting Manual*, a popular handbook that remains a standard source for histories of the Methodist camp meeting; Degen also published Gorham's camp-meeting songbook, *Choral Echoes*.

Under Degen, the *Guide to Holiness* steadily increased its circulation to about sixteen thousand by the Civil War, more than double the average circulation of

American periodicals in that period.[3] The *Guide* benefited enormously from the growing general interest in Christian perfection and especially from its association with one of the movement's leading exponents, Phoebe Palmer. The *Guide* published several articles and letters by Palmer and reported on her expanding activities. By the late 1850s, the regional spread of the magazine's circulation closely resembled that of Palmer's activities. Ontario, Canada led all other regions in the number of subscribers, with New York following at a close second, and Massachusetts at a distant third. This represented the base area for the magazine, with a significantly wide distribution across most other states, including five hundred in Mississippi and even thirty-one in Hawaii.[4]

The *Guide to Holiness* temporarily declined in the early 1860s. The Civil War disrupted production, increased costs, and hindered distribution, while diverting popular concern for its cause. Moreover, Phoebe Palmer, its principle promoter, had departed for a long campaign in the British Isles. At their return, Palmer and her husband Walter found the *Guide* suffering financial losses and "some serious embarrassment." Walter C. Palmer purchased the paper in 1863 to save it "for the good of the cause," moved it to New York, and combined it with the *Beauty of Holiness*, a similar paper edited by Reverend and Mrs. A. M. French.[5] Palmer paid thirteen thousand dollars, representing one dollar for every name on the combined subscription lists of the two papers, although only seven thousand were paying subscribers.[6]

The resulting journal entered a four-year transition period before rising once again among the nation's leading popular monthlies. The new journal first appeared under the awkward title *Guide to and Beauty of Holiness*, later adding *and Revival Miscellany*, before settling on *Guide to Holiness and Revival Miscellany* in 1868. Moreover, with wartime production costs tripling, the Palmers reduced the paper to twenty-four pages and added twenty-five cents to the previous subscription price of one dollar. These efforts combined with the more general economic boom to stabilize the *Guide*'s decline. By 1867 the *Guide* was once again among the nation's leading religious monthlies with thirty thousand subscribers and would soon add another seven to ten thousand, giving it a circulation equal to or larger than that of any Methodist paper of the time. The paper returned to thirty-two pages and showed improvements in illustrations and ornament.

Phoebe Palmer assumed responsibility for the editorial work in 1864, with her son-in-law, Elon Foster, assisting until 1867 when he left to publish an influential four-volume religious literary cyclopedia. Although her husband's name then appeared as joint editor, W. C. Palmer tended almost entirely to the publishing and business end of the enterprise until Mrs. Palmer's death in November 1874. The *Guide to Holiness* experienced its greatest influence under the editorship of Phoebe Palmer. Under Palmer, reports of the New York Tuesday Meetings for the Promotion of Holiness became a regular feature; this coverage fostered their emulation in Methodist homes across the country. Palmer's wide-ranging revival itinerancy also contributed to the content and audience of the *Guide*. Phoebe Palmer regularly preached and spoke in Chicago, in Michigan, in Cincinnati, making other trips to California and into the South, in addition to her established base on the east coast centering around Boston, New York, and Philadelphia. The *Guide* routinely covered her preaching tours and drew new subscribers from among those who heard her speak.

The Palmers also developed an impressive line of book titles that the *Guide* advertised, reviewed, and introduced in digest and serial form. Many of these publications reveal the Holiness movement's subtle but profound shift from a Christocentric to a Pentecostal understanding of the second work of grace. This included three of Mrs. Palmer's books, the most notable being *The Promise of the Father*, quite possibly the first theological rationale for the right of women to preach in the Church. Other notable titles included Asa Mahan's *The Baptism of the Holy Ghost*, T. C. Upham's *Divine Union*, and Mrs. Upham's *Letters of Madame Guyon*, as well as numerous works by James Caughey, an influential Methodist revivalist. Thus, during the Palmer years, the *Guide to Holiness* served at the center of a complexly structured set of activities reciprocally supporting and benefiting from the Palmer's Tuesday Meetings, itinerant revivalism, and book publications.

In 1867 a number of Methodist ministers formed the National Holiness Association (NHA), an organization of Holiness camp-meeting preachers that soon had its own periodical, the *Advocate of Christian Holiness*. Several of these ministers, including NHA president John Inskip, had claimed sanctification under Phoebe Palmer's ministry. Although the Palmers and the NHA each strove to support the other's work, competition with and the different spirit of the more clergy-dominated NHA became immediately apparent. Palmer used the *Guide* to lecture the new association that the doctrine of the second blessing had not been as neglected before their arrival as they seemed to think. For their part, the NHA chaffed at permitting a woman to speak from its camp-meeting pulpits, while Phoebe Palmer's meetings in their prayer tents fully rivaled the main preaching services of the NHA evangelists for attendance and fervor.[7]

Competition with the NHA paper initiated considerable decline in the *Guide*'s circulation even before Phoebe Palmer's death on 2 November 1874. Under husband W. C. Palmer's guidance, the circulation leveled off, with the *Guide* remaining as the leading Holiness periodical, if no longer among the nation's leading religious papers. W. C. Palmer's success at stabilizing the *Guide* may be attributed to the continuation of his former wife's Tuesday Meetings by her sister Mrs. Sarah Lankford, whom Walter soon married, and to the late flowering of his own ministry in the new Holiness camp meetings. From 1878 until his death in 1883, Palmer conducted the daily morning prayer services at the large and prosperous Ocean Grove camp-meeting resort on the New Jersey coast, where he attracted crowds of up to 10,000 in the main tabernacle during the summer months.

Under W. C. Palmer, the *Guide* harshly criticized the new directions of the American Holiness movement. Palmer refused to join, or connect the paper to, any of the emerging holiness associations, stating that the new "Societies for the Promotion of Holiness" looked to him revolutionary and carried at least the appearance of evil.[8] Nevertheless, in July 1880 Dr. Palmer introduced George Hughes, a former editor and member of the National Holiness Association, as his assistant and soon sold half the business to Hughes, who took up its editorial and management responsibilities as Dr. Palmer declined in health. At Palmer's death in 1883, Sarah Lankford Palmer undertook an active partnership with Hughes in the business and editing of the periodical.

The Holiness Almanac and Year Book, published by Palmer and Hughes, included a national directory of Holiness periodicals for 1884, which largely explains the decline of the *Guide* to the close of the century. More than twenty-five Holiness periodicals of varying size and complexion were being issued from areas scattered across the United States, all competing for much the same audience. The list foreshadows both the fragmentation of the Holiness movement into scores of small sectarian groups and also the emergence of Pentecostalism in the twentieth century. All of these papers acknowledged their debt to both the *Guide* and to the Palmers, sometimes as direct antecedents.

Following the death of Sarah Lankford Palmer in 1894, George Hughes assumed editorial control and ownership of the *Guide to Holiness* and its publishing business. Six years later the Pepper Publishing Company of Philadelphia purchased the paper and merged it with another to produce *Consecrated Life and Guide to Holiness*, edited by Clarence B. Strouse. The new publication lasted for only four issues.

Without any institutional progeny, the *Guide to Holiness* and Phoebe Palmer were rapidly forgotten by even the emerging Holiness denominations who had more immediate founders and institutions to memorialize. Thirty years after the *Guide*'s demise, the first scholarly study of the Holiness movement demonstrated no knowledge of the paper or Phoebe Palmer apart from a passing mention by a folk preacher among the Texas Holiness sects.[9] The *Guide to Holiness*, with its East Coast, urban, middle-class, and literate character, did not fit the early academic understanding of the Holiness movement as a frontier religion. More recent studies have found the *Guide to Holiness* helpful in understanding women's history and the histories of Wesleyan theology and of Pentecostalism. Its study would also enrich studies of the cult of domesticity, evangelical spirituality, and the camp meeting.

Notes

1. George Hughes, *Fragrant Memories of the Tuesday Meeting and the Guide to Holiness* (Metuchen, NJ: Scarecrow, 1980), 173–75; John L. Peters, *Christian Perfection and American Methodism* (New York: Abingdon, 1956), 141.

2. Hughes, *Fragrant Memories*, 173–75; Peters, *Christian Perfection and American Methodism*, 141.

3. Frank Luther Mott, *A History of American Magazines* (Cambridge: Harvard, 1957), 1:514. Mott uses 7,400 as the average circulation of American magazines.

4. Charles Edward White, *The Beauty of Holiness: Phoebe Palmer as Theologian, Revivalist, Feminist, and Humanitarian* (Grand Rapids, MI: Francis Asbury Press, 1986), 92–93.

5. *The Beauty of Holiness* began in Delaware, Ohio, in 1849 and moved to Xenia, Columbus, and possibly Cincinnati before arriving in New York City where Palmer purchased and combined it with the *Guide*.

6. White, *Beauty of Holiness*, 93. Harold E. Raser, *Phoebe Palmer: Her Life and Thought* (Lewiston, NY: Edwin Mellen, 1987), 71, 332 n. 183.

7. The NHA did not allow a woman to speak from the pulpit until after Palmer's death, when Maggie Van Cott held services for them in 1876 (*Advocate of Christian Holiness* 7:10 [October 1876]: 292). For Palmer's participation in the NHA camp meetings, see A. McLean and J. W. Eaton, eds., *Penuel; or, Face to Face with God* (New York: W. C. Palmer, Jr., 1869).

8. Hughes, *Fragrant Memories*, 223; Raser, *Phoebe Palmer*, 333; George Hughes, *The Beloved Physician: Walter Palmer, M.D., and his Sunlit Journey to the Celestial City* (New York: Palmer and Hughes, 1884), 243–46.

9. M. E. Gaddis, *Christian Perfectionism in America* (Ph.D. diss., University of Chicago, 1929).

Information Sources

INDEX SOURCES: None.

LOCATION SOURCES: Microfilmed by the American Theological Library Association. Copies of this microfilm are held in a variety of locations, including Asbury Theological Seminary (Kentucky), Drew University (New Jersey), Duke University (North Carolina), Nazarene Theological Seminary (Missouri), Oberlin College (Ohio), and Wheaton College (Illinois).

Publication History

MAGAZINE TITLE AND TITLE CHANGES: *Guide to Christian Perfection* (1839–1845), *Guide to Holiness* (1846–1863), *Guide to and Beauty of Holiness* (1864), *Guide to and Beauty of Holiness and Revival Miscellany* (1865–1867), *Guide to Holiness and Revival Miscellany* (1868–1901). Continued by *Consecrated Life and Guide to Holiness* (four issues, 1901); possibly continued by *Christian Standard and Guide to Holiness*.

VOLUME AND ISSUE DATA: Published monthly. (Old series) 1:1 (July 1839)–264 (June 1861), volumes 16–17 are numbered 18–19. Old series identified by whole numbers 28–264 (October 1841–June 1861). (New series) 7:6 (June 1868)–75:2–3 (August–September 1901); old serial numbering maintained with some irregularities.

PUBLISHER AND PLACE OF PUBLICATION: Merritt and King, Boston (1839–1845); Geo. C. Rand, Boston (July 1846–184?); Waite, Pierce and Co., Boston (184?–1851); H. V. Degen, Boston (1851–1863); Degen and Foster, Boston (1864); Foster and W. C. Palmer, Jr., New York (1868–1883); Palmer and Hughes, New York (1883–1894); G. Hughes, New York (1894–1901); Pepper Publishing, Philadelphia (1901).

EDITORS: Timothy Merritt (1839–1845), D. S. King (1840–1851), H. V. Degen (1852–1863), B. W. Gorham (1854–1863), Phoebe Palmer, Elon Foster, and H. V. Degen (1864), Phoebe Palmer, editor, and Elon Foster, associate editor (1864–1867), W. C. Palmer and Phoebe Palmer (1868–1874), W. C. Palmer (1875–June 1880), W. C. Palmer and George Hughes (July 1880–1883), Sarah Lankford Palmer and George Hughes (1884–1893), George Hughes (1894–1901), Clarence B. Strouse (1901).

CIRCULATION: 2,500–3,000 (1851); over 12,000 (1857–1858); 16,000 (1860); 13,000 (1863); over 30,000 (1867); up to 40,000 (1870–1873).

Steven D. Cooley

GUIDE TO HOLINESS AND REVIVAL MISCELLANY. *See* GUIDE TO HOLINESS

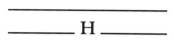

H

HAPPY HOME. *See* CHRISTIAN PARLOR

HAPPY HOME AND PARLOR MAGAZINE. *See* CHRISTIAN
PARLOR

HERALD OF GOSPEL LIBERTY

Christians have struggled to reform the Church since its inception. One of the popular approaches in the eighteenth and early nineteenth centuries was restorationism/primitivism, or trying to recapture earliest Christianity. Glasites, Sandemanians and Haldanes in Great Britain along with the O'Kelly, Stone, and Campbell movements in America, for example, shared the ahistorical concern to purge the Church of traditions, authorities, creeds, and organizations in order to reincarnate the "New Testament church." One of the earliest leaders of American primitivism was the New Englander, Elias Smith (1769–1846). The *Christian's Magazine* and the *Herald of Gospel Liberty* served as Smith's vehicles for popularizing his primitivist vision.

Elias Smith's sensitive soul and inquisitive mind created his independent spirit. Searching for assurance of his righteousness before God, Smith struggled throughout his adolescence with the popular religious systems (Calvinism, Arminianism, and Universalism), but was uncomfortable with them all. Around 1785, Smith found that for which he was looking. Traveling through the woods, he had an accident and was trapped under a log. "While in this situation a light appeared to shine from heaven," Smith recalled. "My mind seemed to rise in that light to the throne of God and the Lamb, and while thus gloriously led, what appeared to my understanding was expressed in Revelation 14:1 ['I looked, and there on Mount Zion stood the Lamb']. My mind was at peace with God through the Lamb of God. My mind was cleansed from all guilt of sin."[1]

Although he found peace with God through this rational conversion experience, the state of American religion still troubled Smith. Doctrinal peculiarities and numerical growth divided the denominations, while concern for social prestige diverted an elitist clergy's attention from the needs of the people. Smith had an idea. What if the laity seized the initiative and stressed their commonalities rather than denominational distinctions? Smith believed that this effort by the common people could literally reunite Christendom. Consequently, on 30 March 1803 Smith and a handful of like-minded friends formed a "church of Christ, to bear the name of Christian, leaving all unscriptural names behind, with everything contrary to the New Testament." Smith's vision spread in New England, and by 1807 fourteen congregations, with over a thousand members, called themselves "churches of Christ."[2]

Toward the goal of Christian unity, Smith founded the *Christian's Magazine, Reviewer, and Religious Intelligencer* in 1805. Smith published the magazine quarterly, and for twelve and a half cents per issue one could read his reflections on Church history and doctrine, the work of the Holy Spirit, the practical application of Christian beliefs, news of revivals around the United States, and selected religious poetry. The fundamental premise of the magazine was the simplicity of the Christian message. In the area of doctrine, for example, Smith believed that Scripture contained only one teaching, "that truth which Christ preached concerning God and man." This included six principles: repentance, faith, baptism (immersion), laying on of hands, the resurrection of the dead, and eternal judgment. These tenets, reasoned Smith, were "so consistent that there is no room for any dispute."[3] One only needed to read perspicuous Scripture and apply the truths.

The journal's mainstay, therefore, was invective against the clergy, who interfered with the people's rights. With the second issue of the *Christian's Magazine*, Smith initiated a column on the history of the clergy, attempting to prove that they were a tyranny. "The word 'clergy' in history," Smith asserted, "describes an order of men in a church, which is ruled by earthly Lords; or in other words, in the church of [the] anti-christ." Since Scripture did not sanction the clergy, they must be a "company of interlopers, who had intruded into society, without any regard to laws, divine or human; and that they were a set of beings who were born only to rule the ignorant and keep them so." Whether one spoke of Roman Catholic, Greek Orthodox, Presbyterian, or Congregational clergy, they were "alike by nature"; they "deprived the people of their rights, which were, liberty and equality."[4]

The despotic priesthood was not alone in its attempt to subvert American liberties, however. According to Smith, Federalists, who advocated tax-supported religion, subsidized the clergy's oppression of the people. One piece of evidence that Smith pointed to was the 1800 Massachusetts statute requiring communities to supply and support a Protestant minister for at least three months of every six-month period. The only justification that Smith could fathom for Massachusetts's tax-supported religion was "the fact [that] in this state were a number of young men too lazy to work, who had been sent to college to be made into ministers; when they came out they were such useless creatures that towns would not employ them.'' A free-market system for the clergy, concluded Smith, would be the most practical solution, for ''were the clergy a useful set of men, there would be no need of a law to oblige people to buy them.''[5] Smith was convinced that once the people were free to exercise their authority on the issue of clerical support, they would extricate themselves from the clergy ''as they did of stamps, loans, direct taxes, and standing armies.''[6]

In 1808 Smith ceased publication of the *Christian's Magazine* and initiated the biweekly *Herald of Gospel Liberty* to expand discussion of religious and political issues. The four-page paper was a gamble for Smith since it was the first religious newspaper and cost one dollar per year. Smith planned to fill the pages with editorials on civil and religious liberty, reprinted sermons, news of revivals and Christian-unity movements, anecdotes, and letters. The first issue on 1 September had around three hundred subscribers, but by 1815 subscriptions had increased to fifteen hundred, reaching twenty states and Canada. Smith's goal in the *Herald* was to educate the common person of their *''unalienable''* right of religious liberty. For Smith this meant the right to determine and implement God's truth for one's self and to worship as one deemed appropriate.

Smith believed that under God and the U.S. Constitution the people were sovereign. But the people could not simply take their authority for granted. ''On the whole,'' Smith warned, ''liberty is nowhere safe in any hands excepting those of the people themselves, who as they have the greatest interest in being free, are natural guardians of their own rights.''[7] This democratic form of government was not merely a wise creation of Americans, it was the ''righteous form of government Jesus Christ taught the people when he preached.''[8] No other nation had been as open to Christ's political teachings of liberty, equality, unity and peace as the United States. This government was ''different from all others on earth: It is from heaven,'' Smith proclaimed. ''The nature of the constitution, and articles of confederation and perpetual union, and the manner in which it was adopted, is a striking proof of its being from God.''[9] Not only America's republican government, but more specifically Thomas Jefferson's Republican party was God's handiwork. After the ''four year scourge'' of the Federalist John Adams, ''our present President Thomas Jefferson was raised up by the King of Kings,'' whose ideas of government and religion were those of Christ. Even though Jefferson was a deist, the evangelical Smith defended him as ''our Divine Emmanuel'' and denounced the opponents of Jefferson as the ''enemies of Christ.''[10] Smith concluded, therefore, that ''almost all who are converted to the Lord are Republicans.''[11]

Since, as republican ideology assumed, the people were the depository of virtue and truth, Smith asserted that the people should exercise their prerogative to simply read and implement Scripture. This action would belie the clergy's arrogance. In the days of the apostles, Smith argued, no one was more esteemed than another. The true religious liberty of the democratic New Testament Church meant that "the sound of Pope, Patriarch, Master, Bishop, Rector, Curate, Parson, Lord Archbishop, Reverend, Doctor, Rabbi with all other names of distinction was no where [sic] heard."[12] In addition, Smith argued that theologians, philosophers, and other academics interpreted Scripture with human designs, codifying their opinions in creeds, catechisms, and platforms. "Real Christians," Smith declared, "believe God has spoken to them by his Son, and that they are bound to hear him in all things, not regarding any of the commands or doctrines of men."[13] Besides, reasoned Smith, it was only common sense that God would make revelation plain. "Is it not a little degrading to the Supreme God," he asked, "to suppose that he himself should institute a religion, and convey it to rational creatures and yet that this revelation should be so vague that we must have the assistance of men to perfect that which is lacking in the work of God? That it must be modelled by political heads; that it needs the labor of Synods, General Assemblies, Councils of fathers to systematize and arrange it?"[14]

With this assertion Smith's vision had come full circle. Once a republican form of government was established for both church and state, the people were empowered to use their liberty. In so doing the people would not only find God's revelation in Scripture for themselves, but would also break the hierarchy's tyranny that had divided Christendom for nearly two millennia. Finally, this rediscovered liberty would unite Christians in a community committed to Christ rather than to doctrines or denominations. Smith admitted that complete consensus was unattainable since "harmony and agreement in every point of doctrine [is impossible] in our present imperfect state of knowledge and understanding."[15] But that was not an impediment to his vision since the foundation of unity was not doctrinal homogeneity. An egalitarian Church would be a tolerant family. "Let every Christian bear and forbear: and be careful not to brand with heresy everyone who may happen to differ from him," he counseled. "Allow to others the same liberty and privilege which we wish to enjoy ourselves, that of free inquiry, of reading, understanding, believing and practicing according to the best light we have, and if we should still differ in some things, let us be careful to retain the unity of the spirit."[16] Furthermore, it was not a Christian's calling to decide for Christ who his followers were. Since all were equal in the Church, all "are accountable to the King, and not to any of his subjects."[17] A united Christendom would naturally form as Christians seized their liberty to think and act for themselves.

In October 1817, Smith announced that he was stepping down as editor of the *Herald*. He stated that his involvement with Samuel Thomson's populist medical theories consumed his time, but the real reason was his shift to Universalism, which alienated him from most of the subscribers of the *Herald*. Smith used the final issue of the *Herald* as an apology for his new-found theological position, ending with an advertisement for the *Gospel Visitant*, which would "contain things important relating to the salvation of all men." In 1827, however, Smith recanted and initiated the *Morning Star and City Watchman*.

After Smith's resignation, Robert Foster became the editor of the *Herald of Gospel Liberty* and renamed it the *Christian Herald*. Others would later use the title and volume numbering of the *Herald of Gospel Liberty*. In March 1930, for example, a journal of religious education and missions, which traced its lineage back to the original *Herald*, merged with the *Congregationalist* and became the *Congregationalist and Herald of Gospel Liberty*. Nonetheless, the period when the *Herald* both represented the ethos of society and had its greatest effect on America's religious history was during the tenure of Elias Smith.

Notes

1. Elias Smith, *The Life, Conversion, Preaching, Travels and Sufferings of Elias Smith* (Portsmouth: Beck and Foster, 1815), 58–59.
2. *Christian's Magazine* 1:1 (1805): 11. The *Magazine* existed for only one volume, and Smith did not include dates on the individual issues.
The "churches of Christ" gathered by Smith became part of the larger "Christian Connection," associated with the leadership of Smith, Abner Jones, James O'Kelly, and to some extent Barton Stone. Those advocates of the Connection who did not follow Stone's 1832 merger with the Campbellites eventually united with the Congregational Church. In 1957 the Congregational Church joined the Evangelical and Reformed Church to form the United Church of Christ.
3. *Christian's Magazine* 1:1 (1805): 15.
4. Ibid. 1:2 (1805): 39, 40–41.
5. Ibid. 1:8 (1805): 284–85.
6. Ibid. 1:7 (1805): 229.
7. *Herald of Gospel Liberty* 1 (15 September 1808): 5–6.
8. Ibid. 1 (22 December 1808): 33.
9. Ibid. 1 (5 January 1809): 37.
10. Ibid. 1 (19 January 1809): 41.
11. Ibid. 1 (10 November 1809): 126.
12. Ibid. 1 (26 May 1809): 78.
13. Ibid. 1 (24 November 1808): 26.
14. Ibid. 1 (8 December 1809): 136.
15. Ibid. 1 (5 January 1809): 39.
16. Ibid. 1 (19 January 1809): 43.
17. Ibid. 1 (15 September 1809): 111.

Information Sources

INDEX SOURCES: Each issue of *Christian's Magazine* contained a table of contents; *Herald of Gospel Liberty* is not indexed.
LOCATION SOURCES: Both titles are available from University Microfilms International in the *American Periodicals Series*.

Publication History

MAGAZINE TITLE AND TITLE CHANGES: *Christian's Magazine, Reviewer, and Religious Intelligencer* (1805–1808), *Herald of Gospel Liberty* (1808–1817). Superseded by *Christian Herald*. *Herald of Gospel Liberty* designation was restored in several later titles, the last of which was *Congregationalist and Herald of Gospel Liberty* (1930–1934).

VOLUME AND ISSUE DATA: *Christian's Magazine* 1:1 (1805)–1:8 (1808); *Herald of Gospel Liberty* 1:1 (September 1808)–8:8 (October 1817). Volume numbering of successor titles has been confused by the many mergers and title changes.

PUBLISHER AND PLACE OF PUBLICATION: *Christian's Magazine*: Elias Smith, Portsmouth, New Hampshire (1805–1808). *Herald of Gospel Liberty*: Elias Smith, Portsmouth, New Hampshire (1808–1809), Portland, Maine (1810–1811), Philadelphia, Pennsylvania (1811–1814), Portland, Maine (1814–1816), Boston, Massachusetts (1816–1817).

EDITOR: Elias Smith (1808–1817).

CIRCULATION: 1,500 (1815).

Richard C. Goode

HERALD OF LIFE AND IMMORTALITY

The *Herald of Life and Immortality* and *Morning Star and City Watchman* were two of the popular religious magazines edited by Elias Smith (1796–1846), a colorful religious radical and democratic populist in early nineteenth-century New England. Smith led an iconoclastic and democratic indigenous New England religious movement, the Christian Connection, which was composed of common people and was self-consciously opposed to clerical elites, ecclesiastical traditions, and theological doctrines (especially Calvinism and Trinitarianism) that the common person could not find in a plain reading of the Bible. Devoting his life to a quest for what he called Gospel liberty, Smith sought to restore the primitive Gospel by circumventing the contingencies of history and replacing the inherited Church with a pristine Christianity of the apostolic period. The restored true Christianity provided in turn the basis for his democratic radicalism with its far-reaching implications for politics, medicine, and other aspects of culture.

Underlying Elias Smith's vision of Gospel liberty was the assumption that the flow of information must be open, lively, bold, and accessible to all, or, put succinctly, communication must be democratic. If Gospel liberty gave to all people the responsibility and ability to be actively involved in church and society, then populist leaders like Smith had to make information available to all so that ordinary people could think and make decisions for themselves. Smith thus made use of any form of communication to spread his radical message, including popular Gospel songs, preaching in fields and city streets, and itinerant traveling; but he was best known for his writing.

In addition to producing many books and inexpensive pamphlets, Smith found journalism to be an effective way to spread his radical ideas. His journalism career began in 1805 with a quarterly entitled *Christian's Magazine, Reviewer, and Religious Intelligencer* and led in 1808 to his biweekly newspaper entitled *Herald of Gospel Liberty*, which cemented his reputation as a publicist of religious and political radicalism. Smith gave much space to accounts of revivals, baptisms, ordinations, religious controversies, and the founding of independent churches that would go only by the name "Christian," in addition to endorsements of the Democratic-Republicans and writings of other religious and republican radicals.

Claiming that "as truth is no private man's property, and as all Christians are under obligations to propagate it, I do also declare, that every Christian has a right to publish and vindicate what he believes,"[1] Smith effectively inverted the elites' learned world of print into a populist organ of democratic sentiments and utilized any device and style that people would find interesting, compelling, and authoritative, including humor, satire, spirited prose, the appeal to common sense, coarse language, and personal attacks against those who disagreed with his message. Although many castigated his writing as erroneous demagoguery, Smith was for common people a folk genius because he spoke their language and appealed to their democratic aspirations with his emphasis on the plain meaning and popular appropriation of the Bible in distinction to a servile acceptance of religious doctrine from the religious elite.

The Christian Connection of New England experienced a crisis in October 1817 when Elias Smith announced in his newspaper that he had adopted the doctrine of universal salvation. This was a shocking development, for though the "Christians" sought to substitute religious experience and Christian character for theology as the test of fellowship, they considered Universalism to be clearly contrary to the Bible and subversive to revivals and the evangelical conversion experience. Smith argued that Universalism was an "advance," a logical conclusion that was true to the literal meaning of the Bible and that followed his rejection of Calvinism, eternal misery of the wicked, and the doctrine of the Trinity.

Having relocated from Portsmouth, New Hampshire, to the Boston area earlier in 1816, Smith became a Universalist minister, leading a short-lived Third Universalist Society in the city and preaching in Scituate and other surrounding areas. Between January 1819 and October 1820, he published the *Herald of Life and Immortality* primarily to defend the doctrine of universal salvation, but also to print sermons, the minutes of Universalist association meetings, religious news, and poetry. Since he believed that Christianity had been dominated by oppressive doctrines of death and destruction, Smith claimed that "it is now time to sound to men the opposite—LIFE and IMMORTALITY," and he chose his title accordingly. With evangelistic zeal, he dedicated his new journal to the proclamation of Universalism, "which declares all are born free and equal, and all equal sharers in the love of him who is good to all, and whose tender mercies are over all his works, and who will have all men to be saved, and come to the knowledge of the truth." Smith's enthusiasm was compounded by the belief that the spread of "impartial religion" would lead to the inauguration of God's kingdom on earth.[2]

Smith believed that his Universalism was in keeping with the popular ideals of the Christian Connection, and he used his *Herald of Life and Immortality* to make appeals to his former colleagues that his new doctrine was a logical result of their joint quest to recover primitive Christianity. Smith continued to rail against the clergy, missionary and educational societies, Calvinism, and other ideas and practices that his "Christian" movement had found contrary to the Bible, but he also used his new journal to accuse the Christian Connection of leaving its original simplicity and acquiring the trappings of a denomination. The organization of Christian "conferences" especially drew Smith's ire, for he believed that the "conferences" were authoritarian and he resented the power they wielded in excommunicating him for his Universalist sentiments.

Begun as a thirty-six-page quarterly at the subscription rate of one dollar per year, Smith hoped that the *Herald of Life and Immortality* would become a biweekly newspaper like his popular *Herald of Gospel Liberty*. It is evident from his comments at the end of each issue, however, that he had great difficulty collecting his subscription money and retaining the enthusiasm of his old audience or gaining the allegiance of a new audience. Smith ceased publication in October 1820, claiming that there was no longer a need for his journal because of the availability of other Universalist magazines and recommending that his readers transfer their subscriptions to the better known *Universalist Magazine* edited by Hosea Ballou.

The *Herald of Life and Immortality* was not a success like Smith's earlier journalism, but it does offer a window to the larger landscape of popular religion in a turbulent period of American history. Besides showing the early affinities between Universalism and popular evangelicalism, the *Herald of Life and Immortality* is of note because it demonstrates how the democratic emphasis of popular Christianity spilled into other areas of life. In a notable statement, Smith made an explicit connection between Universalism, democracy, and botanic medicine:

A *Government*, good for ALL men, must include the whole; and be administered for the good of the whole, without partiality. *Medicine*, to be good, must be such as is suited to the state of ALL. *Religion*, that is pure, must be such as will encourage ALL to deny ungodliness and worldly lusts while ALL are looking for that blessed hope and glorious appearing of the great God, and our Savior Jesus Christ who gave himself for ALL, that he might redeem ALL.[3]

The third link to his democratic radicalism, botanic medicine, came about at the same time that he became a Universalist, when he began practicing medicine according to the system of Samuel Thomson. This popular system was based on plant and steam therapy and was opposed to the bleeding and "poisonous" chemical medicines of "regular" or "mineral" doctors.

With his turn to Universalism and botanic medicine, most of Smith's former colleagues no longer saw him as an ally and began to accuse him of inconsistency. Smith, however, believed that his Universalism and his botanic medicine were consistent with his quest for Gospel liberty. Just as Universalism bestowed the benefits of Christianity to all people, he believed, botanic medicine was democratic because it sought to impart knowledge about the medical properties of natural substances so that common people could take care of their own family's physical ailments, thus circumventing the hegemony, greed, and "poisons" of regular doctors.

From the demise of his *Herald of Life and Immortality* until his death in 1846, the bulk of Smith's energy was given to his medical practice, writing manuals for the self-administration of botanic medicine and managing his own hospital in Boston. He wrote three medical manuals, *The Medical Pocket-Book, Family Physician, and Sickman's Guide to Health* (1822), *The American Physician, and Family Assistant* (1826), and *The People's Book* (1836), and he produced two short-run medical magazines, the *Medical News-Paper* (1822–1824) and the *Medical Tract, and Singular Miscellany* (1830). Linking botanic medicine to democratic radicalism (explicit in the titles of his medical manuals) and popular religion, Smith's medical books and magazines were devoted to defending and imparting knowledge of botanic medicine, attacking regular doctors and state licensing laws that sought to restrict the practice of medicine, exonerating himself from charges of chicanery and advertising his services. Both medical magazines were introduced with the claim that medicine, government, and religion were intimately related, and the magazines included Bible verses on their title pages.

Smith's last journalistic attempt to propagate his popular religion and democratic radicalism appeared in June 1827 with the appearance of his *Morning Star and City Watchman*, a twenty-four–page monthly magazine with the subscription rate of one dollar per year. Although the stated desire of this new magazine, like his past ventures, was to impart biblical knowledge, religious news, and other useful information for common people, much of the *Morning Star* was dedicated to the advocacy of botanic medicine and to the rehabilitation of Smith in the Christian Connection.

Smith continued to advocate in the *Morning Star* a populist understanding of religion, politics, and medicine. In one article, Smith addressed a New York law that restricted the practice of medicine to licensed doctors and concluded that it was "making a *privileged class*, and *order of nobility*; and *aristocracy*—and aiming a blow at the very root of genuine REPUBLICANISM!"[4] In another article, he claimed that the oil by which Church elders were to anoint the sick according to James 5:14-15 was actually a reference to botanical medicine.[5] Smith brought these ideas together into a comprehensive history in his *People's Book*, grouping kings, priests, and regular doctors together as tyrants who usurped the freedom of the people:

The *kings and priests* had the bodies and souls of the people to take care of, as they pretended. There was one thing more needful. Our subjects are liable to diseases, and some must attend to this part; this brought out *Physicians*, but as the people knew how to cure themselves with herbs and roots, the physicians had but little to do, so they made *regular doctors* . . . and a law was then passed that no others should practice within six miles of London, excepting the privilege of giving herb drink. Soon the people forgot their *herb drink* and *roots*, and the physicians marked their drugs in Latin, and as minerals took up less room than vegetables, they were introduced instead of herbs.

Just as true religion is "a matter between God and man" and government is "by the people, for the people," Smith called his fellow Americans through the *Morning Star* and other publications to reject the poisons of the doctors, learn how to administer botanic medicine, and take their medical well-being into their own hands.[6]

Smith also devoted much energy in the *Morning Star* to reestablishing himself in the Christian Connection. He had renounced Universalism and rejoined the "Christians" in 1823 but reverted to the Universalists in 1824. When he began this venture in 1827, Smith again disavowed Universalism and edited the *Morning Star* as an "Elder to the Christian Church." Although he was drawn to Universalism from a belief that it was democratic and consistent with his strong sense of God's providential care, Smith was also repelled by its tendency towards moral inaction and its denigration of the conversion experience.

As the founder of the Christian Connection, a claim asserted in his magazine but contested by others, Smith assumed authority in the *Morning Star* to criticize the Christian Connection for compromising its earlier iconoclasm and purity and for taking on the trappings of a denomination. Specifically, Smith attacked those in the Christian Connection who used the title "Rev." and referred to themselves as "evangelical Unitarians" and the "Christian denomination"; he also criticized the trend toward settled pastorates ("hirelings") and giving greater authority to the state conferences.

Smith claimed that the response to the *Morning Star* exceeded his expectations, and he had agents as far as Tennessee, Indiana, Canada, and Maine. But this magazine never achieved the popularity of his earlier endeavors. Many in the Christian Connection did not trust Smith because of his vacillations between the "Christians" and the Universalists (which continued until he died a Universalist), and the pages of the *Morning Star* became bogged down with controversy over Smith. Almost sixty years old and seemingly exhausted, Smith announced in the last page of the May 1829 issue that he was transferring his subscriptions to the *Christian Herald*, a more moderate and respected "Christian" magazine. Smith thus concluded his checkered but colorful career as an editor of popular religious magazines. Although the *Christian's Magazine, Herald of Gospel Liberty*, *Herald of Life and Immortality*, the medical magazines, and the *Morning Star and City Watchman* varied in format, specific doctrines, audience and success, there was a consistency that ran through them, namely, the popular religion and democratic radicalism of Elias Smith's quest for Gospel liberty.

Notes

1. Elias Smith, *The Life, Conversion, Preaching, Travels, and Sufferings of Elias Smith* (Portsmouth, NH: Beck and Foster, 1816), 403. For a general discussion of Smith and popular Christianity in the early republic, see Timothy E. Fulop, "Elias Smith and the Quest for Gospel Liberty: Popular Religion and Democratic Radicalism in Early Nineteenth-Century New England" (Ph.D. diss., Princeton University, 1992); see also Nathan O. Hatch, *The Democratization of American Christianity* (New Haven: Yale University Press, 1989).
   2. *Herald of Life and Immortality* 1 (January 1819): 2–8.
   3. Ibid. 1 (July 1819): 98.
   4. *Morning Star and City Watchman* 1 (March 1828): 233.
   5. In ibid. 1 (April 1828), Smith added that "the Editor of this work is in possession of this oil or medicine, which will cure when applied, according to the direction given by the Apostle in the text" (280–81).
   6. Elias Smith, *The People's Book* (Boston: B. True, 1836), 19–25.

Information Sources

Herald of Life and Immortality

INDEX SOURCES: *Herald of Life and Immortality* 1:8 (October 1820): 286–88.
REPRINT EDITIONS: American Periodicals Series, 1800–1850, University Microfilms International.
LOCATION SOURCES: American Antiquarian Society (Worcester, Massachusetts), Boston Athenaeum, New York City Public Library, Tufts University (Massachusetts), New Hampshire State Library.

Morning Star and City Watchman

INDEX SOURCES: *Morning Star and City Watchman* 1:12 (April 1828): 285–87.
REPRINT EDITIONS: None.
LOCATION SOURCES: Boston Public Library, University of Chicago, Library of Congress, University of Minnesota, New York Historical Society.

Publication History

Herald of Life and Immortality

MAGAZINE TITLE: *Herald of Life and Immortality* (1819–1820).
VOLUME AND ISSUE DATE: 1:1 (January 1819)–1:8 (October 1820).
PUBLISHER AND PLACE OF PUBLICATION: Publisher unknown, Boston.
EDITOR: Elias Smith (1819–1820).
CIRCULATION: Unknown.

Morning Star and City Watchman

MAGAZINE TITLE: *Morning Star and City Watchman* (1827–1829).
VOLUME AND ISSUE DATE: 1:1 (June 1827)–1:12 (May 1828), 2:1 (September 1828)–2:8 (May 1829).

PUBLISHER AND PLACE OF PUBLICATION: E. Bellamy, Boston (volume 1); Shaw
   and Cushing, Boston (volume 2).
EDITOR: Elias Smith (1827–1828).
CIRCULATION: 300 and 800 (estimated).

Timothy E. Fulop

HERALD OF TRUTH. *See* GOSPEL HERALD

HOME MISSION HERALD. *See* PRESBYTERIAN SURVEY

HOME MISSION MONTHLY MISSIONARY MAGAZINE. *See*
BAPTIST MISSIONARY MAGAZINE

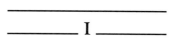

INDIAN SENTINEL

In 1895 the American Catholic Church and the United States Indian Office (later known as the Bureau of Indian Affairs) commenced a twelve-year battle over Church participation in the federally administered system of American Indian education. This confrontation gave birth, in 1902, to the *Indian Sentinel*, a periodical destined to become one of the most important sources for the nation's Catholic Indian missions.

At the center of this controversy lay the constitutional conundrum over federal support for sectarian schools. As early as the administration of Thomas Jefferson (1801–1809) the federal government had recruited the aid of Christian denominations in its program of "civilizing" the country's native American peoples. However, church involvement in United States Indian relations reached its zenith in 1871 with the so-called peace policy of President Ulysses S. Grant, under which selected denominations were awarded oversight of Indian reservations. During this same period the government Indian office contracted with churches to build and staff reservation boarding schools, providing tuition and subsidies (treaty stipulated rations and clothing) for students educated in such facilities.

Among the denominations to receive the government's proposal was the Roman Catholic Church. Although convinced of the anti-Catholic bias of the Indian office, those at the helm of Catholic Indian missions decided to accept the invitation to participate. During the next quarter century the Church, through the Washington-based Bureau of Catholic Indian Missions (BCIM), invested heavily in the construction and operation of reservation boarding schools. However, this period of expansion came abruptly to a halt in 1889 with President Benjamin Harrison's appointment of Thomas J. Morgan as Indian commissioner. Arguing that federal support of Christian Indian schools breached the separation of church and state, Morgan initiated an ambitious program to replace such church-operated facilities with those administered directly by the Indian Office. The two commissioners after Morgan, Daniel M. Browning (appointed in 1893) and William Jones (appointed in 1897), continued their predecessor's campaign to eliminate church participation in federal Indian education. This campaign culminated in a series of congressional acts sanctioning the gradual withdrawal of government funding for denominational schools. Beginning in 1896, the annual allowance for these institutions was decreased by 20 percent, leaving them completely divested of federal support by 1901.

In opposition to the Indian office, the Catholic Church insisted that the appropriations used to finance both sectarian and government reservation schools were not ''public'' monies, but federally administered treaty benefits or ''trusts'' belonging to the Indians themselves. The Church thus submitted that far from safeguarding the separation of church and state, the government's unilateral withdrawal of these funds constituted an infringement of the right of Indian parents to choose a religious education for their children. In 1904 the Catholic hierarchy successfully argued its position before President Theodore Roosevelt, who issued an executive order restoring funds to the Church's Indian schools. However, shortly thereafter, the Indian Rights Association (IRA) challenged this presidential order, commencing a series of suits that culminated in the Supreme Court case of *Quick Bear v. Leupp*. In 1907 the court affirmed the constitutionality of allocating treaty monies for sectarian education, and distribution of these funds to Catholic contract schools was thereby recommenced.

While the Catholic Church was overjoyed with the Court's decision, the twelve years preceding that ruling had been exceedingly lean for its Indian schools. During this period the Bureau of Catholic Indian Missions had been forced to cultivate alternative sources of funding for Indian education. The contributions of such wealthy Catholics as Mother Katherine Drexel, heiress to the Drexel family fortune, constituted one such source. Even more important, however, were the offerings of average Catholics who responded to the Lenten appeals of their parish priests and the features carried in the publications of Church societies. Among these publications, none was more successful in rallying popular sentiment for Catholic Indian education than the *Indian Sentinel*.

Debuting in 1902, the *Indian Sentinel* was distributed annually in English and in German (*Die Indianer Wache*) to members of the BCIM's Society for the Preservation of the Faith among Indian Children. In its ''salutatory'' editorial the magazine asked its readers: ''With the memories of the heroic sacrifices endured to establish our present schools for Catholic Indian children, shall we supinely allow them to fail, and our Indian missions to enter into a dead past ... for the want of generous support?'' Insisting that this could never be allowed to happen, it announced as its own ''high mission'' to help rescue the nation's Catholic Indian wards ''by introducing [the Society] into every household in the land.''[1] To encourage enrollment, the *Sentinel* solicited individuals to organize chapters of the preservation society in their parishes. As a reward for their efforts, society ''promoters'' received certificates, badges, and the opportunity to win a Navajo blanket. Meanwhile, an annual fee of twenty-five cents entitled each chapter recruit to a certificate of membership (available in English, German, Polish, Bohemian, French, Spanish, Italian, Magyar, and Sioux), occasional circulars on matters of import to the Indian missions and schools, and a copy of the *Indian Sentinel*. Members were also extended the opportunity to gain a plenary indulgence, "on the usual conditions," during the feast of the Epiphany and an indulgence of a hundred days by reciting a specified prayer. Through the use of these and other material and spiritual incentives, James Cardinal Gibbons, president of the BCIM, hoped to secure the four hundred thousand sustaining members, the number whose contributions he estimated were needed to underwrite the schools.

During its fifteen-year run as an annual (1902–1916), issues of the *Sentinel* followed a format skillfully designed to mobilize grass-roots support for the Catholic Indian schools. The front cover of each edition carried a photograph of an Indian child or children usually clad in tribal dress. The cover's verso and page one featured letters from elevated members of the American Catholic hierarchy commending the noble work of the preservation society. These acclamations typically were followed by a poem and an essay celebrating the work of a prominent Indian missionary or the progress of the faith among a missionized tribe. Appearing next and constituting the centerpiece of each issue were edifying stories of the origins and present needs of selected Indian schools and reports from missionaries in the field. Issues of the *Sentinel* generally closed with one or more lively editorials presenting the Church's position on issues affecting its Indian missions and schools.

With the cost of operating Catholic Indian schools outstripping private donations and renewed government support, in 1917 the *Sentinel*'s editorial board began publishing the journal as a quarterly. By linking more frequent distribution with a greater use of human interest stories and photographs, the board hoped to attract the one million sustaining subscribers now needed to keep the schools solvent. In reaffirming the *Sentinel*'s fundamental mission, the quarterly's maiden editorial stated that "the Indians have stood in need of guidance and protection ever since they came in contact with the white race."[2] By committing themselves to spiritual uplift and the temporal well-being of the Indians, Catholic missionaries had involved themselves in an unending war with the devil. "Has it never occurred to the reader," the editorial asked, "that Satan seems to have regarded as his very own the Indian races of both Americas, where he had succeeded in his design of thoroughly alienating human creatures from their Creator. . . . How Satan must have raved and sworn to revenge himself upon all who would dare rescue these precious souls from his clutches. . . . So the war for Indian souls will continue. . . . In this struggle missionaries confidently hope to find THE INDIAN SENTINEL a powerful ally and advocate."[3]

The *Sentinel* continued as a quarterly until 1936, when it reemerged as a monthly and so remained until 1956. From 1957 until 1962, when it ceased publication, the journal was distributed bimonthly and finally on a quarterly basis.

The *Indian Sentinel* is an indispensable resource for anyone interested in the history of Catholic education and missions among native North Americans. The unflattering images of Indian societies and religions that fill its pages are a reflection of the paradigm that informed native American missions before the advent of Vatican II. Underlying this paradigm were two basic assumptions regarding the nature of Indian societies and spiritualities. There was first the supposition that Indian lifeways belonged to a stage of human collective life both historically anterior and inferior to that of European and Euro-American nations. Given this assumption, missionaries considered it an essential part of their ministry to train native Americans in the institutions of Occidental society and, thereby, speed them along in cultural advancement. They also believed that once Indian tribes had adopted "civilized" forms of social life, suitable "natural ground" would exist for the planting and germination of the Catholic faith.

Second, Catholic missionaries understood and evaluated native American patterns of worship in the context of an assumed split between "natural" religion, on the one hand, and the revealed Judeo-Christian tradition, on the other. They acknowledged that because of humanity's innate capacity for critical reflection, "natural" religions such as those practiced by the Indians might contain a few grains of truth. The missionaries nonetheless insisted that the major components of such systems were human delusions and devil worship. In view of this perspective, the missionaries' fundamental goal was to replace indigenous religions with Catholic belief and ritual. Correspondingly, contemporary notions that native religions are grounded in authentic revelatory events or that Indians might validly participate in both their tribe's spiritual traditions and Christianity were totally alien to the missionaries' understanding.

In 1978, after a hiatus of thirteen years, the *Bureau of Catholic Indian Missions Newsletter* succeeded the *Indian Sentinel*. It continues today as the official organ of the remaining Catholic Indian missions.

Notes

1. *Indian Sentinel* 1 (1902–1903): 25.
2. Ibid. 2 (Spring 1917): 6.
3. Ibid.

Information Sources

INDEX SOURCES: No indexes published.
LOCATION SOURCES: Widely available in major university, public, and private libraries.

Publication History

MAGAZINE TITLE: *Indian Sentinel* (1902/1903–1962). Succeeded by *Bureau of Catholic Indian Missions Newsletter.*

VOLUME AND ISSUE DATA: 1 (1902–1903)–(1916), published annually; 2 (1917)– 15 (1935), published quarterly; 16 (1936)–36 (1956), published monthly; 37 (1957)–39 (1961), published bimonthly; 40 (1962), published quarterly.

PUBLISHER AND PLACE OF PUBLICATION: Bureau of Catholic Indian Missions, Washington, DC.

EDITORS: William Ketcham (1902–1921), William Hughes (1921–1935), J. B. Tennelly (1935–1966).

CIRCULATION: Unavailable.

Harvey Markowitz

INSTITUTE TIE. *See* MOODY MAGAZINE

INTERPRETER

The religious movement begun by John Wesley in the eighteenth century has always been characterized by its orderly ways. The name "Methodist," applied in derision to Wesley's group at Oxford University, contained enough truth that it stuck. Consequently United Methodists are noted for a strong connectional organization and an approach to faith that emphasizes practical application. United Methodists churches conduct many programs to promote Christian education, missions, evangelism, and the relation of faith to the problems of society. Committees direct each program area.

Since 1969, the United Methodist Church has published a program journal to help Church members direct those programs. That journal is the *Interpreter*, with roots going back to 1955. By 1992, Spanish and Korean editions were also available.

As with cognate journals within other denominations, the *Interpreter* is a "house organ" for its sponsoring agency. Hence, the content of the *Interpreter* focuses narrowly on the United Methodist Church and its objectives at the national and world levels. It assumes that local churches, as part of a "connectional system," share those objectives and welcome assistance in working toward them. The main content consists of information about a variety of programs, with ideas and resources for putting them into effect in each parish. The magazine also carries information about the benevolent funds of the denomination, intended to help each church generate giving for missions, emergency relief, and other causes. Much of the content originates with general boards of the denomination, often called "program agencies." An editorial advisory group represents those boards, working with the editors on content.

Volume numbers for the *Interpreter* continue those of the *Methodist Story*, begun by what was then known simply as the Methodist Church. The first issue

(March 1957) carried a statement of purpose: "We hope that this regular unfolding of the story of what the Methodist Church is doing through its many arms will inspire church workers and strengthen their commitment to the cause we all share. At the same time, it is our aim that the key leadership of every Methodist church shall find here each month information useful in program building and help for their problems."[1] The statement remains an appropriate description.

The *Methodist Story* began with a full-time professional editor, managing editor, and production manager, in addition to a part-time business manager. It began in magazine format, two colors, with two novel features: three-hole punching, so the magazine could be stored in ring binders, and perforated pages, so that the pages could be torn out and passed along to other readers. The magazine format continues with little change except for the addition of four-color printing throughout and discontinuance of the punching and perforation.

Earlier, in 1955, the Evangelical United Brethren Church (EUB) had begun *Spotlight* with similar purposes but in newsletter format. It was put together by volunteers from the staffs of general boards of the denomination and eventually was sponsored by the denomination's program council.[2]

As union in 1968 between the Methodist and EUB denominations approached, staff persons from *Spotlight* and the *Methodist Story* met to plan a combined publication. The first issue of *Methodist Story–Spotlight* was on the desks of delegates to the uniting conference in Dallas in April 1968. The format and professional staff for the combined publication came from the Methodist side; and the staff of the *Methodist Story* moved from Evanston, Illinois, to Dayton, Ohio, to edit the program journal. With the issue for January 1969, the name became the *Interpreter*.[3]

Content continues the parallel traditions of the two initial publications. In fact, two departments have remained with names and purposes unchanged since the first issue. They are "Just Out," reviewing new resources for program work in local churches, and "It Worked for Us," an exchange of ideas supplied by readers.

The *Interpreter* contains columns in each issue for persons who hold specific jobs in local churches. Each column gives practical suggestions for its area of work, often drawing upon the actual experiences of real churches. Frequently the columns cite new resources in print or audiovisuals, accompanied by order blanks. Feature articles are resources in themselves, providing information and suggesting plans for programs. For most years there is a special issue on general program planning for churches. Some of these have been reprinted as planning books.

The *Interpreter* and its predecessors reflect long-standing concerns in the history of Methodist-related periodicals. The *Christian Advocate*, founded in New York in 1826 and once the weekly newspaper with the largest circulation in the United States,[4] had metamorphosed into regional *Christian Advocates* (as many as eight by 1929), each with its own editor and distinct content, but sponsored by the Methodist Book Concern.[5] With a Church union in 1939 these became a single, national, weekly magazine with five regional editions. By the 1950s this journal was trying to serve the needs of both clergy and laity and be a large-circulation subscription magazine. As a paid-subscription magazine, aimed at the person in the pew, the *Advocate* could not be a program journal. Many of the general boards of the Church had already begun to publish their own magazines and newsletters directed toward local churches. There were complaints of a surfeit of publications.

At the 1956 Methodist general conference, delegates approved publication of three denominational periodicals, each with a different purpose. *Together* was to be a monthly magazine for the laity, *New Christian Advocate* would focus on clergy, and a new program journal would take the place of board publications.[6] Thus was born the *Methodist Story*, one of the *Interpreter*'s predecessors.

The EUB Church had a remarkably parallel history with its periodicals. The venerable *Religious Telescope* (1834) and *Evangelical Messenger* (1836) had been combined into the *Telescope-Messenger* at a Church union in 1946. In 1962 that was replaced by a semimonthly family magazine, *Church and Home* (quite similar to, and in 1969 combined with, *Together*). As with the Methodists, a family magazine did not meet program needs. So in 1955, *Spotlight* was started to promote denominational programs.[7]

The *Interpreter* continues the pattern of the *Methodist Story* as a monthly magazine with a July–August combined issue. There have been adjustments at various times reflecting budget problems and changes in reading habits. In 1992 the *Interpreter* was published just eight times. It began with free distribution to persons responsible for conducting local programs, augmented by some paid subscriptions.

Publication in languages other than English began in 1958 when editors became aware of the needs of Spanish-speaking members of the Church. *El Intérprete* began as a joint venture with a Cuban Methodist publication, then was moved to Puerto Rico, and in 1973 was brought into the editorial offices with a Spanish-speaking editor on staff. The purpose of *El Intérprete* is parallel to that of the *Interpreter*, but it is not a translation.[8] Nearly all of the writing originates in Spanish, written by Hispanic American persons. Because it is the only Spanish-language magazine for general circulation in the United Methodist Church, program-related content is supplemented by articles of general interest to Spanish-speaking United Methodists. It is published six times a year.[9]

The 1980s saw a remarkable growth of the United Methodist Church among Korean Americans, and there was a request for a magazine parallel to the *Interpreter* and *El Intérprete* to serve Korean-speaking congregations. In 1990 the governing board of United Methodist Communications, which since 1972 had been responsible for publishing the program journals, voted to establish a Korean-language journal. The editor is Korean American and a United Methodist clergy who is advised by a committee representing the Korean churches. The journal is called *United Methodist Family* and is written entirely in Korean. It is published twice a year.[10]

The *Interpreter* and its companion journals are unabashedly in-house publications. They do not carry editorials nor do they attempt to influence policies of the denomination. They view themselves as a link between the Church at its general level and the parishes where United Methodist Church members experience their church life. In this the program journals appear to be successful, as attested by periodic readership surveys and the continued willingness of the denomination to fund publications that for the most part go to their subscribers free of charge.

Notes

1. W. C. Martin, E. Harold Mohn, and Edwin H. Maynard, "When They Hear the Story," *Methodist Story* 1:1 (March 1957): 2.

2. Edwin H. Maynard, *Keeping Up With a Revolution* (Nashville: United Methodist Communications, 1990), 137.

3. Edwin H. Maynard, "Milestones and Mission," *Interpreter* 26 (March–April 1982): 4–6.

4. Emory Stevens Bucke, ed., *The History of American Methodism* (New York: Abingdon Press, 1964), 1:577–78.

5. *Daily Suggester, 1929* (Cincinnati, New York, and Chicago: Methodist Book Concern, 1929), 18.

6. Edwin H. Maynard, "Getting the Word around about Church Program" (unpublished manuscript, 1986), 5.

7. Maynard, *Keeping Up*, 8.

8. Irene Kenigson, "Treinta Años de El Intérprete," *El Intérprete* 26:3 (May–June 1988): 13.

9. Maynard, *Keeping Up*, 140–41.

10. Ibid, 142.

Information Sources

INDEX SOURCES: With a few exceptions, the last issue of the *Interpreter* each year carries an index for that volume.

LOCATION SOURCES: Bound volumes of the *Interpreter* may be found in the libraries of most United Methodist theological seminaries and some colleges.

Publication History

MAGAZINE TITLE AND TITLE CHANGES: *Spotlight* (1955–1968), *Methodist Story* (1957–1968), *Methodist Story–Spotlight* (1968) *Interpreter* (1969–present).

VOLUME AND ISSUE DATA: 1:1 (March 1957)–present.

PUBLISHER AND PLACE OF PUBLICATION: *Spotlight*: Council of Administration of the Evangelical United Brethren Church, Dayton, Ohio (1955–1963); Program Council of the EUB Church, Dayton, Ohio (1963–1968). *Methodist Story*: Commission on Promotion and Cultivation of the Methodist Church, Evanston, Illinois (1957–1968). *Interpreter*: Division of Interpretation of the Program Council of the United Methodist Church, Evanston, Illinois (1968–1972); United Methodist Communications, Dayton, Ohio (1972–1986); Nashville, Tennessee (1986–present).

EDITORS: *Spotlight*: collective editorship (1955–1968). *Methodist Story*: Edwin H. Maynard (1957–1967), Darrell R. Shamblin (1967). *Interpreter*: Darrell R. Shamblin (1968–1988), Laura J. Okumu (1988–1992), Ralph E. Baker (1992–present). Korean and Spanish editions have separate editors.

CIRCULATION: 286,000 (1992).

Edwin H. Maynard

L

LADIES' REPOSITORY

In January 1841, the Methodist Episcopal Church unveiled a new magazine for Christian women. The *Ladies' Repository* was the brain child of a prominent Cincinnati Methodist layman, Samuel Williams, who believed that the Church had an obligation to provide women with instructive and inspiring reading material. Williams envisioned a magazine of "pure literature" that would serve as a Christian alternative to the widely read *Godey's Lady Book* and to the popular romantic fiction of the day. Through the *Ladies' Repository*, Williams hoped to shield women from the temptations of the secular literary marketplace and to encourage women's intellectual and spiritual growth.

In response to Williams's initiative, the Ohio Conference of the Methodist Episcopal Church agreed to sponsor the magazine and appointed L. L. Hamline as editor. Hamline opened an editorial office in Cincinnati, and arrangements were made to print the magazine both there and in New York. Annual subscriptions, originally priced at two dollars, were sold by Methodist book agents.[1] The men who shaped the *Ladies' Repository* in its early years were committed to publishing a journal of undisputed excellence. Two high-quality steel engravings were included in each issue, and editors maintained a strict standard by which articles were evaluated for publication. Each month, the thirty-two pages of the *Ladies' Repository* were filled with poetry and prose from some of the finest popular writers of the mid–nineteenth-century.

Hamline set the tone of the magazine in the first issue. The goal of the new periodical, he wrote, was "to promote the healthful cultivation of the female mind, and draw it from trifles into its appropriate sphere of privilege."[2] He solicited serious articles on a broad range of issues, giving preference to contributions from female writers, and labored to make eclecticism the defining feature of the *Ladies' Repository*.

In the first issue of the magazine, readers were treated to essays on subjects as diverse as physical science, the birth of Jesus, and the history of the Brazilian monarchy. Brief, plainly written, factual articles on various branches of science regularly appeared in the early years of the *Ladies' Repository*. The magazine's consistent emphasis on science is evidence that a rudimentary knowledge of basic scientific principles was, by the 1840s, an essential part of the education of both men and women in the United States.

Historical pieces, often on religious topics, also were included regularly. Short, descriptive entries on religious figures, symbols, and practices were scattered throughout the early issues, and Christian history, from biblical times forward, was a dominant, although not exclusive, focus. Other articles covered civilizations and historical epochs as distant and distinct from one another as ancient Greece and eighteenth-century Europe. In addition, editors encouraged readers to submit poetry, fiction, and travel essays.

As it entered its second decade, the eclecticism of the *Ladies' Repository* gave way to a somewhat narrower focus on religious topics and the responsibilities of women as wives and mothers. These themes had always been represented in the magazine, but emphasis on them grew throughout the 1850s and early 1860s. Gradually, the *Ladies' Repository* became less concerned with the general education of its readers and more intent upon publishing literature with a religious and moral message.

The didacticism of the magazine is particularly evident in its articles about women. From the beginning, the *Ladies' Repository* tried to provide women with worthy role models by publishing articles on famous wives and mothers. Essays on the mothers of men like John Wesley and George Washington demonstrated to readers that great leaders owed their achievements at least in part to positive maternal influences. Perhaps more importantly, essays like one entitled "Wives of Wesley and Luther" forcefully illustrated how a wife could affect a husband's life for good or ill. In this essay, Luther's wife, Catherine de Bora, is described rhapsodically as a model helpmeet and spiritual partner, while the faults of John Wesley's unnamed wife are carefully enumerated.[3] Prominent women like Phoebe Palmer, the Countess of Huntingdon, and the missionary Ann Judson were also held up as inspiring examples of the transforming power of religious faith.

It was not only famous women who were offered up in this way; ordinary women served this purpose too. Although it was the official policy of the magazine to discourage contributors from submitting obituaries, the editors occasionally made exceptions in order to note the untimely deaths of particularly virtuous and pious women. These articles, usually about young wives and mothers, served a dual purpose: they reminded readers how quickly and unexpectedly death could come, while also demonstrating that ordinary women were capable of living lives of great faith.

Most of the material in later issues of the *Ladies' Repository* reflected the magazine's religious roots, but there were some exceptions. Poetry and prose sometimes honored women like Elizabeth Barrett Browning and Charlotte Brontë, both of whom were known more for their secular literary achievements than for their faith.[4] The secular made its way into the *Ladies' Repository* in other ways, too. Essays on philosophy discussed the thought of men like Immanuel Kant, Voltaire, and Jean Jacques Rousseau, and the words of Thomas Carlyle were invoked by writers who argued against the cause of women's rights.[5]

Although the enfranchisement of women was a public issue of obvious relevance to readers of the *Ladies' Repository*, it was not a frequent topic of discussion.[6] The paucity of material on female suffrage and other issues, like temperance, that were of special interest to women, is striking to the modern reader, but not inexplicable.[7] Until its final years, the *Ladies' Repository* took little notice of current events and issues. Indeed, the most explosive social issue of the nineteenth century, slavery, never received prominent exposure even though the Methodist Church was torn in two by debate over it. In the months between the 1860 presidential election and the outbreak of the war, editors noted, with a sense of foreboding, the potential for conflict, but they printed their comments amid other editorial notes on the final page of the magazine. Throughout the war, editors continued to use this space to condemn, albeit in moderate language, the secession of the Southern states and the institution of slavery. Submissions placed elsewhere in the magazine ignored altogether the tensions at the root of the war, focusing instead on the conflict's tragic human dimension by invoking sentimental images of grief-stricken wives and mothers and suffering soldiers.[8]

The Civil War years were a watershed for the *Ladies' Repository*. The weak postwar economy and a concomitant decline in subscriptions and rise in production costs led to a financial crisis that left the magazine's future in doubt. In what may have been a fatal miscalculation, editors decided to begin marketing the *Ladies' Repository* more aggressively as a general magazine for the whole family. As early as 1858, editors had described the *Ladies' Repository* as a family magazine and organized children's stories into a special section, but the format had never offered anything that was aimed specifically at a male audience. In the postwar years, editors tried to remedy this by adding features like "Art Notes," the "Foreign Department," "Current History," and a column on popular science that they hoped would attract a more general adult readership. Subjects like science and the fine arts had been covered in the magazine's early years, but they had presumed no prior knowledge on the part of readers. The articles of the 1870s, on the other hand, were written for educated men and women who wanted to keep abreast of current developments in a broad range of fields. These changes did nothing to save the magazine, however, and in 1876 publication of the *Ladies' Repository* ceased. The Church immediately replaced it with another magazine, the *National Repository*, but it survived for only four years.

The *Ladies' Repository* is a valuable resource for students of nineteenth-century American popular culture. In its pages, modern readers can follow changes in literary taste and in expressions of religious piety, as well as the development of a new domestic culture. Above all, the *Ladies' Repository* is significant for what it suggests about the ambiguous status of women in mid–nineteenth–century America. The magazine reflects a growing appreciation of women's intellectual potential while also underscoring the persistence of paternalistic attitudes toward women. Women writers were encouraged to publish in the pages of the *Ladies' Repository*; and articles on the classics, science, and theology were included in order to advance the education of women. Still, men developed and controlled the magazine, and men determined what women needed to learn from it. The *Ladies' Repository* was the magazine that male Christians felt the women in their churches needed.

The *Ladies' Repository* was to some extent a pragmatic response to the changes that were occurring in women's lives. Whereas women once had worked in partnership with men to provide the basic goods needed by the family, the duties of men and women were becoming more distinct and removed from one another. The United States moved from an agrarian to an increasingly industrial economy, and the center of economic life moved from the home to the office and factory. Out of this change emerged a new conception of womanhood. As women became less valued for their role in producing household goods, their importance as wives, mothers, and guardians of morality increased.[9]

Increasingly, the home was regarded as a private space in which the nuclear family interacted apart from the larger community. The home was to be a sanctuary to which husbands could retreat at the end of a long day, and it was each woman's responsibility to make it so. Child rearing, traditionally a woman's responsibility, took on added importance with the new emphasis on the tightly knit family circle. Writers emphasized the qualities that made women uniquely qualified to rear children, going beyond mere physiology to include women's inherent capacity for piety, virtue, and tenderness.[10] There was a recognition that piety and virtue in particular were needed if the United States was to produce the kind of citizenry that democracy demanded, and it was a woman's duty to instill these qualities in her children.

In an ironic twist, this circumscription of women's roles gave rise to the increased emphasis on female education, of which the *Ladies' Repository* was a product. Child rearing was viewed as such an essential task, and one so closely tied to the future strength of the republic, that American society accepted the need for female education. In the antebellum years, its learned essays established the *Ladies' Repository* as a unique vehicle for educating women; but once editors recrafted it into a general family magazine there remained little to distinguish it from other popular journals. The *Ladies' Repository* had lost its distinctive style by the 1870s—and this fact, perhaps more than any other, led to its ultimate demise.

Notes

1. The annual subscription rate remained two dollars until the early 1860s, when it was raised to two and a half dollars. In 1864, the rate increased to three and a half dollars, but there were no price increases in the final twelve years of publication. In May 1854, the magazine had eighteen thousand subscribers, and by 1860 this number had reached thirty-four thousand. Six thousand additional subscribers were added in 1861, making it the most successful year in the *Ladies' Repository*'s history. During the war years, subscriptions fell to the 1860 level of thirty-four thousand.

2. *Ladies' Repository* 1 (January 1841): 7.

3. Ibid. 11 (January 1851): 34–35.

4. See Jesse Atherton, "A Review of the Life of Charlotte Brontë," *Ladies' Repository* 17 (December 1857): 734–36; see also Sarepta M. Irish Henry, "Elizabeth Barrett Browning," *Ladies' Repository* 22 (September 1862): 564.

5. A brief but balanced discussion of Kant can be found in Edward Thomson, "Extremes in Philosophy," *Ladies' Repository* 14 (September 1854): 395. J. C. Wells also offered a balanced treatment of philosophy in his essay "Voltaire and Rousseau," *Ladies' Repository* 18 (December 1858): 746–48. Carlyle appears in the magazine several times. On the subject of women's rights he is quoted by the editor in *Ladies' Repository* 14 (March 1854): 140. W. W. Battershall analyzed his views on other matters in "Carlyle and His Religion," *Ladies' Repository* 21 (November 1861): 678–81.

6. See "Talks about the Woman Question I," *Ladies' Repository* 31 (February 1871): 133–37; see also "Talks about the Woman Question II," 31 (March 1871): 212–17.

7. It was not until after publication of the *Ladies' Repository* had ceased that both the temperance and women's-rights movement gained their fullest momentum. Public discussion of both issues began in the antebellum years, but they did not generate the same amount of attention and support in the nineteenth century as they did in the early twentieth century. As noted before, essays on the "woman question" did appear in the magazine, but essays on temperance did not. The destructiveness of alcohol use was illustrated to great effect, however, in stories of long-suffering wives and mothers who tried to save their drunken men from ruin.

8. For sorrowful poems and other relevant literary offerings during the war, see "Burial at Camp" and "Killed and Wounded," *Ladies' Repository* 23 (February 1863): 96, 108; "Woman: The Soldier's Friend," *Ladies' Repository* 24 (May 1864): 305; and "Driven to the War," *Ladies' Repository* 23 (April 1863): 209–12.

9. The changing role of women in American society is discussed in Nancy Cott, *The Bonds of Womanhood: "Women's Sphere" in New England, 1780–1835* (New Haven: Yale University Press, 1977), and in Carl Degler, *At Odds: Women and the Family in America from the Revolution to the Present* (New York: Oxford University Press, 1980). Several valuable essays on this subject are collected in Mary S. Hartman and Lois Banner, eds., *Clio's Consciousness Raised: New Perspectives on the History of Women* (New York: Octagon Books, 1976). Paul E. Johnson has discussed changing family structures and the emergence of an industrial economy in *A Shopkeeper's Millennium: Society and Revivals in Rochester New York, 1815–1837* (New York: Hill and Wang, 1978).

10. For an example of this theme, see the "Letters" column of the magazine's first

issue. In this column, a male writer expressed his support for the new magazine and its goals, commenting on the ''superior place that maternal influence has in the original formation of individual and social character'' (*Ladies' Repository* 1 [January 1841]: 29).

Information Sources

INDEX SOURCES: Each volume contains a general index for the year.
LOCATION SOURCES: Available on microfilm in the American Periodicals Series II. Also available at the Library of Congress, Detroit Public Library, University of Michigan, and Brown University (Rhode Island).

Publication History

MAGAZINE TITLE AND TITLE CHANGES: *Ladies' Repository and Gatherings of the West: A Monthly Periodical Devoted to Literature and Religion* (1841–1848), *Ladies' Repository: A Monthly Periodical Devoted to Literature and Religion* (1849–1872), *Ladies' Repository: A Monthly Periodical Devoted to Literature, Art, and Religion* (July 1872–December 1876).
VOLUME AND ISSUE DATES: 1:1 (January 1841)–36:12 (December 1876). Published monthly. Volumes 28–34 (1868–1874) also numbered as new series volumes 1–14. Volumes 35–36 (1875–1876) also numbered as third-series volumes 1–4.
PUBLISHER AND PLACE OF PUBLICATION: Published in Cincinnati by J. F. Wright and L. Swormstedt (1841–1843), Swormstedt and Mitchell (1844–1847), Swormstedt and J. H. Power (1848–1851), Swormstedt and A. Poe (1852–1859), Poe and Hitchcock (1860–1868), Hitchcock and Walden (1869–1876). Published in New York by G. Lane and C. B. Tippett (1841–1847), Lane and L. Scott (1848–1851), T. Carlton and Z. Phillips (1852–1855), Carlton and J. Porter (1856–1868), Carlton and Lanahan (1869–1872), Nelson and Phillips (July 1872–December 1876).
EDITORS: L. L. Hamline (1841–1843), G. Thompson (1844–1845), B. F. Tefft (1846–1852), W. C. Larrabee (August 1852–January 1853), D. W. Clark (1853–1863), I. W. Wiley (1864–June 1872), E. Wentworth (July 1872–June 1876), Daniel Curry (July–December 1876).
CIRCULATION: 40,000 (1861).

Kathleen Joyce

LADIES' REPOSITORY: A MONTHLY PERIODICAL DEVOTED TO LITERATURE AND RELIGION. *See* LADIES' REPOSITORY

LADIES' REPOSITORY: A MONTHLY PERIODICAL DEVOTED TO LITERATURE, ART, AND RELIGION. *See* LADIES' REPOSITORY

**LADIES' REPOSITORY AND GATHERINGS OF THE WEST: A
MONTHLY PERIODICAL DEVOTED TO LITERATURE AND
RELIGION.** *See* LADIES' REPOSITORY

LADY'S BOOK. *See* GODEY'S LADIES BOOK

LATTER DAY LUMINARY. *See* CHRISTIAN INDEX

LIBERAL JUDAISM. *See* REFORM JUDAISM

LIBERTY

Liberty, a "magazine of religious freedom" published by the Seventh-Day
Adventist Church, commenced publication in 1906 with the warning that "another crisis is at hand" over the fate of religious liberty in America.[1] Measures
proposed in Congress to require businesses in the District of Columbia to close
on Sundays amounted to something less than a national crisis to most Americans. But for Adventists such a law would be an alarming first step toward a
union of church and state and the end of American freedom—which, their apocalyptic beliefs informed them, must inevitably come, but which, some of them
believed with equal firmness, must be resisted in the present.

During a similar "crisis" in the 1880s and 1890s, the Adventist commitment
to a publication advocating religious freedom and the separation of church and
state took shape. When Adventists began publishing *Liberty*'s predecessor, the
American Sentinel, in 1886, maintenance of Sunday as a day set apart by law,
along with Prohibition, was seen by many as crucial to sustaining Anglo-
Protestant cultural preeminence in the face of social changes wrought by rapid
immigration, industrialization, and urbanization.[2] Adventists also regarded Sabbath observance as vital to Christianity, but were convinced that Christendom
at large had gotten the day wrong: the Ten Commandments, they believed,
required observance of the seventh day of the week—Saturday. Imposing the
coercive pressure of law on the minority who adhered to the true biblical Sabbath, said Adventists, constituted violation of the political essence of Protestantism—individual liberty.[3] The Sabbath issue was the starting point for a
broad-ranging advocacy of religious liberty and the separation of church and
state in the *American Sentinel* and then in *Liberty*.

Though Adventists numbered only about twenty thousand in the 1880s, increasing pressures led them to make their voices heard in public debate over
religious liberty. One was the legal harassment that some members were experiencing. In the 1880s and 1890s, over a hundred Adventists were convicted of
violating state Sunday laws, primarily in the South, and many were imprisoned.[4]
At the same time, Adventists were concerned about the activities of the National
Reform Association (NRA), an organization of conservative evangelicals that
emerged in the mid–1860s, with the primary goal of enacting a constitutional

amendment that would "indicate that this is a Christian nation."[5] Laws enforcing the Christian Sabbath would be among those undergirded by such an amendment, and in 1879 the NRA began a drive for a national Sunday law that would
indicate "national recognition of divine sovereignty." Though a relatively small
organization, the NRA gained the support of several other reform organizations,
such as the WCTU, the Prohibition Party, and the American Sabbath Union. A
national Sunday law supported by these groups was introduced in Congress in
1888.[6]

Adventists regarded these developments not simply as a threat to their own
religious liberty, but as the fulfillment of apocalyptic prophecy. Since the 1850s,
they had understood the book of Revelation to forecast both the emergence of
religious liberty in America and its demise. According to their reading, the
American government would enforce religious laws, specifically a national Sunday law, causing the final persecution of the people of God prior to the Second
Coming. Though they believed that these events were sure to occur, Adventists
after the Civil War came to believe that public witness on behalf of religious
liberty was their duty in the interim between the present and the Second Coming.
Liberty must be preserved and the end delayed for a short time for the sake of
the Church's mission.[7]

Thus, in 1886 they launched the *American Sentinel*, an eight-page monthly
(weekly beginning in 1889) first published in Oakland, California (then in New
York City in 1890), designed to reach public officials and other leaders with
articles on civil and religious liberty and on the threats to it posed by the NRA
and allied organization. The *Sentinel* was "devoted to the defense of American
Institutions, the preservation of the United States Constitution as it is, as far as
regards religion of religious tests, and the maintenance of human rights, both
civil and religious."[8] Later that year Adventists formed the National Religious
Liberty Association to coordinate the work of public education and to lobby
legislators.[9]

From its first issue, the *American Sentinel* opposed the concept of the United
States as legally a Christian nation. In resisting legal supports for Protestant
hegemony, including the amendment, Sunday laws, and religious exercises in
the public schools, the *Sentinel* laid down precedents that *Liberty* has followed
to the present day.

Publication of the *Sentinel* lapsed in 1904, but less than two years later the
Church launched *Liberty: A Magazine of Religious Freedom*, a new 6½-by-9½-
inch, thirty-two–page quarterly edited by Leon A. Smith and published at the
denomination's new headquarters in Washington, D.C. Like the *Sentinel*'s, *Liberty*'s circulation was based on having Adventists sponsor subscriptions for
prominent citizens. Reported at 40,000 in 1911, circulation increased to over
130,000 by 1929. After a dip to 51,000 in the midst of the depression, it picked
up again to 175,000 in 1946.[10]

Liberty featured copious illustrations depicting patriotic symbols and portraits
of statesmen and champions of religious freedom in America, highlighting the

magazine's claim to be an upholder of the republic's highest principles. Use of two-color cover designs was introduced in 1909, three-color covers in 1918, and four-color in 1941. The size was enlarged to 8⅜ by 11⅜ inches in 1937.

Beginning in 1909, *Liberty* ran in most issues a "declaration of principles" by the denomination's Religious Liberty Association as the theoretical touchstone guiding the magazine. The declaration claimed that the separation of church and state and religious liberty were based on biblical revelation. Because "love cannot be forced," the "religion of Jesus Christ needs no human power to enforce it." The role of civil government, though separate from religion, was declared to be "divinely ordained" for the purpose of protecting human beings "in the enjoyment of their natural rights and to rule in civil things." In particular, government had the responsibility to protect freedom of worship. Thus, in the Adventist view, the divine purpose was for the state to be secular, not in order to promote the secularization of humanity but to maintain a context for that uncoerced worship that characterizes true religion. The church, stated the declaration, has the responsibility to enter the public arena in an effort to hold the state to its proper role, making use of "every lawful and honorable means to prevent religious legislation, and oppose all movements tending to unite church and state, that all may enjoy the inestimable blessings of civil and religious liberty."[11]

During its first half century, *Liberty* was for the most part in the hands of two editors, Charles S. Longacre (1871–1958) and Heber H. Votaw (1881–1962). Longacre, a minister who acquired a law degree and an M.A. in philosophy and international law while carrying out his church duties, edited *Liberty* from 1914 to 1942 and remained with the publication as associate editor until his death. Votaw was the first Adventist missionary to Burma and superintendent of federal prisons during the administration of his brother-in-law, Warren G. Harding. After Harding's death, Votaw returned to denominational work, serving as associate editor of *Liberty* from 1923 to 1941 and as editor from 1942 to 1954.

Sunday laws remained *Liberty*'s primary concern until the early 1930s since they remained an important part of Protestant efforts to sustain Christian civilization in America.[12] Organizations such as the NRA and the Lord's Day Alliance generated considerable support for repeated initiatives for Congress to enact Sunday laws for the District of Columbia as the first step toward national legislation. *Liberty* editors vigorously opposed such moves, arguing that all Sunday laws, whether disguised as social welfare or softened by exemptions for Saturday observers, have a religious basis and thus violate the separation of church and state. They also pointed to the economic injustice of compelling observers of Saturday, such as orthodox Jews, to refrain from pursuing their livelihood on Sunday.[13] Longacre also spoke against Sunday laws in congressional committee hearings, while *Liberty* circulated petitions for readers to use in gathering signatures to send to their congressmen. Longacre claimed that Adventists had generated seven million signatures in 1927 and 1928 protesting a Sunday law proposed by Representative William Lankford of Georgia.[14] In 1933, *Liberty* could note with satisfaction that none of the nearly 150 Sunday observance bills introduced in Congress since 1888 had succeeded and that Sunday laws were receding on the state level.[15] Adventists still expected a national Sunday law to be the decisive issue in an apocalyptic crisis, but paradoxically that very expectation injected zeal into their effort to hold off the inevitable until the Church's work was done.

Liberty also resisted efforts to strengthen Protestant cultural hegemony through the public schools in the 1920s, speaking out against programs for religious instruction in the public schools and against state laws restricting parochial education. A "100% Americanism" directed against Roman Catholics lay behind an Oregon law passed in 1922 (overturned by the U.S. Supreme Court in 1925) requiring all children ages eight to sixteen to attend public schools. Despite its strong antipapalism, *Liberty* joined with Catholics in protesting this and similar laws in other states.[16] *Liberty*'s stance on Sunday laws and on education contributed to a more thoroughgoing religious pluralism in America at a time when Protestants were resorting to legal measures to retain the historic preeminence that was rapidly slipping away. However, on two other issues, *Liberty* sided with fellow Protestants. Adventists reasoned that Prohibition, rather than being an undue restriction on individual liberty, was mandated by the right to freedom from the social devastation caused by the liquor traffic.[17] *Liberty* also spoke out against the teaching of evolution as fact in the public schools, regarding it as a state-sponsored ideological assault on believers in the Bible and as not true science.[18]

In the 1940s, education became the foremost arena for *Liberty*'s efforts to defend the Adventist interpretation of the First Amendment and has remained so to the present. From *Liberty*'s standpoint, the principle of separation of church and state required battle on two educational fronts: against religious instruction or exercises sponsored by public schools and against state aid to parochial schools. Thus, the magazine joined the ACLU and organizations representing Jews and Baptists in opposing a "released-time" program for periods of religious instruction in the public schools conducted by various religious groups after regular school hours that the Supreme Court struck down in *McCollum v. Board of Education* (1948).[19] But *Liberty* also defended the freedom of children of the unpopular Jehovah's Witnesses not to salute the flag during public-school patriotic rituals.[20]

The issue of state aid to parochial schools, along with moves by Presidents Roosevelt and Truman to establish diplomatic ties with the Vatican, brought Adventists and *Liberty* into more formal cooperation with other Protestants. While Catholic leaders maintained that Catholic schools had a right to their share of tax dollars for education, *Liberty* insisted that any form of state funding to church-related institutions constituted establishment of religion, even that directed to auxiliary services such as busing, which the Supreme Court upheld in *Everson v. Board of Education* (1947).[21] Adventists joined a wide spectrum of

Protestant leaders in forming Protestants and Other Americans United for Separation of Church and State (POAU) in 1948 to counter the political influence displayed by Catholics. Frank Yost, associate editor of *Liberty* and associate secretary of the Religious Liberty Department of the Adventist General Conference, was one of POAU's founders.[22]

A Church historian with a doctorate from the University of Nebraska, Yost was *Liberty*'s editor from 1955 to 1958. His efforts reflect movement on the part of the Adventists toward cooperative action, though they remained in many ways a people apart and consistently declined membership in ecumenical organizations. A trend toward feature articles by non-Adventists that began in the 1930s became even more pronounced in the 1950s. Beginning in 1956, the *Liberty* masthead announced that the Religious Liberty Association advocated "only one doctrine, the doctrine of soul liberty." More than ever, *Liberty* now positioned itself as promoting an interfaith struggle for religious freedom rather than a distinctively Adventist agenda.

In 1959, Roland R. Hegstad, a young minister who began his editorial career with the evangelistic magazine *These Times* in 1955, was appointed editor of *Liberty*, a position that he still held in 1992. Hegstad brought a breezy and provocative style to the magazine. Under his editorship, publication frequency increased from quarterly to bimonthly, circulation increased from about 152,000 in 1958 to about 500,000 in 1975, and the magazine won numerous awards from the Associated Church Press in the categories of general excellence and graphics.[23] Hegstad also sought to make the publication's Adventist identity clearer by running some articles and columns on doctrine and biblical prophecy.[24]

The publication's circulation continued to be based on funds raised from Adventists, who are called upon by Church leaders to do their part for religious liberty by sponsoring free subscriptions to non-Adventists. However, letters from readers suggest that the magazine's appeal to the American ethos through text and images often struck a responsive chord. A judge, for example, wrote in 1972 that he had hung on his wall a *Liberty* cover that reproduced a photo of Iowa state education officials chasing Amish children, who were fleeing into a cornfield, in an effort to force them into public schools.[25]

In the Hegstad era, *Liberty* has continued to advocate separation of church and state as the best means of realizing religious liberty, despite mounting challenges to the separationist stance. In commenting on the retirement of Supreme Court Justice William O. Douglas, Hegstad favorably compared Douglas's staunch advocacy of a "wall of separation" between church and state to Chief Justice Warren Burger's description of a "blurred, indistinct, and variable barrier."[26] Increasing government aid to and regulation of church-related educational and health-care institutions, however, was making it more difficult to keep the barrier sharp, even for Adventists. Beginning in the late 1940s, Adventist institutions began accepting various forms of government aid, despite warnings from the editors of *Liberty* that such action violated the Church's historic stance and that governmental largesse would lead to governmental control.[27]

Liberty in the 1960s and after remained adamant in its opposition to official religious exercises in public schools. In contrast to the views of many conservative Christians, *Liberty* welcomed the Supreme Court's decision barring the use of prayers composed by public-school officials (*Engel v. Vitale*, 1962) as a strengthening of the "constitutional barrier" against state-directed religious practices." Adventists also vigorously opposed the constitutional amendments repeatedly proposed into the 1980s to permit organized prayer in the schools.[28]

The controversy over school prayer most clearly marks *Liberty*'s sharp differences from the New Christian Right (NCR) that emerged in the late 1970s and 1980s. Adventists regarded the NCR's drive for political power and conservative morality as a step toward the repression of individual freedom that they had long expected.[29] Other differences can be seen in *Liberty*'s decidedly cautious stand on legal measures against pornography, despite the editors' outrage, and suspicion of the antiabortion crusade, which brought Catholics and conservative Protestants together in a political alliance that appeared ominous for the religious freedom of dissenting minorities.[30]

While it has tackled numerous complex issues regarding church and state and has often taken the side of unpopular or misunderstood religious minorities, *Liberty* has generally taken a cautious approach regarding the nation's most deeply controversial issues of human rights. Rarely has its commitment to equal rights and liberty led it to forthright stands on behalf of racial minorities and political radicals or to protests over American support for foreign regimes repressing human rights.

For over a hundred years, the Seventh-Day Adventist Church has sustained publication of magazines dedicated to religious liberty. Defense of its own right to be different was the starting point for this action, and all along an apocalypticism that envisions an American conspiracy against their Sabbatarian practices has been at the root of their vigilance. Yet these concerns issued in a broader commitment to the defense of religious liberty for all people.

Notes

1. *Liberty* 1 (First Quarter 1906): 3.

2. Robert T. Handy, *A Christian America: Protestant Hopes and Historical Realities* (New York: Oxford University Press, 1971), 85, 65–94.

3. Ellen G. White, *The Great Controversy* (Oakland: Pacific Press Publishing Association, 1888), 440–50; Eric Syme, *A History of SDA Church-State Relations in the United States* (Mountain View, CA. : Pacific Press Publishing Association, 1973).

4. William H. Blakely, ed., *American State Papers Bearing on Sunday Legislation* (Washington, D.C.: Review and Herald Publishing Association, 1911), 733–34.

5. Cited in Handy, *Christian America*, 100. See also *Dictionary of Christianity in America* (Downers Grove, IL: Inter-Varsity Press, 1990), 800; Henry F. May, *Protestant*

Churches and Industrial America (New York: Harper and Brothers, 1963), 42–43; Dennis L. Pettibone, "Caesar's Sabbath: The Sunday Law Controversy in the United States, 1879–1892" (Ph.D. diss., University of California, Riverside, 1979).

6. Dennis Pettibone, "The Christian Voice, Part II," *Liberty* 76 (March–April 1981): 19–21.

7. Jonathan M. Butler, "Adventism and the American Experience," in *The Rise of Adventism*, ed. Edwin S. Gaustad (New York: Harper and Row, 1974), 173–206.

8. *American Sentinel* 4 (January 1889): 8.

9. *General Conference Daily Bulletin* 3 (25 October 1889): 75–76.

10. See reports on the Religious Liberty Department in *Review and Herald* 88 (2 November 1911): 17; ibid. 107 (9 June 1930): 153; ibid. 123 (13 June 1946): 165.

11. See, for example, "Declaration of Principles," *Liberty* 83:2 (March–April 1988): 31.

12. Sydney E. Ahlstrom, *A Religious History of the American People* (New Haven: Yale University Press, 1972), 915.

13. For example, C. S. Longacre, " 'Reformer' Robbing Peter to Pay Paul," *Liberty* 18 (First Quarter 1923): 108; idem, "Congress Invaded by a Gigantic Religious Lobby," *Liberty* 21 (Second Quarter Extra 1926): 67–74.

14. C. S. Longacre, "The Religious Liberty Association," *Review and Herald* 107 (6 June 1930): 153.

15. "Much-Agitated Question Submitted for National Recovery," *Liberty* 28 (Fourth Quarter 1933): 99; C. S. Longacre, "No Sunday Laws in Wisconsin," *Liberty* 28 (Third Quarter 1933): 67–68.

16. "The Menace of Bogus Americanism," *Liberty* 17 (Fourth Quarter 1922): 117–18; Joseph T. Wayne, "A Danger Signal," *America* 29 (25 December 1920): 226–28.

17. C. S. Longacre, "The Liquor Traffic a Menace to Personal Liberty," *Liberty* 8 (Fourth Quarter 1913): 187–88.

18. L. A. Smith, "Evolution, Christianity, and the State," *Liberty* 20 (Fourth Quarter 1925): 102–3, 121.

19. C. S. Longacre, "U.S. Supreme Court Outlaws Religious Teaching in Public School," *Liberty* 43 (Second Quarter 1948): 28–29.

20. C. S. Longacre, "Should the Flag Salute Be Forced?" *Liberty* 36 (First Quarter 1941): 32–33.

21. Heber H. Votaw, "Adventists Oppose Free Transportation of Parochial School Pupils," *Liberty* (Fourth Quarter 1947): 29.

22. "Frank H. Yost (1894–1958)," *Church and State* 12 (January 1959): 2.

23. M. E. Loewen, "Circulation of Liberty Now Highest in History," *Review and Herald* 145 (29 August 1968): 24; "Public Affairs and Religious Liberty," *Review and Herald* 152 (31 July 1975): 25–26.

24. Roland R. Hegstad, "*Liberty* Learns a Lesson," *Adventist Review* 163 (15 May 1986): 8–10.

25. Robert W. Nixon, "Amish Win," *Liberty* 67 (July–August 1972): 4–6.

26. Roland R. Hegstad, "Justice William O. Douglas," *Liberty* 75 (May–June 1980): 31.

27. "Church-State Relations," *Review and Herald* 145 (26 September 1968): 1–7; Neal C. Wilson, "A New Policy on Government Aid," *Review and Herald* 149 (7 December 1972): 18, 30; Roland R. Hegstad, "Adventists and Government Money," *Liberty* 68 (March–April 1973): 15–21.

28. Roland R. Hegstad, "Supreme Court Decision Misunderstood," *Liberty* 57 (September–October 1962): 32; W. Melvin Adams, "Hearing on Dirksen Amendment," *Liberty* 61 (September–October 1966): 30; Roland R. Hegstad, "Now I Lay Me Down to Sleep," *Liberty* 77 (September–October 1982): 4.

29. Clifford Goldstein, *The "Saving" of America* (Boise, ID: Pacific Press Publishing Association, 1988); Roland R. Hegstad, "Down the Road to a Christian Republic," *Liberty Sentinel* (supplement to *Liberty*, 1980): 2–3.

30. Roland R. Hegstad, "Obscenity and Free Expression," *Liberty* 68 (July–August 1973): 28; Elvin L. Benton, "States Rights and Moral Wrongs," *Liberty* 68 (September–October 1973): 26–27.

Information Sources

INDEX SOURCES: Volumes 51–59 (1956–1964) contain an index in the magazine. Volumes 62–64 (1967–1969) are indexed in the *Index to Seventh-Day Adventist Periodicals*. Volumes 66 (1971–present) are indexed in the *Seventh-Day Adventist Periodical Index*.

LOCATION SOURCES: James White Library, Andrews University, Berrien Springs, Michigan 49104.

Publication History

MAGAZINE TITLE: *Liberty* (1906–present).

VOLUME AND ISSUE DATA: 1:1 (First Quarter 1906)–present. Published quarterly through 1959; published bimonthly from 1960 to present.

PUBLISHER AND PLACE OF PUBLICATION: Review and Herald Publishing Association for the Seventh-Day Adventist Church, Washington, D.C., 1906–1983; Hagerstown, Maryland, 1983–present.

EDITORS: Leon A. Smith (1906–1909), C. M. Snow (1909–1912), W. W. Prescott (1912–1913), C. S. Longacre (1913–1942), Heber H. Votaw (1942–1954), Frank H. Yost (1955–1958), J. Arthur Buckwalter (1959), Roland R. Hegstad (1959–present).

CIRCULATION: 250,000 (1990).

Douglas Morgan

LIBERTY: A MAGAZINE OF RELIGIOUS FREEDOM. *See* LIBERTY

LIBERTY AND CATHOLIC SENTINEL. *See* PILOT (BOSTON)

LIGUORIAN

Liguori, Missouri, is a beautifully serene and comforting place. It is not a town, nor a city, and is not usually listed on a Missouri map. Yet, by special permission of the U.S. postal authorities, it does have a post office that processes over 10 million pieces of mail each year. Located twenty-five miles directly south of downtown St. Louis, Liguori is on the private property of the Redemptorists and is the home of Liguori Publications.

Liguori Publications has grown to be one of the largest Roman Catholic publishing houses in the United States. Among its many products and services today are the *Liguorian* magazine, parish education bulletins, books and pamphlets, audio and videocassettes and various devotional cards, pictures, and articles. But the *Liguorian* was the reason for the founding and development of the publishing house.

The name "Liguori," Italian in origin, is the family name of a bishop and doctor of the Roman Catholic Church, St. Alphonsus Maria de Liguori, who founded a religious community for men in 1732 called the Congregation of the Most Holy Redeemer. Members of this community, known as Redemptorists, have a mission to proclaim the Gospel of Jesus Christ to all people, with a special preference for the economically poor, the spiritually alienated, and the pastorally neglected. They work and live in geographical regions called provinces. The Redemptorists of the St. Louis province owned a theological seminary in Oconomowoc, Wisconsin, called Immaculate Conception College. In 1913, five Redemptorists priests—professors at the seminary—wanted to provide ongoing and more extensive spiritual help and guidance to the faithful of the time. Fathers August T. Zeller, Chris D. McEnniry, J. W. Brennan, B. A. Connelly, and T. Z. Austin presented their proposal to the faculty of the seminary. The minutes of a 15 February faculty meeting at the seminary formally record initial discussion of the project: "To consider issuing a monthly magazine to be called THE LIGUORIAN and devoted to religious purposes."[1]

Shortly after this meeting, one of the founders of the new publication wrote a letter offering a fuller explanation of the goals of the new publication:

Our ideal is a magazine that will afford a new medium to connect us with the people that will offer increased opportunities of working for souls. It will be a popular magazine, a magazine for the ordinary people, treating of subjects that will be of interest to the ordinary reader and written in a popular style. The articles should therefore be comparatively short. They must be striking and interesting.[2]

The provincial superior, Reverend Thomas P. Brown, C.SS.R., approved the new enterprise and provided fifty dollars for financial support. The founding editors inquired among local printers and found that with this money they could get five hundred copies of a forty-eight–page magazine printed. The *Liguorian* began with an Easter issue in March 1913.

However, in the early years subscribers were not easy to find, so the magazine became an in-house organ, with circulation confined mostly to relatives and friends of the midwestern Redemptorists. The magazine did continue to provide some religious instruction and inspiration to its readers, but it also contained many items of Redemptorist interest, such as personnel changes, notices of future events, accounts of the lives of pious Redemptorists who had recently died, and lists of newly ordained priests.[3]

Until this time, editorship of the magazine remained in the hands of the founding professors with Father A. T. "Gus" Zeller, C.SS.R., gradually assuming full editorial responsibility. This was a logical step since Father Zeller wrote most of the articles anyway, often under a variety of pen names.

In the early 1930s a decision was made to eliminate the family news and to make *Liguorian* a magazine of general interest for a national audience, helping people to understand the truths of the Catholic faith and the traditions of the Catholic Church. The magazine would include articles on such topics as prayer and spirituality, marriage and family, Scripture, children and teenagers, self-help and how-to, theology, seasonal celebration, personal experiences, and social-justice issues.

Father Donald F. Miller, C.SS.R., became its editor in May 1932. He also became somewhat of a legend. Besides writing a minimum of three lengthy articles for each issue, he preached numerous missions and retreats, gave lectures, and taught philosophy at the seminary. In addition, he also served as rector of the seminary for six years, encouraging many young seminarians to write for the magazine.

Circulation was still very limited, but during World War II, a dramatic rise in circulation occurred. At this time a pamphlet department was added to the publishing efforts of the seminary. The Redemptorists of the St. Louis province quickly realized that for this "apostolate of the pen" to flourish, a significant move to more adequate and more adaptable quarters was necessary. In late October 1947, Father Donald Miller brought a group of seven Redemptorists from Wisconsin to a site near St. Louis, Missouri. These eight priests—Father Donald Miller, Father John Schaefer, Father Frank Bockwinkel, Father Thomas Tobin, Father Ernest Miller, Father George Corbet, Father Francis Darmady, and Father Louis Miller—founded Liguori Mission House, the enterprise that developed into Liguori Publications.[4] Father Don Miller remained the editor until February 1956.

One month later, Father Matt Huber, C.SS.R. became the next editor of the *Liguorian*. Father Huber's genius was organization, and he took special interest in the mechanical aspects of the magazine—typefaces, margins, page layout, and above all accuracy. In October 1961, he was forced to resign as editor because of serious eye troubles.

Successor to Father Huber was Father Louis Miller, C.SS.R., the youngest of four Miller brothers, all of whom became Redemptorist priests and all of whom were (or are) in some way closely associated with the *Liguorian*. Father "Louie" had a long career as editor, from November 1961 to December 1976. He brought to the *Liguorian* "a freshness of outlook, a sense of history, a deft scholarship, and above all, a deep personal spirituality which infused his writings." He guided the magazine through the turbulent years of the 1960s when the Second Vatican Council and its aftermath shook the Catholic Church. Many of the faithful believed that the bishops ordered a large-scale liberalization and modernization of practices in the Church. During that time Father Louie was simultaneously accused of being too liberal and too conservative, but he was able to make the magazine "an amalgam of sweet reason, true Christian love, and solid devotion and fidelity to the Church." This was recognized in 1969 at a meeting of the American Catholic Bishops and Editors, when the *Liguorian* was singled out by the bishops as worthy of praise, for it presented "a balanced picture of the teachings of the Church and the needs of modern Catholics in today's world."[5]

Father Louis Miller is also credited with inviting responsible lay writers to the *Liguorian*. Up to that time only Redemptorists had been writing. In addition, web presses were purchased and the size of the magazine was changed from 6 by 9 inches to 5 by 8½ inches. Father Miller left the *Liguorian* in December 1976 as its editor, but continued to be involved with the magazine, as a contributing writer, a consultant and advisor, and a spiritual strength.

Missionary Father Gerald Gibbons, C.SS.R., succeeded Father Louie Miller as editor. The first five months showed great promise of a brilliant editorial career for Father Gibbons. However, that career was suddenly terminated when Father Gibbons suffered a fatal heart attack on 1 June 1977. Father Norman Muckerman, C.SS.R., immediately assumed editorship in June 1977. Father Muckerman was a perfect choice, for he had the distinct privilege of knowing and working with all the previous editors. He pledged himself to the challenge of continuing the founders' ideals. He successfully maintained their goal of publishing a Catholic magazine written in a popular style and treating subjects of interest to ordinary people. During his editorship, the *Liguorian* received six awards for general excellence and for best writing from the Catholic Press Association. Father Muckerman was one of the magazine's most visible editors. He is a former president of the Catholic Press Association and a recipient of its prestigious St. Francis de Sales Award.[6]

When Father Muckerman retired in May 1989, Father Allan Weinert, C.SS.R., became editor. Father Weinert's vision as editor is embodied in the new mission statement of the *Liguorian*: "To make spirituality accessible, to attune readers to the spiritual reality that is around them, to find those meeting points between ourselves and our loving God."[7] Father Weinert sought to publish material that treated the mystery of grace and redemption as it came into the ordinary circumstances of human lives. For him the *Liguorian* was not an agent of change but a vehicle to pass on a basic faith and a challenge to grow in quiet and consistent ways.

Recognizing that unsettling matters exist in the Church, Father Weinert has been open to well-researched ventures into areas that are troublesome and unclear but important to the way in which Catholics live. He has invited and encouraged the best writers in the Catholic press to contribute to the magazine. Under his leadership, three fourths of the editorial content of each magazine became composed of commissioned articles. In June 1990, Father Weinert increased the number of pages from sixty-four to seventy-two to provide extra editorial space and more and better graphics. The *Liguorian* continues to gather press awards under Father Weinert's editorship.[8]

The *Liguorian* is firmly committed to orthodox, historic, Catholic Christianity and does not publish anything that departs from Catholic doctrine or teaching. The editorial staff believes that its readers want to know how the Church can help them in those matters most important to them—their families, their work, their own personal growth—as they live out their faith each day in an ever-changing world. The editorial policy commits the staff to providing such materials to the *Liguorian* readers. Each Sunday, Redemptorist priests travel to Catholic parishes throughout the United States to preach about the *Liguorian* and to obtain subscribers. Subscribers are also sought through telephone calls. Subscriptions number more than 365,000.

Notes

1. *Liguorian* 76 (March 1988): 5. Listing of founders provided by Father Allan Weinert, C.SS.R., editor. Father Weinert found the names by searching through the early bound copies of the magazine housed at the Redemptorist residence at Liguori, Missouri.

2. Ibid., p. 5.

3. Ibid., p. 6.

4. Ibid., p. 7. An additional listing of founders of Liguori Publications is provided by Father Allan Weinert, C.SS.R. Framed pictures hang in corridors of Liguori Publications.

5. Ibid., p. 8.

6. Information supplied by Father Allan Weinert, C.SS.R. Framed awards line the halls of Liguori Publications.

7. Liguorian Editorial Policy (1992). Document provided by Father Allan Weinert, C.SS.R.

8. Information supplied by Father Allan Weinert, C.SS.R.

Information Sources

INDEX SOURCES: *Catholic Periodical Literature Index*; *CERDIC* (Université de Strasbourg, Centre de Recherche et de Documentation des Institutions Chrétiennes Bulletin du CERDIC), located in the United States at the Library of University of California, Los Angeles.

LOCATION SOURCES: All volumes are bound. Complete run is located at the Redemptorist residence at Liguori, Missouri.

Publication History

MAGAZINE TITLE: *Liguorian* (1913–present).

VOLUME AND ISSUE DATA: 1:1 (March 1913)–present.

PUBLISHER AND PLACE OF PUBLICATION: Congregation of the Most Holy Redeemer (Redemptorists of the St. Louis Province), Oconomowoc, Wisconsin (1913–1947); Liguori, Missouri (1947–present).

EDITORS: Chris D. McEnniry (1913–1932), J. W. Brennan (1913–1932), B. A. Connelly (1913–1932), T. Z. Austin (1913–1932), August (Gus) T. Zeller (1913–1932), Donald F. Miller (1932–1956), Matt Huber (1956–1961), Louis (Louie) Miller (1961–1976), Gerald Gibbons (1977), Norman J. Muckerman (1977–1989), Allan Weinert (1989–present).
CIRCULATION: 365,000 (1993).

Marti Tomas Izral

LUTHERAN

The *Lutheran* became the magazine of the Lutheran Church in America (LCA) at its inception in January 1963 and continued in that capacity until the LCA ceased at the creation of the Evangelical Lutheran Church in America (ELCA) twenty-five years later.

The title of the magazine was a continuation of the name of the official journal of one of the constituting Churches of the LCA, the United Lutheran Church in America (ULCA). In fact, the title *Lutheran* can be traced in American religious journalism as far back as 1860, and a magazine including the word "Lutheran" in the title first appeared in 1831 with the initial issue of the *Lutheran Observer*.

The first editor of the LCA journal was G. Elson Ruff, who had already served as editor of the ULCA magazine since 1945. He insisted that the new periodical have a distinctive size, and so until the year after his death in 1972 it was published with a unique size of 6⅜ by 9¼ inches. Ruff, however, continued his previous editorial policy, characterized as that of an Old Testament prophet, presenting "the truth plainly and fearlessly and prodding the people of God along the path of righteousness."[1] While this characterization recognized the influence of Ruff's study of the Hebrew scripture, the writer paying him tribute then mixed the metaphor: "He wasn't a gentle shepherd leading his flock, but rather a cowboy who could crack the whip to round up the strays and help keep the flock on the move."[2]

Underneath this aggressive policy there was the hope that the magazine would help in developing a sense of fellowship within the larger company of Christians that the LCA afforded in bringing together Lutherans of German and Scandinavian heritages as well as Church bodies primarily centered in both eastern and midwestern America. In this regard, the magazine assisted the members of the LCA in thinking of themselves as a single Church rather than as a confederation of regional entities. In addition, the attempt was clearly made to publish a magazine with appeal to every member of this Church. To this end the news was written briefly and compactly, composed in the popular journalistic format of the day. Likewise, feature writing was designed to assist the readers in developing their Christian lives. As a result of the success of this program, the subscription list grew rapidly. It was also admitted that "because of the popularity of his editorials and letters to the editor, many subscribers began reading the magazine from the back to the front"[3] since those features came at the back of the issue.

Succeeding Ruff at his death was Albert P. Stauderman, who summarized his stewardship of the magazine at the time of his retirement in 1978 after six years at the helm: "This magazine has been able to demonstrate to those both within and outside the church that the Lutheran way of life makes sense," which he interpreted as meaning that the magazine had "provided impartial information about religion and social issues" and had "allowed differing views to be expressed, thus enabling church members to make decisions based on facts."[4] Tongue in cheek, this Lutheran editor then offered his assessment: "So reading *The Lutheran* may not be necessary for salvation, but it helps."[5]

Stauderman retired "as editor of the most widely circulated denominational periodical in North America"[6] and noted that the most satisfying part of his career, including the long period before he assumed the editorship, was to have watched the role that the magazine played not only in articulating a single Church, but also "in preventing the kind or cleavage in the ULCA and LCA between liberals and conservatives"[7] that plagued some other Lutheran Churches. He asserted: "The magazine has provided a strong base for discussion so that nearly everyone in the church could find something to hold onto. We've been a kind of 'glue' for the church."[8] Yet he did speak out forcefully about the race question and strongly urged the ordination of women and the use of the Revised Standard Version of the Bible in the new hymnbook.

The final editor was Edgar R. Trexler, who in 1986 added a four-page wraparound in Spanish that was provided for members of congregations conducting worship in that language. He also developed the journal as an agent to assist in the creation of the ELCA since merger talks were underway when he took the helm. The success achieved in bringing forth a major feature article in a majority of the issues in the years immediately preceding the 1988 merger was announced at the final convention of the LCA: "The staff believes that the features coverage and editorial comment helped build a favorable climate within the LCA for a positive convention vote and general support for the merger among members."[9]

Trexler then became the editor of the latest incarnation of the *Lutheran* when it began appearing in January 1988 as the Church periodical published by the ELCA. This magazine has a literary genealogy of some forty English language predecessors in the three merging Churches and their forebears, including the *Lutheran Standard*, which had been published continuously since 1842.

With the first issue, the *Lutheran* continued to be the largest denominational periodical published in North America and also the largest Lutheran publication in the world.[10] Four years later, over a million copies were printed and delivered to 70 percent of the homes of ELCA members, helped by having one third of the synods and over four thousand congregations use the synod or congregationwide plan of circulation, so that every home in that synod or congregation received the magazine.[11]

Trexler insisted that the magazine continue much of the material from its more recent predecessors. This was evidenced in feature articles, Bible study, devotional material, theological series, news of the world of religion, a young readers' page, some humor, and the bishop's message. The editor insisted on the seriousness with which reader interest was served: "Your questions are answered and your opinions valued in 'Viewpoint' and 'Letters.' "[12]

Continuing the policy of Ruff as well as Stauderman, Trexler announced to the ELCA Constituting Convention: "The first priority for the magazine is to bond us together."[13] Calling the *Lutheran* an "old friend in a new church,"[14] he reflected the style of Ruff in stating, "Our editorial character will be aggressive but not sensational, open but not indiscriminate, thoughtful but not stuffy, substantive but not obtuse, pastoral but not sentimental," and then asserting, "We'll stretch your horizons occasionally, raise issues that we believe need raising."[15] But then he assured the readers: "When the church has spoken on a topic, our content will reflect those positions."[16]

These characteristics were soon tested over one of the continuing issues in the previous Churches and now in the ELCA—gay clergy. When three male graduates from Pacific Lutheran Seminary, who had been certified for ordination and assigned as pastoral candidates by previous Church bodies, now presented themselves for ordination in the ELCA, they announced their sexual orientation. This soon became a highly controversial issue, and Trexler secured from the bishops of two of the Churches that helped bring about the ELCA articles about how their respective Churches addressed this issue. The editor was prepared to publish these statements when bishops of the ELCA persuaded the authors to withdraw their statements. This prompted Trexler and his associates to bemoan hierarchical interference in the publication of the magazine as the editorial guidelines approved by the ELCA Church Council stated: "The editor is authorized to present . . . articles and statements of opinion reflecting responsible concern for relevant issues. These articles and opinion columns are not to be regarded as official statements of the Evangelical Lutheran Church in America."[17] The discontent that this action underscored motivated the denomination's Church Council in August 1991 to order a review of the magazine because of what some called its "negative tone and slant."[18] This was reported in the magazine, indicating that the Church Council would determine whether the "publication goals are in 'congruence' with ELCA mission goals."[19]

This incident highlighted the difficulty in publishing a national denominational magazine for a constituency of over five million members. The task of bringing together the variety of persons, cultures and points of view was proving to be enormous. So also was the task of personalizing the magazine, so that the individual reader sensed an identity with the Church that the periodical represented. A survey of the readership identified the section entitled "Changes," the listing of new calls or appointments for clergy, as the piece most read by the clergy, while for the laity it was "Letters" that was the second most widely read section following the most popular "Lite Side," the humor page.[20]

Specifically to address the issue of diversity and reader interest, the magazine established a designated correspondent in each of the sixty-five synods within the ELCA. All but two also publish on a regular basis an insert placed in the middle of the magazine for the purpose of accenting more local programs, events, concerns, and persons. Extended coverage is also given annually to the meetings of all synod assemblies.

The magazine has not sidestepped unfavorable news, such as stories of clerical misconduct. These have been dealt with forthrightly, while at the same time trying to be quietly accurate in the reporting, as, for example, in the special report in the 17 July 1991 issue on sexual misconduct charges raised against clergy members.[21] The *Lutheran* has also reflected the opinions of the bishops and the Church Council—for example, in speaking out against the "Desert Storm" war with Iraq.[22] Incidents such as this have at times left the readers with the impression that the magazine acts as the arm of Church authority.

There has been a reduction in the frequency of publication, from an original eighteen issues per year to twelve in 1992, but the later issues have been significantly larger. This was a move brought about by economic necessity.

The editorial staff has taken surveys and has announced it is open to suggestions so that the magazine may be viewed as "a pastoral visit in your home."[23] Recognition is thus being given to the responses of two thirds of the lay readers who want more coverage on people like themselves, family issues, prayer, and spirituality. Moreover, older readers want more traditional articles, which appeared in the previous journals, while younger (under 35) readers want more discussion of controversial moral issues and social problems.[24] Thus, feature articles detail "the life and work of the ELCA, church personalities, 'think' pieces about what Lutherans believe and how belief relates to society, and stories of personal Christian experiences."[25] News articles articulate the rapidly changing world conditions as these affect religion and the events that occur in the United States that also have implications for the Christian community.

There is the continuance of widely accepted sections, such as "Between Us," the column by Walter Wangerin in which he probes the spiritual life with his distinctive literary style. A second column that also began with the first issue is "Since You Asked," where Norma and Burton Everist respond to a wide variety of readers' questions. Another consistent contribution has been several series, written by theological and college faculty, that address biblical and doctrinal issues. Regularly included also are communications from the ELCA bishop, Herbert W. Chilstrom. In January 1989, Linda-Marie Delloff introduced a bimonthly series entitled "Accent on Arts," investigating the relation between art and religion. A year later she began another column, "Accent on Books," alternating with her other column and bringing to the *Lutheran* a segment that had a prominent role in predecessor magazines—namely, a book review section. In 1992 the two columns were merged into a monthly segment. Then, as was true in predecessor journals, a page has been set aside for the comments of the editor.

On 9 November 1992 the Church Council responded to its own investigation begun fifteen months earlier by concluding that the magazine was fulfilling denominational objectives. The council recognized the tension between editorial independence and the *Lutheran*'s function as a house organ and suggested that the tension may well be evidence of evenhandedness. Still the editorial staff was encouraged to be sensitive to the concerns of Church officials.

The Church Council has thus added its voice of support for the magazine as it seeks to fulfill its role as the voice of the ELCA, even in the face of the difficulties in a Church as large, diverse, and diffuse as the ELCA.[26]

Notes

1. *Lutheran* 10:4 (16 February 1972): 6.
2. Ibid.
3. Ibid., p. 9.
4. Ibid. 16:16 (4 October 1978): 34.
5. Ibid.
6. Ibid. 16:17 (11 October 1978): 4.
7. Ibid., p. 6.
8. Ibid.
9. *Minutes of the Closing Convention, Lutheran Church in America* (Philadelphia Board of Publication, 1987), 152.
10. *Lutheran* 1:1 (January 1988): 50.
11. *Reports and Records, 1991 Churchwide Assembly, ELCA* (Chicago: Office of the Secretary, ELCA, 1991), 1:243.
12. *Lutheran* 1:1 (6 January 1988): 50.
13. *Reports and Records, 1989 Churchwide Assembly, ELCA* (Chicago: Office of the Secretary, ELCA, 1989), 1:200.
14. *Lutheran* 1:1 (6 January 1988): 50.
15. Ibid.
16. Ibid.
17. *Reports and Records, 1989*, 1:204.
18. Edgar R. Trexler, *Anatomy of a Merger* (Minneapolis, MN: Augsburg, 1991), 248.
19. *Lutheran* 4:12 (2 October 1991): 34.
20. Ibid. 2:16 (29 November 1988): 24.
21. Ibid. 4:9 (17 July 1991): 22–25.
22. Ibid. 4:2 (30 January 1991): 50.
23. Ibid. 1:1 (6 January 1988): 50.
24. Ibid. 2:16 (29 November 1988): 24.
25. *Reports and Records, 1991* 1:241.
26. *Lutheran* 5:12 (December 1992): 35.

Information Sources

INDEX SOURCES: None.

LOCATION SOURCES: Augsburg Fortress Press, Lutheran School of Theology at Chicago, and others.

Publication History

MAGAZINE TITLE: *Lutheran* (1963–present).

VOLUME AND ISSUE DATA 1:1 (January 1963)–25:18 (December 1987). Published biweekly and occasionally monthly; 1:1 (January 1988)–present, 18 to 12 issues annually.

PUBLISHER AND PLACE OF PUBLICATION: Lutheran Church in America, Philadelphia (1963–1987); Publishing House of the Evangelical Lutheran Church in America, Minneapolis, Minnesota (1988–present).

EDITORS: G. Elson Ruff (1962–1972), Albert P. Stauderman (1972–1978), Edgar R. Trexler (1978–present).

CIRCULATION: 601,023 (1981); 1,250,596 (1988).

Myron Fogde

LUTHERAN CHURCH WORK AND OBSERVER. *See* LUTHERAN OBSERVER

LUTHERAN COMPANION

Swedish immigrants helped organize only one Lutheran Church body in the United States, the Scandinavian Evangelical Lutheran Augustana Synod of North America. Established in 1860, it continued until 1962 when it merged with several other Lutheran Churches to form the Lutheran Church in America. Throughout its life it was well served by two popular denominational magazines: *Augustana*, a Swedish language publication from 1868 to 1956, and the *Lutheran Companion*, the English-language counterpart, published from 1911 to 1962.

The first publication, however, began in 1855, when T. N. Hasselquist, later to become the first president of the synod, set up a press in his own home in Galesburg, Illinois, and issued a newspaper entitled *Hemlandet, det Gamla och det Nya* (*Homeland, the Old and the New*). Designed as a communication among the newly arriving immigrants, it also had distinctly religious concerns. Initially supportive of the new—that is, American—elements appearing in the immigrants' Church, it soon began to question these and to lament the indifference of the Church of Sweden in sending pastors to America.

Eighteen months later, in 1856, a second, definitely religious newspaper, was also begun by Hasselquist under the title *Det Rätta Hemlandet* (*The True Homeland*) with its devotional content often taken from *Pietisten*, edited by C. O. Roesnius in Sweden. For a time these were issued on an alternating basis, and a publication society assumed responsibility when the enterprise was moved to Chicago in 1859. Then four years later, under the title *Det Rätta Hemlandet och Missionsbladet* (*The True Homeland and Missionary Magazine*), a return to a decidedly religious format was again in evidence. This was followed in 1868 by the appearance of *Augustana*, later in 1873 to become the official paper of the synod. This was published for eighty-eight years with some early modifications in title, page size, frequency of issue, and mergers with other journals. *Augustana* was a self-conscious representative of the Church of Sweden in America. Yet Hasselquist, who continued as editor until 1890, wrote in the first issue:

I have long recognized the need of a periodical in which our church problems and conditions in this country can be set forth more thoroughly. As Lutherans we have come from a state church in which the congregations have very little to say in what belongs to the care, order and government of a congregation, have difficulty in learning the privileges and duties, and consequently have only a slight, not to say wrong, conception of these things and still less any experience of them.[1]

Nonetheless, the editor unabashedly proclaimed the synod as a daughter of the Church of Sweden. While in the first decades this was evidenced by a personal relationship between Augustana clergy and the Church of Sweden, in later decades there was a formal institutional relationship as indicated, for example, by the presence of Swedish ecclesiastical authorities at celebrations in 1893 marking the tercentenary of the proclamation of Lutheranism as the faith of the Church of Sweden, and in 1910 the semicentennial of the synod. This relationship and these events received extensive coverage in the periodical.

Unlike the later *Companion*, there was a theological vigor in the early *Augustana*. The pietistic movement in Sweden was now attacked, especially when it came under the leadership of Paul Peter Waldenström (1838–1917). This "new evangelism" was seen as significantly deviating from the theology of the Church of Sweden, particularly in regard to the doctrine of the atonement. This then led *Augustana* to declare against the expression of this in the Mission Friends Movement, which did become the Swedish Covenant Church. However, pietism not affected by "new evangelism" was a staple element in the journal for decades. Combining theological concerns and pietism, Hasselquist was also determined to seek the preservation of the unity of the synod and the Swedish immigrants, leading him to take on a polemical stance when defending against the proselytizing of Swedish immigrants by the Baptists, Methodists, Episcopalians, and Mormons.

The acme of the synod as a Swedish institution occurred just before World War I. After the war, use of the English language became more prominent, and soon the tone of *Augustana* became more nostalgic, underscored in part by a continuing accent on poetry and hymnody.

Within the synod another shift came with the formation of the Association of English Churches in 1908. This institutionalized a movement away from the identity of the synod with Sweden. The first English-speaking congregation dated from 1888 in Rock Island, Illinois, and at nearby Augustana College two English language publications began in 1892: the *Alumnus* and the *Young Observer*. These were journals designed to reach the American-born who were not continuing the Swedish tradition and those Swedish immigrants who did not come to the Midwest or identify with *Augustana*. The publications merged in 1894 to form the *Augustana Journal*, which three years later became the *Young Lutheran's Companion* and which in 1911 became the *Lutheran Companion*, the name it retained until the synod merged with other Lutheran bodies fifty-one years later and the magazine was discontinued.

In the first issue of the *Companion*, it was stated: "Ours is a 'conservation policy,'—to protect the young saplings as the old monarchs of the forest are felled or fall"[2] so "that no serious loss to our church should be incurred by neglect or internecine strife."[3] The *Companion* became the official organ for the English-speaking members of the synod. The subscription list grew slowly, yet the language question was addressed in the first issue with the assumption that the organization of separate English congregations was not the appropriate response to the language transition taking place. Young people would not leave en masse, rather "the drainage of our old congregations will be by the evaporation process, one by one . . . (until) the life blood will be sapped out of the congregation."[4]

Seven years later, in 1918, the synod noted that the immigrants and their children ought to learn English, but stated: "Swedish, as a rich cultural heritage, ought to be preserved as long as possible."[5] However, two years earlier it was stated in *Augustana*: "The primary task of our church is to win our people for the evangelical Lutheran faith, and thereby promote its highest interests for time and eternity, and in order to attain that goal, it must use the language in ways through which the best results may be reached."[6] There was not a basic tension between the two publications, since each maintained that the language most beneficial to the synod should be used. The *Augustana* position was that it perceived clear indications that the synod would lose more than it would gain if the transition to English were accelerated. As late as 1926 *Augustana* declared that "particular situations demand that both languages be used."[7] The *Companion* continued to urge a more rapid transition and a focus on the younger people. It was not until 1930 that the subscription list for the *Companion* exceeded that of *Augustana*—15,316 versus 14,873.[8] When *Augustana* ceased publication in 1956, it had 3,132 subscribers versus 88,345 for the *Companion*.[9]

The *Companion* was definitely a child of *Augustana*. In spite of their ethnic accents, both papers strongly emphasized devotional material, and there was a strong accent on missions—foreign missions being a high priority with the synod. There was always the ever-popular section on local religious news, including anniversary celebrations in congregations. Extremely important to the membership of the synod were the news accounts about pastors, including information about new calls, changes of address, and deaths. These two sections were like the local news items in small-town weeklies and also here served as a bonding between members—so much so that there was enunciated a sense of the Church as a community of people, much like yourself, no matter how geographically scattered. Abetting this was the ever-increasing use of photographs of pastors, lay men and women, new church buildings and celebrations. Another popular feature was the extended coverage of church assemblies, national and regional. The colleges of the synod were constantly kept before the attention of the readers, and the letters to the editor aroused considerable interest. Continuing a tradition from *Augustana* was the *Companion*'s interest in moral issues, even such personal issues as drinking and dancing.

Differentiating the two was the attitude toward the quadricentennial of the Protestant Reformation in 1917. *Augustana* did not support this as an occasion to promote Lutheran unity in America, expecting a rise in Swedish immigration at the conclusion of the war. This did not happen—but not because of the new, restrictive American immigration laws. Rather, Swedes simply no longer came in significant numbers, not even in large enough numbers to fill the recently established quota. The *Companion* saw the observance as an opportunity to push for Lutheran unity and showed interest in the 1918 merger that produced the United Lutheran Church in America, even though it did not include any Scandinavian Church bodies.

This ecumenical interest was seen in a continuing flow of articles urging inter-Lutheran conversations, cooperative endeavors, and new alignments in the United States. On a wider scale, the *Companion* placed the synod in relation to other American denominations and European Churches in addition to the Church of Sweden. In fact, among Lutherans in America, the synod became known for its ecumenical interests, as seen in the *Companion*'s support for the work of the Federal Council of Churches and later the National Council of the Churches of Christ in the United States, as well as the Life and Work and the Faith and Order Movements that led to the formation of the World Council of Churches. *Augustana* joined in covering these ecumenical endeavors.

A major influence in the later years of the *Companion* was its editor, E. E. Ryden (1934–1961). The magazine championed the causes that interested him—and did so at the beginning of the era when half of the synod's congregations used only the English language. In addition to the ecumenical accent, which had been much to the fore in 1923 with the visit to America of the international ecumenist Archbishop Nathan Söderblom of Sweden, there was also a heavy concentration on social issues. Earlier the accent had been antisaloon, but now it was primarily the peace movement. This reflected the continuing strong pacifist influence of Carl Bengston, editor from 1915 to 1934. Catalyzed by his own experiences in World War I and supported by a coterie of like-minded individuals, Ryden provided space for the consideration of this issue even after 1939, continuing to urge a policy of neutrality and peace down to the bombing of Pearl Harbor. By then, the defense of the conscientious objector had become an editorial concern.

The synod was not a body to become entangled in theological disputes as some of the other Lutheran bodies of German and Scandinavian background did in the twentieth century. Moreover, the *Companion* sought not to be dogmatic or to set a theological standard. With its pietistic tradition, it instead placed a strong emphasis on Bible study and was a frequent supporter of the nonsynodical Lutheran Bible Institute in Minneapolis.

In 1930 the American Lutheran Conference was formed by several midwestern Lutheran bodies, and Ryden thought that this might be the beginning of a Lutheran Church that would cross ethnic lines. Later he came to realize that this would not be the case and returned the *Companion* to the traditional interest, dating from as early as 1870, in developing contacts with Lutheran bodies of Germanic background headquartered in the eastern United States. He thus helped to lead the synod's participation in the formation of the Lutheran Church in America in 1962. This was abetted through attempts by the *Companion* and *Augustana* to nurture and sustain a sense of the Church as institution and community in the Augustana synod, a contribution that led to the development of the Lutheran Church in America. The *Companion* was succeeded by the *Lutheran* as the magazine of the new Church.

Notes

1. *Augustana* 1 (18 October 1868): 1.
2. *Lutheran Companion* 19:1 (7 January 1911): 1.
3. Ibid.
4. Ibid., p. 6.
5. *Augustana* 63 (4 July 1918): 432.
6. Ibid. 61 (17 December 1916): 954.
7. Ibid. 71 (25 May 1926): 184.
8. Nils Hasselmo, *Swedish America: An Introduction* (Minneapolis: Bring Press, 1976), 43.
9. Ibid.

Information Sources

INDEX SOURCES: *Augustana* had an annual index; the *Lutheran Companion* had annual indexes from 1917 to 1925 and from 1954 to 1962.

LOCATION SOURCES: Augustana College, Illinois; Gustavus Adolphus College, Minnesota; Lutheran School of Theology at Chicago; and others.

Publication History: *Augustana*

MAGAZINE TITLE AND TITLE CHANGES: *Augustana* (1868–1869), *Rätta Hemlandet och Augustana* (1869–1873), *Augustana, Luthersk Kyrkotidning* (1874–1878), *Augustana, och Missionänen* (1879–1889), *Augustana* (1889–1956).

VOLUME AND ISSUE DATA: 1:1 (October 1868)–102:12 (December 1956). Published semiweekly from 1868 to 1878, weekly from 1879 to 1949, semiweekly from 1950–1955, monthly in 1956.

PUBLISHER AND PLACE OF PUBLICATION: Swenska Boktryskeriet, Chicago (1868–1873); Swenska Lutherska Tryckföreningen, Chicago (1874–1875); A. C. F. de Remee, Moline, Illinois (1876–1877); Swedish Printing Co., Moline, Illinois

(1878–1881); Wistrand and Thulin, Moline, Illinois (1882–1884); Thulin and Anderson, Moline, Illinois (1884); Augustana Book Concern, Rock Island, Illinois (1884–1956).

EDITORS: T. N. Hasselquist (1868–1890), L. G. Abrahamson (1885–1901), S. P. A. Lindal (1891–1912), L. G. Abrahamson (1912–1940), A. T. Lundholm (1940–1956).

CIRCULATION: 21,594 (1914).

Publication History: *Lutheran Companion*

MAGAZINE TITLE: *Lutheran Companion* (1911–1962).

VOLUME AND ISSUE DATA: 19:1 (January 1911)–108:12 (December 1962). Published weekly.

PUBLISHER AND PLACE OF PUBLICATION: Augustana Book Concern, Rock Island, Illinois (1911–1962).

EDITORS: C. J. Sodergren (1911–1915), Carl J. Bengston (1915–1934), E. E. Ryden (1934–1961), Paul E. Gustafson (1961–1962).

CIRCULATION: 96,888 (1960).

Myron Fogde

LUTHERAN OBSERVER

By August 1831 two English papers for Eastern Lutherans had failed: the *Lutheran Intelligencer*, which had been started in Maryland in 1826, and the *Lutheran Magazine*, which began in New York in 1827. A German paper called *Das Evangelisches Magazin* would fold in 1833.

It was hoped that one of the editors of *Das Evanglisches Magazin*, S. S. Schmucker (1799–1873), professor at the recently formed Lutheran seminary at Gettysburg, would edit a new English paper. But his health made that impossible. So John G. Morris (1803–1895), a pastor in Baltimore, agreed to do it "upon the condition that all our brethren would cheerfully assist us."[1]

On 1 August 1831, the first issue of the new paper appeared. Called the *Lutheran Observer*, it was a sixteen-page biweekly of two columns that sold for one and a half dollars. Morris promised to "maintain" the "doctrines of the Reformation . . . as they are substantially taught in the Augsburg Confession; still the Holy Scriptures will be the only rule of our conscience." He noted that the title of the paper bore the "distinctive name of our church" but that the intention was not to be "exclusively partisan." He said, "We desire to hold communion with all who love the Lord Jesus in sincerity."[2]

Morris promoted Gettysburg Seminary, gave anecdotes and advice for Christian living as well as hints to Sunday-school teachers, printed letters, discussed the needs of the Church, ran historical materials, and summarized Church news from far and near. For example, the fourth issue on 15 September 1831 had these topics: a learned ministry, family prayer, true religion, rules for doing good, statistics for religious denominations in the United States, a "convention of colored people,'' the unbeliever's creed, letters, announcements of denominationwide meetings, and foreign news—from Bombay, Ceylon, Persia, Russia, Greece, and Smyrna. This sort of spread, including advertising, was to characterize the *Lutheran Observer* throughout its history.

Morris found the slave trade ''detestable'' and championed the rights of ''people of color.''[3] With even more vehemence and frequency, he denounced the use of strong drink and favored abstinence. Rum was ''the severest kind of slavery.''[4] He was not enamored of ''popery'' and announced its decline in France.[5] As to ''protracted meetings,'' he reported them, but was nervous about their noise and disorder and potential for ''fanaticism.''[6] He allowed ''Melanchthon'' to opine that the ''church should not be like a boat managed by a drunken sailor,''[7] and he printed two articles (not terribly convincing ones) that were titled ''Ruinous Effects of New Measures.''[8]

By the end of the first year there were about seven hundred subscribers and calls for a weekly paper. In the second year the two columns became three, the print was made smaller, and the sixteen pages were compressed into eight; the paper remained biweekly.

In August 1833, Benjamin Kurtz (1795–1865) became editor. Ill health (''hemorrhage from the lungs'') had forced him, after eighteen years, to retire from the ministry. Unlike Morris, who had worked on the paper in addition to his pastoral responsibilities, Kurtz was able to devote all of his time to the *Lutheran Observer.*

His ill health did not seem to deter him. As Morris later said, he ''had no other employment, and was ambitious of success.''[9] He turned the paper into a weekly, renumbered it as a ''new series,'' increased the price to two dollars, and in April 1834 changed the format to four large pages of six columns. In August of 1845 seven columns replaced the six. That format did not change until 1870, well after Kurtz was editor. The paper remained a weekly, with only slight fluctuations in price, through its last issue in 1915.

Kurtz, one of the more controversial figures of nineteenth-century Lutheranism, allowed Morris's concerns about slavery and people of color to recede. He ''sought to maintain a policy of neutrality on the slavery question and refused to print articles about it.''[10] He continued to advocate temperance and made the paper's anti-Catholicism virulent.[11] Mostly, however, he championed revivals without Morris's nervousness about them.

With each issue the reader came to expect something about revivals: ''revival intelligence,'' reports of revivals, how to get them started, why they were needed. The paper was both a ''clearing-house for . . . opinions on new measures'' and a proponent of them.[12] It included many other things as well: reports of marriages (in a column called ''Hymeneal''), obituaries, and religious statistics; devotional and doctrinal materials; articles about any number of topics, such as relaxation, somnambulism, the minister's wife, church news, frivolous conversation, quarreling, family worship; pleas for payments and more subscriptions; market news and grain prices; and advertisements for cure-alls like Houck's Panacea. But it always had revival "intelligence" of some sort.

The most graphic illustration of Kurtz's position—one that has especially intrigued historians—came in an exchange with John Williamson Nevin (1803–1886). Nevin was professor at the German Reformed Seminary in Mercersburg, Pennsylvania. In 1842 William Ramsey preached a trial sermon in the German Reformed Church at Mercersburg, then "issued an altar call . . . When the tumult abated, Nevin told the congregation . . . that while they had got some fairly good exercise they should not assume to have progressed in piety."[13] The following year Nevin expressed himself about these matters in the columns of the *Weekly Messenger of the German Reformed Church*, then put the material together in a pamphlet entitled *Anxious Bench*. Nevin characterized new measures as a Montanist "Phrygian dance," "quackery," "solemn tricks for effect," "justification by feeling rather than faith," the symbol of a false Pelagian system.[14] Against this he juxtaposed the system of the catechism, which involved faithful instruction, the regular administration of word and sacraments, and pastoral visitation.[15]

Kurtz, typically passionate, responded in the *Lutheran Observer* with a series of thirteen articles from 10 November 1843 through 22 March 1844. He sought to argue scriptural and historical authority (including Lutheran and Reformed sources) against Nevin; turned Nevin's central theological and systemic argument into a matter of defining "New Measures" and the "Anxious Bench," accused Nevin of being a theoretical professor and not a parish pastor—and, therefore, not qualified to speak—heaped up examples to show that results speak for themselves, argued that whatever evils attended new measures were minor matters, quoted Jonathan Edwards at length, and said Nevin misunderstood the "German field."

When a majority in the German Reformed Church sided with Nevin, Kurtz pledged space for the minority in the *Observer* and called them "the oppressed."[16] But he did not simply fight those outside his denomination. Lutherans also disagreed with him. The *Lutheran Standard* opposed revivals, and Kurtz carried on a "running feud" with it.[17] When the *Missionary*, edited by William A. Passavant (1821–1894), and the *Lutheran*, edited by Charles Porterfield Krauth (1823–1883), merged with the *Olive Branch* and continued to take on the *Lutheran Observer*, Kurtz attacked the union as polygamous and incestuous and sought to characterize the paper as promoting "a stiff, popish, uniformity."[18]

Though independent, the *Observer* throughout its history always represented the General Synod. Kurtz, with more vitriol than his colleague, supported S. S. Schmucker's calls for an "American Lutheranism" that sought to correct five presumed errors in the Augsburg Confession. These included baptismal regeneration (a topic over which much ink was spilled in the *Observer*), and the real presence of the body and blood of Christ in the Eucharist.[19] By 1855, however, even the General Synod was becoming more attuned to confessional impulses, and the *Observer* "no longer reflected the attitude of its constituency."[20]

Kurtz relinquished his editorial responsibilities in February 1858. In the next several years, F. R. Anspach, George Diehl, Theophilus Stork, and a "committee" edited the paper. Kurtz returned as corresponding editor in February 1861 and again as chief editor in February 1862. In November 1862 he was replaced by Diehl, Stork, and Frederick William Conrad (1816–1898), who pledged to keep the General Synod as their doctrinal basis and to "advocate genuine revivals of religion [and] favor protracted or repeated services of public worship when the indications of Providence call for them."[21]

In July 1869 Conrad emerged as the chief editor, a position that he held until 1898 when V. L. Conrad (his brother) and Sylvanus Stall, who had been associate editors, assumed the post. In 1870, the year in which V. L. Conrad became assistant editor, the format was changed to eight pages of six columns. On the masthead, "Devoted to the Principles and Interests of the General Synod of the Evangelical Lutheran Church in the United States" remained, but the next line—"We are set for the defence of the truth as it is in Jesus"—was changed to Luther's statement at Worms: "Unless with proofs of Holy Writ, or with manifest, clear and distinct principles and arguments, I am refuted, I can and will recant nothing." Though that may sound like a more fiery spirit than before and though disputes continued with the General Council and the *Lutheran and Missionary*, actually the paper was becoming less feisty.

The *Observer* celebrated its "semi-centennial" in 1876, using the founding year 1826 of its predecessor, the *Lutheran Intelligencer*, as its birth date, although 1831 was eventually listed each week above the editor's name. In January 1891 it became sixteen pages of five columns, and in January 1896 there were thirty two pages of two columns. The print was also made easier to read.

In December 1899, M. H. Valentine, son of Gettysburg Seminary's president Milton Valentine, became the editor and served for the last years of the *Observer*'s existence. By then the paper had long since taken on the look of a professional fixture. A serialized story and an honor roll of churches that had increased their pastor's salaries were now part of its fare. It had a different sort of bite from midcentury, arguing about "The Trend toward Socialism" or taking on Colonel Theodore Roosevelt about the abrogation of the treaty of 1832 with Russia.[22] A report of a meeting between the General Council, the General Synod, and the United Synod of the South signaled a period of cooperation and coming mergers.[23] An article on the "Value of Observing the Church Year" pointed to new currents.[24] So did a quotation from Philip Schaff—"Heresy is an Error; Intolerance is a Sin: Persecution is a Crime"—which was printed each week under the editor's names beginning in May 1896. Though he moved to Union Seminary in New York and was a leading American church historian before he died in 1893, Schaff was Nevin's former partner at Mercersburg and had helped forge the Mercersburg liturgical and theological position that Kurtz had found so offensive.

But the *Observer* was still the same paper. It told you about abstinence, the position for healthy sleep, whether football was brutal, and how to avoid the grippe.[25] And—a reflection perhaps of Morris's early concerns or an omen of things to come or both—a place was found for the treatment of "Negroes in Washington" and a defense of their good citizenship "in the work-world and the religious world."[26]

In 1912 the *Observer* reported a resolution of the General Synod that called for establishing a single weekly journal for the synod and conferring with those who were at the time responsible for three separate papers, the *Lutheran Church Work*, the *Lutheran Observer*, and *Lutheran World*.[27] Then it reported a resolution of the board of the Lutheran Observer Association which, because of the support of its friends and readers, said that the association would not sell the *Lutheran Observer* "and that all negotiations looking to that end are hereby terminated."[28] But it was a new day. In February 1915 the board changed its position. Unceremoniously, though with complaints about how the arrangements had been handled, on 22 October 1915 the last issue of the *Lutheran Observer* appeared, and the paper merged into the *Lutheran Church Work and Observer*.

In 1833 Kurtz had lamented that there were only about a thousand subscribers.[29] He was always seeking more and quarreling with those who did not pay up. By 1857 W. J. Mann estimated that Kurtz had increased the circulation to ten thousand subscribers and fifty thousand readers.[30] Mann probably overstated the case. A friend of Philip Schaff and no friend of the *Observer*, he wanted to point to the extent of what he considered the journal's unhealthy influence. In 1876 the *Observer* still needed two thousand more subscribers to reach ten thousand.[31] Albert Stauderman suggests that during Kurtz's tenure the *Observer* reached a plateau of about eight thousand subscribers and stayed there "with remarkable consistency."[32]

At midcentury, when Kurtz was editor, the *Lutheran Observer* championed American Lutheranism. As the century wore on, the periodical took on a broader cast. Throughout its more than eighty years, it mirrored the issues and times that engaged its readers.

Notes

1. *Lutheran Observer* 1:1 (1 August 1831): 1. For a good review of Morris, see Michael J. Kurtz, "John Gottlieb Morris and Nineteenth Century Lutheran Historical Consciousness," in *American Lutheranism: Crisis in Historical Consciousness*, Essays and Reports, 1988, (St. Louis: Lutheran Historical Conference, 1990), 14–28.

2. *Lutheran Observer* 1:1 (1 August 1831): 2–3.

3. Ibid. 1:5 (1 October 1831): 74; see also ibid. 2:1 (1 August 1832): 13 and ibid. 2:13 (1 February 1833): 98.

4. Ibid. 1:18 (16 April 1832): 285.

5. Ibid. 1:10 (15 December 1831): 156.

6. Ibid. 1:24 (16 July 1832): 378; see also ibid. 1:16 (15 March 1832): 249.

7. Ibid. 2:5 (1 October 1832): 33.

8. Ibid. 2:11 (1 January 1833): 81; see also ibid. 2:11 (15 January 1853): 89. With his typical balance, Morris also ran the "Beneficial Effects of 'New Measures,' " in *Lutheran Observer* 2:13 (1 February 1833): 97.

9. John G. Morris, *Fifty Years in the Lutheran Ministry* (Baltimore: James Young, 1878), 138.

10. Donald Sponheim, "A Historical Study of the Issues Raised by New Measure Revivalism in the Lutheran Church from 1831–1850 as Discussed in 'The Lutheran Observer' " (Master's thesis, Luther Theological Seminary, 1969), 4. Kurtz was criticized for this. There were those who could praise the rest of the paper and single out slavery as a glaring omission. See, for example, *Lutheran Observer*, n.s., 26:5 (29 January 1858): 3. F. R. Anspach, one of the *Observer*'s owners and editors, was attacked for being one of the largest slaveholders in Maryland. See ibid., n.s., 30:1 (3 January 1862), [2]. Hereafter, new series is assumed for dates after 24 August 1833.

11. See, for example, *Lutheran Observer* 12:49 (1 August 1845): 122, reports the story of a priest who attacked Calvinists and Lutherans by comparing them to the outer shell and skin of a nut, each of which he peeled off as he spoke. When he got to the nut itself, which was to represent Roman Catholicism, he found it rotten.

12. John E. Groh, "Revivalism Among Lutherans in America in the 1840s," *Concordia Historical Institute Quarterly* 43 (February 1970): 33.

13. Bard Thompson, "The Catechism and the Mercersburg Theology," *Essays on the Heidelberg Catechism* (Philadelphia: United Church Press, 1963), 60.

14. John W. Nevin, *Anxious Bench*, 2d ed. (Chambersburg: Office of the *Weekly Messenger*, 1844), 27–29, 114.

15. Ibid., 132–33.

16. *Lutheran Observer* 21:49 (2 December 1853): 112.

17. Groh, "Revivalism," 31.

18. *Lutheran Observer* 30:3 (17 January 1862): [2]; ibid. 30:28 (11 July 1862): [1].

19. Kurtz summarized his views about these matters in ibid. 28:1 (4 January 1861): 2. He also wrote a book about baptism that was regularly advertised in the *Observer* and that was titled *Arguments Derived from Sacred Scripture and Sound Reason, Exhibiting the Necessity and Advantages of Infant Baptism; and Proving Sprinkling or Affusion To Be the Most Scriptural and Appropriate Mode of Administering It; Together with a Number of Essays on Important Subjects Connected with Baptism* (Baltimore: Publication Rooms, 1840).

20. See Albert P. Stauderman, "First Came the 'Observer,' " *Lutheran* 19:14 (August 1981): 11.

21. *Lutheran Observer* 30:45 (7 November 1862): [2].

22. Ibid. 80:1 (5 January 1912): 14; ibid. 81:1 (12 January 1912): 13.

23. Ibid. 67:1 (6 January 1899): 1, 12.

24. Ibid. 80:3 (19 January 1912): 5.

25. Ibid. 62:1 (5 January 1894).

26. Ibid. 83:10 (5 March 1915): 8.

27. Ibid. 81:1 (12 January 1912): 12.

28. Ibid., p. 13.

29. Ibid. 1:1 (24 August 1833): 175.
30. W. J. Mann, *Lutheranism in America* (Philadelphia: Lindsay and Blakiston, 1857), 33.
31. *Lutheran Observer* 44:1 (7 January 1876): 2.
32. Stauderman, "First Came the 'Observer,' " 11.

Information Sources

INDEX SOURCES: Beginning in 1899, an index for the previous year is included in the final edition of the year.
LOCATION SOURCES: Lutheran Theological Seminary, Gettysburg, Pennsylvania. On microfilm at Luther Theological Seminary, St. Paul, Minnesota, and the archives of the Evangelical Lutheran Church in America, Chicago.

Publication History

MAGAZINE TITLE AND TITLE CHANGES: *Lutheran Observer* (1831–1915). *Weekly Literary and Religious Visitor* was added to *Lutheran Observer* in 1:31 (2 April 1834), switched to *Weekly Religious and Literary Visitor* in 1:37 (9 May 1834), and deleted in 7:27 (5 March 1840).
VOLUME AND ISSUE DATA: 1:1 (1 August 1831)–2:24 (15 July 1833), published every two weeks; new series, 1:1 (24 August 1833)–83:43 (22 October 1915), published weekly.
PUBLISHER AND PLACE OF PUBLICATION: Lucas and Deaver, Baltimore, Maryland; Cloud and Pouder, Baltimore; William Wooddy, Baltimore; Publications Rooms 7, Baltimore; The Religious Press Association, Philadelphia and Lancaster, Pennsylvania.
EDITORS: J. G. Morris (1831–1833), Benjamin Kurtz (1833–1858, 1861–1862), F. R. Anspach (1855–1862), George Diehl (1855, 1862–1866), Theophilus Stork (1862–1870), F. W. Hutter (1866–1870), F. W. Conrad (1862–1898), V. L. Conrad (1870–1899), Sylvanus Stall (1890–1901), M. H. Valentine (1899–1915).
CIRCULATION: About 8,000 (1862).

Paul Westermeyer

LUTHERAN STANDARD. *See* LUTHERAN

LUTHERAN WITNESS

Many religious periodicals are born in the heat of conflict. The *Lutheran Witness* is one such publication. It was begun out of the passionate commitment of one man and his opinions concerning a theological controversy within American Lutheranism. Yet many of these same periodicals lose their way and die as soon as that particular controversy is ended or the efforts of their founder cease. This is certainly not the case with the *Lutheran Witness*, for what began as the vision of one editor grew and flourished far beyond the circumstances of its founding to become the official periodical of the Lutheran Church Missouri

Synod. It attained a large circulation and has a continuous publication history that spans over a hundred years.

The *Lutheran Witness* first began publication on 21 May 1882, with a masthead that read: "Devoted to the interests of the Joint Synod of Missouri and Friends. Edited and published under the auspices of the Cleveland District Conference by C. A. Frank."[1] The paper had its roots in a controversy over the doctrine of predestination, a controversy that divided many conservative midwestern Lutheran groups and led the Ohio Synod to separate from the Missouri Synod. Frank, a Lutheran pastor in Ohio fiercely devoted to the Missouri view, was especially concerned that English-speaking Lutherans were not hearing the "truth" on this issue, for while the Ohio Synod had an English-language publication, the Missouri Synod did not. In 1884 Frank restated his original intent: "Our *Witness* is the only paper in the (English-speaking) world which endeavors to do justice to an unqualified exposition of Lutheran doctrine and practice."[2] The early issues of the *Witness* were filled with articles examining technical points of this theological controversy. As the controversy faded, the Cleveland district felt that the paper had "fulfilled its mission" and in 1884 withdrew its support.[3] Frank, however, continued the paper on his own; the only published notice of this change was a new masthead, "Devoted to the interests of the Joint Synod of Missouri and its Friends," and a short note that indicated that "all communications should henceforth be sent to *Lutheran Witness* . . . Zanesville, Ohio."[4]

Frank's strict confessional Lutheranism (along Missouri lines) was continuously evident in the paper, but so was his concern for the advancement of English-speaking Lutheranism in America. Many Germans, especially in the Missouri Synod, thought that these two concerns were contradictory and that true Lutheranism could be maintained only in the German language. The success of the periodical, however, and its acceptance by the Missouri Synod Lutherans, showed Frank to be correct. C. F. W. Walther, Missouri's leader, warmly praised the *Lutheran Witness*, saying, "Up then, dear brethren who understand English, and hasten to subscribe to this beautiful paper."[5] While polemics were an important reason for initiating the paper, the *Lutheran Witness* also addressed many other areas of religious life, publishing devotionals, church news, edifying stories, and comments on morality. Although the doctrinal material was strictly confessional Lutheran (as defined by the Missouri Synod), other materials were drawn widely from many American sources.[6]

In 1888 Frank donated the paper to the newly formed General English Conference of Missouri, urging that it "let our *Witness* remain essentially what it has been till now, an uncompromising advocate of . . . sound Christian doctrine and practice."[7] The *Lutheran Witness* became the conference's official paper, and Frank was persuaded to remain as editor until 1891. Reverend William Dallman served as editor from 1891 to 1895, and then was replaced by an editorial team from the faculty of Concordia College, at Conover, North Carolina, headed by Reverend George Romoser. This arrangement continued until

1912. During this period, the paper changed its presentation, employing more pictures and graphics and a less ponderous tone, but there was little alteration of editorial substance. Dallman's editorial motto, "Our Father's Faith, our Children's Language," reflected this continuity.[8] The paper evidenced increasing interest in synodical affairs and less in the moral and political issues of the day; on social issues, the paper "followed Frank's editorial thought but fell far short of his thoroughness and frequency of report."[9]

In 1911 the English Synod of Missouri merged into the German Missouri Synod as a nongeographical district of the latter. The *Lutheran Witness* became the official English periodical of the whole synod as a result of this merger. The English district was still represented editorially on the paper, but content was subject to the review and revision by the faculty of Concordia Seminary.[10] The existing editorial committee served until 1914, when the synodical convention elected two new editors, Reverend Martin Sommer of the English district and Reverend Theodore Graebner of the Concordia Seminary faculty. Their editorial partnership (1914–1949) was one of the longest in the history of American Lutheran journalism.[11]

Their tenure saw both tremendous growth and turmoil for the synod and the nearly total transition from German to English. This did not mean, however, a relaxation of the *Lutheran Witness*'s editorial stance. Historian Fred Meuser has observed: "As the Synod became more English, the English church paper . . . became even more polemical than the German . . . (translating) into English the 'siege mentality' of Missouri's earlier period."[12] Nevertheless, this period also saw great growth for the *Lutheran Witness*; its circulation rose from approximately three thousand in 1914 to more than a quarter million in 1949,[13] making it the "second largest Protestant church paper in America" in 1949.[14]

Graebner clearly took the editorial lead, and he exhibited in his contributions a policy similar to that of past editors. Americanization and transition to English were encouraged, but there was no movement from Missouri's particular brand of conservative confessional Lutheranism.[15] Graebner remarked that the *Lutheran Witness* was "a book of Chronicles of the war of a sound Lutheranism against the enemies that sought to encompass the ruin of our Western Zion."[16] During the turmoil of the 1920s and 1930s, Graebner sought to reflect and influence the synod's stance on many issues through the *Lutheran Witness*. For example, the sentiment of many Missouri Synod Lutherans was sympathetic to Germany prior to World War I and World War II, and because of these sentiments they were the target of much hostility and suspicion from their American neighbors. Initially, the *Lutheran Witness* reflected a neutral (if not pro-German) stance. Its editorial policies did shift after the United States entered these wars, but there was an air of resignation in its support for the government. The *Lutheran Witness* has been particularly faulted for its support for Germany and the Nazis in the period leading up to World War II.[17]

On social issues, the *Lutheran Witness* generally followed conservative American Protestantism in opposing dancing, movies, "flappers," women's rights, and the like. One exception came over the question of Prohibition, which the Missouri Synod emphatically opposed. Graebner made it clear that on the basis of Romans 13 Christians were to obey Prohibition, "no matter how unrighteous or unreasonable," but he reserved much venom to hurl at the coalition of conservative Churches that brought about passage of the Eighteenth Amendment. Graebner wrote, "The churches which have put over prohibition . . . look upon the State as the secular arm of the church, which shall enforce obedience to church regulations by the policeman's billy and handcuffs . . . The very spirit of the First Amendment . . . had to be ignored in order to put over the Eighteenth."[18]

From 1939 to 1949, Graebner and Sommer were assisted by members of an editorial committee from Concordia Seminary who functioned as associate editors. These associates continued the paper from 1949 to 1952, when the first full-time editor, Reverend Lorenz F. Blankenbuehler, was called. Blankenbuehler was assisted by Dr. Martin Mueller, who succeeded him as editor in 1960. During Martin's control (1960–1974) the *Lutheran Witness* reached its highest circulation (625,000 copies in 1965).[19] During this period the paper saw an increased use of color and graphics and in May 1965 changed from bimonthly to monthly.

The period after 1960 saw a new freedom in the Missouri Synod, which was reflected in the *Lutheran Witness*. Articles pertaining to new social and political concerns appeared, discussing race relations, social change, Vietnam, and drug abuse, among others. One article on "Love, Truth and Justice" stated, "We are Christian citizens (and must) take our commitment to Christ with us into the political arena"[20]—quite a change from Graebner. A seminary professor, writing on race relations, asserted that Christ's words in Matthew 25 "sound almost as if he had read the Kerner Commission report."[21]

In the early 1970s, a resurgent conservatism took hold of the synod. The new synod president, J. A. O. Preus, sought to purge moderate leaders, leading to a schism in which some moderate Missourians left the synod. These were contentious times in the synod, and the *Lutheran Witness* struggled to provide balanced coverage of these events. President Preus used his access to the *Lutheran Witness* to push his views in a 1974 series entitled "With One Voice." Moderate leaders protested the use of the magazine in a letter to the editor, saying, "We do not believe it helpful, therefore, to publish at this time in our official synodical organ a delineation of the issues which is strongly weighted toward one point of view and which above all casts suspicion on the integrity of other parties in the controversy.[22] But since the paper was the official publication of the synod and the conservatives were in control of synodical power, they used the *Lutheran Witness* to disseminate their view of the situation.

In 1975 Reverend Frank Starr succeeded Martin Mueller as editor of the *Lutheran Witness*, a post that he held until 1979. Upon beginning his duties, Starr reviewed the threefold purpose of the *Lutheran Witness* as he understood it: (1) to teach (honoring and upholding the synodical positions), (2) to promote and support the work of the synod, and (3) to inform readers about events and developments of importance to the synod and its members.[23] In 1979 Starr was succeeded as editor by Reverend Leland Stevens, who served until 1984 and who was in turn succeeded by Reverend David L. Mahsman in 1985.

Over the years, the *Lutheran Witness* has proved to be a close reflection of, and contributor to, the denomination that it represents. It has a long history of service to the Lutheran Church Missouri Synod and to the people of that Church. The *Lutheran Witness* has also been reflective of the men who edited it as they made their way through the events of a rapidly changing world.

Notes

1. *Lutheran Witness* 1:1 (21 May 1882): 1.

2. Ibid. 3:1 (21 May 1884): 4.

3. See Roger L. Sommer, "Witness' Vision," *Lutheran Witness* 86:11 (November 1967): 294.

4. *Lutheran Witness* 3:3 (21 June 1884): 24. For further details see August R. Suelflow, "Synod's Official Organ," *Lutheran Witness* 76:8 (9 April 1957): 188.

5. Quoted in August R. Suelflow, "Tributes and Trouble," *Lutheran Witness* 76:6 (12 March 1957): 140.

6. For an in-depth examination of the history and the editorial practice of the *Lutheran Witness*, see Leland R. Stevens, "The Americanization of the Missouri Synod as reflected within the 'Lutheran Witness' " (Ph.D. diss., St. Louis University, 1986). Stevens was editor of the *Lutheran Witness* from 1977 to 1984.

7. Frank, quoted in H. P. Eckhardt, *The English District: A Historical Sketch* (n.p.: English District of the Synod of Missouri, Ohio, and Other States, 1946), 26.

8. This first appears in the *Lutheran Witness* 10:19 (7 March 1892).

9. Stevens, "Americanization of the Missouri Synod," 123. For an analysis of the editorial policy of this period, see ibid., 82–133.

10. The principles of this agreement were spelled out in the "Cleveland Articles of Union" (1911). See Walter A. Baepler, *A Century of Grace: Missouri Synod, 1847–1947* (St. Louis: Concordia Publishing House, 1947), 253–56.

11. Leland Stevens et al., "A Century of Witness," *Lutheran Witness* 100:1 (January 1981): 4.

12. Fred W. Meuser, "Facing the Twentieth Century," in *The Lutherans in North America*, ed. E. Clifford Nelson (Philadelphia: Fortress Press, 1975), 424.

13. Stevens, "Americanization of the Missouri Synod," 214.

14. Editorial, "Drs. Graebner and Sommer Retire as Editors," *Lutheran Witness* 68:20 (4 October 1949): 319.

15. For more on Graebner, see Jerrald Kort Pfabe, "Theodore Graebner: Apologist for Missouri Synod Lutheranism" (Ph.D. diss., St. Louis University, 1972).

16. *Lutheran Witness* 41:8 (25 April 1922): 129.

17. John G. Mager, "Nazis, Jews, and the War: What the *Lutheran Witness* Said, 1934–45," *American Lutheran* 47 (November 1964): 10–13.

18. [Theodore Graebner], "Prohibition," *Lutheran Witness* 35:4 (23 February 1926): 50.

19. "A Century of Witness," *Lutheran Witness* 100:1 (January 1981): 6.

20. Richard Jeske, "Love, Truth, and Justice," *Lutheran Witness* 86:9 (September 1967): 221.

21. Herbert T. Mayer, "White Racism," *Lutheran Witness* 87:9 (September 1968): 239.

22. Letter to the Editor, *Lutheran Witness* 93:17 (3 November 1974): 425.

23. "What the 'Witness' Does," *Lutheran Witness* 94:1 (5 June 1975): 4.

Information Sources

INDEX SOURCES: Each volume contains its own index, in the last number of the volume or in the first number of the next volume.

LOCATION SOURCES: Best complete set is at the Concordia Historical Society Archives in St. Louis, Missouri, the official archives of the Lutheran Church Missouri Synod.

Publication History

MAGAZINE TITLE: *Lutheran Witness.*

VOLUME AND ISSUE DATA: 1:1 (21 May 1882)–present.

PUBLISHER AND PLACE OF PUBLICATION: Cleveland District Conference of the Lutheran Synod of Missouri, Ohio, and Other States, Cleveland, Ohio (1882–1884); Charles A. Frank, Zanesville, Ohio (1884–1888); English Conference of Missouri, Zanesville, Ohio (1888–1891); English Conference of Missouri, Baltimore, Maryland (1891–1895); English Conference of Missouri, Conover, North Carolina (1895–1911); (German) Evangelical Lutheran Synod of Missouri, Ohio, and Other States, Concordia Publishing House, St. Louis, Missouri (1911–present).

EDITORS: Charles (Carl?) A. Frank (1882–1891), William Dallman (1891–1895), faculty of Concordia College, Conover, North Carolina (1895–1914), Theodore Graebner and Martin Sommer (1914–1949), faculty of Concordia Seminary, St. Louis, Missouri (1949–1952), Lorenz F. Blankenbuehler (1952–1960), Martin Mueller (1960–1974), Frank Starr (1975–1979), Leland Stevens (1979–1984), David Mahsman (1985–present).

CIRCULATION: 1,400 (1883); 4,000 (1914); 200,000 (1944); 300,000 (1949); 625,000 (1965); 400,000 (1991).

Mark Alan Granquist

M

MARYKNOLL

Maryknoll magazine is a monthly publication of the Catholic Foreign Mission Society of America (better known as the Maryknoll Fathers), an organization of Roman Catholic missionary priests established in 1911.[1] In the decades that followed its founding, Maryknoll has sent hundreds of missionaries from the United States to parts of East Asia, Latin America, and Africa. Its magazine has chronicled their experiences.

The mission society was the brainchild of two enterprising priests, James Anthony Walsh (1867–1936) of Massachusetts and Thomas Frederick Price (1860–1919), the first native North Carolinian to be ordained for diocesan service.[2] In Boston, Walsh directed the local chapter of the Society for the Propagation of the Faith, a Catholic body that encourages and funds missionary outreach. Price operated a seminary in North Carolina that trained missionaries for the rural South and published a newspaper, the *Truth*, that was aimed at a non-Catholic audience.

Both had independently envisioned an organization to train and support American Catholic missionaries overseas. At the time, scarcely more than a dozen U.S. Catholics labored in foreign mission fields, most of which were affiliated with European religious orders. Not until 1908 was the United States itself removed from the official list of Catholic mission territories. Hence, their dream called for more than mere administrative talent and financial backing; American Catholics had to be persuaded of the need for missions.

Walsh already had at his disposal a vehicle to assist in mass education. Several years earlier, he and three other clerics in the Boston area had started the Catholic Foreign Mission Bureau. The bureau in turn put out a small magazine with an admittedly "romantic" title, the *Field Afar*. The publication's stated purpose, according to its first issue, was "to deepen and widen in its readers the missionary spirit.''[3] But a second, more substantial challenge followed: to establish somewhere in the United States a seminary dedicated to the formation of priests for foreign missions. Toward that end, the *Field Afar* was filled with news of the accomplishments of Catholic missionaries around the world. The influence of these reports was calculated to "appeal to the heart of an American Catholic."[4]

In 1911, Walsh and Price won approval to start their seminary and the society that it was to serve. They purchased for the campus a large farm on a hilltop near Ossining, New York, and dubbed their surroundings "Maryknoll" in honor of the Blessed Virgin. Maryknoll was probably the first Catholic institution in the United States to be preceded by a popular religious magazine and to be launched because of its emphases. Appeals in the magazine provided the society and its school with a steady stream of donations and students. One of the first Maryknoll priests remembers the *Field Afar* as the society's "bread-winner, the source of practically all our material support."[5] Another member credited the publication with being "the lifeblood of the Society. Without it, there would have been no Maryknoll."[6] Several Catholic young men who perused the periodical as students in parochial schools later found their way to the seminary to study for ordination. One survey in the 1950s revealed that more than half of the new seminarians who enrolled at Maryknoll each year were introduced to the Fathers through the magazine.[7]

Most early numbers of the *Field Afar* reveal the influence of Father Walsh. He wrote much of the copy himself and filled in the rest by reprinting correspondences from active missionaries. The writing style was Walsh's own: "light, breezy, conversational."[8] There were also many more photographs than was typical in magazines of the day. From the beginning, the *Field Afar* was designed to be an illustrated periodical, for the effect of foreign places was primarily visual. "Father Walsh was a great believer in photojournalism long before *Life* made the term popular," observed one Maryknoll Father. "For his magazine, he used all the pictures he could get, and besieged [sic] missioners all over the world for more."[9] To help ensure a plentiful supply of images, Walsh suggested that friends of missionaries buy them cameras as gifts.[10]

In 1918, *Field Afar* incorporated the Maryknoll name into its masthead; in 1957 it dropped *Field Afar* and became *Maryknoll*. Its writers and editors have borrowed a fairly stable formula for editorial content from successful mass-circulation periodicals of all sorts. Walsh was an advocate of what he called "the personal element" in mission publications,[11] and the pages of his magazine furnished constant testimony to this emphasis. Articles were brief, seldom more than two or three pages long. There was a preference for first-person narratives submitted by religious personnel in the field, with occasional reports about Maryknoll's home institutions. Although the themes of the essays were serious, they were usually framed with anecdotes. Text on mission lands was amply illustrated with photographs, particularly ones in which small children were the main subjects. Everywhere the human-interest angle of the story was pushed to the front.

Like many periodicals, *Maryknoll* printed comments from its publisher and letters to the editor. It also compiled stories of amusing incidents from members abroad for a running column labeled "Life in the Missions." A recurring cartoon feature intended to inspire vocations to the religious life—"What One Priest Can Do!" was drawn in a manner nearly identical to that of the famous "Ripley's Believe It or Not!"[12] In addition, *Maryknoll*'s editors were not above exploiting the fascination with the unknown to attract readers. One form of this tactic involved pointing out the humor that came from the juxtaposition of cultures that is a fact of mission life. Accordingly, humorous stories about the awkward adaptation of American sports to foreign settings became frequent features in the magazine.[13] More sensational were stories that highlighted native practices such as shamanism, snake-charming, and hunting a hippopotamus for food.[14]

The effect of *Maryknoll* during the first century was to romanticize the missionary priesthood with scenes from colorful locales and tales of triumph over the dual challenges of physical hardship and spiritual persecution. Its writers rarely departed from an upbeat tone. Their outlook was confident of Catholicism's truth and the advance of that truth to the far corners of the globe. More broadly, *Maryknoll* was optimistic about the course of history as an unfolding of God's will for humanity. Moreover, it was positively triumphal about the leading role that the United States had come to play in the world.[15]

Most of all, the *Maryknoll* message was delivered with a masculine voice. A special type of what Protestants termed "muscular Christianity" would be required to promote the Church's interests around the world, it was implied, and a distinctively American combination of manual labor, participation in competitive sports, and mastery of practical skills guaranteed that Maryknoll men would have it.[16]

Because such an attitude might lead to feelings of cultural superiority, *Maryknoll* scrupulously preached the virtue of international understanding, albeit on Christian terms. As Americans, U.S. Catholics might stand at the head of nations, but they would be less than good Catholics, *Maryknoll* taught, if they did not possess an outward-looking, humble orientation toward the inhabitants of other lands. "The Church's task," instructed one editorial, "is to make Catholics realize the size of the world and the responsibility of the Church for all the people in it."[17]

Cartoon strips in the magazine trumpeted the theological assertion that "Christ came to all the human race." Readers were admonished repeatedly that "we are not worthy of [Christ's] sacrifice or our own Christian heritage unless we are actively interested in every man in every nation on earth."[18] To further this interest, Maryknoll writers produced a series of pamphlets about foreign cultures, under the title *Our Neighbors, the...* that were advertised for sale at modest prices in the back pages of the magazine. *Maryknoll* understanding received a challenge when Chinese Communists harassed, arrested, imprisoned, and killed some missioners. The magazine carefully distinguished the grievances of the Church against the leaders of the Communist Party from its enduring affection for the Chinese people.[19]

By the 1960s, *Maryknoll* had undergone changes that mirrored shifts in wider Catholic thinking about the Church, evangelism, and social development. Largely missing from the magazine were the quaint vignettes of "local color" in mission contexts. Gone too was the reinforcement of traditional piety through sentimental accounts of the resilience of an unadorned faith. Nor were there discussions about the plight of impoverished populations and the attendant need for charity (or the arousal of pity and initiative that they caused). Nearly absent, finally, was any glorification of priests and sisters as "soldiers of Christ" leading the heavenly march of religion against a world of ignorance and unbelief.

Instead, readers of *Maryknoll* were exposed to a new sensitivity to the integrity of indigenous cultures, a new interpretation of the Church's teachings on social justice, and a new call for commitment by the laity to works of service around the world.

Each of these perspectives brought changes in the format and content of the magazine. Articles grew longer, and their topics tended toward greater abstraction. Much was made of the declarations of the Second Vatican Council (1962–1965), Pope Paul VI's 1967 encyclical *Populorum progressio* (*On the Development of Peoples*), and the increasing lay attention to study of Scripture.

This updated philosophy was most evident in how *Maryknoll* presented issues that previously had long been of concern. The worldview of Maryknoll missionaries had moved from one that placed the United States at the center of global affairs to one that was more evenhandedly internationalist. Consequently, rather than emphasizing the difficulty of explaining the Western rituals of Roman Catholicism to foreign cultures, articles in *Maryknoll* defended and even celebrated the adjustment of the liturgy to local circumstances.[20] Rather than recount individual stories of the world's afflicted and forgotten, *Maryknoll* drew popular attention to the problems of foreign aid and trade policies and to their effect on economic development.[21] Lastly, rather than sketch the lives of the society's clerical heroes, *Maryknoll* printed profiles of and interviews with lay Catholics who were agitating for social change.[22] For once lay people were portrayed as other than buyers of annuities, sources of bequests, or sponsors of vocations.

In the post–Vatican II years, the editors of *Maryknoll* even aired (and answered) questions about the efficacy of the customary modes of priestly formation.[23] The "What One Priest Can Do!" cartoon survived, but its sense of admiration for the clergy was transformed into a summons to service. "Maryknoll Needs Young Men to Help People Attain a Place of Dignity in Society" read the revised advertising copy.[24] In 1965, the periodic group interview with Maryknoll seminarians contained just one reference to the magazine itself from a participant who doubted the authenticity of its depictions of a missionary's daily life.[25]

The missionary's role, too, was changing. Now the missionary was to become a collaborator with, if not a subordinate to, the people who were native to the mission site. At approximately this same time, the general chapter of Maryknoll concluded that "pastoral statistics such as large numbers of converts, catechumens, [and] Communions . . . along with sizable attendance at Mass and parish devotions" [i.e., precisely those indices generated directly by the energies of priests] were not "valid criteria of the success of missionary efforts where they exist in *isolation from the demands of Christian witness.*"[26]

With time, the perceived demands of witness propelled *Maryknoll* further to the political left. This drift reached a peak during the 1970s. More and more Maryknollers were advocating new visions of the Church that had been formulated in connection with a "theology of liberation" in Latin America. In 1972 the magazine published excerpts from a translation of a pioneering work by liberation theologian Gustavo Gutierrez (b. 1928).[27] *Maryknoll* also profiled controversial Third World Churchmen like Dom Helder Camara (b. 1909), bishop of Recife, Brazil, and helped to popularize such ethical notions as "social sin," a structural parallel to personal acts of evil.[28] Ultimately, this movement arrived at its logical destination in the title of an essay by a Maryknoll sister who had been a missionary to South America: "Salvation and Liberation Are Synonymous."[29]

Subscribers, many long accustomed to an essentially tame "mission magazine," wrote to *Maryknoll* to complain of a "radical" tilt and an anticapitalist bias in the material published. The editors printed many of these protests. The storm eventually subsided as *Maryknoll* published fewer theological meditations or political analyses and returned gradually to articles that were anchored in specific times and places and that told a story with human interest. Dispatches from the mission fields, often now by "lay associates," have made a resurgence in the magazine. And a link with the society's grand past is preserved by writing about the contributions of elder members of the community.[30]

Trends within the ordained ministry in the Roman Catholic Church have begun to catch up with the Maryknoll Fathers. Ordinations to augment the force of the foreign mission society's approximately seven hundred priests and brothers have dwindled; fewer than ten new priests will have been added to their ranks in the years between 1990 and 1995. Simultaneously, the average age of Maryknoll's members, already high at sixty-three, is rising steeply. Estimates project that by the year 2000 more than half the priests and brothers remaining in Maryknoll will have reached retirement. Yet some things stay the same. The magazine of Maryknoll, now as at the beginning, generates substantial revenue for the society. One recent report states that such sources as missions collections, proceeds from sales of books through Maryknoll's publishing house (Orbis Books), and subscriptions to the *Maryknoll* magazine "account for 80–85 percent of the society's income."[31]

Through the *Maryknoll* magazine, generations of American Catholics first encountered the vast geography and human variety of their world. At the same time, they were reminded of the devotion and sacrifice of those who would hear the call of Jesus Christ to go forth and "teach all nations" the Gospel. For thousands of Catholic lay people, *Maryknoll* has functioned as a religious version of the *National Geographic*, with detailed maps, eye-catching photographs, and compelling descriptions of life in far-off lands. Yet, no matter how exotic the foreign forays of Maryknollers may have seemed, published accounts of their significance invariably returned to the one feature that readers held in common and desired for others: the Catholic faith.

Moreover, as popular conceptions of the position and purpose of the Catholic Church within American society changed, so did the ways in which the American missionaries of Maryknoll engaged the world beyond the borders of the United States. Intentionally or not, their magazine conveyed that story as well.

Notes

1. The author extends his thanks to Sister Mary Grace Rrieger, M.M., Director of the Maryknoll Mission Archives, for her assistance in verifying some of the facts in this entry.

2. Jean-Paul Wiest, *Maryknoll in China: A History, 1918–1955* (Armonk, NY: Sharpe, 1988), 11–13. See also Robert B. Sheridan, M.M., *The Founders of Maryknoll: Historical Reflections* (Maryknoll, NY: Maryknoll Fathers [Catholic Foreign Mission Society of America], 1980).

3. *Field Afar* 1 (1 January 1907): 2.

4. Ibid., p. 3.

5. Raymond A. Lane, *The Early Days of Maryknoll* (New York: McKay, 1951), 146.

6. Albert J. Nevins, *The Meaning of Maryknoll* (New York: McMullen Books, 1954), 326.

7. Ibid., pp. 322–23.

8. Glenn D. Kittler, *The Maryknoll Fathers* (Cleveland, OH: World, 1961), 46.

9. Nevins, *The Meaning of Maryknoll*, 28.

10. "Contribution Box," *Field Afar* 1 (1 January 1907): 15.

11. Quoted in Wiest, *Maryknoll in China*, 22.

12. See "What One Priest Can Do, You Can Do Too!" *Maryknoll, The Field Afar* 49 (May 1955): 24–25.

13. For example, see John F. Donovan, " 'Jom Bowl': China's Basketballers Talk American," *Maryknoll, The Field Afar* 41 (January 1947): 35; James J. McNiff, "Buzz Saw and Boxing Gloves," *Maryknoll, The Field Afar* 41 (May 1947): 1–4; Sister Mary Mark, "Baseball among the Cave Dwellers," *Maryknoll, The Field Afar* 48 (February 1954): 28–29.

14. See Felix Fournier, M.M., "How Witch Doctors Operate," *Maryknoll* 56 (January 1962): 25–28; Mark Bartholomeusz, "Gypsy Snake Charmers of Ceylon," *Maryknoll* 61 (January 1967): 24–26; Alphonse A. Schiavone, "Hippo for Dinner," *Maryknoll, The Field Afar* 46 (June 1952): 4–5.

15. In this vein, see the magazine's publication of an article by Francis Cardinal

Spellman, the archbishop of New York, "America, the World's Good Samaritan," *Maryknoll* 54 (August 1960): 20–23. In conclusion, Spellman contends that "our wondrous, free, and blessed country" is a "symbol of Christly Charity to the world's bereft and exiled" (23).

16. See the description of "The Making of a Maryknoller" in Wiest, *Maryknoll in China*, 30–42.

17. "Look Out for Everybody," *Maryknoll, The Field Afar* 41 (November 1947): 28.

18. "CHRIST CAME TO ALL THE HUMAN RACE," *Maryknoll, The Field Afar* 47 (December 1953): 32–33.

19. See, for example, John J. Considine, "Bishop Ford: 'This Is the Path to True Growth for China,' " *Maryknoll, The Field Afar* 47 (January 1953): 1–5; Albert J. Nevins, M.M., "Red China and the UN," *Maryknoll, The Field Afar* 50 (November 1956): 36–37; Joseph McCormack, M.M., "Five Years in a Red Prison," *Maryknoll* 53 (March 1959): 22–27; Wiest, *Maryknoll in China*, 451. See also Jean-Paul Wiest, "China as Portrayed to American Catholics by Maryknoll Missionaries, 1918–1953," in *United States Attitudes and Policies Toward China: The Impact of American Missionaries*, ed. Patricia Neils (Armonk, NY: Sharpe, 1990), 171–92.

20. See "Editorial: Catholicity Is Not Latinization," *Maryknoll* 61 (July 1967): 34–35; see also "Mariachi Mass," *Maryknoll* 61 (September 1967): 8–13.

21. See Harold Graves, "Beyond Handouts," *Maryknoll* 63 (June 1969): 56–60; see also James P. Colligan, M.M., "Land Reform," *Maryknoll* 64 (February 1970): 36–45.

22. For example, see "Exclusive Interview: Ethel Kennedy," *Maryknoll* 60 (September 1966): 50–54; see also John Bank, "[Cesar] Chavez: Third World Organizer," *Maryknoll* 64 (June 1970): 48–53.

23. "Editorial: Is the Minor Seminary Outmoded?" *Maryknoll* 61 (January 1967): 34–35.

25. David Brown, "A Discussion: Why We Chose Maryknoll," *Maryknoll* 59 (March 1965): 12–16.

26. Quoted in Donald J. Casey, M.M., "Mission Today," *Maryknoll* 61 (October 1967): 15. The emphasis appears in the original.

27. Gustavo Gutierrez, "You Who Are Rich, Become Poor," *Maryknoll* 66 (October 1972): 2–7, from Gustavo Gutierrez, *A Theology of Liberation: History, Politics, and Salvation*, trans. and ed. Sister Caridad Inda and John Eagleson (Maryknoll, NY: Orbis Books, 1973).

28. Raymond M. Boyle, "Dom Helder: A Prophet Besieged," *Maryknoll* 64 (September 1970): 2–13; Peter J. Henriot, S.J., "Social Sin and the Christian," *Maryknoll* 67 (April 1973): 14–17.

29. Sister Patricia O'Mera, M.M., "Salvation and Liberation Are Synonymous," *Maryknoll* 64 (October 1970): 58–59.

30. For example, see James Campion, "Maryknoll's Living History," *Maryknoll* 84 (August 1990): 43–46.

31. Patricia Lefevere, "Maryknoll Budget Woes Beg Big Questions About Vision," *National Catholic Reporter* 29 (5 February 1993): 7.

Information Sources

INDEX SOURCES: Some volumes are indexed in *Catholic Periodical Index* (1930–1933 and 1954–1964) and in *Guide to Catholic Literature* (1940–1944). A card index to the magazine is in the library of the Maryknoll School of Theology, Maryknoll, New York. Since 1953, an annual index has been bound with the volumes stored at the Maryknoll Mission Archives.

LOCATION SOURCES: Complete run available at the Maryknoll Mission Archives (P.O. Box 305, Maryknoll, New York 10545–0305).

Publication History

MAGAZINE TITLE AND TITLE CHANGES: *Field Afar* (January 1907–October 1918); *Field Afar–Maryknoll* (November 1918–December 1936); *Field Afar–The Magazine of Maryknoll* (January 1937–April 1939); *Maryknoll, The Field Afar* (May 1939–December 1956); *Maryknoll* (January 1957–present).

VOLUME AND ISSUE DATA: 1:1 (1 January 1907)–present. Published bimonthly, 1907–1912; monthly, 1913–1923; eleven times per year with July and August issues combined, 1924–1949; monthly, 1949–present.

PUBLISHER AND PLACE OF PUBLICATION: Catholic Foreign Mission Bureau, Boston, Massachusetts (1907–1911); Maryknoll, New York (1911–present).

EDITORS: James Anthony Walsh (1907–1936), James M. Drought (1936–1942), James G. Keller (1942–1943), John J. Considine, (1944), Albert J. Nevins (1944–1969), Miguel F. D'Escoto (1970–1979), Moises Sandoval (1979–1991), Joseph R. Veneroso (1991–present).

CIRCULATION: 740,000 (1992).

Kevin J. Christiano

MARYKNOLL, THE FIELD AFAR. *See* MARYKNOLL

MASSACHUSETTS BAPTIST MISSIONARY MAGAZINE. *See* BAPTIST MISSIONARY MAGAZINE

MESSENGER. *See* A.D.

METHODIST STORY. *See* INTERPRETER

METHODIST STORY–SPOTLIGHT. *See* INTERPRETER

MIDNIGHT CRY

The *Midnight Cry*, published in New York City between 1842 and 1844 by Joshua V. Himes, the antebellum reformer, religious crusader, and Adventist, briefly emerged as one of the most important "Millerite" newspapers of the antebellum Adventist movement. It succumbed to effects of the "great disappointment" on 22 October 1844, the exact day set by Samuel S. Snow for the "second advent," and it ceased publication on 26 December 1844. Yet, however brief its appearance, the *Midnight Cry* exemplified both the power of the American antebellum religious newspaper and the complexities of the Millerite movement that it promoted.[1]

Himes established the office of the *Midnight Cry* at 36 Park Row in New York City in November 1842, and the first issue of the *Midnight Cry* appeared on 17 November. With a masthead trumpeting Adventist fervor—"Write the vision, and make it plain upon tables, that he may run that readeth it"—the *Midnight Cry* aimed "to lay before the public in a cheap and popular form, some of the principal reasons for our faith in the Second Coming of Christ in 1843."[2] Himes intended daily publication for twenty-four issues, "Sundays excepted," to determine the response, and he immediately advertised for sales agents in cities surrounding New York—"Brooklyn, Jersey City, Newark, New Haven, Hartford, Boston, Albany, Philadelphia."[3]

New York City's strategic place in the developing national markets soon allowed the *Midnight Cry* a readership, and then a coverage, far beyond the city. By December 1842, the *Midnight Cry* had printed a letter reporting Adventist successes in Virginia, and by the summer of 1843 the paper regularly reported regional Adventist revivals in Massachusetts, Connecticut, New York, New Jersey, and Pennsylvania. Increasingly, letters described Adventist success in such diverse and distant places as Cleveland, Ohio; La Porte County, Indiana; Wilcox County, Alabama; and Farmington, Mississippi. When volume five commenced in August 1843, the *Midnight Cry* claimed not only to have published 420 quarto pages but to have received 2,600 letters from readers around the nation, many of which were printed as news reports. Little wonder, then, that the early interest in distribution agents had long since given way to lists of mail "subscribers" living far beyond New York whose receipt of the *Midnight Cry* stemmed from the burgeoning success of the U.S. postal system.[4]

From its first to last issue, the *Midnight Cry* exemplified the cohesive eclecticism that characterized the Millerite movement. Himes and his editorial companion, Nathaniel Southard, stuffed every issue with articles that insistently proselytized on the subject of Christ's imminent Second Coming. "Bible dictionaries" interpreted the Bible in Adventist terms; reports of murders, beatings, children's tragedies, and robberies predicted the coming apocalypse; and articles such as "Signs in the Heavens" included drawings of peculiar heavenly sights that foretold Christ's return. The *Midnight Cry* also sometimes printed the sensational charts and diagrams that Himes commissioned for his newspapers that have stereotyped Adventist and millennialist propagandizing ever since, the best known being the drawing of a thickset, bare-chested, bearded Christ, arms folded, staring gloomily at the reader in such diagrams as "A Pictorial Chart of Daniel's Vision" and accompanied by a quotation from Daniel 2:31: "Thou, O king, sawest and behold a great image. This great image whose brightness was excellent, stood before thee, and the form thereof was terrible."[5]

The *Midnight Cry* also cultivated historical sanction, contemporary prejudice, and respectability. It cited a surprising range of religious leaders—the seventeenth-century female Puritan writer, Elizabeth Singer Rowe, as well as John

Wesley and Martin Luther among them—whose views reputedly paralleled those of William Miller and the other Adventists. It printed innumerable anti-Catholic articles attacking "Catholic Schemes" to plant Irish colonies in the American West and alleged Catholic Bible burning in rural New York, and it openly justified the nativist riots in Philadelphia in May 1844 where loyal "Native Americans" had "endeavored to rescue the city from the undue influence which the Catholic Irish have obtained for the last few years."[6] It stressed Jewish conversion as a sign of the Second Coming in a way that forwarded the casual anti-Semitism endemic to nineteenth-century Adventist proselytizing; Jews could never "inherit Palestine," for example, because it "belong[ed] to Christ."[7]

Despite its seeming craft trade and "mechanic" appeal, the *Midnight Cry* also pursued university learning and intellectual respectability, though not always successfully. It trumpeted Adventist commitments among "Oberlin Professors"; and when it recommended and excerpted books and articles by the putative English Adventists Alfred Addis and Reverend T. R. Burks, it pointedly described both as "B.A. of Trinity College, Cambridge, England." Still, the search for respectability had pitfalls. When the *Midnight Cry* reprinted Nathaniel Hawthorne's short story "The Celestial Railroad" in July 1843, it apparently did not realize how thoroughly Hawthorne humorously, and sometimes bitterly, parodied John Bunyon and ridiculed contemporary Adventists who saw themselves on a train to heaven.[8]

Following the "great disappointment," the *Midnight Cry* withered rapidly. Like Himes's other newspapers, through the spring of 1844 the *Midnight Cry* had followed William Miller's lead in predicting only that Christ would return "sometime" in 1843, a strategy that left room for maneuver and allowed for differing views about the timing and effects of the Advent. Indeed, as late as 19 August 1844, the *Midnight Cry* reprinted an article from the *Gospel Standard* by a "Brother Morley" that set the Advent sometime in 1846 or 1847.[9]

But by September 1844 Himes and the *Midnight Cry* had embraced the dramatic prediction of Massachusetts's Samuel S. Snow, previously a minor Adventist figure, that Christ would return on 22 October 1844. George Storrs, one of William Miller's long-time associates, endorsed the view in the 3 October issue; Snow's tract, "The True Midnight Cry," appeared in the 11 October issue; and in the 12 October issue William Miller himself endorsed Snow's calculation—though the same issue also contained a letter from two obscure Rhode Island Adventists worrying that problems in adjusting the "Rabbinical and Caraite calculation of the Jewish year" might push the Advent back to November, a suggestion that editor Nathaniel Southard and publisher Himes rejected.[10]

Two months after the "great disappointment," the *Midnight Cry* ceased publication. It turned to Richard Baxter's *The Saints Everlasting Rest* to open the issue of 31 October and defended Adventists from attacks that they had stolen the money—and even lives—of the gullible. But a letter from G. F. Cox of

Saco, Maine, signaled the Adventists' loss of will and, hence, the paper's demise: "I am glad," Cox told the editors, "that one of your number,—Bro. J. Litch—has now abandoned the idea of ascertaining by any means now known, the specific time of the second Advent of our blessed Lord."[11]

In the 157th and last issue of the *Midnight Cry* on 26 December 1844, the lead story counseled "Patience" and William Miller apologized to followers yet again. Many hoped that the paper would continue, the editors noted, and some now believed that "the Lord will come to receive his children before the date of our next paper . . . Jan. 2, 1845." But if "our pilgrimage is prolonged," then Himes and Southard intended to publish a new paper to be called merely the *Morning Watch*, and this new newspaper indeed appeared on 2 January 1845, though it ceased publication by July after printing only four issues.[12] A vision had indeed been written, but not the one that the *Midnight Cry*'s editors had so confidently predicted in November 1842.

Notes

1. On Himes, see David T. Arthur, "Joshua V. Himes and the Cause of Adventism," in *The Disappointed: Millerism and Millenarianism in the Nineteenth Century*, ed. Ronald L. Numbers and Jonathan M. Butler (Bloomington: Indiana University Press, 1987), 36–58. Other important studies and books on Millerism include Ruth A. Doan, *The Miller Heresy: Millennialism, and the American Culture* (Philadelphia: Temple University Press, 1987); Edwin S. Gaustad, *The Rise of Adventism: Religion and Society in Mid–Nineteenth-Century America* (New York: Harper and Row, 1974); and David L. Rowe, *Thunder and Trumpets: Millerites and Dissenting Religion in Upstate New York, 1800–1850* (Chico, CA: Scholars Press, 1985).

2. *Midnight Cry* 1:1 (17 November 1842).

3. Ibid. 1:15 (3 December 1842).

4. Ibid. 4:11 and 4:17–18 (1 June and 29 June 1843).

5. One of these charts is reprinted in Arthur, "Joshua V. Himes," 44–45; see also "Diagram of Daniel's Visions," *Midnight Cry* 1:2 (18 November 1842).

6. *Midnight Cry* 1:8 (25 November 1842); ibid. 1:17 (6 December 1842); ibid. 5:8 (12 October 1843); ibid. 7:18 (16 May 1844).

7. Ibid. 1:12 (30 November 1842); ibid. 4:16 (22 June 1843); ibid. 5:16–17 (30 November 1843); ibid. 7:11 (28 March 1844); ibid. 7:23 (20 June 1844); ibid. 7:1 (18 July 1844); ibid. 7:5–6 (15 August 1844). Sometimes anti-Catholic and anti-Jewish themes clashed, as in the report that the *Midnight Cry* reprinted from the *Toronto Banner* in its 12 October 1843 issue that expressed sympathy for Jews caught in the alleged revival of the Catholic "inquisition" in Latin America.

8. Ibid. 1:21 (12 December 1842); ibid. 7:2 (25 July 1844). Nathaniel Hawthorne's story appeared in the issue of 14 July 1843, pp. 156–69 (the *Midnight Cry* was consecutively paginated from issue to issue). "The Celestial Railroad" first appeared in *United States Magazine and Democratic Review* 12 (May 1843): 515–23. Hawthorne's interest in Adventism and in "Father Miller" are evident in other stories, including "The Hall of Fantasy," "The New Adam and Eve," and "Earth's Holocaust," all of which were published in 1843 and 1844.

9. *Midnight Cry* 7:7 (22 August 1844).

10. Ibid. 7:11 (19 September 1844); ibid. 7:13 (3 October 1844); ibid. 7:14 (10 October 1844); ibid. 7:15 (11 October 1844); ibid. 7:16 (12 October 1844); ibid. 7:17 (19 October 1844).

11. Ibid. 7:23 (5 December 1844).

12. Ibid. 7:24 (12 December 1844); ibid. 7:25 (19 December 1844); ibid. 7:26 (26 December 1844).

Information Sources

INDEX SOURCES: Some volumes contain an index in the final issue. No index exists for the full run of the newspaper.

LOCATION SOURCES: All surviving issues of the *Midnight Cry* are included in the 60-reel microfilm collection issued in 1977 by University Microfilms International entitled *The Millerites and Early Adventists*, section 5, reel 6. For a guide to this collection, see Jean Hoornstra, *The Millerites and Early Adventists: An Index to the Microfilm Collection of Rare Books and Manuscripts* (Ann Arbor, MI: University Microfilms International, 1978). Full sets are located at Andrews University, Berrien Springs, Michigan; Berkshire Christian College, Lenox, Massachusetts; and Harvard University, Cambridge, Massachusetts. Partial files are located at Aurora College, Aurora, Illinois; and at Yale University, New Haven, Connecticut.

Publication History

MAGAZINE TITLE AND TITLE CHANGES: *Midnight Cry* (1842–1844); succeeded on 2 January 1845 by the *Morning Watch*, which discontinued publication on 24 July 1845.

VOLUME AND ISSUE DATA: 1:1 (17 November 1842)–7:26 (26 December 1844). Published daily and weekly, with some combined issues.

PUBLISHER AND PLACE OF PUBLICATION: Joshua V. Himes, New York, New York, 1842–1844.

EDITORS: Joshua V. Himes (1842–1844), Nathaniel N. Southard (1842–1844).

CIRCULATION: Some historians, including David T. Arthur, have claimed a weekly circulation of 10,000 copies at its height, but actual figures remain unknown.

Jon Butler

MILLENNIAL HARBINGER

In 1809 former Seceder Presbyterian minister Thomas Campbell, then living in western Pennsylvania, proposed creating a journal that would expose the "anti-christian enormities, innovations and corruptions, which infect the christian church."[1] Campbell's statement reflected a pervasive American impulse to cut all ties with the tainted past and restore primitive Christianity. Thomas and his son Alexander joined forces in the 1830s with the reformation begun by Kentucky revivalist Barton W. Stone to create one of the most significant restoration movements in American church history—the Disciples of Christ.[2] Campbell's journal would not become reality, however, for nearly fifteen years when Alexander launched the iconoclastic *Christian Baptist*. That periodical and its successor, the *Millennial Harbinger*, became the chief vehicles for spreading the Campbells' reform ideas.

Acting on medical advice for a severe stomach ailment, Thomas Campbell arrived in Philadelphia from northern Ireland in 1807. His malady was likely brought on by stress from his unsuccessful attempts to reunite the fragmented Church of Scotland. Campbell's unity efforts, however, did not end in Ireland and Scotland. After receiving a ministerial assignment in western Pennsylvania from the Associate Synod, he allowed Presbyterians who were not members of his denomination to commune at the Lord's Table. After a series of trials for this and for denouncing obligatory creedal subscription, he finally cut his ties with Presbyterianism in 1809.

That year Campbell and a group of supporters formed the Christian Association of Washington, Pennsylvania, a society dedicated to studying and promoting Christian unity. Campbell's *Declaration and Address* provided an apology to the public for the group's existence. The document issued a call to Christians of every denomination to unite on the self-evident scriptural truths accepted by all evangelical Christians.

Thomas Campbell's family joined him in America in 1809. His son Alexander, aged twenty-one, enthusiastically accepted the ideas in the *Declaration and Address* and soon moved into a leadership position in the fledgling movement. When the Christian Association became an independent congregation named the Brush Run Church, it called the gifted younger Campbell to be its minister.

The birth of Alexander Campbell's first child in 1812 forced him to reconsider the matter of infant baptism. He concluded that it had no scriptural warrant and adopted the practice of adult immersion. This move prompted the Redstone Baptist Association to invite the Brush Run Church to join. The Church assented in 1813.

Though the Campbells agreed with their Baptist colleagues on adult immersion, they were at odds on many points of doctrine and practice. For the Campbells the issue then became one of determining how they could best spread their reform ideas. Alexander Campbell began to realize the potential of the printed word with the publication of his 1820 debate on baptism with Presbyterian William Walker. In consultation with his father and Walter Scott, evangelist for the Mahoning Baptist Association, Campbell issued the prospectus for a new periodical in the spring of 1823. Originally to be titled the *Christian*, Campbell finally named the paper the *Christian Baptist* to gain a more sympathetic hearing among the Baptist churches.

Campbell purchased equipment for a complete printing operation so that he would be dependent on no one for the paper's production. He set up shop on a creek near his home in Buffaloe (renamed Bethany in 1827), Brooke County, western Virginia. The preface to the first volume was penned on 4 July 1823, and the first issue came off the press on 3 August. It was a small pamphlet-sized paper of twenty-four pages, measuring 4 by 7 inches with a type face of 3¼ by 5¾ inches. The masthead carried the perfect antielitist text: "Style no man on earth your Father; for he alone is your Father who is in heaven; and all ye are brethren. Assume not the title of Rabbi; for ye have only one Teacher: neither assume the title of Leader; for ye have only one Leader, the Messiah" (Matthew 23:8–10).

The paper was Campbell's vehicle for exposing religious error and testing his ideas of reform. He included articles attacking the pretensions of the clergy, the tyranny of creedal tests for fellowship, and unscriptural denominational structures, along with news, letters to the editor, historical sketches, and religious anecdotes.

Perhaps Campbell's most famous jab at the clergy was his satirical "Third Epistle of Peter" that appeared in the July 1825 issue. Purporting to be a translation of an ancient manuscript suppressed by the Council of Nicea, the document advised ministers to use exalted titles, wear rich clothing, eat and drink sumptuously, and cater to the rich. The writer urged, "In all your getting, get money," and he advised that the chief consideration in accepting a call should be the salary: "When ye shall have fleeced the flock, and shall know of another call, and if the flock be greater, or rather if the fleece be greater, then greater be also unto you the call."[3]

The most significant material in the *Christian Baptist* that helped in the formation of the Campbell movement was a thirty-two–article series entitled "A Restoration of the Ancient Order of Things." In these essays Campbell examined Church polity, creeds, worship, the Lord's Supper, and Church discipline. Positions expressed in these articles became marks of the movement. They included weekly communion, rejection of creeds and extracongregational organizations, bishops and deacons in every congregation, and simple orderly worship.

Besides the "Ancient Order" articles, Campbell wrote several other important series. Among them were five articles on the "Clergy" in 1824, nine articles on the "Work of the Holy Spirit in the Salvation of Men" in 1824–1825, ten articles on the "Ancient Gospel" in 1828, and sixteen "Essays on Man in His Primitive State and under the Patriarchal, Jewish and Christian Dispensations" in 1828–1830.

By 1829, however, Campbell had become convinced that the *Christian Baptist* had served its purpose. Afraid that the paper's title was becoming a denominational name for the followers of his reform, he argued that his readers were ready for something less iconoclastic and more constructive than the *Christian Baptist*. Campbell envisioned a new paper to be called the *Millennial Harbinger*. Since he had not yet finished the "Ancient Order" series, he decided to finish volume seven of the *Christian Baptist* as he proceeded with the new paper in January 1830. For seven months of 1830, then, he published both the *Christian Baptist* and the *Millennial Harbinger*.

The *Millennial Harbinger* became the chief vehicle for communication in the Campbellite movement before the Civil War. On the masthead Campbell quoted from Revelation 14:6–7: "I saw another messenger flying through the midst of heaven, having everlasting good news to proclaim." In the opening issue Campbell asserted that the paper's focus would be twofold: to destroy sectarianism, infidelity, and antichristian doctrine and practice and to develop and introduce "that political and religious order of society called THE MILLENNIUM, which will be the consummation of that ultimate amelioration of society proposed in the Christian Scriptures."[4]

In some early pessimistic, almost premillennial, statements, Campbell reflected James West Davidson's afflictive model of progress, that is, that as the Kingdom of God gained ground Satan's resistance would increase.[5] The thrust of his millennial understanding, however, became overwhelmingly positive. He did not attempt to specify dates or precise sequences of events, but he was convinced that the millennial period was near.[6] Campbell, along with many other Americans, believed that in this chosen nation, with God's help, Christians would eradicate earthly problems and usher in the millennial age. In Campbell's view this would result from restoring the primitive Church, which would bring Christian unity and the conversion of the world.[7] The coming of the Civil War, however, greatly diminished Campbell's optimism.

Like the *Christian Baptist*, the *Millennial Harbinger* included correspondence from friends and critics, reprinted articles from other journals, and carried news items concerning the advance of the reform. Particularly interesting are materials dealing with the difficulties of the union with the Churches of Barton W. Stone's Christian movement in the early 1830s.[8]

Campbell also used the *Harbinger* to deal with internal enemies threatening the movement. In 1837 he responded to John Thomas, later founder of the Christadelphians, especially concerning Thomas's insistence on rebaptism of Christians from other groups. In 1853 Campbell lashed out at Jesse B. Ferguson, popular preacher and editor in Nashville, Tennessee, for embracing Unitarianism, Universalism, and Spiritualism. Written debates with David Skinner in 1837–1839 on the doctrines of Universalism and with Barton W. Stone in 1840–1841 on the nature of the Atonement showed Campbell's "orthodoxy" on key Christian doctrines.

Extremely important in the development of the movement was Campbell's discussion of Church cooperation and organization between 1842 and 1849. In August 1849 Campbell called for a national delegate meeting of the Churches of the Reform.[9] Disciples held their first national convention in October 1849. Yet these yearly gatherings were never decision-making bodies, but mass meetings open to all. The first convention created the American Christian Missionary Society with Campbell as its president. Some saw in this society a reversal of Campbell's earlier stance against nonbiblical structures. Missionary societies and the use of instrumental music in worship became hotly debated and eventually divisive issues after the Civil War.[10]

Campbell struggled to keep slavery from fragmenting the movement. He personally opposed slavery and severely chastised slave traders in his earlier writing. When the Methodist and Baptist denominations split over the issue in 1844 and 1845, Campbell wrote an eight-article series titled "Our Position to American Slavery." He concluded that though he regarded slavery as out of harmony with the spirit and genius of the age, "the relation of master and slave is no where condemned in the Holy Scriptures as morally wrong." Furthermore, he contended, "no Christian community can religiously make the simple relation of master and slave a subject of discipline or a term of communion."[11] In the *Harbinger*, he refused to allow inflammatory articles from either side.

One of Campbell's eccentricities is reflected in the way in which he numbered the volumes of his journals. In keeping with the biblical significance of seven as perfection or completeness, he began a new series after every seven volumes. This started with the completion of the seven volumes of the *Christian Baptist* and continued through five series of the *Millennial Harbinger*. Only after he relinquished the journal to his son-in-law W. K. Pendleton in 1864 did this practice stop.

Campbell's active participation in the *Harbinger* gradually diminished in the 1850s with Pendleton taking on increasingly more of the editorial work. He used material from Isaac Errett, who became editor of the *Christian Standard* at its beginning in 1866 and brought in Charles L. Loos as coeditor in 1864. When Campbell died in 1866, supporters persuaded Pendleton to continue the paper because it was the "powerful directing journalistic organ" of their "Reformation."[12]

Yet the days of the *Harbinger*'s prominence were past. Even before Campbell's departure, his "neutral" position on slavery had irritated both Disciples of Christ abolitionists and slavery advocates, especially as sectional tensions increased in the 1850s. When the outbreak of the Civil War disrupted mail service and virtually eliminated the *Harbinger*'s Southern subscription base, the editors were forced to reduce the number of pages per issue from sixty to forty-eight between 1862 and 1866 in order to cut expenses. Though the journal returned to sixty pages in 1867, the editors could never restore the journal to its previous prominence. Pendleton was simply not as dynamic and interesting an editor as Campbell had been. Competition from several weekly religious papers carrying material of a more popular nature had already begun to cut into the strongly theological monthly's support even before the war. Pendleton decided to cease publication at the end of 1870.

The success of the *Christian Baptist* and the *Millennial Harbinger* depended greatly upon and reflected the skill of Alexander Campbell as a religious controversialist and reformer. When Campbell died in 1866 the *Harbinger*'s influence and support were already waning. Yet it and its predecessor had been essential vehicles in the formation and development of a religious reform in which four million Americans today find their roots.

Notes

1. Thomas Campbell, *Declaration and Address of the Christian Association of Washington* (1809; reprint, Lincoln, IL: Lincoln Christian College Press, 1986), 88.

2. The movement was variously known as Disciples of Christ and, with the infusion of the Stone movement, Christian Churches and Churches of Christ. See, especially, Nathan Hatch, *The Democratization of American Christianity* (New Haven: Yale University Press, 1989), 68–81; see also Richard T. Hughes and C. Leonard Allen, *Illusions of Innocence: Protestant Primitivism in America, 1630–1875* (Chicago: University of Chicago Press, 1988), 102–32.

3. *Christian Baptist* 2 (4 July 1825): 243–47.

4. *Millennial Harbinger* 1 (January 1830): 1.

5. Ibid. 4 (February 1833): 49. James West Davidson, *The Logic of Millennial Thought* (New Haven: Yale University Press, 1977).

6. Robert Richardson, *Memoirs of Alexander Campbell* (reprint, Indianapolis: Religious Book Service, 1970), 2:302.

7. See *Millennial Harbinger* 7 (January 1836): 27; see also Richard Hughes, "From Primitive Church to Civil Religion: The Millennial Odyssey of Alexander Campbell," *Journal of the American Academy of Religion* 44 (March 1976): 87–103.

8. See, for example, *Millennial Harbinger* 3 (May 1832): 193–95, 237–38. See also C. Leonard Allen, " 'The Stone That the Builders Rejected': Barton W. Stone in the Memory of the Churches of Christ," in *Cane Ridge in Context: Perspectives on Barton W. Stone and the Revival*, ed. Anthony L. Dunnavant (Nashville: Disciples of Christ Historical Society, 1992), 43–61.

9. *Millennial Harbinger* 3d ser., 6 (August 1849): 475–76.

10. In the 1864 and 1865 *Harbinger*, John W. McGarvey examined the instrumental music issue, concluding that it was not appropriate for Christian worship.

11. *Millennial Harbinger* 3d ser., 2 (June 1845): 257, 262.

12. Charles Louis Loos, "The Harbinger after Mr. Campbell's Death," in *The Millennial Harbinger Abridged*, ed. Benjamin Lyon Smith (1902; reprint, Rosemead, CA: Old Paths 1965), 2:537.

Information Sources

INDEX SOURCES: Each volume of the *Christian Baptist* and the *Millennial Harbinger* contains an index based on article titles. An "Index to the Burnett Edition of the *Christian Baptist*" is appended to the College Press reprint, 1983, Joplin, Missouri. *An Index to the Millennial Harbinger* was published by College Press in 1981. In addition, a fifty-page "Index to the Forty Volumes of the Millennial Harbinger" is included in volume two of *The Millennial Harbinger Abridged* (Cincinnati: Standard Publishing, 1902) and in the final (1870) volume of the College Press reprints of the entire set.

LOCATION SOURCES: Originals of the *Christian Baptist* and its early reprints are rare. Issues may be found in the Disciples of Christ Historical Society, Nashville, Tennessee 37212, and the Center for Restoration Studies, Abilene Christian University, Abilene, Texas 79699. The Gospel Advocate Company of Nashville, Tennessee, reprinted the entire seven volumes in 1955–1956. In addition, at least fifteen editions of D. S. Burnett's one-volume abridgement were published in the nineteenth and early twentieth centuries beginning in 1835. The latest reprint of this version was done in 1983 by College Press, Joplin, Missouri 64802. Reprints of the full forty-one volumes of the *Millennial Harbinger* were done in the 1950s and 1960s by the Old Paths Book Club of Rosemead, California, and in 1976 and 1987 by College Press. *The Millennial Harbinger Abridged* (2 vols.), published in 1902 by Standard Publishing Company of Cincinnati, was itself reprinted in 1965 by the Old Paths Book Club.

Publication History

MAGAZINE TITLE AND TITLE CHANGES: *Christian Baptist* (1823–1830), *Millennial Harbinger* (1830–1870).

VOLUME AND ISSUE DATA: *Christian Baptist* 1:1 (3 August 1823)–7:12 (5 July 1830), published monthly. *Millennial Harbinger* 1:1 (4 January 1830)–7:12 (December 1836); new series, 1:1 (January 1837)–7:12 (December 1843); third series, 1:1 (January 1844)–7:12 (December 1850); fourth series, 1:1 (January 1851)–7:12 (December 1857); fifth series, 1:1 (January 1858)–7:12 (December 1864); 36:1 (January 1865)–41:1 (December 1870); published monthly, with occasional extras.

PUBLISHER AND PLACE OF PUBLICATION: *Christian Baptist*: Alexander Campbell, Buffaloe (name changed to Bethany in 1827), Brooke County, Virginia (1823–1830). *Millennial Harbinger*: Alexander Campbell, Bethany, Virginia (1830–1864); W. K. Pendleton, Bethany, Virginia (1864–1870).

EDITORS: *Christian Baptist*: Alexander Campbell (1823–1830). *Millennial Harbinger*: Alexander Campbell (1830–1864), W. K. Pendleton (1864–1870); Coeditors: W. K. Pendleton (1846–1855, 1857–1864), Robert Richardson (1847–1852, 1856–1857), Archibald W. Campbell (1849–1862), Robert Milligan (1857–1859), Isaac Errett (1861–1862), Charles L. Loos (1864–1870).

CIRCULATION: *Christian Baptist* 3,000 (ca. 1830). *Millennial Harbinger* 15,000 (ca. 1850s).

Douglas A. Foster

MISSION. *See* BAPTIST MISSIONARY MAGAZINE

MISSIONARY. *See* PRESBYTERIAN SURVEY

MISSIONARY SURVEY. *See* PRESBYTERIAN SURVEY

MISSIONARY VOICE OF EVANGELICAL FRIENDS. *See* EVANGELICAL FRIEND

MISSION CALL. *See* REIGN OF THE SACRED HEART

MISSIONS. *See* BAPTIST MISSIONARY MAGAZINE and
AMERICAN BAPTISTS

MISSIONSFÖRBUNDETS UNGDOMSTIDNING. *See* COVENANT
COMPANION

**MONTHLY EXTRACTS FROM CORRESPONDENCE OF THE
AMERICAN BIBLE SOCIETY.** *See* AMERICAN BIBLE SOCIETY
RECORD

MOODY BIBLE INSTITUTE MONTHLY. *See* MOODY
MAGAZINE

MOODY MAGAZINE

Initially appearing in 1891 as a biweekly newsletter entitled the *Institute Tie*, *Moody Magazine* is one of the largest periodicals associated with an educational institution—the Moody Bible Institute. The magazine boasted a 1992 paid circulation figure of 135,000, with a total readership of roughly 400,000. Of these, several thousand come from abroad, reflecting the continuing worldwide influence of the ministries started by the turn-of-the-century evangelist Dwight L. Moody. In its second century of publication, the magazine reflects both the initial concerns of Dwight L. Moody and the changing issues faced by conservative American Protestants in the twentieth century.

Moody Magazine traces its roots to the work of evangelist Dwight L. Moody in urban America during the late 1800s. It is hard to overestimate the importance of D. L. Moody to American Protestantism. At Moody's funeral service, Theodore Cuyler estimated that, on average, Moody spoke to forty or fifty thousand people a week. A biographer has noted that A. T. Pierson's assertion that Moody presented his brand of the Gospel by pen or voice to 100 million people is actually a conservative figure.[1] As a result, revivalist evangelicalism became virtually synonymous with D. L. Moody. Indeed, Moody has been described as the head of a broad evangelical empire that towered over the American religious landscape toward the end of the nineteenth century.[2]

Moody came to prominence during a tumultuous period in American history. Still reeling from the tragedy of the Civil War, the country faced the traumas of industrialization, urbanization, and massive immigration. Between 1860 and 1920 close to 30 million foreigners entered the American work force—a number almost equal to the total population of the country in 1850. These immigrants were often Roman Catholics, who struggled to fit into a decidedly Protestant culture. Many of the immigrants ended up congregated in the slums of the cities. Indeed, the urban population in America doubled from 1860 to 1900. Chicago, which became the center of Moody's activities, was typical, expanding from seventeen buildings in 1833 to a population of almost 2 million in 1900—the fifth largest city in the world. Not surprisingly, overcrowding, low economic standards, and illiteracy gripped the cities. With the rise of industrialization and the massive influx of immigrant workers, class wars erupted. The country was rocked by riots, boycotts, and strikes.[3] D. L. Moody offered one Protestant response to these problems: giving his life to the cause of bringing the Gospel to the urban working class. In fact, a contemporary of Moody, Lyman Abbott, declared, "No man on either side of the ocean has done so much as Mr. Moody to solve practically the problem often and laboriously discussed: How to carry the gospel to non-church goers."[4]

One of the centerpieces of Moody's urban strategy was a Bible training center established in Chicago in 1886. Eventually this school would be known as the Moody Bible Institute. The institute was designed to provide education to the working class. Consequently, all classes were free and open to the public. The goal of the school was to raise an army of volunteers to act between the preachers and the people to get the Gospel directly to the working class. He believed the seminaries tended to educate ministers away from the urban working class. Moody's vision was to fill communities with trained young people who had been taught to take upon themselves the obligations of Christian work so that their example of Christ might pervade their community and make revivals no longer necessary.[5] It was during the early years of the Moody Bible Institute that what is now known as *Moody Magazine* emerged.

Initially titled the *Institute Tie*, the magazine first appeared in 1891 and bore little resemblance to the current publication. Beginning as a brief biweekly newsletter designed to provide updates on events at the institute, it was circulated to a small group of alumni and friends of the school. This initial appearance was short-lived since publication was terminated a little over a year later. However, the periodical reappeared under the same title in September 1900. This time it was edited by A. P. Fitt, Moody's brother-in-law, and was copyrighted as a monthly periodical.

This revived *Institute Tie* reflected many of the same concerns as the initial version. The September 1900 issue reflected these continuing concerns in its threefold rationale for reviving the periodical: (1) the need for a medium to inform donors and friends of the work of the school, (2) the need for a "tie" to unite alumni as they move into fields of service, (3) the need to provide information—Bible studies, and so forth—for those alumni in remote or poverty-stricken areas who have no other resources available. The issue pledged that "articles will never be sought except from those who lecture, teach or are in some other way associated with Mr. Moody's enterprises."[6] The scope of the magazine was to be limited to the "interests of the Institute, its students and work" and it was not to be "a general magazine."[7] This new *Institute Tie* would appear monthly as opposed to its predecessor's biweekly format.

For roughly the next decade, the magazine reflected the aforementioned philosophy, content to publish class offerings at the institute, provide updates on the various departments within the institute, publish alumni news and prayer requests, provide practical tips for leading revivals or prayer meetings, record donations, and publish new hymns and Bible studies. Overall the periodical served as a guide to practical ministry and a source of communication and encouragement for institute alumni and friends.

This focus began to evolve in 1907 with a change of editors. R. A. Torrey and James M. Gray took over as coeditors and established the precedent that the editors in chief were also the presidents of the school. Torrey and Gray moved the focus of the publication from serving the needs of the institute and its alumni to appealing to a more general readership. It would remain true to its aim of servicing and encouraging those in Christian work, but less true to the goal of servicing exclusively those associated with the institute. The magazine took on a more educational focus, seeking to train lay people for Christian service. This change was formally recognized by a name change in 1910. This *Institute Tie* was renamed the *Christian Workers Magazine*.

Under the leadership of Torrey and Gray, the magazine began to reflect the theological and cultural concerns of the emerging fundamentalist movement. Both Torrey and Gray were prominent leaders within fundamentalism, and the periodical often served as their mouthpiece. Consequently, many of the articles assumed polemical tones. Theological liberalism was vigorously denounced, and numbers of apologetic articles appeared. Articles purporting to prove the reliability of the Bible and disprove perceived liberal notions, such as higher criticism of the Bible, began to become more frequent. Typical of this is A. C. Dixon's article entitled "Why I Am Not an Evolutionist."[8]

The magazine also began at this time to propagate dispensational premillennialism: the view that biblical history is quite segmented into epochs, each with their own juridical structure, with the additional proviso that the current dispensation will conclude with the "rapture of the church" and the start of the so-called Great Tribulation. For example, the October 1916 issue contains an article attempting to prove that John Wesley was a premillennialist.[9] Numerous articles appear either defending premillennialism or providing premillennial answers to various questions. Further evidence is the number of articles dealing with prophecy and the advertisements for various prophecy books and charts.

Concerns about the state of the country were also raised, leading the magazine to venture into the political and social arena. The July 1911 issue illustrates these trends. The lead articles included "Godless Schools," "Free Speech Menaced," "The President's Religion," "The Bible and the Nation," and "War and the Panama Canal." Prohibition, woman's suffrage, and the war in Europe were discussed in the October 1916 offering. Indeed, every issue during this time contained several political and social commentaries.

The year 1920 brought another change of title when the *Christian Workers Magazine* was replaced by *Moody Bible Institute Monthly*. James Gray remained as editor, R. A. Torrey having left in 1910. The periodical also assumed a new look, changing from its original 6½ by 9½ inches to its present size of 8½ by

11½ inches. By this point the readership had expanded significantly beyond the environs of the school, reaching a paid circulation of almost twenty thousand by 1921.[10]

As far as content and editorial policy are concerned, the magazine remained largely unchanged. The cover of the initial edition made this clear. It was a cartoon entitled "No Middle Ground—Only A Chasm."[11] In the cartoon, a canyon was used to contrast the irreconcilable differences between seven points of fundamentalist doctrine and modernist doctrine. Subscriptions grew throughout this period to about forty thousand by 1935.[12]

During this time, from 1907 to 1935, the magazine served as a fundamentalist journal, an aid for Christian workers, and an alumni magazine for the school. Thus, each edition contained reports from graduates, tips for ministry, testimonies, Bible studies, and theological, political, and social commentary.

The magazine ran an interesting collection of advertisements throughout this time. They promoted various health aids and "fabulous" new inventions. Among the most amusing was an advertisement for a "miracle" violet ray machine selling for almost eight dollars.[13] Montgomery Ward and other large retailers advertised, along with various small businesses. Most numerous were advertisements for Christian literature or the accoutrements of ministry, such as hymnbooks, choir robes, and portable organs.

The year 1935 marked the beginning of a gradual change in the tone and thrust of the magazine. This change from a polemical journal with a fundamentalist orientation to a conservative devotional journal geared toward practical Christian living would drive the magazine from the 1930s to the present. The beginning of this movement was largely the result of the arrival in that same year of a new president at the institute, Will Houghton. Houghton embarked on an aggressive campaign to increase readership, although the periodical did not back away from its traditional themes. For example, the September 1937 issue still contained articles attacking atheism and modern philosophy and decrying the "alarming trend toward atheism, materialism, communism, and skepticism . . . in our secular institutions of higher learning."[14] Evolution was also repeatedly attacked during this time. However, the magazine moved further into the mainstream, publishing articles geared more toward the conservative Christian public. It also underwent another name change, from *Moody Bible Institute Monthly* to *Moody Monthly*.

This gradual trend toward a devotional journal geared toward practical Christian living and aimed at a general Christian audience continued through the 1940s to the early 1990s. The trend was reinforced by events in the late 1940s. With the death of Will Houghton in 1947, the presidents of the institute became less involved in the day-to-day running of the magazine. Ken Taylor served as interim editor for one year in 1947. He was succeeded by Wayne Christianson in 1949. Christianson had a journalism degree from the Iowa State School of

Journalism. As a result, the articles became more readable, and the magazine began to polish its look. Print type was expanded, and color was added. More energy was invested in producing creative covers, with the first full-color covers appearing in the early 1960s.

Not only did the look change, but the content changed as well. The change, however, was gradual; and the standard collection of tips for ministry, information from foreign mission fields, testimonies, and Bible studies remained. Theologically the magazine remained conservative and largely dispensational in orientation. Intermittent articles on prophecy reflect this approach. There were also still a number of articles reflecting concern over evolution, Biblical higher criticism, and the reliability of scripture. This is especially the case through the 1960s.

Articles from the late 1940s through the 1960s reflect a relatively high degree of theological sophistication. But the number of these kind of articles appears to diminish. In their place appeared columns like "Out of the Mixing Bowl," a monthly devotional thought geared toward women. A monthly section entitled "Teen Focus" was prominent in the 1960s. Articles appeared that dealt with practical issues like parenting and choosing a church. In May 1960, the magazine that had once carried the subtitle "The Christian Service Magazine" now described itself as "The Christian Magazine for All the Family." The magazine still addressed current issues, the most notable being the May 1980 edition dealing with abortion. But the magazine became less polemical and more selective in its choice of subject than during the Gray era. The change then was not so much theological as focal, and consistent throughout was the material designed to aid lay people in Christian work.

The 1990s have seen another name change, from *Moody Monthly* to *Moody Magazine*. This change appears in part to be a belated acknowledgment that the periodical is no longer issued every month, having changed from twelve issues a year to eleven in 1962. Moving into its second century, it has evolved from an internal organ of the Moody Bible Institute to a Christian family magazine. The magazine continues to reflect Dwight Moody's concerns in its tips for ministry for the layperson, practical Bible studies, and moving personal testimonies. Additionally, it reflects the current conservative Protestant approaches to major theological and social issues. After a century, *Moody Magazine* remains an important source of practical teaching and encouragement for conservative Protestant laity.

Notes

1. Stanley Gundry, *Love Them In: The Proclamation Theology of D. L. Moody* (Chicago: Moody Press, 1976), 10. Gundry cites Will H. Houghton and Chas. T. Cook, *Tell Me About Moody* (London: Marshall, Morgan and Scott, 1936), 117. For similar statistical estimates, see J. C. Pollock, *Moody: A Biographical Portrait of the Pacesetter in Modern Mass Evangelism* (New York: Macmillan, 1963), 166, 242, 283–84.

2. George Marsden, *Fundamentalism and American Culture: The Shaping of Twentieth Century Evangelicalism, 1870–1925* (New York: Oxford University Press, 1980), 33–35.

3. Myron R. Chartier, *The Social Views of D. L. Moody and Their Relation to the Workingman of 1860–1900* (Hays, KS: Fort Hays State College, 1969), 5.

4. Dennis D. Olenik, *The Social Philosophy of Dwight L. Moody* (DeKalb, IL: Northern Illinois University, 1964), 29.

5. Olenik, *Social Philosophy*, 34.

6. *Institute Tie* 1 (September 1900): 26.

7. Ibid.

8. *Christian Workers Magazine* 17 (November 1916): 177–79.

9. Ibid., pp. 96–101.

10. *Moody Monthly* 86 (February 1986): 63.

11. *Moody Bible Institute Monthly* 21 (September 1920): cover.

12. *Moody Monthly* 86 (February 1986): 63.

13. Ibid.

14. *Moody Bible Institute Monthly* 38 (September 1937): 10, 11.

Information Sources

INDEX SOURCES: In recent years the July–August issue contains an annual index. Bound cumulative indexes exist for the *Institute Tie*, the *Christian Workers Magazine*, and *Moody Monthly* through 1980. They are available at Moody Bible Institute, Chicago, Illinois.

LOCATION SOURCES: Moody Bible Institute Library and Moody Magazine offices both own a complete set of bound back issues. Both are located in Chicago. Issues are also available on microfilm.

Publication History

MAGAZINE TITLE AND TITLE CHANGES: *Institute Tie* (1891–1910), *Christian Workers Magazine* (1910–1920), *Moody Bible Institute Monthly* (1920–1938), *Moody Monthly* (1938–1990), *Moody Magazine* (1990–present).

VOLUME AND ISSUE DATA: 1:1 (November 1891)–2:6 (February 1893). New Series, 1:1 (September 1900)–present. Published monthly until September 1962. October 1962–present, eleven issues annually; July–August issue combined.

PUBLISHER AND PLACE OF PUBLICATION: A. P. Fitt (1900–1907), James M. Gray and R. A. Torrey (1907–1910), James M. Gray (1910–1934), Will H. Houghton (1934–1947), William Culbertson (1948–1971), George Sweeting (1971–1987), Joseph Stowell III (1987–present); Chicago, Illinois.

EDITORS IN CHIEF: A. P. Fitt (1900–1907), James M. Gray and R. A. Torrey (1907–1910), James M. Gray (1910–1934), Will H. Houghton (1934–1947), William Culbertson (1948–1971), George Sweeting (1971–1987), Joseph Stowell III (1987–present).

CIRCULATION: 135,000 paid subscribers (1992).

Gregg Quiggle

MOODY MONTHLY. *See* MOODY MAGAZINE

MORNING WATCH. *See* MIDNIGHT CRY

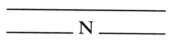

NATIONAL PREACHER

Austin Dickinson (1791–1849), an evangelist who became editor of the American Tract Society's publications in 1827,[1] established the *National Preacher* in 1826 in New York City. In the preface to volume 1, Dickinson eloquently described his aspirations for the new journal. He hoped that these discourses "might reflect light on the desolate places, as well as on the churches of our land. It was thought, also, that this method of introducing Ministers of different sections of the church and of the nation to each other and to the Christian public, might be the means of promoting among good men a more general harmony of feeling and effort, and thus widening and strengthening that band of brotherhood which is to encircle the world."[2] He also thought the journal might be "an item of history" that would enable people of other nations and eras to know something of the sermons of the United States in his era.[3] These three goals manifested themselves in the journal's emphasis on revivalism, in the diversity of the denominational affiliations of the sermon writers, and in the characteristic that held true for most of the journal's history of printing only sermons written by living Americans.

For the first three years of publication, the journal bore the full title of *National Preacher; or, Original Monthly Sermons from Living Ministers*. Beginning with volume 4 (June 1829), Dickinson changed the title to *American National Preacher; or, Original Monthly Sermons from Living Ministers of the United States*. This name was used until 1858, when a succeeding editor, W. H. Bidwell, changed the name to *National Preacher and Village Pulpit. Original—Monthly. From Living Ministers of the United States*. Bidwell called this a new series and in 1858 numbered it volume 1 (sermon numbers began again, too). In 1862 Bidwell changed its name to the *National Preacher and the Prayer-Meeting*, a title that it would hold until publication ceased in

1866. This was called the "third series," but volume numbers continued in sequence.[4] For one brief period, June through December 1837, the journal suspended publication without explanation.

The *National Preacher* was issued monthly, with twenty-four pages, 8¾ by 5½ inches in size. There were no illustrations until 1838, when a steel-plate etching of Jonathan Edwards was placed at the beginning of the new volume. Thereafter, etchings occasionally appeared at the beginning of the new years, often of a noted preacher whose sermon was to appear sometime later that year. In 1858, with the advent of the new series, the publication increased to thirty-two pages; the pages remained the same size.

Journal circulation increased from an average of eight or nine thousand per month in its first year ("upwards of one hundred thousand copies" for the year[5]) to fourteen or twenty-five thousand in its third year.[6] An index was provided at either the beginning or end of every volume.

The format of the journal until 1862 was almost constant: one to three sermons per month. During the first three years fifty-nine sermons were printed. Over time, the length of the sermons gradually decreased; but when the length of the journal increased to thirty-two pages, more than a hundred sermons were printed in a three-year period (1858–1861).

Beginning in 1862, Bidwell began including a number of devotional stories under the title "The Prayer Meeting." On the cover page of the first issue that year he noted, "By the proposed change, we hope to add greatly to the circulation and practical usefulness of the word, and render it a welcome visitor in many families where it is not now taken."[7] Apparently the change did not stimulate sufficient interest; after several notices in 1866 encouraging readers to pay their bills, the journal ceased publication.

The *National Preacher* appeared during a time of strong interest in revivals, stimulated in part by Charles Finney and his "new measures" revivalism that began in Rochester and other areas of upstate New York in the late 1820s and early 1830s. From the outset until 1847, the *National Preacher* drew sermons from persons who came from the larger Reformed tradition, but who represented varying theological perspectives within that tradition.

During Dickinson's tenure as editor (1826–1838), a number of prominent figures had sermons printed. These prominent persons included Nathaniel Emmons, Gardiner Spring, and Enoch Pond, who reflected the theological stance of Jonathan Edwards; Lyman Beecher and Albert Barnes, representatives of the New School Presbyterian theology that followed Nathaniel William Taylor's efforts to redefine Calvinist ideas of sin and conversion; Bennet Tyler, president of Dartmouth College and an opponent of Taylor; Archibald Alexander, founder of the Princeton tradition of scholastic Calvinism, and a student of his, William B. Sprague; and Francis Wayland, a leading Baptist who was president of Brown University.

Many sermons were evangelistic in tone. A good example is Beecher's sermon preached before the American Board of Missions in 1827 and titled "Resources of the Adversary, and Means of Their Destruction."[8] Others were directed more toward encouraging the Christian to duty, such as Francis Wayland's 1830 address before the American Sunday School Union entitled "Encouragements to Religious Effort."[9] Other sermons addressed issues such as Christian duty, scriptural authority, and prayer.

Under Darius Mead's two years as editor (1839–1841), the journal had some truly prestigious authors, including Jeremiah Day, president of Yale; Ebenezer Porter, president of Andover Seminary; and Horace Bushnell, a noted pastor whose distrust of revivalism (which he said worked against Christian nurture) made him controversial in the late 1840s. A wide variety of sermons were printed during these years. For example, Horace Bushnell's "American Politics"[10] was separated by only a few months from a sermon on temperance, which promised its readers the following: "Whether it is right to use intoxicating drinks at the present day."[11]

During Walter Bidwell's first stint as editor (1841–1847), the practice of including a diversity of sermons continued. Notable among these were several sermons by Horace Bushnell, including "Unconscious Influence," "Barbarism the First Danger," and "The Great Timekeeper."[12] The Reverend David Coe gave an interesting sermon entitled "War as a Means of Settling National Disputes."[13] In this sermon he discussed the morality of the war that looked likely with England (over the disposition of the territory of Oregon) and concluded that this "war which threatens us would be dishonorable, impolitic, and useless."[14]

Although the official editorial policy did not note a change in emphasis, after 1847 the journal became increasingly devotional and revivalistic. Few sermons before this time addressed social issues such as slavery or women's rights, but after 1847 the sermons were much less attuned to national politics and events. For example, although the outbreak of the Civil War generated three sermons on the conflict (all calling for loyalty to the country and defining the war as a rebellion) in the June issue of 1861, subsequent volumes ignored the hostilities. After 1847, moreover, few of the writers came from the academy, and none was of the status of the earlier academicians.

By the time of the introduction of the "Prayer Meeting" in 1862, the tone of the journal had changed considerably. Emotional appeals for salvation or support of revivals increasingly dominated the content of the sermons. Simply put, many Presbyterian and Congregationalist clergy had become less interested than their forebears in the technical points that had once generally divided American Calvinists into three theological clusters: the followers of Jonathan Edwards, the adherents of Taylor's revisions, and strict Presbyterian traditionalists. Refined theological distinctions gave way to more devotional interests.

The *National Preacher* in its time communicated a sense of unity of purpose among preachers at the same time that it attempted to be a positive example to them. For the modern reader, it lends a wealth of material toward an understanding of what sermons of the nineteenth century were like. Broadly speaking, one may find sermonic illustrations of the theological issues and divisions in the early nineteenth century and of the devotional ethos of the later period after 1847. Some sermons show an exemplary brilliance of style and content, but all of them reflect the theological concerns of the time—issues such as revival, morality, the authority of Scripture, the missionary effort, prayer, and temperance.

Notes

1. A biographical sketch of Dickinson's life may be found in *The Annals of the American Pulpit*, ed. William B. Sprague (New York: Robert Carter and Bros., 1857), 2:674–77.

2. *National Preacher* 1 (1826–1827): iii.

3. Ibid.

4. It seems that the editor was somewhat unsure of how he wanted to describe this new series. For example, the title page to volume 5 (1862) read "Vol. V," but the monthly issues indicated "Third Series, Vol. I." Further, in 1864 the title page read "Vol. VII," but the monthly issues indicated "Vol. XXXVIII," referring to the whole series.

5. *National Preacher* 1 (1826–1827): iii.

6. Ibid. 3 (1828–1829): i.

7. Ibid., n.s., 5 (January 1862): magazine cover [also known as Third Series, 1].

8. Ibid. 2 (October 1827): 65–80.

9. Ibid. 5 (August 1830): 33–48.

10. Ibid. 14 (December 1840): 189–204.

11. Ibid. 14 (February 1840): 17–32.

12. Ibid. 20 (August 1846): 179; ibid. 21 (September 1847): 197–219; ibid. 18 (January 1844): 1–9.

13. Ibid. 20 (March 1846): 62–72.

14. Ibid., p. 69.

Information Sources

INDEX SOURCES: Each volume contains its own index. At the end of volume 11 (1836–37) a complete index of sermon titles to date was printed, but the preachers' names were not listed. A separate index was published in 1865, covering the period from 1826 to 1864. It lists the titles and authors in consecutive order and includes both a topical index arranged alphabetically and a Scripture index. This index can be found at the beginning of the reprint of the *National Preacher* in *The American Periodical Series, 1800–1850.*

LOCATION SOURCES: The most accessible copy of all volumes is available in *The American Periodical Series, 1800–1850* (Ann Arbor, Michigan: University Microfilms, Inc., 1946–1978), microform, reels 1087–90.

Publication History

MAGAZINE TITLE AND TITLE CHANGES: *National Preacher; or, Original Monthly Sermons from Living Ministers* (1826–1829); *American National Preacher; or,*

Original Monthly Sermons from Living Ministers of the United States (1829–1857); *National Preacher and Village Pulpit. Original—Monthly. From Living Ministers of the United States* (1858–1861); *National Preacher and the Prayer-Meeting* (1862–1866).

VOLUME AND ISSUE DATA: 1:1 (June 1826)–31:12 (December 1857); new series, 1:1 (January 1858)–new series, 9:12 (December 1866); published monthly (not published between June and December 1837).

PUBLISHER AND PLACE OF PUBLICATION: New York, New York. There is no evidence of organizational ownership or support.

EDITORS: Austin Dickinson (1826–1838), Darius Mead (1839–1841), Walter Hilliard Bidwell (1841–1847), James Manning Sherwood (1848–1849), Francis Channing Woodworth (1850), James Manning Sherwood (1851–1852), Eber Carpenter (1853–1856), Walter Hilliard Bidwell (1857–1866).

CIRCULATION: 8,000–9,000 (1826–1827); 14,000–25,000 (1828–1829).

Allen S. Davidson

NATIONAL PREACHER AND THE PRAYER MEETING. *See* NATIONAL PREACHER

NATIONAL PREACHER AND VILLAGE PULPIT. ORIGINAL—MONTHLY. FROM LIVING MINISTERS OF THE UNITED STATES. *See* NATIONAL PREACHER

NATIONAL PREACHER; OR, ORIGINAL MONTHLY SERMONS FROM LIVING MINISTERS. *See* NATIONAL PREACHER

NATIONAL REPOSITORY. *See* LADIES' REPOSITORY

NEW CHRISTIAN ADVOCATE. *See* CHRISTIAN ADVOCATE

NORTH AMERICAN REVIEW

From 1815 to 1940, the *North American Review* offered readers articles on literature, economics, politics, culture, and religion. Although printed by a variety of publishing houses and under the direction of twenty-one different editors during its 125-year history, the *Review*'s story can be set within two periods. For purposes of analysis, then, this essay considers first the journal's story from its origins in Boston up to 1877, when publication shifted to New York City. It assesses its time in New York down to its discontinuance in 1940.

In 1815 an association of men, including Judge Willard Phillips, President John Thornton Kirkland of Harvard College, and Professor Edward T. Channing, also of Harvard College, started a literary periodical that they called the *North American Review and Miscellaneous Journal*. This association chose William Tudor as editor because of his "social and literary accomplishments" and his aspirations. Like the founders, Tudor believed that since "the citizens of the United States are not yet emancipated," there was a need for a national journal to elevate American scholarship to "the great standards of learning."[1]

A perusal of an index for the periodical covering 1815 and 1877 shows a decided dependence upon English writers and English topics during this first phase. In fact, there are nearly as many articles dealing with England as with North America.[2] During this first phase, Tudor and subsequent editors faced the quandary of a commitment to American letters but with a sense that English literature was insufferably superior. An article in the inaugural issue entitled "The United States and England" reveals the frustration. After providing an overview of England's press, the *Review*'s essayist castigated England's *Quarterly Review* for its condescending criticism:

It was in this work, published under these auspices, that forty-five pages of the number for January of last year, were devoted to the most laboured, revolting libel on the United States; involving the general and state governments, the whole nation from north to south, and from east to west—their character and conduct, moral, social and political, in one wide covering of profligacy, brutality and crime. . . . That a work pretending to high literary character, and only noticing politics incidently, should be made use of, to carry into every library in England a collected mass of calumny and falsehood against a whole nation, and this at a period of extreme irritation arising out of war; that such a movement should be seized, and such means employed, to endeavour to make hostility and hatred immortal, is the offence that moves our indignation.[3]

This lengthy statement reveals not only a subtle pride in American scholarly achievement, but also the ponderous verbosity that often gave the *Review* "an encyclopedic dullness." Looking back on its first fifty years, an article in the hundredth volume of the *North American Review* evaluated the journal's dilemma with scholarship. According to John Gorham Palfrey, seventh editor of the *Review*, "Boston was then a place . . . of simple habits and tastes." While the city's intellectuals "esteemed learning and literary opinion," they were really culturally isolated and, therefore, provincial.[4] The *Review* drew most of its contributors from this base. Many were young, paid sparingly for their work, and overly committed elsewhere. Such factors hindered the *Review*'s avowed goal "to hold up a high standard of thought, of learning, of style, and . . . to improve . . . the public taste."[5]

Palfrey himself illustrated these problems. While editor, Palfrey admitted to "lecturing and teaching eleven times every week," serving as "one of three Sunday preachers" at Harvard, and preparing "two volumes of an elaborate treatise on the Hebrew scriptures." Because of these commitments, he did not always read submitted manuscripts. This practice became an embarrassment for Palfrey in 1838 when he printed an article on the life and death of Marie Louise, although the ex-empress of France was still alive and did not die until 1847.[6]

Despite such difficulties, the first editors established the *North American Re-*

view as a prestigious journal. Even Britain's *Edinburgh Review*, always more friendly to American institutions than the *Quarterly Review* was, said that the Boston periodical was "by far the best and most promising production of the press of that country that has ever come to our hands."[7] Under the editorship of Jared Sparks (1824–1830) and Alexander Hill Everett (1830–1836), the *North American* reached the high point of its influence during the first phase of its journalistic history. Its circulation peaked at over three thousand in 1830 and hovered near that mark until 1865. By then the editors had eliminated much miscellaneous matter, had moved from a bimonthly to quarterly publication, and had begun paying a dollar per page for printed manuscripts. Although its circulation was small, the quarterly was considered by a few knowledgeable Americans as "the property of the nation."[8]

Its pages treated European topics as well as U.S. political problems. The one major exception to the latter category was the review's avoidance of the slavery issue. When the editors chose to deal with the subject, as in a review of *Uncle Tom's Cabin*, they accepted the view that the African was "naturally the servant of the white man."[9] Nonetheless, during these years the *North American* was written with "great spirit, learning, and ability"[10] through its successful solicitation of renowned contributors, such as former President John Adams, Senator Daniel Webster, and Caleb Cushing.

The decade after the American Civil War was a time of struggle for the quarterly. Despite the editorial efforts of James Russell Lowell (1863–1872) and Henry Adams (1873–1877), the *Review*'s circulation declined to less than four hundred subscribers. Limited distribution perpetuated annual deficits. Moreover, the journal had acquired a reputation as an unprofitable "relic" that wasn't "lively" and that had "no particular opinion on any particular topic." Too often the "Old North," as "that singular fossil" had come to be called, published the essays of "unknown and fifth-rate writers."[11] While the *North American* ossified during its last few years in Boston, competition grew as new monthly magazines and better newspapers were founded. A new generation could not wait for a quarterly's circumspectly formulated opinions on events more than three months old. The *North American* recognized that fewer people could "find time to read the careful essay on matters which have been already discussed and settled by the daily or monthly press."[12]

During these years when "its business affairs declined" and the periodical was "past helping by anything short of radical change," Allen Thorndike Rice bought the *North American Review* for three thousand dollars. "Wealthy, energetic and lively-minded," Rice reanimated the "Old North" with a new format and new ideas, thus beginning the second and more forceful phase of its journalistic career.[13] In 1878 Rice moved the periodical to New York City, ending the influence of Bostonians who were Harvard graduates. A year later he made the *Review* a monthly magazine that closely followed current events and welcomed all opinions on contemporary controversies. Rice also introduced the symposium format that simultaneously presented variant views and attitudes on one issue. The revitalized *North American Review* initiated this successful format with a forum on the controversial presidential election of 1876.

The most popular and polemical debate to be printed in the pages of the journal was a religious symposium that began in 1877. Such provocative topics as "What is inspiration?" and "An Advertisement for a New Religion by an Evolutionist" began the series. In just a few years the religious debate developed a personal tone; individual authors would explain "Why I am a Unitarian," "Why I am an Agnostic," and even "Why I am a Heathen." During the 1880s this symposium, with its personal dimension, timeliness, and forcefully stated arguments, attracted attention in both the United States and Britain. The British *Review of Reviews* asserted that the *North American* "is up to date, on the nail, and much more alive than any other American magazine. . . . It is the one serious periodical that can be found in reading rooms in every state and territory, and . . . is especially influential in the States of the Mississippi valley, that constitute the great heart of the American republic."[14]

The main focus of the religious symposium centered on the Field-Ingersoll-Gladstone controversy. The dispute commenced in late 1881 when two lawyers, Jeremiah Black, defending Christianity, and Robert Ingersoll, ridiculing it, presented side-by-side articles in the *Review*'s pages. Early the next year the debate erupted into a sensational quarrel because in the final number of 1881 the *North American* had published only one perspective, an article by the resolute agnostic Ingersoll. The editor of the *Chautauquan* found this scandalous and proclaimed that "the *North American* has sold out to Mr. Ingersoll" and predicted that the publication would have a sizable subscription loss.[15] The contrary happened; subscriptions increased from seventy-five hundred in 1880 to seventeen thousand in 1889.

A few years after this, Reverend Henry Field reopened the symposium's debate when he declared Ingersoll's beliefs to be "utterly without reason" and excoriated Ingersoll's "slashing" style. In November 1887 the *North American* published Ingersoll's defense. The agnostic attempted to turn the table on his Christian critic, arguing that an objective reading of the Bible "has forced itself upon my mind not only that it is not inspired, but it is not true."[16] The tripartite debate was made complete when editor Rice drew the Englishman William Ewart Gladstone into the contest. This was a major coup for Rice because Gladstone was a respected statesman and former prime minister. In July 1888 Rice completed the flourishing religious symposium with an array of articles that commented upon the Field-Ingersoll-Gladstone controversy. In this concluding symposium Frederick R. Coudert noted the effectiveness of scorn in a country where the law was liberal and self-restraint was lax. He asked "whether the Lord's Prayer may be abolished and the Sermon on the Mount derided into general contempt, without changing the whole structure of our moral and social world."[17]

Upon Rice's death in 1889, Lloyd Bryce bought the magazine and became the managing editor until 1896. Under Bryce's direction subscriptions peaked at seventy-six thousand in 1891. At this time the monthly sold for five dollars per year. Bryce continued the successful methods used by Rice. For example, he ran a symposium in 1892 on Irish home rule with the Duke of Argyll and with Gladstone, once again prime minister, as contributors. Although religion was still discussed in the *North American*, Bryce cultivated "a sophisticated type of essay on contemporary social life, manners, and fad."[18] During 1891, for instance, the magazine ran numerous articles with an appeal to women, such as "Why More Girls Do Not Marry," "Why Women Marry," and "Married Women in Fiction."

After Bryce's departure, the *North American Review* was purchased in 1899 by the creative and energetic Colonel George Harvey, who had made a fortune in electric railroads and who also owned *Harper's Weekly*. He maintained ownership until 1926 and during much of that period also acted as editor. Under Harvey's guidance, the *Review* gave increasing attention to politics. In 1904 Harvey added a "World-Politics" department that drew correspondence from the leading European capitals on major issues of the day. Furthermore, beginning in 1912 the *North American* opened each number with an editorial on domestic issues. Harvey zeroed in on that year's U.S. presidential election and endorsed Woodrow Wilson in the race with William Howard Taft and Theodore Roosevelt. Harvey wrote in a direct, terse style, easily comprehensible by Americans with an elementary education: "The election of [Theodore] Roosevelt would be a national calamity of incalculable magnitude." "If it were possible to re-elect President Taft, what would be the use?" "A prime reason for installing a Democratic administration . . . is to be found in the character of its candidate."[19]

No longer was the review without "particular opinions on any particular topics." Under Harvey's direction the *North American* took clear sides on political issues. In 1916 when Harvey reversed his earlier support for Wilson, he set forth the journal's political purpose:

If it [the free press] does not lead, it is because it chooses to follow; it is because it does not know that no office is so great as that of molding opinion which makes parties and Presidents; that no patronage is so powerful as the just fear of an unquailing criticism brought home to every word and every act of every public man, and commending its judgment to the intelligence and the conscience of every citizen.[20]

Then after the United States had entered World War I, Harvey explained America's mission in the same direct terms. Until Germany surrendered, "our chief duty before God and man," the editor thundered, "is to KILL HUNS."[21]

Beneath the political bombast, however, problems had begun to appear. By 1924 circulation had dropped to thirteen thousand, and the format was changed from a monthly to a subscription quarterly that sold for four dollars per number. Since the journal was no longer available at newsstands, sales dropped even more. By 1926 when Harvey relinquished the *North American Review* to Walter

Mahoney, the quality of material had diminished. The once successful symposium format also lacked luster. In 1925 the *Review* ran a symposium on Prohibition that presented both sides, but the content was inferior to what Rice had procured for the journal forty years earlier. Now the articles were short, averaging only four pages of large print, and were written by unknowns. This formed quite a contrast to the nineteenth century when, despite a ponderous writing style, the content was at least substantive.

This trend continued through the 1930s, the last decade of the *North American*'s career. The pages were filled with lightweight articles, quite often short fiction pieces. Two that appeared in February 1930, for example, were "The Seven Little Foxes" and "Miss Loop," which was a "portrait of a good soul." During those final years the editors introduced a section entitled "Stuff and Nonsense," which the editor said was "a Monthly Magazine of No Importance with Matter Pertinent and Profound, and Weightily with Those of No Consequence Whatever."[22] Topics in this department such as "Where's Your Hat?" show that "Stuff and Nonsense" really was "of no Consequence Whatever." Although the *North American* reviewed drama, music, art, cinema, and books, the once-distinguished journal had lost its purpose. The last number, Winter 1940, carried some poetry and a few inconsequential articles, varying in length from five to fifteen pages.

Although the periodical had a bleak demise, its first hundred years were quite distinguished. The January 1876 issue, which celebrated America's centenary, illustrates that high quality. That particular issue opened with long but significant essays on "Religion in America" and "Politics in America," which remain insightful. During the *Review*'s prime, its authors were often New Englanders distinguished in literature and local public affairs. Despite a brief period of floundering after the Civil War, editors like Rice, Bryce and Harvey significantly built the *North American* into a "scintillating and lively journal" by presenting contrasting opinions on economic, political, religious, scientific, and social problems. For a time prominent persons in their fields willingly offered essays on issues of current interest. The *Review*'s period of journalistic prominence, 1880–1920, paralleled the coming of age of the United States between the Civil War and World War I. Until the *North American* lost its moorings in the 1920s and 1930s and was eclipsed by newer magazines like *Time*, it served as a solid forum of American thought.

Notes

1. *North American Review* 100 (January 1865): 317.
2. William Cushing, *North American Review, 1815–1877* (Cambridge: John Wilson and Son, 1878), 3–5, 34–35.
3. *North American Review* 1 (May 1815): 65.
4. Ibid. 100 (January 1865): 315–30.
5. Ibid., pp. 329–30.

6. Ibid., pp. 324–25.

7. Frank Luther Mott, *A History of American Magazines, 1850–1865* (Cambridge: Harvard University Press, 1938), 2:231.

8. Ibid., p. 232.

9. Ibid., p. 242.

10. Ibid., p. 231.

11. Ibid., p. 243.

12. *North American Review* 100 (January 1865): 329.

13. Mott, *American Magazines*, 2:249, 260–61.

14. *Review of Reviews* 3 (June 1891): 588.

15. *Chautauquan* 2 (December 1881): 185.

16. *North American Review* 145 (November 1887): 474.

17. Ibid. 147 (July 1888): 36.

18. Mott, *American Magazines*, 2:255.

19. *North American Review* 196 (October 1912): 447, 433, 435–36.

20. Ibid. 204 (October 1916): 481.

21. Ibid. 208 (July 1918): 15.

22. Ibid. 229 (February 1930): 250.

Information Sources

INDEX SOURCES: *General Index*, 1815–1826 (Boston, 1827); William Cushing, *Index*, 1815–1877 (Cambridge, 1878); *Supplementary Index*, 1878–1880; indexed in *Poole's, Poole's Abridged, Reader's Guide, Annual Library Index, Cumulative Index, Jones' Index, Review of Reviews Index, Engineering Index, Dramatic Index.*

LOCATION SOURCES: A combination of bound copies and microfilm can be found at Buswell Memorial Library, Wheaton, Illinois.

Publication History

MAGAZINE TITLE AND TITLE CHANGES: *North American Review and Miscellaneous Journal* (1815–1821); *North American Review* (1821–1940).

VOLUME AND ISSUE DATA: 1 (May 1815)–249 (Winter 1940). Volumes numbered on a semiannual basis with the following exceptions: 8 (December 1818-March 1819), 9 (June-September 1819), 184 (4 January 1907–19 April 1907), 185 (3 May 1907–16 August 1907), 186 (September-December 1907), 222 (September 1925-February 1926), 223 (March 1926-February 1927), and 224 (March-December 1927). 10 (1820)–30 (1830) also known as new series 1–21.

PUBLISHER AND PLACE OF PUBLICATION: Wells and Lilly (1815–1816); Cummings and Hilliard (1817–1820, 1824); Oliver Everett (1821–1824); Frederick T. Gray (1825–1828); Gray and Bowen (1828–1831); Charles Bowen (1832–1836); Otis, Broaders, and Company (1837–1838); Ferdinand Andrews (1840–1841); David H. Williams (1842); Otis, Broaders and Company (1842–1847); Charles C. Little and James Brown (1848–1852); Fields, Osgood, and Company (1878–1880); A. T. Rice (1881–1889); Lloyd Bryce (1889–1894); North American Review Publishing Company (1895–1915); North American Review Corporation (1915–1940). Published in Boston (1815–1877) and New York (1878–1940).

EDITORS: William Tudor (1815–1817); Jared Sparks (1817–1818); Edward Tyrrel Channing (1818–1819); Edward Everett (1820–1823); Jared Sparks (1824–1830); Alexander Hill Everett (1830–1835); John Gorham Palfrey (1836–1842); Francis Bowen (1843–1853); Andrew Preston Peabody (1853–1863); James Russell Lowell (1863–1872), with Charles Eliot Norton (1863–1868), E. W. Gurney (1868–1870), and Henry Adams (1870–1872); Henry Adams (1872–1876), with Thomas Sergeant Perry as assistant editor (1872–1873) and Henry Cabot Lodge as assistant editor (1873–1876); Allen Thorndike Rice (1877–1889); Lloyd Bryce (1889–1896); David A. Munro (1896–1899); George B. M. Harvey (1899–1926); Walter Butler Mahoney (1926–1935); John H. G. Pell (1935–1939); Joseph Hilton Smyth (1939–1940).

CIRCULATION: 3,200 (1830); 400 (1872); 7,500 (1880); 17,000 (1889); 76,000 (1891); 13,000 (1924).

George Sochan

NORTH AMERICAN REVIEW AND MISCELLANEOUS JOURNAL. *See* NORTH AMERICAN REVIEW

NORTHWESTERN PILOT. *See* Pilot

NORTHWEST FRIEND. *See* EVANGELICAL FRIEND

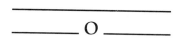

OKLAHOMA METHODIST. *See* UNITED METHODIST
REPORTER

OLD AND NEW. *See* CHRISTIAN EXAMINER

ORTHODOX OBSERVER

Archbishop Athenagoras Spyrou arrived in New York in 1931 with a daunting commission from the ecumenical patriarchate of Constantinople: to reconstruct the Greek Orthodox archdiocese of North and South America. The Church had been splintered by a decade of turmoil—polarized parishes, lawsuits, riots in churches, and rival hierarchies—that reflected bitter political conflicts in Greece.

In addition, the members of the ten-year-old archdiocese were sprinkled thinly across a vast continent, with only a few major clusters of Greek immigrants in New York, Boston, and "Chicagopolis."

A tall, imposing figure, Athenagoras was up to the task. He had won his reputation in Greece by boarding, under fire, an Italian warship that was bombarding the seat of his diocese. Traveling incessantly for more than a decade, he gathered the fragments of the Greek Church in the United States and Canada into a centralized archdiocese.

Despite perpetual difficulties in raising money, Athenagoras wanted to publish an Orthodox magazine to help forge a sense of community and to offer Orthodox nourishment on a continent dominated by "Protestants and Papists." The first *Orthodox Observer* (*O Orthodoxos Paratiritis*) was mailed from New York on 25 November 1934.

The twice-monthly, twelve-page magazine was printed on 8-by-10-½-inch paper stock. Its sole editorial language was Greek, and its first editor was Athenagoras Cavadas, an energetic and inquisitive priest. The magazine, he noted, was not the first Greek Orthodox periodical "to see the light in America."[1]

Cavadas chose an irenic tone for the *Observer*. Its early volumes touched lightly on the activities of the hierarchy. "This periodical is being sent to you, the holy clergy and the respected People," he wrote. "It is intended that power and grace will flow from this effort."[2]

Each issue included Cavadas's column of sermons, "The Pulpit," editorials, and national and international Orthodox news. Priests and lay leaders made up the presumed audience, and accounts of the lives of the saints and articles on Orthodox doctrine were staples. Advice on parish administration also appeared frequently since Greeks were accustomed to a state church and neither the clergy nor the laity was familiar with fund raising, budget making or other aspects of voluntary organizations.

Very quickly, the *Observer* took up several themes and issues that would dominate its pages for decades. The largest was the challenge of establishing Orthodox Christianity "in the sea of America." For the first immigrant generation, it seemed impossible—and wholly undesirable—to separate Greek and Orthodox identity. The preservation of both identities and their transmission to a new generation of "Hellenic youth" were vital concerns. Some, like Bishop Kallistos of San Francisco, faced the challenge optimistically, but many others feared American permissiveness. Their anxieties found expression in articles such as the 1934 piece on "Contemporary Dangers Facing Youth from the Movies."[3]

While the *Observer* was an official publication, it quickly became a forum for Greek Americans. Second only to the organization of new parishes, the provision of Greek education for children was the most pressing institutional concern. In December 1934, for example, Dimitrios Papantoniou of Stamford, Connecticut, offered concrete advice to those planning Greek schools.

Debates on assimilation and loyalty to Greece evoked the highest flights of rhetoric. Dimitrios Tsambadas of Erie, Pennsylvania, expressed the most common view during the 1930s, namely, that Greeks could be good Americans while still preserving their religious and ethnic identity. "American culture does not cast down everything out of love of America," he argued in 1935. Other immigrants had shown the proper path. "They preserve their church and teach their language. Let us observe the Germans, the Scandinavians, the Irish, the French, the Polish, and the rest. Papists and Protestants, the others preserve the foundations of their communities."[4]

Cavadas was intensely curious about America and often wrote positively about American culture. When Jane Addams died in 1935, he printed dispatches describing the mourning of the Greek community on Chicago's West Side, where merchants closed their stores during Addams's funeral. In November 1935, he wrote a long essay on "American Puritanism," interpreting the role of Calvinism in American culture.

The files of the *Observer* from this and subsequent periods are a rich and underutilized source for the history of Greek Orthodoxy in America. Under Cavadas and his successors, the magazine carried dispatches from communities, photographs of new churches, festal sermons, hierarchical encyclicals from New York and Constantinople, discussions of communal issues, and practical articles. The column "Church Life" chronicled the travels of Archbishop Athenagoras, who always seemed to be on a train going somewhere.

When Cavadas was assigned to organize a theological seminary in 1938, he was replaced by another Greek-born priest, Germanos Polyzoides, who made few major changes in the *Observer*. The magazine, however, took on a more staid and official character and stuck closer to Greek matters.

World War II, however, loomed over everything. Cut off from Greece, Greek Americans filled the columns of the *Observer* with expressions of dread about the Axis occupation. The war had other tangible effects. In 1942, newsprint replaced higher-grade paper stock for the duration. The English language also made its debut in the recurring headline "Greek Orthodox American Heroes," placed over accounts celebrating (in Greek) the prowess of Greek American soldiers.

From the late 1940s to the early 1970s, *Observer* editors tended to serve only brief terms. But the magazine passed two major milestones in 1950. It shifted to a monthly publication schedule and printed its first English-language article. Under the headline "In Honor of Gen. James Van Fleet," Archbishop Michael offered a typically Greek tribute to the American general who had assisted the royal government during the Greek civil war. "His name is already written in letters of gold in the history of Greece. Nay his name is engraved on every Greek heart," the archbishop declaimed.[5]

The *Observer* continued its push toward acculturation, announcing in December 1950 that an English-language section would be included henceforth in every issue even though none of the staff wrote in English comfortably. The pioneering December 1950 edition reflected this delicate problem. While Anne Anthony, one of the first female contributors, wrote an article on Christmas observance in Greece, most items were scavenged from other sources, including the polemic entitled "Why Santa Claus?" that had been lifted from the Salvation Army's *War Cry*.

During the late 1940s and 1950s, the focus of the *Observer* remained fixed largely on the activities of the national Church and its growing institutions, although the magazine remained a forum for the discussion of the challenges of life in America. Increasingly, these involved the tensions felt by Greek families moving out of immigrant isolation. In 1952, for example, one of the archdiocesan priests, Father Joseph G. Vasiliou, singled out Greek American converts to evangelical Protestantism as a singular threat to Greek Orthodoxy. "Zealous fanatics," especially Seventh-Day Adventists, Jehovah's Witnesses, and fundamentalists, he complained, were attacking Greek Orthodoxy. "There is no reason for any Orthodox to seek spiritual satisfaction in any other church. If he really hungers for it, he can find it in the faith of his fathers."[6]

During the 1950s, the youth so frequently discussed by earlier correspondents broke into the *Observer*'s pages themselves. Anastasia Lebaris contributed a two-part article in 1951 about the dilemma faced by the "suffering second generation" of Greek American women, who felt torn between American social pressures and their parents' indestructible belief that "dating is an unacceptable social act."[7]

While most of them spoke Greek, the rising generation contributed chiefly to the English columns of the *Observer*. The magazine attracted American-born writers who would become fixtures on the Orthodox scene, including Fathers Eusebius Stephanou and Anthony Coniaris, as well as John Rexine, a classicist and a prolific book reviewer.

By the early 1960s, the English section of the magazine was larger and livelier than its Greek counterpart. In a crucial symbolic act, the English pages were quietly transferred from the back of the magazine to the front. Increasingly, articles in Greek were restricted to press releases from abroad, official news from the archdiocese, sermons, and encyclicals.

News coverage focused on the activities of Archbishop Iakovos Coucouzes, on the efforts of the archdiocese to expand its institutions, such as Holy Cross School of Theology in the suburbs of Boston, and on exciting developments in the ecumenical movement. Both Athenagoras Spyrou, the ecumenical patriarch since 1949, and Iakovos were deeply involved in ecumenical activities.

The *Observer* reached its peak from 1967 to 1971 under the editorship of Father Nicon Patrinacos, probably the most talented Greek Orthodox journalist ever active in America. A former dean of Holy Cross seminary and founder of the *Greek Orthodox Theological Review*, Patrinacos looked forward to the emergence of a Church that was both authentically Greek Orthodox but also rooted in American culture.

"We are determined," Patrinacos wrote in 1967, to make the *Observer* "a tribune reflecting the mind and doings of our Church in the Americas" as it "searches for self-confidence and for an authoritative cornerstone to lean on in this rapidly changing world."[8]

Under Patrinacos, the magazine issued ambitious theological supplements, delved into the ecumenical and civil-rights movements, and reviewed serious books. His column, "Editor's Notebook," offered the most trenchant, reform-oriented commentary in the history of the magazine. Careful reform, he argued, could revitalize a Church at risk of irrelevancy. "Orthodoxy in America is indeed in danger of being dogmatically and culturally leveled and of ultimately being effaced by absorption," he wrote in 1969.[9]

A liberal, Patrinacos hoped that American Orthodoxy could make a self-conscious and selective transition out of its ethnic context. He was unusually open to the possibility of adjusting Church traditions to contemporary problems. He embraced social-scientific methods of studying the Church and its history and, very controversially, advocated liturgical reform. He argued that English should be allowed to take over gradually as the chief liturgical language and, more explosively, that the liturgy itself be pruned of accretions in order to reflect the Church's earliest liturgical traditions.

His proposals enraged conservatives and perhaps especially members of the new wave of Greek immigrants who had begun entering the United States after 1965 and who wanted the church to serve them as a safe haven. Patrinacos was widely identified with reform proposals authorizing a bilingual liturgy approved by the archdiocesan clergy-laity conference in 1970. Vigorously condemned by newspapers in Greece and in America, the changes were struck down by the ecumenical patriarchate in 1971.

Soon afterwards, Patrinacos left his editorial post, and the *Observer* was drastically reshaped. On 20 October 1971, it returned to its original, twice-monthly format and appeared as an eleven-by-fifteen-inch tabloid newspaper of twenty pages. Sent to every family that paid parish dues, its circulation jumped from a few thousand to a hundred thousand copies. An editorial described the changes as the result of a three-year-long search by the Archdiocesan Council for a more effective way of reaching the faithful.

The focus of the *Observer* changed significantly. It abandoned the sort of reflection and debate of issues that characterized the Patrinacos years and devoted itself to covering the official news of the archdiocese, especially Archbishop Iakovos' activities. The paper also emphasized coverage of congregations, printing pages of news briefs and photographs of parish life. Larger amounts of advertising helped to support the costs of the new venture, and the perennial language question was handled by inserting the Greek pages in the middle of each issue.

The letters to the editor and "question" columns remained popular and attracted vigorous participation. Debates over the language issue, the importance of seeking American converts, relations with other religious groups, and the role of pious practices such as fasting bubbled up frequently and were often carried on over many issues.

During the 1970s and 1980s, the *Observer* covered the Church's increasingly complex and troubled relations with its partners in ecumenical dialogue, the financial strains of institutional expansion, and the rearrangement of the Church's administrative structure. A monthly supplement entitled "Youth Challenge" began publication in 1976.

The *Observer* remains the largest and most widely distributed Greek Orthodox publication in the United States. And although perhaps limited in certain respects by its official role, it is still the best place to take the pulse of Greek Orthodoxy in the Americas.

Notes

1. It was preceded by the *Ecclesiastical Herald*, published by the short-lived St. Athanasios Seminary in New York, and the *Voice of Orthodoxy*, published in Chicago. Both

had brief runs during the 1920s. The *Russian-American Orthodox Messenger* predated Greek efforts.

2. *Orthodox Observer* 1:1 (25 November 1934): 3.

3. Bishop Kallistos of San Francisco, "H Neolaia kai to Mellon," *Orthodox Observer* 1:1 (24 November 1934): 5; idem, "Oi Suyxronoi kindinoi tis neolaias ek tou kinimatografou," *Orthodox Observer*, 7.

4. Dimitrios Tsambadas, *Orthodox Observer* 1:2 (9 December 1934): 5.

5. Archbishop Michael, "In Honor of Gen. James Van Fleet," *Orthodox Observer* 15:1 (January 1950): 2.

6. Father Joseph G. Vasiliou, "Keeping the Faith," *Orthodox Observer* 17:5 (May 1952): 12.

7. Anastasia S. Lebaris, "Cultural Integration—A Problem, Pt. 1," *Orthodox Observer* 16:10 (October 1951): 17–19.

8. Nicon D. Patrinacos, "To Our Readers," *Orthodox Observer* 33:6 (June 1967): 142.

9. Nicon D. Patrinacos, "Editor's Notebook: Orthodoxy in America," *Orthodox Observer* 35:9 (September 1969). For a multipart series on the social-scientific study of religion and liturgical reform, see idem, "Orthodoxy through the Social Sciences? Yes!" *Orthodox Observer* (August 1969–January 1970).

Information Sources

INDEX SOURCES: Each volume from 1935 to 1948 contains an index, typically in the final issue for each year. Later issues are not indexed, although each issue from 1948 to 1971 contains a table of contents. The twice-monthly tabloid newspaper format published since 1971 is not indexed.

LOCATION SOURCES: A complete run is held in the Cotsidas-Tonna Library of Hellenic College/Holy Cross Greek Orthodox School of Theology in Brookline, Massachusetts. Microfilming the *Observer* is under consideration.

Publication History

MAGAZINE TITLE: *Orthodox Observer* (1934–present).

VOLUME AND ISSUE DATA: 1:1 (11 November 1934)–present. Published twice monthly until 15:23 (15 December 1948). Published monthly from 15:24 (January 1949) to 39:9 (September 1971). Published as a fortnightly tabloid newspaper, (20 October 1981–present).

PUBLISHER AND PLACE OF PUBLICATION: Greek Orthodox Archdiocese of North and South America, New York, New York.

EDITORS: Archimandrite Athenagoras Cavadas (1934–1938), Archimandrite Germanos Polyzoides (1938–1948), Archimandrite Athenagoras Kokkinakis (1948–1950), Phocas Angelatos (1950–1954), Emmanuel Hatziemmanuel (1954–1961), Basil Vasiliades (1962–1966), Panos B. Peclaris (1966–1967), Nikon D. Patrinakos, (1967–1971), P. J. Gazouleas (1971–1989), James Goulding (1989–present). English-language editors: Arthur Dore (1962–1967), James Couchell (1971–1981),

Evanthia Allen (1986–1987), Peggy Johnides (1987–1988). Greek-language editors: Costa Delayannis (1989–present).
CIRCULATION: 135,000 (1992).

Andrew H. Walsh

OUR DAILY BREAD

No one knew in 1938 that from Dr. Martin R. De Haan's Detroit Bible Class, carried on 50-watt WEXL, there would evolve a devotional that now attracts 7 million readers. Among the most surprised, no doubt, was Dr. M. R. De Haan himself, who began his career as a country doctor, traveling on dusty roads south of Grand Rapids, Michigan. Then in October 1921, a prolonged hospital stay convinced him that at thirty years old, his spiritual life needed attention. Although he had grown up in the Christian Reformed faith, he cited this as his conversion date.[1]

A restlessness for ministry began to fester in his heart, but M. R. De Haan continued in his medical practice. Then in the spring of 1922, after work one day, he announced to his wife, "Mother, I can't go on any longer," and he slid his medical bag across the kitchen floor.[2] He then sold his practice and enrolled in the Western Theological Seminary of Holland, Michigan.

De Haan was ordained in the spring of 1925, and he assumed the pastorate of Calvary Reformed Church in Grand Rapids. His evangelistic messages attracted a growing audience; within a year, a new building program ensued.

With the start of his preaching career also came his involvement in broadcasting. Traditionally, Calvary Reformed Church aired Sunday morning services, and thus De Haan's raspy voice was heard over the air waves.

However, De Haan's theological views disturbed some Reformed leaders. He attacked the 1920s issue of modernism, defending the literal interpretation of Scripture; and unlike many of his Reformed colleagues, he leaned toward pretribulation premillennialism. De Haan saw amillennialism as " 'a cancerous curse' of Bible teaching [that grew] out of 'spiritualizing scriptures.' "[3] De Haan also concluded that he could no longer preach infant baptism.

Tension wedged itself between him and the Grand Rapids classis of the Reformed Church of America. "He was a man of strong ideas," explained nephew Dennis De Haan, current editor of *Our Daily Bread*. "Often times it takes a man like that to begin a ministry."[4]

From his pulpit on Sunday, 3 March 1929, De Haan announced that he and sixteen other men had broken with the classis: "These men have not only resigned from Calvary Reformed Church but also from the Reformed Church in America. They have organized a new church which will be known as the Calvary Undenominational Church. . . . They have called me to be pastor of the new church and I have accepted."[5]

For ten years, De Haan pastored the new Church, which grew to nearly two thousand members. Radio facilities were moved to Calvary Church, and soon radio programs were added. Along with two Sunday sermon broadcasts, there aired a request program and a late evening "heart-to-heart" talk. De Haan realized that the church's radio ministry was its "greatest outstanding domestic missionary work."[6]

But once again contention erupted. When three board members fired the music director without De Haan's consent, De Haan disbanded the deacon board. Several retaliated by pressing legal action against him. Because of failing health and "conscientious scruples about going to law about a church matter," De Haan resigned in May 1938.[7]

While De Haan recovered his health, a friend encouraged him to broadcast a Bible class. On 4 September 1938, the Detroit Bible Class, renamed the Radio Bible Class in 1941, aired live over Royal Oak's station, and thus began De Haan's third and final career change.

More and more, letters poured in requesting a written copy of the half-hour weekend messages, so the Detroit Bible Class began to print De Haan's messages in sermon booklets. This held true until 1956, when an employee of Radio Bible Class, radio personality Henry Bosch, approached De Haan with an idea. Bosch recalled, "I said, 'People don't have time to sit down and read a whole sermon. A lot of them won't do that.' "[8]

Bosch believed that the listeners needed more than the sermon booklet. People needed daily contact with the Bible—a need that a daily devotional would fill. Thus was born the idea for *Our Daily Bread*.

With De Haan and Bosch as cocontributors, twenty-seven thousand copies of *Our Daily Bread* rolled over the presses in April 1956. The booklets were printed on eight 6½-by-4¼-inch sheets of paper, folded into sixteen pages, with no illustrations except for a one-color cover photo.

Each monthly issue appeared in a similar format. A suggested Scripture reading of ten to twenty verses, started in September 1956, came below the title. Then a short verse in italics followed. A story, analogy, or a life-related incident formed the text that ran approximately 250 words. After the text, a four-lined poem, often the work of Bosch, would appear. Each devotional ended with a sentence-long thought that "was supposed to be . . . one last clinching statement to capture [the text] in a single sentence."[9]

Text topics were drawn from such themes as hope, trials, faith, salvation, and obedience. These topics were dispersed throughout the monthly editions so that there would be "a healthy mixture of comfort, challenge and conviction."[10]

Today the basic elements are the same for *Our Daily Bread*. The booklet itself has been shortened to 6¼ by 4¼ inches, and now the cover features a full-color picture, framed in a white border. Except for stylistic revisions, the only other changes include a plan for Scripture readings to cover the complete biblical text yearly and a shortened daily message. Current texts run approximately two hundred words. Large print editions were issued beginning in January 1976.

Originators De Haan and Bosch formed several principles that continue to govern the devotional. First of all, the coeditors wanted to express theological truths in everyday language and life. Stories of life-related incidents were used to convey richer spiritual meaning.

This was a special gift of Dr. De Haan, for he drew analogies from whatever he saw. His fishing friend, Clarence Carlson recalled: "He could look at anything in nature and come up with a story that had to do with redemption. Whether it was a fish, a tree, or an animal, he could see the handwriting of God and its relationship to the Word of God."[11] Current editor Dennis De Haan cited this as a key to the devotional's success. "Everybody loves a story," he noted. "If you can tell a story that has interest to the young child then it will also be of interest to the older adult."[12]

Each booklet was to be distinctly Christ-centered as well. "The ultimate answers to the spiritual needs of people is fundamentally found in Christ," explained Dennis De Haan.[13] Although the devotionals were aimed at Christians, each contained at least one call for conversion. The articles were written to be "understandable for new believers and offering challenge for mature believers."[14]

Third, every article was to rest on a solid biblical foundation. To ensure this today, a four-person committee evaluates the material before any editing is done. The committee asks the question: Does the central theme of this article find support in the Scripture that the writer has attached to it?

Another guideline suggested avoiding all denominationally offensive subjects. Instead of discussing such issues as baptism or dispensationalism, the articles addressed basic Christian truths. Bosch wrote:

A devotional guide is designed to reach the widest possible circle of readers without compromising the truth. As most orthodox and evangelical assemblies and individuals are agreed on 90% of their creed, it is deemed wise on our part not to enter into controversial subjects which might wave a red flag and so hinder our reading reaching the masses with the main message of God's comfort and salvation.[15]

Because of this principle, Our Daily Bread drew a widely cross-denominational audience. Readership extended from mainline denominations, such as Presbyterian, Baptist, Catholic, and Pentecostal Churches.

In the same way that it did not target a specific denomination, the new devotional did not target a specific audience age group. Its subtitle proclaimed it as "An Aid to Daily Devotions and the Family Altar." Being a family devotional opened the door to a wide range of ages. Dennis De Haan explained, "There's a sense in which Our Daily Bread has almost gone contrary to that philosophy [of target audience]. It's worked partly because everybody loves a story. . . . That has been the bridge."[16]

In recent years, though, Our Daily Bread's editors have narrowed down the target audience. Now they characterize their readers as theologically conservative, twenty-five years old, and older high-school graduates from all social and economic levels.

Since the 1970s, international demand has enlarged *Our Daily Bread*'s audiences. The Radio Bible Class has met global needs by opening headquarters in Canada, Australia, England, Nigeria, Swaziland, and Manila. Currently, the international mailing list holds the names of 125,000 individuals and groups.

At the booklet's inception, it was also decided not to make public appeals for funding, although the nonprofit organization did rely on giving from individuals and group members. At request, individuals or groups were placed on the mailing list. Considered a "member," those listeners would receive a package of information about Radio Bible Class; however, no demands for money were made. An exception to the rule appeared on the title page of the May to November 1956 issues. A line read: "Additional copies 15 cents each, 8 for $1.00." To educate readers of its other ministries, Radio Bible Class has printed information on the back cover of *Our Daily Bread* since January 1969.

Along with the member mailing lists for individuals, quantity mailing lists for groups or businesses also existed. Churches, restaurants, hospitals and doctor's offices have often made the devotionals available to patrons. Because of this, Bosch wanted to produce a booklet that did not look too "Christian": "The books are not to look too religious, so words like 'sermon,' 'meditation' and so forth should not appear on the cover. . . . The first article of the book, for example, should not have a title that is too pious, or religious sounding— that would turn someone off."[17]

To encourage a wider readership, the devotionals avoided mention of public policy. Dennis De Haan explained this guideline: "We will generalize in the sense of urging upon our readers the importance of balancing the devotional inner world of our relationship to the Lord with the importance of social concern and justice. But we don't get into political parties. We try to keep the basic principles before the reader so that they will make choices based on the candidate's stand for truth."[18] Just as *Our Daily Bread* did not promote one denomination, it did not support one political group over the other.

Over the years, the editorial and writing staff has branched out. Although the first issues listed Dr. De Haan and Bosch as coeditors, the editorial responsibilities rested solely on Bosch. In 1957, Clair Hess, director of publications for Radio Bible Class and then managing editor, aided Bosch with the in-house production. Dennis De Haan, assistant editor since 1973, replaced Bosch in 1981 when the editor retired. Then in 1988 the editorial responsibilities were restructured to include the positions of editor, senior editor, managing editor, staff editor, and assistant editor. To limit editorial demands, in the 1970s, staff writers were added, totaling seven in 1992.

Now under the leadership of the third generation of De Haans, the daily devotional still reflects the original guidelines. Often nicknamed the "bread and butter" of Radio Bible Class, *Our Daily Bread* has the widest circulation of any of the organization's literature. Few foresaw this success when the 1938 broadcast over a 50-watt station aired, carrying the teachings of Dr. M. R. De Haan.

Notes

1. James R. Adair, *M. R. De Haan: The Man and His Ministry* (Grand Rapids, MI: Zondervan Publishing House, 1969), 62.
2. Ibid., 64.
3. Ibid., 75.
4. Dennis J. De Haan, interview with author, Grand Rapids, Michigan, 16 June 1992.
5. Adair, *De Haan*, 80.
6. Ibid., 83.
7. Ibid., 86.
8. Henry G. Bosch, interview with author, Grand Rapids, Michigan, 7 July 1992.
9. De Haan interview.
10. Ibid.
11. Adair, *De Haan*, 137.
12. De Haan interview.
13. Ibid.
14. Ibid.
15. Undated memorandum by Henry G. Bosch, on file, Radio Bible Class, Grand Rapids, Michigan.
16. De Haan interview.
17. Undated memorandum by Bosch.
18. De Haan interview.

Information Sources

INDEX SOURCES: Topical indexes are published in monthly and quarterly editions since June 1992.

LOCATION SOURCES: The best daily devotionals were collected in the following four volumes: *Our Daily Bread: 466 Devotional Meditations* (1959), *Bread for Every Day: 366 Devotional Meditations* (1962), *Our Daily Bread Favorites: 366 Devotional Meditations* (1967), *Our Daily Times With God* (1988). All were published by Zondervan Publishing House of Grand Rapids, except for the last which was printed by Discovery House. Radio Bible Class, Grand Rapids, Michigan, has the complete collection of all published issues of *Our Daily Bread*.

Publication History

MAGAZINE TITLE: *Our Daily Bread* (1956–present).

VOLUME AND ISSUE DATA: Monthly issues ran from April 1956 to February 1982. These monthly issues were discontinued until June 1990; since then they have been sent only to members. Bimonthly issues began in April–May 1982 and ran until January–February 1987. Quarterly editions, started in March–May 1987, remain available. Large print editions have been printed since January 1976.

PUBLISHER AND PLACE OF PUBLICATION: Radio Bible Class, Grand Rapids, Michigan, 1956–present.

EDITORS: Henry G. Bosch (1956–1981), Dennis J. De Haan (1981–present).

CIRCULATION: Approximately 7 million (1992).

Cynthia L. Beach

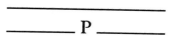

PACIFIC

"A host of preachers without the aid of a religious literature, and a printed medium of diffusing truth, would be like an army with a trumpet and sword only, but without artillery."[1] With that declaration, the *Pacific* was launched on 1 August 1851 in San Francisco, California. The weekly's Congregationalist and New School Presbyterian supporters had high hopes for the paper's effectiveness in the task of Christianizing Gold Rush–era California.

In 1848 and the years immediately following, the Northern Baptists, Northern and Southern Methodists, Episcopalians, and Old School Presbyterians, along with New School Presbyterians and Congregationalists, sent home missionaries to northern California. The task of these official and unofficial Church workers was to offer the Christian gospel to the thousands of temporary and longer-term residents of San Francisco and the gold-mining regions of the Sierra Nevada. These representatives of Protestantism also brought a distinct nineteenth-century evangelical culture with them that found expression in the institutions that they established in the San Francisco area.[2] In addition to churches, they organized regional mission societies, reform societies, benevolence organizations, and educational institutions; they also published religious periodicals.[3]

The *Pacific* is significant as a particularly stable and articulate example of a host of Far West–based denominational periodicals that have generally been neglected by American religious and communications historians. From the mid–nineteenth century through the first third of the twentieth, such periodicals provided their clerical and lay readership with religious news, opinion, and literature that both mirrored and sustained a religious identity with a regional twist.

Behind the founding of the *Pacific* were aspirations for shaping more than just the Anglo-American Protestant religious community of California. The paper "will advocate the great doctrines of the gospel," wrote the editors in the inaugural issue. They also had an eye on the cosmopolitan and secular society around them, which they hoped to change. The ''sanctity of the Sabbath'' and ''obedience to the laws of God and man'' were also promised as guides to editorial policy. ''The field of politics it will avoid—but any crooked policy will be very likely to fall its way. It promises to let no body [sic] alone; because it is the advocate of that which is needful to every one.''[4] Congregationalist and New School Presbyterian assumptions of social and cultural order were derived from a New England conception of ''ordered liberty'' that entailed, in the words of historian David Hackett Fischer, the ''freedom to order one's own acts in a godly way—but not in any other.''[5] Timothy Dwight Hunt, one of the four founding editors of the *Pacific*, made the cultural aspirations explicit in his words to a New England Society meeting in 1852: ''Sons and daughters of New England! You are the representatives of a land which is a model for every other ....*Here* is *our* Colony. No higher ambition could urge us to noble deeds than, on the basis of the colony of Plymouth, to make CALIFORNIA THE MASSACHUSETTS OF THE PACIFIC.''[6]

Hunt himself was the earliest of the *Pacific*'s founders to arrive in San Francisco. As a New School Presbyterian, he had been in the Hawaiian Islands since 1844 as a missionary under the American Board of Commissioners for Foreign Missions (ABCFM). New School Presbyterians, a distinct grouping between 1837 and 1870, supported interdenominational Protestant voluntary societies such as the ABCFM. The discovery of gold in California lured virtually all of Hunt's island parishioners away in 1848. Hunt followed them, arriving in San Francisco in October 1848. Protestant citizens of the city invited him to stay. His interdenominational worship services functioned as the first Protestant church in San Francisco.

After other clergy arrived and organized denominational churches in 1849, Hunt organized the remainder of his congregation into the First Congregational Church, even though he was a New School Presbyterian.[7] This crossing of denominational lines was common with Congregationalists and New School Presbyterians of the era because of the Plan of Union adopted in 1801. The plan was an agreement of cooperation on the home mission field, overseen between 1826 and 1861 by the American Home Missionary Society (AHMS). Clergy of either group were encouraged to work with those of the other denomination, and crossovers and mixing of the denominational affiliations of clergy and new congregations were allowed.

Hunt and AHMS missionaries Samuel H. Willey and John W. Douglas, New School Presbyterians, and Joseph A. Benton, a Congregationalist, started the *Pacific*, with Douglas as editor. In 1863, the Presbyterians withdrew their support of the periodical because the New School and the Old School were in the process of reuniting.[8] The *Pacific* then became, in effect, the Congregationalist periodical for California, but with a strong and enduring pride in its interdenominational origins.

During the latter half of the nineteenth century, the periodical was typically between eight and sixteen pages. Sermons and addresses by resident pastors or by visitors to the region frequently appeared in the *Pacific*, and even after 1863 it provided news of more than just Congregationalist events. The paper also eventually offered conventional fare for the Protestant family. For example, the 3 October 1888 issue contained "My Story," serialized from the *Christian Weekly*; a poem entitled "A Strike"; a page called the "Children's Corner" that contained stories, riddles, and information deemed of interest to children; another page, entitled "Gleanings," that featured lengthy quotations from the likes of Scottish novelist George MacDonald and southern evangelist Sam Jones; and the week's Sunday-school lesson.[9]

It also regularly offered religious opinion upon local developments and needs. Up to 1896, various groups of coeditors shaped the paper. Editorials were normally unsigned and the divisions of work unspecified, so that evaluating the particular contributions of each editor for this period is virtually impossible. The *Pacific*, though, took a predictably northeastern- (even New England-) colored, editorial stance on a number of issues. During the 1850s, for example, the periodical was a persistent voice for public schools, for "no state can be wise in its government, pure in office, happy in private life, successful in enterprise, and respected by others, unless she has an educated and virtuous people."[10] It also was vociferous, but ultimately unsuccessful, in advocating the reinsertion of Bible reading into the public-school program (1855–1856, 1858–1859). The *Pacific* was outspoken against any moves in the state by those who supported slavery. The editors believed that they had uncovered a plot for the advancement of slavery behind the call for a constitutional convention in 1852.[11]

Twice, in 1851 and 1856, middle-class business leaders and their supporters in San Francisco formed vigilance committees to punish criminals and, particularly in the second instance, to "cleanse" the city government. The *Pacific* did not get under way until the first committee had largely completed its work. The editors did not, however, hesitate to support the second vigilance committee.[12]

After the Civil War, San Francisco continued to function as the socially and culturally dominant metropolitan center for northern California. While the rawness of the 1850s was gone, economic developments and continuing immigration made for a cosmopolitan society that was disconcertingly secular in the eyes of the *Pacific* and its readership. The editors of the periodical and other Anglo-American Protestant leaders eagerly welcomed the work of mass evangelists, hoping that urban revivalism would provide the fulcrum for tipping San Francisco and the surrounding region in a more godly direction. Evangelist D. L. Moody made two visits to the San Francisco Bay area, first in 1880–1881 and later in 1888–1889.[13] The *Pacific* provided extensive coverage of each of Moody's campaigns. "We have as fair a land as the sun shines upon," opined the *Pacific* prior to Moody's first visit, "but a wicked, God-forgetting people in general. Let this enterprising, intelligent people turn away from their sin and misery to the service of the living God, and difficulties will vanish, and this coast, that we love, will become a heaven below.''[14] Moody came and went, as did others, but the *Pacific*'s millennially charged hopes for the religious regeneration of the region remained unfulfilled.

The 1890s were a turbulent decade throughout the United States. Economic depression and politically insurgent laborers and farmers were the most visible signs of deeper social and cultural changes that were underway. Anglo-American Protestant unity showed increasing signs of strain over responding to modernity in the decades surrounding the turn of the century.

The *Pacific* became a voice for moderate theological liberalism and social progressivism, especially after 1897. In that year, William W. Ferrier (1855–1945) took over the editorship of the periodical. Ferrier gave the *Pacific* the indelible stamp of his own personality. Born in Indiana and educated at Otterbein College and Lane Theological Seminary in Ohio, he had edited newspapers for several years before assuming Congregationalist pastorates in Washington and California. Once he took up the *Pacific*, he labored to ensure the periodical's financial stability by founding a printing company. By 1906, the Publishing Company of The Pacific produced not only the *Pacific* but also the *California Christian Advocate* (Methodist Episcopal), the *Pacific Methodist Advocate* (Methodist Episcopal, South), and the *Pacific Presbyterian*. The San Francisco fire and earthquake of April 1906 destroyed his publishing facilities, but the local Congregationalists, led by Ferrier, rebuilt the printing company, which continued to print the paper until Ferrier's retirement at the end of 1919.[15]

Ferrier presided over the final two decades of the *Pacific*'s life as a weekly "religious and family paper." The periodical's circulation was relatively small—sixteen hundred in 1910—but Ferrier maintained the paper at between sixteen and twenty pages per week. Typical issues in 1906 and 1916, for example, featured a poem on the cover, religious news of the San Francisco area and the Pacific Coast, and reading material for children, in addition to Ferrier's and others' editorials and reports.[16]

In addition to the disaster of the 1906 earthquake and fire, Ferrier's tenure saw the rebuilding of the city and the celebration of the rebuilding with a world's fair, the Panama-Pacific International Exposition of 1915. Ferrier, like his fellow editors of other denominational periodicals in the region, exhorted his readership to rebuild spiritually as well as materially. He vigorously supported the efforts to convict San Francisco political and business leaders of graft (1906–1909), and he cheered on the Social Gospel movement and the moralism of political progressivism. When major interdenominational Protestant events occurred in San Francisco, such as the International Sunday School Convention (1911), the Gipsy Smith evangelistic campaign (1911–1912), and a convention of the Men and Religion Forward Movement (1912), the *Pacific* enthusiastically covered them. When theological conflict erupted, first among the Presbyterians over the Old Testament critical views of San Francisco Theological Seminary professor Thomas F. Day (1910–1912), and later over the liberal Christology of Charles F. Aked, pastor of First Congregational Church, San Francisco (1914), Ferrier took the liberal side, expressing concern that attacks on Aked were motivated by a desire "to weaken the influence of Protestant Christianity in San Francisco and California—as well as the forces working for certain great moral reforms."[17]

The Great War, however, proved to be a turning point, not just for Europe and the United States, but also for the *Pacific* and other West Coast denominational periodicals. The war itself made paper scarce and costly, undermining the tenuous financial base of such periodicals. More importantly, the success of daily newspapers in winning a broad general readership, together with centralizing trends in Protestant denominations, undermined the already dwindling support for regional religious periodicals such as the *Pacific*.[18]

The *Pacific* ended weekly publication with its 26 September 1918 issue, citing as the immediate cause that their printer was "hard-pressed by the exigencies of the war."[19] With the December 1919 issue, W. W. Ferrier relinquished the editorship. Under E. Clarence Oakley and other successive editors, the *Pacific* continued in name, but there was no attempt to sustain its previous size, frequency, or scope. In 1920, the publication rapidly shrank to eight pages. In frequency, it has remained monthly for most of its life. In scope, the periodical narrowed. No longer did it offer regular editorial opinion on the events and developments, whether religious or not, of its time and place. Neither did it seek to provide "family" reading material or church school lessons, as it had in earlier decades.

The February 1965 issue illustrates the substantive change from the *Pacific* of 1851–1919. The four pages featured various announcements of concern to the clergy and laity of the Northern California conference of the United Church of Christ (UCC) : the annual conference meeting, a conference leaders' retreat, the twenty-fifth anniversary of the Orinda Community Church, the need of Church World Service for blankets, and several opportunities for overseas work. In addition, there was a column of news on various UCC congregations and clergy and two brief stories, one on a mural painted by the youth of Eden Congregational Church in Hayward, the other on the newly appointed publications general secretary of the UCC.[20]

In effect, after 1919 the distinctive regional and inter-Protestant opinion and reportage of the *Pacific* came to an end. Much the same happened with other Far West denominational weeklies and monthlies in the wake of World War I.[21] The demise of regional Protestant journals was symptomatic of widespread cultural and structural developments within, as well as external to, the old-line Protestant community.[22] Regrettably, these changes also drew shut some revealing windows into the life and thought of the Anglo-American Protestant religious community on the Pacific Coast.

Notes

The author wishes to thank Oscar C. Burdick and Dr. Harland E. Hogue at the Graduate Theological Union Library, Berkeley, California, and Richard C. Norberg, Arthur Pritchard, and the Northern California Conference History Committee, United Church of Christ, for their indispensable aid with this article.

1. *Pacific* 1 (1 August 1851) : 2.

2. For a classic study of the Anglo-American Protestant culture, see Robert T. Handy, *A Christian America: Protestant Hopes and Historical Realities*, 2d ed. (New York: Oxford University Press, 1984).

3. Excluding the *Pacific*, the major Anglo-American Protestant denominational periodicals based primarily in California during the later nineteenth century and the early twentieth century are included in the list that follows. Northern Baptists: *Pacific Banner* (Sacramento, published weekly, 1852–1853), *Pacific Recorder* (San Francisco and Sacramento, published semimonthly, 1854–1855; weekly, 1855–1856), *Baptist Circular* (Sacramento, published irregularly, 1858–1860), *Evangel* (San Francisco, published semimonthly, 1860–1874), *Pacific Baptist and Evangel* (San Francisco, published semimonthly? 1874–1875), *Pacific Baptist* (San Francisco, published semimonthly? 1875), *Pacific Evangel* (San Francisco, published semimonthly? 1876–[1881]), *Herald of Truth* (San Francisco, published semimonthly, 1880–1889), *Southern California Baptist* (Los Angeles, 1887–1893), *Leader* (San Francisco, published weekly, 1888–1893), and the *Pacific Baptist*, with which the *Southern California Baptist* and the *Leader* merged in 1893 (as the *Baptist Beacon*: Salem, Albany, and Portland, Oregon; published monthly; 1877–1885; then issued as the *North Pacific Baptist*: Portland, Oregon; published monthly; 1886; and issued as the *Pacific Baptist*: Portland and McMinnville, Oregon; published semimonthly; 1887–1889: published weekly, 1889–1919); Christian Church (Disciples of Christ): *Western Evangelist* (San Francisco, published monthly, 1858–1863), *Christian Teacher* (San Francisco, published monthly, 1864–1866), *Pacific Gospel Herald* (Santa Clara, published weekly, 1867–[1870]), *Bible Expositor* (San Francisco, published monthly, 1871–1875), *California Christian* (Colusa, published monthly, 1875–[1880]), *Pacific Church News* (San Francisco, published monthly, 1881–1883), *Christian Church News* (Sacramento, published monthly, 1883–1884; published semimonthly, 1884–1886; published weekly, 1886), *Christian Independent* (Oakland, frequency unknown, 1886–?), *The Truth* ([Oakland], frequency and years unknown), *Christian Herald* (data unknown), *Pacific Christian* (San Francisco, published weekly, ?–1911), *Christian Church News* (Healdsburg, frequency unknown, 1913–1916), *Christian Endeavor Messenger* (Vallejo, published monthly, 1909–1919), *Christian Messenger* (Vallejo, San Jose, San Francisco, Berkeley; published monthly, 1919–1962), *Letter to the Ministry* (place unknown, published monthly, 1962–1970), *Good News* (place unknown, published quarterly, 1975–present); Methodist Episcopal Church: *California Christian Advocate* (San Francisco, published weekly, 1851–1932); Methodist Episcopal Church, South: *San Francisco Christian Advocate* (San Francisco, published weekly, 1852), *Christian Observer* (San Francisco, published weekly, 1852–1853), *Pacific Methodist* (Stockton and Sacramento, published weekly, 1856; San Francisco, published weekly, 1857–1862), *Christian Spectator* (San Francisco, published weekly, 1865–1871), *Pacific Methodist* (San Francisco, published weekly, [1871]–[1901]), *Pacific Methodist Advocate* (San Francisco, published weekly, [1883]–1934); New School Presbyterian: *Pacific* (San Francisco, published weekly, 1851–1863); Old School Presbyterian: *Watchman* (San Francisco, published monthly, 1850), *Pacific Expositor* (San Francisco, published monthly, 1859–1862); Presbyterian Church, U.S.A.: *Occident* (San Francisco, published weekly, 1868–1900), *Pacific Presbyterian* (San Francisco, published weekly, 1902–1914); Protestant Episcopal Church: *Pacific Churchman* (San Francisco; published monthly,

semimonthly, weekly, monthly, 1866–present). The foregoing list is as accurate and complete as sources currently allow. No single source provides information on the religious periodicals of California; however, two indispensable sources for the nineteenth-century beginnings of the religious press are Wesley Norton, '' 'Like a Thousand Preachers Flying': Religious Newspapers on the Pacific Coast to 1865,'' *California Historical Quarterly* 56 (1977): 194–209, and Clifford Merrill Drury, *California Imprints, 1846–1876, pertaining to Social, Educational, and Religious Subjects* (n.p.: privately printed, 1970).

4. *Pacific* 1 (1 August 1851): 2, quoted in Kenneth L. Janzen, ''The Transformation of the New England Religious Tradition in California, 1849–1869'' (Ph.D. diss., Claremont Graduate School, 1964), 96.

5. David Hackett Fischer, *Albion's Seed: Four British Folkways in America* (New York: Oxford University Press, 1989), 202, 205.

6. Timothy Dwight Hunt, *Address Delivered before the New England Society of San Francisco* (San Francisco: Cooke, Kenny, 1853), 20.

7. Clifford Merrill Drury, *William Anderson Scott: "No Ordinary Man"* (Glendale, CA: Arthur H. Clark, 1967), 161.

8. Kenneth L. Janzen, ''The Transformation of the New England Religious Tradition in California, 1849–1869'' (Ph.D. diss., Claremont Graduate School, 1964), 93–95, 233–234.

9. *Pacific* 37 (3 October 1888): 3, 6–8.

10. Ibid. 1 (10 October 1851): 2.

11. Ibid. 1 (16 January 1852): 2.

12. Ibid. 5 (9 October 1856): 1.

13. Douglas Firth Anderson, ''San Francisco Evangelicalism, Regional Religious Identity, and the Revivalism of D.L. Moody,'' *Fides et Historia* 45 (Spring–Summer 1983): 44–66.

14. *Pacific* 29 (25 August 1880): 4.

15. *Who Was Who, 1943–1950*, 1950 ed., s.v. ''Ferrier, William Warren''; *Pacific* 68 (25 April 1918): 9–13; ibid. 69 (September 1919): 20.

16. *Pacific* 56 (24 January 1906); ibid. 66 (6 July 1916). The *Pacific*'s circulation is compared with that of other West Coast–based denominational periodicals in *Pacific Presbyterian* 9 (21 July 1910): 3–4.

17. *Pacific* 64 (25 March 1914): 2. For a detailed critical account of the early twentieth-century Bay Area and the Anglo-American Protestant community, see Douglas Firth Anderson, ''Through Fire and Fair by the Golden Gate: Progressive Era Protestantism and Regional Culture'' (Ph.D. diss., Graduate Theological Union, 1988).

18. Anderson, ''Through Fire and Fair,'' 952–55.

19. *Pacific* 68 (26 September 1918): 2.

20. *Pacific* 114 (February 1965).

21. Anderson, ''Through Fire and Fair,'' 952–55.

22. Martin E. Marty, ''The Religious Press,'' in *Encyclopedia of the American Religious Experience: Studies of Traditions and Movements*, ed. Charles H. Lippy and Peter W. Williams (New York: Scribners, 1988), 3:1697–1709, provides an important and recent overview of religious periodicals, but the general rise and fall of regional Anglo-American Protestant periodicals has yet to be addressed by historians of American religion. Regarding the passing of regionally based Protestant journals, see William R. Hutchison, ed., *Between the Times: The Travail of the Protestant Establishment in Amer-*

ica, 1900–1960 (Cambridge: Cambridge University Press, 1989), and David W. Lotz, ed., *Altered Landscapes: Christianity in America, 1935–1985* (Grand Rapids, MI: Eerdmans, 1989); both works provide excellent background on some of the currents of social and religious modernization that must be taken into account in any future analysis.

Information Sources

INDEX SOURCES: Clifford M. Drury prepared an index for 1851–1869, available in microform at the Graduate Theological Union Library, 2400 Ridge Road, Berkeley, California 94709.

LOCATION SOURCES: Virtually complete files are available at the Pacific School of Religion Archives, Graduate Theological Union Library, 2400 Ridge Road, Berkeley, California 94709.

Publication History

MAGAZINE TITLE: *Pacific* (1851–present).

VOLUME AND ISSUE DATA: 1:1 (1 August 1851)–68:39 (26 September 1918), published weekly; 68:40 (October 1918)–118:12 (December 1968), published monthly; 119:1 (January 1969)–122:5 (Fall 1972), published irregularly; 123:1 (Winter 1973)–134:1 (Summer 1985), published quarterly; 134:2 (December 1985)–present, published monthly.

PUBLISHER AND PLACE OF PUBLICATION: Congregational General Association of California and the Presbytery of San Francisco (New School), 1851–1863; Congregational General Association of California, 1863–1879; Northern California Congregational Conference, 1879–1962; United Church of Christ, Northern California Conference, 1962–present; San Francisco, California.

EDITORS: J. W. Douglas (1851–1855); coeditors Isaac H. Brayton and S. V. Blakeslee (1855–1858); James H. Warren (1858–1862); coeditors J. A. Benton (1863–1879), George Mooar (1863–1879), W. C. Bartlett (1863–1879), and E. C. Bissell (1864–[1879]); coeditors S. S. Smith (1879–1896) and John Kimball (1879–1896); J. A. Cruzan (1897); William W. Ferrier (1897–1919); E. Clarence Oakley (1920–1923); William J. Minchen (1924–1930); Harley H. Gill (1932–1950); William D. Pratt (1953–1960); Richard C. Norberg (1960–1975); John Deckenback (1975); Jack Smith (1976–1978); W. Evan Golder (1978–1985); David J. Jamieson (1986); Paul and Jan Chafee (1986–present).

CIRCULATION: 4,000 (1856); 1,600 (1910).

Douglas Firth Anderson

PARTNERS. *See* WORLD VISION

PENTECOSTAL EVANGEL

The *Pentecostal Evangel* traces its immediate origins to July 1913, when J. Roswell Flower and his wife, Alice, began publishing a Pentecostal weekly magazine out of their home in Plainfield, Indiana. The Flowers were in their early twenties—independent Pentecostal evangelists working in cooperation with others to extend news of the Pentecostal revival around the world.

Many Pentecostal publications existed in 1913, but most were published monthly or less often. It would be difficult to exaggerate the importance of such publications to the emergence and growth of Pentecostalism. Virtually every thriving Pentecostal center produced a publication carrying devotional and teaching articles, poetry and hymnody as well as reports of the progress of the revival and testimonies to its transforming power in people's lives. These magazines created and sustained a growing network of widely scattered Pentecostals. They gave people a sense of participation in a larger movement and shaped their understanding of what Pentecostals believed and how they related to the larger culture. The many Pentecostals who lived far from Pentecostal congregations and felt marginalized in local religious settings depended on such publications for news and teaching and often subscribed to several of them. Most were free or available at nominal cost.

The Flowers saw a place for a weekly publication oriented toward families and began producing an eight-page magazine that they mailed to an initial list of about a thousand readers.[1] They set the subscription price at one dollar.[2] Like other Pentecostal magazines, the *Christian Evangel* mirrored and shaped the deepest longings of the common people who were its readers. In that sense, it was a popular magazine, written in the language of the people and dedicated to reporting and advertising events that concerned the daily lives of ordinary men and women.

The perceptions of common identity and purpose that created a religious movement out of scattered ministries were cultivated assiduously by editors like the Flowers. Periodicals like theirs helped blend regional expressions of Pentecostalism into a coherent movement. Within a year of the Azusa Street revival's beginning in April 1906, the start of modern Pentecostalism, periodicals began transforming an unlikely event into an extraordinary evangelistic outreach.[3] In a real sense, these publications shaped Pentecostalism. They also sustained it as it encountered opposition, and they kept it from becoming mired in a provincial morass. They mediated influence from one culture to another by reporting and commenting on issues and events in widely diverse Pentecostal centers. Their numbers suggest that people widely stereotyped at worst as illiterate and at best as little concerned with the printed page in fact invested heavily in print media and were fundamentally shaped as a people by the printed word.

In April 1914, J. Roswell Flower played a leading role among the three hundred Pentecostals who participated in the gathering in Hot Springs, Arkansas, that created the Assemblies of God. He donated the magazine and its mailing list to the Assemblies of God.[4] The new organization chose as its first chairman E. N. Bell, a pastor from Malvern, Arkansas, who also edited a Pentecostal magazine, *Word and Witness*. A popular pastor and camp-meeting speaker, Bell had issued a monthly publication entitled *Apostolic Faith* since 1908. In 1911, he had merged his mailing list with that of another minister, M. M. Pinson, and had adopted for his publication the name of Pinson's paper, *Word and Witness*. He charged a nominal subscription fee, but made the paper available to any who could not pay. When Bell resigned his pastorate to devote his full time to the Assemblies of God, he began publishing *Word and Witness* as an Assemblies of God monthly magazine.[5]

The *Christian Evangel* and *Word and Witness* were published from the denomination's first headquarters in Findlay, Ohio, from July 1914 until March 1915, when the headquarters and printing operation moved to St. Louis. The weekly magazine was renamed the *Weekly Evangel* in March 1915 to avoid confusion with another publication also based in St. Louis, *Christian Evangelist*. Bell served as editor until October 1915 when he was replaced by the newly elected denominational chairman, J. W. Welch.[6]

In January 1916, subscriptions reached five thousand, *Word and Witness* was discontinued, and the *Weekly Evangel* was expanded to sixteen pages. After American entry into World War I in April 1918, the *Weekly Evangel* was published biweekly for the duration of the war.[7]

In June 1918, the Assemblies of God moved its headquarters and publishing plant to Springfield, Missouri. E. N. Bell returned to the editor's desk and began an influential question-and-answer column. The magazine was considered the "voice" of the General Council of the Assemblies of God, but during the denomination's early history, its editor wielded significantly more control than his successors would. During World War I, for example, the *Evangel* reflected the constituency's lack of consensus on participation in war.[8] Into the 1920s, it was addressed to everyone in sympathy with Assemblies of God teaching and practices—to Apostolic Faith and Pentecostal people everywhere.

The *Evangel* was nonetheless important to the growing sense of common identity and purpose among Assemblies of God adherents. It carried many personal testimonies as well as reports of revival meetings and camps. These not only kept readers aware of the progress of the movement but also popularized the names of evangelists whose efforts seemed particularly successful. Those whose sermons and writings were featured also gained visibility that translated into status within the constituency. Denominational leaders perceived the *Evangel* as a fund-raising tool: Each subscription, they calculated in 1919, brought in five dollars per year for foreign missions. Soliciting *Evangel* subscriptions, then, facilitated the realization of other denominational goals.[9]

From 1921 until 1949, except for one year, Stanley Frodsham edited the *Pentecostal Evangel*. Frodsham had migrated from Britain to the United States. He wielded considerable influence through the *Evangel*, especially by reporting on the progress of Pentecostalism in Great Britain and by introducing the writings and ministries of various British Pentecostals to American readers. Frodsham's style of spirituality embraced mystical elements, was nurtured by a network that included numerous independent Pentecostal ministries, and was always significantly broader than the Assemblies of God. Occasionally at odds with elected denominational leadership over both his personal views and his inclination to feature his British friends, Frodsham nonetheless managed to use the pages of the *Evangel* to serve denominational interests as well as to serve some of his own broader interests.[10]

On 21 December 1932, the *Evangel* first printed a motto that has been on the masthead of every issue since: "Not by might, nor by power, but by my spirit, saith the Lord."

During the 1930s, two Canadians, Robert Cunningham and Gwen Jones, joined the *Evangel* staff. The presence of these Canadians working with a British-educated editor undoubtedly influenced the writing style and the perspectives on Pentecostalism featured in the magazine. Personally and culturally they represented experiences significantly different from those of many of their readers whose lives were spent in Arkansas, Texas, and the Southwest.

In December 1947, with circulation approaching a hundred thousand, the *Pentecostal Evangel* for the first time raised its subscription price—from a dollar to one and a half dollars per year.[11] When Stanley Frodsham retired in 1949, his long-time associate, Robert Cunningham, became editor. A change in the selection process for the editor was perhaps significant in indicating increasing denominational control over content. Cunningham was appointed to his post and was directly responsible to the denomination's executive presbytery. In contrast, early in his tenure, Frodsham had been elected editor of the *Pentecostal Evangel*. Early in the denomination's history, the *Evangel* editor had been considered a denominational executive. Meanwhile, the *Evangel* office had become training ground for people who went on to other headquarter offices to edit and produce the growing line of literature offered by the Gospel Publishing House.

In August 1951, the *Evangel* went to offset printing. Five years later, the sixteen-page magazine doubled in size and the subscription price was raised to two and a half dollars per year.[12] As denominational programs proliferated, an increasing percentage of magazine space was devoted to reporting and promoting their progress, and proportionately less space was given to general Pentecostal news. Each issue of the *Evangel* generally featured testimonies, letters, a popular question-and-answer column by longtime denominational leader Ernest S. Williams, missionary news and teaching articles.

By 1969, circulation was approaching two hundred thousand. Gospel Publishing House purchased a four-color press in 1970. By then, the first *Evangel* issue of each month was called the "international edition" and was issued in sixteen pages. This edition had less denominational news and was designed as a witnessing and advertising tool. From September 1970, it was printed in full color.[13]

A popular feature during the middle decades of the century was a weekly article on the Sunday-school lesson written by J. Bashford Bishop. This commentary was on the lesson scheduled in the adult curriculum that was published by the Assemblies of God and was used in the vast majority of Assemblies of God congregations. It represented the degree of shared experience in denominational life at midcentury.

By 1979, circulation had reached close to three hundred thousand. A new press further modernized the *Evangel*'s look in 1981, when sixteen pages of every issue began to appear in full color. By the time that Robert Cunningham retired as editor in July 1984, the *Evangel* looked very different from what it had when he assumed his duties thirty-five years earlier. Richard G. Champion, who had joined the *Evangel* staff as managing editor in January 1964, replaced Cunningham and brought to the *Evangel* a different view of the editorial task. Rather than regard himself primarily as a writer, he and his team crafted other people's words to fit the *Evangel*'s mission.

In recent years, circulation has inched closer toward three hundred thousand. Like many other of the early Pentecostal publications that have survived, the *Evangel* has become exclusively a denominational organ. This has redirected—though not entirely displaced—its earlier ability to sustain a sense of interdenominational and international network and family. It targets a far narrower audience than it once did and promotes a significantly more restricted agenda—especially, perhaps, since the publication of an article by Gordon Fee published in 1979. This article, entitled "The 'Gospel' of Prosperity: An Alien Gospel," generated more reader response than any other article in recent years.[14] The *Evangel* seldom features individual's views on controversial questions: Whenever it does, reader response is quick, divided, and voluminous.

The *Evangel* is distributed in the military and in prisons and hospitals. Occasional "spiritual life editions" as well as "international editions" address specific audiences, but the *Evangel*'s primary function is to facilitate communication among adherents of the Assemblies of God and especially from the headquarters to the constituency.

Notes

1. Alice Reynolds Flower, *Grace for Grace* (Springfield, MO: privately printed, 1961), 59–60.

2. *Christian Evangel* 1:1 (9 July 1913): 1.

3. *Apostolic Faith*, September 1906, was the first issue of this monthly publication.

4. Flower, *Grace for Grace*, 60.

5. Edith L. Blumhofer, *The Assemblies of God: A Chapter in the Story of American Pentecostalism* (Springfield, MO: Gospel Publishing House, 1989), 1:133, 280.

6. Ibid., 281–82.

7. "When It Happened," *Pentecostal Evangel* 3869 (3 July 1988): 5.

8. Blumhofer, *Assemblies of God*, 344–55.

9. *General Council Minutes*, 1919, 11.

10. Faith Campbell, *Prophet with a Pen* (Springfield, MO: Gospel Publishing House, 1974).

11. "When It Happened," 7.

12. Ibid., p. 9.

13. Ibid., p. 9.

14. *Pentecostal Evangel* 3398 (24 June 1979): 4–8.

Information Sources

INDEX SOURCES: The *Evangel* has published an index annually since 1988. The Assemblies of God Archives in Springfield, Missouri, has an *Evangel* author and title index since 1917, with more extensive indexing available for the years since 1950.

LOCATION SOURCES: The *Evangel* office at the Assemblies of God headquarters in Springfield, Missouri, has a full run of paper copies of the *Evangel*. The Assemblies of God Archives in Springfield, Missouri, has a microfilm copy as well as a substantial paper collection.

Publication History

MAGAZINE TITLE AND TITLE CHANGES: *Christian Evangel* (1913–1915), *Word and Witness* (1911–1915), *Weekly Evangel* (1915–1919), *Pentecostal Evangel* (1919–present).

VOLUME AND ISSUE DATA: Published weekly until April 1918; biweekly until March 1923; weekly since March 1923.

PUBLISHER AND PLACE OF PUBLICATION: The General Council of the Assemblies of God, Plainfield, Indiana (1913–1914); Malvern, Arkansas (1911–1914); Findlay, Ohio (1914–1915); St. Louis, Missouri (1915–1918); Springfield, Missouri (1918–present).

EDITORS: J. R. Flower (1913–1914), E. N. Bell (1911–1915, 1918–1919), W. Welch (1915–1918), J. T. Boddy (1919–1921), Stanley Frodsham (1921–1928, 1930–1949), Harold Moss (1929–1930), Robert C. Cunningham (1949–1984), Richard Champion (1984–present).

CIRCULATION: 270,000 (1990).

Paul B. Tinlin

PILOT

William Bell Riley was a dominant figure in American fundamentalism in the first half of the twentieth century. In the 1920s he marshaled fundamentalist forces into crusades against modernism in the Protestant denominations and evolutionism in the public schools. When checked at the national level, the indefatigable Riley turned to the local level. Using his Northwestern Bible School of Minneapolis as the base of operations, Riley and his followers created a powerful fundamentalist network in the upper Midwest. Crucial to this great enterprise was Northwestern's magazine, the *Pilot*.[1] While it scarcely outlived Riley, this periodical played an important role in promoting fundamentalism at the regional and national levels.

The *Pilot* began in November 1920 as a mimeographed student newspaper that was designed "to promote interest in school activities" among the students and to "give added incentive to literary efforts on [their] part."[2] For its first two years, the paper came out biweekly, varying from issue to issue in page size and number. Early issues consisted almost solely of student-written articles.

Over time, however, faculty members and fundamentalists outside Northwestern contributed an increasing number of articles. *Pilot* readership, hence, began to change, from students to alumni and, as one writer grandiosely noted in 1929, then to "Christian people everywhere." This audience shift wrought other changes. By the autumn of 1922 the *Pilot* had become a standardized monthly magazine, with eight typeset pages per issue. The length increased to twelve pages in 1925, sixteen pages in 1927, and thirty-two pages in 1930; in the latter year, circulation surpassed the one thousand mark.[3]

Still, Northwestern students continued to edit the *Pilot*. Of course, there was always faculty and administrative supervision, primarily in the person of Marie Acomb, dean of women, English department chair, and the force behind the founding of the *Pilot*. When, in 1930, the periodical went to a twelve-month schedule, Acomb's role expanded, as she (assisted by Helene Rensch) assumed editorial charge of the summer issues. But the most important shift away from student control came in 1932 with the absorption of the *Christian Fundamentalist*. Founded and edited by William Bell Riley, the *Christian Fundamentalist* was the official publication of the World's Christian Fundamentals Association (WCFA). While Riley did not say so publicly, it seems likely that his decision to discontinue this periodical grew out of a realization that the WCFA had irreversibly declined in influence. Whatever the reason for the cessation of the *Christian Fundamentalist*, the fact that it was absorbed by the *Pilot* not only increased the latter's circulation but also hastened the termination of student control. The end came in 1934, when Marie Acomb Riley (she had married the fundamentalist patriarch in 1933) and Helene Rensch were appointed full-time managing editors of the *Pilot*.[4]

Of course, in keeping with his dominant role at Northwestern, William Bell Riley had final authority over the publication. In 1943, four years before his death, he acquired the title to match his power, when he became editor in chief. Still, his wife, now with the title of associate editor, retained much authority at the *Pilot*. This magazine really was a Riley concern.

From the mid–1920s on, editors of the *Pilot* repeatedly made the point that this magazine was, first and foremost, a "Bible Study Magazine." This meant that in virtually every issue lengthy articles expounded upon biblical passages and themes. While these pieces were often devotional in tone, they were also written from a fundamentalist perspective; among other things, this meant strong emphases on biblical inerrancy and dispensational premillennialism. Many of these articles were written by Northwestern administrators and faculty, including Robert Moyer, C. W. Foley, and William Bell Riley. But contributors also included, as Marie Riley stated, "men of note in the Bible world," including Henry A. Ironside, Robert G. Lee, F. J. Miles, and Harry Rimmer.[5]

The *Pilot* was much more than simply a Bible study magazine. In keeping with other fundamentalist Bible schools of the time, Northwestern served as a surrogate institution for conservatives who were disaffected with schools of their own denominations. In this regard, Northwestern provided local fundamentalists a host of services, including a continuing education program for church laypersons. The *Pilot* was Northwestern's most important quasi-denominational effort. Along with the aforementioned articles on the Bible, the *Pilot* supplied fundamentalist ministers with sermon outlines and illustrations and detailed advice regarding church administration, including how to advertise, how to impose restrictions to keep moviegoers and smokers from being admitted to membership, and how to keep all the members busy in the Lord's work. Despite all this attention to ministers, however, fundamentalist laypersons were not forgotten in the *Pilot*. The magazine provided them with inspirational stories, detailed Sunday school lessons, and numerous suggestions for youth and music workers.[6]

Northwestern itself was the focus of much attention in the *Pilot*. Interspersed with the Bible studies and the suggestions for church workers were reports on events at the school, advertisements encouraging prospective students to consider enrollment in the program, and pleas for contributions. Moreover, the *Pilot* kept remarkably close tabs on graduates who were involved in church-related vocations, frequently imploring them to "keep in touch with the home base."[7] Many did, and the alumni pages were filled with information as to their activities and movements. This publicity and support probably helped keep many Northwesterners at their isolated, low-paying posts.

Much of the preceding discussion fits in the context of Northwestern's position at the center of a fundamentalist network in the upper Midwest. But the *Pilot* had a national circulation, with subscribers in every state of the Union by the early 1940s.[8] William Bell Riley had much to say to these readers. During the 1920s Riley used the *Christian Fundamentalist* as a primary vehicle to convey his views to his supporters. He did not cease speaking to them when the national crusades collapsed and the WCFA journal was absorbed by the *Pilot*. Virtually every issue of the *Pilot* from 1932 to 1947 included Riley's extended comments regarding contemporary religious affairs in the United States. Many of these observations were contained in the column "Facts for Fundamentalists." Here a reader could, for example, find Riley commending fellow Bible institute presidents for their schools' high enrollments, excoriating Northern Baptist "middle-of-the-roaders" for enabling modernists to control the denomination, and attacking Protestant organizations for so readily joining the World Council of Churches.[9]

Riley also used this column and the *Pilot* in general to promote a vicious brand of anti-Semitism. Perhaps out of a desire to secure a scapegoat for the demise of the national fundamentalist crusades, by the early 1930s Riley had completely accepted the notion of an international Jewish-Bolshevik conspiracy that was actively seeking global domination. As articulated in *Pilot* articles such as "The Blood of the Jew vs. the Blood of Jesus" and "The Jewish Web for the Gentile Fly," Riley asserted that the Jews had perfected their scheme in communist Russia, with its economic collectivism and its state-imposed atheism; in the United States, the Jewish-controlled Roosevelt administration was moving America closer to the day of Gentile enslavement.[10] Besides his own writings,

Riley also included articles by other prominent anti-Semites, including Elizabeth Dilling and Elizabeth Knauss. When Joseph Cohn, a Jewish Christian leader, took Riley to task for a particularly nasty series of Knauss articles, Riley primly responded in the *Pilot*: "Our advice to Joseph is to be silent, and especially not to charge falsehood to a woman who writes as intelligently and faithfully . . . as Elizabeth Knauss is doing."[11]

W. B. Riley died in 1947. Acceding to Riley's deathbed wishes, Billy Graham replaced Riley as president of Northwestern. At first, Riley's choice appeared to have been a brilliant one. Not only did the magnetic young evangelist attract a record number of students to Northwestern, but under his leadership the *Pilot* reached its peak circulation of approximately thirty-five thousand.[12] Graham was editor in chief, but running of the magazine was left to managing editor Gerald Beaven. Marie Acomb Riley remained on the editorial staff. While the *Pilot* of the Graham years was similar to the Riley *Pilot*, production quality was slicker, and content was a little more moderate, including editorial criticism of anti-Semitism.[13]

The early successes of the Graham presidency were misleading. Graham was rarely at the school, concentrating more on his skyrocketing career as a revivalist. Moreover, the administration of the school was badly divided, with a significant minority who criticized Graham for being too moderate and who desired a school that promoted a more militant, separatist fundamentalism. Graham resigned in 1952 to concentrate full-time on evangelism, taking with him *Pilot* editor Beaven (who became his director of crusade planning). A management committee assumed control of Northwestern, including control of the *Pilot*. In response to financial problems left behind by Graham, the committee immediately reduced the periodical from thirty-two to twelve pages, in the process eliminating the colored front and back covers and other publication niceties.[14]

In late 1953 Richard Elvee was appointed president of Northwestern; he also became *Pilot* editor, with Stan Cook as managing editor. In January 1954 the editors announced a plan to increase gradually the size of the *Pilot*, which they did, until it reached its maximum of forty-eight pages in February 1956. (Three months later it was back down to thirty-two pages.) While returning the magazine to a more sophisticated format, they also eliminated any alumni news and most other details about Northwestern, apparently in an effort to make the magazine more attractive to its national audience.[15]

While these changes may have been unwise, it was not format modifications that doomed the *Pilot*. In 1956 the infighting at Northwestern exploded into open warfare, with the disaffected militants seceding to create their own institutions. The greatly weakened Northwestern, struggling for its institutional life, could not afford to maintain a national magazine. In May 1956, with no previous warning in the *Pilot* and without reference to the administrative battles, Northwestern president Richard Elvee informed the readership that "we are no longer able to underwrite the publication of the *Pilot*."[16]

After thirty-six years of publication, the *Pilot* was no more, a victim of the fundamentalist-neo-evangelical strife that would rent the national fundamentalist movement in the late 1950s. While the *Pilot* lasted, however, it was an important means by which William Bell Riley could communicate with his national following and an essential link between Northwestern Bible School and the hundreds of churches in its fundamentalist orbit in the upper Midwest.

Notes

1. In January 1944, the *Pilot* was renamed the *Northwestern Pilot*. For the purposes of consistency, all references to this periodical in the text of the article will use the *Pilot* as title. For more on Riley and Northwestern Bible School, see William Vance Trollinger, Jr., *God's Empire: William Bell Riley and Midwestern Fundamentalism* (Madison: University of Wisconsin Press, 1990).

2. "Why?" *Pilot* 1 (17 November, 1920): 1.

3. "Subscribe Now!" *Pilot* 10 (November 1929): 47; "The *Pilot* Celebrates Tenth Birthday," *Pilot* 10:6 (March 1930): 169.

4. "The President of Northwestern," *Pilot* 13:1 (October 1932): 3; *Pilot* 14:10 (July 1934): 290.

5. "The President of Northwestern," *Pilot* 13:1 (October 1932): 3; "A New Department," *Pilot* 16:9 (June 1936): 259; Marie Acomb Riley, "From the Editor's Desk," *Pilot* 22:1 (October 1941): 3.

6. M. A. Riley, "From the Editor's Desk," *Pilot* 22:1 (October 1941): 3; John Lundberg, "Do You Let Your People Know?" *Pilot* 24:3 (December 1943): 69; L. C. Masted, "The Successful Church," *Northwestern Pilot* 25:9 (June 1945): 265–66, 280.

7. "Don't Forget to Write," *Pilot* 8:4 (January 1928): 15.

8. Marie Acomb Riley, "From the Editor's Desk," *Pilot* 22:1 (October 1941): 3.

9. William Bell Riley, "Facts for Fundamentalists," *Pilot* 14:2 (November 1933): 58; William Bell Riley, "Facts for Fundamentalists," *Pilot* 19:4 (January 1938): 110–11; William Bell Riley, "Facts for Fundamentalists," *Pilot* 20:9 (June 1940): 267–68.

10. William Bell Riley, "The Blood of the Jew vs. the Blood of Jesus," *Pilot* 15:2 (November 1934): 24–26; William Bell Riley, "The Jewish Web for the Gentile Fly," *Pilot* 15:5 (February 1935): 124; William Bell Riley, "Facts for Fundamentalists," *Pilot* 15:12 (September 1935): 311–12.

11. Elizabeth Knauss, "Communism as Glimpsed Behind the Scenes in Sovietland," *Pilot* 13:1 (October 1932): 20–22; Elizabeth Knauss, "Communism and the Protocols," *Pilot* 13:2 (November 1932): 40–41; Elizabeth Knauss, "Communism and the Illuminati," *Pilot* 13:3 (December 1932): 77–78; Elizabeth Knauss, "Communism and the Jewish Question," *Pilot* 13:9 (June 1933): 271–72; William Bell Riley, "Facts for Fundamentalists," *Pilot* 14:5 (February 1934): 143. It should be noted that as American entry into World War II neared, Riley ceased making blatantly anti-Semitic remarks in the *Pilot* or elsewhere. The evidence indicates, however, that this was due more to fear of government prosecution for aiding the enemy than to a change of heart regarding the Jews.

12. John Pollack, *Billy Graham: The Authorized Biography* (Grand Rapids, MI: Zondervan, 1967), 45; Billy Graham, "Annual Report to the Board of Directors of the

Northwestern Schools,'' *Northwestern Pilot* 29:10 (July 1949): 299; *Northwestern Pilot* 31:4 (January 1951): 111.

13. ''Pilot Editorials,'' *Northwestern Pilot* 29:8 (May 1949): 231. A more sustained attack on anti-Semitism appeared in the post-Graham periodical: Orval Watts, ''Is Communism a Jewish Conspiracy?'' *Northwestern Pilot* 33:9 (June 1953): 98–99, 105–6. Perhaps not surprisingly, William Bell Riley escaped censure in these articles.

14. Letter from Gerald R. Beaven to author, 19 July 1992; ''Letter from the Management Committee,'' *Northwestern Pilot* 32:7 (April 1952): 219.

15. ''In and Around the Word,'' *Northwestern Pilot* 34:4 (January 1954): 1, 10.

16. Richard Elvee, ''To all *Pilot* Readers,'' *Northwestern Pilot* 36:8 (May 1956): 5.

Information Sources

INDEX SOURCES: Beginning in the 1940s, some of the volumes have partial indexes. An incomplete index of William Bell Riley's writings in the *Pilot* exists in the William Bell Riley Archives, Northwestern College Library, Roseville, Minnesota.

LOCATION SOURCES: The best copies of all volumes are held in the William Bell Riley Archives, Northwestern College Library, Roseville, Minnesota.

Publication History

MAGAZINE TITLE AND TITLE CHANGES: *Pilot* (1920–1943); *Northwestern Pilot* (1944–1956). On occasion, ''A Bible Study Magazine'' or ''The Bible Study Magazine'' would appear on the cover, but this did not occur with any consistency.

VOLUME AND ISSUE DATA: 1 (17 November 1920)–36 (May 1956). Published monthly.

PUBLISHER AND PLACE OF PUBLICATION: Northwestern Bible School (which became Northwestern Bible School and Evangelical Theological Seminary in 1935, and Northwestern Schools in 1944), Minneapolis, Minnesota, 1920–56.

EDITORS: A series of student editors (1920–June 1934); Marie Acomb Riley, managing editor, with Helene Rensch and then Irene Woods assisting and with William Bell Riley as de facto editor in chief (July 1934–October 1943); William Bell Riley, editor in chief, with Marie Acomb Riley as associate editor (November 1943–December 1947); Billy Graham, editor in chief, with Gerald Beaven as managing editor (January 1948–July 1950); Gerald Beaven as editor (August 1950–July 1951); Richard White as managing editor (July 1951–March 1952); the management committee as de facto editorial group (April 1952–October 1953); Richard Elvee as editor and Stan Cook as managing editor (November 1953–May 1956).

William Vance Trollinger, Jr.

PILOT (BOSTON)

The *Pilot* is the oldest Catholic journal in the United States and the oldest continuing newspaper in Boston. The paper first appeared as the *Jesuit* on 5 September 1829. After a period of false starts and varying names, however, it finally embarked on its uninterrupted course of publication on 28 January 1838. Since 1908 it has been the official organ of the archdiocese of Boston.

The history of the *Pilot* began in the summer of 1829 when Bishop Benedict Joseph Fenwick, bishop of Boston, was on a visit to Hartford, Connecticut. In July of that year Francis Taylor began publishing a Catholic weekly paper called the *Catholic Press*. Bishop Fenwick was impressed by Taylor's paper and upon his return to Boston founded the *Jesuit* on 5 September 1829. Reverend Thomas J. Flaherty served as the paper's first editor (1829–1833).

Bishop Fenwick originally intended the *Jesuit* to be devoted exclusively to religious topics and, in fact, to link all the paper's topics together in such a way as to form a complete demonstration of the Catholic faith. This severe theological diet understandably failed to attract a sufficient number of subscribers, and so, in October 1831, after two years of publication, Fenwick was persuaded to change the name of the paper to the *United States Catholic Intelligencer* and to try what other Catholic editors had already done: to introduce secular, particularly Irish, news into the paper. The new format still did not work, however, and so the paper reverted back to its original name with the opening issue of 1834. By then Fenwick had concluded that managing a newspaper demanded far too much time. Hence, he sold the paper in 1834 to Henry L. Devereux, his publisher, and Patrick Donahue, an employee.

Devereux and Donahue immediately changed the character of the paper to concentrate on Irish American interests, even while they continued to provide much Catholic Church news. Their publication first appeared in 1835 as the *Literary and Catholic Sentinel*, but at the beginning of the following year they renamed it the *Boston Pilot*, a title that evoked the name of the *Dublin Pilot*, then the chief organ of Daniel O'Connell and his movement. The owners also offered a second reason for the nautical choice of title: the paper would do its best to ''pilot'' readers through rough waters and the rocks of doubt and error.[1]

Devereux and Donahue at first engaged as editor George Pepper, a man of irascible and violent temper known for his bombastic and vituperative pen.[2] To restrain Pepper, the owners in 1836 appointed John Stephen Bartlett as coeditor, but later that same year both men unexpectedly resigned to establish their own journal. This paper, called the *Emerald Isle*, quickly put the *Boston Pilot* out of business, and the paper ceased publication on 7 January 1837 because of financial difficulties. Pepper's sudden death on 1 April 1837, however, brought the *Emerald Isle* to an end in just three months. A year later, on 28 January 1838, Donahue, now sole proprietor and editor, revived the *Boston Pilot*, which now embarked on an uninterrupted course of publication to the present.

The paper was successful for a variety of reasons: Donahue's business acumen; the establishment in 1840 of Boston as the U.S. terminus of the transatlantic Cunard Lines; and most important, the phenomenal increase in the number of Irish immigrants, many transported on Cunard ships during the two decades before the Civil War. At the end of 1838 the *Boston Pilot* had 680 subscribers, but by 1844 that number had increased to more than 7,000. In 1859 Donahue changed the name of the paper to its present title, the *Pilot*, dropping "Boston" from the designation. By 1866 the *Pilot* was the foremost Catholic journal in the nation, with over 100,000 subscribers and a circulation throughout the United States and Canada.

In the early years, the *Pilot* was primarily a newspaper for the Irish immigrants caught between two worlds. Although they had physically broken their ties to the Old World, they were not yet part of the New World. The paper, therefore, served to interpret the alien political, social, and economic environment in which the newcomers found themselves and to keep them informed of the land they had left behind. It was both their advocate and their defender in this strange new society. The *Pilot* soon came to be known as the "Irish Bible" of the nineteenth-century American.

In 1844 the newspaper engaged its first editor with literary talent, Thomas D'Arcy McGee, who later became a founding father of the Dominion of Canada. That same year also witnessed a particularly tumultuous presidential election in which the Whig vice presidential candidate, Theodore Frelinghuysen, had apparently allied himself with persons publicly attacking the Roman Catholic Church. The *Boston Pilot* threw itself into the campaign against the Whigs, stirring up a backlash against Irish Catholics throughout the country. The *New England Reporter*, another Catholic publication originally begun in Lowell, Massachusetts, but by 1844 headquartered in Boston, attacked the *Boston Pilot* for its partisan politics and declared that the *Boston Pilot* did not represent the opinion of the majority of Irish Catholics or of the Catholic Church in the United States. The *New England Reporter* helped to mitigate anti-Catholic and anti-Irish resentment during the campaign. The Whigs, in fact, went on to win Massachusetts in the campaign, only to be defeated in the national election.

The episode caused a furious battle between the *Boston Pilot* and the *New England Reporter*. Bishop Fenwick, the founder and original owner of the *Boston Pilot*, canceled his subscription. Partly as a result of the controversy, in 1847 Bishop John Bertrand Fitzpatrick, who succeeded Fenwick, approved the establishment of another paper, the *Boston Catholic Observer*, as the official newspaper of the Boston diocese. Its founding editor was Reverend Nicholas J. O'Brien of East Boston. The policies of the new paper were distinctly Catholic: to instruct people in the Catholic faith, to describe the activities of the Catholic Church throughout the world, and to avoid political matters (except those relating to Ireland).[3] Poor fiscal management, however, caused the paper to cease publication in less than three years. The *Pilot* absorbed the failed diocesan paper.

Even with its new acquisition, the *Boston Pilot* continued to pursue an independent editorial policy. Donahue did not convert the paper into the official organ of the Boston diocese. Still, with the permission of Bishop Fitzpatrick, Donahue appointed Reverend John Roddam of Quincy as the first priest to edit the paper. Roddam was also the first Boston priest to have been educated in Rome. In 1858 Reverend Joseph M. Finotti succeeded Roddam as editor and transformed the paper into a scholarly and literary journal.

The *Pilot* continued to grow after the Civil War. By 1872 it had more than 103,000 subscribers, and Donahue was considered the wealthiest and most influential Catholic layman in New England. But 1872 brought an avalanche of misfortunes. The great Boston fire of 9–10 November 1872 destroyed his offices at Franklin and Hawley streets. Ten days later, after having moved to Cornhill, another fire destroyed his new offices, for a total loss of more than $350,000. The 1872 collapse of the insurance companies left Donahue to absorb the loss alone. Undaunted, he continued publication, only to be burned out a third time on 30 May 1873. That final loss, combined with the great financial panic of 1873, forced Donahue into bankruptcy in 1876.

To assist Donahue in paying his creditors, Archbishop John Williams and John Boyle O'Reilly, Donahue's editor since 1870, purchased the *Pilot* in 1876 for twenty-nine thousand dollars. Williams was majority owner with three-quarters interest; O'Reilly held one-quarter. In purchasing the paper, Williams promised that he would eventually dispose of his share in the best interests of Donahue.

O'Reilly, now as partial owner, continued as editor, pursuing an independent policy, even though the archbishop was the majority owner. The paper remained the leading Irish American journal in the nation. A man known for his charming personality, O'Reilly was a literary scholar, orator, and poet who published several volumes of verse. On his death in 1890, Williams purchased his one-quarter interest in the paper from the heirs and then sold the paper back to the financially recovered Donahue on 20 December 1890. Donahue remained in charge of the paper until his death on 18 March 1901 at the age of ninety.

In 1902 James Jeffrey Roche purchased controlling interest in the *Pilot* from Donahue's widow. Roche was a personal friend of Theodore Roosevelt, whom he strongly supported in the presidential election of 1904. Because of that support, Roche was severely criticized for his "desertion to Republicanism." In 1905 Roche received a political appointment from Roosevelt and sold his interest in the paper to Donahue's son, Patrick M. Donahue, who appointed Katherine E. Conway as editor. Conway was a woman of considerable literary accomplishment whose fiction and poetry won her the Laetare Medal from the University of Notre Dame.

Unfortunately, serious literary quality has never been a guarantee of financial success. When William Henry O'Connell became archbishop of Boston in August 1907, the *Pilot* was in serious financial trouble for several reasons. First, the steady stream of Irish immigrants, long the paper's backbone of support, had begun to slacken. Second, the increasing assimilation of Irish Americans into the larger society also caused the *Pilot*'s nationwide circulation to wane as its readers turned to American rather than to Irish American journals.[4] Finally, the emergence of official diocesan newspapers elsewhere in the country contributed to the paper's decline. As a result, in May 1908 the paper's net worth stood at just $20.02.

Archbishop O'Connell was well aware of the importance of a Catholic press.

Convinced that the Boston archdiocese, celebrating its centenary in 1908, had emerged as a leader in the Catholic Church in the United States, O'Connell wanted a "good, readable Catholic paper" that would represent the interests of the archdiocese. He sought a newspaper that would "publish, diffuse, and defend Catholic doctrines and principles, the pronouncements of the Holy Father and of the American hierarchy, and to build up sound, well-informed, and alert Catholic opinion."[5]

To accomplish this goal, O'Connell set out to purchase the *Pilot*. He engaged James T. Murphy, a former newspaperman and securities broker, to buy the paper from the Donahue family for five dollars a share, considerably more than the stock was worth. He announced the acquisition of the paper on 14 September 1908 and completed the purchase the next month. As president and chancellor of the newspaper, Archbishop O'Connell appointed his nephew, Rev. James O'Connell, as treasurer and Reverend David J. Toomey as director of the Diocesan Press. With the purchase Archbishop O'Connell restored to the Boston archdiocese what it had originally established and once again made the paper the official organ of the archdiocese. Transformed into a diocesan weekly, the *Pilot* as an immigrant journal had come to an end.

The *Pilot* remains the official organ of the archdiocese of Boston. Since 1944 three archbishops have succeeded as titular publishers of the paper: Richard Cardinal Cushing (1944–1970), Humberto Cardinal Medeiros (1970–1983), and Bernard Cardinal Law (1984–present). In 1993 Reverend Peter V. Conley was editor in chief; Leila H. Little, editor; and Valerie E. M. Elmore, managing editor. The newspaper is published every Friday except for the first two weeks of July and the last week of December. Its 1993 circulation was approximately forty thousand.

For the period when the *Pilot* was an Irish American immigrant journal, it offers rich materials on the Irish American reactions to politics and reform, especially on issues such as nativism, abolitionism, the Civil War, and the immigration of other ethnic groups. The paper was a militant champion of the working class during the last quarter of the nineteenth century.

The *Pilot* also serves as a barometer of the increasing assimilation of Irish immigrants into the New World. In the two decades before the Civil War, the *Pilot*'s defensive tone reflected the insecurity of the Irish minority. But as that minority moved into the mainstream of society in the three decades following the war, the *Pilot* reflected the growing confidence of the Irish, a confidence that was sometimes characterized by a Gaelic chauvinism.[6] As the process of assimilation neared completion (1888–1908), the paper reflected a balanced sense of pride.

Since 1908 the *Pilot* has been the official organ of the archdiocese of Boston, presenting religious news and information for readers within the archdiocese of Boston and throughout the United States and the world. The paper diffuses news about the Roman Catholic Church in the archdiocese of Boston, New England, the United States, and the world but also includes news of an ecumenical and interfaith nature. In addition, the *Pilot* carries secular news stories, particularly as these affect religion and the Catholic Church. As the oldest Catholic journal in the United States and the oldest continuing newspaper in Boston, the *Pilot* provides a wealth of information about the religious and cultural history of nineteenth-and twentieth-century America.

Notes

1. *Pilot* 150 (7 September 1979): 13.
2. Pepper often referred to the Pilgrim fathers as ''that atrocious and impious band of sanguinary and ignorant fanatics'' 1 *Sentinel*, (30 May 1835): 3.
3. Robert H. Lord, John E. Sexton, and Edward T. Harrington, *History of the Archdiocese of Boston* (New York: Sheed and Ward, 1944), 2: 344.
4. Francis Robert Walsh, ''The 'Boston Pilot': A Newspaper for the Irish Immigrant, 1829–1908'' (Ann Arbor, MI: UMI Dissertation Services, 1991), 189.
5. Lord, Sexton, and Harrington, *History* 2: 355.
6. Ibid., vii.

Information Sources

INDEX SOURCES: The *Pilot* is not indexed.
LOCATION SOURCES: The best copies of all volumes are available on microfilm at the Archives of the Archdiocese of Boston, 2121 Commonwealth Avenue, Brighton, Massachusetts 02135. Recent issues are available from the *Pilot* Publishing Company, 49 Franklin Street, Boston, Massachusetts 02110-1381.

Publication History

MAGAZINE TITLE AND TITLE CHANGES: *Jesuit* (1829–1831, 1834), *United States Catholic Intelligencer* (1831–1833), *Literary and Catholic Sentinel* (1835), *Boston Pilot* (1836–1858), *Pilot* (1859–present).
VOLUME AND ISSUE DATA: 1:1 (5 September 1829)–present. Published weekly.
PUBLISHER AND PLACE OF PUBLICATION: Bishop Benedict Joseph Fenwick (1829–1834); Henry L. Devereux and Patrick Donahue (1834–1837); Patrick Donahue (1838–1876, 1890–1901); Archbishop John Joseph Williams and John Boyle O'Reilly (1876–1890); James Jeffrey Roche (1902–1905); Patrick M. Donahue (1905–1908); William Cardinal O'Connell (1908–1944); Richard Cardinal Cushing (1944–1970); Humberto Cardinal Medeiros (1970–1983) Bernard Cardinal Law (1984–present). All in Boston, Massachusetts.
EDITORS: Thomas J. Flaherty (1829–1833), George Pepper (1834–1836), George Pepper and John Stephen Bartlett (1836), Patrick Donahue (1838–1844), Thomas D'Arcy McGee (1844–1849), John Roddam (1849–1858), Joseph M. Finotti (1858–1870), John Boyle O'Reilly (1870–1890), Patrick Donahue (1890–1901), James Jeffrey Roche (1902–1905), Katherine E. Conway (1905–1908), James T. Murphy (1908–1909), David J. Toomey (1909–1918), Mark Driscoll (1918–1929), Edward Campbell (1929–1932), Francis Quinn (1932–1942), John S. Sex-

ton (1942–1948), Francis P. Moran (1948–1952), Francis J. Lally (1952–1972), John J. Grant (1972–1981), A. Paul White (1981–1987), Philip Lawler (1987–1989), Leila Little (1989–1991), Peter V. Conley (1991–   ).
CIRCULATION: 680 (1838); 7,000 (1844); 100,000 (1866); 40,000 (1993).

Norman P. Bolduc

PITTSBURGH CATHOLIC

A ribbon of type under the masthead of the *Pittsburgh Catholic* proclaims it as America's oldest Catholic newspaper in continuous publication.[1] It is a proud boast, certainly nowadays when the weekly is dealing from strength not only as the official, church-owned organ of the diocese of Pittsburgh but also as a publication with a circulation in excess of 116,000.[2] That is a robust figure, although in publishing longevity, numbers are not necessarily synonymous with preeminence. The *Pittsburgh Catholic* has known times of brilliance and large influence. But it has also passed through dark journalistic nights and, in fact, for many years was the number two Catholic paper in its own denominational bailiwick.

The *Pittsburgh Catholic* was founded in 1844 under the aegis of Pittsburgh's first bishop, Michael O'Connor, who saw a newspaper as a tool for defending and preserving the faith and for uniting an estimated thirty-five thousand Catholics spread across a diocesan area that then consisted of 21,151 square miles. The idea for the paper did not originate with O'Connor, however. The impetus came from a "fair-minded non-Catholic [printshop owner] who admired the bishop's spunk, and had a nose for business," A. A. Anderson.[3] Shortly after the Roman Catholic Diocese of Pittsburgh was erected in 1843, Anderson sent a Catholic journeyman printer of his, P. F. Boylan, to O'Connor suggesting that the new diocese could be advantageously served by a Catholic newspaper. O'Connor concurred, and on 16 March 1844, the first issues of the *Pittsburgh Catholic* rolled from the presses for six hundred subscribers for one dollar a year.

Curiously, the name of the first editor has not survived, though quite a bit is known about the selection of the paper's name. *Pittsburgh Catholic* has a relatively innocent ring today, but the name was chosen as a proclamation that would affirm "something of the militant character" O'Connor intended the publication to have.[4] The name was proposed by Herman Berg of Butler, Pennsylvania, one of the paper's seventy-eight, five-dollars-a-head founder-subscribers. Reflecting on that time, Monsignor Charles Owen Rice, labor activist and writer, has noted that *Catholic* was then a "fighting word" around Pittsburgh, and the combining on the paper's masthead of the denominational name with that of the dominant city of the region served notice that Catholics intended to take a bold place in western Pennsylvania culture, then dominated by Scotch-Irish Presbyterians.[5]

The new paper, under independent, as distinct from diocesan, ownership, was predictably aggressive, taking on local issues, challenging the presumptions of the pro-nativist Know Nothing movement, and keeping a careful eye peeled for "fake or apostate priests and phony ex-nuns"[6] who might have been making the rounds, a common scam of the times. When the Civil War erupted, the paper was strongly pro-Unionist and featured in its pages the writings of Orestes A. Brownson, the convert-apologist who was also a zealous abolitionist. The paper's positions cost it considerable support among a readership distressed by the military draft and the war's heavy casualties. In fact, reader resistance was such that the paper's chief editorial writer, Father James Keogh, quit and returned to Philadelphia.

Under pressure, the paper retreated from secular controversy but also encountered the first challenge to its position of privilege in the diocese. The challenge came from a group of priests and laity who, contending the *Pittsburgh Catholic* was not "progressive enough,"[7] transformed an Irish publication named the *Hibernian* into the *Catholic Journal*. The *Catholic Journal*, however, backed the wrong side in a tumultuous 1876 diocesan dispute and lasted only a little more than a year. No copies of the paper are known to survive.

The next challenge was far more serious and nearly overwhelmed the *Pittsburgh Catholic*. This challenge originated in the 1920s, when the German-language Catholic paper *Der Beobachter* (*The Observer*) switched to English and took the title the *Catholic Observer*. "Vigorous reaction"[8] to issues surrounding the Ku Klux Klan, Prohibition, and the 1928 presidential candidacy of Alfred E. Smith, the first Catholic presidential nominee of a major American political party, propelled the paper in prominence and circulation. The *Observer* moved well ahead of the *Pittsburgh Catholic*, which, besides being editorially weak, was underfinanced and underpromoted.

The *Catholic Observer*'s success was credited to its editor, James Costin, a fiery writer with a relish for controversy and a willingness to grapple with issues. An overzealous attack on a prominent Catholic supporter of Herbert Hoover, Smith's presidential opponent, cost Costin his job, but he did not have to look far for another. The *Pittsburgh Catholic* signed him on as editor in 1929, and he quickly restored life to the paper. Economic security continued to be elusive, however, and life was precarious for the *Pittsburgh Catholic*. The *Catholic Observer*, still editorially strong, prospered at its rival's expense. It had the advantage of a busy job shop, a factor that became of increasing financial importance as the depression deepened. The diocese of Pittsburgh was a bystander in the struggle between the two papers, though not a totally disinterested one. In fact, in the late 1940s, the diocese attempted a friendly takeover of the *Pittsburgh Catholic*, but it was never concluded.[9]

By now the *Pittsburgh Catholic* was under the editorship of John B. Collins, a layman of theological sophistication and strong social conscience. Collins's viewpoint was progressive. He supported the New Deal agenda, pro-labor priests, including the increasingly controversial Rice, and the pacifist Catholic Worker movement led by social activists Peter Maurin and Dorothy Day. Rice, indeed, was a regular in the paper, and his column and that of Collins brought it national attention but not affluence. The *Pittsburgh Catholic* remained a chancy operation.

From the beginning, the *Pittsburgh Catholic* had the approval of the bishops of Pittsburgh. Occasionally they used it as the official organ of the diocese to announce clergy appointments, Lenten regulations, and the like. Ownership, though, remained in private hands. From 1844 to 1899, individuals owned the paper. Then, in 1899 a proprietorship known as the Catholic Publishing Company took control. The company's stockholders were all Catholics, and editorial policies were reliably Catholic. Still, the diocese grew increasingly anxious for a newspaper that was its in fact as well as theory.

By the mid-twentieth century, the Pittsburgh diocese had shrunk in geographical size from Bishop O'Connor's time, yet it was a major American diocese with a Catholic population approaching eight hundred thousand, nearly 40 percent of the populace in a six-county area of southwestern Pennsylvania. Population numbers virtually demanded that the diocese have its own newspaper. Thus, in July 1954 the diocese arranged to purchase the *Pittsburgh Catholic*.[10]

A nonprofit corporation was established under the legal entity Pittsburgh Catholic Publishing Associates. Its charter outlined its purpose:

To promote and maintain a high standard of ethics and morals in reading, viewing and listening practices of members of the Catholic faith and of the public generally; to print and publish, distribute and disseminate pamphlets, periodicals, books, newspapers, bulletins, programs and other written or printed instruments and spoken or visual information; to explain the teachings and practices of the Catholic faith; to give news and information on matters of local and general interest; and to acquire or use such facilities and property as may be necessary or desirable for carrying out its aims.[11]

The sweeping statement of intentions notwithstanding, the business of the corporation since 1954 has been almost exclusively a newspaper, the *Pittsburgh Catholic*.

Under its new ownership, the paper continued as a weekly, but the format was changed from tabloid to full-size sheet, and a new editor was placed in charge. He was John Ward, a man with twenty-five years' experience in daily journalism in Pittsburgh. Collins was not included in the reorganization, which, in Rice's words, was "just as well"; he theorized that Collins would not have fit into "the bland, conservative"[12] style of the Pittsburgh diocese of the 1950s. Nor was Rice himself part of the new arrangement. "I was too hot for the gelid conformism that prevailed," he wrote.[13] The "new" *Pittsburgh Catholic* debuted 16 September 1954.

The paper's mode under Ward was "churchy" in the style of then-current American Catholicism. It was a time of great institutional expansion. The pews were filled, and there was large participation in Church programs and apostolates. But it was not the day of an assertive laity. The Church's hierarchical structure was firmly in place, and ecclesiastical decisions flowed down to a people responsive to authority. The *Pittsburgh Catholic*, cautious in contrast to its immediate past, reflected the tenor of the times, and it flourished. It had typographical polish and, thanks to a diocesan-mandated parish quota system, a burgeoning circulation. It also had the field to itself, for the *Pittsburgh Observer*, unable to compete against diocesan ownership, quickly faded, then disappeared altogether.

The appointment in 1959 of Bishop John J. Wright of Worcester, Massachusetts, to head the Pittsburgh diocese set the *Pittsburgh Catholic* on yet another editorial course. The paper's editorship was vacant in 1959, Ward's having gone to Miami to launch a Catholic paper there, so Wright brought with him to Pittsburgh the editor of his paper in Worcester, John Deedy. As part of the same move, Rice was rehabilitated and restored as a columnist.

Like Ward, Deedy came from a daily newspaper background, and, given a free hand by Wright, he steered the paper in liberal editorial directions on the great issues of the 1960s: civil rights, the war in Vietnam, and Vatican II. From the earliest stages of the Vietnam conflict, the *Pittsburgh Catholic* was outspoken in opposition to the war, some of its editorials being reprinted by the *Worker*, the publication of the Communist Party, and quotes from some of Rice's columns making their way to Radio Hanoi. Changes in the Church were covered "with ardor,"[14] as were developments in the heating Catholic debate over artificial means of birth control. The paper's liberal leanings created a tension between Wright and Deedy, but Wright did not interfere in editorial decisions. The tension resolved itself when Deedy left in 1967 to become managing editor of *Commonweal* magazine in New York.

Terry F. Brock was hired from the *Critic* in Chicago as the *Pittsburgh Catholic*'s new editor, and if anything he proved even more avant-garde than Deedy. Brock stayed only two years, however, leaving to join the staff of the newly founded *National Catholic Reporter* in Kansas City, Missouri. About the same time, Wright departed for Rome, where he became a cardinal in the Roman Curia.

Since then the diocese of Pittsburgh has been headed by Bishops Vincent M. Leonard (1969–1983), Anthony J. Bevilacqua (1983–1988), and Donald W. Wuerl (1988–present). The *Pittsburgh Catholic* at the same time has come under the direction of a succession of editors, all professionally trained and developed in the Pittsburgh area. Thomas O'Neill moved from the Pittsburgh *Post-Gazette* to head the paper from 1970 to 1981. Robert Medler of the *New Castle News* took over from 1981 to 1987, and in 1988 William P. Fodiak, a onetime assistant editor at the *Pittsburgh Catholic,* resigned a teaching position at Duquesne University to return to the paper as editor. Fodiak departed in 1993 and was succeeded by Michael J. Aquilina, editorial supervisor of a Pittsburgh-area high-technology company.

Those changes in bishops and editors inevitably resulted in changes in the editorial directions. Ideologically, they have been mostly in conservative directions. Rice, then in his eighties, was still a columnist in 1992, his opinions on the paper's "op-ed" page as lively and provocative as ever. Otherwise, the paper came to reflect a wider Church mood, one originating in Rome, for greater internal orthodoxy and respect for hierarchical authority. The paper's news columns report straightforwardly, but some weeks the editorial page features across its upper half a column by the bishop of the diocese, a practice that tends to clericalize the paper and overlay its principal opinion and ideas page with officialness. Editorials can be presumed to mirror official diocesan policy, especially on larger issues. This is a departure from the 1960s and earlier, when bishop and editor occasionally were poles apart.

Closer ecclesiastical guidance and supervision ensure political and social unity between ecclesial and editorial offices, as well, perhaps, as dogmatic orthodoxy, although, despite its controversial positions on social issues, the *Pittsburgh Catholic* maintained a dogmatic correctness throughout its history.

The paper's current modus operandi was expressed in a "mission statement" published in 1992:

The purpose of the *Pittsburgh Catholic* is:
To provide its readers with full, fair and accurate news and information about the Church.
To help Catholics understand the mission and teachings of the Church and their role in the Church and community.
To provide a forum for an expression of views in a manner consistent with the teachings of the Church and the principle of respect for others.
To serve as an instrument of evangelization.[15]

Notes

1. For many years, the article "The" was incorporated into the newspaper's title but was dropped after the change of ownership and reorganization of 1954. For purposes of convenience the newspaper will be referred to throughout this essay by its present title, *Pittsburgh Catholic*.

2. *Catholic Press Directory, 1991* (Rockville Centre, NY: Catholic Press Association, 1991), 64.

3. Monsignor Charles O. Rice, *Pittsburgh Catholic* 145 (2 February 1990): 5; first of a series of four columns on the newspaper's history running on successive weeks.

4. Archival material, *Pittsburgh Catholic*, 135 First Ave., Suite 200, Pittsburgh, PA 15222.

5. Rice, *Pittsburgh Catholic* 145 (9 February 1990): 5.

6. Ibid.

7. Ibid.

8. Ibid. 145 (16 February 1990): 5.

9. Ibid. 145 (23 February 1990): 5.

10. *Pittsburgh Catholic* 111 (22 July 1954): 1.

11. Ibid.

12. Rice, *Pittsburgh Catholic* 145 (23 February 1990): 5.

13. Ibid.
14. Ibid.
15. *Pittsburgh Catholic* 148 (10 July 1992): 5.

Information Sources

INDEX SOURCES: The *Pittsburgh Catholic* is not indexed. The newspaper is on microfilm, and bound volumes exist for the years 1844–1968 and 1989 onward.
LOCATION SOURCES: Microfilm of the *Pittsburgh Catholic*, 1844 to date, is available at the newspaper's office (135 First Avenue, Suite 200, Pittsburgh, Pennsylvania) and at the library of Duquesne University in Pittsburgh. Existing bound volumes are stored in the diocesan archives at Synod Hall, 125 N. Craig Street, Pittsburgh, Pennsylvania.

Publication History

MAGAZINE TITLE AND TITLE CHANGES: The *Pittsburgh Catholic* (1844–1954); *Pittsburgh Catholic* (1954–present).
VOLUME AND ISSUE DATA: 1:1 (March 1844)–present. Published weekly.
PUBLISHER AND PLACE OF PUBLICATION: P. F. Boylan, owner and publisher (1844–1847); Jacob Porter and Henry McNaughton, owners and publishers (1847–1849); Jacob Porter, sole owner and publisher (1849–1889); Catholic Publishing Company, corporate owner and publisher (1889–1954); Pittsburgh Catholic Publishing Associates, nonprofit corporation bearing approval of the Roman Catholic Bishop of Pittsburgh (1954–present). The newspaper has been published from various addresses in Pittsburgh. Current address: 100 Wood Street, Suite 500, Pittsburgh, Pennsylvania 15222–1922.
EDITORS: The name of the first editor has not survived. For many years the newspaper was run by a board, with five laymen in charge of gathering and writing news stories and priests writing the editorials. Recent editors include Francis P. Smith (1923–1929), James Costin (1929–1939), John B. Collins (1939–1954), John J. Ward (1954–1959), John G. Deedy (1959–1967), Terry F. Brock (1967–1970), Thomas O'Neill (1970–1981), Robert Medler (1981–1987), William P. Fodiak (1988–1993), Michael J. Aquilina (1993–present).
CIRCULATION: Over 116,000.

John Deedy

PLAIN TRUTH

In February 1934 Herbert W. Armstrong began publishing the *Plain Truth*. Since that time the *Plain Truth* has served as the Worldwide Church of God's official publication.

Armstrong credited his wife, Loma, with kindling his interest in religion.[1] He began his professional ministerial career in 1931, when the Oregon Conference of the Church of God ordained him to the ministry. Unfortunately, the Church of God in the 1930s was wracked by strife over doctrinal issues, particularly the nature of Church government and whether or not modern Christians were compelled to observe Old Testament feasts. Armstrong, who had already espoused Sabbatarianism, sympathized with the minority and helped form the Church of God (Seventh-Day). He began building a congregation in Eugene, Oregon, in 1933, but more doctrinal division resulted in another schism in 1937, and Armstrong disassociated himself from the Church of God (Seventh-Day). Nevertheless, he continued his local ministry as well as a radio ministry, "The Radio Church of God." Shortly after World War II, Armstrong and his wife moved their operation to Pasadena, California, and in 1968 his Church adopted the Worldwide Church of God as its official name.

The Worldwide Church of God claims to have roots in the first century. Scholars are more inclined to see its origin in Stephen Mumford's Seventh-Day Baptist Church of 1671. Mumford insisted that his congregation observe Saturday as its Sabbath, a teaching that the Adventists and related groups adopted in the mid-nineteenth century. In fact, J. Gordon Melton classifies the Worldwide Church of God with other "Adventist Family" groups in *The Encyclopedia of American Religions*.[2] In addition to its Sabbatarianism the Worldwide Church of God maintains other unique doctrinal positions. Much like other groups within the Church of God movement, the Worldwide Church of God teaches a non-Trinitarian interpretation of the Godhead. They practice baptism by immersion, the Lord's Supper, and foot washing as their three Church ordinances. They also refuse to observe most holidays, especially Easter and Christmas, because they believe them to be steeped in paganism.[3]

Generic similarities between the Worldwide Church of God and other Churches of God, however, end here. The Worldwide Church of God observes such Old Testament festivals as "Passover and the days of Unleavened Bread, Pentecost, Trumpets, the Great Last Day, and The First Day of the Sacred Year."[4] Moreover, among the most unusual features of Worldwide Church of God theology is the doctrine of British or Anglo-Israelism. According to this doctrine, the ten northern Israelite tribes were scattered abroad in 721 B.C. Herbert W. Armstrong believed that these tribes wandered into Western Europe. He also believed these tribes left evidence of their presence. For example, he understood the names "Denmark" and "Danube" to be evidence of the presence of the Tribe of Dan. While different interpreters associate different tribes with particular European locations, many believe Ephraim and Manesseh represent England and the United States. This notion stems from their esteemed positions in the eyes of Israel and Joseph (see Genesis 48 and 50).[5] The *Plain Truth* frequently carries stories dedicated to these topics.

Armstrong worked closely with his son Garner Ted Armstrong throughout most of his ministry. But by the 1970s the Worldwide Church of God faced numerous internal problems, most notably scandal involving Garner Ted Armstrong. The younger Armstrong was ultimately disfellowshipped from the Church, whereupon he founded the Church of God International.[6] Other rival groups have also formed, largely from doctrinal issues and personality conflicts.

Among these splinter groups are the Associated Churches, Inc., the Congregation of Yah, and the Twentieth Century Church of God.[7]

The Worldwide Church of God is engaged in numerous mission projects. For example, they have operated Ambassador College since 1947. Originally established in Pasadena, California, the college in 1964 opened a second campus in Big Sandy, Texas, about one hundred miles east of Dallas. The two campuses were merged in 1989, and as of 1993 the full-time enrollment numbered about 1,150.[8] Another Worldwide Church of God mission effort is "The World Tomorrow" television program, which they describe as a "public affairs" show. This program originally aired in 1934 as a radio program but went to a television format in 1955. The program is broadcast weekly throughout the United States, Canada, the Caribbean and Austrialia.[9] Yet another of the Church's ventures is the Ambassador Foundation, which was established in 1975. Official Church material describes this organization's purpose as simply "to promote international understanding between peoples."[10] This group generally engages in benevolent functions.

The Worldwide Church of God uses the *Plain Truth* as a means to propagate its theological beliefs and promote its organizational ventures. However, the magazine's scope is much broader than mere polemics. The magazine's mission statement says the Church preaches Christ's Gospel and "announces that redemption and salvation are available through Christ."[11] Moreover, according to the official publications from the Worldwide Church of God, the purpose of the magazine is "to make the teachings of the Bible interesting, understandable and relevant to the personal lives of its readers."[12] Personal interest stories are staple features in the *Plain Truth*. The magazine itself is about thirty pages in length, and in appearance it does not differ significantly from more journalistically oriented magazines. However, the Worldwide Church of God sends the *Plain Truth* free of charge to those interested in receiving it. It is also available free in public places such as supermarkets. Financially, the magazine is supported primarily by the offerings of the Worldwide Church of God's membership. Contributions are accepted but not solicited. When Herbert W. Armstrong died in January 1986, he was succeeded by Joseph W. Tkach as the denomination's pastor general. As such, he leads most Worldwide Church of God ventures, including acting as editor in chief of the *Plain Truth*. The magazine has continued to grow under Tkach's leadership. As of 1993 some 2.3 million people subscribed to the *Plain Truth*, which is published in English, French, Spanish, Italian, German, Dutch, and Norwegian. In addition to the *Plain Truth*, the Worldwide Church of God also publishes *Good News*, *Youth*, and *The Worldwide News*.

Notes

1. Walter R. Martin, *The Kingdom of the Cults* (Minneapolis: Bethany Fellowship, 1977), 295.

2. J. Gordon Melton, ed., *The Encyclopedia of American Religions*, 3d ed. (Detroit: Book Tower, Gale Research, 1989), 525.

3. Ibid., 526.

4. Melton, "Worldwide Church of God," *Encyclopedia*, 526.

5. Ibid., "British Israelism," 84.

6. Ibid., "Worldwide Church of God," 525–26.

7. Ibid., "Associated Church, Inc.," 518; "Congregation of Yah," 520; "Twentieth Century Church of God," 524.

8. "Fact Sheet," Ambassador College, Big Sandy, Texas, U.S. Rev. 2–93. Available from the Worldwide Church of God.

9. "Fact Sheet," The World Tomorrow Television Program, U.S. Rev. 2–93. Available from the Worldwide Church of God.

10. "Fact Sheet," Ambassador Foundation, U.S. Rev. 2–93.

11. "Mission Statement," *Plain Truth* (found in each issue).

12. "Fact Sheet," *Plain Truth*, U.S. Rev. 2–93. Available from the Worldwide Church of God.

Information Sources

INDEX SOURCES: Each issue has a table of contents, but there is no cumulative index for the magazine.

LOCATION SOURCES: The Worldwide Church of God maintains a complete run of *Plain Truth* at its headquarters in Pasadena, California.

Publication History

MAGAZINE TITLE: *Plain Truth* (1934–present).

VOLUME AND ISSUE DATA: 1:1 (February 1934)–present.

PUBLISHER AND PLACE OF PUBLICATION: Herbert W. Armstrong, Eugene, Oregon (1934–1947); Pasadena, California (1947–present).

EDITORS: Herbert W. Armstrong (1934–1986); Joseph W. Tkach (1986–present).

CIRCULATION: 2.3 million (1993).

Keith Harper

POST-AMERICAN. *See* SOJOURNER

PRESBYTERIAN

For over a century the *Presbyterian* defended the conservative position and attacked innovation whenever Presbyterians argued over doctrinal issues, which was almost weekly. It began defending the Old School Presbyterian position against what it saw as the heretical Congregational New England theology of New School Presbyterians. It ended over a century later, in merger with *Presbyterian Life* (a new official denominational magazine), still actively conservative, if less combative. The *Presbyterian* was, as its editor declared in a retrospective published during the magazine's centennial in 1931, "continuously conservative in spirit'' throughout its six thousand issues.[1] In its pages historians will be able to trace all of the denomination's intense theological battles, its growth, the development of boards and programs, and other issues of interest, especially Presbyterian efforts at self-definition and at characterizing their relationship to the broader American culture.

The fusion of the Scotch-Irish and New England strains in American Presbyterianism affected the magazine as much as it did the denomination. The magazine stressed the importance of both intellectual grappling with doctrine and the engagement of the heart. The magazine sometimes slipped into doctrinal formalism but was unlikely to advocate the religion of the heart zealously. The magazine saw itself as loyal to the denomination's creeds and the Presbyterian form of Church government. Although they actively sought balance between authority and liberty, editors more often sided with those who liked good order and favored stronger ecclesiastical authority.

The *Presbyterian* began publication in Philadelphia, in 1831 in the heart of Old School Presbyterian territory (joining other Philadelphia weeklies, including the *Saturday Evening Post* and the *Friend*). It was one of the many religious newspapers introduced after the mechanization of presswork came to the United States through the cylinder press in the mid–1820s.[2] Its founders were Presbyterian ministers and laymen, including Ashbel Green, who had served as moderator at the general assembly in 1824 and edited the ultraconservative *Christian Advocate*, and who offered to divide any profits earned between the board of education and the board of missions of the Presbyterian Church.[3] With initial subscriptions costing $2 ($2.50 postpaid), the weekly was priced for a broad audience. It soon raised the rates by fifty cents but held that cost steady for decades. It quickly developed a significant network of sales agents. While most were in Pennsylvania, New Jersey, and New York, within a few months of its founding there were agents as far west as Illinois and into the South, including five solicitors each in Kentucky and Tennessee, four in North Carolina, and one in Alabama.[4]

The first issues were edited by John Burtt, a Scottish immigrant, and were four pages measuring seventeen by twenty-eight inches. Burtt edited the weekly for a little over a year and was followed by James Alexander, a future professor of Church history at Princeton and the son of eminent Presbyterian theologian Archibald Alexander. William Engles became editor in 1834 and remained in that post until he died in 1867. He also directed the denomination's board of publications for twenty-five years, although the *Presbyterian* remained financially independent throughout its existence.

In its first years the *Presbyterian* devoted much energy to opposing Lyman Beecher, Albert Barnes, the *New York Evangelist*, and other leading voices in New School Presbyterianism. From the start, the magazine went after fellow Philadelphian Barnes, pointing to his New England theology tendencies (particularly his denying the imputation of Adam's sin and rejecting the idea that the Atonement served as a substitutionary sacrifice only for the elect). While the

Old School party lost in the General Assembly each year from 1831 to 1834, the defeats only made the *Presbyterian* more determined. The magazine cheered the Old School victory of 1835 and mourned the loss in 1836, when the Presbyterian General Assembly overturned the synod of Philadelphia's suspension of Barnes. It took "real pleasure" in announcing in 1836 that popular revivalist Charles Grandison Finney and five others had formed a Congregational association—that they had "laid aside the garb of Presbyterianism."[5] It not only covered the expulsion of New School Presbyterians by the Old School in 1837 but supported Old School leaders with regular attacks on the new party and by aiding conservative consolidations after the General Assembly meeting.

In addition to articles on doctrinal and "practical" religious matters, the paper also included biographical sketches of religious figures, essays on church history, a smattering of devotional poetry, and information about religious work. It occasionally offered biographies of Westminster Divines and in the 1830s reprinted articles from other papers, including the *Christian Advocate*, *Baptist Repository*, and *Presbyterian Review*. It included literary material because of what it saw as the relevant connection between sound learning and intelligent piety. Occasional columns described the foreign lands where Christian mission work took place. While the paper paid attention to events other than Presbyterian assemblies, it tried to avoid discussion of local and party politics. The editor hoped to "impart a Christian character" in reflections on political, literary, and scientific matters.

In the 1840s the *Presbyterian* printed agricultural advice and excerpts from the *Scientific American*, reported on cholera epidemics, and gave news from congregations. It provided interesting perspectives on the westward migrations, including the growth of cities like Chicago, especially when it chronicled the building of new churches. It also discussed social reform and social activism, especially aid to the poor and immigrants, and described technological advances and medical innovations during the 1840s. It paid attention to the gold rush of 1849, describing it "as clearly marked by the Providence of God as any other of the stirring movements of the age."[6] Its foreign correspondence in 1848 included reports about the squalor and poverty in Manchester, England, and essays on the famine in Scotland.[7]

The *Presbyterian* covered the split of the Old and New schools into northern and southern camps at the time of the Civil War. After the reunion of the two northern schools, it pushed Church unity while maintaining a conservative stance. Editorial content continued to focus on denominational work, including that among the "freedmen" (the *Presbyterian* can be a helpful source in tracing northern Protestant work among African-Americans in the South after Reconstruction). It continued to give prices for farm products, news from other denominations, and general religious subjects and developed children's and Sunday school columns. In 1874 it expanded from eight to sixteen pages and added a cover advertising sheet providing four pages of display advertising.[8] John Wanamaker's retail stores became one of the magazine's principal advertisers by the early 1880s.

The *Presbyterian* followed denominational heresy trials after the Civil War as closely as it had before, observing with great interest the accusations against David Swing in 1874 and Charles Briggs in 1893. It began paying close attention to Briggs in the 1880s, showing suspicion of his teachings, especially his writings in the *Presbyterian Review*. In the 1900s it watched the proposed reunion with Cumberland Presbyterians cautiously, suspicious that Arminianism might creep into the denomination along with ninety thousand new adherents. The *Presbyterian*'s coverage of women in the denomination increased after Clara Alexander gained increased editorial responsibility in 1901, in addition to her work as treasurer of the publishing company. Although more extensive coverage began after the Civil War and continued to develop during the 1870s, when a separate women's board was created, reports on the activities of Presbyterian women increased at the turn of the century.

By 1920, issues were typically thirty-two pages long, except for occasional summer numbers half that size. Generally, issues in the first decades of the twentieth century contained editorials, comments on timely topics, Sunday school lessons, reflections for the midweek services and young people's prayer meetings, reports on the successes of overseas and home mission activities, correspondence from synods and presbyteries around the nation, and news from denominational colleges and seminaries. The magazine included book reviews, a smattering of mediocre poetry, and moralist fiction. In addition, individual issues were dedicated to topics like the Sunday school and budgets. During the early 1920s, it stated its motto on the masthead: "Contending for the Faith once delivered to the Saints." Its editorials covered both internal Church matters, like the controversy surrounding Harry Emerson Fosdick, and social issues. Clarence Macartney launched the conservative counteroffensive to Harry Emerson Fosdick when the *Presbyterian* published his "Shall Unbelief Win?" as a response to Fosdick's "Shall the Fundamentalists Win?"[9] Macartney, pastor of Philadelphia's Arch Street Church and a member of the magazine's editorial board, led the charge against Fosdick and the liberals.[10] It printed articles by Princeton Seminary professors and occasionally published their formal addresses, often reprinted from the *Princeton Theological Review*. The magazine also ran articles by William Jennings Bryan and other notable Presbyterian public figures and included essays on Presbyterian history by Lefferts Loetscher. During the early 1920s the *Presbyterian* engaged in theological debate with the liberal *Presbyterian Advocate* about the authority of the Bible and the legitimacy of traditional creeds like the Westminster Confession and, from the *Presbyterian*'s view, the infiltration of "rationalism" among Presbyterians. The *Presbyterian* opposed what it saw as an attempted takeover of Presbyterian publishing houses, seminaries, colleges, and pulpits by a group that it likened to Old Testament Midianites, entering the ranks of the pious and violently overthrowing long-standing traditions with new meanings for old concepts.[11] It supported J. Gresham Machen's view that Christianity and liberalism were essentially different religions, and it declared there could be no peace without victory.[12]

Editor Samuel Craig left the *Presbyterian* in 1930 because, he claimed, the *Presbyterian* had ceased to be the true defender of the faith.[13] W. Courtland Robinson, himself a staunch conservative, became the new editor of the *Presbyterian*. Craig's fellow directors of the Presbyterian Publishing Company claimed they dismissed him because of differences over what the magazine should be. The majority of directors wanted to maintain the *Presbyterian* as a family paper that diffused knowledge and nurtured the spiritual development of its readers. Its role as conservative stalwart in theological debate had been a secondary aim for much of its existence, and the directors wanted no change, nor did they want the magazine to become an "organ of protest" that was "dominantly controversial in its contents."[14] They also rejected Craig's proposal to tie the magazine to the newly founded, ultraconservative Westminster Seminary. In a comment to readers in the first issue after Craig left, the *Presbyterian* referred to "an increasing volume of protest" from people who, while sympathetic to the magazine's editorial stance, objected to the unbalanced character it assumed at the end of the 1920s.[15] When Craig left, Machen, Maitland Alexander and Walter Buchanan also left as members of the editorial advisory board.[16] (Machen and Alexander had joined the journal's staff with Craig when the editorial board expanded during the heat of battle in 1923.[17]) The editors of the *Presbyterian* hoped it would serve as an umbrella organ for theologically conservative Presbyterians and regretted the division in their ranks.

During the Great Depression the *Presbyterian* was reorganized, and its Board of Directors was enlarged to include wealthy laymen like J. Howard Pew. For a time it described itself as "an evangelical weekly" but eventually settled on "a religious weekly." It remained staunchly conservative and loyal to the denomination, opposing the schism that developed in 1936 and 1937. It refused to support the Independent Mission Board (set up by conservatives) and noted that conservatives had plenty of work to do inside the Presbyterian Church as it stood. While it opined that "Ours is an inclusive Church," it also predicted that "the Conservative is going to feel increasingly like a step-child."[18] In the mid–1930s it cheered neo-orthodoxy and praised Reinhold Niebuhr's critique of theological liberalism. Yet, it also took some odd steps for a Presbyterian journal, reprinting essays from some surprising sources. For instance, it published articles by Arno C. Gaebelein (without additional comment) on prophecy and arranged to reprint articles from *Our Hope* on a regular basis during World War II. These articles represent a shift in editorial thinking about eschatology. Traditionally amillennial, the *Presbyterian* allied itself during World War II with a dispensationalist premillennialism that it and most traditional Presbyterians had rejected earlier. As in earlier years, during World War II it continued to run articles submitted by the denomination's publicity department and announcements from Church agencies such as the board of Christian education. Facing declining readership and increased costs, the *Presbyterian* was reformulated in October 1946.[19] Its hope to remain as an independent voice within the denomination died in the spring of 1948, despite the best efforts of an again-expanded

Board of Directors and the energy of its editors, and the magazine merged with *Presbyterian Life*.

Historians using this periodical will find no easy shortcuts; there is no index to annual volumes. They will, however, be rewarded by patient examination of its contents. It is an invaluable source for historians of American Presbyterianism and for those interested more broadly in American religion and culture.

Notes

1. W. Courtland Robinson, "Old Loyalties," *Presbyterian* 101:6 (5 February 1931): 1.

2. William S. Pretzer, "The Quest for Autonomy and Discipline: Labor and Technology in the Book Trades," in *Needs and Opportunities in the History of the Book: America, 1639–1876*, ed. David D. Hall and John B. Hench (Worcester, MA: American Antiquarian Society, 1987). Pretzer also provides an excellent historiographical essay at the end of his article that is helpful in following the developments in the magazine's printing and technology.

3. This was asserted in the first issue and from then on proclaimed on the newspaper's masthead. See the *Presbyterian* 1:1 (16 February 1831): 1.

4. *Presbyterian* 1:16 (1 June 1831): 1.

5. Ibid. 6:16 (23 April 1836): 62.

6. Ibid. 19:27 (7 July 1849): 106.

7. Ibid. 18:31 (29 July 1848): 121.

8. The new format began with 44:10 (7 March 1874).

9. *Presbyterian* 92:28 (13 July 1922) and ibid. 92:29 (20 July 1922).

10. Bradley Longfield, *The Presbyterian Controversy: Fundamentalists, Modernists, & Moderates* (New York: Oxford University Press, 1991).

11. See, for instance, the editorials in *Presbyterian* 92:1 (5 January 1922): 6 and *Presbyterian* 92:2 (12 January 1922): 6–7.

12. "The Gravity of the Issue," *Presbyterian* 93:50 (13 December 1923): 3.

13. "Comments and Timely Topics," *Presbyterian* 100:22 (29 May 1930): 12.

14. "To Our Readers," *Presbyterian* 100:6 (6 February 1930): 5.

15. Ibid.

16. Compare the mastheads on the issues of 30 January 1930 and 6 February 1930.

17. "The Presbyterian's Announcement," *Presbyterian* 93:52 (27 December 1923): 5.

18. "Editorial," *Presbyterian* 106:26 (25 June 1936): 3.

19. The makeover was described in an editorial in *Presbyterian* 116:15 (17 April 1946): 3, 5.

Information Sources

INDEX SOURCES: None.

LOCATION SOURCES: The publication is available on microfilm from the American Theological Library Association. OCLC indicates nearly two dozen libraries holding the microfilm editions.

Publication History

MAGAZINE TITLE AND TITLE CHANGES: *Presbyterian* (1831–1925; 1926–1948); *Presbyterian and Herald and Presbyter* (11 June 1925–13 May 1926).
VOLUME AND ISSUE DATA: 1:1 (16 February 1831)–118:15 (26 June 1948). Published weekly from 1831 to 24 January 1948, biweekly from 7 February 1948 to 26 June 1948.
PUBLISHER AND PLACE OF PUBLICATION: Russell and Martien, later known as Wm S. Martien and Co., and Alfred Martien and Co. (1831–1873); Mutchmore and Co. (1873–1899); Presbyterian Publishing Company, Philadelphia, (1904–1946); Presbyterian Publishing Company, Chillicothe, Missouri (1947–1948). Beginning in April 1836, the *Presbyterian* was published in both New York and Philadelphia. This arrangement continued through the nineteenth century. They added the New York office in order to increase circulation, thinking that it might reach 10,000–15,000.
EDITORS: John Burtt (1831–1832); James W. Alexander (1832–1834); William M. Engles (1834–1867); John Leyburn (1852–1861); Matthew B. Grier (1861–1899); E. E. Adams (1870–1872); Samuel A. Mutchmore (1873–1898); William W. McKinney (1884–1905); Robert Alexander (1899–1901); Edward B. Hodge (1905–1906); Walter A. Brooks (1906–1912); David S. Kennedy (1911–1926); Samuel G. Craig (1915–1930); William Courtland Robinson (1930–1934); Stewart M. Robinson (1934–1946); Jarvis Morris (1946–1948).
CIRCULATION: est. 10,000 (1850); est. 80,000 (1925); est. 14,000 (1948).

David O. Yntema

PRESBYTERIAN GUARDIAN. *See* PRESBYTERIAN JOURNAL

PRESBYTERIAN JOURNAL

In May 1942 the inaugural issue of the *Southern Presbyterian Journal* described itself as "a Presbyterian monthly magazine devoted to the statement, defense and propagation of the Gospel, the faith which was once for all delivered to the saints." The *Journal* was headquartered in Weaverville, a small town in the mountains of western North Carolina. It was owned and operated by what would become known as the "Weaverville crowd," a group of ministers and prominent laymen in the Presbyterian Church in the United States (PCUS), commonly called the Southern Presbyterian Church. The masthead was quick to remind its readers however, that "the Journal has no official connection with the Presbyterian Church in the United States."

The first editor of the *Journal* was Reverend Henry B. Dendy, a local minister. But the inspiration and guiding editorial light was Dr. L. Nelson Bell. Known to many as the father-in-law of evangelist Billy Graham, Bell had recently returned to the United States after serving twenty-five years as a medical missionary in China. He founded the *Journal* because he believed the denomination needed a conservative voice that would awaken southern Presbyterians to the liberal trends in the Church and call them back to traditional Presbyterian standards and evangelical faithfulness.

The magazine was originally published monthly for a $1.00 per year subscription. With World War II, the *Journal* began publishing twice monthly and in 1950 became a weekly with a subscription rate of $2.50 per year. The format included letters, editorials, articles, Sabbath school lessons, a young people's department, "women's work," Church and world news, and book reviews. Articles were primarily devotional and polemical, yet for a "popular" magazine, they were frequently quite scholarly in nature. In 1946, for instance, the *Journal* arranged for Edward J. Young, professor of Old Testament at Westminster Theological Seminary, to write a series of forty articles on the Old Testament from a conservative perspective, which was later published by Eerdmans as *An Introduction to the Old Testament.* In 1948 Morton H. Smith authored studies on the Westminster Standards, and in the mid–1950s one could find a regular column by Reformed philosopher Gordon Clark. Consistently the magazine offered defenses of the historic Reformed position on the sacraments, baptism, prayer, missions, predestination, and evangelism.

The overriding polemical concerns were ecclesiastical and involved the related issues of theological subscription of Church officials to the Westminster Standards and the question of the proposed union of the PCUS with the Northern Presbyterian Church, the United Presbyterian Church in the USA (UPUSA). Throughout the 1940s and early 1950s a stream of editorials and articles argued against union. While some have suggested that southern opposition to union was racially motivated, the *Journal* opposed union primarily for theological reasons. An early representative article was entitled "Church Union" by W. Calvin Wells.[1] Wells, a representative on the General Assembly's permanent committee on cooperation and union pointed out that the proposed plan for union did not guarantee the rights of congregations to elect not to enter the union and that the home and foreign mission agencies of the Southern Church were not consulted about the plan of reunion. But the thrust of his article was that "the purity of doctrine" would not be safeguarded, given the extent of liberal leadership in the Northern Church.

Wells called attention to the Auburn Affirmation, a statement signed by over a thousand ministers in the UPUSA that insisted that the full inspiration and inerrancy of Scripture, the virgin birth of Jesus, his sacrificial death, bodily resurrection, and the working of miracles were simply theories to which one did not have to subscribe in order to be a minister in good standing in the Presbyterian Church. He further noted that the General Assembly refused to adopt an overture to declare that these five fundamentals were indeed involved in the ordination vows to which ministers subscribe. Wells pointed out that Dr. Henry Sloane Coffin, professor at Union Theological Seminary and then moderator of the General Assembly, rejected the requirement that ministers and other officeholders accept the Bible as the word of God, the only infallible rule of faith and practice, and receive the Westminster Confession of Faith "as containing the system of doctrine taught in the Holy Scriptures.'' As a result of this type of steady and constant opposition, the *Journal* was able to rally southern conservatives and lead the defeat of the plan for Church union in 1955.

Beginning with the 7 October 1959 issue, the magazine changed its name to the *Presbyterian Journal*, moved its editorial offices down the road to Asheville, and, more important for the future of the *Journal* as well as the PCUS, received a new editor: G. Aiken Taylor, the pastor of First Presbyterian Church of Alexandria, Louisiana. Taylor, while studying for a Ph.D. at Duke University, gained a reputation as being a ''controversial figure,'' in part, because of his conservative stance in an ecclesiastical battle of national notoriety, the ''Charles M. Jones'' case. Jones was deposed by the action of the Orange, North Carolina, presbytery as pastor of Chapel Hill Presbyterian Church, and the action was upheld by a margin of one vote by the General Assembly of the PCUS.

Taylor was alarmed that the vote was so close after a commission had discovered that Jones did not hold to the doctrinal position of the Church and that *Presbyterian Outlook*, another southern publication, repeatedly spoke of the way Jones was being persecuted by the Orange presbytery. Taylor became convinced that the leadership of the Church was misrepresenting their intentions and attempting to take the Church in directions rank-and-file members of the Church would not approve.[2] While he would continue the *Journal*'s attempt to expose the liberal aims of much of the Church leadership, he also believed that the periodical's effectiveness would require a slight change in focus.

Prior to Taylor, the emphasis in the *Journal* had been on expression of opinion rather than reporting of facts. Without diminishing the editorial role of the magazine, Taylor wanted to improve news reporting. He thus brought with him from his church in Louisiana a young professional journalist, Arthur Matthews, as editorial assistant. Taylor and Matthews were aware that the *Journal* had a bad reputation, especially among ''liberals,'' as merely being a flag-waver, a banner, or a persuasion sheet. It was not generally taken to be a reliable source of information. They sought to remedy the perception by changing the format to include three or four pages of straight news, often by reporting on developments in the National Council of Churches and covering ecclesiastical matters in other Presbyterian and Reformed churches. Through its reporting and endorsement of other conservative organizations and events such as the Intervarsity Urbana Missions Conference and the National Association of Evangelicals, the magazine helped make conservative southern Presbyterians more aware of movements in the broader evangelical community.

By elevating the news function of the *Journal*, Taylor helped to bring more respect for the magazine both inside and outside the Southern Presbyterian Church. During the 1960s and early 1970s, the *Journal* could proclaim that its circulation of forty-three thousand made it the leader among independent Presbyterian magazines. With increased popularity came significant criticism. The *Journal* became a prime target for attacks from the liberal opposition.

But the *Journal* was more than just a magazine. Largely through its annual

"Journal Day," a conference for supporters held each August in Weaverville, the *Presbyterian Journal* became a rallying flag for conservative Presbyterians. The most enduring impact of the magazine was as a catalyst for the formation of a number of independent organizations of Southern Presbyterians. These organizations were originally constituted to reform the denomination, but, increasingly, many became convinced that reform was impossible and that separation from the PCUS was necessary. The *Journal* thus became the communication arm of a conservative separation movement.

In 1971 at "Journal Day," the *Journal*'s Board of Directors, along with three other independent organizations, formed a steering committee to plan and promote the formation of a new church. This action prompted the resignation of Bell, who was passionately opposed to separation. In his final editorial, "A Layman and His Church," Bell stated that "No one could feel more deeply the presence and effects of theological liberalism in the Church than I do." But after noting that this " 'liberalism' exhibits an unbelievable intolerance towards those of us who are evangelicals," Bell argued that "the battle must be fought on a higher level than that of an organizational issue and that a division of the Church will not solve the problems caused by liberalism."[3]

Taylor and the *Presbyterian Journal*, on the other hand, took an active role in the separationist movement. Although the magazine received no official support from the new denomination, the Presbyterian Church in America (PCA), many of its old supporters came to believe that the *Journal* was its de facto denominational magazine and therefore disassociated themselves from it. Ironically, while Bell was serving as moderator of the PCUS in 1972, Taylor used the *Journal* to provide a weekly voice expressing why a new church was necessary, how it would be formed, and what shape it would take.

But Taylor was also concerned that the separation movement not lead to the creation of another purely regional denomination and therefore led the *Journal* away from a narrowly defined ecclesiastical focus and toward a more ecumenically conservative Reformed one. Thus, by 1975 the masthead described the purpose of the *Journal* as "Seeking to promote a rising reformation in God's church according to the whole counsel of God commonly known as the Reformed faith; to encourage and assist Reformed conservatives in the UPUSA, the PCUS and the PCA; and to report on activity in other Presbyterian and Reformed bodies." The *Journal* clearly did not want to aggravate tensions between conservatives who chose to separate and those who remained within their denominations. But subscriptions were declining (to twenty-five thousand by 1975 and twenty-one thousand by 1977) not only because those who refused to separate quit supporting the *Journal* but also because many of those who did, believed the *Journal* had accomplished its mission and was now superfluous. The broader focus could not compensate for this loss.

In 1979 the *Presbyterian Journal* incorporated the *Presbyterian Guardian*, a magazine founded by J. Gresham Machen. Partly because of the *Journal*'s support, the Reformed Presbyterian Church Evangelical Synod (the denomination of Francis Schaeffer) merged with the PCA in 1982. In 1983 Taylor resigned to become president of Biblical Theological Seminary; however, he died shortly afterward on 6 March 1984. Commenting on his death, Joel Belz, acting editor, noted that the *Journal* under Taylor's editorship was of necessity cast in a defensive mode. But now, he suggested, a new task was ahead.

Agreeing on essentials, many of us are blessed to be in an ecclesiastical generation where the battle for the purity of the church, while not taken for granted, is for the time being primarily behind us. Because others have fought that battle, we are freer than they were to examine Christian perspectives on matters like family life, economics, and justice—in short, the lordship of Christ over all of life.[4]

Subscriptions, however, continued to decline. By 1986, under the editorship of William Barker, the *Journal* decided to publish every third week. The *Journal*'s last publication was on 18 March 1987. But the second generation of the "Weaverville Crowd" had not exactly died. In 1981, under the direction and leadership of Joel Belz, the *Journal* launched "It's God's World," a weekly children's reader modeled as a Christian alternative to the popular "Our Weekly Reader," a project that not only turned a profit but would exceed the volume of the *Journal*. The corporation, Presbyterian Journal, Inc., soon changed its name to God's World Publications, Inc., and then launched the adult current events magazine *World*, a decidedly nonecclesiastical, broadly evangelical adult "news magazine from a Christian perspective" that currently has a circulation of twenty-four thousand.

What began as an ecclesiastical magazine dedicated to reforming the Southern Presbyterian Church eventually proved to be the catalyst for a separatist movement from that denomination. It then transformed itself into a popular voice of conservative Reformed theology and finally, after ceasing publication, spawned a widely read national conservative evangelical newsmagazine.

Notes

1. *Southern Presbyterian Journal* 2:12 (April 1944): 7–18.
2. Author's interview with Mrs. Georgia Settle, 23 September 1983.
3. *Presbyterian Journal* 30:18 (1 September 1971): 13.
4. *Presbyterian Journal* 42:47 (21 March 1984): 3.

Information Sources

INDEX SOURCES: None.
LOCATION SOURCES: A complete set of all but a few magazines is held in the Historical Center for the Presbyterian Church in America, Covenant Seminary, St. Louis, Missouri.

Publication History

MAGAZINE TITLE AND TITLE CHANGES: *Southern Presbyterian Journal* (1942–1959); *Presbyterian Journal* (1959–1987).

VOLUME AND ISSUE DATA: 1:1 (May 1942)–45:16 (March 1987).

PUBLISHER AND PLACE OF PUBLICATION: Weaverville, North Carolina (1942–1959); Asheville, North Carolina (1959–1987).

EDITORS: Henry B. Dendy (1942–1959), G. Aiken Taylor (1959–1982), Joel Belz (acting editor) (1982–1984), William S. Barker (1984–1987).

CIRCULATION: 43,000 (late 1960s); 25,000 (1975); 21,000 (1977); 14,000 (1985); 12,000 (1987).

Keith Pavlischek

PRESBYTERIAN LIFE. *See* PRESBYTERIAN

PRESBYTERIAN OF THE SOUTH

''Do you ask where 'The Presbyterian of the South' stands and for what its testimony and work will be given? It hesitates not a moment to reply that it stands for the old faith and for our Church. Its purpose is to maintain the principles and standards of the Presbyterian Church in the United States, to do its part to preserve the integrity and doctrine of that Church.''[1] So began a statement describing the rationale for a weekly paper launched in 1909 to serve the membership of the Presbyterian Church in the United States, the largest Presbyterian denomination concentrated in the South. Until 1944, when the magazine was superseded by *Presbyterian Outlook*, which still continues as a weekly, *Presbyterian of the South* reflected the concerns of Southern Presbyterian leaders. It also mirrored the changes that gradually came to the denomination.

Presbyterian of the South was born through the merger of three papers that had served more narrow regional constituencies: *Central Presbyterian*, published in Richmond; *Southwestern Presbyterian*, based in New Orleans; and *Southern Presbyterian*, long a voice of ''deep South'' Presbyterianism originating in Charleston. Its first editorial board included the editors of those three papers, although Thornton S. Wilson, as managing editor, was most directly responsible for overseeing production from its founding in 1909 until 1915.

From the outset, *Presbyterian of the South* aimed to reach a wide audience. It was never a journal for clergy and religious professionals but was targeted to Presbyterian families. As such, it rarely offered scholarly articles that would appeal only to the theologically sophisticated. Rather, its contents aimed to strengthen the bonds among Southern Presbyterians by reporting on missionary activity, actions of the General Assembly, and news of local congregations and regional presbyteries. This sense of denomination as large, extended family is most readily observed in profiles of individual congregations, denominational agencies, and mission projects that became the lead feature in 1910 and remained such until 1915, when editorial comment took over the front page.

Equally prominent was the desire of the paper to nurture personal piety through commentary on denominational Sunday school lessons, regular features for children and youth, and columns for family devotion, departments that remained integral to the publication throughout its history. As a newspaper, however, *Presbyterian of the South* also provided capsule summaries of both religious and secular news—regional, national, and international. As well, it carried an array of advertisements from secular businesses in Richmond, Charleston, and New Orleans, only gradually replacing them with advertisements primarily for religious goods and services.

The claim that *Presbyterian of the South* would advance the ''old faith'' meant that a theologically and socially conservative stance undergirded the periodical, a stance advocated in the nineteenth century by such theological giants of Southern Presbyterianism as James Henley Thornwell and Thomas Smythe. This position was presented in one of the few serious theological pieces to appear early on, a two-part series by prominent pastor Benjamin Morgan Palmer on ''The Church, a Spiritual Kingdom.''[2] The idea of the ''spirituality of the church'' was a hallmark of Southern Presbyterianism. Ostensibly based on the theological claim that as the earthly representation of a heavenly, spiritual kingdom of God, the Church should remain aloof from politics and public issues that were the proper domain of government, the idea of the ''spirituality of the church'' had actually served to allow Southern Presbyterians to avoid dealing directly with the matter of slavery in the nineteenth issue. Slavery was a matter of the public domain and thus removed from the proper sphere of the Church. In time, advocates of the ''spirituality of the church'' used the doctrine as a way to insist on support for the strict separation of church and state but also to view ethics exclusively in terms of individual behavior. When Robert B. Kerr replaced Wilson as managing editor in 1915, for example, an editorial comment noted that *Presbyterian of the South* would continue to be ''strictly orthodox'' in doctrine and a firm advocate of the ''entire separation of Church and State.''[3]

This distancing of the Church from social issues proved difficult to maintain, and one of the striking changes in the tone of *Presbyterian of the South* over time is its gradual willingness to address problems and concerns in the public domain. At first, most reference to social issues was presented without analysis or endorsing a particular position, even when treating such a passionate concern as temperance. Then when analysis did occur, it tended to cast social problems in terms of threats to personal morality. For example, a 1912 series on immigration by Juan Gonzalez, who also wrote a number of anti-Catholic pieces in the early years, argued a nativist position on the grounds that immigrants promoted immoral behavior, a problem compounded by their association with labor and their concentration in northern cities.[4]

Perhaps the first symbolic challenge to a narrow understanding of the ''spirituality'' of the Church came with the election of Woodrow Wilson as president of the United States in 1912. The son of a Southern Presbyterian pastor and seminary professor, Wilson was lauded as a "Christian gentleman" in an editorial note following his election. The same issue featured as its cover story a reprint of an address by Wilson on the "Importance of Bible Study."[5] Offering a comment on Wilson challenged the conviction that the Church should remain aloof from the political sector, but featuring an essay by Wilson on a traditional religious theme allowed the periodical to straddle the fence. The outbreak of World War I furthered the liberalizing trend, despite the fear voiced just after the United States declared war on Germany in 1917 that now there would be "too much" war news.[6] In the New Year's issue of 1919, *Presbyterian of the South* even printed the text of a proclamation by President Wilson on the necessity of providing relief for areas devastated by the war.

The crisis in the 1920s over the teaching of evolutionary theory in the public schools also moved *Presbyterian of the South* away from a narrow interpretation of the "spirituality" of the Church. In 1925, for example, an editorial note argued that citizens had a right to determine what would be taught in the public schools and should act to prohibit teaching of Darwin's theories. Yet, the rationale given was a religious one. Such activity would not be interfering in the sphere of politics but would promote scriptural precept.[7] But the major shift came when renowned Presbyterian historian Ernest Trice Thompson became an editorial associate in 1931, the same year *Presbyterian of the South* absorbed the Charlotte, North Carolina-based *Presbyterian Standard*.[8] In 1933, at Thompson's urging, a department called "Round Table" debuted. This feature contained open discussion of vital issues, both social and religious, by a number of Presbyterian pastors and professors. As Thompson would later note, the "Round Table" allowed the social mission of the Church to become prominent.[9]

Positions taken on intramural Church issues and other matters reveal similar liberalizing trends. In 1908, the year before *Presbyterian of the South* began publication, several Protestant bodies agreed to cooperate with one another through the newly formed Federal Council of Churches, the forerunner of today's National Council of Churches. While the Presbyterian Church in the United States alternated between joining the Federal Council and withdrawing from it, at first editorial comment in *Presbyterian of the South* was wary of such ecumenical ventures. Because the Federal Council echoed the more liberal Social Gospel movement in its adoption of a social creed and in its calls for Church involvement on behalf of labor, commentary in *Presbyterian of the South* was critical of the council. In keeping with the separation of church and state inherent in the doctrine of the "spirituality" of the Church, the paper argued that the denomination had no business trying to influence the legislative process to advance the cause of labor.[10] But by 1919, one discerns not only a general support for ecumenical activity but also for a possible merger with other Presbyterian bodies to avoid duplication of activity.[11] After the appearance of "Round Table" in 1933, writers more openly supported such endeavors. Curiously, however, the economic ravages of the Great Depression received scant attention in the journal, other than an occasional lament that giving to denominational programs had declined to such an extent that mission work especially was often in danger of serious cutbacks.

"Round Table" writers would also address a number of other theological matters that were formerly taboo. When application of critical methods of analysis to Scripture in the later nineteenth century began to challenge orthodox doctrines, Southern Presbyterians saw themselves as a bastion of traditional teaching. In 1913, Thomas Converse, one of the editors, railed against attacks on the doctrine of the virgin birth, warning that departure from orthodox views would lead to further schism within Christendom.[12] By the late 1930s, contributors to "Round Table" were routinely endorsing modern scholarship and calling for rethinking traditional doctrinal formulation.

Indeed, by the early 1940s, *Presbyterian of the South* had moved so much in a moderate, if not liberal, direction editorially that more orthodox Southern Presbyterians felt that it no longer reflected the "old faith" that its founders had pledged to promote. Hence, as a reaction in 1941 there appeared a staunchly conservative periodical bearing the name *Southern Presbyterian Journal* (later, simply *Presbyterian Journal*). But by then the nearly forty persons who lent their names as editorial associates to *Presbyterian of the South* were already rethinking the nature and purpose of their weekly. In 1943, Aubrey Brown took over the editorial reins with an eye to a complete revamping of the periodical that would lessen even more its regional focus. The following year, *Presbyterian Outlook*, without reference to its regional base, though still published in Richmond, issued its inaugural number, superseding what had been a major voice of Southern Presbyterianism for thirty-five years.

If change in editorial stance and liberalizing trends marked the history of *Presbyterian of the South*, much about the weekly remained constant. Throughout its history, the periodical was a major conduit for disseminating news of local Church activity, presbytery and synodical agencies and programs, and the work of the General Assembly of the denomination. Excerpts from sermons of prominent pastors and brief book reviews always dotted its pages, as did regular features for children, youth, and, from the 1920s on, adult men's and women's groups. Occasional pieces on aspects of Presbyterian history would appear, along with profiles of prominent figures in Presbyterian life. There would also be obituaries extolling the work of clergy and distinguished laity who had died. Overall, the bulk of the content remained consistently centered on religious nurture, strengthening the faith of individual believers and building stronger Church programs so that the "old faith" would endure.

Notes

1. *Presbyterian of the South* 1 (6 January 1909): 2.
2. B. M. Palmer, "The Church, a Spiritual Kingdom," *Presbyterian of the South* 3 (15 February 1911): 1–3, and 3 (1 March 1911): 2–3.

3. *Presbyterian of the South* 84 (16 June 1915): 2. Volume numbering is confusing. In 1912, the periodical announced that it would adopt a new numbering scheme that regarded the first volume of the *Charleston Observer*, its oldest predecessor title founded in 1826, as the proper first volume. Hence issues in 1913 appeared as volume 89. But all issues in 1914 were identified as part of volume 88, and those in 1915 as volume 84. Beginning in 1916, volumes are numbered in sequence until 1923, when issues are identified variously as part of volumes 93, 97, and 98; in 1924, issues appear as part of either volume 97 or 98. Beginning again in 1925 with volume 99, numbering occurs in sequence.

4. The series commences in *Presbyterian of the South* 4 (28 August 1912).

5. Woodrow Wilson, "The Importance of Bible Study," *Presbyterian of the South* 4 (13 November 1912): 1, 11; editorial note, *Presbyterian of the South* 4 (13 November 1912): 9.

6. Editorial, *Presbyterian of the South* 86 (11 April 1917); Ernest Trice Thompson, *Presbyterians in the South* (Richmond: John Knox Press, 1973), 3: 249. Thompson notes, however, that the paper would not directly endorse the formation of the League of Nations after the war since the League was construed as a political project.

7. "Tennessee's Evolution Case," *Presbyterian of the South* 99 (17 June 1925): 3.

8. In retrospect, some of the groundwork had been laid by Walter L. Lingle, Jr., who served on the editorial staff from 1923 until 1931, though Lingle was clearly more moderate than liberal.

9. Thompson, *Presbyterians*, 3: 507.

10. "The Federal Program," *Presbyterian of the South* 4 (7 August 1912): 11.

11. See the highly positive report of the meeting of the Federal Council in Atlanta in "The Federal Council of the Churches in America," *Presbyterian of the South* 98 (17 December 1924): 9, 16.

12. Thomas E. Converse, "To Guard Against Future Schisms," *Presbyterian of the South* 89 (26 March 1913): 11.

Information Sources

INDEX SOURCES: None.

LOCATION SOURCES: The Department of History, Presbyterian Church in the United States of America, Montreat, North Carolina, has a nearly complete run as do Union Theological Seminary (Richmond, Virginia), Columbia Theological Seminary (Decatur, Georgia), and many other southern Presbyterian colleges.

Publication History

MAGAZINE TITLE: *Presbyterian of the South*.

VOLUME AND ISSUE DATA: 1:1 (1909)–4:52 (1912), 89:1–52 (1913), 88:1–52 (1914), 84:1 (1915)–118:52 (1943); issues in 1923 listed variously as volumes 93, 97, and 98; issues in 1924 listed variously as volumes 97 and 98; two issues numbered 12 in 1916; occasionally volume numbering crosses calendar years so that 52 numbers will complete a volume. Published weekly.

PUBLISHER AND PLACE OF PUBLICATION: The Presbyterian Co., Atlanta, Georgia (1909), Richmond, Virginia (1910–1943).

EDITORS: Thomas E. Converse (1909–1914), James P. Smith (1909–1914), E. B. McCluer (1909–1919), George Summey (1909–1919), Thornton S. Wilson (managing editor, 1909–1915), A. A. Little (1914–1923), Robert Hill (1914–1919), Robert B. Kerr (managing editor, 1915–1919), William S. Campbell (1919–1937), Walter L. Lingle (1923–1931), Ernest Trice Thompson (1931–1943), Aubrey Brown (1943); others listed from time to time as associate editors or editorial associates.
CIRCULATION: Unknown.

Charles H. Lippy

PRESBYTERIAN STANDARD. *See* PRESBYTERIAN OF THE SOUTH

PRESBYTERIAN SURVEY

The *Presbyterian Survey* serves as the official magazine of the Presbyterian Church (U.S.A.). Since its founding, it has changed substantially in name, format, and emphasis.

The *Presbyterian Survey* originated as a magazine of the Presbyterian Church in the United States (PCUS). This denomination, popularly known as the "Southern Presbyterian Church," emerged from the divisions within American Presbyterianism resulting from the sectional hostilities of the Civil War. After the war, the PCUS came to include a membership of approximately five hundred thousand in thirteen southern states.[1]

In 1867, the Church's General Assembly authorized the executive committee of foreign missions to begin publication in Nashville of a monthly paper called the *Missionary*, which promoted the Church's foreign mission work. In 1889, the executive committee of home missions began a concurrent monthly concentrating on the missionary work within the southern states themselves, the *Home Mission Herald*. In November 1911, these two magazines were combined into the *Missionary Survey*, published in Richmond, Virginia. Although the primary focus of this publication continued to be both foreign and home missionary work, material related to Christian education, ministerial relief, and religious publications was included as well. By 1924, however, Southern Presbyterians wanted to broaden the scope of the magazine still further, and in April of that year, the *Missionary Survey* was enlarged and renamed the *Presbyterian Survey*.[2]

Since 1924, the *Survey* has been published under the authority of the General Assembly, and its purpose has been to educate and inform lay members about the work of the wider denomination.[3] Until the 1950s, the editors of the *Survey* were drawn from Church agencies and served only part-time on the magazine itself.[4] The magazine's content is not theological, strictly speaking, but promotional, inspirational, and practical. Although the format, content, and size have changed over the years, that basic purpose has not.

In the 1920s and 1930s, the *Presbyterian Survey* retained much of its predecessors' chief focus on home and foreign missions. With 517 missionaries serving nine missions in six countries (China, Japan, Korea, Belgian Congo, Brazil, and Mexico), the Southern Presbyterians had a higher percentage of foreign missionaries in the field than any other southern denomination.[5] The home mission field included work among "the colored population" of the South, the poor whites of Appalachia, Native American tribes from Oklahoma to Florida, Hispanics in Texas, and, perhaps most interesting, Jews in Baltimore and Italians in Kansas City. Both home and foreign missionaries wrote monthly in the *Survey* about their work and experiences in schools, hospitals, churches, orphanages, and training institutes. A complete listing of the names and mailing addresses of the Church's missionaries was frequently included in the back of the issue. Births, deaths, serious illnesses, personal news, and even birthdays were reported regularly, on the assumption that the Southern Presbyterian Church was an extended family where it was possible for most of the members to know one another. Indeed, because of the Church's relatively small size and geographically compact location, the early *Survey* sometimes had the intimate feel of a small-town newspaper, albeit one that consciously strove to provide a window on the larger world for its readers.

Until 1938, the *Presbyterian Survey* also contained regular formal departments for the woman's auxiliary, the juniors, and the men of the Church. Most of these articles were written either by pastors or by Church agency employees and consisted of inspirational stories, informative articles, and suggested programs for monthly meetings on mission topics based on articles contained in the current issue of the *Survey*. The magazine also offered book reviews, brief news items, accounts from meetings of the General Assembly, and information on the work of other Church agencies.

Women clearly made up the largest readership and provided the most support for the early magazine.[6] The woman's auxiliaries conducted subscription drives for the *Survey* in the local churches,[7] used large sections of the magazine for their programs, and, indeed, often kept the mission fields alive through their annual "birthday gift" to the Church, a fund-raising effort promoted extensively in the pages of the *Survey*.[8]

The most significant early editor of the *Survey* was Harriet Blackford Williams. Although listed either as managing or assistant editor to a series of editors in chief throughout her tenure from 1927 to 1944, Williams shaped both the tone and content of the *Survey* for almost twenty years. Her personal concern for "the sick and needy and sorrowing around the world" was reflected in the pages of the *Survey*, and she found her personal calling in "unfolding to her readers the pressing spiritual needs which the Executive and Promotional Agencies of [the] church [were] organized to serve."[9]

In 1938, the *Survey* underwent a significant change in format, a partial response to the drastically declining subscription rate brought about by the Great Depression.[10] Reduced in size from sixty–four to forty–eight pages, the magazine eliminated separate departments in an effort to promote a more holistic view of Church work.[11] Although the *Survey* still highlighted the Church's missionary activities, the new *Survey* reflected an increased emphasis on the home and family, especially on the family's role in the religious training of the young. This format was continued with slight modifications into World War II and the 1950s. Features on family life,[12] the educational ministries of the Church,[13] individual home mission congregations, and Presbyterian colleges increasingly began to squeeze out articles on overseas missions.

Despite the postwar baby boom and a membership explosion within PCUS in the 1950s, *Survey* subscriptions remained relatively stagnant. Circulation had been 38,000 in 1924,[14] and by the mid–1950s it had increased to only 45,840.[15] A dissatisfied General Assembly took steps to increase circulation and make the *Survey* a more effective means of communication for all of the Church's agencies. In 1953, an independent Board of Directors was created,[16] and for the first time, three full-time professional staff members were hired.[17] The board and staff turned the *Survey* into a true denominational force.[18] At the same time, throughout the 1950s, the *Survey* experimented with several formats and began to assume something close to its present configuration. Increasing emphasis was placed on feature stories, ''news'' of interest, and practical helps for congregational work. Much less was written about overseas missions, while the ''home mission'' field seems to have shifted primarily to the suburbs. In June 1959, Ben Lacy Rose began the longest running column of the magazine, a question-and-answer column entitled simply ''Q and A,'' which he maintained for more than thirty years. Answering the questions of ordinary Presbyterians with a mixture of wit, grace, sternness, and compassion as the situation required, Rose's column was consistently one of the magazine's most popular features.[19]

The creation of a congregational ''every family plan'' finally caused circulation to explode. In November 1957, the annual subscription rate was cut in half to one dollar,[20] and in 1958, circulation nearly quadrupled to more than 161,000.[21] By 1960, it was over 227,000, and subscribers numbered nearly 250,000 when the *Survey* moved its offices from Richmond to Atlanta in 1962.[22]

Without question, the most dramatic years of the *Survey*'s existence were the 1960s. The *Presbyterian Survey* had contended from its earliest days that a distinct and careful separation must exist between church and state, a notion historically identified with the PCUS. But such did not necessarily preclude the Church from taking a stance on certain social issues.[23] For example, in the 1920s and 1930s, the *Survey* had supported Prohibition.[24] It also endorsed the peace movement between the two world wars.[25] It regularly printed articles and news from the southern-based Commission on Interracial Cooperation[26] and included numerous articles regarding the white South's obligation to find Christian-based solutions to ''the daily more complicated Negro problem.''[27] In the late 1940s and early 1950s, these articles led to more challenging ones designed to confront white Presbyterians' most basic assumptions about race relations.[28]

By the mid–1960s, the South was in turmoil over the issue of civil rights, and the *Presbyterian Survey* was right in the middle of the controversy. Editor

Ben Hartley, who had been appointed in June 1959,[29] and associate editor Frances Furlow drew on the *Survey*'s progressive tradition and attempted to make the magazine a prophetic voice during this crisis for Southern Presbyterians. Hartley warned as early as 1961 that the *Survey* would print "disturbing ideas, [and] conscience-pricking opinions," rather than focusing on "sweetness and light."[30] Complaints began to come in that the *Survey* often presented only one side of an issue.[31] A special issue on race relations was already in the works when Dr. Martin Luther King, Jr., was assassinated in April 1968; the editors called in a panel of black Presbyterian pastors to write "kindly if possible, belligerently if necessary, what the white Christian must know in order to deal with white racism, which is, after all, the cause of the crisis."[32] The result was the June 1968 special edition entitled "Love Shall Overcome," featuring a cover photo from King's funeral.

The reaction was explosive. Angry readers canceled subscriptions. The *Survey*'s editors initially received the backing of the General Assembly,[33] but as circulation continued to plummet, the General Assembly called for a change of format and new direction for the magazine. On 22 September 1969, the *Survey*, reduced to sixteen pages, became a "semi-monthly magazine of news, forum, and interpretation" and abandoned its more prophetic focus. A chastened editor Hartley stated that in its new form the *Survey* would deal "more with facts, less with opinion; it will report more community level church life, do less reflecting on vast, complex issues . . . [W]e are certain that essential truths can be translated to words in print in such fashion that very, very few readers will be alienated."[34] Such alienation, however, mirrored more widespread tension within the denomination over issues of integration and civil rights for African-Americans.

The changes in format and retreat from addressing controversy did not halt the decline in circulation.[35] Finally, in February 1971, with circulation down to 140,000, editors Hartley and Furlow were dismissed,[36] and the *Survey* ceased to function as an autonomous denominational agency.[37] By 1973, circulation had fallen below 110,000.[38]

John Allen Templeton, who became editor in September 1971, took steps to ease the *Survey* back to its original function "as the prime communications-promotional-interpretive medium of the church."[39] He self-consciously attempted to make the *Survey* a "reconciling agent" for the splintering Church.[40] He returned to a monthly publication schedule in January 1972. The magazine's size gradually increased and began to shift back to its former format of features, articles, program resources, Church news, and inspirational items. For the first time in years, the foreign mission work of the Church was recovered and highlighted on a regular basis. William P. Lamkin, named editor in 1978, and Vic Jameson, who assumed the role in 1983, continued the magazine along the same lines, though articles on abortion, homosexuality, and issues of peace and justice indicated that the *Survey* once again had become a magazine that "thrives on debate."[41]

In 1983, the Southern Presbyterian Church merged with the United Presbyterian Church in the U.S.A. to form the Presbyterian Church (U.S.A.), and *Presbyterian Survey* became the official magazine of the new Church. In late 1983, 240,000 copies of the *Survey* were distributed for three issues, more than half of them going to former subscribers of *A.D.*, which had been the general-interest magazine of the United Presbyterian Church. Paid circulation of the *Survey* rose from 113,000 in July 1983[42] to almost 200,000 in 1986, but circulation dropped rather steadily after that, to a level of about 120,000 in 1992.[43]

Today, the *Presbyterian Survey* is published ten times a year, with combined January–February and July–August issues. A 192-page special issue appeared in 1988 to commemorate the bicentennial of the first General Assembly of Presbyterians in the United States, and in that year, the offices of the *Survey* moved to Louisville, Kentucky. Under editor Ken Little, who was appointed in 1991 upon Jameson's retirement, the *Survey* has continued to offer itself as more of a congregational resource than a general purpose religious magazine, but the content has remained essentially unchanged since the late 1970s. The magazine's primary audience remains older laypeople of the Church, and it is still read by more women than men.[44] But the *Survey*'s mission continues to be as first elucidated in 1924: to ensure that there "is no excuse now for uninformed Presbyterians."[45]

Notes

1. *Presbyterian Survey* 16 (April 1926): 197.
2. Ibid. 28 (April 1938): 195.
3. Ibid., p. 195.
4. Ibid. 74 (June 1984): 47.
5. Ibid. 16 (April 1926): 198.
6. See notes regarding the "Reading Contests" held to encourage Presbyterian men to read "at least two articles" in the *Survey* a month in *Presbyterian Survey* 16 (May 1926): 260. See also *Presbyterian Survey* 14 (August 1924): inside back cover; 16 (April 1926): 195 and (January 1926): 1.
7. See, for example, *Presbyterian Survey* 16 (May 1926): 260; 24 (September 1934): 532.
8. *Presbyterian Survey* 28 (May 1938): 280.
9. Ibid. 34 (September 1944): 331.
10. Ibid. 24 (June 1934): 337; 26 (May 1936): 262.
11. Ibid. 28 (April 1938): 195–96.
12. See, for example, articles related to children, parents, marriage, and the war in *Presbyterian Survey* 32 (July 1942): 321 and 32 (August 1942): 353; 34 (August 1944): 303; 35 (December 1945): 429 and (September 1945): 303; 36 (August 1946): 323.
13. *Presbyterian Survey* 32 (June 1942): 257 and 32 (May 1942): 214; 35 (September 1945): 301.
14. *Presbyterian Survey* 14 (September 1924): 587.
15. Ibid. 74 (April 1984): 48.

16. Ibid. 47 (September 1957): 5.

17. Ibid. 74 (June 1984): 47.

18. Ibid. 70 (November 1980): 2.

19. Ibid. 49 (June 1959): 49.

20. Ibid. 47 (September 1957): 5.

21. Ibid. 49 (April 1959): 2.

22. Ibid. 74 (June 1984): 48.

23. See ibid. 22 (August 1932): 453–54. (Volume 22 is labeled incorrectly throughout 1932 as volume 23.)

24. See, for example, *Presbyterian Survey* 16 (January 1926): 13 and 16 (December 1926): 713; 24 (June 1934): 327.

25. See comments on the motives behind World War I in *Presbyterian Survey* 16 (July 1926): 411; 20 (February 1930): 70–71; 24 (June 1934): 327.

26. See, for example, *Presbyterian Survey* 22 (May 1932): 266; 26 (August 1936): 453. (Volume 22 is incorrectly labeled throughout 1932 as volume 23.)

27. Quotation is from *Presbyterian Survey* 14 (April 1924): 267. See also *Presbyterian Survey* 16 (April 1926): 211; 22 (June 1932): 361–62. (Volume 22 is incorrectly labeled throughout 1932 as volume 23.)

28. *Presbyterian Survey* 39 (October 1949): 456. See also ibid. 47 (August 1957): 5.

29. Ibid. 49 (June 1959): 4.

30. Ibid. 51 (July 1961): 4. See also ibid. 59 (May 1969): 6, where Hartley conceded that "the possibility that substantial numbers (and perhaps on occasions a majority) of the members of PCUS do not agree with some of the more progressive positions of *Survey*," but this did not change his editorial policy.

31. Ibid. 50 (August 1960): 4.

32. Ibid. 58 (June 1968): 3.

33. The General Assembly voted down a requirement that would have required that the "other side" of controversial issues be given a voice in the magazine as well, but the *Survey*'s "Board of Directors, editors, and staff were requested to continue to exercise diligence and discretion in its editorial policy" (*Presbyterian Survey* 58 [August 1968]: 20).

34. Ibid. 59 (July–August 1969): 4.

35. See letters from disappointed subscribers in ibid. 59 (8 December 1969): 20. See also *Presbyterian Survey* 60 (9 March 1970): 8; 61 (22 February 1971): 13.

36. Ibid. 61 (22 February 1971): 8.

37. Ibid. 61 (12 July 1971): 3–4. (The volume number on this issue is incorrectly labeled volume 60.)

38. Ibid. 74 (June 1984): 48.

39. Ibid. 61 (20 September 1971): 20.

40. Ibid. 68 (January 1978): 4.

41. Ibid. 76 (July–August 1986): 2.

42. Ibid. 74 (June 1984): 48.

43. Letter from Catherine Cottingham, managing editor, *Presbyterian Survey*, to the author, 17 June 1992.

44. Ibid. 25 August 1992.

45. *Presbyterian Survey* 28 (April 1938): 195.

Information Sources

INDEX SOURCES: *Presbyterian Survey* began its own yearly index in December 1954.
LOCATION SOURCES: All issues from 1924 to date are available in microform from
   University Microfilms International.

Publication History

MAGAZINE TITLE AND TITLE CHANGES: *Missionary* (Nashville) (1867–1911) and
   Home Mission Herald (1889–1911) were combined into *Missionary Survey* (Richmond) (1911–1924). In 1924, *Missionary Survey* was renamed the *Presbyterian
   Survey.*
VOLUME AND ISSUE DATA: *Missionary Survey* 1:1 (November 1911)–14:3 (March
   1924). *Presbyterian Survey* 14:4 (April 1924)–present. Published monthly, except
   for 22 September 1969 to January 1972, when it was a semimonthly from September to June and a monthly in July and August. Currently published 10 times
   a year, with combined January–February and July–August issues. Issues for 1932
   are mislabeled volume 23 instead of 22.
PUBLISHER AND PLACE OF PUBLICATION: The General Assembly of the Presbyterian Church in the United States (1924–1983); the General Assembly of the
   Presbyterian Church (U.S.A.) (1983–present). Richmond, Virginia (1924–1962);
   Atlanta, Georgia (1962–1988); Louisville, Kentucky (1988–present).
EDITORS: Sarah Lee Vinson (managing editor, 1924–1927); Harriet Blackford Williams
   (managing and assistant editor, 1927–1944); Gilbert Glass (1930–1934); John L.
   Fairly (1934–1949); Holmes Rolston (1949–1954); Marea Yount Stratton (assistant
   editor, 1949–1952); William Thompson (1952–1959); Frances Furlow (associate
   editor, 1956–1971); Ben Hartley (1959–1971); John Allen Templeton (1971–1978)
   William P. Lamkin (1978–1983); Catherine Cottingham (managing and associate
   editor, 1982–present); Vic Jameson (1983–1991); Ken Little (1991–present).
CIRCULATION: 38,000 (1924); 161,000 (1958); 250,000 (1962); 110,000 (1973);
   200,000 (1986); 120,000 (1992).

Susan Wilds McArver

PRESENT TRUTH. *See* ADVENT REVIEW

PROPHETIC TIMES

   The year 1863 witnessed the crucial battles of Vicksburg and Gettysburg,
turning points in the Civil War. It also witnessed the advent of a new periodical
that interpreted present-day events so that people might prepare themselves for
the premillennial return of Christ. However, the paper did not focus primarily
on occurrences in the United States. Its gaze rested on Europe and found in
continental events the signs of Jesus' impending return. It wondered in print
whether Louis Napoleon might be the personal Antichrist and watched and reported on any movement that might indicate a restoration of the Jews to Palestine, a condition that had to be fulfilled prior to the return of Christ. The serial

was called the *Prophetic Times*, and it was edited by Joseph Seiss, a Lutheran clergyman.

Joseph Augustus Seiss was born near Graceham, Frederick County, Maryland, 18 March 1823, the son of John and Eliza (Schuler) Seiss. After study at Gettysburg College, he received his ministerial license from the Lutheran synod of Virginia in 1842 and served congregations in Virginia, Maryland, and Pennsylvania. Seiss enjoyed a wide reputation as a preacher and published several volumes of sermons. From his pen also issued works on *Luther and the Reformation*, a number of hymn and devotional books, and the *Children of Silence*, on the deaf. He contributed to the *Lutheran Quarterly*, *Evangelical Review*, and *Lutheran Church Review* and edited the *Lutheran and Missionary* for more than a decade. He was the most published Lutheran author of the nineteenth century.

Seiss's first exposure to the issue of the millennium resulted from the appearance of the Millerites while he was a pastor in Shepherdstown, West Virginia, in 1842–1843. The preaching of William Miller's followers caused great concern among Seiss's parishioners, and, in order to comfort them, he studied the biblical doctrine of Christ's return. From this point on, he held to the doctrine of the premillennial return of Christ. Further, his lifelong opposition to postmillennialism, the view that a period of peace and prosperity will occur prior to the Second Advent, stems from this period.[1]

Although Seiss published a number of works that dealt with millennial themes,[2] his growing conviction of Christ's imminent return compelled him to publish a cross-denominational paper that would spread the news of the Second Advent to readers in the United States. To this end, Seiss, along with Richard Newton of Philadelphia (Episcopalian), George Duffield of Detroit (New School Presbyterian), John Forsyth of Newburg, New York (Dutch Reformed), E. E. Reinke of Olney, Illinois (Moravian), Robert Adair of Philadelphia (New School Presbyterian), and William Newton of Gambier, Ohio (Episcopalian), began to publish the *Prophetic Times* in 1863.[3]

The paper was futurist in orientation; it argued that the prophecies of Scripture had yet to be fulfilled. It looked for the restoration of the Jews to Palestine and the translation, or rapture, of the Church. In this respect it may have drawn some of its ideas from the theology of John Nelson Darby and the Plymouth Brethren, the so-called dispensationalists, although Seiss specifically rejected Darby's thought on the Atonement and felt that denominations were legitimate expressions of the one true Church.[4]

Seiss sought a broad representation of traditions in the *Times*; his paper was to be "not at all denominational or sectarian."[5] Seiss was quite sensitive to the charge that the millenarian doctrine that he espoused was late to the theological scene and spared no effort in proving that the early Church, especially the early Church fathers, had, in fact, held to the same position.[6] He appealed more than once to Irenaeus, but his favorite early father was Justin Martyr. Justin, Seiss argued, was not a solitary figure in the early Church who held to a unique idea of his own creation; Justin's views represented those of the Church of the earliest periods. Hence, the premillennial doctrine of Christ's return that Seiss found in Justin's writings was the orthodox position. From this he drew several conclusions. First, the entire orthodox Church received the premillennial doctrine in unity. Second, the Christians of the early period believed that their eschatology was the same as Christ's, which he had handed down to his apostles. Thus, any person who did not receive this doctrine or disputed its truth was to be labeled a schismatic. The question to which Seiss often returned was, "If millenarianism were not taught to the churches by divine teachers, who did communicate it to them?" Seiss countered the arguments of his opponents by stating that orthodoxy assumes that the doctrines of Christ were "fixed and unalterable." How, then, he asked, could this doctrine have arisen in the context of an orthodox Church, which, by nature, "repels innovation upon the ancient faith of the church?" The truly orthodox Church would not abide teachers who abandoned the faith once delivered. Hence, those who argued that premillennial thought is doctrinally aberrant should reconsider their charges. In attacking the doctrine, they came close to denying the very truth they sought so hard to maintain.[7]

According to Seiss, the orthodox Church of the earliest periods held to the doctrines that the *Times* confessed: the appearance of a personal Antichrist, the restoration of the Jews to Palestine, the material nature of the new heavens and new earth, and the translation of the saints. In the first number of the *Times*, Seiss and his fellow editors outlined what they believed. Regarding the personal Antichrist, Seiss confided to his readers that "without undertaking, therefore, to decide positively that Louis Napoleon is the personal Antichrist of the Last Days, we have no hesitation in saying that we are strongly inclined to believe that he is the man who is to figure in this remarkable capacity. Events will very soon show whether this belief is founded in truth or not."[8] On the restoration they believed that "the house of Israel, or Jewish race, shall again occupy their own land, and hold the first place among the nations, under their proper King, the Son of David, forever." On the nature of the new heavens and earth, they stated that "the earth, and the heavens enveloping it, are to be renovated by Him who is to have the dominion; that the heavens and earth which are now shall be made to pass away into new heavens and earth, in which righteousness shall dwell: as the natural man by regeneration is made into the new man, being renewed in the image of the Creator." Finally, on the translation of the Church, they held that "the saints shall rise first, and, together with such of the living as shall be accounted worthy of such honor, be received up into the glorified state, to share with Christ in his subsequent dealings with the world, in ridding it of sin and sinners, and in bringing it back from the curse to everlasting peace and blessing."[9]

In essence, the periodical served as a vehicle to instill a sense of community in the growing movement in the United States of believers in the premillennial advent. It did this primarily in two ways. First and foremost, Seiss offered to his readers a history. Premillennialism was not to be seen as a theological innovation; it was the doctrine of the earliest Church. Second, Seiss used the paper as a forum to instruct his readers in the doctrine. He recommended quality new works on millennial themes, enabling his readers to be well-read scholars in the doctrine of the last things. Yet the real purpose of the paper was to make this material available directly to the readership. The *Times* offered articles, usually of moderate length, that required the readers to devote themselves to serious thought. Seiss divided the serial into three sections: "Special Contributions," "Selections," and "Editorial." "Special Contributions" acted as a forum for the latest opinion on the imminent return of Jesus. Commentaries, for example, on "Characteristics of the Last Days" and "Calamities in 1866" helped readers to know "More About Our Times."[10] "Selections" included both original articles for the *Times* and reprints from various sources. In this section Seiss offered his readers the opinions of the Church fathers, Luther and the Reformers, and many modern divines on the doctrine of Christ's return. Sources of reprints included a wide variety of denominational papers and demonstrated the ecumenical breath of the enterprise.[11] The "Editorial" section of the *Times* served as a forum for the editors' views. It was to this section that readers would turn if they needed to know exactly what the editors believed. Here Seiss spelled out his views on the topics that he felt were most crucial.

Critics charged that the premillennial system was pessimistic in outlook. Seiss responded by striving invariably to let the good news of the Gospel message triumph over the more negative aspects of the doctrine. He wanted his readers to rejoice in the Lord always. As long as the Lord continued to spare the world from the tribulations to come, he stated, then all God's people should sing "Hosanna in the highest!" The offer of salvation remained open to all people, and the Savior maintained communication with his people through the Word and ordinances. Most important, though, readers should daily expect the coming of the Savior, for in this expectation all believers will find comfort. "Is our religion after all so frail a thing, that faith must dread to take the very blessedness for which it prays and hopes! Nay, reader, sing Hosanna! Blessed is He that cometh! Hosanna in the highest!"[12]

However, Seiss likely did not feel like rejoicing when he considered the financial condition of the *Times*. Money troubles plagued the enterprise from its inception. Time and again Seiss reminded his readers of the serial's desperate need for funds; his subscribers always seemed to be in arrears.[13] When the situation became overly critical, Seiss would print two issues of the *Times* together, although this was very unpopular with his readers.[14] Yet, the paper was a labor of love for Seiss; he served as its editor for twelve years without compensation.[15] Eventually, however, the financial burden became too much for Seiss alone to bear. When his predictions of Christ's return in 1866 and 1870 did not materialize, and when Louis Napoleon suddenly fell, his confidence diminished, and he decided to terminate his editorship of the *Times*.[16]

In his final editorial, "The End of This World," Seiss rehearsed the doctrine to which he had dedicated himself. He refused to summarize the work of the serial; that had been done by others. Instead, he took the opportunity to testify one final time to the spirit and ideas that had driven his paper for more than a decade. The imminence of the end remained most prominent. "Reminders of the approaching end are again plentiful about us. On all sides there are symptoms and preintimations of it . . . all our church lessons for the season point forward to the sounding of the last trump and the end of the world itself."[17] Yet, as this terrifying day approached, one could look forward to God's new work of creation on behalf of believers, that is, a regenerated humanity and a new heavens and earth. "The Scriptures . . . give us several most significant intimations, that the *new* heavens and *new* earth are not *other* heavens and *another* earth . . . but that these same heavens, and this same earth, delivered, renewed, refined, purged, and refitted, shall be the abode of everlasting righteousness."[18] With these words the *Prophetic Times* ceased publication.

John G. Wilson resurrected the *Times* the following year, renaming it the *Prophetic Times and Watchtower*. The second series ran from 1875 to 1878 and was followed by a third series form 1879 to 1880. However, with the name change came a change of editorial attitude. While Seiss did, on occasion, publish in the serial, the previous broad denominational representation disappeared in the list of contributors. The paper took on a sectarian flavor and lost its ecumenical character.[19]

Notes

1. In "A New Publication," *Prophetic Times* 6 (July 1968): 168, Seiss argued that these teachings are "full of Chiliasm, and Chiliastic promises and hopes, of the most earthly, carnal, coarse and secular sort." See also "Our Enterprise: Remarks and Explanations," *Prophetic Times* 1 (January 1863): 13.

2. For example, *The Last Times* (Baltimore: T. Newton Kurtz, 1856) and *The Parable of the Ten Virgins* (Philadelphia: Smith, English, 1862).

3. Later, in December 1866, Seiss listed members of the editorial group: C. Colegrove of Sardinia, New York (Baptist), L. C. Baker of Camden, New Jersey (Old School Presbyterian), B. B. Leacock of Harrisburg, Pennsylvania (Episcopalian), and Samuel Laird of Lancaster, Pennsylvania (Lutheran). Even with all of these men on the masthead, Seiss assumed the bulk of the editorial labors.

4. See Ernest R. Sandeen, *The Roots of Fundamentalism: British and American Millenarianism 1800–1930* (Chicago: University of Chicago Press, 1970), 94–99.

5. A phrase Seiss employed on the inside front cover of many numbers of the *Times* (e.g., see *Prophetic Times* 9 [December 1871]). He made certain that his readers knew that the *Times* would have "no connection whatever with the erratic and irresponsible men usually claiming attention on these themes." Instead, they came "before the public as accredited ministers of orthodox churches, with no motives other than fidelity to the truth and to the souls of men, and the desire 'to show unto God's servants the things which must shortly be done' " ("Our Enterprise: Remarks and Explanations," *Prophetic Times* 1 [January 1863]: 12).

6. In "A Word About Ourselves," *Prophetic Times* 7 (December 1869): 190, he

argued that his position was "not the heat of imagination—not morbid fancy—not tumid idiosyncracy—not fanatical feeling—not hasty and unconsidered wish to be singular."

7. "Assaults on Millenarianism," *Prophetic Times* 11 (July–August 1873): 110–16.

8. "The Antichrist: Will It Be Louis Napoleon?" *Prophetic Times* 1 (February 1863): 21.

9. "Our Enterprise: Remarks and Explanations," *Prophetic Times* 1 (January 1863): 13–14.

10. W. Cadman, "Characteristics of the Last Days," *Prophetic Times* 2 (September 1864): 129–31; Cadman, "Calamities in 1866," *Prophetic Times* 5 (February 1867): 21; Cadman, "More About Our Times," *Prophetic Times* 8 (March 1870): 26. Articles in this section for the most part were written specifically for the *Times*. The quality and nature of the views expressed in this section varied widely. It was the first section of the magazine and perhaps the first read by its subscribers. As a result, Seiss had to warn his readers that the position taken by the authors was their own and did not necessarily reflect that of its chief editor ("The Signs of the Times," *Prophetic Times* 7 [1869]: 133): "We do not hold ourselves responsible for all that appears in the department 'Special Contributions.' "

11. Articles from the *Western Episcopalian, The Rainbow, Earth's Eventide*, and many others appeared in the paper.

12. "The New Year," *Prophetic Times* 10 (January 1872): 16.

13. "A Word to Our Readers," *Prophetic Times* (1869): 133.

14. "A Word About Ourselves," *Prophetic Times* 7 (November–December 1869): 190.

15. "One More Year!" *Prophetic Times* 11 (November–December 1873): 192.

16. Ibid. Seiss was not alone in his disappointment. The place of Louis Napoleon in the premillennial system absorbed many interpreters. Michael Baxter was preeminent among these, publishing numerous works on prophecy, most importantly, *Louis Napoleon, the Destined Monarch of the World and Personal Antichrist*, 3d ed. (Philadelphia: Wm. S. & A. Martien, 1866) and *Coming Wonders Expected Between 1867 and 1875: Explaining the Future Literal Fulfillment of the Seals, Trumpets, Vials and Other Prophecies of Revelation and Daniel, Within the Final Seven Years* (London: S. W. Partridge, 1867?). See also Sandeen, *Roots*, 60, 97–98.

17. "The End of This World," *Prophetic Times* 12 (November–December 1874): 186.

18. Ibid., p. 189.

19. Seiss's unusual view on the nature of the new heavens and new earth may have influenced the thought of Charles Taze Russell, founder of Jehovah's Witnesses. See M. James Penton, *Apocalypse Delayed: The Story of Jehovah's Witnesses* (Toronto: University of Toronto Press, 1985), 18. The National Union Catalog notes that the periodical *Words of Reconciliation* "supersedes the Prophetic Times and Watchtower" (*National Union Catalog* 673:643).

Information Sources

INDEX SOURCES: Most volumes include a table of contents that lists article titles for the three divisions of the serial, along with page numbers. Names of authors are not supplied. Initials are often provided in the body of the serial at the end of articles. Extractions from larger works carry the author's name at the beginning of the piece, along with the source of the reprint.

LOCATION SOURCES: An almost complete set of the *Prophetic Times* was compiled and microfilmed by the American Theological Library Association. Missing from the three-reel set are 1:6 and the third series. The reels are available as ATLA S0196. Hard copies of the serial exist at Lutheran Theological Seminary at Philadelphia, Lutheran Theological Seminary at Gettysburg, Presbyterian Historical Society at Philadelphia, and the Chicago Public Library, among others. Most lack various numbers and/or volumes.

Publication History

MAGAZINE TITLE AND TITLE CHANGES: *Prophetic Times* (1863–1874); *Prophetic Times and Watchtower* (1875–1880).

VOLUME AND ISSUE DATA: 1:1 (January 1863)–12:12 (November–December 1874); New Series 1:1 (January 1875)–4:12 (December 1878); Third Series 1:1 (January 1879)–2:12 (December 1880). Published monthly, with some numbers published together.

PUBLISHER AND PLACE OF PUBLICATION: W. Z. Harbert, Philadelphia, Pennsylvania (1863–1874); C. Sherman and Co., Printers, Philadelphia, Pennsylvania (1875–1880).

EDITORS: Joseph A. Seiss (editor in chief, 1863–1874), Richard Newton, John Forsyth, E. E. Reinke, Robert Adair, and William Newton (coeditors, 1863–1874), George Duffield (coeditor, 1861–1868), C. Colegrove, L. C. Baker, B. B. Leacock, and Samuel Laird (coeditors, 1866–1874); John G. Wilson (1875–1880).

CIRCULATION: Unknown.

Lawrence Rast

PROPHETIC TIMES AND WATCHTOWER. *See* PROPHETIC TIMES

PURSUIT. *See* EVANGELICAL BEACON

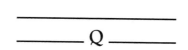

QUARTERLY EXTRACTS. *See* AMERICAN BIBLE SOCIETY RECORD

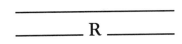

R

RATTA HEMLANDEDT OCH AUGUSTANA. *See* LUTHERAN
COMPANION

RECORDER. *See* CONGREGATIONALIST

REFORM JUDAISM

Reform Judaism is currently the official publication of the Union of American
Hebrew Congregations (UAHC), the oldest cooperative organization of Jewish
congregations in the United States. This journal is actually the descendant of a
rather large family of magazines published by the Reform movement for nearly
a century.

Established in 1873, the UAHC's primary objective was to coordinate support
for the founding of a rabbinical seminary—the Hebrew Union College in Cincinnati, which opened in 1875. During its first decade of existence, the Jewish
congregations constituting the UAHC were not all Reform in practice. In fact
by 1879, 118 congregations belonged to the Union—an impressive number but
by no means the majority of all the synagogues in the United States. Many of
these UAHC congregations were traditional in their ritual practice. However, as
Isaac Mayer Wise (1819–1900), founding president of the Hebrew Union College, became increasingly perceived to be in alignment with the Reformist wing
in American Judaism, the traditionalist congregations began to distance themselves from the Union and its college. By 1886, they had lent their support to
the establishment of a new rabbinical school in New York, and thereafter the
UAHC and the Hebrew Union College gradually became, de facto, Reform
institutions.

Although the organization's primary raison d'être was to serve as patron of
a rabbinical seminary, the UAHC's original constitution also authorized the new

union "to provide for and advance the standard of Sabbath-schools for the instruction of the young" and "to aid and encourage young congregations by [furnishing] material and spiritual support."[1] Over the years, this charge prompted the UAHC to develop a diverse array of administrative services for its member congregations in areas such as religious education, congregational organization, sisterhoods, brotherhoods, youth activities, synagogue administration, and social action. The Union also began distributing a wide variety of publications relating to Jewish education and congregational activity from its earliest days of existence.

The UAHC published its first national newsletter, *The Union Bulletin*, in 1911 with the hope that the quarterly would serve "as a means of bringing the friends of the Union into closer touch with its activities." *The Union Bulletin* was sent to each member of every congregation affiliated with the UAHC—approximately twenty-three thousand homes. It contained brief articles describing the Union's various organizational activities, news of the Hebrew Union College, and a few concise essays on contemporary issues.[2]

The Union Bulletin was renamed *Union Tidings* in December 1919. Initially, the change in name did not signify any noteworthy innovations, with the exception that in September 1924 the magazine began to appear monthly, except in July and August. Readers could still find a summary of the proceedings of the UAHC's Executive Board, the annual report of the Board of Governors of the Hebrew Union College, and lists of donations to the UAHC and its budgetary expenditures. In addition, each issue contained a brief article or two describing the activities of the Union or the college. Throughout 1929, for example, *Union Tidings* regularly trumpeted the successes of the five million-dollar endowment campaign on behalf of the Hebrew Union College.[3]

In January of 1930 the contents of the *Union Tidings* began to undergo revision. The editors increasingly devoted more space to editorials on serious topics of contemporary interest, such as "The Jew and Christmas," "How Shall Modern Jews Study the Bible?" and "Religion and Theology." Concomitantly, less space was given to reports on the UAHC's budget and its organizational structure. In short, the publication slowly began to transform itself from a prosaic organizational bulletin to a magazine that appealed to the broad interests of the contemporary Reform Jew.[4]

Due to the Depression, probably, the Executive Board of the Union decided to terminate the publication of *Union Tidings* in June 1930. Believing, too, that the practice of subscribing to a local or national Jewish paper was widespread among its constituents, the leadership of the UAHC asserted that the general Anglo-Jewish press would serve as a better medium of publicity for the Reform movement than their own in-house magazine. In their notice of discontinuance, the editors urged the UAHC membership to subscribe to the general Jewish press: "If you are interested in news of the Union, in the progress of our religious life, in the furtherance of every good cause—then subscribe for a Jewish paper."[5]

The Union's departure from Jewish journalism on a national scale did not last long. Within a few years, the UAHC again began to publish *two* service-oriented magazines for its constituents: the *Jewish Teacher* and the *Synagogue Service Bulletin.*

The *Jewish Teacher*, a quarterly magazine for Jewish religious schools, appeared in November 1932. Issued by the Union's Department of Synagogue and School Extension and edited for many years by the influential Jewish educator Emanuel Gamoran (1895–1962), the *Jewish Teacher* promised to provide a forum for "stimulating and fruitful exchange of opinions and experiences between rabbis, educational directors of temples, and teachers, on the many problems of the Jewish school." Each edition contained several articles of pedagogic interest as well as a book review section. The journal held to this format for more than three decades. A second publication, the *Synagogue Service Bulletin* (later renamed *The Synagogue*), was issued monthly and contained an exchange of views by congregational officers relating to synagogue activities.[6]

In May 1943, the UAHC reentered the larger arena of general Jewish journalism. *The Synagogue* was absorbed into a new monthly journal entitled *Liberal Judaism*, jointly published by the UAHC and the Central Conference of American Rabbis (CCAR), which promised to provide readers with a "realistic approach to the questions of the day." With its absorbing illustrations and well-written essays on Jewish life in all parts of the world, this new journal marked a significant departure from most of its predecessors, which tended to focus primarily on the institutional life of Reform Judaism. Appealing to "young and old, rabbi and congregant, the religious and the unsynagogued," *Liberal Judaism*'s self-proclaimed objective was to respond to the challenge of new conditions that would "affect the course of Judaism and the destiny of America."[7]

Under the editorial direction of a dynamic young UAHC executive, Rabbi Alexander Schindler (b. 1925), the *Jewish Teacher* became *Dimension* in 1966. Promising no fundamental alteration of content and approach, Schindler nonetheless introduced a "symposium" feature, a series of articles on a single theme that were subsequently made available for distribution in reprint form. Symposium topics such as "Fundamental Questions in Contemporary Jewish Theology," "The Jewish Family in a Changing Society," and "The Middle East Crisis" provided subscribers with timely reading. By appending a "Study Guide" at the end of each issue, *Dimension* made a serious attempt to serve both teacher and nonteacher in one publication. "In the final analysis," the editors noted, "not just teachers but all congregational leaders are involved in the educative process."[8]

Liberal Judaism became a quarterly journal entitled *American Judaism* in 1951 and, in 1967, it merged with *Dimension* to create *Dimensions in American Judaism*—a true amalgam of its two parents. This publication continued to offer its popular "symposium" feature together with topical essays on issues of Jewish and general concern. *Dimensions in American Judaism* also included a section on contemporary Jewish arts and literature.[9]

In September 1972, *Reform Judaism* replaced *Dimensions in American Judaism*. While maintaining that the objectives of the new journal remained unchanged from those of its predecessor, the editors promised readers "fresh insight." *Reform Judaism* fashioned itself as "a cutting edge into unexplored regions of Reform Judaism: keeping our nearly 1,000,000 readers informed of the programs and thinking going on in our movement; dealing with matters of general interest that affect Jews; presenting all of these in readable style, to entertain and enlighten."[10]

Reform Judaism has clung, more or less, to a tripartite format dealing with issues related to the world and Judaism, the Reform movement, and the activities of the UAHC itself. Essays on topics such as "Jews & Blacks," "Israel and the U.N.," and "Pollard Revisited" keep readers abreast of issues of contemporary Jewish concern. At the same time, *Reform Judaism* provides the UAHC membership with a valuable source of information of particular interest to Reform Jews.

From the earliest stages of its history, the UAHC sought to inform its members of the organization's activities. In time, however, some believed that a movementwide magazine should aspire to be more than a mere house organ; the association's journal could be a useful educational resource as well as an entertaining medium. The history of the UAHC's magazines is, in effect, the mediation of these hopes. The current format of *Reform Judaism* represents only the most recent attempt to reconcile these two goals under the cover of one magazine.

Notes

1. Sefton D. Temkin, "A Century of Reform Judaism in America," *American Jewish Yearbook* 74 (1972): 3–75.

2. *The Union Bulletin* 1 (April 1911): 1.

3. *Union Tidings* 9 (June 1929): 1.

4. Ibid. 10 (January 1930): 2.

5. Ibid. (September 1930): 2.

6. *Jewish Teacher* 1 (November 1932): 1–2; *The Synagogue Service Bulletin* 1 (September 1933): 1.

7. *Liberal Judaism* 11 (May 1943): 2.

8. *Dimension* 1 (Fall 1966): 2.

9. *American Judaism* 1 (November 1951): 3; *Dimensions in American Judaism* 2 (Fall 1967): 3. Two smaller publications of UAHC affiliates were also absorbed by *American Judaism* at this same time: *The Jewish Layman*, the journal of the Brotherhoods of the UAHC, and *Topics & Trends*, the journal of the Sisterhoods.

10. *Reform Judaism* 1 (September 1972): 2.

Information Sources

INDEX SOURCES: Unfortunately, no general indexes are available for any of the periodicals mentioned in this article.

LOCATION SOURCES: The best collection of all volumes is at the Klau Library of the Hebrew Union College-Jewish Institute of Religion, Cincinnati, Ohio.

Publication History

MAGAZINE TITLE AND TITLE CHANGES: *The Union Bulletin* (1911–1917); *Union Tidings* (1919–1930); *Jewish Teacher* (1932–1966); *The Synagogue* (1933–1951); *Liberal Judaism* (1943–1951); *American Judaism* (1951–1967); *Dimension* (1966–1967); *Dimensions in American Judaism* (1967–1972); *Reform Judaism* (1972–present).

VOLUME AND ISSUE DATA: *The Union Bulletin* 1:1 (April 1911)–7:9 (November 1917); *Union Tidings* 1:1 (December 1919)–10:7 (September 1930); *Jewish Teacher* 1:1 (November 1932)–34:4 (April 1966); *The Synagogue* 1:1 (September 1933)–19:1 (June 1951); *Liberal Judaism* 11:1 (May 1943)–19:1 (June 1951); *American Judaism* 1:1 (November 1951)–16:3 (Spring 1967); *Dimension* 1:1 (Fall 1966)–1:4 (Summer 1967); *Dimensions in American Judaism* 2:1 (Fall 1967)–6:3 (Spring 1972); *Reform Judaism* 1:1 (September 1972)–present.

PUBLISHER AND PLACE OF PUBLICATION: *The Union Bulletin*, UAHC, Cincinnati, Ohio (1911–1917); *Union Tidings*, UAHC, Cincinnati, Ohio (1919–1930); *Jewish Teacher*, UAHC, Department of Synagogue and School Extension, Cincinnati, Ohio (1932–195?); New York, New York (195?–1966); *The Synagogue*, UAHC, Cincinnati, Ohio (1933–1951); *Liberal Judaism*, UAHC and the Central Conference of American Rabbis, Cincinnati, Ohio (1943–1951); *American Judaism*, UAHC, Cincinnati, Ohio (1951–1967); *Dimension*, UAHC, New York, New York (1966–1967); *Dimensions in American Judaism*, UAHC, New York, New York (1967–1972); *Reform Judaism*, New York, New York (1972–present).

EDITORS: *The Union Bulletin*, Rabbi George Zepin (1911–1917). *Union Tidings*, Rabbi George Zepin (1919–1930). *Jewish Teacher*, Emanuel Gamoran (1932–1958), Rabbi Eugene B. Borowitz (1958–1962), Rabbi Alexander Schindler (1963–1966). *The Synagogue*, Rabbi Jacob B. Schwarz (1933–1953), Rabbi Eugene J. Lipman (1953–1961), Albert Vorspan (1957), Myron Schoen (1957–1968). *Liberal Judaism*, Louis Rittenberg (1943–1950). *American Judaism*, David Resnick (1951–1952), Rabbi Samuel M. Silver (1952–1960), Paul Kresh (1960–1967). *Dimension*, Rabbi Alexander Schindler (1966–1967). *Dimensions in American Judaism*, Rabbi Alexander Schindler (1967–1969), Jack D. Spiro (1969–1972). *Reform Judaism*, Ruth A. Buchbinder (1972–1976), Aron Hirt-Manheimer (1976–present).

CIRCULATION: *The Union Bulletin*, 22,000 (1912). *Union Tidings*, unknown. *Jewish Teacher*, unknown. *The Synagogue*, unknown. *Liberal Judaism*, unknown. *American Judaism*, unknown. *Dimension*, unknown. *Dimensions in American Judaism*, unknown. *Reform Judaism*, 290,000 (1992).

Gary P. Zola

REIGN OF THE SACRED HEART

Scores of new Roman Catholic religious orders arose during the nineteenth century. Often inspired by one of the increasingly popular Christocentric or Marian devotions, many of these communities were devoted to combating secularism in the Western culture, responding to social and economic conditions created by the Industrial Revolution, and promoting the renewed imperialism of that century. Such is the context for the work of Father Leo Dehon, a priest of the diocese of Soissons, France, who founded the Congregation of the Priests of the Sacred Heart in 1878. Dehon's purpose in establishing his community was twofold: reclaiming men and women lost to secularism or the harshness of the industrial order and sending laborers into mission fields. The congregation attracted recruits from most European countries; Sacred Heart fathers and brothers entered mission fields in Africa, Indonesia, and Scandinavia. In 1923 Father Mathias Fohrman came to the United States to work among the native American peoples of South Dakota. He was joined later by Fathers John Emonts and Charles Prantauer.

Determined to structure a stable community in the United States, the community acquired an abandoned hospital in Ste. Marie, Illinois, and opened a house of formation and mission appeals center there. Subsequent houses were founded in Hales Corners, Wisconsin (later the community's national headquarters) and Donaldson, Indiana. Additional missions and seminaries opened as finances and personnel improved.

Early on, Father John Emonts, a German, laid plans for a periodical to inform interested Catholics about the community's work and to solicit funds to support it. Thus was born the progenitor of the *Reign of the Sacred Heart,* a pamphlet-sized periodical known as the *Mission Call.* The idea of having a mission magazine was anything but original. Virtually every major religious community in the United States with missions had a magazine to appeal for support. A gifted writer, Emonts knew that most cognate magazines dwelt on missions to the Far East.[1] Sacred Heart missions in Africa, Finland, Sumatra, and Latin America, as well as among the Native Americans of South Dakota, would offer a refreshing change. The *Mission Call*'s first number, in January–February 1929, directly addressed this concern: "What! Another Mission Magazine? . . . We answer that there is always room for more, as the Mission Cause is such a noble and important cause." More to the point, Emonts observed, "The Fathers of the Sacred Heart needed a medium, a medium which would enable them to win even greater numbers of friends."[2]

Until 1944, the bimonthly was published in pamphlet form. Throughout its history, the magazine never had a full-time editor or staff. Emonts served as editor until 1933 and established the magazine's basic format: a regular article encouraging devotion to the Sacred Heart, short pieces about the life and needs of students at the order's formation houses, and lengthy accounts from the missions. Emonts emphasized work in Africa, drawing on his prior experience as a missionary there. Appeals for "pagan children relief" also appeared regularly.

By late 1929, the operation and Emonts were transferred to the new Hales Corners facility. The magazine was costly, however, and with the onset of the Great Depression, the size of the magazine was reduced to just a few pages. Emonts was replaced by the provincial superior of the community, Richard Kiefer, who kept the magazine alive. Though he kept Emont's basic format, he embellished it with reports from a Benedictine nun who worked with the priests in South Dakota and a section on international Church news. In 1937, the magazine was able to return to its original length.

In 1942, Father Charles Keilman and Father Charles Talsky assumed the editorship. They introduced short stories in 1942. The magazine expanded its size in 1944 and started monthly publication. During World War II, there was emphasis on patriotism and on regular appeals for war bonds. Keilman and Talsky's names disappear from the masthead after 1943, and it is difficult to ascertain who handled editorial duties. In 1948, the energetic Father George Pinger took over as editor of the magazine, working with a group of dedicated young priests, including James Alexander, Peter Miller, Martin Porter, and Michael Noonan.

This editorial staff determined to revitalize a magazine that was stagnant and afflicted by low circulation. The priest in charge of direct mail appeals, an innovation the Sacred Heart fathers began in the late 1940s, complained that the *Mission Call* was "antiquated" and that its "unattractive form would not entice the potential Catholic reading public." His concern opened the door to change.[3] After consultation with other editors and with specialists from Marquette University's School of Journalism, Pinger transformed the *Mission Call* into a family magazine called *COR*. Pinger explained the reasons for this change in a letter to his superior: "We are of the opinion that the Priests of the Sacred Heart must contribute to the formation of the Catholic American family. Too long have we been concentrating on receiving from them. Now we must become benefactors to our benefactors—and what better gift can be given them than the Sacred Heart?"[4] Latin for "heart," *COR* debuted in March 1949.

The differences from the *Mission Call* were palpable. The size and format assumed a more professional form. Pinger expanded the use of short stories and solicited pieces from many Catholic writers, including Anne Tansey and Margaret Colville. Features on timely subjects such as the fate of the Church in communist China, Catholic Action, race relations, American church leaders, and family issues appeared regularly. Popular Catholic writers such as Daniel Lord and Eddie Doherty were frequent contributors. Pinger, who doubled as vocation director for the Sacred Heart fathers, wrote articles about various Sacred Heart apostolates around the country. Occasionally, the *Catholic Digest* or some other Catholic weekly reprinted articles from *COR*.

In late 1955, the superior general of the Sacred Heart Fathers, Alphonse Maria Lellig, suggested changing the periodical's name to *Reign of the Sacred Heart*.

"Fr. General argued," editorial board minutes reported in June 1955, "that we would be in accordance with the magazines in other provinces who have the same name on their magazines."[5] Consequently, the first issues of *Reign of the Sacred Heart* appeared in January 1956, explaining that "this title, more understandable than *COR* to the average layman, is also more expressive of the underlying purpose of the magazine, to promote the Apostolate of the Sacred Heart, to make the Sacred Heart of Jesus better known and loved throughout the world."[6]

In 1955 Pinger and his coworkers began to organize issues around a theme related to some aspect of devotion to the Sacred Heart of Jesus. Peace was the topic in 1955. In 1956, the notion of victimhood informed the magazine. In 1957, power was the theme, and the next year the eleven passions of Thomistic theology became the focus. In 1958, the twelve promises of the Sacred Heart to St. Margaret Mary Alacoque highlighted each issue. But the same mix of feature articles, fiction, and fund-raising appeals constituted the magazine.

Despite these changes, the magazine had financial difficulties. Conflict with the order's fund-raising department hampered efforts to boost circulation. Costs probably always exceeded income from subscriptions. Yet, the magazine won third place for general excellence from the Catholic Press Association in 1961. That same year, Pinger turned over the editorship to Father Howard Melzer.

Melzer continued Pinger's policy of thematic issues, but he was also aware that the audience of *Reign of the Sacred Heart* had become more middle-class and more suburban. Articles such as Antoinette Bosco's reflections on suburban living reflected the changed demographics of American Catholicism. Moreover, the election to the presidency of Catholic John F. Kennedy elicited William O'Toole's "What Is the Effect of a Catholic in the White House for the Suburbanite?"[7] Themes mirroring middle-class concern for health, family unity, leisure, and crime began to appear.

Melzer also began to give the magazine more of an editorial punch and to comment on public issues. The first issue of 1962 highlighted the word *reign* in the periodical's title and included under the masthead: "Promoting devotion to the Sacred Heart and Social Justice." Articles encouraging devotion to the Sacred Heart remained but seemed out of step with the increased social commentary.

Reaction to the new approach was muted until Melzer raised the subscription rate from two dollars to three dollars per year. The magazine lost eight hundred subscriptions. Others were unhappy with his defense of the Kennedy administration and interracial justice. One disgruntled subscriber wrote: "You have wandered far from the spiritual message that Catholics expect in their magazines by going into other fields."[8] Another wrote: "For a long time I have enjoyed 'Reign' and have looked forward eagerly to its arrival. However, since it has become a political journal under the new editor who chose to offend a part of its readership, I am not interested."[9]

In 1965, Melzer relinquished editorial reins to layman Frank Wessling. A devotee of the specialized Catholic Action movements, Wessling had written extensively for the magazine, including a series on Pope John XXIII's social encyclical *Mater et Magistra.* Wessling reconfigured both format and content, devoting the magazine almost exclusively to social justice issues. Its design and style reflected none of the devotionalism of even Melzer's reign and rarely spoke about either Sacred Heart missions or devotional life, which received less official emphasis after Vatican II.

In 1967, the format was altered once again. When Wessling found another job, the Sacred Heart Fathers turned over production to fund-raiser Father Linus Merz, who reduced the size to a small pamphlet and abandoned social commentary and family reporting. Instead, the magazine was directed at benefactors and dealt almost exclusively with the work of the Sacred Heart fathers. It continues in this form and since 1987 has appeared bimonthly.

The evolution of *Reign of the Sacred Heart* is similar to that of other magazines begun by Catholic religious orders for fund-raising, publicity, and the promotion of particular devotions. Many began in the 1920s, weathered the Depression, reformed themselves after World War II, and experienced a period of expansion and popularity in the postwar period. After Vatican II, a number then fell victim to rising costs of production or the dearth of members willing to assume responsibility for overseeing publication. Magazines were often replaced by newsletters, and the field of Catholic journalism was left to the Jesuits' *America,* the Claretians' *U.S. Catholic,* and the Franciscans' *St. Anthony Messenger.* Promoting devotion became the province of *New Covenant* and *Our Sunday Visitor,* both published by Sunday Visitor Press.

Notes

1. Emonts was particularly adept at translating his mission experiences into fictionalized accounts, including one book entitled *The Witch Doctor of the Bahiri,* trans. Francis Scheper (Sainte Marie, IL: Society of the Priests of the Sacred Heart, n.d.).

2. *Mission Call* 1 (January–February 1929): 1.

3. Pinger, Alexander, Miller, Porter, and Noonan, letter to Reverend and Dear Father Provincial, Feast of St. Francis de Sales (1950).

4. Ibid.

5. Editorial board minutes, 13–16 June 1955, Archives of the Priests of the Sacred Heart of Jesus.

6. *Reign of the Sacred Heart* 28 (January 1956): title page.

7. Ibid. 33 (April 1961): 26–28.

8. Letter of Mrs. Leo Hassler of Staples, Minnesota, *Reign of the Sacred Heart* 34 (August 1962): 1.

9. Letter of Mrs. Mary Hatfield, *Reign of the Sacred Heart* 35 (January 1963): 1.

Information Sources

INDEX SOURCES: None of the issues is indexed.

LOCATION SOURCES: The only complete collection of *Reign of the Sacred Heart* can be found at the Archives of the Priests of the Sacred Heart, P.O. Box 289, Hales Corners, Wisconsin 53130-0289.

Publication History

MAGAZINE TITLE AND TITLE CHANGES: *Mission Call* (1929–1949); *COR* (1949–1956); *Reign of the Sacred Heart* (1956–present).

VOLUME AND ISSUE DATA: 1:1 (January–February 1929)–present. Published monthly, with some numbers published together.

PUBLISHER AND PLACE OF PUBLICATION: Priests of the Sacred Heart, Sacred Heart Monastery, Hales Corners, Wisconsin.

EDITORS: John Emonts (1929–1933), Richard Kiefer (1933–1942), Charles Keilmann and Charles Talsky (1942–1948), George Pinger (1948–1961), Howard Melzer (1961–1965), Frank Wessling (1965–1967), Linus Merz (1967–1985), Brian McCullough (1985–present).

CIRCULATION: 523,000 (1993).

Steven M. Avella

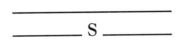

S

ST. JUDE. *See* U.S. CATHOLIC

SALVATIONIST. *See* WAR CRY

SECOND ADVENT REVIEW AND SABBATH HERALD. *See* ADVENTIST REVIEW

SOJOURNERS

In the early summer of 1971, seven students answered a notice posted on the bulletin boards at the Trinity Evangelical Divinity School in Deerfield, Illinois, offering free housing for the summer in exchange for a paint job. Once they moved in, the group referred to their new summer residence as the "Jolly Green Giant house," since the owner, a radio disc jockey, provided the infamous "ho, ho, ho" for the oversized purveyor of vegetables. Besides painting, their summer activities included putting together the first issue of what would later become *Sojourners*.

Each of the seven had scraped together one hundred dollars to cover publication expenses. When the content of the journal reached a satisfactory form, several of them stayed up all night typesetting and proofreading in the dilapidated office of an underground Chicago newspaper. Their childlike excitement for the project overshadowed any frustration they might otherwise have experienced because of their work space, largely defined by an archaic typesetter, deafening band noise emanating from the singles' bar immediately beneath them, and the regular passing of the elevated train just fifteen feet outside the nearest window.

The seven students, all male, had met the year before. In the time since, their protests concerning the Vietnam War and other of the group's activities had already attracted the attention of the Federal Bureau of Investigation (FBI) and caused the seminary's dean to express concern about the declining status of financial gifts to the traditionally conservative evangelical seminary. These reactions only reinforced the solidarity forming among these individuals.

The idea for the magazine had grown slowly out of the group's general dissatisfaction with traditional forms of church and a growing belief that seminary was irrelevant to the work that lay ahead of them. They gathered regularly at Bill's Pub, "where the peanuts were free and the beer two dollars a pitcher." One night the waitress had difficulty finding a place to deposit the beer because she found them "all bowed in intense prayer, hands locked across their table."[1] These were not average evangelicals. Soon they began to forge a common vision that, since those days, has provided a considerable catalyst for change within the evangelical community.

With the seven hundred dollars collected for the first issue, the group paid for the printing of thirty thousand copies. With no mailing list in hand, they decided to have some of the group head west, while others headed east, each individual hand-delivering copies to colleges, universities, seminaries, and churches encountered along the way. Published initially as a sixteen-page quarterly tabloid on newsprint, the first issue announced a subscription cost of "$2.00 or whatever you can to help cover our expenses."[2] The cover carried a post-Crucifixion depiction of Jesus robed with an American flag with the words " . . . and they crucified him" printed beneath it. The image conveyed the meaning that American Christianity, because of the complete surrender of the Church to American culture, had crucified Jesus anew.

As exemplified by its initial name, the *Post-American*, the magazine asserted its belief that Christians in America needed to assume a radical stance about the American status quo, "an American system that we regard as oppressive; a society whose values are corrupt and destructive." Jim Wallis, the journal's first and continuing editor, summarized the perspective and mission of the magazine in the final words of the lead editorial of that first issue:

Christians must be active in rejecting the values of our corrupt society, radical in our resistance and activism against the injustice of a racist society, warfare state, and materialistic system. We must be people of God, "salt and light," those of a new order who live by the values and ethical priorities of Jesus Christ and His kingdom. We must be radical disciples applying the comprehensive Christian message to all areas of life, culture, and human need—committed to reconciliation, justice, peace and faith which is distinctly Post-American.[3]

To describe the history of *Sojourners* accurately, one must recognize that the magazine itself grew out of a particular community; for the most part, it has been rooted in the inner history of that community. In the beginning, the community was small and mostly interested in producing literature to challenge the "cultural captivity of the church." The *Post-American* provided a focal point for the individuals associated with it, and a deeper sense of their community with each other started to grow.

In the spring of 1972, around a dozen members of the growing group, now including married couples and single women, made a deliberate commitment to live together in an apartment building and work toward justice in an impoverished area of north Chicago. The students among them, who were alienated by their experiences in school, left the seminary. "Doing theology," as they put it, was more important than learning it. They formed a nonprofit corporation, the Peoples' Christian Coalition, in order to provide a legal organization for both the magazine and the number of community ministries that grew up around it. Though neighborhood ministries were formed and experienced a measure of success, and though the magazine continued to mature in terms of both its reputation and its content, the initial experiments at community failed miserably over the next two years.

Upon reflection, the editors decided the cause for failure resulted from the dominant belief that the key to community rested in finding the proper structure for it. Members of the community argued over competitive structural visions. Ego struggles became prominent, and the community slowly degenerated, until, finally, it disbanded altogether. Jim Wallis and Joe Roos constituted the only staff for the magazine during the months after the fragmentation. Depressed about their failure but carrying on, even though they felt they had little to say to their readers anymore, they moved in 1974, along with three others, into Uptown, a poor, racially mixed community on the north side of Chicago. In Wallis's words: "There was a real gulf between our concern for healing and justice in the world and the brokenness of the life that we shared with one another. In our apartment we didn't talk of community or use the word. We just felt a desperate need to turn to God in a way we had never done before. We just began to pray together."[4]

While in Uptown, a contrite spirit enabled some of the old members to return, and several new members joined the group. In the summer of 1975, largely because of an encounter with Graham Pulkingham, minister at the Church of the Redeemer, a conservative Episcopal parish in Houston, Jim Wallis and the others decided they needed to give as much attention to the pastoral dimensions of their lives together as they gave to their prophetic ministry. At the same time, Uptown found itself in the midst of a transformation as numbers of young, upwardly mobile types moved into the area, rapidly displacing the poor. As a result of these changes both within the neighborhood and within their own understanding of ministry, Wallis and about fourteen other adults, accompanied by four children, decided in the fall of 1975 to move the whole base of their operations to Washington, D.C., "an environment characterized by urban conflict and the idolatry of political power."[5] Such a location suited their newfound interest in wedding more carefully the pastoral dimensions of Christian faith to the prophetic aspects of Christian witness.

In addition to the decision to move, the editorial staff decided to change the name of the magazine from the *Post-American* to *Sojourners*. The rationale behind the change explained that the original name had been "too narrow" and too easily misunderstood. *Sojourners*, on the other hand, was "one of the central biblical metaphors for the people of God who are to live in the world as strangers, pilgrims, aliens, and sojourners because of their loyalty to the kingdom of God, because of their identity as those who have entered into a new order of things."[6] The name, with its inherent sense of being on a journey, captures well the essence of the magazine and the people associated with it. Spearheading a movement more than founding an institution, *Sojourners* and its community have changed considerably over the years.

In the early years, editorial arrogance and antiestablishment self-righteousness marred the magazine's call for a radical form of Christianity. The editorial staff seemed blind to their own cultural limitations and believed wholeheartedly that their approach to faith, the life of the Christian, the work of the Church, and the radical interpretation of social questions marked a new turning point in the history of Christianity. In short, they took themselves a bit too seriously. Perhaps this weakness was also a strength. There seems little doubt that passion for their mission and for their own sense of self-importance saw them through times when lesser-committed people would most surely have given up.

Early issues of the magazine condemned the American church for its sanctioning of civil religion, U.S. involvement in Vietnam, and economic and racial oppression. The duplicity of the Church in these matters made the established Church a lost cause, needing to be replaced by something else. The magazine sought the recovery of the Gospel and the renewal of the prophetic tradition willing to apply the teachings of Jesus as a judgment on the circumstances of contemporary life.

After failing in their own communal experiment, the editorial staff assumed genuine humility and an awareness of their own involvement in human sinfulness. They came to a more sophisticated understanding of the struggles of the Church in history. They began to see connections between their own renewal movement and the actions of other Christians through time. They appreciated more fully the revival movements of eighteenth-century England and nineteenth-century America as those movements witnessed against industrial exploitation and slavery. In seeking connections with the Franciscans, Anabaptists, and other renewal movements, these editors found new ways to affirm the history and life of the Church.[7] The resistance demanded by the magazine took on a new form, one more anxious to celebrate what it means to be the people of God in the world.[8]

The move to Washington in the fall of 1975 symbolically points to the emergence of a more mature magazine. The staff added a professional art director, a book review editor, a copy editor, and a film and arts editor. The graphic design and readability of *Sojourners* improved considerably. New departments, called "The Crucible," "Common Life," and "Seeds," attempted to address happenings and events in the life of the Church and local Christian communities in a way lacking in previous years. As a result of a direct mail campaign conducted in 1976, subscriptions soared from five thousand to twenty-five thousand by the end of 1977, a phenomenal accomplishment. From 1978 to the mid–1980s, the number of subscribers grew to just over fifty thousand, though the figure is closer to thirty thousand at this writing.

The drop may be the direct result of a tough economy. The magazine has always had a basic appeal to readers in low-income brackets, those who suffer most when the economy turns sour. It may also have something to do with the consistency and forcefulness of the magazine's message. Lindsey McLaughlin, a staff member at the magazine in the early 1980s, once posted the following sentence, under the title of "The Sojourners Dilemma," on the office bulletin board: "Editors should avoid articles that are repetitive, redundant, and say the same things over and over, but repetition is the key to social change."[9] Though the statement was posted, no doubt, with a tongue-in-cheek mentality, it actually may have offered a prophetic insight into why subscriptions have fallen off so drastically in recent years.

Sojourners's readership has always been varied and ecumenical. The magazine's cutting-edge social stance, accompanied as it is by a certainty of faith's relevance to public issues, attracts a fairly impressive readership from mainstream Protestantism. The magazine's historical concern, as it began to appear in the late 1970s, for contemplative spirituality, in the tradition of Thomas Merton, and for a socially active spirituality, reminiscent of Dorothy Day's Catholic Worker movement, continues to bring it a good number of Catholic readers. Its essentially conservative theology hooks many evangelical Christians, just as its joining of this element to an active quest for social justice attracts many other evangelicals who hunger for these types of connections. Its deep respect for the Mennonite tradition, especially its pacifist witness, and the regular contributions of John Howard Yoder to its pages have also won the allegiance of a good many Anabaptist readers.

The editors have accumulated a list of contributors who no doubt have helped to cultivate the magazine's loyal ecumenical audience. Though most of these contributors have been within the ranks of an arguably "evangelical" theology, broadly considered, their denominational allegiances and backgrounds are quite varied. Included among this group, in addition to Yoder, are Clark Pinnock, the only seminary professor at Trinity to back the early enterprise, Senator Mark O. Hatfield, Richard Pierard, William Stringfellow, Dale W. Brown, John R. Stott, Donald W. Dayton, Dan Berrigan, Walter Brueggemann, Virginia R. Mollenkott, Will Campbell, Henri Nouwen, Allen Boesak, and Garry Wills. In the last few years, the list of contributing editors has begun to include minorities and women, James H. Cone and Rosemary Radford Ruether, for example, who are less directly connected to evangelical roots than earlier persons on the list. The social voice of protest associated with *Sojourners* is well known. Though a latecomer (1971) as an official protest organ concerning Vietnam, the magazine quickly became a powerful voice against the war. It joined the battle for minority civil rights and supported women's rights from its beginning, though its awareness and acceptance of the full implications of "evangelical feminism" have been somewhat slower in developing.[10] The evangelical theological perspective behind the magazine no doubt contributes to this tardiness. Most certainly, evangelical foundations have made it difficult for editors to take strong stances with regard to issues of sexuality, particularly homosexuality, which they failed to mention substantively until the mid–1980s, when treatment clearly fell along conservative lines, angering some of the magazine's readers.[11] Though the magazine in July 1991 finally treated all sides of the issue, the editors themselves begged the question of where they personally stood on homosexuality.[12]

Unwillingness to take a stand is most unusual in the magazine's history. Found sprinkled throughout its pages are cogent criticisms of a capitalist economy and perceptive analyses of both the political situations in Latin America and the inadequate American response to them. Nuclear energy and nuclear weapons, global hunger, urban decline, gun control, the death penalty, tax resistance, human rights, sanctuary, apartheid, and countless other such topics have regularly graced these pages. On each of these issues, the magazine has argued the side generally associated with a "liberal" social viewpoint.

Editors continue to grow in their awareness of both new issues and the widening implications of old ones. The last decade has brought ecological concerns to the front burner, finally resulting in the magazine's use of recycled paper and soy-based ink. More recently, the editors have discovered the importance of nutrition and now regularly offer a column on food, entitled "Simple Feast," emphasizing an "environmentally rooted perspective."[13]

Since its arrival in Washington in the fall of 1975, the community's ministries have shifted from an emphasis on providing services to one of active, systematic political engagement with a view toward the empowerment of the oppressed. Beginning with the development of a large day-care ministry for neighborhood children and a major food program, the ministry of the community has expanded into a complete Neighborhood Center Building and the formation of a housing union to fight "gentrification" (wealthy displacement of the poor) in Washington's neighborhoods.

The *Sojourners* community in Washington, D.C., has consistently been concerned to practice what it preaches. Associates of the magazine have regularly conducted protest marches or vigils and have tried to withhold the portion of their taxes designated for weapons or defense. In years past, most salaries at the magazine were well below taxable rates. Everyone directly related to the *Sojourners* community lives fairly simply, occasionally sharing resources and income. The magazine remains supported mostly by reader donations and subscriptions and rarely has enough money in the bank to last three weeks.[14] With falling subscriptions, monetary pressures are reaching serious proportions. In response, the magazine has issued a recent call to its readers to "join" the *Sojourners* network rather than simply "subscribe" to the magazine.

Mounting financial pressure has renewed editorial emphasis on the long-held truism that *Sojourners* is "more than a magazine." The goal of *Sojourners* in the 1990s is to make the "extended community" it has always touted more of a connected reality, in terms of both the development of a truly national ministry (not the same as a "national organization") and an accompanying, wide-ranging base of financial support for its various manifestations, including, of course, the magazine. As Wallis put it in an early 1992 essay:

Sojourners is more than a magazine; we are a community-based network with the feel of a family.
Sojourners doesn't want to become a national organization; we want to help link the organizations who [*sic*] could be working together more fruitfully.
Sojourners certainly doesn't want to become a new denomination; we want to help unite the forces of radical renewal in all of them. *Sojourners* isn't the movement; we want to serve one—connect it, nurture it, and help prepare for its fuller emergence.[15]

Few objective observers could deny the influence this magazine has exercised in the last twenty years, especially in the nurturing of the social conscience and activity of the evangelical community. Perhaps, however, the most significant dimension of *Sojourners'* work resides elsewhere. One could argue that the real contribution of this periodical has resulted from its mid–1970s shift away from advocating faithful Christian resistance to culture as a strategy in and of itself toward the more reflective posture of defining an active Christian resistance born of personal and communal spiritual discipline and emerging from the midst of a responsible Christian community. The greatest contribution of the journal probably lies in its ability to hold concern for both spirituality and political action together. Its popular appeal results from a growing ability to demonstrate, more explicitly than most other religious journals, that worship and ethics belong together, that personal healing and pastoral nurture in a community are inevitably connected to the "prophetic imperatives of biblical faith."[16]

Notes

1. Joyce Hollyday, "A Little History," *Sojourners* 10:9 (24 September 1981): 24.
2. See *Post-American* 1:1 (Fall 1971): back page.
3. "Post-American Christianity," *Post-American* 1:1 (Fall 1971): 2.
4. "Crucible of Community," an interview, *Sojourners* 6:1 (January 1977): 18.
5. Jim Wallis, "The Move to Washington, D.C.," *Post-American* 4:7 (August–September, 1975): 4.
6. Jim Wallis, "Sojourners," *Post-American* 4:8 (October–November, 1975): 3.
7. These types of connections are expressly made in Jim Wallis, "Ten Years," ibid. 4; and 10:9 (August–September 1991): idem, "For Still the Vision Awaits Its Time: Reflections on Sojourners' 20 Years," *Sojourners* 20:7 (August/September 1991): 12.
8. See, for example, "Crucible of Community," 21.
9. Hollyday, "A Little History," 26.

10. See, for example, Jackie Sabath, "From Principles to Partnership: A History of Male-Female Relationships at Sojourners," *Sojourners* 9:7 (July 1980): 19–21.

11. See Richard J. Foster, "God's Gift of Sexuality," *Sojourners* 14:7 (July 1985): 14–19; the Sojourners Community, "Listening Together," *Sojourners* 15:11 (December 1986): 37. See reader response during the months between these two particular issues.

12. See *Sojourners* 20:6 (July 1991).

13. Jim Wallis, "The New Year at Sojourners," *Sojourners* 21:1 (January 1992): 4.

14. See Joe Roos, "Keeping the Vision Afloat," *Sojourners* 20:7 (August–September 1991): 12.

15. "Keeping Faith, Doing Justice, Building Community," *Sojourners* 21:2 (February–March, 1992): 17.

16. Wallis, "Self-Portrait of a Church in the City," *Sojourners* 6:1 (January 1977): 3.

Information Sources

INDEX SOURCES: *Religious Periodicals, Religion Index One, Christian Periodical Index, Current Christian Abstracts, CERDIC, Media Review Digest, Political Science Abstract, Human Rights Internet Reporter, Peace Research Abstract, Alternative Press Index, Family Resources Database*, and *Religious and Theological Abstracts*.

LOCATION SOURCES: Available on microfilm from the American Theological Library Association, 820 Church Street, Suite 300, Evanston, Illinois 60201–3707, and from University Microfilms International, 300 N. Zeeb Road, Ann Arbor, Michigan 48106.

Publication History

MAGAZINE TITLE AND TITLE CHANGES: *Post-American* (1971–1975), *Sojourners* (1976–present).

VOLUME AND ISSUE DATA: *Post-American*: 1–4 (1971–1975), number of issues per year varies; *Sojourners*: 5 (1976–present), number of issues per year varies (usually ten issues).

PUBLISHER AND PLACE OF PUBLICATION: Institute of Christian Thought, Deerfield, Illinois (1971–1973); The People's Christian Coalition, Chicago, Illinois (1974–1975); Washington, D.C. (1976–June 1977); Joe Roos, Washington, D.C. (July 1977–present).

EDITOR: Jim Wallis (1971–present).

CIRCULATION: 30,000 (mid–1992).

Mark G. Toulouse

SOUTHERN PRESBYTERIAN. *See* PRESBYTERIAN OF THE SOUTH

SOUTHWESTERN CHRISTIAN ADVOCATE. *See* UNITED METHODIST REPORTER

SOUTHWESTERN CHRISTIAN RECORDER. *See* CHRISTIAN
RECORDER

SOUTHWEST FRIEND. *See* EVANGELICAL FRIEND

SPIRIT OF MISSIONS

For a century the pages of the *Spirit of Missions* revealed the changing nature
of the Episcopal Church's identity. Founded in 1836 at a formative moment in
the Church's life, the *Spirit of Missions*' content evolved as Episcopalians
adapted their Church to the shifting course of American society. Succeeded in
1939 by *Forth*, which was followed, in turn, by the *Episcopalian* in 1960, the
Spirit of Missions served as the first and longest-standing publication designed
to express the Episcopal Church's official mind. Indeed, the appearance of this
monthly journal was evidence that the Episcopal Church had emerged from its
colonial past and revolutionary rubble to achieve a secure American presence.

The Episcopal Church reached North America as a colonial outpost of the
Church of England. Between 1607 and 1776 the Church achieved admirable
levels of parish organization in most colonies and, in such places as Virginia
and South Carolina, considerable diocesan organization in becoming a colonial
religious establishment. New England Anglicans were notable for their success
in planting the church of the Crown amid a Puritan establishment. But overall
North American structure was lacking, and colonial bishops were never chosen.
The Church technically remained under the authority of the bishop of London,
a linkage that crippled the Church after the American Revolution.[1] Until it could
distinguish itself from English control, but not English precedent, the Church's
American future seemed dim.

In the wake of the American Revolution, articulate individuals, such as Samuel Seabury and William White, combined to create an American structure. The
Episcopal Church would be led by bishops overseeing the various dioceses and
meeting regularly in their own house, but governed bicamerally through a triennial general convention. Elected clergy and lay representatives from each diocese would share legislative authority with their bishops in a structure much
like that of the American Congress.[2] Nevertheless, the creation of a national
structure did not endow the Episcopal Church with national purpose. That sense
of purpose emerged over the first third of the nineteenth century, culminating
in the appearance of the *Spirit of Missions*.

Mission was the idea that lent Episcopalians an American identity. In 1821
the general convention produced a constitution officially naming the Church
"The Domestic and Foreign Missionary Society of the Protestant Episcopal
Church in the United States of America." Church leaders, following the example
of English missionary societies, determined that the Church must be no mere
confederation of dioceses but a nationally organized mission body. The general
convention also created a thirty-member Board of Missions and, in 1835, the

post of missionary bishop, who was authorized to organize the Church in large frontier areas. Jackson Kemper, the first missionary bishop, became one of the Episcopal Church's great leaders. For a generation he led the Church's growth in what became Illinois, Indiana, Missouri, Iowa, and Wisconsin. Kemper embodied the Episcopal Church's American identity in that he was both bishop and missionary. Thus, he stood for ancient precedent, which the Episcopal Church construes in a catholic way, and he represented the challenge of the American environment, especially the necessity of adapting to the American frontier.[3]

Initially, the spirit of Episcopal missions was broad and undifferentiated. It was not restricted to America, because Episcopalians felt they shared a global responsibility with their English counterparts, as Anglican mission grew generally. Over time, American Episcopalians sensed that certain mission fields, notably Africa, were not their prerogative, because of the solidification of British imperial control. What made their missionary style truly American, from an Anglican point of view, was that the bishops were elected—as opposed to the British and colonial system of Crown appointment—and that the American Church was, since the American Revolution, governed synodically. Again, synodical rule grew gradually in British colonial territories, for example, New Zealand and Australia and South Africa, and emerged very slowly in England itself. American Episcopal polity was from the beginning synodical and popular. American Episcopalians were the first Anglicans to adapt English governance to democratic circumstances.[4]

The first half of the nineteenth century was a period of rapid growth. Along with the new dioceses created by westward missionary expansion, the Church founded schools and colleges across the continent. Episcopalian missions went beyond making converts or mere numerical growth. The Church viewed itself as an ecclesiastical ethos seeking to infuse Christian values into national life. The appearance of the *Spirit of Missions* in 1836 represented the achievement of a national sense of Episcopal mission. The Church "is the trustee for the world," the pages of the *Spirit of Missions* declared in 1856. "All parts of the world are now open to the missionaries of the cross, and we are invited to enter and occupy them."[5] Episcopalians determined to seize this opportunity to preach the Gospel throughout the world.

Before the American Civil War, the pages of the *Spirit of Missions* illustrated the wide scope of Episcopal missions and the effort's increasing organization. Lists of subscribers, some individuals but many local and parish committees, suggest that this work began at the grass roots. The *Spirit of Missions* took care to note local committee activity and to reprint missionary sermons from regional meetings. The magazine served as a meeting ground for mission, juxtaposing committee business with missionary reports from the domestic and foreign fields. Foreign missions were a high priority between 1836 and 1865. Missions to Greece, Persia, Africa, and China were newly organized and actively reviewed. In each case, energetic individuals began Episcopal worship services and elementary schools. Bibles and religious tracts for distribution were shipped by the domestic board, and plans to translate religious materials into the local idiom advanced. Foreign missions achieved a high profile, though the scale of this work remained small.

Domestic missions along America's burgeoning frontier received just as much attention. "I want words adequately, to express my sense of the liberality and kindness which the Committee have manifested in the appropriations made to this diocese," wrote Bishop James Otey of Tennessee in the journal's second issue.[6] Domestic work from the start had features unlike foreign work. In frontier areas, Episcopalians who had migrated westward were often found, though often in small numbers. The Church sought out the "leading citizens" in new towns and quickly identified local resources for building churches and inaugurating programs. Native Americans, especially in the upper Midwest, attracted special interest as missionaries labored to translate the Bible and the Book of Common Prayer into indigenous languages. Reports of this work appeared monthly in the *Spirit of Missions*, concluding with pleas for additional funds and missionary clergy.

The American Civil War received scant mention in the *Spirit of Missions*. The Church experienced an unofficial split during the conflict but reunited seamlessly within months of the peace and rededicated itself to mission. Nevertheless, changes in the direction of the Church's work began to appear in the *Spirit of Missions*. The scope of the Church's work in Africa receded to focus upon Liberia, where a teacher training college grew impressively. "An important branch of missionary work is to train natives as *teachers, interpreters,* and *catechists,* who can take charge of out-stations, as well as assist the foreign missionary." Thus, the Church paved the way for an indigenous church with its own leadership.[7] In China a similar deepening of commitment was apparent as Samuel Isaac Joseph Schereschewsky, Episcopal missionary, translated the Bible into Mandarin, a major step in the search for an indigenous Chinese Christianity. John Liggins and Channing Moore Williams made the Church one of the first Protestant denominations to reach Japan, where it achieved cultural influence far beyond its numbers. Meanwhile Episcopal work in Greece and Persia declined.

The domestic mission effort became diversified in the late 1860s as programs for freed slaves in the South emerged. On the pages of the *Spirit of Missions*, one reads of the Freedmen's Commission of the Episcopal Church. With the end of hostilities, Episcopalians awakened to the social and religious needs of millions of people. "Never was so large a body of men placed in a condition so critical, both as to themselves and as to the nation of which they are part." The southern social system under which they labored was morally corrupt, but slaves had been freed without regard for their economic survival. "A free and yet ignorant and debased race cannot exist in the vitals of the body-politic without the most fearful risks." Episcopalians created schools to equip this uprooted population for skilled jobs.[8] Across the South a number of schools appeared, several of which (St. Paul's, St. Augustine's, and Voorhees) remain as distinguished colleges.

By 1872 a variety of domestic groups required the Church's ministry. In a missionary sermon highlighted in the *Spirit of Missions*, Bishop J. B. Kerfoot of Pittsburgh cited the changing face of national life and urged that there was "much more we *could* and ought to have done as a Church in conquering this land." Episcopalians, the journal revealed, felt their mandate was to adjust the Anglican form of worship and governance to the values and procedures of American political democracy. Kerfoot noted that sixty thousand Chinese persons were now in America; "in some way the Church, as well as the Nation, must meet this strange fact of Chinese immigration. Strange, indeed, are the lot and the resulting duties of this nation. Men of almost every race settle among us."[9] Soon reports of Episcopal work among these immigrants appeared in the *Spirit of Missions*.

"The long and sad tale of civil, social and religious mismanagement and wrong in the history of our Indian tribes need not be gone over now," Kerfoot added. "It is . . . more inspiring to say that in this thing the Nation as well as the Church seems really awakening to our common duty; that even this arousing of the national mind and conscience is due largely to faithful monitions going out from this Church."[10] Episcopalians called for equitable treatment of native Americans and became influential in work among the Sioux and Navajo.

In many cases this effort was staffed by the Episcopal Church's women. Church work by and among women became prominent in the second half of the nineteenth century. Citing ancient example, the *Spirit of Missions* called for "the restoration of a ministry of women, in due subordination to the higher ministries of the Church."[11] Perhaps the most apparent change in the conduct of Episcopal Church mission in the late nineteenth century was the organization of work led by women and the high profile given this effort. Monthly columns in the *Spirit of Missions* told of women's ability to raise funds and to create new programs. Restricted in the ways they could exercise leadership, Episcopal women became teachers and social workers, often using existing parishes as bases, sometimes breaking ground in new foreign and domestic mission fields. By the early twentieth century the Church's mission relied heavily upon women's initiative.

The rapid development of the women's auxiliary at the national level gave evidence of a process that reshaped the entire Episcopal Church. The *Spirit of Missions* began with a concern to unite Episcopalians in a shared sense of mission. By the end of the twentieth century the Church had become a centralized organization prizing professional training among its leaders. A gradual shift was under way, as monthly speeches and reports revealed. Mission became less the prerogative of lonely individuals breaking ground in new locales and more the product of elaborate programs run by highly organized committees responsible to staff persons at the Church's New York offices. Mission ceased to be a shared spirit and became routinized programs operating according to standards derived from business and government. Monthly news in the journal's pages tended to be official reports of fund-raising and administration. The Church had become a complex organization.

However, Bishop Kerfoot's concern to make the Church ethnically diverse remained a primary goal. The *Spirit of Missions* affords insightful perspective on America's changing social conditions from the late nineteenth to the early twentieth centuries. Month after month, astute reports on urban slums, industrial conditions, and changing immigration patterns appeared. The Church's concerns were of impressive scope. One reads of early ministry to Hispanic populations, in the Caribbean, and among Alaskan Eskimos. Occasional questions were raised about American influence in Cuba, Puerto Rico, and the Philippines. Calls for ameliorative foreign and domestic policies were common features of monthly news. Mission became a counterpoint to the Church's accommodation to the business world. Identification with diverse cultures assured Episcopalians that they adequately represented the breadth of God's creation.

For a century the *Spirit of Missions* traced the changing face of the Episcopal Church's mission. Its format featured reports of committee activity and news of missionary advance. By the end of the 1930s, however, a different format seemed required. Episcopalians, like most Americans, had less time to read and required a magazine rather than a journal. Larger print, more photographs, fewer pages, and bold headlines replaced the *Spirit of Mission*'s roughly fifty pages of vertical columns containing elaborate reports with few illustrations. Yet, its successor, *Forth*, promised to continue what had been set out a century before: the Episcopal conviction that mission sustains a living body, the Church.

Notes

1. See John Woolverton, *Colonial Anglicanism* (Detroit: Wayne State University Press, 1984).

2. See Frederick V. Mills, Sr., *Bishops By Ballot* (New York: Oxford University Press, 1978).

3. See James Thayer Addison, *The Episcopal Church in the United States, 1789–1931* (Hamden, CT: Archon, 1969).

4. See William L. Sachs, *The Transformation of Anglicanism* (Cambridge, England: Cambridge University Press, 1993).

5. *Spirit of Missions* 1:12 (November–December 1856): 529.

6. Ibid. 1:2 (February 1836): 82.

7. Ibid. 29:5 (May 1864): 118.

8. Ibid. 31:1 (June 1866): 43.

9. Ibid. 37:1 (January 1872): 12.

10. Ibid.

11. Ibid. 37:2 (February 1872): 91.

Information Sources

INDEX SOURCES: Each volume contains a thorough index. A general index, published in 1902, covers 1836–1902.

LOCATION SOURCES: A complete set of the *Spirit of Missions* can be found at the Archives of the Episcopal Church, at the Episcopal Seminary of the Southwest, Austin, Texas. Virtually complete sets may be found at the Virginia Theological Seminary, Alexandria, Virginia, and at the General Theological Seminary, New York City.

Publication History

MAGAZINE TITLE AND TITLE CHANGES: *Spirit of Missions* (1836–1938); absorbed by *Forth* (January 1939).

VOLUME AND ISSUE DATA: 1:1 (January 1836)–103:12 (December 1938). Published monthly.

PUBLISHER AND PLACE OF PUBLICATION: Episcopal Church, New York City offices. No one person served as publisher.

EDITORS: None listed (1836–1922); Robert F. Gibson (June 1922–November 1923); G. Warfield Hobbs (December 1923–1939).

CIRCULATION: Unknown.

William L. Sachs

SPOTLIGHT. *See* INTERPRETER

SUNDAY MAGAZINE. *See* CHRISTIAN LIFE

SWORD OF THE LORD

Following a series of highly visible public embarrassments of fundamentalists in the 1920s (most notably in the Scopes trial at Dayton, Tennessee, in 1925), fundamentalists spent the decade of the 1930s regrouping. That regrouping took the form of establishing new institutions for education and new publishing enterprises for the dissemination of the fundamentals of the Christian faith. In 1934 evangelist John R. Rice launched one such enterprise with his weekly newspaper, *Sword of the Lord.*

Rice grounded his position and that of his newspaper on two essential pillars. First, he firmly believed in soul winning. The greatest need of the Church and of individuals, he thought, was fundamental faith in Jesus Christ. Meeting that need entailed "a vigorous defense of the faith, active soul winning, great New Testament-type local churches going abroad to save multitudes, having fervent love for all of God's people."[1] The second pillar, inseparable from the first, was the admonition to "earnestly avoid compromise in doctrine of yoking up with unbelievers."[2] The forty-six years Rice spent as editor and publisher of *Sword of the Lord* from the inception of the newspaper in 1934 until his death in 1980 were ardently devoted to the upholding of those two pillars.

Rice used the paper not only as a forum for his views and those of like-minded Christians but also to publicize the hundreds of books he authored and published under the aegis of Sword of the Lord Publications and to promote "Sword of the Lord" Bible conferences and retreats. In conjunction with the latter, Rice's paper ran a regular feature highlighting his own schedule of revival meetings as well as those of other acceptable itinerating evangelists, presumably so that readers could take note of appearances in their area and bring their friends and neighbors.[3]

The acceptability of the evangelist was a crucial consideration. The "vigorous defense of the faith" and the earnest avoidance of compromise inevitably led to controversies between Rice and other fundamentalists. Rice's newspaper at no time shrank from controversy, often taking positions illustrating the axiom that the best defense is a good offense. As a result, issues of *Sword of the Lord* tend to alternate between an emphasis on gentle nurture and strident polemic.

In the realm of gentle nurture, *Sword*, which is still being published, contains such regular columns as "With the Evangelists: Reports from America's Outstanding Soul Winners," "This Week's Illustrations and Quotes," and "For Young People—Miracles of Science." Rice's own column and the articles he contributed often emphasized the positive aspects of redemption and offered to believers comforting words of assurance in addition to providing the schedules of evangelistic events where their faith might be bolstered.

Rice's concerns extended to the pastors who subscribed to his paper as well. *Sword* ran a series of contests in the 1950s inviting pastors to contribute evangelistic sermons. Another contest sought "Sermons on Vital Public Issues." In addition to offering the honor of seeing the sermon printed in *Sword of the Lord*, the public issues contest carried a total of sixteen hundred dollars in prizes; in 1954 the winner of the evangelistic sermon contest received a cash prize of one thousand dollars.[4]

Another creative invitation enlisted pastors as salesmen of the paper. In an effort to push the circulation of the paper above the two hundred thousand mark, the 16 April 1954 issue advertised a subscription campaign offering special low subscription rates to all preachers who presented *Sword of the Lord* to their congregations.[5]

The enlistment of pastors and the various offerings of comfort to the afflicted gave *Sword of the Lord* a personal tone. Readers were brought near to John R. Rice by means of his counsel to them. In addition, Rice's editorials often contained references to home and heart clearly intended to contribute an air of intimacy to the newspaper. Thus, Rice often reported family events to his readers in much the same way that such events would be covered by a small-town newspaper. In the same issue that announced the subscription drive, for example, Rice reported on the marriage of his fourth daughter. With no small measure of parental pride, Rice reported, "All of our six daughters were won to Christ by the time they were six years old."[6] Such intimate matters, intimately reported, contribute to the personal style of the paper. John R. Rice was in control, but his control could appear benign, even pastoral. It is abundantly clear that Rice viewed his readership as a kind of extended congregation, for which he felt the desire and the calling to be a pastoral leader.

If the intimate nurturing articles reflect Rice's desire to provide comfort for the afflicted, his polemical attacks on any and all forms of "compromise of the faith" reflect his desire occasionally to afflict the comfortable. Among fundamentalists, the desire for purity has often led to rapidly changing alliances and startling turnabouts concerning individuals "gone astray" and institutions that have sacrificed the faith. As historian George Marsden has put it, fundamentalists have existed as a "loose, diverse, and changing federation of co-belligerents united by their fierce opposition to efforts to bring Christianity into line with modern thought."[7]

It is difficult to overestimate the degree of the changes that have taken place from time to time among fundamentalists, and perhaps no periodical better illustrates the acrimonious nature of those changes than *Sword of the Lord*, especially during its heyday in the 1940s and 1950s.

John R. Rice was among the founders of the National Association of Evangelicals in 1942, but by the end of the 1950s he self-consciously kept his distance from the "neo-evangelicals." Rice was a friend, promoter, and defender of Billy Graham when Graham began his public ministry, but by 1957 Graham was a target of Rice's invective. Rice was once a friend of Bob Jones and his university, but they, too, fell out from one another in the 1970s. Thus, even as *Sword of the Lord* demonstrated a consistent pastoral care for its readers, it also exhibited a consistent caution in determining just who its friends were and where they could be found.

Perhaps the most startling turnabout concerned Graham. Graham was on the "co-operating board" of *Sword of the Lord* through most of the 1950s, and Rice presented glowing accounts of Graham's crusades until the fateful New York City crusade of 1957. In a well-documented move, Graham decided to include representatives of groups involved in the National Council of Churches in planning and administering the crusade. Such cooperation amounted to a yoking with unbelievers, in Rice's view.[8] Rice's abrupt hostility toward Graham is all the more stunning when one considers the vigor with which Rice had defended Graham in the mid-1950s. One issue of *Sword* in 1956 featured a front-page headline declaring "Modern Critics Beset Fundamentalist Billy Graham."[9] Early in that same year, Rice noted a "modernist" attack on Graham: the modernists in question were those on the staff of the *Christian Century*.[10]

As noted, Graham was not the only object of Rice's scorn. In a matter-of-fact tone, the issue defending Graham against his "modern critics" also reported on the demise of a publishing house. That publisher had shown the temerity to publish a work known to bear the "curse of God." Considering some of the authors who were writing in the 1950s and some of the books published then, one would expect to see a secular publisher of some secular work. Instead, the accursed work is *True Christianity*, a book written by the longtime president of theologically conservative Dallas Theological Seminary, Lewis Sperry Chafer. Rice reported that the publisher, Dunham Publishing House, made a fateful decision in accepting the book for publication. The book bears its curse because of Chafer's "ultra-Calvinist" theology and because of Chafer's stance against evangelism and evangelistic preaching. According to Rice, Dunham Publishing House was doomed to become the fourth publisher victimized by the curse upon the book.[11]

Rice's polemics could be vitriolic and personal, but, in general, Rice steered clear of political issues. There are exceptions to his reticence to inject political issues into the pages of *Sword*. Some are predictable: anger and shock at Supreme Court decisions on such matters as prayer in public schools and abortion and expressions of concern over the general moral decay of the nation. Similarly, it is not surprising that anticommunist rhetoric figures prominently in the 1950s. On the other hand, Rice's cautionary article on the legal landmark *Brown v. Board of Education* was a more drastic departure from the usual political quiescence. The decision was viewed as unnecessary by Rice, who feared that the decision signaled further government interference in such matters. Rice, like many of his readers, feared the potential for such outside agitation.[12]

For Rice, political quietism was prudent, since there was trouble enough in matters of religion. Whether the concern was dancing at Furman, Stetson, or Florida Baptist Universities; the drift of the ''old-line'' denominations toward modernism; the accuracy of the Revised Standard Version of the Bible; or any of literally dozens of other matters crucial to the foundations of the faith, Rice had little trouble finding alarms to raise to the attention of his readers.

Rice's propensity for sensing the drift of former friends away from the faith has been reciprocated by other fundamentalist leaders. In 1977 and 1978, Rice exchanged barbs with Bob Jones III when Jones expressed alarm over Rice's amicable relationship with such Southern Baptists as W. A. Criswell. The Southern Baptist Convention was, according to Jones, apostate, and Rice had to be shunned on account of his association with members of the group. Much as Graham's supporters did in the 1950s, Rice protested his innocence but was unable to appease Jones.[13]

Rice's death in 1980 came at a time when fundamentalism had again gained notable visibility in public life. Ironically, one of the leaders in the political activism of the ''new fundamentalism'' was Rice's protégé, Jerry Falwell. If Rice's pupil was more politically active than his mentor, his newspaper also showed an enhanced sense of political awareness under new leadership. The publisher retained the name *Sword of the Lord* and showed an increased willingness to wield the sword in the arena of public combat but by 1982 had to cut back to an every-other-week schedule of publication.

The circulation of a publication so linked with vitriolic rhetoric and so apt to find fault with a former ally is bound to fluctuate. The paper enjoyed its heyday in the 1950s. Before the turnabout concerning Billy Graham, circulation neared 250,000. At the time of Rice's death in 1980, it was about 135,000. Today, the circulation is about 120,000. Subscribers to *Sword of the Lord* may have been attracted initially to the folksy, parish-pastor style of John R. Rice, viewing Rice as someone close to them. Since Rice's death and coinciding with the politicization of fundamentalism, the readership has hovered at or near the same level, either because *Sword* is known as a purveyor of fundamentalist truth or because of continued loyalty and devotion to the memory of John R. Rice. Ultimately, there may be no difference between the two, since Rice's legacy is a legacy of earnestly contending for the faith as he understood it without compromise and with no loyalty greater than his loyalty to Christ.

Notes

1. John R. Rice, *I Am a Fundamentalist* (Murfreesboro, TN: Sword of the Lord Publications, 1975), 15.

2. Rice, *I Am a Fundamentalist*, 15.

3. There have been and are more features than those listed, but those listed are representative of the nurturing tone and Rice's overall emphasis on evangelism.

4. The winning evangelistic sermon for 1954 was by Merrill Tenney and was printed in the 9 April 1954 issue.

5. The details of the offer appear in *Sword* 21 (16 April 1954): 5.

6. Ibid. 4.

7. George M. Marsden, *Fundamentalism and American Culture: The Shaping of Twentieth Century Evangelicalism, 1870–1925* (New York: Oxford University Press, 1980), 4.

8. The year 1957, approximately, marks the emergence of "neo-evangelicalism," characterized by Graham, out of the broader, if loosely connected, group that emerged in the 1930s from the apparent wreckage of fundamentalism in the 1920s. See George Marsden, *Reforming Fundamentalism: Fuller Seminary and the New Evangelicalism* (Grand Rapids, MI: Eerdmans, 1987), especially 162–71; Joel A. Carpenter, "From Fundamentalism to the New Evangelical Coalition," in *Evangelicalism and Modern America*, ed. George M. Marsden (Grand Rapids, MI: Eerdmans, 1984).

9. *Sword* 23 (6 April 1956): 1.

10. "Modernists Attack Billy Graham," *Sword* 23 (27 January 1956): 2.

11. "Another Publisher Publishes Attack on Evangelism, Gets Ready to Go Broke," *Sword* 23 (6 April 1956): 2. The names of the publishers done in by the curse are not revealed in the article.

12. Rice argued that the decision in *Brown* was not alarming except insofar as some might try to use the decision to impose "forced associations" between the races.

13. See Bob Jones III, *Facts John R. Rice Will Not Face* (Greenville, SC: Bob Jones University Press, 1977); John R. Rice, "Here Is Historic Fundamentalism," *Sword* (22 September 1978): 7.

Information Sources

INDEX SOURCES: No index exists.

LOCATION SOURCES: The most readily available source is the microfilm collection prepared by the American Theological Library Association.

Publication History

MAGAZINE TITLE: *Sword of the Lord* (1934–present).
VOLUME AND ISSUE DATA: 1:1 (1934)–present. Published weekly 1934–1982, twice
      monthly since 1982.
PUBLISHER AND PLACE OF PUBLICATION: John R. Rice, Dallas Texas (1934–
      1940); Wheaton, Illinois (1940–1963); Murfreeboro, Tennessee (1963–1980);
      Curtis Hutson, Murfreesboro, Tennessee (1980–present).
CIRCULATION: 120,000 (1992).

W. Russell Congleton

SYNAGOGUE. *See* REFORMED JUDAISM

SYNAGOGUE SERVICE BULLETIN. *See* REFORMED JUDAISM

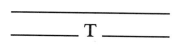

T

TEACHER'S COMPANION. *See* COVENANT COMPANION

TEXAS CHRISTIAN ADVOCATE. *See* UNITED METHODIST REPORTER

TEXAS CHRISTIAN ADVOCATE AND BRENHAM ADVERTISER. *See* UNITED METHODIST REPORTER

TEXAS METHODIST. *See* UNITED METHODIST REPORTER

TEXAS WESLEYAN BANNER. *See* UNITED METHODIST REPORTER

TODAY'S CHRISTIAN WOMAN

I asked the Lord to send me a friend. Little did I know He would send you. I've been a Christian almost three years, and I have many questions. Maybe now I'll find some answers.[1]

This was one woman's response to the first issue of *Today's Christian Woman* when it was published in the summer of 1978. Since then, *Today's Christian Woman* has striven to serve in that role of a friend to Christian women. This goal was still primary in the minds of the editors at the end of the 1980s. "We see TCW as a friend who comes to visit you every couple of months, just to talk and maybe help you cope with life a little better," wrote *Today's Christian Woman* editor Rebecca Grosenbach in 1989.[2] This philosophy of helping is still present in the current issues as evidenced by the large number of self-help articles, columns, and departments.

Today's Christian Woman was conceived and produced by three men. During the latter half of the 1970s, Jerry Jenkins, editor of *Moody Monthly* magazine at the Moody Bible Institute of Chicago, had been thinking about the need for a magazine designed exclusively for Christian women. "I was a dreamer in my late twenties, an entrepreneur with no cash. I sensed a gap in the magazine market, an itch begging to be scratched. Among the most successful periodicals in the secular marketplace were magazines for women. No counterpart existed in the Christian field."[3]

One day Jenkins received a telephone call from Hugh Barbour, vice president and co-owner of the Fleming H. Revell Company in Old Tappan, New Jersey, a publisher of Christian books. Barbour told Jenkins that he and his brother, William R. Barbour, Jr., had been thinking about publishing a Christian woman's magazine. Jenkins agreed to help them and became the editor and publisher for the first two issues. His home in Deerfield, Illinois, served as the editorial office.[4]

With permission from Moody Bible Institute, Jenkins used the pseudonym of Jerry Bruce, Jenkins's first and middle names. This eliminated the conflict and confusion of Jenkins's being listed concurrently as the editor of two evangelical periodicals. The agreement included the understanding that *Today's Christian Woman* would not compete for *Moody Monthly*'s advertisers. This was really not a problem because at the beginning the new magazine contained no advertisements except for Revell's products.[5]

Jenkins employed free lancers to design the magazine and write the feature articles, several of whom were current students and alumni of the graduate communications department of Wheaton College. The *Christian Woman* was the first title selected for the new publication. It was changed to *Today's Christian Woman* when it was discovered that another magazine already was using the title *The Christian Woman*.[6]

The first issue of *Today's Christian Woman* appeared in time to be introduced at the July 1978 convention of the Christian Booksellers Association. This was crucial because the marketing strategy called for this new publication to be sold in Christian bookstores. The new magazine was one of the most talked about new products among the several thousand bookstore owners and publishers in attendance.

The first two issues were double-size, 144 pages, printed on quality paper with heavy glossy covers. The finished product had the feel of a coffee-table book. It had *Time* magazine dimensions (10⅞ inches by 7¾ inches).

Anita Bryant appeared on the four-color cover of the premiere issue, starting a tradition that has continued of featuring a well-known evangelical Christian woman on almost all the covers.[7] Dr. James Dobson, however, appeared on one cover with his wife, and Michael Smith barely made it on the front of the November–December 1993 issue, which featured his wife. The cover story in the first issue was titled "America's Love-Hate Relationship with Anita Bryant." The special sections included "Plants," "Budget," "Decorating,"

"Crafts," "Nutrition," "Beauty," "Bible Study," and "Book Excerpt." The two most popular features proved to be a special black-and-white photo feature, "A Celebration of Children," and an article on gardening. How-to and personality articles were prominent. Eleven women and six men authored the material in the initial issue.[8]

William R. Barbour, Jr., president of Revell, welcomed the readers of the first issue. He informed them that all the women featured in the articles and the authors in the new magazine would be Christians. He also noted that not every article would be overtly Christian but that each issue would be a publication that readers would be proud to have in their homes. "If, when you are finished, you have been enriched and feel better about the role to which God has called you—whether it be as a single, a wife, a mother, a career mother, or a combination of those—then we will have done what we set out to do."[9]

After its paternal beginnings, *Today's Christian Woman* has been edited exclusively by women. After Jenkins produced the first two issues, he decided to stay full-time with *Moody Monthly*. The magazine's editorial offices were moved to Revell's corporate offices in New Jersey. At that time, 1979, Dorianne R. Perrucci became editor. She served in that position from the fall of 1979 through the winter/spring issue of 1980.

Starting with the summer 1980 issue, the editorial offices of *Today's Christian Woman* moved to Washington, D.C., and Fleming H. Revell asked Dale Hanson Bourke to become the editor. Her eight-year tenure is the longest among all the editors of the magazine. As president of her company, Publishing Directions, Bourke brought to the magazine the expertise she had already acquired in publishing both Christian and secular products. David W. Shultz was the publisher at this time, and his marketing and advertising acumen helped get the magazine on a sound financial footing.

When Bourke assumed the editorship in 1980, she was well aware of the milieu in which the Christian woman had been living in the previous decade. "The seventies held a lot of negative manifestations of feminism. Christian women were looking for a magazine they could identify with, one that understood they couldn't relate to some of the values that permeated women's magazines. They also wanted a Christian magazine that was just for them."[10]

After Christianity Today, Inc., acquired *Today's Christian Woman* in 1988, the editorial offices moved west to Carol Stream, Illinois, where *Christianity Today* had earlier relocated from Washington, D.C. Four more women have edited the magazine since the magazine's return to metropolitan Chicago: Sharon Donohue (1988), Rebecca K. Grosenbach (1989–1990), Julie A. Talerico (1990–1993), and Ramona Tucker (1994–present). Talerico brought her experience gained at *Redbook* and *Woman's Day* magazines.[11]

From the smorgasbord of subjects in its first issues, *Today's Christian Woman* has developed a more focused four-part editorial formula that has been well received by its readers. This formula is based on a Christian woman's relationships. The four specific areas are the relationships of a Christian woman with her children, her husband, her God, and herself.[12] These topics are carried to the readers mainly by four types of feature articles in the editorial well: first-person, how-to, personality, and interview.

Since its birth, *Today's Christian Woman* has regularly brought its readers articles on friendship, marriage and family, biblical principles for daily living, and personal growth. Also, in recent years it has dealt with some of society's most sensitive and troublesome subjects. These have included abortion, extra-marital affairs, acquired immunodeficiency syndrome (AIDS), alcoholism, eating disorders, divorce, rape, sexual harassment, wife abuse, and world hunger.

When William Barbour introduced the first issue, he identified the original target audiences: the single woman, the wife, the mother, the career woman, or any combination of these categories.[13] By 1990 the editors had categorized their readership in the following roles: married women, homemakers, women with children, working women, and single women. From its inception *Today's Christian Woman* has carefully researched its readership. Major readership surveys were conducted in 1984, 1987, and 1990 to get reader reaction to content and a profile of the magazine's audience. This research has shown a rise in the median age of the readers from 37.5 in 1984 to 40.9 in 1990. The median income of the magazine's subscribers rose only 3 percent from 1987 to 1990. The percentage of subscribers with children under the age of eighteen declined 14 percent during the same three-year span.[14] The 1990 survey found that the typical, nearly forty-one-year-old subscriber is married and has one child living at home. She works outside the home, and her income, combined with her husband's totals a relatively low thirty thousand to forty thousand dollars. She has not finished college but hopes to do so.[15] The average subscriber takes her Christian faith seriously. She identifies herself as a ''born-again'' evangelical Christian and attends church regularly with her family. She became a Christian before she was seventeen and now is active in her church, singing in the choir or teaching a Sunday school class. She and her husband give one thousand dollars annually to their church and related Christian ministries. She has daily devotions, and each year she participates in at least one group Bible study. She is becoming more open-minded concerning the roles of women in society and approves women in the clergy. She never drinks alcoholic beverages.[16] The factor of the reader's race does not appear in the demographic profiles. Perhaps the editors assume that most of the subscribers are white suburbanites.

From the start *Today's Christian Woman* has won awards for excellence. The photo feature on children won a first-place award in that category in the Evangelical Press Association's annual contest. For two years in a row (1982, 1983) the magazine was awarded the gold medal for graphic arts excellence in the neographics competition.[17] That level of recognition by secular and evangelical evaluators has continued to the present.

Jenkins was right in 1978 when he felt that a niche existed in evangelical publishing that needed filling. *Today's Christian Woman* has grown from an initial run of 50,000 to 350,000 in 1993. Harold Smith, a vice president of Christianity Today, Inc., predicts circulation to reach 400,000 in 1994.[18]

During its first fifteen years, *Today's Christian Woman* went from a quarterly publication to bimonthly, the median age of its readers increased nearly four years, the sales price increased one dollar, advertising became a major source of financing, the percentage of woman authors increased, and the emphasis on gardening and home decorating faded.

But, as the 1990 survey indicates, *Today's Christian Woman* continues to serve its original purpose as it arrives in the homes of the subscriber every other month. "When TCW arrives in her home she considers it to be like the visit of a good friend. She finds TCW to be more enjoyable and useful than most secular magazines that she reads," the report on the 1990 survey concluded.[19]

Notes

1. "A Festival of Friends," *Today's Christian Woman* 1 (July–August 1978): 6.

2. Rebecca K. Grosenbach, "Inside TCW," *Today's Christian Woman* 11 (January–February 1989): 4.

3. Jerry Jenkins, "In the Beginning," *Today's Christian Woman* 10:4 (July-August 1988): 6.

4. Ibid.

5. Ibid.

6. Ibid.

7. *Today's Christian Woman* 1 (Fall–Winter 1978–1979): cover.

8. William R. Barbour, Jr., "Welcome to Today's Christian Woman," *Today's Christian Woman* 1 (July–August 1978):1.

9. Ibid., 1.

10. Sharon Donohue, "Can a Woman Have It All?" *Today's Christian Woman* 10 (July–August 1988): 34.

11. Rebecca Grosenbach, "Inside TCW," *Today's Christian Woman* 11 (January–February 1989): 4.

12. Phone interview with Harold B. Smith, vice president of Christianity Today, Inc., 13 November 1993.

13. *Today's Christian Woman* 1 (Fall–Winter 1978–1979).

14. *Today's Christian Woman 1990 Subscriber Profile* (August 1990): 47, 48.

15. Ibid.

16. Ibid.

17. David W. Shultz, "*Today's Christian Woman* Wins Graphic Arts Medal," *Today's Christian Woman* 5:2 (Summer 1993): insert.

18. Phone interview with Harold B. Smith, vice president of Christianity Today, Inc., 13 November 1993.

19. *Today's Christian Woman 1990 Subscriber Profile* (August 1990): 48.

Information Sources

INDEX SOURCES: None.

LOCATION SOURCES: A complete run can be found at Christianity Today, Inc., 465 Gundersen, Carol Stream, Illinois 60188.

Publication History

MAGAZINE TITLE AND TITLE CHANGES: *Christian Woman* (1978); *Today's Christian Woman* (1978–present).

VOLUME AND ISSUE DATA: 1:1 (Fall/Winter 1978–present. Published quarterly until November 1983, when bimonthly publication began.

PUBLISHER AND PLACE OF PUBLICATION: Fleming H. Revell Company, Old Tappan, New Jersey (1978–1980), and Washington, D.C. (1980–1988) Christianity Today, Inc., Carol Stream, Illinois (1988–present).

EDITORS: Jerry Bruce Jenkins (1978); Dorianne R. Perrucci (1978–1980); Dale Hanson Bourke (1980–1987); Sharon Donohue (1988); Rebecca K. Grosenbach (1989–1990); Julie A. Talerico (1990–1993); Ramona Cramer Tucker (1994–present).

CIRCULATION: 400,000 (1994).

Glenn Arnold

TRUTH SEEKER

In 1873 a drought struck eastern Illinois. As crops died, people flocked to churches to pray for rain. A seed salesman in Paris, Illinois, questioned the value of this practice, and he got into a debate with two clergymen over praying for rain. When the local newspaper carried the ministers' opinions but refused to print the salesman's counterarguments, he determined to found his own magazine where he could express himself as he pleased. He promised that in his paper all opinions would receive a fair and equal hearing.

The seed salesman was DeRobigne Mortimer Bennett, and the paper he started was the *Truth Seeker*, which quickly became the dominant voice of popular atheism, commonly called Freethought. In the latter nineteenth century, Freethought was the most radically progressive religious movement in the United States, at least according to its adherents. Descendants of eighteenth-century Deists, freethinkers championed freedom of thought and natural morality against the shackles of superstition and clerical domination. They believed that irrational creeds and unscientific beliefs must be repudiated for the United States to progress confidently into the modern era. Embracing rationalism, freethinkers hoped to usher in the modern era when the light of human wisdom would conquer the forces of darkness.

Freethinkers were not the only people advocating these ideas in the late nineteenth century. Liberal Christians likewise supported reason, technology, and new scientific developments. However, while liberals sought to reconcile the Church with modern culture, freethinkers questioned the necessity of Christian belief in the modern world. In the conflict between the Church and modernity, freethinkers jettisoned the Church. Evangelists of a gospel of progress, freethinkers were in the vanguard of a movement to replace Christianity with a humane religion more consonant with modernity. They provided organized, articulate voices of what it meant to be a secular American.

The years 1860–1900 formed the "golden age of Freethought." Robert Ingersoll, the most famous infidel in the country, and others lectured to large crowds. Freethinkers organized into local, state, and national groups, the most important of which were the Free Religious Association, founded in 1867, and the American Secular Union, founded in 1876 as the National Liberal League. These groups agitated for the complete separation of church and state, viewing Roman Catholicism, the National Reform Association, and the Woman's Christian Temperance Union as their primary opponents.

Freethinkers founded Liberal University in Silverton, Oregon, a town called Liberal, in Missouri, and secular churches that met weekly for singing, lectures, and support. Freethought periodicals mushroomed; Freethought publishers and tract societies churned out books and pamphlets. A cottage industry grew, selling Freethought calendars, paperweights, spoons, and jewelry.

Initially strongest in the Boston-to-New York corridor, by 1885, Freethought groups existed in thirty-five states. By 1900, Chicago had replaced New York as the center of Freethought activity. Strong state groups also existed in Indiana, Kansas, and Oregon. Freethinkers were overwhelmingly white, middle- or lower-middle class, and self-educated. Although homogeneous socially, they had varying religious backgrounds. Some had parents who were devotees of Thomas Paine; others had Unitarian or Transcendentalist backgrounds. The majority came from evangelical Protestant families.

D. M. Bennett's journey to atheism was circuitous, but not atypical. Born in 1818 in Springfield, New York, he grew up as a devout Methodist and was interested in religious questions. At fifteen he joined a Shaker community but left in 1845 to marry Mary Wicks. In 1848 he encountered Freethought and began to doubt the truths of Christianity. He studied Thomas Paine's *Age of Reason* and became just as aggressive an atheist as he had been a Methodist and Shaker. Bennett pursued a number of careers before launching the *Truth Seeker*. He was a druggist in St. Louis, Cincinnati, and Kansas City; manufactured bricks on Long Island; worked in a nursery in Rochester, New York; and was a partner in a seed business in Paris, Illinois, when he engaged in the prayer controversy that sparked his journalistic career.[1]

Bennett began the *Truth Seeker* as a monthly magazine in Paris in September 1873. The first issue stated that the new periodical was "devoted to Science, Morals, Free Thought, Free Enquiry and the Diffusion of Liberal Sentiments [*sic*]."[2] That issue carried the "Nine Demands of Liberalism," a list of principles for separating church and state and the closest thing to a Freethought creed. In 1874 the paper moved to New York City and adopted a new heading; it was now "devoted to Science, Morals, Free Thought, Free Dicussion [*sic*], Liberalism, Sexual Equality, Labor Reform, Progression, Free Education, and What Ever Tends to Emancipate and Elevate the Human Race" and "opposed to Priestcraft, Ecclesiasticism, Dogmas, Creeds, False Theology, Superstition, Bigotry, Ignorance, Monopolies, Aristocracies, Privileged Classes, Tyranny, Oppression and Everything that Degrades or Burdens Mankind Mentally or Physically."[3]

In New York, the *Truth Seeker* thrived. In 1876 it became a weekly and began carrying reports of meetings of Freethought organizations, particularly the Manhattan Liberal Club, New York State Freethinkers Association, and National Liberal League/American Secular Union. With a newsy tone, it chronicled the activities of freethinkers, serialized Freethought novels, and printed pithy, argumentative pieces on controversial issues. It attracted prominent supporters such as Robert G. Ingersoll and Elizabeth Cady Stanton. A prolific writer, Bennett published his own books, among them *The World's Sages, Infidels and Thinkers* (1876) and *A Truth Seeker Around the World* (1882).

Bennett gained fame as a Freethought martyr when he was arrested in 1878 for violating the Comstock Act, a federal antiobscenity law passed in 1873 that banned the distribution of obscene material through the mail. Sponsor and enforcer of this legislation was Anthony Comstock, secretary of the New York League for the Suppression of Vice and a government special agent. Believing that antagonism toward the Church was blasphemy, Comstock targeted freethinkers. Given their scientific views, which prompted them to discuss sexuality with an un-Victorian candor, Freethought advocates were an easy mark. Bennett was arrested after Comstock, using a fictitious name, ordered ''Cupid's Yokes,'' a pamphlet on marriage and contraception. He spent a year in prison and died less than three years later in 1882. His celebrated trial and prison term gained publicity for the *Truth Seeker.*

Eugene Macdonald succeeded Bennett as editor of the magazine, continuing until his death in 1909. During these years, the paper flourished and reached its circulation peak of approximately nine thousand in the last decade of the century. It became the leading journal of Freethought. It eliminated its unwieldy heading in favor of the simpler masthead, ''a Journal of Freethought and Reform,'' and added illustrations and photographs.[4] Through the ''Children's Corner,'' a regular column, it emphasized strengthening Freethought in the next generation.

In its pages radicals of all kinds debated women's suffrage, spiritualism, temperance, labor, Darwinism, anarchism, industrialization, and dress reform. It agitated for antiobscenity laws (to replace the Comstock Act), free speech, spelling reform, antivivisection, moral purity, and contraception. Although its articles lacked concrete strategies for action, the *Truth Seeker* projected optimism and confidence in the ability of rationalism to solve humanity's problems.

After Ingersoll's death in 1899, many freethinkers felt they had lost their champion, and the movement began to change. The *Truth Seeker* devoted more space to obituaries and less to reports of lectures and meetings. Younger, more radical leaders promoted anarchism and socialism, challenging the movement's unstated faith in democracy and capitalism. While the *Truth Seeker* was still the leading atheist periodical, it lost its hopeful tone in the face of increasing fragmentation and impending war. Dynamic discussion gave way to complaining. Edited by George Macdonald following his brother's death, the magazine looked backward more than forward.[5]

Its readership began to decline. Rather than cease publication altogether, in 1930 Macdonald changed the paper from a weekly to a monthly. Charles Smith became editor in 1937, succeeded by James Hervey Johnson in 1964 after Smith's death. Under Smith and Johnson, the paper became more conservative and advocated white supremacy along with atheism. While Northern European ethnocentrism had been an implicit theme since the paper's founding, its open racism and xenophobia offended many readers. In recent years its circulation has declined to less than a thousand.[6] Since 1989 James W. Prescott has been the editor, and circulation has begun to rebound.

During its heyday in the 1880s and 1890s, The *Truth Seeker* popularized Freethought and legitimated it as an (ir) religious movement. It helped to dispel the stereotype of the ignorant "village atheist" by promoting a coherent rationalist philosophy. Through rationalism, freethinkers sought to usher in a secular millennium of peace and prosperity. Although there were disagreements about this vision, vitality pervaded the movement. The *Truth Seeker* articulated the controversies surrounding this vision and embodied this vitality. In giving voice to a heretical minority, the *Truth Seeker* stabilized Freethought as a viable movement rather than a collection of dissenters. It promoted community among people who believed in individualism so strongly that they could agree on virtually nothing. The 1873 drought in Paris, Illinois, brought unexpected rain.

Notes

1. On Bennett, see Samuel Putnam, *400 Years of Freethought* (New York: Truth Seeker, 1894), 694–98; George Macdonald, "Passing the First Half-Century Mark," *Truth Seeker* 50 (1 September 1923): 553–70.
2. *Truth Seeker* 1 (September 1873): 1.
3. Ibid. 1 (January 1874): 1.
4. Ibid. 8 (1 January 1881): 1.
5. George MacDonald, *Fifty Years of Freethought*, 2 vols. (New York: Truth Seeker, 1929) is a good example of this tendency to romanticize the *Truth Seeker*'s history.
6. Marshall Brown and Gordon Stein, *Freethought in the United States: A Descriptive Bibliography* (Westport, CT: Greenwood Press, 1978), 70–71, 76.

Information Sources

INDEX SOURCES: None.
LOCATION SOURCES: The Library of Congress and the New York Public Library have the most complete runs.

Publication History

MAGAZINE TITLE: *Truth Seeker* (1873–present).
VOLUME AND ISSUE DATA: 1:1 (September 1873)–present. Published monthly,

1873–1874; semimonthly, 1874–1875; weekly, 1876–1929; monthly, 1930–present.

PUBLISHER AND PLACE OF PUBLICATION: D. M. Bennett, The Truth Seeker Company, Paris, Illinois (1873–1874); New York, New York (1874–1964); San Diego, California (1964–present).

EDITORS: D. M. Bennett (1873–1882); Eugene Macdonald (1882–1909); George Macdonald (1909–1937); Charles L. Smith (1937–1964); James Hervey Johnson (1964–1989); James W. Prescott (1989–present).

CIRCULATION: 9,000 (1894–1896).

Evelyn A. Kirkley

U

UNION BULLETIN. *See* REFORM JUDAISM

UNION TIDINGS. *See* REFORM JUDAISM

UNITED CHURCH HERALD. *See* A.D.

UNITED METHODIST REPORTER

Today the *United Methodist Reporter* claims to be the largest religious newsweekly in the United States and the oldest continuous religious publication in the United States. However, its present name dates only from 1981. The *United Methodist Reporter*, which at the end of 1991 claimed a circulation of 451,347 and served the United Methodist churches of thirty-six annual conferences in twenty-eight states, was previously known as the *Texas Methodist*, which indicates that the newspaper has its roots deep in the religious history of the state of Texas. The story of the *United Methodist Reporter* is, indeed, a typically Texan story with an amalgam of Wesleyan evangelical commitment, southern social conservatism, entrepreneurial derring-do, and financial and numerical success.

The story begins in Brenham, Texas, in 1847, less than two years after the Lone Star Republic had joined the United States. In January of that year, Reverend Robert B. Wells, Methodist pastor at Brenham, issued the first edition of the *Texas Christian Advocate and Brenham Advertiser*, which was partly a church paper and partly secular, as its name implied. Wells was short on cash, short on time, and long on pro-slavery sentiment. By August 1847 he wrote in his journal, "Did not journalize last week. Too busy. No help in office."[1] Later in the same year Wells turned the presses over to his father-in-law, Reverend Orceneth Fisher, who moved the operation to Houston and continued to publish the paper under the title of the *Texas Christian Advocate* until the summer of 1848.

In the fall of 1848, a group of preachers and laymen at the Rutersville camp meeting decided to bring the paper under the control of Methodism's Texas annual conference. The name was changed to the *Texas Wesleyan Banner*, and Reverend Chauncey Richardson became editor. Richardson continued the paper's strong editorial voice in favor of slavery. Once, when a rival denomination charged that Texas Methodists were abolitionists, Richardson replied, "On this subject, the M.E. Church, South, is like Caesar's wife: above suspicion."[2]

The paper, however, could not rise above continuing financial difficulties. By 1854, there had been four new editors, a new location—Galveston—and another new (old?) name, the *Texas Christian Advocate*. The eighth editor of the paper, Reverend C. C. Gillespie, finally began to bring some stability to the project. Coming to the paper in 1854, Gillespie was popular with his readers for advocating the idea that slavery was not incompatible with Christianity, and by 1858 the circulation of the *Texas Christian Advocate* was up to forty-one hundred.

Lurking in the near future was war. A Union naval blockade of Galveston harbor made newsprint and other printing supplies hard to get, and in December 1861 new editor J. E. Carnes printed two final issues on wallpaper and then packed up all the printing equipment and moved it to Houston for storage. The *Texas Christian Advocate* would not publish again until December 1864.

Following the war, operations resumed in Galveston, and the paper began to enjoy a fairly steady prosperity. Under the editorial guidance of Reverend I. G. John and the publishing leadership of Louis Blaylock and William A. Shaw, the paper grew to enjoy a circulation of thirteen thousand by 1876. These were rough years on the Texas frontier, and a casual perusal of *Christian Advocate* headlines from this period indicates that Texas Methodists were not exactly preoccupied with weighty matters of academic theology: "New York Dogs," "Does Sheep Raising Pay?" "A Word to the Stockmen of Texas," and "Genesis of Thunder Storms." Some of the products advertised during these years were also quite remarkable, such as "Koskoo," a patent medicine guaranteed to cure "bad dreams, confusion, failing of the memory, mental depression, confusion of ideas, noises in the ears, hesitation in answering questions, twitching of the face, insanity, impotency, apoplexy, etc., etc."[3]

After the Civil War, northern churches had to wrestle with problems of immigration, labor violence, and increasing urbanization. Such issues were largely unknown during this time in Texas. What the *Texas Christian Advocate* did do, however, was launch vigorous editorial crusades on issues of private personal morality. Saloons, gambling, and prostitution were three of the favorite Methodist targets during these years of the "wild West," and the *Christian Advocate* had its editorial campaigns on all three.

In 1887 the paper, which four years earlier had come under the direct supervision of an editorial board composed of representatives of the five English-speaking conferences of the Methodist Episcopal Church, South in Texas, was moved from Galveston to Dallas. In this fast-growing and centrally located city, under the distinguished editorship of Reverend George C. Rankin, the *Texas Christian Advocate* enjoyed probably its greatest years. When Rankin died in 1915, both houses of the Texas legislature passed memorial resolutions, and twenty-seven newspapers ran eulogistic editorials.

The first half of the twentieth century saw various ups and downs for the paper. The Great Depression of the 1930s badly hurt both advertising and circulation, and in 1931 the paper was renamed the *Southwestern Advocate* and broadened to serve Oklahoma and New Mexico as well as Texas. In 1949, the *Southwestern Advocate* actually disappeared from view for a time, although it continued to exist as a special "News of the Southwest" section of the *Christian Advocate* published in Chicago. Finally, in 1952, the *Texas Christian Advocate* reappeared as a weekly paper serving Texas Methodism. This phoenixlike rebirth set the stage for the phenomenal growth and transformation of the paper that were about to occur.

Three outstanding religious journalists succeeded one another at the newspaper between 1958 and 1991: Reverend Carl Kieghtley, Jon Kinslow, and Reverend Spurgeon Dunnam III. Each made his own contribution in such a way that what was in 1958 a regional, denominational newspaper with a circulation of eighteen thousand and a fairly parochial vision had become by 1991 a publication with a global view of the church that had a readership of nearly half a million.

Kieghtley came first, serving as editor from 1958 to 1967. He had the initial, pioneering idea to transform the four-page *Texas Christian Advocate* into a publication that could individualize some content to target a particular readership while having much material that would be common to all editions of a given issue. Each issue would contain three identical pages of general religious news and editorial opinion, but the cover page would feature news of a particular annual conference or local church, varying from edition to edition. In this way, Kieghtley reasoned, each edition of the paper could have its own regional identity. This idea has become very popular in secular journalism today and is used by publications such as *USA Today* and the *Wall Street Journal*. In 1958, however, it was revolutionary. In 1960 Kieghtley changed the name of the paper one more time to the *Texas Methodist* and in 1961 published the first conference edition of the paper—for the Texas Conference. In 1963, five annual conference editions of the *Texas Methodist* were launched, and in 1965 the first local church editions came out.

Carl Kieghtley left the paper in 1967 and was succeeded by Jon Kinslow, a Methodist layman with a background in secular journalism at the *Dallas Morning News*. Kinslow's view was, not unreasonably, that a newspaper should report the news. However, the secular news in 1967 and 1968 (civil rights, Vietnam, political assassinations) had controversial theological implications for the churches.

Under Kinslow's leadership, the *Texas Methodist* reported and editorialized on all this news, which made clergy leadership uncomfortable. In what Kinslow saw as an attempt to reassert clergy control over the paper, the Methodist Communications Council of Texas and New Mexico was founded in June 1968. Although the communications council had a much broader and more positive purpose than simply controlling the newspaper, a dispute broke out immediately between Kinslow and the council, with the result that Kinslow resigned the editorship in March 1969.

Kinslow's replacement was debated among the members of the communications council, who eventually settled upon a young United Methodist pastor, Reverend Spurgeon Dunnam III. Dunnam, reared in Methodist parsonages in the Texas Conference and a graduate of Texas Wesleyan College in Fort Worth, had begun to work at the *Texas Methodist* as a copy editor while still a seminary student at Perkins School of Theology at Southern Methodist University. He was an unknown quantity at the time of his promotion to editor in 1969, but Dunnam soon revealed dynamic qualities of leadership that catapulted the *Texas Methodist* into the forefront of popular religious journalism in the United States.

Dunnam was a social and theological liberal, but a fiscal conservative. He was a workaholic entrepreneur who always answered when opportunity knocked, and opportunity knocked often at the door of the *Texas Methodist* between the years of 1969 and Dunnam's unexpected death in 1991. He had gained a vision of the universal Church from Albert C. Outler, his seminary professor at Perkins who was an official Protestant observer at the Second Vatican Council in Rome. Dunnam was committed to a fuller realization of Kieghtley's earlier journalistic vision of regional editions of the *Texas Methodist.*

In 1970, the first out-of-state conference edition of the *Texas Methodist* was produced by Dunnam for the Rocky Mountain Annual Conference. In 1973, the *United Methodist Reporter* began as a "wholly owned subsidiary of *The Texas Methodist.*"[4] Annual conference and local church editions began to be added at a whirlwind pace, such that by 1978 the total weekly circulation of the *Texas Methodist/United Methodist Reporter* stood at 464,854. In 1981, the Communications Council of Texas and New Mexico voted to bow to the new reality: the *Texas Methodist* officially became the *United Methodist Reporter.*

Still, Dunnam pushed forward at a frenetic pace. In March 1981, a new ecumenical weekly newspaper, the *National Christian Reporter*, was launched. In 1983, a biweekly tabloid, the *United Methodist Review*, was begun. Also in 1983, the National Conference of Christians and Jews sold the financially ailing Religious News Service to the *United Methodist Reporter.*

Regional publications were begun for other denominations: the Christian Church, Disciples of Christ; the Evangelical Lutheran Church in America; the Presbyterian Church (USA); the United Church of Christ; and the Roman Catholic dioceses of Dallas and Fort Worth. In 1987, the *United Methodist Reporter* foundation was established, with the goal of raising $14 million for a new Dallas headquarters for the newspaper. In 1991, the monthly tabloid the *United Methodist Record* was added to this exploding list of publications.

At the end of November 1991, the untimely death of Spurgeon Dunnam rocked the world of religious journalism. Just months before, Dunnam had been traveling in Africa, Germany, and Russia. His guiding vision of a truly global, ecumenical church had seemed to be coming into ever-sharper focus as Nelson Mandela walked free and the Berlin wall fell.

In late 1992, John Lovelace was named as the new editor of the *United Methodist Reporter*. A new position of publisher was created and filled by Reverend Ronald Paul Patterson, thus recognizing that the executive and editorial duties of such a major news operation can no longer be performed by one person. A new era began. The frontier is no longer in the cotton fields or the range land of antebellum Texas. But a new frontier of world community is just opening up, and the *United Methodist Reporter* is active on that frontier as a dynamic example of practical ecumenism.

Notes

1. Walter N. Vernon, Robert W. Sledge, Robert C. Monk, and Norman W. Spellman, *The Methodist Excitement in Texas* (Dallas: Texas United Methodist Historical Society, 1984), 96.

2. Ibid., 97.

3. Ibid., 135.

4. Robert L. Robertson, "Unpublished Report to the Board of the United Methodist Communications Council of Texas and New Mexico," 1981, 5.

Information Sources

INDEX SOURCES: Some volumes are self-indexed in the last issue of the volume. Some issues from 1850–1854, 1857–1870, and 1872–1881 are abstracted in *Texas Methodist Newspaper Abstracts*.

LOCATION SOURCES: Partial collections are in the following libraries: Emory University, Garrett Theological Seminary, New York Public Library, Duke University, Drew University, Texas State Library in Austin, and the University of Texas. The most complete collection is located in the Bridwell Library of Perkins School of Theology, Southern Methodist University, Dallas, Texas. The Bridwell collection is available for purchase on microfilm.

Publication History

MAGAZINE TITLE AND TITLE CHANGES: *Texas Christian Advocate and Brenham Advertiser* (1847); *Texas Christian Advocate* (1848); *Texas Wesleyan Banner* (1848–1854); *Texas Christian Advocate* (1854–1931); *Southwestern Advocate* (1932–1949); *Texas Christian Advocate* (1952–1960); *Texas Methodist* (1960–1981); *United Methodist Reporter* (1981–present).

Texas Christian Advocate merged with *Oklahoma Methodist* to form *Southwestern Advocate*, January 1932.

Southwestern Advocate merged with *Christian Advocate*, March 1949. Suspended publication December 1861–December 1864 and July 1940–Fall 1940.

VOLUME AND ISSUE DATA: No issues of *Texas Christian Advocate* are known to survive. *Texas Wesleyan Banner* 1 (1 February 1849)–5 (1 July 1854). *Texas Christian Advocate* 1:1 (18 August 1854)–78:20 (31 December 1931). Publication suspended, 1862–1864. *Southwestern Advocate* 78:21 (7 January 1932)–95:41 (24 February 1949). Appeared as a supplement to *Christian Advocate*, March 1949–May 1952. *Texas Christian Advocate* 99:1 (29 May 1952)–106:40 (11 March 1960). *Texas Methodist* 106:41 (18 March 1960)–127 (1981). Known as *Texas Methodist/United Methodist Reporter*, 1973–1981. *United Methodist Reporter* 128:1 (1981)–present.

PUBLISHER AND PLACE OF PUBLICATION: Publisher unknown, Brenham, Texas (1847); publisher unknown, Houston, Texas (1848); Joint Committee of Ministers of the Texas and East Texas Conferences for the Methodist Episcopal Church, South, Houston, Texas (1849–1854), Galveston, Texas (1854–1861); Blaylock Publishing Co., Galveston, Texas (1864–1887); Dallas, Texas (1887–1923); Reverend George S. Slover, Dallas, Texas (1924–1926); Harben-Spotts Co., Dallas, Texas (1926–1934); Southwestern Advocate Publishing Co., Dallas, Texas (1935–1949); Christian Advocate, Chicago, Illinois (1949–1952); Texas Christian Advocate for the Joint Board of Publications, Fort Worth, Texas (1952–1960); Texas Methodist, Fort Worth, Texas (1960–1965); Texas Methodist and All Church Press, Irving, Texas (1965-1969); All Church Press, Dallas, Texas (1970–1972); Newspaper Division of the United Methodist Communications Council, Dallas, Texas (1972–1981); Newspaper Division of the United Methodist Communications Division (1981–present).

EDITORS: Robert B. Wells (1847); Orceneth Fisher (1848); Chauncey Richardson (1849); George Rottenstein (1852); Simon B. Cameron (1853); J. A. Hancock (1853); C. C. Gillespie (1854); J. E. Carnes (1858); H. B. Philpott (1865); I. G. John (1866); George W. Briggs (1884); James Campbell (1888); Thomas R. Pierce (1894); George C. Rankin (1898); W. D. Bradfield (1915); Andrew J. Weeks (1918); P. E. Riley (1922); E. V. Cole (1930); Andrew J. Weeks (1931); editorial committee (1939); H. M. Whaling (1942); E. A. Hunter (1946); J. Daniel Barron (1948); Carl Kieghtley (1958); Jon Kinslow (1967); Spurgeon Dunnam (1969); John Lovelace (1992).

CIRCULATION: 4,100 (1858); 13,000 (1876); 20,500 (1926); 18,000 (1958); 464,900 (1978); 425,300 (1992).

George L. Procter-Smith

UNITED STATES CATHOLIC INTELLIGENCER. *See* PILOT (BOSTON)

UPPER ROOM

On the initiative of Methodist women from Texas, the *Upper Room* was first published in the spring of 1935. Since then the daily devotional guide has served Christians worldwide. The little magazine has been called a "twentieth century miracle" because of its rapid growth and its large circulation.[1] The *Upper Room* is published in sixty-six editions and in forty-four languages, with a circulation of well over 2 million copies each issue. The purpose of the devotional guide is to have its readers join a worldwide fellowship of prayer each day.

In 1934, a proposal was made by women in the Philathea Class of Travis Park Methodist Episcopal Church, South in San Antonio, Texas, to the denomination's Board of Missions. These women, led by Mrs. Seth A. Craig, perceived an urgent need for daily devotions in Christian homes. Their concerns, along with suggestions for a prayer guide, were presented to the Board of Missions at its 13 December 1934 meeting in Nashville, Tennessee. At that meeting the board accepted the recommendation to publish a devotional guide, and it assigned oversight of the task to one of its own members, Grover C. Emmons. A booklet containing a daily Scripture reading, a text, a short meditation, a prayer, and a devotional "thought for the day" was developed by Emmons in such a way as to fit all on one page per day.[2]

Former editor J. Manning Potts has recounted how the new religious magazine got its name.[3] With a format developed and contents secured for the first issue, all was ready for the printing press except for one detail: the magazine had no name. At a conference in Richmond, Virginia, Emmons heard a minister preach on the story of Pentecost in which Jesus's disciples met for prayer in an "upper room" and consequently decided on the name, the *Upper Room*. The inspiration came not a moment too soon, as a copy of the first issue had already gone to the printer without a title. Editor Emmons quickly sent the name to the Nashville press by telegraph. From 1935 until 1940, when the Board of Missions moved to New York, the *Upper Room* was published by the Committee on Evangelism, Hospitals, and Homes of the Methodist Episcopal Church, South. In 1940, production was transferred to the Commission on Evangelism, later the General Board of Evangelism of the Methodist Church.

At its creation, the *Upper Room* was intended to aid Christians in private devotional life; given changes among the Methodist churches, the magazine soon served to help unify the Methodists in a more public way. The Methodist Church had been divided for years by region, by the Civil War, and by the debate over slavery. In 1939, unification among a number of Methodist bodies was achieved. At this same time circulation for the new devotional magazine shot sky-high. During the unification process, denominational leaders encouraged use of devotional literature to build common ground and to promote a feeling of solidarity. For instance, the department of spiritual life of the Woman's Division of Christian Service "furnished suggestions and resources and urged each local church society to develop a group who would meet together periodically for Bible study, prayer, and meditation." Leaders specifically promoted use of the *Upper Room* to link local groups together in common prayer and devotion.[4]

Beyond serving a unifying role for Methodists in the late 1930s, the *Upper Room* reached early in its history for a larger, ecumenical audience, even as it sought ways to express Christian piety during the age of the Depression and World War II. Economic disaster, social problems, and the crisis of war were matters that lay beyond denominational boundaries. From the outset, the *Upper Room* was intended to be nonsectarian in character. This pluralistic intention, more than any other factor, has led to the devotional guide's accessibility, its adaptability, and its popularity well beyond the bounds of American Methodism.

Printing 100,000 copies of the first issue was at the time considered to be highly ambitious, but the early issue sold out. More copies were printed of subsequent issues: 160,000 of the second, and 211,000 of the third. Within three years, circulation topped 1 million. In 1937 a Hindustani edition was published; in 1938, requests for Spanish and Korean translations were approved. Soon after, in 1940, a Braille and a Portuguese edition became available.[5] Today, the *Upper Room* is published in forty-two languages and sixty-three editions and is circulated in 125 countries.

In the United States, the magazine is available in several editions: Braille, cassette, large print, and small (original size). Page dimensions are 6¼ by 8 inches, folded in half to make pages measure 4 inches. One page of the large-print edition measures 10¾ by 8 inches. The magazine is self-supporting. It receives no funds from any national church agency. The *Upper Room* also publishes books (twenty to twenty-five per year) and three other magazines: *alive now!* (1971), a thematic (as opposed to daily) devotional magazine for adults; *Pockets* (1981), a children's magazine; and *Weavings: A Journal of the Christian Spiritual Life* (1986), a serious journal with in-depth articles about the spiritual life.

The words *unifying, connective, ecumenical,* and *popular* describe the history, design, and editorial purpose of the *Upper Room,* rehearsed on the front page of each issue in the phrase, "Interdenominational, International, Interracial." These inclusive terms point to the worldwide identity, production, and readership of the magazine. Indeed, local groups produce most of the foreign editions. The *Upper Room* is popular in the fullest sense of the term: it communicates human concerns simply, generally, and widely. The popular international character is also evident in the magazine's biblical exegesis, as well as in the thematic focus of the meditations printed in each issue.

The *Upper Room* "attempts to be consciously international in order to reflect the diversity that is part of the family of God."[6] Its readers are "part of a worldwide fellowship every day," and the magazine staff is acutely conscious of this fact. The *Upper Room*'s readers have developed a personal relationship to the magazine; many readers have read it daily for fifty years. Consequently, devoted readers often feel a personal investment in the devotional guide; when the magazine makes a change in page layout, readers often send letters and raise questions about the new format.

The personal character of the writing style has made for strong feelings of reader ownership. This personal quality allows people to tell their own stories to each other, stories that strengthen personal faith and provide a way for readers to stand in solidarity with each other. Titles for daily meditations include "More than a Mother," "Not Alone," "Thinking of You," and "Grandfather's

Jacket."[7] One writer found joy in the face of an old friend. Another, almost overcome by the dark and gloomy morning weather, discovered a full-arched rainbow and thus the creator, God. A father is visited by his adult son, who left after some bitter, discouraging remarks; the father, trying to sleep, listened to a religious radio program, recalled his own unpleasant words, and resolved to use his words instead to express the faith felt in his heart. The personal nature of the writing in the *Upper Room* speaks directly and powerfully; it is perhaps the secret of the magazine's popularity.

The inclusive, personal, and popular character of the magazine can also be seen in the variety of contributing authors, in its selected topics, and in editorial considerations regarding translation. Readers are invited to contribute pieces on announced themes. Each daily meditation is thus written by a different person, often from a different country. Most contributors are not writers by profession. Thus, entries tend to be heartfelt, written in ordinary language in a conversational style, and on easily accessible topics. Editors read submissions, considering how they will relate to a cross-cultural audience. The best entries speak broadly on common concerns. Culture-bound entries, for instance, on "dating" or "Little League baseball," may not reach print, because of the limitations of these and other such topics to the culture of the United States. Likewise, though more dramatic, a meditation on "dieting" may well be inappropriate, especially in the Third World. However, the very best of culture-bound meditations will be accepted for publication if the power of the message transcends the regional character of the topic. Those in charge of non-English editions may choose not to print pieces deemed inappropriate, however. These cases are exceptional; in general, editorial policy reflects the greater desire for a common daily program of thought and prayer, whenever possible.

A second editorial concern regards wordplays: "presents" for "presence" may enliven an entry on God's gifts, but the pun is lost in translation and thus avoided. Biblical passages used for the daily reading must be similar in several translations of the Holy Bible, because the editors cannot expect all translators or readers to have the same text. These concerns highlight the ways in which the popular audience shapes the content of the devotional guide.

The *Upper Room* is published six times per year, bimonthly. The regular edition is printed at 2 million copies for each issue, while there are approximately 250,000 copies of the large-print issue. Estimates of 8 million for the daily audience include readings in group settings and communication through radio broadcast. Given its ambition and its popularity, the *Upper Room* is truly a "twentieth-century miracle."

Notes

1. G. Ernest Thomas, *A Twentieth Century Miracle* (Nashville: Upper Room, 1972), 5.

2. For the early history of the *Upper Room*, I have relied upon Brooks B. Little, "*The*

Upper Room," *The Encyclopedia of World Methodism*, ed. Nolan B. Harmon, 2 vols. (Nashville: United Methodist Publishing House, 1974), 2: 2400.

   3. Little, "*Upper Room*," 2400.

   4. Emory Stevens Bucke, ed., *The History of American Methodism*, 3 vols. (New York and Nashville: Abingdon Press, 1964), 3: 564.

   5. Other language editions include Chinese, 1947; Armenian, 1949; Ilocano, Tagalog, Australasia, Swedish, and Norwegian, 1950; Japanese and India (English), 1951; Greek, Italian, Hindi, and Urdu, 1952; Telugu, Arabic, and Thai, 1953; British Isles, Persian, Hungarian, Finnish, and Russian, 1954; Cebuano, Gujarati, and Tamil, 1955; French, 1956; Burmese and Talking Book, 1957; Burma (English, Marathi, Sinhalese), 1958; Kannada, 1959; Malayalam, 1960; Danish, 1961; Bengali, Santhali, and Pampango, 1962; and German, 1965 (Little, "*Upper Room*," 2400).

   6. Telephone conversation with Mary Lou Redding, managing editor of the *Upper Room*, 29 July 1992.

   7. *Upper Room* 58 (July–August 1992).

Information Sources

INDEX SOURCES: None.
LOCATION SOURCES: The *Upper Room*, 1908 Grand Avenue, Nashville, Tennessee 37202-9929.

Publication History

MAGAZINE TITLE: *Upper Room* (1935–present).
VOLUME AND ISSUE DATA: 1:1 (April–May–June 1935)–13:3 (October–November–December 1947), Published quarterly. Published bimonthly as of 14:1 (March–April 1948).
PUBLISHER AND PLACE OF PUBLICATION: The Upper Room, Inc., Nashville, Tennessee.
EDITORS: Grover C. Emmons (1935–1944); Roy H. Short (1944–1948), J. Manning Potts (1948–1967), Wilson O, Weldon (1967–1975), Maxie D. Dunnam (1975–1982), Rueben P. Job (1982–1984), Janice T. Grana (1984–present).
CIRCULATION: Regular edition: 2 million (1992); large-print edition: 255,000 (January–February 1993).

John Kloos

U.S. CATHOLIC

   U.S. Catholic, the monthly magazine published in Chicago, Illinois, by the Claretians, has undergone several incarnations that have changed it radically, yet somehow it has achieved a continuum. The Claretians, a Roman Catholic congregation of priests, brothers, and students for the religious life, are the source of that continuum. Founded in Spain in 1849 by St. Anthony Claret, the Claretians (formally the Congregation of Sons of the Immaculate Heart of Mary) have taken publishing as an essential part of their mission since their founding.

A native of Spain, Anthony Claret was a many-talented man who became a Catholic priest and then a bishop and whose wide-ranging apostolic labors encompassed serving as confessor for Spanish Queen Isabella and as archbishop of Santiago in Cuba. He was a tireless preacher who wrote numerous books and pamphlets.

Following in the footsteps of their founder, the Claretians in the United States began in 1935 to publish a monthly magazine called the *Voice of St. Jude.* Basically an external house organ, the *Voice* had as its primary aim the spreading of word about Catholic devotion to the apostle St. Jude. Seven years previously, the Claretians had established in Chicago a shrine or place of particular devotion and prayer to St. Jude, and the *Voice* was to be its mouthpiece. Filling a thirty-two-page monthly magazine required more substance than that. Substance was supplied by articles and stories that depicted the missionary work of the Claretians.

The *Voice of St. Jude* continued as an external house organ until 1948, when it changed radically, if not really dramatically, into a thirty-two-page general interest Catholic magazine with something of a family orientation. The description "something of" is appropriate because the "new" *Voice* began with a meager editorial budget and a single editor whose full-time job was as rector of a seminary in a small town some miles from Chicago. The eclectic contents of the magazine were garnered from other publications, often without the permission of the publications of origin. Assembling and laying out the contents were done by employees of the publication's printer, tasks they accomplished rather well.

The newly appointed publisher of the *Voice* was a dynamic priest named Father Joachim DePrada, to whom it was immediately evident that this half-hearted, amateurish publication needed professional improvement. In 1949 he hired a lay general manager, and two years later, at the behest of the latter, he added a full-time editor, James O'Gara, who had been cofounder and editor of *Today,* a Catholic student magazine and a widely applauded publication. O'Gara brought editorial professionalism to the *Voice* immediately, and although his editorial budget continued to be meager (e.g., authors of feature articles received a stipend of thirty-five dollars), the *Voice* achieved a degree of respectability.

Beginning in the late 1940s, the *Voice* became, for the first time, a paid subscription magazine. Some subscriptions were sold by mail, but most came from door-to-door sales by a small cadre of agents, men and women whose earnings were based strictly on commissions from their sales. This small cadre worked from the Chicago office of the *Voice* but were independent agents rather than employees of the magazine.

In 1951, *Vincentian,* another Catholic magazine, sold by a similar but far larger sales organization, decided to discontinue door-to-door subscription sales. The Claretian publishers of the *Voice* took over the sales organization, comprising more than one hundred field agents operating from nine district offices. The paid circulation of the *Voice* soon soared, reaching as high as 140,000. But the lion's share of each subscription payment went to the field agents and their crew managers. *Voice* officials held the erroneous assumption that many of these subscribers would renew by mail and/or be targets for fund-raising. Such assumptions were erroneous since subscribers tended to renew in the same way that they subscribed originally.

At the *Voice* editorial desk, James O'Gara had accomplished much, but after one year the prestigious Catholic magazine, *Commonweal*, made him an offer he could not refuse, to be its managing editor. Before leaving, O'Gara, Father DePrada, and the general manager and executive editor, Robert E. Burns, employed Donald J. Thorman as managing editor.

A prodigiously energetic man, Thorman in the four years of his tenure succeeded in improving the *Voice* substantially. Perhaps most important among his achievements was his success in persuading a number of competent freelance writers to become contributors. In this he was helped by the fact that he and Burns were able to gradually increase the stipends for their authors. When Thorman left Chicago in 1956 to become managing editor of the Catholic magazine, *Ave Maria*, and subsequently editor-publisher of the *National Catholic Reporter*, he was replaced by Robert Ostermann, who served as managing editor until 1960.

The early 1960s proved to be watershed years for the *Voice* and its successor magazine, *U.S. Catholic*. First to receive attention were the matter and manner of subscription selling. It was possible for the Claretian publishers to tolerate the large army of door-to-door agents as long as the cost of publishing the *Voice* was low. In the early 1950s actual printing and distribution costs were less than the subscription price. Thus agents could receive their commissions without hurting the magazine's financial base. But as costs increased, subsidy became necessary to meet operating costs and commission payments. When the subsidy became unreasonable, the decision was made to close the field offices and discontinue field selling. The result was that the magazine's circulation declined rather abruptly. The publishers of the *Voice*, however, never regretted this decision.

Editorially in the early 1960s, there was a growing realization that additional rebuilding was in order. The magazine had achieved widespread approval from its subscribers and publishing peers alike, but it continued to be an anomaly. Its name had been shortened from the *Voice of St. Jude* to *St. Jude* in the late 1950s. But the name continued to have little relation to its content. In substance, the magazine had continued to grow in its professionalism, but the style, design, graphics, and layout left much to be desired. Glenn Heinlein, artist and art director for a leading Chicago ad agency, had begun to assist the editors with these matters in the late 1950s, but the limitations of the magazine itself limited him.

So, in 1963, executive editor Burns proposed to the Claretian publishers a bold plan that would increase the editorial budget substantially, add pages, allow better graphics and inside color, and, not incidentally, change the magazine's name to *U.S. Catholic*, a preemptive title suggested by editorial consultant Richard Frisbie. The Claretian publishers accepted these proposals with grace and enthusiasm, aware that they were committing themselves to large and continuing subsidy for their new magazine.

The first issue of *U.S. Catholic* appeared in September 1963 and was received with wide enthusiasm. Art director Heinlein, considered by his colleagues as a genius, now had room for his dramatic use of graphics, color, titles, and white space. Expressions of opinion were printed on colored stock of quality different from the body stock on which reporting articles were printed. An opinion feature called "Sounding Board," individuals' opinions on various subjects, was carried over from the old magazine, but added to it was a new "Feedback" feature. A computer selection of the magazine's readers received a questionnaire based on the "Sounding Board" well in advance of the latter's publication. Replies to the questionnaire were then tabulated and published with the "Sounding Board" opinion piece. This and other features, such as an expanded letters to the editor department named "You May Be Right" (after the reply sent by H. L. Mencken to all his reader correspondents), allowed *U.S. Catholic* to describe itself as "the magazine that carries on a continuing correspondence with its readers."[1]

In this latest incarnation, the editors of *U.S. Catholic* boldly confronted a genre of publishing that many Catholic publications have adopted, communicating the teachings of the Church in an authoritative, deductive manner (a style that might be described flippantly as a "now hear this" approach). With the support of their Claretian publishers, the editors of *U.S. Catholic* raise significant questions rather than supply answers, especially final answers. Some of the magazine's readers remain restless with this approach, asking for the clear-cut answers that had been offered to them in the past. But the majority of readers have made it clear that they welcome being treated as adult Christians capable of serious reflection, of thinking for themselves.

Since 1963, *U.S. Catholic* has been acclaimed in its field, as witnessed by awards for both editorial and promotional excellence from the Catholic Press Association, the Associated Church Press, and the Religious Public Relations Council.

In the past several decades the magazine has broadened its circulation base by offering subscriptions as an option for subscribers to discontinued magazines such as *Look*, the original *Life*, and a number of other publications, such as the Catholic monthly *Sign*.

In its October 1968 issue *U.S. Catholic* announced:

With this issue, a highly respected name appears in conjunction with *U.S. Catholic* on the cover and masthead. In 1953, when Edward Rice and Robert Reynolds began to publish *Jubilee*, the future for Catholic magazines seemed unlimited—at least for magazines like *Jubilee*. The first of the Catholic magazines to emphasize and use photojournalism creatively, *Jubilee* revolutionized its field and made imitators of most of us.

We expect the merger of *Jubilee* and *U.S. Catholic* to graft on to the newer magazine the creative spirit of *Jubilee*'s founders and the dedication of its loyal subscribers. And if the future of Catholic magazine publishing doesn't seem as unlimited as it did in 1953, those of us who are convinced that Catholic magazines do have a necessary part to play cannot but be encouraged by the joining of *U.S. Catholic* and *Jubilee*.[2]

The unwieldy title, *U.S. Catholic and Jubilee* continued as the magazine's logo through the December 1971 issue.

One noteworthy occasion in the history of *U.S. Catholic* came in December 1967, when the magazine editorially was among the first publications to call the war in Vietnam "immoral." This outspoken statement generated some favorable correspondence from readers, but when a recap of the editorial appeared in the *New York Times*, the editors received many angry letters and other hate mail from this wide readership. Interestingly, when *U.S. Catholic* repeated its editorial position two years later, the growing American disenchantment with the war was reflected in an almost total absence of negative mail. This latter editorial was acclaimed the best of its kind by the judges of both the Associated Church Press and the Catholic Press Association.

In 1979 the Claretians worldwide resolved to dedicate themselves to "a preferential option for the poor"[3] and to the social justice challenges inherent in that statement. In order to be faithful to this commitment of their publishers and yet not to unbalance the general interest nature of *U.S. Catholic*, an editorial decision was made to spin off another magazine to be devoted solely to social justice issues, especially those that confront individuals and small groups rather than institutions. This magazine, called *Salt*, is published by the Claretians ten times annually.

Notes

1. "Media Kit" (Chicago: Claretian Publications, 1993).
2. Robert E. Burns, Editorial, *U.S. Catholic and Jubilee* 34 (October 1968): inside front cover.
3. *Proceedings of the Claretian General Chapter* (Rome: Claretian General Curia, 1979), 101-103.

Information Sources

LOCATION SOURCES: *U.S. Catholic* and its predecessors are not self-indexed. They are indexed in the *Readers' Guide to Periodical Literature* and the *Catholic Periodical Index*. Back issues are available on microfilm, University Microfilms, Ann Arbor, Michigan.

INDEX SOURCES: Bound volumes of all issues published are available at the offices of the publisher.

Publication History

MAGAZINE TITLE AND TITLE CHANGES: *Voice of St. Jude* (1935–June 1961); *St. Jude* (July 1961–August 1963); *U.S. Catholic* (September 1963–September 1968, January 1972–); *U. S. Catholic and Jubilee* (October 1968–December 1971).
VOLUME AND ISSUE DATA: 1:1 (January 1935)–present.
PUBLISHER AND PLACE OF PUBLICATION: Claretian Publications, Chicago, Illinois.
EDITORS: James Tort (1935–1944); Joseph Puigvi (1944–1948); Joachim DePrada (1948–1958); Robert J. Leuver (1958–1972); Mark J. Brummel (1972–present).
CIRCULATION: 50,000.

Robert E. Burns

U.S. CATHOLIC AND JUBILEE. *See* U.S. CATHOLIC

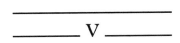

V

VINCENTIAN. *See* U.S. CATHOLIC

VIRTUE

Evangelical Protestant Christianity in twentieth-century America took institutional form primarily in special-purpose parachurch organizations. These became the primary agents for spreading the evangelical Gospel. As the popular base of evangelicalism expanded after World War II, many evangelicals felt a need for special organizations dedicated not to spreading the Gospel but to nurturing the lives and faith of those already within the evangelical fold. Evangelicals set up their own institutions that directly paralleled secular organizations found in the larger culture. The trend became particularly evident in the 1970s, when evangelical entrepreneurs started scores, perhaps hundreds, of new non-evangelistic enterprises with an explicit Christian orientation. These encompassed virtually every area of modern life: professional associations, popular avocations, education, leisure, family life, health, arts and entertainment, and publishing.

The 1970s were also when the women's movement became prominent. As social attitudes concerning women's roles and activities shifted, career and educational opportunities previously closed to women opened up. Legislation and court decisions redressed many inequalities under the law, and the equal rights amendment came close to ratification. Governmental restrictions on birth control became unthinkable, and the Supreme Court judged abortion to be a constitutional right, though later decades brought much controversy and some greater regulation of abortion.

Some American women, however, found that the women's movement did not represent their interests or understand their needs. Officially, groups like the National Organization of Women affirmed the legitimacy of religion, monogamy, motherhood, and homemaking for those who freely chose them. In its popular voice, however, the women's movement seemed to some to denigrate these choices, for they equated the encouragement for women to take up careers outside the home with a view that saw traditional motherhood as an impediment to self-fulfillment.

Virtue magazine was a product of both the growing evangelical interest in ministries of nurture and popular discontent among evangelicals with the presumed ideological narrowness of the women's movement. Devi Titus founded *Virtue* in 1978 as an alternative forum for Christian women who had chosen to make home and family their center of concern. Titus's husband, Larry, was the pastor of Bethesda Christian Center, a large, independent charismatic church in Wenatchee, Washington. Backed by the church and with some advice from Jamie Buckingham, a well-known charismatic pastor and writer, Titus and several other women in the congregation launched the magazine in glossy, full-color format. The first issues had no advertising, and women in the Church wrote most of the articles. Within a year they had a mostly regional, paid circulation of over ten thousand.

In 1979 Bethesda Christian Center began to have severe financial difficulties. The magazine itself had run up a $180,000 debt, and the church was forced to consider putting it up for sale. Titus called in William Carmichael, editor of the charismatic periodical *Logos Journal*, as a consultant. Despite the magazine's debt and its unpolished style, Carmichael and his wife, Nancie, were highly impressed with the intense loyalty demonstrated in readers' letters. *Virtue* seemed to have its finger on the pulse of evangelical women who found themselves unrepresented by the women's movement and therefore outside one of the currents cascading through American culture.

Virtue's difficulties came at a propitious time for the Carmichaels. William Carmichael had been commuting to New Jersey from his home in Sisters, Oregon, to work on *Logos Journal* but had finally concluded that the arrangement was unworkable. *Virtue* offered a way to remain in the Christian periodical business and stay in Oregon. As a result, the Carmichaels bought the magazine and moved it to offices near their home in 1980. The Carmichaels came to their new project out of a background in the "classic Pentecostalism" of the Assemblies of God. William Carmichael had pastored churches in that denomination before he went to *Logos Journal*. The reorganized *Virtue* began publication with a total staff of five, including the Carmichaels and editor Laurie Masten, who had worked for the magazine in Wenatchee. For articles, they helped nourish a network of freelance Christian writers, virtually all women, many of whom lived in the Pacific Northwest.

To meet *Virtue*'s pressing financial needs, the Carmichaels mortgaged their house and then mailed a letter to all subscribers asking them to help save the magazine by renewing for a year in advance. They also began to seek revenue from advertising, but this proved more difficult than they had anticipated. Many organizations catering to the Protestant evangelical subculture were reluctant to advertise in a magazine with a charismatic pedigree. This fear was gradually overcome, partly because the charismatic movement gained wider popular acceptance and partly because the Carmichaels diminished the magazine's charismatic tone. By the late 1980s the magazine was generating substantial advertising revenue, primarily from religious book publishers and record companies.

When the Carmichaels acquired *Virtue*, they felt that continued reader loyalty would be the key to the magazine's success. To keep centered on their audience's needs and concerns, the Carmichaels established an editorial board made up of women who were representative of their readers. In the early 1980s the Carmichaels perceived their audience to be mainly Christian homemakers who needed affirmation in the path they had taken. Most editorial content was designed to do this, helping them along the way in their spiritual lives and family relationships.

There were two major shifts in *Virtue*'s editorial policy during the Carmichaels' tenure as publishers. The first was initiated by Becky Durost, who became editor in 1985. Durost was, at the time, an unmarried career woman, and, of course, the other members of the magazine's mostly female staff were career women as well. Durost realized that large numbers of evangelical women in America held jobs outside the home—some out of necessity, although others did so by choice. They shared many of the values of the full-time homemakers who comprised the bulk of *Virtue*'s readers, yet they faced a different set of challenges every day. Durost's intuition was borne out by reader surveys. In 1980, 35 percent of a core group of *Virtue* subscribers worked outside the home. By 1990, 65 percent of these same women had outside jobs. This change led to the addition of career women to the editorial board for the first time and to the inclusion of articles of interest to working Christian women. Under Durost's editorship, *Virtue*'s writers began to seek out the common threads linking young to middle-aged evangelical women, whether married or single, mothers or childless, working primarily inside or outside the home.

The second shift was set in motion by the results of focus group meetings and reader surveys completed in 1990. Throughout the 1980s, *Virtue* urged its readers to take up active Christian ministry outside their homes. The magazine urged women to help the homeless in their communities, to work for better education for their children, to fight drug and alcohol abuse, to visit prisoners, to be more creative and active in church affairs, and to consider a host of other service activities. Nevertheless, the surveys contained something of a surprise for the editorial staff. *Virtue*'s readers seemed to be saying that their lives were already overworked and overstressed. Mothering, working, and maintaining family relationships left them little energy or time for other activities. This discovery led to fewer articles about Christian service and more aimed at deepening readers' spiritual lives. In theological terms, it represented a subtle shift from a focus on works to a focus on grace. This editorial change was accompanied by a design change, as the magazine dropped its modern style, added more color, and took on a nostalgic Victorian look.

Most columns and articles continued to be written by women. Many were freelance writers, but a few prominent in the evangelical subculture, including Luci Swindoll, Joni Eareckson Tada, Jill Briscoe, and Stormie Omartian. Each issue had one or more profiles of, or interviews with, evangelical women, many of whom were well known and all of whom had noteworthy life experiences or careers in ministry. *Virtue* occasionally carried articles by male contributors who were widely known in evangelical circles, such as Jamie Buckingham, Walter Wangerin, and Michael Card. Regular features included letters from readers; book, music, and video reviews; and columns on spiritual life, health, home management, Christian service, and men's viewpoints on marriage and family.

Virtue's paid circulation climbed from 10,000 in 1979 to 114,000 in 1991. It began as a bimonthly, increased to ten times yearly in 1986, then scaled back to bimonthly publication by 1991. Its success allowed the Carmichaels to take on other projects. They organized women's conferences throughout the Pacific Northwest. In 1982 they began a women's prison ministry that involved visiting and evangelizing women in the state prison systems of Oregon and Washington. The Carmichaels also used the issues explored in *Virtue* as a springboard for three books they coauthored between 1984 and 1989.

By the end of the 1980s, *Virtue* occupied an established niche in the marketplace, and the Carmichaels began to think seriously about starting a second periodical—a parenting magazine for evangelical Christians. In 1988 they raised the capital to begin *Christian Parenting Today* through a partnership agreement with David C. Cook Publishing, a for-profit subsidiary of the David C. Cook Foundation of Elgin, Illinois. The agreement organized both magazines under the corporate name of Good Family Magazines and gave Cook the option to purchase them both. Cook exercised the option that year. By 1992 a third magazine had been purchased, *Parents of Teens*, and Bill Carmichael had taken a position with Cook as Director of Development for Family Life. Nancie remained with *Virtue* as an adviser and columnist, and Rocky Gilmore took over as publisher. *Christian Parenting Today*, meanwhile, after just four years in existence, became the highest-circulation commercial periodical in the evangelical world. Only its inability to attract secular advertisers capped its paid circulation at 250,000.

Under Devi Titus, *Virtue* perceived its audience to be composed strictly of evangelical Christian women who were full-time homemakers. The magazine focused on typical homemaker concerns, such as family, food, fashion, and home decorating, and articles on these topics often (but not always) had some religious content. Special features more often discussed spiritual matters, always in nonsectarian fashion. The first issues read much like a general 1950s women's magazine, but with a charismatic flavor. For the most part, *Virtue* did not attack feminism, although its editorial viewpoint assumed attitudes and values at variance with those championed by the feminist movement. Contrary to the women's movement's promotion of self-assertion and gender equality, articles assumed that motherhood and homemaking were the standard for a satisfying life (although there were occasional articles for single women and single mothers) and that women performed a complementary and supportive function for their husbands. Most writers held the view, common in evangelical circles, that men were properly the spiritual and temporal leaders of the home and wives were to submit to their husbands' leadership. *Virtue*'s writers placed a high value on Christian institutions (families, churches, schools, and parachurch agencies) as shelters in which Christianity and its values could be protected and nourished.

During the years Nancie and William Carmichael published *Virtue,* the magazine retained much of this same vision. A more egalitarian vision for marriage prevailed, but marriage and mothering were still accorded high importance in every issue. However, *Virtue* no longer treated marriage and motherhood as the sole norm for Christian womanhood. Columnists, editorial board members, and women profiled in the magazine's feature articles came to include single women, childless women, career women, and divorced women. Columns and articles increasingly dealt with their special concerns. *Virtue* never wavered in its unequivocal opposition to abortion but offered compassion, not condemnation, to women who had had abortions. Nor did it lose its conviction that Christian faith is essential to human wholeness, primarily through a belief in the Gospel's power to heal broken emotions, relationships, and lives. Many of *Virtue*'s articles centered on how to deepen one's relationship with God, and most other articles, whether profiles of women with interesting careers in ministry or suggestions for improving a marriage, had an explicitly Christian frame of reference. Most issues also ran an evangelistic sidebar directed at women who were experiencing problems in their lives, inviting them to write if they had questions about making a decision to follow Jesus. Under the Carmichaels, *Virtue* tried to steer away from promoting either self-abnegation or self-assertion and toward encouraging self-acceptance.

Over the years, *Virtue* expanded its audience from evangelical homemakers to a more diverse spectrum of evangelical women. This made it easier to increase circulation, though the shift cost it a few homemaker-readers along the way. The magazine profiled African American and Latino women more frequently toward the end of the 1980s and in 1992 added an African American to the editorial board. On the issue of schooling, *Virtue* remained neutral, offering support for those who sent their children to public schools, as well as those who sent their children to Christian schools or who schooled their children at home. Its primary mission became affirming and supporting evangelical women from all circumstances and all walks of life.

Information Sources

INDEX SOURCES: None.

LOCATION SOURCES: Copies of all issues are available from *Virtue*, P.O. Box 850, Sisters, Oregon 97759.

Publication History

MAGAZINE TITLE: *Virtue* (1978–present).

VOLUME AND ISSUE DATA: 1:1 (September-October 1978)–present. Published variously from six to ten issues per year; currently, six times yearly.

PUBLISHER AND PLACE OF PUBLICATION: Devi Titus, Wenatchee, Washington (1978–1980); William and Nancie Carmichael, Sisters, Oregon (1980–1992); Rocky Gilmore, Sisters, Oregon (1992–present).

EDITORS: Devi Titus (1978–1980), Laurie Masten (1980–1982), Clare Forward (1982–1983), Lee Zanon (1983–1985), Becky Durost Fish (1985–1990), Marlee Alex (1990–present).

CIRCULATION: 130,000 (1991).

Michael S. Hamilton

VOICE OF ST. JUDE. *See* U.S. CATHOLIC

W

WALTHER LEAGUE MESSENGER

Issued eleven times per year from 1892 continuously through 1963, the *Walther League Messenger* documents the history of the International Walther League—an independent youth auxiliary representing at its peak a network of over five thousand congregations primarily affiliated with the Lutheran Church–Missouri Synod.[1] Full of local society correspondence, convention reports, program news, and religious articles, the journal was also a means to educate young German Americans and, later, Americanized Lutherans about every major issue and debate in their culture and beyond. Published independently and not under the control of the denominational structure of the Missouri Synod, the *Messenger* was at liberty to comment upon questions such as suffrage, war, sexuality, race, ecumenism, and much more. The journal is an outstanding primary source of Lutheran lay piety, in general, and of young people's religion, in particular, for the late nineteenth and most of the twentieth centuries.

In fact, the publication preceded the organization and was instrumental in its founding. The first masthead read *Der Vereinsbote* (The Society Messenger), and the lead article by Reverend August Senne of Buffalo outlined why German American Lutherans needed a national youth organization. "True union makes strength," Senne argued, pointing to guilds, labor unions, and denominational synods as examples.[2] The journal was published almost entirely in German. Advertisements helped defray the cost, including one from "Schorr Bros. Hardware, Roofing, Tinware, and General Jobbing," which ran upside-down for all of 1892. *Der Vereinsbote* also contained sermons, essays on Church history, and articles filled with practical information about organizing a young people's society. Almost every issue included some kind of pitch for the new League. For instance, "A Word to Parents" warned German-speaking mothers and fathers about the glut of cheap, trashy reading material in the English language. The not-so-subtle message was that parents should subscribe to *Der Vereinsbote*, conveniently published in a nine-by-twelve-inch format on newsprint by Buffalo Lutherans F. W. Burow and Sons Printers.[3] More substantively, *Der Vereinsbote* served to announce and report upon the annual League conventions—the first of which was held 20–24 May 1893 in Buffalo, New York (the name of Walther League, after the founder of the Missouri Synod, C.F.W. Walther, was chosen at the 1896 convention).

Walther Leaguers had inherited a learned tradition from the founder of Lutheranism, and thus in 1893 the first "series" of articles in the paper introduced young readers to the colleges of the Synodical Conference: Concordia Colleges at Sherman Park, New York, Conover, North Carolina, Ft. Wayne, Indiana, and St. Paul, Minnesota, along with St. John's College, Winfield, Kansas.[4] Each article was accompanied by a photo of the school. Most of the articles in *Der Vereinsbote* stressed education in some way. Articles on Church history, notably Luther, were especially common. Luther was held up as an example for youth; his work as a scholar was highlighted; a Luther-fest was recommended; Luther's death was remembered.[5] Philip Melanchthon, another Lutheran reformer, also was discussed in two long articles, and the birthday of Katharina von Bora, Luther's wife, was covered.[6]

But the journal featured even more practical articles. Rev. Adolf T. Hanser, editor of the journal from 1892 to 1913, asserted that "true education consists not in having crammed into your head all manner of studies, nay, it consists in using it, when it will do good. Use it then in your society . . . to help your neighbor forward."[7] *Der Vereinsbote* therefore included frequent articles about leadership skills, parliamentary procedure, and suitable "entertainments" for a Lutheran young people's society.

In 1900, subscriptions to *Der Vereinsbote* cost twenty-five cents, but the fee was often hard to collect. The first general field secretary, Fred A. Klein, argued that

Vereinsbote is the official organ of the League. It is the medium through which all societies are kept in touch with each other. It brings to you entertainment, instruction, news from friends far away twelve [*sic*] times a year in a neat shape and form and in return the League expects of you "Twenty-five Cents." And still we hear grumbling, complaint, of all kind. Do you know of another way of keeping the business part of the League alive?[8]

Klein was the first, not the last, to issue such an appeal for Leaguers to support their journal.

Still, the publication grew to thirty-six pages by 1900, and by 1910 *Der Vereinsbote* was over fifty pages per issue—an average maintained throughout the remainder of its history. A typical page from the back of the publication in 1912 contained ten ads, from four different lumberyards, an insurance agent, a chicken farmer ("Let Lutherans patronize Lutherans!"), a physician, a pharmacist, a jeweler, and a business college.[9] In 1914, one organization took up a half-page ad on the back cover that it would keep through much of the history of the publication: "Aid Association for Lutherans, Appleton, Wis. Established in 1902. A Mutual Beneficiary Society for Lutherans in the Synodical Conference. A Good, Live, Progressive Organization."[10] "Advertising rates cheerfully furnished upon application to Business Manager," the editors always alerted readers.

A new, more pious content, along with a more modern magazine format and greater use of English, came along with the transfer of the publication's headquarters from Buffalo to Milwaukee in 1913. Each issue now began with an article devoted to a religious topic, such as "The Life of Jesus," "Heaven," "Repentance," "Justification," "God," "Creation," and so forth. The changes were made by an editorial board that had three clergy—Reverend Charles Buenger of Kenosha and Reverends William Dallmann and Herman Steege of Milwaukee—and one layman, A. A. Grossmann of Milwaukee. Grossmann was the managing editor. Still, piety did not keep the *Messenger* from controversial topics. World War I divided the German American community, and the *Messenger* documented how Walther Leaguers began a campaign to demonstrate their loyalty to the U.S. cause. "Walther Leaguers, Attention!" ran the headline to one article. "The Biggest Opportunity for Service is Knocking At Your Door. Our Lutheran Soldier and Sailor Boys Need Weapons. GET BEHIND THIS CAMPAIGN."[11]

Even more significant was the end of German as the official language of the publication. Over the years the amount of English material in *Der Vereinsbote* had grown well beyond the one-column "English Corner," which had first been published in 1902. When the United States declared war on Germany, the editors initially decided to print two separate versions of the journal: one completely in English to be shipped overseas and another in both German and English for readers in the States. All of the issues of the *Walther League Messenger* after March 1918, however, were completely in English. One editor shed no tears: "We often thought no one read the German department anyhow."[12] The official line was more chagrined: "To confuse the nation's grievance against the German government as a grievance against the German language is utterly silly and displays a lack of understanding for the principles because of which America has gone to war."[13]

By 1920, the Walther Leaguers had, through their conventions and publication, initiated a number of Progressive-like projects. Most notably, after a lengthy debate the Leaguers had voted in 1900 to allow women as voting delegates to their convention, twenty years before women could vote for president of the United States. The Leaguers also, through the *Messenger*, learned of the importance of sanatoria for the treatment of tuberculosis and, through the columns of their publication, advertised for and saw founded a Lutheran Sanatorium in Wheat Ridge, Colorado (the project continues under independent ownership as Lutheran General Hospital, Denver, and Wheat Ridge Ministries, Chicago).[14] Finally, through the pages of the *Messenger* the Walther Leaguers established and propagated a twelve-hundred-city "hospice" system, which was a cross between the Young Men's Christian Association (YMCA) network and

Jane Addams's Hull House, to provide housing and boarding for German American Lutherans relocating to cities.

In 1920 the Walther League hired its first full-time director and editor of the *Messenger*—Reverend Walter A. Maier. The Harvard-trained preacher became, arguably, the most significant Lutheran in American public life during the period. Founder of "The Lutheran Hour" radio ministry in 1923, Maier used the *Walther League Messenger* in a similar fashion to propagate his rhetorically bombastic version of the Christian Gospel, which he tailored to the conflicts and circumstances of American life. Between 1920 and 1945 the *Messenger* was, in many ways, Maier's voice in print. He wrote the lead article and a lengthy news and opinion column in nearly every issue.

Consequently, all of Maier's strong opinions find expression in the magazine, published with color covers after 1935. He supported the Leaguers' involvement in innovative camping ministries, encouraged Lutherans to enroll at Valparaiso University (purchased by a group of Missouri Synod laity in 1925), and, of course, printed favorable reviews of his radio broadcasts. Maier also notably increased the international coverage of the journal, including a missionary's field report in almost every issue. Furthermore, the *Messenger* documents Maier's virulent oppositions: to lodges and secret societies; to "unionism" (ecumenism); to modernism, evolution, the flappers, and jazz; to Catholicism (he followed Luther in calling the pope the Antichrist); and to Zionism (like many German Americans he supported Hitler early in the Nazi leader's rise to power but eventually repudiated anti-Semitism as anti-Christian).

Still, through the correspondence and ancillary articles the *Messenger* continued to record lay voices alongside Maier's. On Prohibition, for instance, one correspondent noted that "the first temperance society in America was formed in New England. Every member had to bind himself to the following pledge: 'We the undersigned, believing in the evil effects of strong drink, do hereby pledge ourselves on our sacred honor that we will not get drunk more than four times a year: Muster Day, Fourth of July, Thanksgiving, and Christmas.' "[15] The subtle point was that a moral matter such as alcohol consumption was best left to individual conscience.

In 1923, the national office launched a "Subscription Campaign" (the first of many) with the motto "A Messenger in Every Home." The drive worked and gained about ten thousand new readers for the *Messenger*, boosting subscriptions to about thirty thousand total.[16] The League also diversified its publishing efforts. Three new journals appeared—*The Bible Student* in 1922, *The Concordia Junior Messenger* in 1923, and *Worker's Quarterly* in 1929. All were short-lived, with the exception of *Worker's Quarterly*, which continued until 1967 to provide program guides, suggestions for "mixers," and advice on social service projects for local societies. In 1937, the *Messenger* spun off another new publication, *The Cresset*, which continues to be published by Valparaiso University.

During World War II, the *Messenger* reported on Lutheran soldiers overseas, served as a guide for local activities on "the home front," and functioned to advise Lutherans on controversial questions of the time. For instance, one article said that "one question was constantly asked" by the Leaguers: " 'Please Tell Us: Should We Marry Now or Wait Till After the War?' "[17] Maier resigned as editor in May 1945. "I have sensed," he explained, "an unmistakable opposition to my editorial policy, particularly in regard to the menace of atheistic communism."[18] In October, the *Messenger* ran a one-page "Appreciation" of Dr. Maier. Until his death in January 1950, these were almost the last words written by or about this man in the publication he had expanded to a distribution list of seventy thousand in 1945.[19] The rift in perspective between Maier and the new editorial committee of the *Messenger* foreshadowed a troubled future for the Walther League, for its church body, and for American culture in general (the Missouri Synod suffered schism in 1974 over many controverted religious and cultural questions).

Beginning in September 1946, Rev. Alfred P. Klausler took over as editor, a position he held until 1963 (he also served as coeditor of *Arena* from 1964 to 1967). Klausler liked controversy. He still included articles on traditional topics such as the Bible, Missouri Synod history, missions, and 4-H leaders and sports heroes, but, increasingly, "hot" issues also found their way onto the pages of the *Messenger*. For instance, reviews of films, trade books, musical recordings, and television (after 1949) were added. Klausler had a keen eye for "scoops"—a notable journalistic coup was an exclusive interview with Walter Reuther, president of the United Auto Workers and a member of the Missouri Synod.[20] More than any other issue, though, eradication of racism became the cause championed by the Walther League publication after 1946. "The *Messenger* hopes to hit, and hit hard, any manifestations of racial discrimination in the Christian church," new editor Klausler announced.[21] He kept his word.

Throughout the 1950s and 1960s, the *Messenger* attained a high degree of journalistic professionalism, which was recognized when it received two Associated Church Press awards in 1951 and 1961 as one of the top religious publications in the country.[22] In 1955, the journal switched from its nine-by-twelve-inch format to a more convenient (and economical) four-by-six-inch size. All of the currents of popular culture found their way into the *Messenger*. For instance, a correspondent from the Rainier, Maryland, Walther League society reported in 1953 on their "Roman Banquet," later immortalized as the fraternity "toga party."[23] Another article from 1957 asked, "What about Elvis Presley?"[24] Throughout the 1960s, the issues of racism, atomic weapons, women's rights, ecumenism, and other controverted topics received extensive coverage. Often, the *Messenger* took stances—especially on ecumenism—far beyond the official Missouri Synod position.

Despite its excellence, beginning in the late 1950s the *Messenger* had a hard time getting and keeping subscribers. Subscription campaigns thereby became a nearly annual affair, but as editor Klausler recalled, "those damnable subscription campaigns . . . never accomplished anything."[25] By 1963 the decision was made to end the *Messenger* as an independent publication, and the Walther League staff agreed to cooperate with the youth board of another Lutheran denomination to publish *Arena*. (The agreement was with the American Lutheran Church [ALC]; *Arena One* was a joint publication of the Walther League, the ALC, and the Lutheran Church in America [LCA]. The ALC and LCA, along with a small group of Missouri Synod congregations, many of whom had roots in the Walther League, formed the Evangelical Lutheran Church in America in 1988.)

During the long, slow death of the Walther League between 1968 and 1977, one or another publication continued to report on Walther League events, but none of these publications achieved the success of the *Messenger* (*Bridge*, for instance, was reduced by 1977 to a four-page mimeographed newsletter). Nevertheless, the *Walther League Messenger* had for over seventy years provided a significant body of Lutheran young people with a forum to express their hopes and dreams, fears and longings. The *Messenger* had reported on nearly every major event and controversy in American history between 1892 and 1963, had articulated the characteristic Lutheran theological emphases on Scripture, grace, faith, and education, and had served as witness to the gradual acculturation of German Americans.

Notes

1. See Jon Pahl, *Hopes and Dreams of All: The International Walther League and Lutheran Youth in American Culture, 1893–1993* (Chicago: Wheat Ridge Ministries, 1993).

2. August P. Senne, "*Was Wir Wünschen*" ["What We Wish"], *Der Vereinsbote* 1:1 (August 1892): n.p., translation by Jill Norton.

3. "*Ein Wort an Eltern*" ["A Word to Parents"], *Der Vereinsbote* 1:7 (December 1892): n.p.

4. See *Der Vereinsbote* 3:7 (January 1895); 6:3 (October 1897); 6:5 December 1897); 6:10 (May 1898); 7:10 (May 1899). The Synodical Conference was an association of doctrinally conservative Lutheran Synods, of which the Missouri Synod was the largest.

5. "Luther als Vorbild für die Jügend" ["Luther as Example for Youth"], *Der Vereinsbote* 2:5 (November 1893); "Luther in Marburg," ibid. 3:4 (October 1894); "Die Lutherfeier: am 10 Nov, dem Geburtstage Luther" ["The Luther-fest: November 10, the Birthday of Luther"], ibid. 4:2 (September 1895); "Luther's Tod" ["Luther's Death"], ibid. 4:7 (February 1896).

6. "Philip Melanchthon," *Der Vereinsbote* 5:6–7 (January–February 1897); "Katharina von Bora," ibid. 7:7 (February 1899).

7. *Der Vereinsbote* 7:11 (June 1899).

8. Ibid. 13:2 (September 1904): 19.

9. Ibid. 21 (December 1912): 51–52.

10. *Der Vereinsbote: Walther League Messenger* 22 (February 1914).

11. Ibid. 26 (August 1917): 1.

12. C. Buenger, "Our War Work," *Walther League Messenger* 26 (March 1918): 236.

13. "To Our Readers," ibid., p. 235.

14. Heinrich G. Merz, "*Denver, Colorado, als Krankenasyl*," *Der Vereinsbote* 12 (November 1903): 31. See also *Der Vereinsbote* 12 (December 1903): 39.

15. *Walther League Messenger* 28 (January 1920): 223.

16. "Announcing a Nationwide Campaign," November 1923, Concordia Historical Institute Walther League Collection. See also "The Voice of the People," *Lutheran Witness* 43 (15 January 1924): 24.

17. " 'Please Tell Us: Should We Marry Now or Wait Till After the War?' " *Walther League Messenger* 50 (April 1942): 436.

18. "Walter A. Maier to Executive Board of the International Walther League, Mr. Henry W. Buck, President," 25 May 1945, Walter A. Maier papers, Concordia Historical Institute, St. Louis, MO. See also Walter A. Maier, "The New Year—For Christ or Communism?" *Walther League Messenger* 53 (January 1945): 190; especially, "Who Is Un-American?" *Walther League Messenger* 53 (April 1945): 280, printed just a month before his resignation.

19. "An Appreciation," *Walther League Messenger* 54 (October 1945): 23.

20. Robert Ihde, "Labor Leader," *Walther League Messenger* 56 (April 1948): 8.

21. "Editorial Window," *Walther League Messenger* 55 (September 1946): 15.

22. See *Walther League Messenger* 58 (June 1950): 22; ibid. 67 (June 1959): 41.

23. "League Mirror," *Walther League Messenger* 61 (July 1953): 31–32.

24. Frederick Pralle, "Elvis Presley?" *Walther League Messenger* 65 (February 1957): 20–21.

25. Alfred P. Klausler to Leonard Ramming, personal letter, 10 August 1972, Concordia Historical Institute, 801 DeMun Avenue, St. Louis, Mo.

Information Sources

INDEX SOURCES: Unknown.

LOCATION SOURCES: Concordia University Library, River Forest, Illinois, has 2–71 (1894–1963).

Publication History

MAGAZINE TITLE AND TITLE CHANGES: *Der Vereinsbote* (1892–1918); *Walther League Messenger* (1919–1963); merged with *Arena* (1963–1965), *Arena One* (1966–1967), *Edge* (1967–1968); continued as *Bridge: The Walther League* (1968–1977).

VOLUME AND ISSUE DATA: *Der Vereinsbote*: 1:1 (June 1892)–21:11 (June 1913). *Der Vereinsbote/Walther League Messenger* 22:1 (August 1913)–26:6 (January 1918). *Walther League Messenger* 26:7 (February 1918)–71:1 (July 1963). *Arena* 72:2 (September 1963)–74:9 (June 1966). *Arena One* 1:1 (January 1967)–1:9 (October 1967). *Bridge* (May 1973–August 1977), mimeographed newsletter.

PUBLISHER AND PLACE OF PUBLICATION: Published by the International Walther League. Published in the home of Adolf T. Hanser, Buffalo, New York (1892–1913); the home of A. A. Grossmann, Milwaukee, Wisconsin (1913–1920); 6438 Eggleston Avenue, Chicago, Illinois (1920–1943); 875 N. Dearborn Street, Chicago, Illinois (1943–1963).

EDITORS: Adolf T. Hanser (1892–1913); Editorial Committee (see text), Managing editor: A. A. Grossmann (1913–1920); Walter A. Maier (1920–1945); Alfred P. Klausler (1946–1963).

CIRCULATION: Unknown.

Jon Pahl

WAR CRY

On a brisk winter night, while a heavy fog shrouded the London streets, William Booth readied his next salvo in the war against sin. A successful street evangelist, Booth had severed his ties to the Methodist New Connection when criticized for his enthusiastic revivalistic techniques. Assisted by his wife, Catherine, and a handful of volunteers, Booth had mobilized an evangelistic and mission team that he had christened the Salvation Army. Now, on 27 December 1879, Booth was preparing the *War Cry*, a four-page, five-column broadsheet, to publicize his campaign to save "wretches" in the city's humblest, hungriest streets.

Why a weekly *War Cry*? Because the Salvation Army means more war.... And why more war? Because the cry of slaughtered millions rises up louder and louder to heaven crying to our inmost souls, with incredible violence, to arise and fight more furiously than ever for the salvation of our fellows from the forces of evil which are dragging them drunken, befouled, degraded, wretched, down to an eternity of woe.[1]

The launching of the *War Cry*, like the Salvation Army, is a colorful example of the transatlantic Holiness movement that swept through the United States and Great Britain during the latter decades of the nineteenth century. William and Catherine Booth, influenced by American revivalists, including James Caughey, Charles Finney, and Phoebe Palmer, believed the power of the Holy Spirit, unleashed in revival, could sanctify and perfect the human heart. Moreover, like the American perfectionists who preceded them, the Booths soon realized that preaching the Gospel to the poor was not enough.

In 1865, after leaving the Methodists, the Booths first took their message to London's East End, where, organized as the Christian Mission, they preached in tents, cemeteries, stables, theaters, and saloons. Their aim was to reach the urban poor, whose plight was largely ignored by respectable churches. In the course of their street-corner evangelism, the Booths saw the debilitating effects of alcohol and poverty on the human soul. Convinced they could not win sinners who were addicted to drink or overwhelmed by need, the Booths began providing humanitarian aid—food, shelter, and rehabilitation—for alcoholics, prostitutes, and criminals, as well as for the poor.

While Booth's work was largely ignored among the genteel classes, he developed a following among the disfranchised, the working classes, and young idealists. Not all slum residents welcomed the Christian message, however, since the outdoor evangelists were frequently pelted with eggs, tomatoes, and refuse. Neither a theologian nor a creedalist, Booth believed in using whatever technique worked to save the unconverted. He encouraged the newly saved to preach to sinners; he staged pageants and theater performances to attract spectators; he rewrote the words of popular tunes to make them become religious hymns; and he even jettisoned the sacraments, which he decided were confusing to new Christians and an unnecessary temptation for reformed alcoholics. Even Booth's decision in 1878 to change the organization's name was pragmatic. He abandoned the colorless Christian Mission for the Salvation Army, a designation that capitalized on the public's infatuation with the military. The new name also provided marginalized converts with a sense of belonging, of having a righteous mission and a sanctified identity.

The *War Cry*, which debuted a year after Booth adopted the name Salvation Army, was not Booth's first publication. In 1868, he started the *East London Evangelist* to spread word of his Christian Mission. The paper was bought out by a Christian publishing house, Morgan and Scott, and it was edited by Booth. Two years later, Booth changed the paper's name to the *Christian Mission Magazine*. Booth proved to be a less than ideal editor. He was overextended, and his prose tended to be dull. Fortunately, he had attracted a talented writer, George Scott Railton, whose work gave the publication the requisite zest. Although well educated and raised in a comfortable family, Railton understood Booth's crusade to reach common folk and, mindful of the fascination with the military, encouraged the movement to adopt martial language. Soon after his appearance on the scene, the Mission's name became the Salvation Army. At first, the organization's monthly periodical was called the *Salvationist*, but Army leaders soon realized they needed a name that would reach the unconverted rather than those already saved. The last issue of the *Salvationist* announced its successor. William Nicholson stated the aim of the publication: ''We shall try to give the news from every station, and we shall open columns in which remarkable occurrences of every sort, stories of destruction as well as salvation, terrible as well as glorious deaths, disgraceful failures as well as magnificent successes, may be recorded, omitting, of course, names when advisable.''[2]

The *War Cry*'s initial run of seventeen thousand was on double sheets, 19 by 13.5 inches. It sold for a halfpenny and proved popular with the reading public. By 1880, the weekly newspaper, which had a short run as a biweekly, reached a circulation of two hundred thousand. The *War Cry* had more in common with its Fleet Street competitors than with religious publications. The Army paper was more interested in crusading than debating. Its editors also had a knack for spotting a good story. Working with W. T. Stead, a noted investigative journalist, Booth led the *War Cry* to champion the protection of young girls through a petition to raise the age of consent for marriage. The newspaper also spoke out for free speech and the rights of women to speak in public.

Before long, the Salvation Army and its newspaper, hawked on the city streets by young recruits, were fixtures in Victorian England, and its soldiers were eager to take the fight abroad. In 1879, Eliza Shirley, a teenage zealot, received Booth's guarded permission to begin the work in Philadelphia, where her parents were moving. When the Shirleys met with success, Booth decided to send over his protégé, Railton, and ''the Hallelujah Seven,'' seven female soldiers. Railton and the ''lassies'' brought a large consignment of newspapers with them on the cruise across the Atlantic, but Railton soon realized he would need an indigenous newspaper to publicize the Army's work in the United States.

On 15 January 1881 Railton published the first edition of the *War Cry* outside

England. The paper was printed in St. Louis, where Railton had moved to begin the Army's western campaign. Newspaper sales were slow, and Railton slept on unsold copies in his cellar office when he worked through the night. The American edition was similar to its British counterpart. The newspaper used a six-column format and reported on news of the Army's advances in American cities. Railton dismissed "theory" in the first issue, observing, "The world has ten thousand times too much of that already. Let us force war."[3] Railton's duties prevented the *War Cry* from keeping to a regular publication schedule, and initial editions appeared sporadically. In the summer of 1882, a group of San Francisco Bay area Holiness men, inspired by the British *War Cry*, published four issues of their own. More than a year later, in November 1883, an official West Coast *War Cry* was launched. Throughout the 1890s, editions of the paper appeared in Swedish, German, and Chinese.

Railton, called back to England, passed the paper to local hands, and, by the early 1880s, editions appeared weekly. The paper, which had moved from St. Louis to Philadelphia, found its home, along with the Army's American headquarters, in New York. There, throughout the 1880s, it reflected late Victorian design aesthetics. The paper's small type and six-column format were increasingly relieved by the playful use of graphics. For example, the front page might feature a four-column-deep announcement that resembled a circus poster with its use of banner headlines displayed in a profusion of type faces, sizes, and settings, announcing "Monster Gatherings!" "Marching Multitudes!" "Hurricanes of Salvation and Waves of Glory!"

By the late 1880s, the newspaper adhered to a sixteen-page format with semiregular features. These included reports from the battlefield, a competition list (noting which units sold the most issues of the *War Cry*), "Come Home!" (announcements of missing persons), the "Little Soldiers'" page (later dubbed "Junior's Corner"), army songs, poems, a woman's column (sometimes called "Woman Warriors Column" and later "Mrs. Booth's Diary"), and a column called "Red Hot Religion" (a catchall that included occasional essays, aphorisms, anecdotes, and news from across the nation). As some of these features changed, so did the design. The type went to four columns, and the graphics, which included steel engravings, took over more and more of the front page until it became an illustrated cover. These illustrations often depicted Salvation Army officers, especially women, doing good deeds. They also picked up on seasonal themes: fall issues frequently showed a young woman gathering sheafs of wheat; New Year's was a variation on Father Time; Memorial Day was a cemetery scene.

The paper's nameplate also went through various configurations. The basic elements were the logo *War Cry and Official Gazette of the Salvation Army*, the folio line, and the Army insignia, a shield inscribed with the motto "Blood and Fire." The initial straightforward design became increasingly ornamental as eagles, banners, flags, and the Statue of Liberty were used to signify the interwoven ideals of liberty, democracy, and Christianity. By the turn of the century, the nameplate returned to the simple, uncluttered style that had graced the paper's earliest editions.

The newspaper stressed reportage. One editor, advising writers in a box addressed "Reporters, Please Note," wrote "When writing reports, please state what actually took place. . . . Remember this, write a report that will interest more people than yourself. No sermons."[4] Mixed in with reports from the field were cautionary tales such as the lead piece on 7 January 1888, entitled "The Speculator." This article, illustrated with a dramatic engraving of a young man in an office surrounded by money bags and a copy of the War Cry, addressed the problem of youth who have "lost sight of the principal object in life, forgotten God and turned to the things of the world for that satisfying power and love which the world can never give."[5] Inspirational items such as songs, poems, and exhortations from William and Catherine Booth filled the rest of the newspaper with an occasional essay dealing directly with a theological topic, most usually, Holiness, for "The doctrine of Holiness is the bulwark of The Salvation Army. It is the rock formation upon which the Salvation structure is built."[6]

The newspaper focused on Salvation Army news to the exclusion of most other current events. Only if the outside world impinged on the Army's actions were secular events mentioned (e.g., Salvation Army work in disaster relief, World Wars I and II, the Depression). However, the Army was not oblivious to its surroundings and its mission. In the late 1890s, the American commander, Frederick Booth-Tucker, wrote a series of articles about conditions in New York slums based on his incognito expeditions. The newspaper also tried to report on events within the Army. The 2 May 1896 edition of the War Cry contained a special supplement on the resignation of Commander and Mrs. Ballington Booth. The Booths, popular with the American public, resigned over differences with William Booth and his eldest son, Bramwell, Ballington's older brother and Army superior. The supplementary section reprinted the letters between members of the Booth family detailing the disagreements without offering any editorial comment.

Over the years, the War Cry has been consistent in its evangelical ideals despite changes in form and content. By the second decade of the twentieth century, there was a growing tendency to present the history of the Salvation Army through profiles of the Booth family and other early leaders as well as chronicles of past crusades as part of the journalistic mix. During the tenure of Commander Evangeline Booth, William Booth's daughter and head of the American Army from 1904 to 1934, covers frequently featured photographic montages of Army officers.

In succeeding decades, War Cry coverage diversified. There were more reports on secular news and news from other religious organizations. Inspirational articles became a larger part of the mix, along with theological expositions. In 1927, the national War Cry split into four regional publications as a result of the Army's expansion and recognition of regional differences. In 1969, the decision was reversed, and the four War Crys became one national magazine again. Each region of the Army still maintains its own newsletter.

The War Cry of the 1990s reflects change and continuity. Differences underscore the "graying" of the Army and its transformation from a persecuted band of raucous street evangelists to a well-respected and successful Christian evangelical and humanitarian organization. The similarities between past and present issues of the *War Cry* demonstrate the Army's ongoing commitment to evangelism and religious activism. By the 1990s, the publication was an 8½-by-11-inch, full-color magazine. Its 9 May 1992 cover was a color photograph of a snowcapped mountain surrounded by majestic trees and rushing white water. At the bottom of the page were the words, "When I look down from lofty mountain grandeur. . . . Then sings my soul. . . . How great Thou Art!'' and the inner side cover recounted the history of the popular hymn "How Great Thou Art.'' Subsequent articles included a poem, a Bible study, and inspirational pieces on learning to forgive, following God's plan for one's life, and extending love to others. The magazine's centerpiece was a lengthy feature on the Army's advances in Korea, and additional stories spotlighted national Army events and an African American Salvation Army husband and wife team.

The *War Cry*, more than a century after its debut on a cold winter's day, has editions worldwide. Weekly circulation tops 2 million, and the paper succeeds, notwithstanding prohibitions on carrying such journalistic staples as crime, sex, astrology, or racing tips. The newspapers do not, as William Booth dictated, accept advertisements. Yet they continue to thrive. That may be because the *War Cry*, despite changing incarnations because of time and place, keeps faith with its initial premise: "Remember Calvary! Comrades, remember that agony of love to you till your hearts beat, and your brains throb to do more for Him who has called you to his glory, and to virtue. . . . Aha we shall conquer! To that end let The War Cry go everywhere. Quick!''[7]

Notes

1. (British) *War Cry* 1 (27 December 1879): 1.
2. Col. William Nicholson, *The Romance of The War Cry* (London: Salvationist Publication and Supplies, 1929), 10.
3. Edward H. McKinley, *Marching to Glory* (San Francisco: Harper and Row, 1980), 35.
4. *War Cry* 327 (7 January 1888): 6.
5. Ibid., p. 1.
6. Ibid. 761 (2 May 1896): 11.
7. (British) *War Cry* 1 (27 December 1879): 1.

Information Sources

INDEX SOURCES: None.
LOCATION SOURCES: Salvation Army Archives, National Headquarters, Alexandria, Virginia.

Publication History

MAGAZINE TITLE: *War Cry* (1881–present).
VOLUME AND ISSUE DATA: No. 1 (17 January 1881)–present. Published weekly until 1985, then biweekly.

PUBLISHER AND PLACE OF PUBLICATION: Salvation Army: Chicago (1881–1965); New York (1965–1981); Verona, New Jersey (1981–1991); Alexandria, Virginia (1991–present).

EDITORS: George Scott Railton (1881), Thomas Moore (1881–1884), Frank Smith (1885–1887), William H. Cox (1888–1898, 1902–1914), William Brewer (1899–1902), W. F. Jenkins (1915–1920), Alfred Gilliard (1967–1969), Robert Thomson (1970–1971), William Burrows (1972–1978), Ralph Miller (1979), Henry Gariepy (1980–present).

CIRCULATION: 525,000 (1993).

Diane Winston

WATCHMAN. *See* WATCHMAN-EXAMINER

WATCHMAN-EXAMINER

The first two decades of the twentieth century that led to the popular use of the term *fundamentalist* were years of intense struggle for conservative evangelicals. Two of the most sensitive issues for conservative evangelicals were those of evolutionary science and biblical criticism. The evangelical paradigms of Baconian inductive science and commonsense philosophy had given way to Darwinism and skepticism by the late nineteenth century, thereby creating for evangelicals an intellectually threatening atmosphere.[1] Fundamentalists within this atmosphere developed what R. Laurence Moore has referred to as an outsider mind-set, in part a result of intellectual insecurity.[2]

At the forefront of the fundamentalist-modernist controversy were denominational battles, which for fundamentalists were battles to ensure doctrinal purity while at the same time to rid some of the major denominations of modernists. Denominations that were affected by this warfare included the Methodist Episcopal Church, Disciples of Christ, Protestant Episcopal Church, and the Southern Presbyterian Church. The most intense fighting, however, took place in the Northern Presbyterian and Northern Baptist denominations.[3] The *Watchman-Examiner* played a significant role throughout the 1920s and 1930s in the crusade to purify the Church of modernistic influences. The first editor of the *Watchman-Examiner*, Curtis Lee Laws, coined the phrase *fundamentalist* in 1920, meaning one who was prepared ''to do battle royal for the Fundamentals.''[4]

The first issue of the *Watchman-Examiner* was published on 4 September 1913 with a circulation of more than one hundred thousand.[5] The *Watchman-Examiner* resulted from the consolidation of two separate Baptist periodicals, the *Examiner* from New York and the *Watchman* from Boston. Both periodicals had impressive histories in terms of their service to the Baptist community. The *Watchman* was established in 1819, and the *Examiner* in 1823.

The editors of both magazines believed it to be in the best interests of the Baptist denomination to consolidate the two periodicals so as to have one strong representative voice rather than two independent voices. The editors of the *Watchman* stated, ''For many years leading men in our denomination have felt that the *Watchman* and the *Examiner* should consolidate.'' The rationale for this union was further justified by the observation that since the subscribers to both magazines lived within the same geographical region, it would be more practical to combine.[6] Financial distress has often been the basis for the collapse of certain publishing companies, yet, as the editors of the *Watchman* pointed out, "The *Watchman* was not in financial straits." Instead, the desire was to take the strengths of both papers and combine them.[7] The question of financial distress also was not present in the last issue of the *Examiner*, but editors assured its readers, "The past year has been its best year for many years." Subscriptions apparently increased by fifteen hundred in a four-month period.[8]

Merger occurred relatively smoothly. Editorial offices of both magazines remained the same; the *Watchman* stayed in Boston, the *Examiner* in New York. There was also an office for a special New England edition in the Boston office of the *Watchman*. Curtis Lee Laws was elected to be the editor in chief of the *Watchman-Examiner*, not only because of his experience as the editor of the *Examiner* but also because he was a younger man than the editors of the *Watchman* and apparently more fit for the pressures of the new job.[9] The consolidation was greeted with magnanimous praise from clergy and laity throughout the United States. Letters of praise also came from numerous other periodicals such as the *Standard*, the *Baptist Commonwealth*, and the *Brooklyn Eagle*.[10]

The *Watchman-Examiner* was printed on 8½ by 14 inch paper from 1913 until 1915, when it changed to 8½ by 12 inches. It was folded into approximately twenty to thirty pages every issue. Within a few years of the first publication, the pages of the magazine had a large W and E at the top of each page, with the date nestled in between the W and E. The design would eventually be changed to read "The Watchman-Examiner" at the top and in the middle of each page, with the date either to the right or the left of the title heading. The cover was adorned with a leafy-designed trim, and subtitled beneath the *Watchman-Examiner* was "A National Baptist Paper." The cover usually featured a photograph of a prominent Baptist leader or an occasional photograph of a landscape or drawing. The magazine was published weekly with subscription rates of $2.50 per year from 1913 to 1947; $3 per year from 1947 to 1959; and $4 per year from 1959 to 1970. In 1964 it became a biweekly magazine.

The overall focus of the *Watchman-Examiner* stayed fairly uniform throughout all fifty-eight volumes. Attention was given primarily to issues of concern to Baptists. Reports on Baptist events throughout the United States and the world were given in an editorial fashion, as were discussions of such issues as the Christian and political liberty, creationism versus evolutionism, sermon outlines for pastors, Christian education, poems, and anecdotal stories. Included in each issue were special columns for children ("Children's Corner") and for missionaries ("Of Missionary Interest"). The magazine was a most appropriate avenue for advertisements for Bible schools, Christian publishing companies, and mission organizations. Reflective of its appeal to a popular audience were advertisements that attempted to mix business and Christian convictions such as the one for the Fleet Fur company. In a convincing manner the ad read:

Fleet asks you to believe all that he says. You need "The Watchman-Examiner" first, and Fleet Furs next. Dr. Curtis Lee Laws assures us that "The Watchman-Examiner" is the best advertising medium because it reaches the best people. Fleet has known Dr. Laws for years and he has always made good. We believe in "The Watchman-Examiner" and we know the Baptist denomination will help it to make good and the Fleet will help too.[11]

During the time that Laws was editor in chief (1913–1938) the Northern Baptist Convention was caught in the midst of the fundamentalist-modernist controversy of the 1920s and 1930s. During this period the *Watchman-Examiner* became not only a source of information for Baptists but also a popular periodical for fundamentalists of many different varieties.

At a time when fundamentalists felt as though they were losing ground against modernism, the *Watchman-Examiner*, along with other evangelical periodicals, encouraged its readers to hold to their beliefs. The Northern Baptist Convention was one of the major denominations involved in the struggle against modernism. As chief editor, Curtis Lee Laws focused on keeping the Northern Baptist Convention in the hands of the evangelicals.[12] He was outspoken about the fact that the *Watchman-Examiner* would in no way "seek to be neutral" but would stand "for the conservative position." Laws said the magazine even played a role in promoting the 1920 "Buffalo Conference on Fundamentals."[13] But as active as Laws was in the fight to preserve the Northern Baptist Convention from modernism, Grant Wacker has shown that "Laws was as far from fundamentalists like William Bell Riley as he was from modernists like Shailer Mathews." The difference between Laws and Riley had to do with how the two viewed the inspiration of Scripture. Laws was not as dogmatic as Riley on the inspiration of the Bible. He believed that Christians who attempt to defend biblical authority by means of the "verbal-mechanical . . . theory of inspiration" are as misguided as Christians who agree with Friedrich Schleiermacher in believing that "Christian Consciousness" was the basis of authority. Oddly enough, Laws was responsible for coining the term *fundamentalist* and was at the same time convinced that biblical authority could not be proven through dogmatism.[14]

Laws retired from his post as editor in chief in 1938, turning over the reigns to John W. Bradbury, his personal choice for a successor. Laws remained as a consultant with the title of president and publisher. His retirement came at his own request, as he felt that he no longer had the strength to deal with the tasks of the job.[15] The magazine continued to carry the banner for the interests of fundamentalists within the Baptist denomination. Editorials covering such issues as the evils of liquor and the dangers of the Roman Catholic Church could be found in the *Watchman-Examiner* as late as 1950.[16] The popular level at which the magazine was published remained the same for years to follow, with the continued emphasis on the practical application of the faith to the lives of the everyday believer.[17]

John W. Bradbury retired as editor in 1964, passing the editorial baton to Dr. Lawrence T. Slaght. Bradbury assured the readers that the *Watchman-Examiner* would continue in its commitment to the Gospel and to informing and encouraging Christians about the issues surrounding their faith.[18] The *Watchman-Examiner* was published until 1970, when, as Slaght acknowledged, it was going bankrupt. He intimated that everything was going well at the magazine "except the cash flow." Despite a 154 percent increase in paid subscriptions over an eighteen-month period and a consistent pattern of advertising, the magazine still had problems overcoming financial obstacles. When the editors of *Eternity* magazine heard of the financial distress of the *Watchman-Examiner*, they leant their support to help save it, yet to no avail.[19] The *Eternity* editors told the Board of Directors of the *Watchman-Examiner* that if the magazine had to close its operation, they would "honor the subscription commitments and provide *Eternity* magazine month by month to their readers." Eventually, the board of the *Watchman-Examiner* turned the subscription list over to *Eternity*.[20] *Eternity*, along with *Christianity Today*, had become a publication outlet for the post–World War II new evangelicals and had established itself as an opponent of separatistic fundamentalism.

The *Watchman-Examiner* provided the same kind of service and function as the *Sunday School Times*, *Serving and Waiting*, *Signs of the Times*, *Revelation*, *Moody Monthly*, the *Baptist Bulletin*, and many others. It provided specifically for the needs and sentiments of Baptists but also for conservative evangelical Christians from many other denominations. The subject matter that the *Watchman-Examiner* covered was, for the most part, the same as that of these others. It appealed to a popular constituency that valued Christian virtue and morality and feared the evils of modernism. It was an attractive outlet for those who identified themselves as fundamentalists. It kept them informed as to what was happening in the Baptist denomination; it reinforced for them the old-fashioned values of conservative evangelicalism and gave spiritual encouragement for dark times. More than its appeal to a popular audience, however, the *Watchman-Examiner* helped to play a historic role in the development and nurturing of American fundamentalism.

Notes

1. Theodore Dwight Bozeman, *Protestants in an Age of Science: The Baconian Ideal and Antebellum American Religious Thought* (Chapel Hill: University of North Carolina Press, 1977); Mark A. Noll, "Common Sense Traditions and American Evangelical Thought," *American Quarterly* 37 (Summer 1985): 216–38.

2. R. Laurence Moore, *Religious Outsiders and the Making of Americans* (New York: Oxford University Press, 1986), 165.

3. Timothy P. Weber, "Fundamentalism," in *Dictionary of Christianity in America*, ed. Daniel G. Reid, Robert D. Linder, Bruce L. Shelley, and Harry S. Stout (Downers Grove, IL: InterVarsity Press, 1990), 461–65.

4. Curtis Lee Laws, "Convention Side Lights," *Watchman-Examiner* 8 (1 July 1920): 834.

5. The circulation figure of one hundred thousand was actually published in the last issue of the *Watchman* (21 August 1913), two weeks before the first issue of the *Watch-*

man-Examiner (4 September 1913). The actual number of subscribers to the *Examiner* is not available. The assumption is that circulation most definitely exceeded one hundred thousand once the two periodicals were combined.

6. *Examiner* 91 (28 August 1913): 1100; *Watchman* 95 (14 August 1913): 7.

7. *Watchman* 95 (14 August 1913): 7.

8. *Examiner* 91 (28 August 1913): 1100.

9. *Watchman* 95 (14 August 1913) 7.

10. *Watchman-Examiner* 1 (4 September 1913).

11. Ibid.: Back cover. (Advertisement for the "Fleet" fur company of New York.)

12. Grant Wacker, *Augustus H. Strong and the Dilemma of Historical Consciousness* (Macon: Mercer University Press, 1985), 143.

13. John W. Bradbury, "Curtis Lee Laws, D.D., LL.D.: An Appreciation," *Watchman-Examiner* 124 (18 July 1946): 747–49.

14. Wacker, *Augustus H. Strong*, 143–44.

15. *Watchman-Examiner* 28 (4 January 1940): 7.

16. "Liquor Has No Rights" and "Assault on Protestantism," *Watchman-Examiner* 38 (19 May 1950): 489.

17. Rev. Homer F. Yale, "Intercessory Prayer," *Watchman-Examiner* 28 (5 September 1940): 954–55.

18. John W. Bradbury, "A Fond Farewell," *Watchman-Examiner* 52 (9 April 1964): 271.

19. Russell T. Hitt and William J. Petersen, "Announcement," *Watchman-Examiner* 58 (19 March 1970): 192.

20. Lawrence T. Slaght, "A Letter to My Friends," *Watchman-Examiner* 58 (19 March 1970): 165.

Information Sources

INDEX SOURCES: Unknown.

LOCATION SOURCES: The entire collection of the *Watchman-Examiner* (volumes 1–58) can be found at the library of Northern Baptist Theological Seminary in Lombard, Illinois. Moody Bible Institute has a partial collection, as do Grand Rapids Baptist College and William Tyndale College.

Publication History

MAGAZINE TITLE AND TITLE CHANGES: *Watchman-Examiner* (1913–1970). Consolidated from two independent periodicals, the *Watchman* (1819–1913) and the *Examiner* (1823–1913).

VOLUME AND ISSUE DATA: 1:36 (4 September 1913)–58:6 (19 March 1970). Published weekly.

PUBLISHER AND PLACE OF PUBLICATION: Published by the *Watchman-Examiner* Company Inc., New York, New York, and Boston, Massachusetts (1913–1920); published in New York, New York (1920–1966); published in Somerset, New Jersey (1966–1970).

EDITORS: Curtis Lee Laws (1913–1938), John W. Bradbury (1938–1964), Lawrence T. Slaght (1964–1970).

CIRCULATION: Over 100,000 (1913).

David L. Russell

WATCHTOWER

In 1879, "Pastor" Charles Taze Russell, a Pittsburgh evangelist, launched the publication of *Zion's Watch Tower and Herald of Christ's Presence*. This magazine was to be the central organ of a burgeoning new religious movement now numbering about 3 million members. The movement, popularly known as Jehovah's Witnesses, still depends on the bimonthly publication of the *Watchtower* as the main tool in recruiting new members and the authoritative expression of its doctrine and policies.

The movement traces its origins to 1870 and an independent Bible study group in which Russell was a participant. Russell, long a Bible student, had developed radical Adventist opinions, which he began to share through a series of Bible studies. Adventist fervor ran high at the time, with thousands of independent Bible study groups seeking the Scriptures and the headlines for signs of the return of Christ. A dispute with a colleague, N. H. Barbour, led Russell to initiate his movement formally in 1872. Russell's students accepted from the first that part of their role was the distribution of the growing body of writings by Russell. The growth of the movement required a regularized publication of Russell's views, a need met by the founding of *Zion's Watch Tower* in 1879. Two years later Russell organized his followers into Zion's Watch Tower Tract Society, a group dedicated to funding and distributing the publication. The work of the society spread and grew dramatically. In 1909, Russell moved the headquarters from Pittsburgh to Brooklyn, New York, where they have remained except for a brief period during World War I. Russell continued to write most of the material in *Zion's Watch Tower*, although he was assisted by various people, including his wife, Maria Russell.

When Russell died in 1916, Joseph F. Rutherford, a lawyer and occasional judge from Missouri, succeeded him. Rutherford rapidly transformed the movement from a loose-knit collection of Adventist Bible students to an autocratic movement, single-mindedly committed to spreading its doctrines. Under Rutherford, adherents first came to be called Jehovah's Witnesses in 1931. Rutherford also turned the bimonthly magazine, now called *Watchtower*, to its modern purpose. He took the lead in applying the principles of business and marketing to the society as it sought to spread its message. *Watchtower* was the central and authoritative expression of that message. Rutherford is also credited with founding another publication, *Golden Age*, in 1918, while he was in federal prison for alleged violations of the Espionage Act. Charges arose from his urging of his followers to refuse to serve in the military, exposing him to the charge of giving aid and comfort to the enemy. He was later released. *Golden Age* soon became *Awake!*, the companion to *Watchtower*. Each is published twice monthly, on alternating weeks. *Awake!* contains the society's commentary on contemporary issues, while *Watchtower* retains its role as the main outlet for doctrine and official positions of Jehovah's Witnesses. Under Rutherford, *Watchtower* began serving as an instrument of evangelism, presented by adherents to prospects in house-to-house preaching. It also provides the basis for a weekly study meeting attended by the faithful.

Rutherford's death in 1942 left the organization in the hands of Nathan H. Knorr. His innovations were fewer, consisting chiefly in an increasingly anonymous character for publications of Jehovah's Witnesses, including *Watchtower*. All articles are without attribution, representing the voice of Jehovah as spoken through the organization. At Knorr's death in 1977, Frederick W. Franz assumed leadership of Jehovah's Witnesses. *Watchtower* has retained its form and function with little change in recent years.

The publication history of *Watchtower* is quite simple. It was first issued in 1879 by Charles Taze Russell as *Zion's Watch Tower and Herald of Christ's Presence*. Under Rutherford the name was changed several times, finally becoming the *Watchtower Announcing Christ's Kingdom*, which is still the official title. The magazine is published every two weeks, at the middle and end of the month, and has been issued continuously since its founding. Initial circulation figures are hard to find, but by 1903 there were twenty thousand copies distributed for each edition. The number had grown to nearly 2 million by 1956 and over 18 million in 1990 in 106 different languages. While there are no formal attributions for authors or editorial staff, members of the central leadership group of Jehovah's Witnesses prepare and issue *Watchtower* from the New York headquarters.

The content and themes of *Watchtower* reflect the history and beliefs of Jehovah's Witnesses. The earliest issues set forth the millennialist interpretations of the Bible of Charles Taze Russell. After his death Rutherford and the new leadership substantially revised the interpretation of history and modified the organization of the movement. The changes were announced in *Watchtower*. In more recent years, the contents of *Watchtower* have continued to reflect the views of the group's leaders about the broad themes of theology and organization. These changes include such matters as the revised predictions about the coming kingdom, as well as more mundane changes in requirements for dress or behavior. Members are generally discouraged from going back to earlier editions of the magazine because of the danger of confusion or "stumbling."

The most prominent feature of *Watchtower* is its general worldview. It describes history as a great war between Jehovah and Satan. In this war, humanity can be divided into two groups, those who are on Jehovah's side and those who are opposed and therefore on the side of Satan. As in any war, the most important task is loyalty and obedience to one's leaders. *Watchtower* depicts the Witnesses as "Jehovah's Organization," established for the purpose of bringing people to the winning side and thereby saving them from utter destruction.[1] It insists that the work is "well organized under the leadership of the Lord himself," a hierarchical structure directed by Jehovah through his appointed leaders.[2]

Loyalty to Jehovah supersedes all other loyalties or commitments. *Watchtower* has repeatedly reminded its readers that their loyalty to Jehovah is more important than responsibility to family, church, friends, or country.[3] To this end, it encourages the young not to marry, demands that adherents sever ties with other religious groups on pain of disfellowship, strives to convince readers to limit their associations to other group members, and severely constrains any entanglement with politics or government.

Millennialism is another persistent theme in *Watchtower*. Jehovah's Witnesses believe that the great conflict will soon end with the overthrow of Satan and the present world order. Since 1918, *Watchtower* has insisted that "millions now living will never die." This general viewpoint has been augmented by specific predictions of the end. In a careful reckoning of biblical dates and prophecies, *Watchtower* announced the end of history would occur in 1976.[4] Earlier editions had predicted Armageddon in 1914 and 1956. Disappointment in the failure of such predictions has led to occasional declines in circulation for *Watchtower*, although the general pattern of growth has persisted, as do the predictions of the coming end of the world.

Other regular themes in *Watchtower* arise directly from these first two. The magazine frequently admonishes its readers to abstain from participation in civic affairs as they belong to the present, Satan-dominated world. It warns against any effort to improve society, explaining that to "join in with this world's programs of reform, preaching the 'social gospel' instead of the Kingdom good news, places one at enmity with God."[5] Instead, Witnesses are urged to publish the news of the Kingdom and to obey Jehovah explicitly. For this reason they refuse blood transfusions, referring to biblical prohibitions about ingesting blood. The same concern for obedience explains the constant admonitions against military service, saluting the flag, and other indications of loyalty to anything besides Jehovah.

Watchtower continues to hold its central importance for Jehovah's Witnesses. They study it in weekly meetings and distribute it in house-to-house evangelism. It remains the most authoritative statement of the doctrine and beliefs of the movement, providing a vital connection between Witnesses around the world. Despite this in-house importance, however, it is lightly regarded except among the faithful. Other traditions view the scholarship as suspect, resting upon an overly simple and literal reading of the text. Outside scholars have complained that the chronologies and predictions are often forced, perhaps because of the Witnesses' conviction that history revolves around their movement.[6] Thus, *Watchtower* will probably remain at the center of the conflict between Jehovah's Witnesses and the rest of the world order.

Notes

1. *Watchtower* (1 February 1932): 87.
2. *Ibid.* (15 January 1942): 61.
3. *Ibid.* (1 July 1961): 401.
4. *Ibid.* (1 February 1955): 95.
5. *Ibid.* (15 August 1960): 488.
6. See, for example, W. C. Stevenson, *The Inside Story of Jehovah's Witnesses* (New York: Hart Publishing Company, 1967).

Information Sources

INDEX SOURCES: None.
LOCATION SOURCES: The Watch Tower Bible and Tract Society, Brooklyn, New York, maintains a complete collection.

Publication History

MAGAZINE TITLE AND TITLE CHANGES: *Zion's Watch Tower and Herald of Christ's Presence* (July 1879–December 1907); *Watch Tower and Herald of Christ's Presence* (January 1908–October 1931); *Watchtower and Herald of Christ's Presence* (15 October 1931–December 1938); *Watchtower and Herald of Christ's Kingdom* (January 1939–February 1939); *Watchtower Announcing Christ's Kingdom* (March 1939–present).
VOLUME AND ISSUE DATA: 1:1 (1879)–present. Annual volumes of 24 numbers each; published semimonthly on the first and fifteenth of each month.
PUBLISHER AND PLACE OF PUBLICATION: Charles Taze Russell, Pittsburgh, Pennsylvania (July 1879–1891); Zion's Watch Tower Tract Society, Pittsburgh, Pennsylvania (1891–1907); Watch Tower Bible and Tract Society, Pittsburgh, Pennsylvania (1908–1909); Watch Tower Bible and Tract Society, Brooklyn, New York (1909–present).
EDITORS: Charles Taze Russell (1879–1916), Joseph F. Rutherford (1916–1942), Watch Tower Bible and Tract Society (editing and authorship anonymous) (1942–present).
CIRCULATION: 20,000 (1903); 1,950,000 (1956); 18,000,000 (1990).

Michael R. McCoy

WATCHTOWER AND HERALD OF CHRIST'S KINGDOM. *See* WATCHTOWER

WATCH TOWER AND HERALD OF CHRIST'S PRESENCE. *See* WATCHTOWER

WATCHTOWER AND HERALD OF CHRIST'S PRESENCE. *See* WATCHTOWER

WATCHTOWER ANNOUNCING CHRIST'S KINGDOM. *See* WATCHTOWER

WAYMARKS IN THE WILDERNESS: A MONTHLY JOURNAL OF SCRIPTURAL STUDIES, LITERARY OBSERVATION, AND CURRENT HISTORY. *See* WAYMARKS IN THE WILDERNESS AND SCRIPTURAL GUIDE

WAYMARKS IN THE WILDERNESS: A SERIES OF ESSAYS ON PROPHECY, CHRISTIAN DOCTRINE, AND HISTORY. *See* WAYMARKS IN THE WILDERNESS AND SCRIPTURAL GUIDE

WAYMARKS IN THE WILDERNESS AND SCRIPTURAL GUIDE

In mid-nineteenth-century America, *Waymarks in the Wilderness and Scriptural Guide* popularized the new Protestant theological movement of dispensational premillennialism. Such diverse groups and figures as Adventism and William Miller, the Shakers and Mother Ann Lee, and the Mormons and Joseph Smith reflect the heightened millenarian interests sweeping across America and Great Britain at this time. The roots of this particular millenarian movement go back to John Nelson Darby (1800–1882), the leader of the Plymouth Brethren movement in Great Britain and Europe. Various traditions have long believed that Jesus Christ will return to this world to establish a kingdom that will last for one thousand years or a millennium. Scholars have debated whether Darby's contribution was an innovation or a reworking of this premillennial eschatology.

Three features distinguish Darby's futurist or dispensational premillennialism. Most important is his division of history into seven distinct periods or dispensations. The sixth dispensation concluded with the Resurrection and ascension of Jesus Christ. The final dispensation will be inaugurated at Christ's return and establishment of the one thousand-year reign. The present time, the "church age," stands between these two dispensations. At the beginning of a seven-year period of tribulation immediately preceding Christ's return, believers both dead and alive will be "raptured" or taken up to heaven. At the end of the seventh year, Christ, in the company of all believers, will return and establish the millennial kingdom. The second distinguishing element was the literal interpretation of the Bible. Third, Darby maintained that most of the Old Testament prophecies concerning Israel were not fulfilled in the creation of the Church but still await fulfillment at a future date.

Disillusioned with the perceived spiritual decadence of the established Church, Darby and his Plymouth Brethren followers departed to form their own nondenominational fellowships. The movement grew quickly in Great Britain and Europe during the 1830s. Eventually, some members immigrated to the United States. In America at that time, the dominant Protestant eschatology was postmillennialism. This view taught that Christ will return after, not before, the one thousand-year period of peace. A minority of Protestant ministers, however, espoused a "historic" premillennial eschatology. Historic premillennialists, less literal than Darby in their biblical interpretation, held that prophecies concerning Christ's return would be fulfilled within present history, not in some future dispensation. But dispensational premillennialism slowly gained advocates among American Protestants.[1]

James Inglis, the chief editor of *Waymarks in the Wilderness*, was one such advocate. Born in Greenlaw, Berwickshire, Scotland, in 1813, Inglis immigrated to America in 1848. After his conversion that same year, he privately prepared for the ministry. A short time later he became the pastor of the First Baptist Church of Detroit, where *Waymarks in the Wilderness* began the first of three periods of publication. The first two attempts lasted no more than a year each. Later, in 1864, the periodical began a sustained period of publication that concluded with Inglis's death.

In the first series, Inglis was joined by two other pastors—his brother, David, and John Hogg—as editors. The full title expressed their lofty ambitions for the publication: *Waymarks in the Wilderness: A Monthly Journal of Scriptural Studies, Literary Observation, and Current History.* "The title of this journal," the authors wrote, "intimates that it aims rather at the edification and comfort of Christians, than at distinctions and influence in the world." Wearied with "the rivalries and conflict of the times," the editors wanted to refresh the souls of their readers with the "divine truths" of the Bible, especially Christ's imminent return. The "divine truth" of premillennialism, in both its dispensational and "historic" forms, brought together authors from six denominations in the first issue. In the antebellum period, abolition, temperance, and missions often united Protestants of various traditions. A common theological conviction, not social action or evangelism, united Protestants in the premillennialist movement. As the premillennialist movement grew in postbellum America, it continued to cut across denominational lines.[2]

The first issue of *Waymarks* appeared in May 1854. Printed in Detroit, the monthly periodical appeared on one sheet of paper, cut and folded, 8½ by 5⅛ inches, with solid ten-point type from front to back, in double columns, and averaged thirty-two pages a number. No illustrations or charts appeared in its pages, and authors' names were omitted. The final issue offered a cumulative title index. The cost of a yearly subscription was one dollar. In the August 1854 issue, some encouraging reviews of the work from other religious periodicals and secular presses were printed. For example, the *Detroit Tribune* commented that "the general reader, as well as the religious public, will find much in it to instruct and interest them in regard to the truths of Christianity."[3]

According to the editors, *Waymarks* was "designed to occupy middle ground between the learned and critical, and the popular and superficial" religious periodicals of the day.[4] Brief lessons from Church history, biblical expositions, doctrinal explanations, and poetry constituted the majority of the articles. While roughly 40 percent of these articles express clear premillennialist sentiments, other topics (e.g., Christianity in Armenia, Islam) also received attention.[5] Although the editors favored dispensational premillennialism, they did not focus solely upon the subject. At this point in the movement's history, the differences between dispensational and "historic" premillennialism did not prevent advocates of the different positions from cooperating. In addition to pieces by dispensational premillennialists such as British Plymouth Brethren leader S. P. Tregelles, the periodical published many by nondispensational premillennialists.

For example, *Waymarks* reprinted a sermon by George Duffield, a leading antebellum historic premillennialist.[6] *Waymarks* also tried to distance its millenarian views from those of William Miller, who predicted that Christ would return around 1843. In one article, the author not only repudiated the "Millerites'" eschatology but also impugned their orthodoxy.[7] An occasional news analysis drew out the premillenarian implications of world events. Events in Europe, not the fear of impending civil war, were the subject of such commentaries: "A general review of the state of affairs in Europe will . . . satisfy both the apathetic and sanguine that a crisis for mankind is approaching; the civilization of the age is imperilled, and consequences most extensive and lasting must result to the whole race."[8] In spite of premillennialism's expectation of society's gradual moral decay, some articles in *Waymarks* expressed the opposite view. "Influences of Christianity on Public Morality and Institutions," for example, outlined the social benefits of a society dominated by evangelical Christians. Writing amid the growing crisis over slavery, one author argued that many instances in history teach that Christianity had led to its abolition. The same was happening in his day: "It is because christianity [*sic*] has created a public conscience and has awakened sentiments which vice can not entirely silence, that Uncle Tom's Cabin shook the 'peculiar institution' of slavery to its very centre [*sic*]."[9] Inexplicably, *Waymarks* temporarily ended publication in April 1855.

After moving to Saint Louis, Inglis briefly revived the publication. He renamed it *Waymarks in the Wilderness: A Series of Essays on Prophecy, Christian Doctrine, and History*. It began monthly publication in January 1857. *Waymarks*'s single-column text in the same 8½-by-5⅛ inch size with solid ten-point type gave the periodical a new appearance. The periodical resembled a scholarly journal, such as *Biblical Repertory and Princeton Review*, with its longer articles and average sixty-four-page length. Theological treatises and biblical expositions, many devoted to premillennialist topics, dominated the work. Articles listed the authors' names. The final issue provided a cumulative title index. Inglis, now the sole editor, may have been appealing to a more academic audience, but again the periodical ended publication without explanation after nine issues.

In 1864 Inglis again resumed publication of the periodical in New York City, where he had taken another church. He renamed it *Waymarks in the Wilderness and Scriptural Guide* and served as its sole editor. Propagating the message of premillennialism was Inglis's expressed intent: "The exposition of the prophetic Scriptures is the prominent object of the enterprise, under the conviction of those engaged in it that the coming of the Lord draws near, and that the church is in her proper attitude when waiting for that event."[10] *Waymarks* measured 7 by 4½ inches in size, with a single column of text in solid ten-point type. After Inglis hired James Colles to assist him in 1870, the periodical was slightly larger, 7½ by 4½ inches. The first three volumes issued numbers six times a year and averaged 500 pages in length. The final five years had quarterly issues that ranged between 245 and 400 pages. This new series cost thirty cents an issue.

Authors in *Waymarks* continued to include both historic premillennialists and dispensational premillennialists.[11] Also, Inglis began to print pieces by younger dispensational premillennialists, including L. C. Baker, William R. Nicholson, and George S. Bishop.[12]

Over the course of its eight-year publication, premillenarian concerns increasingly dominated the new series, especially in its more strident advocacy of dispensational premillennialism. Early proponents like Inglis accepted Darby's eschatology but rejected other aspects of his teaching, most notably his insistence on separating from the denominations. Despite having published articles by some of the leaders of the Plymouth Brethren, Inglis went to great length to distance his publication from close association with Darby. Inglis articulated only a qualified commitment to Darby's theology: "So far from being 'the doctrinal representative of the Plymouth Brethren,' while we gratefully owe our indebtedness to them under God for the testimony they have borne to our standing in Christ and the hope of our calling, we have been constrained to testify against nearly everything in their theology which distinguishes them from the other men of God."[13]

The two most common subjects of articles in *Waymarks* expressed the narrower dispensationalist orientation of the periodical in this final period of publication. Many articles discussed the imminent second advent of Christ. Inglis wrote in 1866, "Judging by the letters of inquirers, one of the most common difficulties which those whose progress is embarrassed by the influence of old misconceptions encounter, is found in tracing the relation of truths and the order of events." To readers trapped in the "wilderness" of this world, Inglis willingly offered them a "scriptural guide" to the upcoming events.[14] To one who genuinely believed that Christ's return was imminent, "the signs of the times" or detailed discussions of prophecy may have been very comforting. The second most popular topic concerned personal holiness.[15] While the moral condition of the world around them may have been collapsing, readers were encouraged to experience personal victory over their own sin.

The analysis of current events reappeared in the pages of *Waymarks* in 1866, but the American Civil War was conspicuously absent from these news commentaries. This stemmed, in part, from premillennialism's literal interpretation of the Bible. Since North America did not play a role in the prophecies concerning Christ's return, but the surviving remnant of the old Roman Empire did, events in the United States were inconsequential. A detailed examination of the political developments in Europe in the aftermath of the Crimean War (1854–1856) led Inglis to suggest in 1866 that a ten-nation federation would emerge and thus fulfill the prophecies of the book of Daniel.[16]

The publication of *Waymarks* came to a close with Inglis's death in 1872. "Its discontinuance," a friend assured its readers, "shall be found in the day of Christ to have been as necessary for His glory and the interests of His church (and these, blessed be His grace, are one) as was the removal of our brother himself."[17] Although Inglis did not live to see the premillennialist movement emerge as a major force within the Protestant community, *Waymarks* helped to popularize its theology and provided its early leaders with the opportunity to publish their views.

Notes

1. Several helpful introductions to dispensational premillennialism's origins in Great Britain and America and theology are available: C. Norman Kraus, *Dispensationalism in America: Its Rise and Development* (Richmond: John Knox Press, 1958), 13–56; Ernest R. Sandeen, *The Roots of Fundamentalism: British and American Millenarianism, 1800–1930* (Chicago: University of Chicago Press, 1970; reprint, Grand Rapids: Baker Books, 1978), 3–103; Timothy P. Weber, *Living in the Shadow of the Second Coming: American Premillennialism, 1875–1982* (rev. ed., Chicago: University of Chicago Press, 1987), 9–26; George M. Marsden, *Fundamentalism and American Culture: The Shaping of Twentieth-Century Evangelicalism 1870–1925* (New York: Oxford University Press, 1980), 43–62.

2. "Preface," *Waymarks* 1 (1854): 1, 2.

3. "Opinions of the Press on the 'Waymarks,' " *Waymarks* 1 (August 1854): 128.

4. "Preface," *Waymarks* 1 (1854): 2.

5. "Life of Mohammed," *Waymarks* 1 (August 1854): 99–105; "Christianity Among the Armenians," *Waymarks* 1 (November 1854): 204–8.

6. "Ministerial Fidelity—George Duffield's Charge at the Installation of H. Niell at Second Presbyterian in Detroit," *Waymarks* 1 (December 1854): 243–47.

7. "Millenarianism—What Is It?" *Waymarks* 1 (December 1854): 247–53.

8. "The Old World in 1854," *Waymarks* 1 (May 1854): 25.

9. "Influence of Christianity on Public Morality and Institutions," *Waymarks* 1 (October 1854): 181.

10. "The Close of 'Waymarks in the Wilderness,' " *Waymarks* 10 (1872): 387.

11. George Duffield, "The Cherubim," *Waymarks* 1 (1864): 103–26, 241–52; S. P. Tregelles, "The Revelation," *Waymarks* 8 (1870): 193–216, 313–36.

12 See, for example, L. C. Baker, "The Mystery of Creation," *Waymarks* 8 (1870): 54–72; William R. Nicholson, "The Hidden Manna," *Waymarks* 8 (1870): 115–31; George S. Bishop, "The Question of the Second Advent," *Waymarks* 9 (1871): 73–96.

13. *Waymarks* 10 (1870): 187, as quoted in Sandeen, *Roots of Fundamentalism*, 101.

14. "The Prospects of the Church," *Waymarks* 4 (1866): 269–91.

15. See, for example, "Sanctification," *Waymarks* 2 (1865): 197–219, 376–401, 464–86 (summary of *God's Way of Holiness* by the Scottish Dispensationalist leader, Horatius Bonar); *Waymarks* 3 (1866): 6780.

16. "European Prospects," *Waymarks* 4 (1866): 302–12.

17. "The Close of the 'Waymarks in the Wilderness,' " *Waymarks* 10 (1872): 382.

Information Sources

INDEX SOURCES: Each volume contains its own index, which lists the article titles either alphabetically or chronologically.

LOCATION SOURCES: The fullest collection is held at Speer Library, Princeton Theological Seminary: 1 (1854–1855); 2 (1857); n.s. 1 (1864)–6 (1868), 8 (1970)–volume 10: 1, 2, 4 (1872). For other holdings consult the Union List of Serials.

Publication History

MAGAZINE TITLE AND TITLE CHANGES: *Waymarks in the Wilderness; a Monthly Journal of Scriptural Studies, Literary Observation, and Current History* (1854–1855); *Waymarks in the Wilderness: A Series of Essays on Prophecy Christian Doctrine and History* (1857); *Waymarks in the Wilderness and Scriptural Guide* (1864–1872).

VOLUME AND ISSUE DATA: 1:1 (May 1854)–1:12 (April 1855), published monthly; 2:1 (January 1857)–2:9 (September 1857), published monthly; n.s. 1:1 (1864)–10:4 (September 1872), volumes 1 through 3 published bimonthly and volumes 4 through 10 published quarterly.

PUBLISHER AND PLACE OF PUBLICATION: James Inglis, Detroit, Michigan (1854–1855); James Inglis & Jones, St. Louis (1857); James Inglis, New York (1864–1869); James Inglis & James Colles, Jr., New York (1870); James Inglis, New York (1871–1872).

EDITORS: James Inglis (1854–1855, 1857, 1864–1872); Coeditors: David Inglis (1854–1855) and John Hogg (1854–1855).

CIRCULATION: Unknown.

Paul C. Kemeny

WEEKLY EVANGEL. *See* PENTECOSTAL EVANGEL

WEEKLY LITERARY AND RELIGIOUS VISITOR. *See* LUTHERAN OBSERVER

WEEKLY RELIGIOUS AND LITERARY VISITOR. *See* LUTHERAN OBSERVER

WESLEYAN JOURNAL. *See* CHRISTIAN ADVOCATE

WESTERN CHRISTIAN ADVOCATE

As the political life of Abraham Lincoln was getting under way in the General Assembly of Illinois and Honoré Balzac published his wonderful work *Le Pere Goriot*, the Methodists were trying their hand and their pen at a new venture. The big cities of the East had a multitude of information sources. Newspapers and other print outlets were in abundance. In the years between 1790 and 1830, more than six hundred religious periodicals were established.

But the burgeoning West had very few. Local forums for discussion and debate were limited. In 1832 Frances Trollope, the mother of novelist Anthony Trollope, in her *Domestic Manners of the Americans*, spoke of the growth of factions and sects within the American religious scene. She lamented the ''tyranny of religion'' in the fledgling country she toured. Even though ''sects,'' as she described them, were growing, the West was growing as well, and the Methodists wanted to have a voice in their wilderness.[1]

Change came in 1834. It brought a local Methodist voice in the West. In Cincinnati, Ohio, the "Queen City," the local Methodist conference began publishing the weekly *Western Christian Advocate*. Called into being by an act of the Methodist general conference in 1832, it began as a simple four-page paper at a cost of two dollars per year, if paid in advance. As the paper grew in circulation, eventually reaching over thirty-five thousand in the 1870s, it grew in size. The *Advocate* eventually grew to eight pages; three pages were used for advertisers, such as Ivory Soap and Queen City National Bank.

In Cincinnati, this city on a hill, as Mrs. Trollope described it, the Methodists sought to be a light on a hill. This new Methodist organ bore the name of its New York sibling, which was one of the first to have national circulation, with a parochial praenomen. The *Western Christian Advocate* was by no means parochial. It desired to have broad appeal and wanted to reach the masses that were flooding the West.

The founders of the *Western Christian Advocate* were clear concerning its mission. They set forth a threefold purpose in its inaugural issue. They sought to publish a weekly newspaper because of the growing population in the West. They realized that there were nearly 5 million people living west of the Alleghenies. In the twenty years between 1810 and 1830 the population had tripled. An eastern paper transported West simply would not suffice. The intellectual climate and experience in this land were quite different from the culture of the East, crossing the Cumberland Gap was still an arduous trip, and it was less costly to produce something in the West than it was to purchase it and then transport it.

Another purpose lay in the needs of the Church. In 1834 the Methodists had 230,000 members west of the Alleghenies. The Church, through its local ministry, could not easily minister to, and educate, its congregants, along with converting the immigrant, the lawless, the irreligious, and the "heathen." Presbyterian Lyman Beecher, an ardent nativist, wrote *A Plea for the West*, which called for greater work among those in the frontier. The *Western Christian Advocate* answered that call and went to work to serve many of the needs found in the West. It offered an outlet to educate, a means of debate, and a witness to the unconverted.

Cincinnati Methodists lived in a city that was the gateway to the West and that lay on the banks of the mighty Ohio, a prime avenue for travel to the massive Mississippi River. Travel that could have taken days or weeks was pruned to much less. Because it was a travel hub, Cincinnati played host to many seekers. These people were not always seekers of religion, but of prosperity and happiness as well. Mrs. Trollope likened Cincinnati's inhabitants to busy bees seeking "that honey of Hybla, vulgarly called money."[2] To the Methodists, many of these seekers were seen as enemies of Christianity, and the

Western Christian Advocate was a means of fighting them. The local Methodists saw a need for spiritual warfare.

The founders of this Methodist organ had two objectives. They predominantly sought the salvation of the world "through [the] advancement of the pure and undefiled religion of the Lord Jesus Christ." Their "grand object [was] . . . the . . . eternal salvation of a lost world."[3] Evangelism was primary.

A secondary goal was the promotion of the interests of the Methodist Episcopal Church. First came salvation, then indoctrination for these Methodists. The doctrines advanced were theological and social. Being near the South and on the road to freedom, Cincinnati's Methodists warned of the evils of slavery, along with other evils. In 1837 the *Western Christian Advocate* appealed for funds to purchase the freedom of James Thompson, who sought to do mission work among the Indians.

The founders had made plain their purposes and also outlined the means of accomplishing their task. They sought to fulfill their goals by announcing that the "principal aim of the *Western Christian Advocate* will be to explain and defend the grand and distinguishing truths of the gospel."[4]

The *Western Christian Advocate* reported on various sorts of topics in sections called departments, including temperance, revival intelligence, missionary intelligence, children's, miscellany, and Sunday school. The paper spoke to literary and everyday concerns as well. This is exemplified in its farmers' department and poetry section. The poetry was often of a religious nature, with titles like "The Dying Infidel" and "God Is Love." This paper spoke to the mind, heart, and soul.

The *Western Christian Advocate* also promoted the missionary cause. In one sense, each of its sections was essentially a missionary report. In every department, from temperance to Sunday school, the conversion of souls was central.

Education was another means to fulfill the magazine's mission. The farmers' department gave advice on how to raise crops, while the parents' department counseled on how to raise children. As with the missionary cause, each department was a method of education of the mind and soul.

A cornerstone of Methodist work in Cincinnati was temperance. Editor and, later, bishop, Matthew Simpson fought for it within the pages of the *Western Christian Advocate*. Temperance reformation was a means to advance the Gospel, according to the Methodists. Liquor stunted the spiritual and social growth of individuals and the nation. Many groups within American Christianity fought this social evil. Groups like the American Tract Society spent large portions of their resources battling for temperance. They all believed that liquor robbed mothers of their sons, wives of their husbands, and children of their fathers, because liquor often brought abandonment.

The Western Book Concern, the publishing arm of the Methodist Episcopal Church, began as the Cincinnati branch of the New York Book Concern in 1820 and was separately incorporated in 1839, five years after it began printing the *Western Christian Advocate*.

The *Western Christian Advocate* produced a long line of important Methodist leaders from its editorial ranks. Since the General Conference, the governing body of the Methodist Church, elected the editors, the editorship often was a stepping-stone, or a proving ground, for future bishops. Its first editor was Thomas Asbury Morris. Morris held this position for over two years, from the *Advocate*'s founding until June 1836, when he left because of his election to a bishopric. Charles Elliott succeeded Morris. Elliott edited and coedited this paper for more than sixteen years. Elliott took the experience he had gained in Cincinnati with him when he moved to Pittsburgh to become editor of the *Pittsburgh Christian Advocate*, another local conference paper founded in 1833. Elliott later guided the *Central Christian Advocate* in St. Louis through the Civil War years. It is most certain that the antislavery tone of the *Western Christian Advocate* was developed by Charles Elliott. Frank Luther Mott in his multivolume work on American magazines recounts that Elliott "sustained the antislavery cause in a border state with vigor."[5] However, it subsided with later editors.

As well as an editor, Elliott was an author. He wrote such works as *Sinfulness of American Slavery Proved from Its Evil Source* and an introduction for *Experience of German Methodist Preachers*, since Cincinnati was a center of German Methodism. Elliott later returned to the editorship of the *Western Christian Advocate* and then moved on to the presidency of Iowa Wesleyan College.

In his first years as editor of the *Western Christian Advocate*, Elliott shared his responsibilities with Leonidas Lent Hamline, who also worked with him on Adam Miller's *Experience of German Methodist Preachers*. Hamline helped establish the German newspaper *Christliche Apologete* and became a bishop in the Methodist Episcopal Church in 1844. As editor of the *Western Christian Advocate*, Hamline did not want to bring divisiveness to a paper that was situated in a prime location reaching into Virginia, Kentucky, and Missouri. Hamline was outspoken on some issues, such as the authority of the General Conference, though he never directly criticized individuals. He sought to preoccupy himself with the same task that took him into the ministry: missions. Hence Hamline steered clear of many issues to keep the focus of his paper on missions.

Matthew Simpson took over the editorship in 1848, replacing Charles Elliott. Simpson, a cousin of Ulysses Simpson Grant, was considered a foe of southerners. Under Simpson the *Western Christian Advocate* ended its practice of printing articles borrowed from other newspapers such as the *Zion's Herald* and *Alton Observer*. The paper took on correspondents, paid the writers of articles, and included block illustrations. With these new additions the length of Simpson's editorials shrank. This change brought about much criticism from his detractors.

In essence Simpson transformed the *Western Christian Advocate* from a collection of stories from other papers to an organ dedicated to fighting the "sinfulness of American slavery." This approach greatly contrasted with the moderate position of past editors. But by Simpson's time the *Western Christian*

Advocate had mainly a northern audience because of the implementation of the "Plan of Separation" that split the denomination into the Methodist Episcopal Church and the Methodist Episcopal Church, South. At the time of the separation there were five Methodist periodicals, including the *Western Christian Advocate* and *Christliche Apologete*, which both originated from the Western Book Concern. Simpson also brought back one of the original purposes of the periodical, being a messenger of Methodism, not a battleground between Methodism and other denominations and sects.

When Simpson was elected bishop in 1852, his predecessor, Charles Elliott, was reappointed editor, a post he held until 1856, when Calvin Kingsley took over. Called a "war" editor, Kingsley guided the *Western Christian Advocate* through the tumultuous early 1860s until he was elected a bishop in 1864.

John M. Reid, whose editorials showed strong patriotism for the North, was appointed to replace Calvin Kingsley and served through the years of Reconstruction. Reid is often viewed as less than moderate. He stated that whites and blacks tend toward separation and that the northern Methodists would be free from many perplexing questions if they were to withdraw into their own congregations.

Reid was succeeded by Stephen Mason Merrill in 1868. Under Merrill, editorials became quite political. He did not warmly receive the candidacy of U. S. Grant for president. He also printed a front-page editorial denouncing the Supreme Court's decision in the case of Lambdin P. Milligan,[6] a civil rights case presented to the Court, which ruled that civil liberties were in force during times of war and peace and that civil courts could call to account other tribunals, like the military tribunal that found Milligan guilty of treason. Merrill also advocated the disfranchisement of the Confederates and the pursuit of holiness. Merrill realized that the black Methodists wanted churches of their own, possibly because of the history of white oppression.

Merrill eventually played a role in the commencement of dialogue with the Methodist Episcopal Church, South and the advancement of the "Plan of Union" through his work on denominational wholeness and solidarity, *Organic Unity*, which was published in 1891.

Later editors continued the work of their earlier compatriots. In 1887 an editor lamented the low level of sermon publication by Methodist preachers, counting them on one finger. In the 1890s these Methodists were still battling the "social evils" like bicycling on the Sabbath and card playing.

The *Western Christian Advocate* was a uniquely western vehicle for change. Through its various editors it sought to change and impact lives, either theologically, religiously, or socially. Whether the subject was John Wesley or slavery, the pages of the *Western Christian Advocate* were a voice for the Methodists in a changing world.

Notes

1. Frances Trollope, *Domestic Manners of the Americans*, 2 vols. (London: Whittaker, Treacher, and Co., 1832), 1: 150.
2. Ibid., 61.
3. *Western Christian Advocate* 1:1 (2 May 1834): 1.
4. Ibid.
5. Frank Luther Mott, *A History of American Magazines* (Cambridge: Harvard University Press, 1938), 1: 67 n.
6. Lambin P. Milligan, *The Milligan Case*, ed. Samuel Klaus (New York: Da Capo Press, 1972).

Information Sources

INDEX SOURCES: Beginning in 1834 until at least 1849 (the large gap of issues inhibits a more precise year), the last issue of each volume contained a partial index. The deletion of the index most likely occurred during Matthew Simpson's restructuring of the newspaper's style.

LOCATION SOURCES: Volumes for the years 1834 to 1888, inclusive, are contained in the American Periodical Series, based on the combined holdings of the Library of Congress, State Historical Society of Wisconsin, Indiana University, Southern Methodist University, and Garrett Evangelical Theological Seminary. This microfilm edition has gaps between 14 April 1843 (9:468) and 8 January 1868 (35:2).

Publication History

MAGAZINE TITLE AND TITLE CHANGES: *Western Christian Advocate*; absorbed into the *Christian Advocate: Western Edition* in 1929.

VOLUME AND ISSUE DATA: 1:1 (2 May 1834)–95:43 (22 February 1929); published weekly.

PUBLISHER AND PLACE OF PUBLICATION: (General Conference of the Methodist Episcopal Church) Charles Holliday and John F. Wright (1834–1836), John F. Wright and Leroy Swormstedt (1836–unknown), Poe and Hitchcock (1868–1880), Hitchcock and Walden (1880–unknown). Published in Cincinnati.

EDITORS: Thomas A. Morris (1834–1836), Charles Elliott and W. Phillips (1836), Charles Elliott (1836), Charles Elliott and Leonidas Lent Hamline (1836–1841), Charles Elliott (1841–1848), Matthew Simpson (1848–1852), Charles Elliott (1852–1856), Calvin Kingsley (1852–1864), J. M. Reid (1864–1868), S. M. Merrill (1868–1872), Francis S. Hoyt (1872–1884), J. H. Bayliss (1884–1889), David H. Moore (1889–1900), Levi Gilbert (1900–1916), Ernest C. Wareing (1916–1929).

CIRCULATION: 20,000 (1836); 20,000 (1848); 23,520 (1869); 25,000 (1872); 35,000 (1879).

David B. Malone

WESTERN RECORDER

In 1834, Kentucky Baptist churches were recovering from the defection of one-third of their members to Alexander Campbell, an outspoken critic of missions, salaried clergy, theological education, Sunday schools—any practice or belief he did not find explicitly sanctioned in the Bible. His "disciples" eventually united with Barton W. Stone's "Christians" to form the Disciples of Christ. Suspicious that the nascent association of Kentucky Baptists would overreact to the Campbellites by usurping local church autonomy, James Wilson, a physician in Shelbyville, Kentucky, began publishing the *Baptist Banner* in 1834. "The object of this paper," Wilson told his readers, "is to receive and disseminate religious intelligence, in relation to the condition and prosperity of our Redeemer's Kingdom; with as much other useful and literary matter as circumstances will admit of."[1] Wilson's paper did "receive and disseminate religious intelligence," but it also generated and goaded issues of its own along the way.

The "literary matter" Wilson included often provided relief from the *Baptist Banner*'s overwhelmingly sober copy, as the following filler illustrates:

We have heard a rumor says the Mobile Register, that the Siamese Twins have had a falling out with each other, and that a duel would have ensued sometime since, but the parties could not agree upon the distance. The quarrel originated from the interference of Chang, in a love intrigue of his twin brother Eng. It is to be hoped the affair will be so adjusted as to prevent a division between friends hitherto so closely united.[2]

Wilson's blend of religious and secular copy drew enough subscribers to attract a buyer in the *Baptist Banner*'s second year. In 1839, the *Baptist Banner* was merged with the *Western Pioneer*.

The *Baptist Banner and Western Pioneer* quickly became the dominant Baptist newspaper in the South and Southwest, even though its finances were always precarious. It had several columns of advertising, much of which promoted such patent medicines as George's Vegetable Pills and H. Eastman's Elixir of Health. However, credit subscriptions caused it to lose money. Until 1843, the newspaper sold for three dollars in advance or four dollars at the end of the year. Too many people chose the second option without paying the bill. Even when it began charging a flat two dollars in advance, the paper lost money. Publisher-editor William C. Buck lost fifty thousand dollars so he sold the *Baptist Banner and Western Pioneer* in 1850. The name was changed to *Western Recorder* the following year.[3]

Although the *Baptist Banner and Western Pioneer* aligned itself with the Southern Baptist Convention when it formed in 1845, the paper studiously avoided arguments over slavery. Mostly, the paper refuted paedobaptists, evangelicals who accepted the sprinkling of infants as a legitimate means of baptism. One issue of the *Baptist Banner and Western Pioneer* offered five hundred dollars to anyone in the United States who could find "*one* instance in the New Testament where John the Baptist, any apostle or preacher, baptized a person by *sprinkling* or *pouring*. And FIVE HUNDRED DOLLARS to any person . . .

who will produce a solitary example in the New Testament of the baptism of an unconscious infant by the authority of Jesus Christ or his apostles.''[4] It never had to pay up.

However much they condemned departures from believers' baptism by immersion, Southern Baptist ministers through the mid-nineteenth century routinely exchanged pulpits with paedobaptist ministers. A series of articles in the *Tennessee Baptist* on the theme ''Ought Baptists to Recognize Paedobaptist Preachers as Gospel Ministers?'' blasted this cooperation. The articles argued that paedobaptist societies are not churches of Christ because they do not follow believers' baptism by immersion, so their sermons, their communions, and even their occasional baptisms by immersion were illegitimate. *Western Recorder* editor John L. Waller responded to the *Tennessee Baptist* articles by concluding that these views ''are not the views of Baptists, past or present. These views are something new under the Sun.''[5] Waller's editorial raised the ire of James Robinson Graves, editor of the *Tennessee Baptist*. Rallying his followers to Proverbs 22:28 (''Remove not the ancient landmark which your fathers have set''), Graves nearly took over the Southern Baptist Convention (SBC) in the mid–1850s. ''Landmark Baptists'' eventually made a formal break in 1905 to form what would become the American Baptist Association, leaving Southern Baptists with a legacy of local Church autonomy, rejection of non-Baptist immersions, and resistance to ecumenical cooperation.[6] (Graves and his followers almost took over the SBC in the 1850s, and their issues were debated throughout the rest of the century, but by the early twentieth century it was clear that they were a minority in the SBC. Hence the break half a century later.)

The Civil War silenced all but five Southern Baptist newspapers. The *Western Recorder* was one of the five survivors, although it published only eight issues between September 7, 1861, and March 15, 1862. The only Southern Baptist paper to ignore the war in its columns, the *Western Recorder* was filled with articles and correspondence on religious subjects, news from the churches and associations, poetry, and advertising. This neutrality was prudent: Kentucky remained in the Union, even though Confederate support prevailed in the southern portion of the commonwealth. The *Western Recorder* did not criticize the government until Reconstruction, when it attacked Missouri's requirement that ministers testify that they had always been loyal to the United States.

As the twentieth century approached, the Southern Baptist Convention expanded its operations through auxiliary organizations. Sunday schools grew, and women's groups and the Baptist Young People's Union formed. *Western Recorder* editor T. T. Eaton, alarmed at the relative liberalization of women's roles within the Church and the increasing part the national convention played in the affairs of local churches, crusaded against most of the auxiliary groups.

Eaton's opposition to auxiliary organizations set him against William H. Whitsitt, president of Southern Baptist Theological Seminary in Louisville. As a seminary trustee, Eaton had supported Whitsitt's selection as president in 1895. However, Whitsitt championed the Baptist Young People's Union and published

an entry in *Johnson's Universal Cyclopaedia* that pointed out that English Anabaptists, through whom Southern Baptists traced their lineage to the apostles,
did not commit themselves to immersion until 1641.[7] Portraying Whitsitt as less
than wholly Baptist, Eaton was able to summon Landmark elements to force
Whitsitt to leave the seminary.

Eaton was able to challenge Southern Baptist thought and practice because
the *Western Recorder* was an independent paper. The General Association of
Baptists in Kentucky endorsed the *Western Recorder*, but the paper was ultimately responsible only to its readers and advertisers, who kept it in business.
Steps to trim the *Western Recorder*'s influence began in 1897, when Baptist
auxiliary enthusiasts and Whitsitt supporters began publishing the *Baptist Argus*
(renamed the *Baptist World* in 1905) with approval from the state association.
The association took the ultimate step of solidifying editorial support in 1919,
when it purchased the *Baptist World*, the *Kentucky Mission Monthly*, and the
Western Recorder and merged them under the name of *Western Recorder*. Since
then, the *Western Recorder* has been a house organ under the authority of a
twelve-person Board of Directors elected by the Kentucky Baptist Convention.
The loss of editorial independence was compensated by financial security, with
support coming from individual and Church subscriptions, advertising, donations, and an annual allocation of Cooperative Program funds from the Kentucky
Baptist Convention.

Convention ownership has not always produced timid editing, though. Under
the outspoken direction of Victor I. Masters, the *Western Recorder* earned the
nickname "Western Disturber."[8] Masters, for example, attacked the social gospel as "one of the 'lame-duck' spiritual bastards sired by the evolution theory."[9]
He even opposed federal regulation of the labor of children under eighteen years
of age on the grounds that work was a better developer of character than schools
should it become necessary to choose between the two.[10]

Similarly, the *Western Recorder* in a later era criticized the support for racial
segregation and the opposition to equality between blacks and whites that prevailed in other Southern Baptist newspapers. Editor C. R. Daley, Jr., wrote:
"The most segregated school today is the Sunday School and the most segregated hour of the week is 11 A.M. on Sunday. Other denominations are speaking
to the issue. Southern Baptists have been mostly silent or defensive for segregation. Can we come to our God-given destiny in this manner?"[11]

Nevertheless, as the *Western Recorder* and other Southern Baptist newspapers
passed from private to convention ownership, a process completed in 1950 when
the Baptist General Association of Virginia bought the *Religious Herald*, they
questioned convention policies and practices less and devoted more space to
news of the churches, their respective state conventions, and the agencies of the
Southern Baptist Convention. They have relied heavily upon Baptist Press, the
news-gathering agency of the Southern Baptist Convention that was begun in
1946. This process of centralization worried Daley, who argued that Southern
Baptist newspapers required editorial independence in order to speak propheti-

cally: "As a trend in denominational centralization continues, the state papers that have any independence could provide an important ministry of constructive criticism and critical evaluation of denominational directions. This would produce some tension, but would be profitable to the denomination and to the denominational paper."[12]

The danger to editorial independence posed by denominational control is stronger now than ever. Baptist Press's efforts during the past two decades to report fully and impartially the step-by-step takeover of the 15-million-member Southern Baptist Convention by fundamentalists have stirred the anger of the fundamentalist hierarchy, who continue to scrutinize the news service to ensure that it conforms to a rigid biblical literalism.[13] Because many editors are still theologically moderate and journalistically professional, control of the thirty-nine state papers with a circulation, mostly weekly, of 1.5 million, is not yet complete. But the convention's leaders permit little diversity on theological and social issues, so no Southern Baptist newspaper is likely to lead a movement of dissent within the denomination. More likely, any spirited editorializing and reporting will endorse the beliefs and desires of the Southern Baptist leadership.

Notes

1. *Baptist Banner* 1:8 (28 November 1834): 1.
2. "A Duel,"*Baptist Banner* 1:8 (28 November 1834): 2.
3. Claude Windell Smith, "A History of Southern Baptist State Newspapers" (Ph.D. diss., University of Missouri, 1968), 329–30.
4. "A Premium of $1,000!!!" *Baptist Banner and Western Pioneer* 4:196 (7 February 1839): 2.
5. "Baptist High-Churchism," *Western Recorder* 21:38 (20 September 1854): 2.
6. Ellen M. Rosenberg, *The Southern Baptists: A Subculture in Transition* (Knoxville: University of Tennessee Press, 1989), 32–35.
7. "Baptists," in *Johnson's Universal Cyclopaedia*, new ed., 1 (New York: D. Appleton and A. J. Johnson, 1898), 489–93.
8. Erwin L. McDonald, *Across the Editor's Desk: The Story of the State Baptist Papers* (Nashville: Broadman Press, 1966), 97.
9. "Social Service Salvation, the Bastard Child of Evolution," *Western Recorder* 96: 32 (12 May 1921): 9.
10. "Kentucky Refuses Approval of Socialistic 'Child Labor' Amendment," *Western Recorder* 100:6 (11 February 1926): 11.
11. "Three Burning Issues," *Western Recorder* 139: 22 (3 June 1965): 4.
12. McDonald, *Across the Editor's Desk*, 119–20.
13. Charles Austin, "The History and Role of the Protestant Press," in *Reporting Religion: Facts & Faith*, ed. Benjamin J. Hubbard (Sonoma, CA: Polebridge, 1990), 111.

Information Sources

INDEX SOURCES: The Southern Baptist Theological Seminary in Louisville has a card catalog for the *Baptist Banner* beginning in 1834 through the *Western Recorder* of 1902. *Western Recorder Index*, 1974 to date, is located at the Southern Baptist Theological Seminary as well as other Southern Baptist colleges and seminaries. One annual retrospective volume is published every year.

LOCATION SOURCES: Bound and microfilm issues are at the Southern Baptist Theological Seminary and the Filson Club in Louisville, Kentucky.

Publication History

MAGAZINE TITLE AND TITLE CHANGES: *Baptist Banner* (1834–1839); *Baptist Banner and Western Pioneer* (1839–1851); *Western Recorder* (1851–present).

VOLUME AND ISSUE DATA: Begun as a biweekly on 12 September 1834 and changed to a weekly in October 1835; only eight issues published from 7 September 1861 to 15 March 1862; now published every week minus one in July and another in December.

PUBLISHER AND PLACE OF PUBLICATION: James Wilson, Shelbyville, Kentucky (1834); J. H. Ramsdell, Shelbyville, Kentucky (1835); Louisville, Kentucky (1836–1837); J. H. Ramsdell and Thomas B. Walker, Louisville, Kentucky, New Albany, Indiana, and Nashville, Tennessee (1838–1840); J. H. Ramsdell, Thomas B. Walker, and William C. Buck, Louisville, Kentucky (1841); J. H. Ramsdell, Thomas B. Walker, William C. Buck, Thomas B. Greenley, and John Russell, Louisville, Kentucky (1842–1848); J. H. Ramsdell, Thomas B. Walker, William C. Buck, Thomas B. Greenley, John Russell, and A. W. La Rue, Louisville, Kentucky (1849); J. H. Ramsdell, Thomas B. Walker, Thomas B. Greenley, John Russell, A. W. La Rue, J. L. Waller, and R. L. Thurman, Louisville, Kentucky (1850–1857); Joseph Otis, Louisville Kentucky (1858–1861); A. S. Worrel, A. C. Caperton, J. S. Coleman, Louisville, Kentucky (1861–1872); A. C. Caperton, Louisville, Kentucky (1873–1887); Harvey, McFerran, and Co., Louisville, Kentucky (1887–1919); Kentucky Baptist Convention, Louisville, Kentucky (1919–1956); Middletown, Kentucky (1956–present).

EDITORS: James Wilson (1834–1835); John L. Waller (1835–1839); John L. Waller and J. M. Peck (1839–1841); William C. Buck (1841–1850); John L. Waller, R. L. Thurman, and A. W. LaRue (1850–1851); John L. Waller and Charles D. Kirk (1852); R. L. Thurman, S. H. Ford, T. J. Fisher, John L. Waller (1853); S. H. Ford, S. W. Lynd, William M. Pratt, A. W. LaRue, A. D. Sears, L. Fletcher, J. M. Bennett, J. W. Warder, and W. C. Duncan (1854–1856); Norman Robinson (1857); Joseph Otis (1858–1861); S. H. Ford (1861–1863); Charles Y. Duncan (1864); Alfred C. Graves and Jonathan C. Waller (1864–1865); R. M. Dudley (1866–1867); R. M. Dudley and J. W. Rust (1868); A. S. Worrell and A. C. Caperton (1868–1871); J. S. Coleman, A. S. Worrell, A. C. Caperton, W. W. Gardner, and George Varden (1872); A. C. Caperton (1873–1887); Thomas T. Eaton (1887–1907); J. M. Weaver (1907); C. M. Thompson (1907–1909); John William Porter (1909–1921); Victor I. Masters (1921–1942); John D. Feeeman (1942–1945); Revel Tipton Skinner (1946–1957); Chauncey R. Daley, Jr. (1957–1984); Jack D. Sanford (1984–1989); E. Marvin Knox (1990–present).

CIRCULATION: 51,000 (1992).

John P. Ferré

WIND BELL

The *Wind Bell* started as a monthly mimeographed newsletter of the San Francisco Zen Center on 2 December 1961. Its first issue carried a poem titled "Wind Bell" by Eihei Dogen (1200–1255), the founder of the Soto Zen school in Japan:

Hanging by his mouth
His whole body is his mouth
East West South and North Wind
He does not care
Always, he talks in many ways
About Prajnaparamita[1] for others
Tsu chan tsun ryan
tsu chin ryan[2]

As a newsletter it was basically a one-or two-page information sheet with an occasional reprint of a short talk by the Zen Center's founder, Suzuki Roshi, who arrived at Sokoji Temple on Bush Street in San Francisco's Japantown to serve the local Japanese Soto Zen congregation in May 1959. At first only a few Western students came—young people, schoolteachers, and painters. Suzuki Roshi emphasized "way-seeking mind" (always seeking one's spiritual path), a "big open attitude" (recognition of a reality that cannot be fully grasped), and *zazen*, or seated meditation. In August 1962 Zen Center was formally incorporated with the state of California.

By 1966 the Zen Center had grown into a stable practicing community, and Suzuki Roshi felt that the time was right to look for some land for a retreat center. Tassajara was purchased in 1967 and named Zenshinji (Zen Mind/Heart Temple). It became the first training temple outside Asia, and students arrived in great numbers.

The *Wind Bell* grew, too. It became a several-page printed booklet published every other month and began to include articles by scholars and visiting teachers as well as general information and news about Zen worldwide. In the fall of 1967 it expanded to an eighty-page issue focused on Tassajara and the need for a training monastery, fund-raising, and other news about Zen in America.

With the opening of Tassajara in 1969 as a large center in San Francisco separate from the Japanese community and the purchase in 1972 of Green Gulch Farm, which included an organic farm and garden, a retreat center, and a meditation hall open to the public, the Zen Center achieved its current form as the first large, predominantly non-Asian Buddhist institution in America.

Richard Baker had founded the *Wind Bell* at Suzuki Roshi's suggestion and served as editor from 1961 to 1967. While Baker was in Japan from 1968 to 1971, Gary Snyder, Tim Buckley, Peter Schneider, and Katherine Thanas edited issues. Baker brought an American spirit to the magazine.

From 1971 to 1983 the *Wind Bell* appeared infrequently. In 1971 Richard

Baker became Suzuki Roshi's successor as abbot of Zen Center. He continued as *Wind Bell* editor, but time constraints on his schedule led to sporadic publication. During this time the content of the *Wind Bell* tended to be mostly about the Zen Center, with a sprinkling of other news and articles about Buddhism outside the institution. It only occasionally had a table of contents, but each issue included reprints of lectures by Suzuki Roshi, who died in December 1971, and by the then-current abbot, Richard Baker Roshi.

In 1983 and again in 1987 the behavior of the abbots came under close scrutiny because of charges of ethical misconduct. Both of these situations were discussed in the *Wind Bell*, which attempted as fair and as neutral a presentation of the facts as can be offered in an emotionally charged situation. The question was how to be supportive of all the parties involved while maintaining harmony and telling the truth as honestly as possible. The resolution of these discussions was the resignation of the abbot in 1983 and the addition of a second abbot in 1987.

Since 1983 several stylistic changes have been made. In 1984 Michael Wenger became editor and continued until 1990. He put the *Wind Bell* on a regular publication schedule and opened the scope of the magazine to include more emphasis on general Buddhist issues. The *Wind Bell* comes out twice a year, once in the spring and once in the fall. The regular printing schedule of the magazine has kept a flow of information coming from the institution. The addition of a table of contents in 1986 made the magazine more accessible, giving the reader an overview. Also in 1986 the length of each issue was fixed at forty-eight pages. The standardizing of the size maximized the periodical's cost efficiency, met reader expectations, and gave the editors a new creative challenge. In the fall of 1986 Zen Center's twenty-fifth anniversary was celebrated with a special issue of sixty-four pages.

Since 1983, the *Wind Bell*, while reporting Zen Center events, has also dealt with Buddhism as a whole and with the issues of American Buddhism. Questions such as ethics, family practice, art, children, ethnic Buddhism, and the like were addressed. Also included have been articles by scholars such as Carl Bielefeldt, Robert Buswell, Robert Thurman, and Masao Abe, as well as religious leaders from other traditions such as U Silananda, Thich Nhat Hahn, and Lama Govinda. Work by, and interviews with, such artists as Mayumi Oda, Kaz Tanahashi, Gordon Onslow Ford, Natalie Goldberg, and Laurie Anderson have also been featured. A yearly financial statement was also printed, as well as a listing of related Zen groups throughout America. Reprints of Suzuki Roshi's lectures continue to be a staple of the magazine. After the two-abbot leadership format was instituted in 1987, the current abbots have alternated in preparing a lecture for each issue. The *Wind Bell* logo, which was calligraphed by the famous Japanese painter Taiji Karyokawa in the mid–1960s, has been a continuing trademark of the publication. The *Wind Bell* has featured rough vellum textured paper as well as fine black-and-white photographs by Robert Boni, Dan Howe, Barbara Lubanski, and others. One of the artistic tensions has been the texture of the paper versus the quality of the photographic reproductions. Laurie Schley, who took over as editor in 1990, has continued to widen the scope with issues featuring art, children growing up at the Zen Center, and Mitsu Suzuki, tea teacher and the wife of founder Suzuki Roshi.

The *Wind Bell* is clearly both the publication of the San Francisco Zen Center as well as a national Buddhist subscription magazine. It is not sold on newsstands, but over forty-five hundred copies are mailed to Zen Center members and subscribers. The question of a balance between how much of the magazine should be devoted to the Zen Center and how much to Buddhism in a wide sense is under continuing discussion. Whatever its description, the *Wind Bell* talks in many ways.

Notes

1. The wisdom gone beyond wisdom.
2. The sound of the bell.

Information Sources

INDEX SOURCES: None.

LOCATION SOURCES: The best copies of all volumes are at Zen Center, 300 Page Street, San Francisco, California 94102.

Publication History

MAGAZINE TITLE: *Wind Bell* (1961–present).

VOLUME AND ISSUE DATA 1:1 (December 1961)–present. Published monthly, 1961–1966; appeared sporadically, 1967–1982, and twice yearly, 1983–present.

PUBLISHER AND PLACE OF PUBLICATION: Zen Center, San Francisco, California (1961–present).

EDITORS: Richard Baker (1961–1967, 1972–1983); Tim Buckley, Peter Schneider, Gary Snyder, and Katherine Thanas (1968–1971); Michael Wenger (1984–1990); Laurie Schley (1990–present).

CIRCULATION: 5,000 (1993).

Michael Wenger

WITTENBURG DOOR. *See* DOOR

WORD AND WITNESS. *See* PENTECOSTAL EVANGEL

WORLD ORDER

Realization of a global community is the unifying aspiration of the Baha'i faith. *World Order*, a Baha'i journal, reflects this mission. Its pages stress the oneness of humanity and the belief that the spiritual teachings of Baha'i prophet-founder, Baha'u'llah, are consistent with those of Judaism, Christianity, Islam, Buddhism, and other world religions. *World Order* publishes pieces that express this vision.

World Order first appeared in 1935, uniting two previous publications, the *Baha'i Magazine* and *World Unity*. The National Spiritual Assembly of the Baha'is of the United States and Canada, the governing body of the two countries, called on Horace Holley and Stanwood Cobb to edit the journal.[1] In "The World as Organism," the first editorial of the publication, Holley described human history as a prolonged battle between warring organizations, groups based on, and divided by, religions, races, nationalism, or economic policies and class:

Today these historic forms of differentiation, though still exerting powerful influence, are rapidly retreating before the rise of one all-encompassing distinction which appears to be truly organic. This vital differentiation between human beings now increasingly manifest is that which sets apart those who view the world of humanity as an organism and those who accept it as a constant and necessary struggle between self-sufficient and sovereign groups.

What has happened is that destiny has brought about a mysterious condition in the development of mankind which compels each individual, consciously or unconsciously, to choose between loyalty to the [human] race, and loyalty to one or another rebellious group. . . .

[We] assert the need of a truly inclusive and universal loyalty capable of uniting together the people of good will, the people who are concerned with the safety and welfare of the [human] race, who understand that the only vital issue is peace and world order, without regard to the older and superficial differences of race, nation, class and creed.[2]

Baha'is believe that the "universal loyalty" capable of uniting humanity was made manifest in the words and life of Mirza Husayn 'Ali (1817–1892), a Persian who became known as Baha'u'llah. Baha'u'llah, translated as "Glory of God," is considered by Baha'is to be the latest in a succession of prophets, including Abraham, Moses, Krishna, Zoroaster, Buddha, Jesus, and Mohammed, whom Baha'is acknowledge, respect, and study as manifestations of God. Each of these prophets delivered a message that contained features corresponding to the social and spiritual needs of the time, place, and people and that advanced human civilization. Baha'is believe that all religions are one, that all of the previous prophets were equally inspired, but that Baha'u'llah's revelation heralds the process that will lead to "a new world order," a global, spiritually based civilization.

World Order was created to provide "a public teaching medium" to represent the faith of Baha'u'llah in the Americas and

to expound the Message upon which human regeneration and universal peace depends. . . . [T]he magazine . . . seek[s] to clarify for the general public the vital elements which enter into the World Order of Baha'u'llah—the oneness of religion, true race amity, the harmony of religion and science, the union of East and West, the attainment of world community based upon world federation as explained by the Guardian.[3]

"The Guardian" is Shoghi Effendi, the great grandson of Baha'u'llah. The spiritual and administrative leader of the Baha'i faith from 1921 to 1957, Shoghi Effendi, used the term *world order* to describe the Baha'i cause, as did Baha'u'llah. The journal editors adopted the term as the publication's title.

In 1949, Shoghi Effendi asked the editors of *World Order* to suspend publication for two years and suggested that subscribers send their annual fees to the fund for completion of the Baha'i House of Worship in Wilmette, the only Baha'i temple in North America. This "emergency action" was intended to last only two years, but in 1950 Shoghi Effendi advised postponement of publication of the magazine until after the dedication of the building in 1953. Because of financial constraints, it was not until 1966 that *World Order* resumed publication.

Originally, the magazine was published monthly; however, *World Order* is now published quarterly under the direction of an editorial board selected by the National Spiritual Assembly of the Baha'is of the United States. It seeks articles that explore various facets of the Baha'i faith. Some issues are general in content, while others follow a theme for which articles are solicited. Throughout its history, the essence of *World Order* has remained the same. The editors of the twentieth-anniversary issue of the magazine noted, "*World Order* is more than ever committed to peace, the equality of races, the equality of sexes, universal education, the abolition of extremes of poverty and wealth, and all the other principles of the Baha'i Faith that are the indispensable prerequisites of a universal and spiritualized civilization."[4]

Frequently, *World Order* articles stress the importance of the institution of the family as the foundation of society. Another common topic is the use of Baha'u'llah's method of decision making and conflict resolution, known as "consultation." This method requires respect for diverse views, encourages the broadest possible participation, and emphasizes the primacy of the common good over individual interests. Many of the articles published in the 1980s concerned the persecution of Baha'is in Iran by Muslim extremists.[5] Works written by non-Baha'is are also accepted, usually on subjects such as the relation of science to religion and comparative religion. A sample of the titles published between 1966 and 1986 reveals the diversity of subjects dealt with in *World Order*: "A View of World Order" by then Canadian prime minister Pierre Elliott Trudeau; "California Coast Redwoods" by Richard St. Barbe Baker; "The Institutionalization of Religion" by Jalil Mahmoudi; "Anthropology and Education" by Zdenek Salzmann; "Anne Frank: The Child and the Legend" by Rosey E. Pool; "The Economy of a World Commonwealth" by John Huddleston; "Health, Nutrition and the Future of Children" by Elizabeth L. Bowen;

"Some Aspects of Baha'i Expressive Style" by Alessandro Bausani; "The Poor in America: A Visionary Assessment" by June Thomas.

Baha'i local spiritual assemblies are encouraged to use sample copies of the magazine to teach others about the Baha'i faith and about humanity's increasing interdependence and multiculturalism. The magazine has a scholarly, thoughtful tone. Many articles, written according to academic standards of style, are composed by professors and poets.

Some Baha'i critics of the journal find the magazine too intellectual or highbrow, arguing that *World Order* should be less stylistically complicated and contain more spiritually inspiring articles. One reader wrote that the publication is written by and for university professors only. "When a rank-and-file Baha'i (like myself), or a casual reader in the Public Library opens this dignified and beautifully made-up Baha'i magazine . . . expectantly, and hopes to find some inspiration in its pages, he or she will be disappointed."[6] *World Order*'s editors argue that the journal strives to achieve widespread use, educate Baha'is and explain the Baha'i faith to outsiders. The editors stress that no single method of expressing the Baha'i message appeals to all audiences.

World Order articles are regularly translated into Italian, French, Dutch, German, and Finnish. The magazine has subscribers in more than sixty countries. Subscriptions in the United States are ten dollars per year. All single copies are three dollars.

Notes

1. *Baha'i News* 90 (January 1935): 8.
2. *World Order* 1 (1935): 1–2.
3. *Baha'i News* 90 (January 1935): 8.
4. *World Order* 21 (Fall 1986–Winter 1987): 2.
5. Ibid. 16 (Spring 1982): 1.
6. Ibid. 21 (Fall 1986–Winter 1987): 4.

Information Sources

INDEX SOURCES: An index for volumes 1–9 of the quarterly was published separately. Indexes for volumes 10–13 appeared in the summer issue of the respective volumes.

LOCATION SOURCES: A complete collection of *World Order* is available for use at the National Baha'i Archives in the House of Worship in Wilmettte, Illinois.

Publication History

MAGAZINE TITLE AND TITLE CHANGES: *World Order.* United two predecessor publications, the *Baha'i Magazine* and *World Unity.*

VOLUME AND ISSUE DATA: 1:1 (1935)–14/15: (1949), published monthly; 1:1 (1966)–present, published quarterly.

PUBLISHER AND PLACE OF PUBLICATION: National Spiritual Assembly, Wilmette, Illinois.
EDITORS: Horace Holley and Stanwood Cobb (1935–1949); Firuz Kazemzadeh (1966–present).
CIRCULATION: 1,761 (1936); 3,200 (1967); 1,500 (1992).

Bruce Dorries

WORLD TOMORROW. *See* CHRISTIAN CENTURY

WORLD UNITY. *See* WORLD ORDER

WORLD VISION

In 1947 a young evangelist affiliated with Youth for Christ began a historic series of religious rallies in mainland China, leading thousands of people to faith in Christ. Bob Pierce had joined Youth for Christ only a few years before but had proven a persuasive preacher and teacher. When Generalissimo Chiang Kai-shek asked Youth for Christ to send an evangelist, the organization chose Pierce.[1]

Just months prior to the communist takeover in China, Pierce had an experience that dramatically changed the course of his life. While visiting the off-shore island of Amoy, he preached to a group of young Chinese girls during a stop at a Dutch Reformed mission compound. At the conclusion of his talk, he exhorted the girls to go home and tell their parents they were now Christians. The next morning, missionary Tena Hoelkeboer introduced Pierce to White Jade, a young girl whose parents had beaten her unmercifully that afternoon for accepting the foreigner's religion. Disowned by her parents, White Jade was now in essence an orphan, and the missionaries did not have funds to help her. "What are you going to do?" Hoelkeboer challenged Pierce, holding White Jade before the shocked evangelist. Pierce gave Hoelkeboer five dollars, all the money he had left.

That incident so affected Pierce that he began looking for other opportunities to show the tangible love of Christ to outcast people such as orphans, widows, and the handicapped outside the United States. It was his conviction that an evangelistic proclamation of God's love should be coupled with good deeds. In postwar America, evangelical Christians roundly debated the implications of this social gospel, and Pierce found himself squarely on the side of those arguing for an integration of evangelism and good works.[2]

Pierce's commitment to helping the poor solidified in Korea, where he went to preach in the early 1950s. Each time Pierce returned to the United States, he challenged churches to help care for the thousands of orphans he met while roaming the Korean countryside. In 1950, he founded World Vision as a vehicle for channeling funds to Korean orphanages and missions groups.

Pierce was a pioneer in the use of films to raise money from American churches, many of which during the early 1950s were still highly suspicious of this "devil's medium."[3] When he decided his ministry needed a magazine, he looked for someone who could re-create the highly visual, action-oriented communication approach of film in a print format. The first such effort was compiled by Frank Wolfe, a Portland *Oregonian* newspaper artist. It was called *Going with God* and was "a beautiful, visually pleasing magazine with lots of pictures and minimal copy. It was the best thing to date."[4] Three editions of the pictorial magazine, coupled with Pierce's commentaries, were published between 1952 and 1957.

In 1957, Pierce asked Larry Ward, formerly with *Christianity Today*, to become his editor and create a more substantial periodical. The first issue of *World Vision Magazine* appeared in June 1957. It was a twelve-page, 8½-by-11-inch periodical with a color cover and expansive inside photos in black and white. The subhead explained that the magazine was published "in the interests of world evangelization." Editor Ward said the publication was needed because "the burgeoning ministry of World Vision, with new fields opening continually and new needs to be presented, made it imperative that we find some fuller means of presenting what God is doing on the mission fields of the world."[5] Most of these early issues carried features on missionaries receiving World Vision assistance, news, and notes on World Vision's work and an article by Pierce, usually a transcribed version of a sermon or an ABC radio network report he frequently produced.

With the fourth edition, December 1957, Ward attempted to move the magazine from being simply a World Vision mouthpiece to a periodical of wider importance. A special report on leprosy highlighted this issue. Ward promoted the piece with a subhead, "Please Read This Special Research Report Prayerfully, Carefully." The presentation was factual and straightforward, with a minimal amount of hyperbole about the dreaded disease.[6] As such, the piece represented the best of a genre of stories that would occasionally appear in the magazine, stories providing readers with educational material on issues affecting Third World development.

The leprosy article foreshadowed a move to the coverage of broader issues that began in earnest in November 1958, when the magazine began publication on a monthly basis. Ward spelled out the editorial content: challenging devotional articles, helpful how-to articles for Church members, photo features that "will take you to the very heart of far-flung mission battlefields of the world," personal testimonies, opinion articles, prayer requests, and book reviews.[7] This issue also ushered in a new design: fewer front page bleed photos and smaller inside photos. In those early days of *World Vision*, the enemy was poverty, and the cause of that poverty was the devil himself, coming in the guise of godless communism. Often it was difficult for Ward to tell in this era of the cold war and McCarthyism if the antidote to communism was "freedom" or "Christianity.'' After a visit to China, Ward filed an ABC radio story that he later transcribed for the magazine. In this visit to the island of Quemoy, he used language that would make both McCarthy and Edward R. Murrow proud:

This is Larry Ward, reporting for World Vision from Kinmen Island in the Formosa Straits. You may know it better as Quemoy.
Yes, this is one of those battle-scarred little islands in the narrow straits between Formosa and the mainland colossus of Red China. . . . I am here on Quemoy today for one reason—to remind you as American and Canadian Christians to pray for your brothers and sisters in this, one of the real trouble spots of the world.

Ward described visits with Nationalist Chinese soldiers and members of several small churches. He also related an incident in which he received a Kinmen Memory Badge, a gift to guests to remind them to pray for the island's residents. Ward continued: ''Well, I wear that badge. I wear it proudly . . . because I am proud to be identified with those who stand here so courageously.'' He concluded by asking readers to ''pray for three brave little churches.''[8] During these early days, Ward established an editorial mix that remains a hallmark of the magazine to this day: first-person stories, biographical features, missions reports, and commentaries from the president.

In February 1964, *World Vision Magazine* went to a subscription basis and began accepting advertising from Christian companies and colleges. Under the leadership of new associate editor Donald Gill, the magazine set as its goal ''seeing and serving the Christian World Mission.'' A 9½-by-11½-inch format was adopted, a heavier cover stock was used, and length expanded to thirty-two pages. Much of the content focused on the work of other mission agencies, moving the magazine out of the category of ''house organ.'' Reflecting on the success of this venture a year after its inception, editor Paul S. Rees commented that the magazine had ''put on a new face and fared forth in a new and simpler dress.'' He added that some readers disapproved of the changes, including the further decline in the number of photos and the inclusion of ''high-hat'' articles. But he countered that the new format was designed in part to ''challenge our brains to think.''[9]

As the magazine de-emphasized articles on World Vision's work, several smaller newsletters were developed and mailed to the organization's supporters during the period between 1963 and 1971. The broader reporting of evangelical missions' work and the introduction of paid subscriptions may have been prompted by the organization's financial difficulties and the editorial philosophy of its new executive vice president, Ted W. Engstrom. In 1963, Engstrom, formerly the head of Youth for Christ, was given a mandate by Pierce and the increasingly restive World Vision board to help the organization achieve a firmer financial foundation. He undertook a number of cost-cutting measures, which reportedly angered Pierce, who by now was suffering from ill health.[10] In 1964 the board granted Pierce a medical leave of absence, and the founder resigned in 1967.

The organization and its magazine entered a new era in 1969, when W. Stanley Mooneyham, a former advance man for the Billy Graham Evangelistic Association, was appointed president. Mooneyham used the magazine as his personal pulpit to exhort Christians to respond to the needs of hurting people in trouble spots like Vietnam, Cambodia, and much of Africa.

At the end of 1971, as the organization's scope increased internationally, *World Vision Magazine* and its newsletters were merged into a new publication, simply called *World Vision*. The experiment with subscriptions ended with the first issue of 1972. At that time, Frank Farrell was appointed editor. Executive vice president Engstrom noted that the magazine would highlight World Vision's work—particularly with refugees—and would also emphasize more the organization's support for evangelism, "with special assistance being given to national evangelists, crusades, and evangelistic thrusts."[11] The magazine itself was downsized, usually running twenty-four pages, and printed on a thinner paper stock than was used for the subscription-based publication.

During the Mooneyham era, most of the feature stories were written by the president and were eyewitness reports of his travels to areas of greatest need. Many of the stories were compellingly photographed by Mooneyham's son, Eric. Beginning with the Mooneyham era, the "enemy" became not communism, but a mélange of natural and human-made disasters to which World Vision responded. Mooneyham's articles of three thousand plus words, at least twice as long as most of Pierce's, were written in a first-person style, often beginning with a story about an encounter Mooneyham had with a victim. This victim's story gave a human name and face to poverty and to the scope of the problem, the need, and World Vision's response. In Shaba Province, Zaire, Mooneyham relayed the horror of civil war through the eyes of an old man; in Ethiopia, starvation from drought was told through the experiences of Amila, a shriveled up grandmother who exhorted the president to bring her food, not promises of food.

Like Bob Pierce before him, Mooneyham burned out, resigning from the organization in 1981. He was replaced as president by Engstrom. During the six-year period Engstrom ran World Vision, the magazine relied on a series of lead stories written by staff members and by celebrities who were increasingly drawn to the organization as they hosted one-hour fund-raising specials for World Vision on television. Articles focused almost exclusively on the efforts of World Vision, a concession made to marketing staff who lobbied for the magazine to help them raise money. The number of educational articles declined further. Under the editorship of David Olson (1978–1987), the magazine was broken into separate editions, one geared toward pastors and leaders, one toward child-care sponsors, and another toward people who responded principally to disaster-related direct mail appeals.

In June 1987 Bob Seiple, former president of Eastern College, became World

Vision's president. He ordered a complete review of the magazine's editorial efforts. In evaluating the magazine, consultant Ron Wilson noted: "Several years ago World Vision moved its magazine toward a marketing approach. Now, however, besides measuring its effectiveness on the basis of donor performance, we want to give more attention to the educational function of the magazine." Wilson concluded that instead of several editions of one magazine, what was needed were two separate magazines: an educational magazine, *World Vision*, and a more visual publication for child-care sponsors, eventually named *ChildLife*.[12] Wilson argued, and Seiple agreed, that *World Vision* should serve to challenge, motivate, and educate not only donors but leaders of Christian opinion. Further, the focus should be on issues related to the Third World, not just World Vision project work. The second publication would be for "the vast image-oriented audience. They process information intuitively and spontaneously, in a mosaic, with emphasis on images. They are not primarily readers and are not comfortable with linear and word-based communication."[13] The December 1987-January 1988 issue of *World Vision*, the first under editor Terry Madison, featured all photos in color, including a full-bleed cover rendition of an oil portrait of Chuck Colson, president of Prison Fellowship. Colson's story on "The Decline in Human Dignity" set a tone for future stories addressing the need for changes not only in America's values but in its approach to a variety of social issues at home and abroad. Seiple noted in his introduction: "We must speak for those who have no voice, for the 15 million children a year who die in physical and spiritual darkness. . . . As God gives us courage, and as He gives us truth, we commit this magazine to 'go, stand and speak,' and to inform, educate, prod and promote the church to its task of reconciliation."[14]

In the late 1980s, then, *World Vision* recaptured the vision of its earlier glory as a missions-minded magazine challenging donors and friends of the organization. Other publications were created as "house organs" to promote other aspects of the organization. Throughout its history, *World Vision* has been both a "house organ" and a broader missions-minded publication, shaped largely by its president, its editors, and the marketing realities of the times. While its editorial focus has swung like a pendulum, it has throughout the years played a key role in promoting the growth of Bob Pierce's dream into what is today a $260-million-a-year organization working in more than one hundred nations.[15]

Notes

1. Norm Rohrer, *Open Arms* (Wheaton, IL: Tyndale House, 1987), 43.

2. Rohrer, *Open Arms*, 47–51.

3. John Hamilton, "An Historical Study of Bob Pierce and World Vision's Development of the Evangelical Social Action Film" (Ph.D. diss., University of Southern California, 1980), 7.

4. Telephone interview with Larry Ward, founding editor of *World Vision Magazine*, 4 May 1992.

5. Larry Ward, "Editor's Notes," *World Vision Magazine* 1 (June 1957): 2.

6. "A Special Report on Leprosy," *World Vision Magazine* 1 (December 1957): 4.

7. "From the Editor," *World Vision Magazine* 2 (November 1958): 2.

8. Larry Ward, "Report from Quemoy," *World Vision Magazine* 4 (December 1960): 4.

9. Paul S. Rees, "One Year After," *World Vision Magazine* 9 (March 1965): 3.

10. Rohrer, *Open Arms*, 92.

11. Ted W. Engstrom, "A New Thing . . . ", *World Vision* 16 (January 1972): 2–3.

12. Ron Wilson, "Prospectus for Two World Vision Donor Publications," World Vision internal memo, 9 July 1987. In 1991, a further division was made in *ChildLife*: a magazine called *Partners* aimed at people responding to direct mail appeals. *ChildLife* remained a publication for child-care sponsors.

13. Wilson, "Prospectus," 4.

14. Robert A. Seiple, "Those Who Refuse to Be Silent," *World Vision* 31 (December–January 1988): 3.

15. "World Vision Fact Card," June 1992, prepared for internal use by World Vision staff.

Information Sources

INDEX SOURCES: The Magazine Department at World Vision keeps a computerized index.

LOCATION SOURCES: Both Fuller Theological Seminary and World Vision Magazine Department have complete runs.

Publication History

MAGAZINE AND MAGAZINE TITLE CHANGES: *World Vision Magazine* (June 1957–December 1971); *World Vision* (January 1972–present).

VOLUME AND ISSUE DATA: 1:1 (June 1957)–present. Published bimonthly from June 1957 to October 1958; monthly from November 1958 to May 1984; bimonthly June–July 1984–present.

PUBLISHER AND PLACE OF PUBLICATION: World Vision, Inc., Los Angeles, California (1957–1964); Monrovia, California (1964–present).

EDITORS: Larry Ward (1957–1963); Norman Rohrer (1963); Paul S. Rees (1963–1971); Frank Farrell (1972–1977); David Olson (1978–1987); Terry Madison (1988–present).

CIRCULATION: 220,000 (1992).

Ken Waters

WORLD VISION MAGAZINE. *See* WORLD VISION

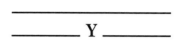

YOUNG LUTHERAN'S COMPANION. *See* LUTHERAN COMPANION

YOUTHCAST. *See* CAMPUS LIFE

YOUTH FOR CHRIST MAGAZINE. *See* CAMPUS LIFE

— Z —

ZION'S WATCH TOWER AND HERALD OF CHRIST'S PRESENCE. *See* WATCHTOWER

Appendix: Magazines by Focus or Religious Direction

PERIODICALS REFLECTING THE ADVENTIST AND MILLENNIALIST TRADITION

Adventist Review

American Millenarian

Liberty

Midnight Cry

Waymarks

PERIODICALS REFLECTING THE ANGLICAN AND EPISCOPAL TRADITION

American Church Monthly

Christian Advocate

Spirit of Missions

PERIODICALS REFLECTING THE BAPTIST TRADITION

American Baptist

Baptist Bulletin

Baptist Missionary Magazine

Christian Index

Watchman-Examiner

Western Recorder

PERIODICALS REFLECTING THE CONGREGATIONALIST-UNITED CHURCH OF CHRIST TRADITION

A.D.

Congregationalist

Connecticut Evangelical Magazine

Pacific

PERIODICALS REFLECTING THE DISCIPLES OF CHRIST AND CHURCHES OF CHRIST TRADITION

Christian Messenger

Millennial Harbinger

PERIODICALS REFLECTING EASTERN, ORIENTAL, OR NON-WESTERN TRADITIONS

Back to Godhead

Wind Bell

World Order

PERIODICAL REFLECTING THE FREE RELIGION TRADITION

Truth Seeker

PERIODICAL REFLECTING THE JEHOVAH'S WITNESS TRADITION

Watchtower

PERIODICALS REFLECTING THE JEWISH TRADITION

American Hebrew

American Israelite

American Jewess

Reform Judaism

PERIODICAL REFLECTING THE INTERESTS OF AFRICAN AMERICANS

Christian Recorder

PERIODICALS REFLECTING THE INTERESTS OF RELIEF, SOCIAL SERVICE, AND BIBLE DISTRIBUTION AGENCIES

American Bible Society Record

Child's Paper

Sojourner

War Cry

World Vision

PERIODICALS REFLECTING THE INTERESTS OF WOMEN

Daughters of Sarah

Godey's Lady's Book

Ladies' Repository

Today's Christian Woman

Virtue

PERIODICALS REFLECTING THE LUTHERAN TRADITION

Lutheran

Lutheran Companion

Lutheran Observer

Lutheran Witness

Walther League Messenger

PERIODICAL REFLECTING THE MENNONITE TRADITION

Gospel Herald

PERIODICALS REFLECTING THE METHODIST AND WESLEYAN TRADITION

Christian Advocate
Interpreter
United Methodist Reporter
Upper Room
Western Christian Advocate

PERIODICAL REFLECTING THE MORMON TRADITION

Ensign

PERIODICALS REFLECTING A NONDENOMINATIONAL PROTESTANT PERSPECTIVE

Army and Navy Messenger
Campus Life
Christian Century
Christian Fundamentalist
Christian Herald
Christian Life
Christianity Today
Church Advocate
Decision
Door
Eternity
Moody Magazine
National Preacher
North American Review
Our Daily Bread
Prophetic Times
Sword of the Lord

PERIODICAL REFLECTING THE ORTHODOX TRADITION

Orthodox Observer

PERIODICAL REFLECTING THE PENTECOSTAL TRADITION

Pentecostal Evangel

PERIODICALS REFLECTING THE PRESBYTERIAN AND REFORMED TRADITION

Presbyterian
Presbyterian of the South
Presbyterian Survey
Southern Presbyterian Journal

PERIODICALS REFLECTING THE REVIVALIST HERITAGE

Bridal Call
Guide to Holiness
Herald of Gospel Liberty
Herald of Life and Immortality

PERIODICALS REFLECTING THE ROMAN CATHOLIC TRADITION

Catholic Near East
Catholic New York
Columban Mission
Columbia
Indian Sentinel
Liguorian
Maryknoll
Pilot
Pittsburgh Catholic
Reign of the Sacred Heart
U.S. Catholic

PERIODICAL REFLECTING THE SOCIETY OF FRIENDS' TRADITION (QUAKERS)

Evangelical Friend

PERIODICAL REFLECTING THE UNITARIAN-UNIVERSALIST TRADITION

Christian Examiner

PERIODICALS SPONSORED BY OTHER AGENCIES AND ASSOCIATIONS

Campus Life
Christian History
Covenant Companion
Evangelical Beacon
Guideposts
Plain Truth
World Vision

Index

Page number in **bold** indicate main entries.

About the Editors and Contributors

P. MARK FACKLER is associate professor, Department of Communications, at Wheaton College. He is co-author of *Media Ethics: Cases and Moral Reasoning* and *Good News: Social Ethics and the Press* and contributes articles to professional magazines and journals.

CHARLES H. LIPPY is the Leroy A. Martin Distinguished Professor of Religious Studies, University of Tennessee at Chattanooga. A specialist in the history of religion in the United States, he is coauthor of *Christianity Comes to the Americas, 1492–1776*. He is editor of *Religious Periodicals of the United States* and *Twentieth-Century Shapers of American Popular Religion*.

DOUGLAS FIRTH ANDERSON is an assistant professor of history at Northwestern College. He has written numerous scholarly articles and is coauthor of *Pilgrim Progression: The Protestant Experience in California*.

GLENN ARNOLD is a professor of journalism at Wheaton Graduate School. He has written *How to Write Award Winning Articles*.

STEVEN M. AVELLA is an associate professor of history at Marquette University. His scholarly focus is on Catholicism. He is the author of *Catholicism Chicago Style* and is currently studying Catholics and their role in American foreign policy.

J. MARTIN BAILEY is a minister in the United Church of Christ and has recently retired as associate general secretary of the National Council of Churches. His most recent book is *The Spring of Nations*.

CYNTHIA L. BEACH is assistant professor of English and speech at Cornerstone College, Grand Rapids.

KURT BERENDS is currently studying the use of Scripture during the American Civil War.

EDITH BLUMHOFER is the director at the Institute for the Study of American Evangelicals at Wheaton College. She had two books published in 1993—*Restoring the Faith: The Assemblies of God, Pentecostalism and American Culture* and *Aimee Semple McPherson: Everybody's Sister.*

NORMAN P. BOLDUC is vice chancellor and director of priestly life and ministry of the Roman Catholic Diocese of Manchester. He is currently researching Langdon Gilkey and Edward Farley on the truth and meaning of theological statements. He was ordained in 1979.

GLENN BROWN is currently researching American Christian communities and their relationship to public policy.

JAMES F. BUNDY is pastor at Galewood Community Church (United Church of Christ) in Chicago. He is adjunct faculty at Elmhurst College and has authored *Fall from Grace: Religion and the Communal Ideal in Two Suburban Villages.*

ROBERT E. BURNS was executive editor of *U.S. Catholic* and general manager of Claretian Publications from 1949 to 1984. He has authored *The Examined Life* and *Catholics on the Cutting Edge.*

JON BUTLER is professor of American studies and history and religious studies at Yale University, and earned his Ph.D. from the University of Minnesota. He has written *Awash in a Sea of Faith: Christianizing the American People* and *The Huguenots in America: A Refugee People in New World Society.*

KEVIN J. CHRISTIANO is associate professor of sociology at Notre Dame and is currently a visiting scholar with the Canadian Studies Center at Duke University. He has authored numerous articles in sociology of American religion. He has also completed a biography of Pierre Elliot Trudeau, former prime minister of Canada.

TIMOTHY T. CLYDESDALE is completing his dissertation in sociology at Princeton University. His research interests include the sociology of religion, American cultural analysis, and American religious history.

W. RUSSELL CONGLETON is studying the Quakers in twentieth-century America, especially their relationship to Herbert Hoover.

STEVEN D. COOLEY is a visiting professor of history at the University of Dayton.

LARRY V. CRUTCHFIELD is the author of *The Origins of Dispensationalism: The Darby Factor* and *The Early Church Fathers and Abortion*. He is a freelance writer.

ALLEN S. DAVIDSON is currently pursuing studies in religion, especially correlations between American Christian and Egyptian Islamic fundamentalism.

JOHN DEEDY edited the *Pittsburgh Catholic* from 1959 to 1967. He was founding editor of the *Catholic Free Press* of Worcester in 1951 and managing editor of *Commonweal* from 1967 to 1968. He has authored twenty books.

TIMOTHY J. DETWILER is divisional chair and associate professor of communication arts at Cornerstone College. His research interests include religious media, technology, and society.

DENNIS C. DICKERSON is the Stanfield Professor of History at Williams College and is historiographer of the African Methodist Episcopal Church. He has written numerous articles on African-American religious history.

BRUCE DORRIES teaches communications at the University of Missouri, where he has received several awards for teaching. He is currently pursuing ethnographic and narrative studies of women and their work in contemporary soup kitchens.

LARRY ESKRIDGE is assistant director of the Institute for the Study of American Evangelicals at Wheaton College. His interests are in mass media, popular culture, and American evangelicalism.

JOHN P. FERRÉ is associate professor of communication at the University of Louisville. His most recent scholarly work is *Good News: Social Ethics and the Press*. His current research interests are the history and ethics of mass media in the United States.

MYRON FOGDE is professor of religion at Augustana College. He has written books on religion in frontier Montana.

DOUGLAS A. FOSTER is associate professor of church history and the director of the Center for Restoration Studies at Abilene Christian University. His research interests center around minimizing religious conflict. He has studied the Church of Christ and its place in the American religious scene.

TIMOTHY E. FULOP is visiting assistant professor at Harvard University. His primary interest is American religious history.

MICHAEL T. GIROLIMON has published several articles and essays in journals and magazines, including *Paraclete* and the *Journal of Religious History*. He is currently studying American evangelicalism and fundamentalism and has also studied the charismatic renewal in the Presbyterian Church (USA).

RICHARD C. GOODE is instructor of history at Lipscomb University. He has written for *Religion and American Culture* and *Encyclopaedia of the Wars of Colonial America*.

STEPHEN R. GRAHAM is associate professor of American church history at North Park Theological Seminary.

MARK ALAN GRANQUIST has served as pastor in Bethel Lutheran Church, Rochester, Minnesota.

MICHAEL P. GRAVES is the chair of the school of communication studies at Regent University. He has authored several studies in Quaker culture and rhetoric.

MICHAEL S. HAMILTON is program coordinator at the Pew Evangelical Scholars Program and the Pew Younger Scholars Program at the University of Notre Dame.

KEITH HARPER has published several articles on Baptist history. He is currently assistant professor of history at Mississippi College.

CHRISTOPHER D. HUDSON is project editor at the Livingstone Corporation, Carol Stream, Illinois.

MARTI TOMAS IZRAL is associate professor of communications at Loyola University. She has written on media literacy and religious communication.

RONALD A. JOHNSON is assistant professor of communications at Sterling College. His studies include the interface of technology and theology.

KATHLEEN JOYCE will join the religion department at Duke University in 1995 and has completed studies in American Catholic history, Catholics and health care in the twentieth century, and other issues associated with religion and medicine.

PAUL C. KEMENY has published several articles on church history and is currently studying the religious character of Princeton University between 1868 and 1928.

RICHARD KERN is professor of history at the University of Findlay. He has written *John Winebrenner: 19th Century Reformer* and *Findlay College: The First Hundred Years.*

EVELYN A. KIRKLEY is assistant professor of American church history at Colgate Rochester Divinity School/Crozer Theological Seminary.

JOHN KLOOS is professor of religious studies at Illinois Benedictine College. He is the author of *A Sense of Deity: The Republican Spirituality of Benjamin Rush, M. D.* His areas of research include American religious history and world religions.

ROBERT H. KRAPOHL is assistant professor and reference librarian in the Jesse H. Jones Library at Baylor University. His academic interests are in dispensationalism and John Nelson Darby.

KATHRYN LONG is visiting assistant professor of history at Wheaton College.

ROXANE SALYER LULOFS is professor of communications at Azusa Pacific University. Her latest work is *The Social Construction of Forgiveness.*

SUSAN WILDS McARVER is studying Southern church history in America.

MICHAEL R. McCOY is the author of several publications in religious and philosophical history. He is retired from careers at both Ferrum College and Union College of Kentucky.

COLLEEN McDANNELL is associate professor of history at University of Utah. She has authored *Heaven: A History* and *The Christian Home in Victorian America: 1840–1900.*

MARGARET M. McGUINNESS is associate professor and chair of the department of religion at Cabrini College. She is currently involved in a project involving American Catholics in the holy land and is the book review editor of *Records of the American Catholic Historical Society.*

DAVID B. MALONE is assistant to the head of Special Services at the Wheaton College Archives and Special Collections.

HARVEY MARKOWITZ last served as assistant director at the Newberry Library in Chicago.

EDWIN H. MAYNARD served as writer, editor, and communication administrator for the United Methodist Church. He is past president of the Associated Church Press.

JOSEPH B. MODICA serves as chaplain and assistant professor in biblical studies at Eastern College. He is ordained in the Christian and Missionary Alliance church.

R. ALBERT MOHLER, JR., is president of the Southern Baptist Theological Seminary, Louisville, Kentucky. He has written and edited numerous works, including *Karl Barth and Evangelical Theology.*

DOUGLAS MORGAN has completed studies in the history of Christianity, with an emphasis on American religious history.

RUTH MORRIS has written freelance articles for Christian periodicals and newsletters.

RICHARD A. MORROW is on the faculty of Antioch University.

DAVID MULDER teaches at Columbia College in Chicago. He has published *The Alchemy of Revolution* (1990).

JON PAHL teaches American religious history in the theology department at Valparaiso University. He is currently studying religious youth and violence in religion and is the author of *Paradox Lost: Freewill and Political Liberty in American Culture* and *Hopes and Dreams of All.*

KEITH PAVLISCHEK works with Evangelicals for Social Action. His most recent publication is *John Courtney Murray and the Dilemma of Religious Toleration.*

RODGER M. PAYNE is assistant professor of religious studies at Louisiana State University. A specialist in American religion and culture, he focuses his research on colonial and antebellum religion, spiritual autobiography, and the story of American Catholicism.

P. JEFFREY POTASH is associate professor of history at Trinity College. He is author of *Vermont's Burned-over District: Patterns of Community Development and Religious Activity, 1761-1850.*

GEORGE L. PROCTER-SMITH is the author of *Religion and Trade in New Netherland* and is campus minister and professor of philosophy and ethics at Navarro College.

GREGG QUIGGLE is assistant professor of theology at Moody Bible Institute, Chicago. He is developing a history of the influence of fundamentalism at Moody Bible Institute.

TODD J. RASMUSON is an assistant professor in speech communication at Bethel College where he serves as chair and director of forensics. He has currently been appointed with Mission Moving Mountains in Tanzania and will serve in community development.

LAWRENCE RAST is pastor of Ascension Lutheran Church, Madison, Tennessee.

ROBERT H. REID, JR., is the editor of the *Christian Recorder* and general officer of the African Methodist Episcopal church. He is ordained in the AME church, and is the author of *Irony of Afro-American History: An Overview of AME History and Related Documents.*

ROGER ROBINS is adjunct professor of history at Grand Valley State University. He is pursuing studies in American Pentecostalism and has published articles in the *Journal of American Culture* and *Anglican and Episcopal History.*

DAVID L. RUSSELL is instructor of philosophy at Oakland Community College. He has written numerous articles and taught American history at William Tyndale College.

WILLIAM L. SACHS is Rector of St. Stephen's Episcopal Church in Richmond, Virginia. He is author of *The Transformation of Anglicanism* and of *One Body: Renewal Movements in the Church.*

GEORGE SOCHAN is a lecturer in the department of history at Loyola University and Wheaton College. His research interests include the role of the church in modern society and public education in England in the twentieth century.

MARK B. SORVILLO is pastor of Presentation Church in Chicago. He teaches part-time in church history at Mundelein Seminary and Barat College.

STEPHEN R. SPENCER is professor of systematic and historical theology at Dallas Theological Seminary. He is a contributor to *Encyclopedia of the Re-*

formed Faith, Later Calvinism: A Geography, and *Broadman Handbook of Church Historians.*

DOUGLAS A. SWEENEY has published several essays on American evangelicalism.

RICHARD S. TAYLOR is chief of technical services, Historic Sites Division, Illinois Historic Preservation Agency.

LAWRENCE THOMPSON is head of special services for Buswell Library at Wheaton College.

PAUL B. TINLIN is senior pastor at Evangel Assembly of God, Schaumburg, Illinois. He has authored *Business Meetings: Confusion in the Church* and several magazine articles.

JAY M. TODD is managing editor of *Ensign*, a monthly periodical of the Church of Jesus Christ of Latter-day Saints and is the author of books and articles about the Latter-day Saints.

JESSE T. TODD, JR., is studying pluralism in the modern era and religion in urban American communities.

MARK G. TOULOUSE is professor of the history of Christianity and associate dean at Brite Divinity School at Texas Christian University. He is writing a book addressing the relationship between Christian commitment and issues in American public life since the 1950s.

WILLIAM VANCE TROLLINGER, JR., is associate professor of history at Messiah College. He is author of *God's Empire: William Bell Riley and Midwestern Fundamentalism.*

THOMAS A. TWEED teaches in religious studies at the University of North Carolina-Chapel Hill. He recently authored *The American Encounter with Buddhism, 1844–1912: Victorian Culture and the Limits of Dissent* and has contributed to several books and journals.

ANDREW H. WALSH is completing studies in the history of American civilization. He is a visiting lecturer in religion and American studies at Trinity College.

ANNALEE WARD is assistant professor of communication arts at Trinity Christian College. She has published articles in religious magazines and is pursuing research in communications and theology at Regent University.

KEN WATERS is associate professor of journalism at Pepperdine University. He has served as an international journalist and director of public relations for World Vision International.

MICHAEL WENGER is president of the San Francisco Zen Center. He is author of *33 Fingers: A Collection of American Zen Koans*.

PAUL WESTERMEYER is professor of church music at Luther Northwestern Seminary. He has served as editor of *The Hymn* quarterly. Many of his works relate to theological, musical, and liturgical intersections.

DIANE WINSTON has studied the nineteenth-century urban church, women in the Salvation Army, religion, and the media and African-American Pentecostalism. She has been a religion writer for the *Dallas Times Herald*.

PETER WOSH is director of archives and library services at the American Bible Society in New York. He is finishing a book titled *The Business of Benevolence: The Institutionalization of the American Bible Society*.

DAVID O. YNTEMA teaches American history at Wayne State University.

GARY P. ZOLA is national dean of admissions and student affairs and dean of alumni relations at Hebrew Union College–Jewish Institute of Religion in Cincinnati. He is working on *Isaac Harby of Charleston*.